KILLING
RASPUTIN

The Murder That Ended
The Russian Empire

MARGARITA NELIPA

WILDBLUE
PRESS

WildBluePress.com

KILLING RASPUTIN published by:
WILDBLUE PRESS
P.O. Box 102440
Denver, Colorado 80250

WILDBLUE PRESS is registered at the U.S. Patent and Trademark Offices.

ISBN 978-1-942266-68-6   Trade Paperback
ISBN 978-1-942266-65-5   eBook

Interior Formatting/Book Cover Design by Elijah Toten
www.totencreative.com

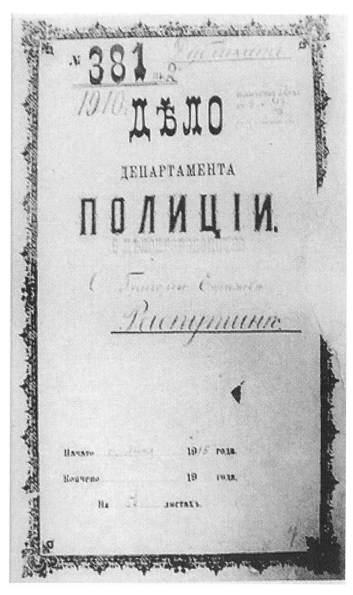

Police Delo File No. 381 (6th Department) with Grigorii Efimovich Rasputin's name written on the front cover. The case was activated in December 1916 and terminated in (March) 1917. The folder contains 56 pages.

TABLE OF CONTENTS

NOTES on SOURCES

My disbelief that a British secret agent was implicated in murdering Grigorii Rasputin gave me the determination to study all the original material related to this murder case, then test that disclosure against the book *To Kill Rasputin*.[1]

Prior to 1924, a few publications appeared in print before the Soviet censors sealed access to its archives. The first book published on the subject of Rasputin's murder was the purported diary penned by Vladimir Purishkevich,[2] who took part in Rasputin's murder. His book appeared in 1918 in Kiev during the Civil War in Southern Russia. During 1917, when the Provisional Government was in power, material that had been previously subject to censorship was published. Parts of the secret investigation that was conducted by the District Court and the gendarmes appeared in the journal *Byloye* (*Past Times*). Other associated material was published in special issue booklets, newspapers *Russkaya Volya* (*Russian Will*), *Rech* (*Speech*), and *Birzheviye Vedomosti* (*Stock Exchange Record*), to mention just a few.

Alexander Blok (poet and lawyer) wrote the second book.[3] He collated all the transcripts from the Extraordinary Commission of Inquiry that sat from March to October 1917, which studied the criminal deeds of the former regime, and examined Rasputin's influence over Nikolai II and if he compromised the imperial government. Among the team of investigators was Vladimir Rudnev. Rudnev resigned his job and returned to Ekaterinoslav in Southern Russia. Fearing for his life and in order to protect his work, he decided to submit his Final Report (dated 28 March 1919) to General-Major M. Nechvolodov on 31 March 1919, with rights to publish his conclusions abroad. Within months, Rudnev's papers became a historic public record in a Russian émigré journal called *Dvuglavii Orel* (*Double-headed Eagle*) in 1920 under the title *Pravda o Tsarskoi Sem'i i Temnikh Silakh* (*The Truth About the Tsarist Family and the Dark Forces*).[4] That publication, of which pertinent details appear in this book, refuted all accusations construed against Grigorii Rasputin.

After the Bolsheviks came to power, the Commission of Inquiry's work ceased; the effect of any valuable information that might have been brought before the panel was silenced. In the same way, Rudnev's published conclusions did not accord with the Bolshevik political objectives, which meant his exposé was suppressed in the Soviet Union. After Vladimir Lenin died in January 1924, access to all government archives and libraries was curtailed. That action ensured that private research stopped. As a result, any major studies relating to Rasputin and the imperial era appeared abroad in cities where émigrés had relocated. Those émigré authors may be categorized as being either favorable, uncommitted, or antagonists of Rasputin and the imperial regime. On the other hand, because they offered diverse impressions about Rasputin's character and what conditions might have led to his murder, their publications, with their intrinsic biases, added to the complexity of evaluating the truth about the historic and forensic questions concerning Rasputin's murder.

Before the Soviet government tightened control over its archives, it published multi-volume compendiums, titled *Krasnii Arkhiv* (*The Red Archives*) from 1922 until 1941, as well as *Padeniye Tsarskogo Regima* (*The Fall of the Tsarist Regime*) from 1924 through 1927. Though the first series uncovered a collection of letters written by Grand Duke Dmitri Pavlovich in 1928,[5] and then three years later, published several excerpts from Nikolai Mikhailovich's diary,[6] few Soviet historians had the opportunity to conduct independent research regarding the *Delo Rasputina* (*The Rasputin Case*).

To maintain government control, all proposed publications required approval by its censors, who themselves were monitored by a network of security agencies such as the NKVD and its later identity, the KGB. Excluding the series of Soviet encyclopedias and occasional journal articles that touched on Rasputin's death, only a few biographic books saw the light of day towards the end of the Soviet era. One such example was Mark Kasvinov's *Dvadtsat tri Stupeni Vniz, a* 1989 book whose title translates as *Twenty-three Steps Down.*[7] To succeed, Kasvinov had to toe the communist party's version of imperial history by inserting political content that vilified the imperial era. The title itself denoted the decline of Nikolai II's twenty-three year reign and offers one example of that political objective.

With the collapse of the Soviet government and easing of political censorship, Russian playwright and historian Edvard Radzinsky became one of the first who was able to examine the concealed archival documents concerning Nikolai II and his reign. Radzinsky's account of the imperial family's murder appeared in 1992.[8] During the course of his research, Radzinsky came across material relating to Grigorii Rasputin and realized how many historic documents the government held in its repositories.[9] Radzinsky noted that Grigorii Rasputin's autopsy report was held in the archives until the 1930s, but during his search, that document was missing. During the early 1990s, a journal maintained by Rasputin (more akin to personal reflections than a diary of events) was found in the archives of the former Senate and Synodal building. Much later, Radzinsky discovered a folder at the Political History Museum (located in the former residence of the imperial ballerina Mathilde Kschessinskaya). It was labelled *Delo Rasputina*, Case No. 573, and titled *Sledstviye po delu ob Ischeznovenii Grigoriya Efimovicha Rasputina* (Investigation in the matter of the disappearance of Grigorii Efimovich Rasputin). That folder contained police photographs taken during the secret investigation conducted during Nikolai II's reign. The sight of those images piqued Radzinsky's interest to continue his research into Rasputin's life and death in an attempt to understand some truths that have eluded historians.

Radzinsky also gained permission to access the Yusupov family archive that, at the time, was held at the Political History Museum. It contained correspondence between Felix Yusupov and his mother, Zinaida, as well as letters Felix had written to his wife Irina. That correspondence revealed how the plot to murder Rasputin had developed and also exposed the socialite's loathing for Rasputin. During his visit to Paris, Radzinsky met Mstislav Rostropovich (the famous cellist and conductor), who, as agreed earlier in Moscow, handed him a folder. The folder contained original documents amounting to five hundred pages from the 1917 Extraordinary Commission of Inquiry. The papers were hand-signed by those who had submitted their testimonies before the presiding commissioner, Nikolai Muravyev. Returning the file to Russia, Radzinsky (and Rostropovich) ensured it was placed with the corresponding files already held in the Russian State Archives in Moscow. Radzinsky's efforts saw the release of his second book *The Rasputin File* in Russia and abroad during 2000.

Other writers showed interest in Rasputin. Ivan Nazhivin, who died in 1940, published his narrative about Rasputin in 1923 in Berlin, and was only made available in Russia in 1995.[10] Valentin Pikul faced political opposition from Brezhnev's agents after he completed his handwritten biographic novel in 1975. *Lenizdat* press declined to publish it, forcing the author to serialize the work in the journal *Nash Sovremenik* (*Our Present*), though copies vanished from library shelves. Pikul's work finally appeared in book form in 1989,[11] notwithstanding the government's past condemnation for going against the Soviet interpretation of history "and the genius of Lenin," by aligning himself with the style of émigré authorship "by giving his own opinions," as customary in the West. Soviet dissident Andrei Amalrik, who died in 1980, was one of the first to write a scholarly political portrait about Rasputin. Though incomplete, his widow Gyuzel Amalrik ensured its posthumous publication in 1993,[12] even though a translation had appeared in France during 1982.

Then in 1990, the Soviets allowed the publication of a book titled *Svyatoi Chert* (*Holy Devil*) that contained a few testimonies sourced from the 1917 Extraordinary Commission of Inquiry. Once the communist regime dissolved in 1991, Russian historians, using their newly found political freedom, sought out their archives. One significant finding came to light after Artur Chernyshov gained permission in 1991 to search through the Tyumen District State Archives (GATO). He found the records from the Bogoroditskoi Church in Pokrovskoye village, the birthplace of Grigorii Rasputin. That register contained the register of births, deaths, and marriages of the Rasputin family. Chernyshev published some of those pages in 1992, revealing Rasputin's date of birth.[13] In 2016, I accessed the same register from GATO and am the first person in the West to provide photographic evidence of Rasputin's birth particulars.

Interest in Rasputin and his imperial connections was not a new topic, but what had evolved ten decades after his death was the direction the research had taken. In 2000, a Russian historian, Oleg Shishkin published *Ubit' Rasputina* (*To Kill Rasputin*), in which he announced that the head of the British Secret Service, Sir Samuel Hoare, was implicated in Rasputin's murder. He expanded on that notion in 2004 in his second book, *Rasputin Istoriya Prestupleniya* (*Rasputin History of a Crime*). One year later, in 2005, British author Andrew Cook had advanced Shishkin's idea one step further in his book *To Kill Rasputin: The Life and Death of Grigori Rasputin*, promoting the view that a British Intelligence Officer was involved in murdering Rasputin. To advance their explanations as to who murdered Rasputin, both writers relied on the 1998 French publication *Raspoutine est Innocent*[14] by Alain Roullier.

Few authors have ventured beyond the two primary accounts of the murder provided by the murderers themselves, Felix Yusupov and Vladimir Purishkevich. Grand Duke Dmitri Pavlovich, who co-conspired to murder Rasputin, did not leave a memoir but did write letters to his imprisoned father. Diaries penned by various members of the imperial family proved invaluable to give a broader understanding about this criminal case.

This book is a fully revised and updated edition of my earlier work, *The Murder of Grigorii Rasputin: A Conspiracy that Brought Down the Russian Empire,* published in 2010.[15]

INTRODUCTION

Grigorii Rasputin was murdered one hundred years ago, on 16/17 December 1916. Though this homicide draws interest, no one will ever know the entire truth of what happened at the Yusupovskii Palace, or who flung his corpse over the Petrovsky Bridge that night. All that can be done is to exercise common sense with the available evidence. Notwithstanding the complication that some documents, which formed part of the secret investigation, were destroyed, there is ample material, as well as a set of forensic photographs that have helped me reconstruct this crime.

After Lenin came to power, the Soviet regime was content to allow the myths about Rasputin to stand. The government's philosophy to circumvent or control facts relating to imperial history, along with its use of heavy censorship, affected what appeared in print inside the Soviet Union. This attitude introduced several problems for historians. By discrediting the last emperor, all questions related to Rasputin's murder became a subject filled with falsehoods. Fortuitously, key individuals, including the former prosecutor, police, and a few former imperial ministers, who fled abroad after March 1917, published various details about the murder.

My approach to reveal the truth

This is effectively three books in one in this fully revised edition. The first component is a biography about a controversial figure in Russian history, the second is a cold case review of a notorious murder, and, lastly, an explanation that connects Rasputin's murder with the social and political circumstances surrounding the downfall of the Russian empire. This book principally relies on original sources that stem from imperial Russia.

The biographic study in **Chapters One and Two** reveal facts with several photographs published for the first time in the West. Rasputin's life is described, focusing on his interactions with the imperial family, all the while as hostilities against him escalated among members of the Romanov family and polite society. In 2010, I was the first in the West to reveal details from the church's secret Consistory investigation (begun in 1907) into Rasputin's purported link to the prohibited *Khlyst* sect. Though Rasputin maintained a wide circle of followers, he also weathered several attempts upon his life. Within this toxic milieu, several powerful politicians swayed others to get rid of him. Denunciations uttered against Rasputin in the State Duma explain why the Russian Empire headed towards the February Revolution.

The second part of this book examines Grigorii Rasputin's murder as if it were a cold case. As a former medical scientist with fluency in the Russian language, I had the opportunity to access and examine a large volume of original material, including police depositions, police photographs, and an autopsy record, as well as the Duma's Stenographic Records and newspaper articles that appeared at the time in Petrograd. I am the first person to translate and have published the testimonies taken during the secret 1916 investigation. In similar fashion, the statements recorded during the 1917 Extraordinary Commission of Inquiry, and the inquiry conducted by special investigator Nikolai Sokolov were used. This material enables the reader to go through the original evidence themselves, which reveals the course of events that led to Rasputin's murder. Most photographs, including the excerpt of Rasputin's Birth Notification, appear in this edition for the first time.

To interpret this particular crime, it was necessary to establish why so many people wanted Rasputin to die. In so doing, the circumstances that contributed to discrediting a person whom few Russians knew outside of St. Petersburg/Petrograd had to be determined. It was important to ascertain how a "man of God" (as described by Nikolai II) became a popular figure among some members of the Romanov family, then accepted by the imperial family, but within a few years was accused of being an evil monk.

Although **Chapter Three** begins with the presumed disappearance of Rasputin, questions such as why eminent Russians agreed to kill him receives attention. The chapter compares the accounts written by two self-confessed accomplices and examines the factors that triggered their scheme. Its success necessitated the assistance of other persons, including the offer of legal support once the deed happened. The British Embassy knew of the conspiracy, despite the face-to-face repudiation made to Nikolai II by Ambassador George

Buchanan. The fact that their Intelligence Service in Petrograd received the autopsy report is telling. **Chapter Four** clarifies the political and social factors that led to Grigorii Rasputin's murder, while **Chapters Five, Six** and **Seven** explain the course of events that led to finding Rasputin's corpse. Given the three day police investigation, the published testimonies provided by eyewitnesses, in addition to the letters and diaries of key individuals, add strength to the fact that certain members of the Russian aristocracy had a direct hand in conspiring to murder Rasputin. Similarly, Nikolai II's diary and Alexandra Fyodorovna's letters disclose their own perspectives about the events as they emerged once they learnt about the murder, as do the diary entries penned by Grand Dukes Nikolai Mikhailovich and Andrei Vladimirovich, which historians tend to overlook. My evidence goes against the myth that Felix Yusupov unreservedly decided to eliminate Rasputin.

Chapter Eight explains Professor Kosorotov's observations regarding the autopsy he performed, and at the same time dispels the present-day falsehood that a British military weapon discharged the last gunfire. My methodical explanation dismisses the myth that Rasputin ingested cyanide; that itself refutes the suggestion provided by two of the co-conspirators. In 1993, a team of forensic pathologists in Moscow had the opportunity to examine the 1916 forensic photographs, in conjunction with assessing Felix Yusupov and Vladimir Purishkevich's accounts of the murder. Their decisions, which appeared in *Ogonek* (*Small Flame*), are mentioned in **Chapter Eight**, while my own forensic assessment appears in **Appendix E**.

All the same, the cumulative evidence led to one conclusion: A group of Russians, rather than a British agent, had murdered Grigorii Rasputin using Russian weaponry.

Though the imperial family attended Rasputin's funeral, **Chapter Nine** reveals why the Provisional Government decided to exhume and dispose of his remains within days of its coming to power. The disposal process signified a divergent period in religious thinking, in that the new administration was resolute that Rasputin's remains had to disappear. Likewise, Rasputin's killers and the syphilitic woman, Khioniya Guseva, who almost succeeded in killing Rasputin in 1914 (**Chapter One**), were granted amnesties. **Chapter Ten** explains how Nikolai II reacted towards the murderers, against the determination of his extended family who sought not justice but compassion for two of their own who were responsible for conspiring and murdering Rasputin. The Conclusion provides a startling link that ties it to the first part of Chapter One.

The efforts of Russian historians—Oleg Platonov, Alexander Bokhanov, Artur Chernyshov, Sergei Fomin and Andrei Tereshuk—have revealed that Grigorii Rasputin was not the man as described by Western historians. I hope that this book will be a testimony that reveals why Rasputin, a smart, semi-literate *muzhik* (not an ordained monk) was maligned; not only by the clergy, the journalists and politicians, but most predominantly by the highest echelons of Petrograd aristocratic society. Regardless of the motive that prompted the murder and the unlawful disposal of Grigorii Rasputin's remains, to use Nikolai II's words:

Никому не дано право заниматься убийством

(Nobody has the right to participate in murder)

Note on the Dates and Names Used

The dates in this book, unless otherwise indicated, follow those used in the documents. All the events fall into the period before the calendar was changed to the New Style (Gregorian calendar) in February 1918. The Russian names reflect the Cyrillic style as close as possible to the original, rather than using equivalent English names, such as substituting Nikolai for Nicholas.

ACKNOWLEDGEMENTS

Appreciation is extended to my husband Graham and especially our daughter Lisa, who re-visited Russia with me in order to help with material for this book. I owe special thanks to my friend and President of the SEARCH Foundation, Peter Sarandinaki as well as Steve Jackson for giving me the opportunity to present the final words about Grigorii Rasputin.

I dedicate this book to my late parents, Anna Dmitriyevna and Pyotr Emelyanovich Nelipa.

CHAPTER ONE
The Siberian Who Crossed Several Boundaries

Birth and Marriage

The Pokrovskoye Church Register No.3, kept in the Tyumen District State Archives, reveals that Grigorii Efimovich Rasputin was born on 9 January 1869[16] in the settlement Sloboda Pokrovskoye. Father Nikolai Titov baptized the baby one day after his birth, on 10 January, and registered the names of both godparents: his uncle, Matvei Yakovlev Rasputin, and a local girl, Agafia Ivanovna Alemasova (DOCUMENT No. 1). Observing orthodox custom, the parents named their newborn son Grigorii after St. Gregorius Nyssenus,[17] whose name was listed in the church calendar for that day. Grigorii's parents, who had married in 1862, were Efim Yakovlevich and Anna Vasiliyevna. Though the family was not well off,[18] the young couple had a dozen cows and eighteen horses on their own land.[19] The Rasputin family could trace their origins in the local region as far back as the seventeenth century, and like many inhabitants, their origins derived from the same ancestors.

This Siberian community (eighty kilometers north of Tyumen) lies on the left bank of the Tura River. Tyumen, which was the first settlement built in Siberia, is 2,318 kilometers from Moscow by rail. Although Pokrovskoye lacked a railway, it was part of the ancient Siberian trail that linked the center of Russia with the most remote towns of Siberia. Tobolsk Museum records reveal this region enjoyed a robust cultural and economic lifestyle.[20] It also had a darker side. Fyodor Dostoyevsky and Leo Tolstoy noted it as the area where political prisoners were exiled, the first of whom arrived in 1593.[21] When local historian Vladimir Smirnov examined the Pokrovskoye records for the year 1869, he found that it was part of the commercial water-trading route, made up of 172 households, supporting close to one thousand inhabitants. The community offered a small school, a post office, an administration building that included the police, and its own church.[22]

The Rasputin surname is common in Siberia. It derived from the word *rasputiye*, which means "crossroads" and originated from the description given to the people of their community, who lived "at the parting of the roads,"[23] which provided access to either Tyumen to the west or to Tobolsk in the northeast. Though the current custodian of the present Rasputin Museum, Marina Smirnova,[24] accepted Matrena Rasputina's explanation of her father's surname, it was unfortunate that those who began to malign Grigorii sneered at it. Sounding similar, they preferred to link the surname with the word *rasputsvo* (debauchery).[25] British Ambassador George Buchanan, like many others in St. Petersburg,[26] supposed that the surname Rasputin was Grigorii's nickname[27] because of his alleged dissolute lifestyle. Few knew that the surname appears in the 1762 Tyumen Church Register.[28] French author Henri Troyat, without the benefit of searching local church records, provided a third possible derivation for the Rasputin surname: the Russian word *rasputivat,* meaning "to disentangle."[29]

Church records indicate that other than his sister Feodosiya, Grigorii (the fifth child) was the only one to survive to adulthood in his family. Not remarkable for that era, Grigorii's mother experienced nine live births, but had to suffer the death of most of her children.[30] Growing up as a typical villager, Grigorii's education was non-existent. Initially, Grigorii helped his father tend the animals, while, as a living, Efim loaded goods on barges and river boats in summer, while driving carts in winter.[31] As Grigorii matured, the church, with its traditions and observance of holy days and Lenten periods, swayed his outlook on life. It has been claimed that throughout his formative years, Grigorii favored discussing truth-seeking matters, rather than help tend his father's animals.[32] Soon enough, Efim grasped that Grigorii (who suffered ill health during his first twenty-eight years) was of no help to him, more so after Grigorii began to distinguish himself by reciting passages from the Bible. In future years, this familiarity enabled Grigorii to gain a favorable reputation among ordained clerics. In 1915, he was unjustly accused of stealing horses by the Tyumen newspaper *Sibirskaya Torgovaya Gazeta* (*The Siberian Commercial Newspaper*), which his daughter Matrena raised in her memoirs, saying the tale had evolved from her community's bygone notoriety and that the label had stuck unjustly against her father. Rasputin sent the editor (Krylov) a telegram demanding immediate proof as to "where, when and from whom I stole horses?"[33] In response, the editor retracted his accusation using a tiny font conceding that he had no proof.

The Church Register shows that on 22 February 1887[34], Grigorii, aged eighteen, married Paraskeva (Praskovya) Fyodorovna Dubrovina[35] (Photo 2), who grew up in the adjacent settlement of Dubrovnoye, some nine miles east of Pokrovskoye. Similar to his father's situation, Grigorii's wife was older. Traditionally, village men preferred to marry younger girls for their strength to work in the fields and care for the home, rather than for their attractiveness.[36] The couple met while they were both partaking their own pilgrimages at the Abalak Znamensky Monastery, which was located seventeen miles from Tobolsk.[37] Grigorii courted Praskovya for half a year before their marriage.[38] Records indicate Praskovya had seven live births. The first child, Mikhail, born on 29 September 1888, died from scarlet fever before his fifth birthday, on 16 April 1893. The last child, Paraskeva, was born in 1903 but died in the same year of her birth, on 20 December.[39] Only three children survived into adulthood. When Efim Rasputin became a widower after his wife's death on 30 January 1906, he continued to live in the outbuilding located next to Grigorii's house on the family's property until his death in 1916.[40]

The newspaper *Rech* reveals[41] that in 1906, Rasputin purchased a two-story house from a pilot, Kuzma Zubov, for 1,700 rubles, money he attained from undisclosed sources in St. Petersburg. Photo 1 shows a large two-story dwelling with one façade alongside the street, while the rear of the property faced the Tura River [the significance of the photograph is revealed in the Conclusion]. Typical for the region, the building was of solid timber construction and its design reflected the local style with its tin roof and elegantly carved window frames. The first level, with four rooms, housed the family and their housekeeper, while the four rooms on the second level provided quarters for out-of-town guests after the house was renovated in 1909.[42] In 1920, the remaining member of Grigorii's family, his son Dmitri, faced eviction by order of the local Executive Political Party. The local inhabitants benefited by the distribution of the Rasputin household bits and pieces (some of these are now exhibited at the Rasputin Museum). In later years, the house served the community initially as a hospital, then as a school until the 1970s. Finally, in February 1980, Moscow handed down an instruction to demolish the house overnight.[43] The land remains vacant today.

The Emergence of a New *Strannik* in Siberia

A *strannik* is a religious wanderer who formed an integral part of the rural Russian Orthodox practices. The term became part of the vocabulary of villagers in Siberia where they first appeared. The villagers saw these wanderers as possessing an in-depth knowledge of the scriptures, setting them apart from the ordinary peasant. The *strannik* had a wiser understanding of life and practiced higher moral standards as dictated by the canonic principles of the church.[44] Such a person was never ordained within the church, an event that enabled one to officially enter the order as a priest and carry distinct responsibilities in relation to the church and its worshippers. Rasputin never declared that he was anything other than one of the many *stranniki* whose sole purpose was "to advocate God's word."[45] Unlike a *staretz*, who was always a monk, devoting his life to prayer in solitude and silence, Rasputin's marriage precluded him from that calling.[46] It is important to note that Nikolai II always described Rasputin as a *strannik*.

In 1892, after Grigorii had turned twenty-three, his life transformed. He left his marital home and began a pilgrimage. No documents exist that reveal what motivated this change. His initial journey took him to the St. Nikolayevsky Monastery (the same route when he was fifteen years old[47]). It was located on a knoll in Verkhoturye, on the left bank of the Tura River, through which all commercial supplies passed from European Russia to Siberia. Verkhoturye was situated some three hundred and thirty miles from Pokrovskoye.[48] Established in 1604, the monastery offered lodgings for pilgrims and had an almshouse that operated until 1917. (After 1939, its cells were used to imprison juveniles.[49]) Though the monastery prohibited women, it gave special dispensation for the empress to visit its main church in 1914 with her ten-year-old son Alexei. The monastery was the spiritual center of orthodoxy in the Urals, as well as the repository of relics attributed to the holy man and miracle worker, St. Simeon Verkhotursky. Rasputin's behavior changed. In addition to venerating the saintly relics or engaging in religious topics, the monks taught him to read and write. When Grigorii returned home (the date remains uncertain), indicating his piousness, he gave up eating meat and, for a short time, stopped drinking alcohol.[50]

After this first pilgrimage, Grigorii realized what his vocation ought to be. One month later, he embarked on his next pilgrimage.[51] This approach repeated itself for the next couple of years, walking some twenty-five miles each day.[52] After visiting all the local monasteries and *Sibirsk* eparchies [an administrative division under the authority of the Metropolitan], Grigorii's spiritual journeys took him to Valaam, Odessa and the Troitse-Sergiev Monastery and catacombs in Kiev.[53] In 1893, he visited the orthodox monastery at Mt. Athos in Greece. By 1900, the inhabitants held that he was a *strannik*. Grigorii walked under all weather conditions, in order to visit and pray within the walls of the holy sites spread around Russia, before spending time in Jerusalem in March 1911.[54]

The idea of going on a pilgrimage was not alien to Russian Orthodoxy. Over a hundred years ago, the majority of orthodox faithful believed it was their sacred duty to attempt at least one pilgrimage during their lifetime. If visiting the Holy Land was out of the question, then a prominent monastery was a satisfactory alternative. Unlike the religious wanderers, the aristocracy and members of the imperial family used carriages and similar conveyances.

Always considering Pokrovskoye as his family home,[55] Grigorii's return generally coincided with the harvest season. In 1902, after a two-year absence, his popularity soared because the inhabitants accepted his piety and liked listening about exotic foreign lands.[56] Matrena Rasputina believed that although her mother grieved over Grigorii's long absences, she was nonetheless proud that her husband was "the elect of God."[57] Predictably, the less-than-worldly locals sought out Rasputin's spiritual counsel. In a humble way, life itself was Rasputin's philosophy that embraced simplicity. People who favored his explanations were the ones who came to him,[58] an approach that continued to the last days of his life.

Despite the innocence of the gatherings held inside his home, village priest Pyotr Ostroumov lodged a formal complaint with Bishop Anthony in Tobolsk. After Grigorii received a stern warning, those private meetings ceased. However, the interruption affected Rasputin to the point that he became disenchanted and before long, he walked to Kiev, some two thousand miles away. Following this pilgrimage, Grigorii arrived at the Kazan Monastery in 1904, where he met Father Superior Gavril (Zyryanov). Gavril provided Grigorii the opportunity to meet the Kazan Bishop, Khrisanf (Khristofor Shetkovsky). Impressed with his demeanor and approach to the faith, Bishop Khrisanf handed Rasputin a referral that was directed to the Rector of the Theological Academy in St. Petersburg, Bishop Sergii (Ivan Stragorodsky).[59] Rather than returning home, Grigorii understood he had to visit Russia's capital city.

The First Footstep in St. Petersburg

One newspaper reported[60] that Rasputin, aged thirty-five, reached the capital on foot in autumn 1904.[61] St. Petersburg and its surrounding region had a population well over one million residents.[62] For Russia, the year 1904 was associated with several significant events. 26 January saw the start of the war with Japan, an event that created its own military burden with the humiliating defeat at Port Arthur and the tragic death of Admiral Makarov in March.[63] Though the major event for the imperial dynasty was the birth of the heir to the throne on Friday, 30 July.[64] Politically, 1904 was the last year of absolute autocratic rule by the emperor. The emergence of the State Duma following the 1905 October Manifesto would, after a decade, provide a public platform for a few delegates to spur both Rasputin's demise and the monarch's downfall.

Rasputin's mission in St. Petersburg was twofold: meet with the miracle worker, Father Ioann of Kronshtadt, and acquire donations to construct an annex for his vilage church, the Church of the Blessed Virgin.[65] Grigorii believed that St. Petersburg, with all its affluence, would be the best place to collect the much needed aid.

Not being a priority at the time, the visit had nothing to do with finding a good school for his six-year-old daughter Matrena (who, with her sister Varvra, were enrolled in a St. Petersburg *gymnasia* in 1910).

Pilgrims who came to St. Petersburg customarily headed for the Alexandro-Nevskaya *Lavra* (a designation for the highest-ranked monasteries), located on the outskirts of the city, to receive food and lodgings.[66] On this site in 1703, Peter I decreed that a permanent monument was to be constructed to commemorate the Russian victory against the Swedish invaders. The tribute turned out to be a monastery bearing the name of Alexander Nevsky, who won the Battle of Neva in 1240.[67] Six months before Peter I's death, Alexander Nevsky's relics were transferred from Vladimir (near Moscow) to St. Petersburg.[68] This *lavra* was the center of orthodoxy in St. Petersburg and rated third in order of spiritual importance in Russia. (The most elite was the twelfth century *Kievo-Pecherskaya Lavra* in Kiev, followed by the *Troitse-Sergiev Lavra*, located in Sergiev Posad.) As a Theological Academy,[69] the *Lavra* served as the ecclesiastical educational center of the St. Petersburg eparchy. Here, Rasputin immersed in his first obligation, kneeling in prayer before the blessed relics and lighting a two-kopek candle[70] inside the Trinity Cathedral before announcing his arrival.

After learning about his Grigorii's life, the Rector of the Academy, Bishop Sergii, impressed by the young *strannik* sitting before him, arranged a meeting between Rasputin and the unofficial imperial spiritual advisor, *Archimandrite* (Archpriest) Feofan (Vasilii Bystrov), the professorial inspector of the Academy, and seminarian student Veniamin (Ivan Fedchenkov).[71] At their first meeting, thirty-one-yearold Feofan thought that while the Siberian *muzhik* (peasant man) who sat before him was not book-smart, he had an unusual understanding about the essence of spiritual suffering only gained through personal consciousness.[72] Monk Iliodor (Sergei Trufanov), who was also present, described Rasputin's appearance in this way:

> "*Grigorii was wearing a plain, cheap, grey color jacket …his pockets were blown out like a pauper's …the pants were like the jacket … tucked under rough men's boots …*

hair was roughly combed …his beard barely resembled a beard …glued to his face … his hands were rough and soiled, under the long nails there was dirt. His body gave off an unpleasant odor." [73]

After this encounter, Rasputin walked thirty-nine miles to Kronshtadt on Kotlin Island in the Gulf of Finland (a naval town, almost as old as St. Petersburg) specifically to attend a liturgy at the St. Andreev Monastery Cathedral. At the end of the service, he sought the blessing from the venerable Archpriest, Father Ioann. This cleric was renowned for his unique manner in consoling the faithful and working among the poor. Matrena described how Father Ioann sensed the devout sincerity of the peasant who came to his liturgy dressed in rags.[74] Allegedly, he told Rasputin, "God granted you many gifts help people, be my right hand."[75] For the faithful, this was the greatest honor coming from the highest moral authority in Russia. It was rare to bless a *strannik* before the congregation and predictably, details regarding this incident spread all over St. Petersburg and eventually reached Pokrovskoye. [Proof about this encounter appeared in *Rech*, No. 52, on 23 February 1912.]

By 1905, Rasputin was seen as a man who possessed a simple but intense religious commitment in a manner not seen in St. Petersburg before. His knowledge concerning the scriptures stunned every cleric who met him. Despite Rasputin's poor literacy skills, his chief asset was his memory.[76] According to one deposition submitted by Mikhail Rodzianko (the former president of the imperial Duma) during the Extraordinary Commission of Inquiry in 1917, a secret Council of Bishops meeting decided that Rasputin was suitable to provide "clear, simple, credible answers to questions posed by Her Majesty" concerning the church.[77] Matrena said that her father was encouraged by Feofan, Bishop Hermogen, and the monk Iliodor to enter the imperial court in the interests of the Russian people, who were in spiritual crisis because (unlike the peasants in the provinces) many aristocrats preferred arcane mysticism rather than practice their faith.[78]

Later that year, Feofan invited Rasputin to accompany him on his regular visit to Grand Duke Nikolai Nikolayevich (Nikolasha), who was married to a Montenegrin, Grand Duchess Anastasia (Stana)

Nikolayevna.[79] Aron Simanovich,[80] who would become Rasputin's secretary, claimed that Anastasia and her sister Militsiya firstly met Rasputin at the Mikhailovskii Monastery in Kiev sometime in 1905. [Though which of the two monasteries bearing this name in Kiev is unknown.[81]] Simanovich said the sisters often chatted with the *strannik* and after they heard he could cure hemophilia, they immediately invited him to come to St. Petersburg. Though the sisters knew about Alexei's hemophilia,[82] the information was a State secret. Most probably, during Rasputin's first visit to their Sergievka residence, both sisters relished talking with their newly found Siberian guest. Despite holding regular evening séances, they became far more allured when acting as hosts to Rasputin. The encounters indisputably became the starting point when his supposed mysticism materialized.[83] Nikolai II's 1905 diary reveals that the sisters were regular visitors to the palace where they enthusiastically discussed the merits of this *strannik*.

The *Strannik* Meets the Imperial Family

Following much persuasion on her part, Grand Duchess Militsiya Nikolayevna invited Nikolai II and his wife Alexandra Fyodorovna to drink tea, with the intention they meet the St. Petersburg phenomenon. Nikolai II's diary entry confirms the date of their first meeting:

> **1905. 1 November. Tuesday:** *Cold windy day ... At 4 p.m. went to Sergievka. Drank tea with Militsiya and Stanok.* [We were] *introduced to a man of God – Grigorii from the Tobolsk Province.*[84]

For the imperial couple, their meeting with Rasputin at the time was no different to meeting any other "man of God." This first encounter proved to be a pleasant social occasion. It followed the dreadful events experienced during the year: the uprising by the Putilov factory workers in January, the terrorist assassination of his uncle, Grand Duke Sergei Alexandrovich, in February, and the relinquishing of Port Arthur after signing a peace treaty following the Russo-Japanese War in September. However, the most terrible misfortune that befell the imperial couple was their private turmoil knowing their son, and heir to the throne, Alexei suffered from hemophilia. Only their intense faith through prayer offered the parents temporary solace and calm. To them, Rasputin mirrored the all-embracing image of the ordinary man, devoid of pretensions. It was a potent blend not seen in the court.

Six months would pass before Nikolai II and Alexandra Fyodorovna would again meet Rasputin. On 18 July 1906, Nikolai II, using an exclamation mark, appeared impressed by his next arranged encounter, noting:

> **1906. 18 July. Tuesday:** *During the evening were at Sergievka and saw Grigorii!* [85]

Militsiya had apparently warned Rasputin that he must never visit the court alone. Feofan confirmed at the Commission of Inquiry in 1917 that Militsiya had indeed attempted to warn Rasputin. She was mindful of the many diverse temperaments inside the court and understood that Rasputin's presence would provoke not only envy, but it would cause a surge of unsolicited intrigue.[86] Unperturbed by the warning Militsiya had given, Rasputin arranged an exclusive audience with their majesties. Using his own initiative, a telegram sent in his name requested an audience so he could present them an icon depicting St. Simeon of Verkhotursky.[87] [The Sokolov investigators found this icon inside the Ipatiev house after the shooting of imperial family and their entourage.[88]] Granting an audience, Nikolai II recalled the visit this way:

> **1906. 13 October. Friday:** *Grigorii arrived at 6.15 and brought us a St. Simeon of Verkhotursky icon. He saw the children and chatted with us until 7.15.* [89]

Deeply touched by the magnitude of the gift, the family permitted Rasputin to stay longer and as a special consideration, he met the imperial children. Alexei was still recovering from his most recent hemophiliac episode and this evening was restless, unable to sleep. Rasputin sensed that the tired youngster needed pacification. While the children listened to the stranger's fairytales, Alexei calmed down.[90] However, the reason why that soporific effect came about escaped the empress. She instead assumed that Rasputin was Alexei's savior[91] and thus began to recognize that before her stood a true "man of God." For the next ten years, Alexei's parents upheld their loyalty towards Rasputin until the day they had to bury him. In 1932, Prince Mikhail Baryatinsky claimed that if Alexandra's faith had been less extreme, she would never have allowed Rasputin near her ailing son.[92]

From 1907, while Rasputin's visits were irregular, he became important to the family's spiritual needs, while *Protopresviter* (Court rank) Ioann Yanishev continued to be the family's cleric until his death in June 1910. When summoned by telephone, all the security procedures every visitor needed to observe upon arrival were set aside. Entering the palace by the secondary entrance rather than presenting himself in the central reception hall, Rasputin walked directly into the room occupied by Maria Vishnyakova, the children's nanny, whose duty was to escort him to the imperial apartment.[93] This practice prevented his visits being logged into the *Kamer-Furyerskii* Ceremonial Journal. Nikolai II's diary for 29 March 1909 says Rasputin had arrived unexpectedly,[94] nowadays confirms the *strannik*'s unique standing. When this preferential treatment became public, it facilitated the condemnation of Rasputin and the denigration of Nikolai II. Pavel Pereverzev, Minister of Justice in the Provisional Government, argued that this single privilege caused many to think "that only absolute holiness" in the form of a "simple Siberian *muzhik*" could be placed higher above "earthly authority."[95] Pereverzev and other critics, who never had cause to visit the court, knew nothing about the purpose of Rasputin's visits.[96]

Rasputin's first visit to St. Petersburg was successful. He was blessed by Ioann of Kronshtadt (with whom he maintained contact) and received a five thousand rubles[97] donation, provided by the Montenegrin sisters, for the renovation of the Pokrovskoye church. The major unanticipated happening was meeting the imperial family. Given his newly acquired celebrity, Rasputin no longer had to live in the *Lavra*'s damp cell. Up until May 1914, supporters offered him lodgings and material possessions. Rasputin received furniture, carpets, food, porcelain and money. The fur coat and hat made from beaver skins were special gifts from the Jewish community. Rasputin helped everyone who came to his door, irrespective of their religious persuasion. Jewish merchants were regular visitors to his apartment. Thus, to assist with housekeeping, Rasputin brought Ekaterina and Evdokiya Pecherkini with him from Pokrovskoye, whilst Akilina (or

Akulina) Laptinskaya, a trained nurse, dealt with bookkeeping.[98]

One can agree that Rasputin would have felt self-confident about his new "sphere"[99] after aristocrats sought his attention, despite his raw speech and simplistic opinions. Aware that her brother, the emperor, always considered Rasputin a *muzhik*, Grand Duchess Olga Alexandrovna explained that if other circumstances had prevailed, Rasputin's public behavior would have been intolerable.[100] Indeed, Nikolai II was routinely photographed, but prohibited pictures of himself with Rasputin, a situation that did not apply to his family (Photo 3).

A Name Change

On 15 December 1906, a handwritten petition was submitted to the Imperial Chancellery, in which there was a plea to modify Grigorii Rasputin's surname to Rasputin-*Novy*.[101] Though some authors mistakenly claim that Rasputin added the word *Novih* (the Siberian variant), the petition seen by this author used the Russian word *Novy*. Why did Rasputin take this step? Radzinsky stated that shortly after Rasputin's audience with the emperor, Alexandra Fyodorovna was "upset about the unpleasant sounding name … inappropriate to the character of the holy man."[102] I doubt that Alexandra Fyodorovna inferred this in the manner suggested. Tereshuk suggested that the imperial family gave Rasputin the incentive to change his surname,[103] after Rasputin allegedly heard two-year-old Alexei shout *novy* (new) when he first set eyes on the *strannik* during one of his visits. Bokhanov disbelieved this clichéd tale, stressing that because Rasputin was not "a friend of the imperial family" in 1906, the adjustment had nothing to do with them.[104] Registers show that seven families had the same surname in Pokrovskoye.[105] Knowing that Grigorii repeatedly returned home, Heresch's suggestion[106] that Rasputin wanted a "new beginning for himself" seems incongruous.

However, the petition addressing Nikolai II (as was customary in all such petitions) provides the reason for the modification of the surname, in that "the surname may create possible misunderstanding."[107] With little imagination, Rasputin applied a simple variation to his surname because he sought to dissociate himself from one Pokrovskoye relative also named Grigorii

Rasputin. The petition was approved by the Chancellery of the Imperial Court on 15 December 1906 and the registration of the modified surname occurred in Pokrovskoye on 7 March 1907.[108] The submission revealed that the modified surname was unique to Grigorii and his descendants.[109] Although Grigorii began to sign his name in the new style, his surname Rasputin persisted as it was before the petition.

Encounters with Alexei – the Heir to the Throne

Throughout the summer of 1907, Alexandra Fyodorovna came to believe that Rasputin's presence was important. After Alexei, then aged three, fell during playtime, his injury developed into a medical crisis. Given that Professor Evgenii Botkin was unable to alleviate the pain, optimism for Alexei's recovery had vanished. Only then, Alexandra Fyodorovna remembered Rasputin and sought his presence. Rasputin arrived very late in the night and began to pray. By morning, Alexei's temperature had decreased and the swelling in his leg had reduced.[110] Once the medical crisis abated, Alexandra Fyodorovna linked Rasputin's prayer vigil with the alleviation of Alexei's condition. Her reliance upon Rasputin became absolute since her *sunbeam* had survived.[111] Since no one could explain that Alexei's recovery was just his own body healing naturally, Rasputin's intercession appeared to be miraculous. *Ober-Gofmeisterina* Narishkin-Kurakina, holding the most senior position in Alexandra Fyodorovna's court, however, saw this matter differently, saying Rasputin "influenced the empress mainly through his insistence on her guilt in regard to her son's illness."[112]

Rasputin's Duty for the Good of the Empire

Rasputin acknowledged that his primary role was simply "…to calm the parents. And this I was able to do."[113] Alexei's English tutor, Sidney Gibbes, thought that Rasputin had no official position in the palace, though he did infer the empress responded to Rasputin's "presumed miracle-working" abilities, which had involved a "hypnotic suggestion to alleviate the Tsarevich's suffering."[114] Throughout his ten years at the court, physician Evgenii Botkin saw Rasputin once. Botkin noted that Rasputin, wearing a cassock, looked like a regular priest sitting in Alexei's classroom.[115] Alexei's guardian and tutor, Pierre Gilliard, recalled that Rasputin appeared by Alexei's bedside on three occasions between 1 January 1914 and December 1916. In fact, Rasputin's attendance was a such a secret matter, the imperial children never named him. Though Gilliard likewise saw Rasputin once, he provided this portrayal:

> *"He was very tall, his face was emaciated, and he had piercing grey-blue eyes under thick bushy eyebrows. His hair was long, and he had a long beard peasant like. He was wearing a Russian smock of blue silk drawn in at the waist, baggy black trousers, and tall boots."*[116]

Rasputin did have a role in the court. He became the spiritual confidant to the imperial family. Most gatherings, especially after the war started, took place in Anna Taneeva's (Vyrubova) stone cottage, located on Tserkovnaya *Ulitsa*, 2,[117] for which the Ministry of the Imperial Court paid two thousand rubles per year.

Both Nikolai II and his wife referred to Rasputin with quaint familiarity as *nash Drug* (our Friend) or just simply Grigorii. In return, Rasputin called them *Papa* and *Mama*.[118] This circumstance arose because as a *muzhik*, Rasputin saw the emperor and empress as the father and mother of the Russian people. [This was indeed the common view of the peasantry, who comprised over eighty percent of the population]. Notably, the imperial family used *ty* (you) rather than the formal *Vy* (Thou).[119] Rasputin's straightforward manner and cumbersome peasant expressions affirmed to the family that he characterized the "voice of the people."[120] Rasputin skillfully explained complex church dogma by transforming it into convincing simplicity. He communicated spiritual affection, pacification, faith and hope. These qualities, complemented by his pilgrimage sketches, resonated well for this family.[121]

In less than two years, Rasputin started to enjoy freedoms not accorded to any others because the *strannik* gave the imperial family rare moments of solace and inner joy. It was as simple as that. Few bothered to understand how essential such moments were for this family's wellbeing. The following extract in Nikolai II's diary confirms that happiness:

1907. April 6. Friday: *After tea we went to the other side on the next level and there we had the joy to see and speak with Grigorii!*[122]

Even so, his extended family failed to respect his insistence in communicating privately with Rasputin.

The Tobolsk Ecclesiastic Consistory Local Takes Action Against the *Khlyst* Allegations

The First Investigation

After Rasputin returned to Pokrovskoye in May 1907,[123] he discovered that the local priest had undergone questioning and that the church had searched through his family home's contents. This incident happened following an allegation, which claimed Rasputin belonged to the *Khlyst* sect and that he had spread the cult's dogma in Pokrovskoye.

Marked SECRET, the Inquiry, as written on the Consistory Folder (now archived in Moscow), began on 1 September 1907. It was set into motion after Bishop Antony (Karzhavin) of Tobolsk signed an *Ukaz* (Order) on the same day.[124] Pyotr Ostroumov and Father Fyodor Chemagin filed their complaint with Bishop Antony seeking his resolution.[125] The background to the complaint relied on the fact that the *Khlyst* sect was banned and thus the State was intent on finding adherents. Despite its beginnings in the seventeenth century, the orthodox church found it to be an abhorrence. The *Khlyst* conducted group sexual activity and self-flagellation. These acts, performed in a somnambulistic state of ecstasy, were inspired through song, which supporters believed would offer them spiritual deliverance from their sins.

Much earlier, on 23 July 1906, Tyumen policeman Vyshnevsky submitted a report that Rasputin received guests from St. Petersburg on 9 July, including Father Yaroslav Medved, who tutored Grand Duke Nikolai Nikolayevich's children. Vyshnevsky added they engaged in "reading the holy book and singing."[126] That report lay dormant until Bishop Antony had to activate the Inquiry ten months later, to determine if Rasputin was a *Khlyst*. The process involved:

- ► The inspection of the Rasputin household.
- ► The questioning of family members and their visitors.
- ► The questioning of Pokrovskoye residents and the clergy.

To begin with, over two days in January, thirteen people closely associated with Grigorii underwent questioning by Father Nikodim Glukhovtsev. They included Grigorii's wife, father, Akilina Laptinskaya, and the two Pecherkin women, Evdokiya and Ekaterina, who ran the Rasputin household. Glukhovtsev questioned Grigorii Rasputin first;[127] he described his lifestyle, adding that he was rarely home and only received guests who were his friends, and when he greeted or farewelled his women guests, he kissed them on the cheek. Rasputin concluded his testimony saying he had given up drinking, did not smoke tobacco, and had become a vegetarian. His father Efim declared that their guests from Russia [Siberians tended to distinguish their location as being beyond the Russian boundary] only came to sing traditional prayers or else read and interpret text from the Bible. He added that Sundays were devoted to visits from their family.[128] Paraskovya declared that for most of the year her husband Grigorii was away in Russia where he prayed. When relatives visited on festival days, they sang spiritual songs and read from the Bible.[129] Akilina Laptinskaya revealed that guests who came to his home wanted to glimpse Grigorii's "lifestyle [and] listen to his teaching."[130]

On 4 January 1908, three more people submitted to questioning. Their statements did not differ markedly from each other except for the one given by a woman who claimed Rasputin "kissed [me] on the cheek" after Rasputin invited her to watch the prayer session. [The investigator in the File Document No. 27 negated this accusation.] One twenty-five-year-old man admitted that he did not know Rasputin well, and the second witness, who lived across the street, heard the singing of prayers and said Rasputin did not exhibit any public indiscretions with his female guests.[131] By contrast, the other village priest, Chemyagin, testified, "Grigorii stands in church absentmindedly" and "kisses various women."[132]

Rasputin had the right to respond to his accusers. He testified that the gossip accusing him of being a *Khlyst* was "not right" and that he "went to the *banya* (bath house) well before the women."[133] After questioning various witnesses, it was obvious there was no evidence indicating that *Khlyst* sexual orgies occurred in the Rasputin household. In fact, the Inquiry revealed the family led simple, pious lives as Orthodox Christians. The Inquiry affected the church more, costing it 46 rubles and 60 kopeks.[134]

On 5 May 1908, the Inquiry, though said to be "conducted too formally," established:

▶ All the rooms were decorated with icons or images of a religious nature.

▶ Six guests were visiting from Russia and two servants were present on the day of the investigation.

▶ The upper level of the house conveyed a town image (for city guests); the lower level had a peasant image (for family living). No compromising material was found.[135]

Enhancing Rasputin's character, on 1 June 1908, the Tobolsk Eparchy acknowledged: "the Christian from ... Pokrovskoye ... Grigorii Novy for donating to the school church."[136]

Given these unremarkable findings, underlying factors had swayed this Inquiry to take place. Who was responsible? Anna Taneeva testified at the 1917 Extraordinary Commission of Inquiry that the main instigator was Grand Duchess Militsiya Nikolayevna.[137] More recently, Radzinsky proposed that Militsiya "wanted to put Rasputin in his place."[138] Once the Consistory verdict was handed down in mid-1908, the Montenegrin sisters were no longer welcomed in Alexandra Fyodorovna's court. This alienation strained relationships between the empress and the Nikolayevich branch of the family, enabling the sisters in turn to vilify the empress at social events. Grand Duke Nikolai Nikolayevich altered his attitude towards the emperor by initiating moves to purge Rasputin.[139] The perception that he instigated the Inquiry[140] lacks merit and ignores the fact that given an opportunity, he failed to act on Vyshnyakov's grievance. His transfer to Tver (near Moscow) in January 1910,[141] almost two years later, was probably connected to his failures regarding the conduct of the Inquiry he oversaw. All in all, the 1907-1908 Inquiry exposed the malice of the two Pokrovskoye priests, who seemingly were guided by envy regarding a local villager made good.

Filing a complaint suggesting Rasputin aligned with the *Khlyst* sect was the first hostile act impugning Rasputin's character.

The Second (Secret) Investigation

Sometime during the summer of 1908, Alexandra Fyodorovna invited Feofan to travel to Siberia and discover the truth about Rasputin. Her request indicated an element of doubt. Feofan examined all the documents from the Tobolsk Inquiry but failed to find anything of interest. Feofan assured the empress that Rasputin was a true orthodox believer.[142] Possibly related to this episode, Feofan was promoted as the Bishop at the Simferopol and Tavricheskaya Eparchy in the Crimea in 1910.[143]

The Third Investigation

The newly installed Bishop of Tobolsk and Siberia, Alexei (Molchanov), activated the Consistory matter on 19 September 1912.[144] He travelled to Pokrovskoye to meet Rasputin and discuss issues relating to faith and his life in order to make his own determination.[145] Firstly, Pyotr Ostroumov was asked to repudiate his 1907 statement.[146] In so doing, he conceded that the Rasputin household did not conduct *Khlyst* ceremonies and that he did own orthodox prayer books, a Russian-language Bible and icons, which the family displayed prominently in various rooms.

On 31 October 1912, Bishop Alexei concluded that Grigorii Rasputin was unequivocally "an Orthodox Christian" possessing exemplary "spiritual leanings (who) sought the truth of Christianity." Most importantly, there was no evidence that Grigorii was ever involved with the *Khlyst*. Bishop Alexei found that Rasputin participated "in decorating his village church and school." Additionally, Bishop Alexei added a *post scriptum* to the Consistory Folder, on 3 November 1912, that stated:

> *"The Tobolsk eparchy authority in this matter played their hand with all the enemies of the Throne of the Russian*

Tsar and His August Family.... Before initiating this matter, its consequences should have been considered."

Bishop Alexei added one document composed by Pyotr Ostroumov (plus three other clerics) to the file on 9 November 1912. It disclosed that Grigorii Rasputin handed over all received donations to his local church. The year-by-year statements revealed that Grigorii Rasputin at no time kept any handouts for his home and that everything had been passed on, benefiting the church and the community. The Report revealed "that Christian Grigorii Efimovich-*Novy*":

▶ During **1906** in **October**, affixed a gold cross to a church icon weighing nine *zolotniks* (1 *zolotnik* is 4.25 gm).

▶ During **1907** in **April**, Grigorii-*Novy* gave five thousand rubles for the construction of the proposed church annex.

▶ During **1908** in **November**, donated an 84% gilded cross weighing over one pound, plus a cross adorned with precious stones valued at ninety rubles.

▶ During **1909** and **1910**, Grigorii-*Novy* donated to the church four silver *lampadi* [incense burners] weighing over four pounds, besides other church paraphernalia.[147]

On 12 November 1912, the Tobolsk Ecclesiastical Consistory panel[148] declared that Grigorii Rasputin-*Novy* was an Orthodox Christian and that the *Delo* (Matter) is closed. The Consistory members submitted their verdict with a cover note (File Document No. 48) to the Tobolsk *Ober-Procurator*, Pyotr Damansky, the same day. Despite the sympathetic conclusions reached, in addition to the 128 pages created during the investigation, the harm that Bishop Alexei warned against proved irreparable. Hence, to seal the File, Nikolai II requested the St. Petersburg Synod transfer the Consistory File into its archive.[149] [It is difficult to grasp why Ambassador George Buchanan claimed Rasputin had belonged to an "offshoot of ... the *Khlyst*," which he believed fitted him well since he was supposed to have held a fascination for women.[150]]

One related *Khlyst* issue

One would have thought that the Tobolsk Ecclesiastical Consistory Investigation would have put an end to the matter. The issue had resurfaced from an unexpected quarter. According to the recollections of a Tobolsk seminarian, M. Andreev, in 1913 Father Alexander Yurievsky read out his lecture before the final year class of thirty students. It proved to be an exposé of Rasputin's early life.[151] Yurievsky stressed that the only reason why Rasputin had turned to the "god-prayers" had to do more with his contrition following his horse-thieving episodes. This fictitious story created a dual problem. It found its way into the media and was read by the St. Petersburg intellectuals, who considered that this was the evidence they needed. Since it originated from a Siberian religious facility, it seemed authoritative and thus useful to prove how Rasputin was sullying the prestige of the throne. Yurievsky's lecture included details how women had sought salvation through sexual activity during their hypnotic séances with Rasputin acting as their facilitator. When Yurievsky approached Bishop Alexei about his work, he saw his three-month project vanish in the open fire. Notwithstanding Bishop Alexei's effort, that exposé had beforehand percolated beyond the seminary walls. Clearly, Yurievsky was guilty for disseminating falsehoods about a man he most likely never met.

The Fourth Inquiry

Given the Commission of Inquiry's purpose (related report in **Appendix C**), one investigator examined the Tobolsk Ecclesiastical Consistory File in 1917 to see if it contained evidence that revealed the likelihood of his *Khlyst* association. By then, the file contained 48 documents. On 31 October 1917, one new page was added, declaring that the judicial investigator for the Provisional Government's Extraordinary Commission of Inquiry opened the file.[152] Professor Ilya Gromoglasov, from the Moscow Theology Academy, read the file documents and was unable to find evidence that Grigorii Rasputin was associated with the *Khlyst*. [Today, the file archived in GARF, the State Archives of the Russian Federation, provides a glimpse into the Rasputin family's way of life in Siberia and some of the people who knew him.]

Attempts Against Rasputin's Life

The First Attempt – the Day of Denunciation

Soon after Prime Minister Pyotr Stolypin's assassination in Kiev on 2 September 1911, the secret regarding Rasputin's presence at the Palace received exposure.[153] Rasputin returned to St. Petersburg at the beginning of November. His arrival triggered complaints, which were passed on to the new *Ober-Procurator* of the Holy Synod, Vladimir Sabler. The most repugnant grievance spoke about the *strannik*'s sexual relations with the empress. Bishop Hermogen (Georgii Dolganov, Photo 4) from Saratov, who happened to be visiting the capital, decided to take the matter into his hands after the Synod deemed to denounce Rasputin and force him to leave St. Petersburg. After confiding with monk Iliodor (Photo 4), both feared that Rasputin was humiliating and contaminating the emperor's "anointed name."

On 13 December, Hermogen and Iliodor consulted Ivan Sheglovitov (Minister of Justice). Several suggestions emerged during the lively conversation as to how they could deal with Rasputin. One foolish scheme raised by Iliodor involved confining Rasputin under lock and key, then depriving him telephone access, until he understood how much he was damaging the throne. Iliodor noticed that Sheglovitov remained in deep thought after he next proposed burning Rasputin's house that contained imperial gifts, letters and photographs in order to erase his imperial links.[154] Sheglovitov considered all suggestions and was most interested in confining Rasputin inside a room for an unspecified period, which was equally ridiculous, because that action would not have been a persuasive technique to ensure he left the city.

Three days later, on 16 December 1911, Iliodor invited Rasputin to accompany him for a get-together with Bishop Hermogen. The *izvochik* (drayman) took them to the Yaroslavsky Synodal House on Nikolayevskaya (now Lieutenant Schmidt) Embankment 39[155] on Vasilevskii Island. It transpired that Hermogen was not alone in the red reception room. It later emerged there were three strangers who were supposed to witness the humiliation and denunciation process.[156] The first observer was forty-five--year old Dmitri (Mitya) Kozelsky. Described as an epileptic with only one functional arm, Mitya lived at the Theology Academy.[157] Mitya's credentials were suitable for this special task because, according to Iliodor, Rasputin evidently displaced him as a favorite of the imperial court and left him without a pension, which was untrue. Ivan Rodionov, the second witness, was a writer who thrived on gossip and notably did not like Rasputin.[158] The third man, Chernyshev, was a merchant whose link with this group is unknown.

The tone of the invitation was set after Rodionov began to criticize the extravagance of the warm fur hat and coat Rasputin was wearing. Rasputin was wise enough to understand that this visit was not going to be amicable. Heresch claimed that when Rasputin entered the room, one of them had attempted to grab his genitals, while Alex de Jonge claimed that Mitya had grabbed Rasputin's penis in an attempt to pull it off after his verbal flare-up.[159] The latter scenario is undoubtedly fiction,[160] since Iliodor wrote that all the witnesses were sitting when Rasputin entered the room, and only Hermogen and he were standing.[161]

The tactics after Rasputin entered the room were comical. Dmitri shuffled towards the guest, grabbed his cuff with his good hand and yelled out "Godless" at the cowering figure of his hapless victim. He then admonished Rasputin for having sexual relations with the empress. Mitya ended his unexpected outburst by pledging firmly that he will destroy the *strannik*. However, the torment was not over. It was now Hermogen's turn to act. Grasping his large pectoral cross in one hand, facing Rasputin, Hermogen berated his prey at the top of his voice and angrily demanded that he must cease all sexual relations involving the empress and never enter the palace again. A litany of abuse ensued. Rasputin was accused of "ruining the sovereign and His family, and permitting the newspapers to trample in the dirt His holy name."[162] Under duress, Rasputin was forced to 'confess' his fictitious sins. Temper frayed, Hermogen began to assault Rasputin, beating him about the head with his bronze cross and repeatedly crying out the word *devil*.[163] Still holding onto the frightened *strannik*, Hermogen then dragged Rasputin inside the cathedral. In the heat of the moment, Hermogen had apparently attempted to smother Rasputin, but Mitya intervened. Taking advantage of the ensuing hesitancy, Rasputin freed himself from Hermogen's clutches and escaped out of the cathedral, down the stony path and out into the street.[164] Radzinsky dramatized these 'proceedings,' claiming a sabre was used,[165] but there is no evidence to suggest that such a weapon was on hand. Iliodor also sensationalized the incident, stating that Rasputin's eyes appeared bloodied and "wild looking."[166] At any rate, the overwhelmed clergy decided that they "would fight to the end."

Rasputin, undoubtedly demoralized by his ordeal, promptly sent a telegram to Nikolai II in which he declared that Hermogen and Iliodor had attempted to take his life by choking him to death.[167] General Gerasimov, Head of the *Okhrana* (the secret police), claimed that Rasputin had embellished the incident and had deceived the emperor into believing that his life was in mortal danger.[168] Rasputin had no reason to cover up such a performance. The most incredible aspect about those raucous proceedings was that all the active participants firmly believed in the lies that they helped to create. The idea about Rasputin's guilt came soon after Iliodor's last visit to Pokrovskoye where he decided to steal a satchel of letters addressed to Grigorii and signed by the empress.[169] Mitya and Iliodor customized the correspondence especially for these proceedings and it was this 'evidence' that was to constitute their proof.

Hermogen, knowing that Rasputin would not remain quiet about the incident, sent a telegram to the emperor requesting an audience. Nikolai II denied the request. Instead, Nikolai II appealed to the Synod *Ober*-procurator, Vladimir Sabler, that Hermogen had to face immediate dismissal and banishment from St. Petersburg. Sabler arranged Hermogen's relocation to the monastery in the small settlement of Zhirovitz (Smolensk District). Therefore, on 23 January, at 11 p.m., Hermogen, with Mitya in tow, was escorted by the *Okhrana* (overseen by General Gerasimov[170]) to the Warsaw railway station, where he boarded the midnight train. [A document held in the Tobolsk Archives reveals that on 23 July 1918, a group of Bolsheviks bound and forced Hermogen off a riverboat. Hermogen drowned close to the riverbank, purportedly in front of Pokrovskoye.[171]]

Nikolai II's second edict concerned Iliodor. One week later, gendarmes escorted Iliodor from his hiding place on the outskirts of the city all the way to the Florishchev Hermitage[172] (near Suzdal). Iliodor could not leave the enclosure and to ensure that the edict took full effect, a guard sat in a nearby cell.[173] Instead of the more comfortable quarters Iliodor would have been entitled to receive, he was put in a cold, damp room with a clay floor and a small window enclosed by a metal grille. The only adornment was a damaged brick stove. After the first year of his confinement, Iliodor became more exasperated after the Synod denied his appeal. [Iliodor failed to realize that Sabler was powerless to act against the will of the emperor]. On the night of 19/20 November 1912, Iliodor wrote his resignation. To distance himself completely from his vocation, Iliodor renounced God, his faith in the church, and lastly, lambasted Rasputin, whom he labeled *Svyatoi Chert* (Holy Devil). Crafting a dramatic exit, he signed his name using the blood that seeped from his arm that he lanced with a razor.[174] Being too obtuse to recognize his misfortune was all due to his own act of betrayal against his former friend, Iliodor always blamed Rasputin for his plight. Vladimir Kokovtsov (Minister of Finance) deduced that this incident, because of its intrinsic scandalous overtures, had elevated Rasputin's public profile.[175]

The Second Attempt Against Rasputin's Life

In January 1914, the police received a deposition from Ivan Sinitsyn, who identified himself as a former disciple of Iliodor. He stated that Iliodor had begun to plan a "number of terrorist acts" to end Rasputin's life, one of which arose in the latter months of 1913. To prove his sincerity, Ivan submitted several incriminating letters written by Iliodor, which revealed Khioniya (Geronya[176]) Guseva received a large sum of money. On 2 February, Sinitsyn contacted the police, this time telling them about his fear that Trufanov had threatened to murder him for his betrayal.[177] Ivan died mysteriously after eating fish later that same day.[178] Ivan Nemkov, who once belonged to Trufanov's conspiracy group, submitted his deposition, stating[179] he urged them to "gather money to organize

Rasputin's murder." Nemkov added that a "former gendarme was involved in collecting the money and that the collected sum of 150 rubles was passed over to Guseva." Since no actual Russian law was broken, the police ignored the information.

Weeks before Germany declared war on Russia, a person attacked Rasputin in front of his home, less than twenty-four hours after he had returned from St. Petersburg. According to the Tomsk District Court File,[180] the offence occurred at four o'clock in the afternoon on 29 June 1914, when Rasputin was leaving his house to respond to a telegram at the postal-telegraphic office.

Khioniya Guseva, a thirty-three year old seamstress from Tsaritsyn, confronted Rasputin and stabbed him with a dagger that was concealed under her skirt. Wounding her victim in the abdomen, she lunged again, to inflict a mortal injury. Among the large crowd strolling along the main street, twenty-six year old Stepan Podshivalov restrained the stranger by taking hold of her, falling to the ground during the scuffle. At the same time, she threw her dagger into Rasputin's yard (later retrieved for future evidence).

As soon as Guseva was led inside the police station, she promptly acknowledged her guilt to Alexei Izosimov. Guseva's police depositions show that she admitted she had intended to kill Rasputin because she believed that he was the 'antichrist.' Guseva stated that she had met Rasputin in 1910, when he was visiting Iliodor in Tsaritsyn.[181] In the interim, the police placed Guseva into a psychiatric facility in Tyumen. There, the two doctors concluded that Guseva suffered from the effects of tertiary or late-stage syphilis.[182] Guseva's appearance (Photo 5) shows a nasal deformity that exaggerated her coarse, peasant appearance. On 24 February 1915, under Statutes 9 and 1454 of the Criminal Code, the Tobolsk District Court sat and heard expert opinion regarding Guseva's mental status. Doctor Orlov declared that although "during the assault Guseva acted in an abnormal hysterical state," she was "aware of her act." The court resolved that Guseva had to submit to further assessment at the Tomsk Psychiatric Clinic.[183]

The Tobolsk Court handed down its decision on 20 June 1915, at which the magistrate declared that Guseva became "severely affected" by Iliodor's expulsion from Tsaritsyn, she was insane and that she had committed the crime influenced by an idea that was religious and political in character. Subsequent to the attack, Rasputin was carried inside his house. The prognosis was poor.

Various rumors spread from Tobolsk suggesting that someone had murdered Rasputin. A newspaper article concerning Rasputin's health only added to the confusion. On 1 July 1914, *Rech,* under the prominent caption *Izvestiya za den'* (News of the Day) on page one, announced that Rasputin had been "severely injured."[184] However, on page three[185] of the same edition, there was a brief account of the events in Pokrovskoye. Towards the end of that second article, the text of "a new evening telegram" alleged "Rasputin had passed away." *Russkoye Slovo* more cautiously announced: "Rasputin rumored to have died."[186] The news motivated Count Witte to send Bishop Varnava (in Tobolsk) a telegram saying that he "read about the murder of the *staretz*"[187] and feared the scandal that such an event would cause. The next day, 2 July 1914,[188] the headline news on the front page of *Rech* repeated the news, "Rasputin passed away from an introduced wound."

Soon after hearing the news, Georgii Sazonov, a family friend living in Petrograd (he put up Rasputin temporarily in his family apartment), sent Matrena a telegram asking for details about the attempt on her father's life. Her response appeared in the evening 1 July edition of *Novoye Vremya* (*New Times*). Matrena stated that her father's condition was satisfactory and that the doctors were expecting to move him to Tyumen, while the attacker was under guard in Pokrovskoye.[189] In the same issue, Tobolsk Bishop Varnava communicated that "The Lord God will save his faithful slave."[190]

The Slow Process Towards Full Recovery

The local community doctor Veniamin Vysotskii was the first person to render emergency aid to Rasputin. All he could do was apply a dressing to stem the blood flow. Surgeon Alexander Vladimirov declared at the Inquiry that he received a telegram at four o'clock in the afternoon (29 June) from the Rasputin family requesting medical assistance. Departing with *feldsher* (primary carer) Praskovya Kuznetsova and one assistant, they reached Pokrovskoye late at night. They found Rasputin "lying in his home in bed with (unspecified) dressing over the abdomen." Removing the dressing, Vladimirov found "a cut wound ... three fingers (lying across the body) above the pubis ... and that part of the intestine had taken on a cherry-red color." Vladimirov was stunned that the intestines remained intact. The attending *feldsher* firstly cleaned the area before Vladimirov closed the wound using metal brackets and then covered the area with gauze. Grigorii now required emergency care at the Tyumen City Hospital rather than home-based care. In the meantime, Rasputin was drifting in and out of consciousness.

Within twenty-four hours of the incident, Nikolai II requested that his Minister of the Court, Vladimir Frederiks, arrange for *Leib-Medik* Professor Roman Vreden (from the Military Medical Academy) to travel to Tobolsk and send back "objective medical information" concerning the injury sustained by the patient.[191]

On 3 July, accompanied by his wife, father and children, Rasputin was placed onto a stretcher and brought onboard the riverboat, which steamed towards Tyumen. Upon arrival at the Tyumen Clinic (wooden barracks built in 1913[192]), the physicians were unsure if Rasputin would survive. The wound measured two centimeters and one centimeter wide with clean, straight margins. [Dr. Nikolskii testified that the "straight sharp ends of the wound" indicated the assault was made by "a sharp pointed weapon."] On 4 July, using chloroform, Vladimirov surgically repaired the internal tissue damage (the bladder was intact) and sealed the wound with an *aseptic bandage*, which the staff changed daily. For close onto a week, Rasputin drank only fluids. Vladimirov's medical report (held in the Tyumen District State Archives) reveals that the mesentery (a membrane that anchors the small intestine to the back of the abdominal wall) was *grazed*. Had the dagger penetrated the intestines, then the injury would have been fatal. By the 17 July, the incision was covered with epidermal tissue, indicating wound-healing. Overall, the wound was not large but it had serious consequences if poorly treated. Given that Rasputin wore several layers of clothing, Guseva's lunge with the dagger was done with extreme force. On 6 July, the *Sibirskii Listok* (*Siberian List*) reported that Rasputin's injury was not perilous (as had *Birzheviye Vedomosti* [193] in St. Petersburg). *Leib-Medik* (Court Physician) Vreden reported to the palace that Rasputin's condition was satisfactory and that the hemorrhaging from the laceration was reducing (Photo 6).

On 9 July, Dr Vladimirov sent *Leib-Medik* Evgenii Botkin a full report that described the injury and the medical care taken. [Vladimirov received a generous one-off payment of one thousand rubles on 24 July and granted the civil rank (VIII) of Collegiate Assessor]. Although the recovery process took several weeks, Rasputin's condition had stabilized by the end of the month. This circumstance allowed *Leib-Medik* Vreden to return home. Rasputin was discharged from Tyumen Hospital on 17 August and by the end of September, he was fit enough to return to Petrograd.

The Legal Process Related to the Stabbing Committed by Khioniya Guseva

The local police began their investigation by taking a number of depositions (34 persons underwent questioning). Evdokiya Pecherkina (aged forty) worked as a housekeeper in the Rasputin household for eight years. Her deposition provided several credible details about Guseva's behavior prior to the attack. Pecherkina stated that around 10 a.m. on Saturday morning (28 June), she was home alone when a woman dressed in a black shawl had tapped on the window three times. Covering her nose with one hand, the woman said that she was from Astrakhan and wanted to seek Rasputin's goodwill because of her illness. Then she asked when Rasputin would return to Pokrovskoye, to which Pecherkina replied that she did not know and asked the woman to go away. When Rasputin returned home later that same night, the stranger was not outside. On the following day, Sunday 29 June, Pecherkina saw the same woman at three o'clock in the afternoon, sitting on the porch of the local store located fifty paces from the house (DOCUMENT No. 2). Five minutes after Pecherkina returned, she heard the crowd shouting outside, "Grigorii Efimovich has been knifed by a woman!"[194] Pecherkina saw that one man had removed the dagger from the same woman she had met earlier, and now, with hands seized behind her back, the housekeeper saw her being led away. Pecherkina said that Rasputin, covered in blood, had sustained a single wound to the abdomen. His pants and shirt had ripped where the dagger had penetrated his body. Belatedly, Pecherkina added that when she saw the same stranger sitting on the porch, moments before the attack, she noticed that the woman had a dagger (not saying where it was located). If true, Pecherkina failed to make a link between the dagger and the stranger's earlier intent to seek out Rasputin.

Rasputin managed to provide clearer details of the attack on the following day just before he lost consciousness,[195] after which time everyone assumed he was close to death. In the first of two police depositions, he claimed that the assailant was a stranger to him. Just as he was about to give her charity from his *portemonnee* (wallet), the woman lunged at him with dagger in hand. After striking once, she then ran after her victim and attempted to strike again. Rasputin said he believed that Iliodor sent this woman to murder him, since Iliodor had written derogatory articles about him and sent complaints to the Synod. Rasputin added that Iliodor became neurotic after he renounced God and the church. Four years earlier, after the former monk visited him in Pokrovskoye, he noticed that "an important letter" (from the empress) vanished. Rasputin said that he was certain Iliodor passed it over to "higher powers." (Government officials who modified the text used that version as their proof that Rasputin was having an affair with the empress.)

In the second deposition,[196] dated 9 August 1914, Rasputin provided proof of the pathological behavior Iliodor directed against him. He testified that he had recognized both the signature and expressions used in a note sent to him from St. Petersburg by someone who signed the communication as *Uznik* (a prisoner, inferring Iliodor in the Hermitage). That note stated the following:

"I am the winner in this battle, and not you, Grigorii!
... I am telling you... I – am your nemesis!"

The investigators compared that signature with one signed *Iliodor* from another letter and established Rasputin's truthfulness. One more letter, found among Guseva's possessions bore the same styled signature, stated that they "will bless Grisha" in their own way. *Uznik* was Iliodor. The police had solved the case concerning the assault committed by Khioniya Guseva.

Undistracted by this failure, Trufanov's revulsion against Rasputin persevered unabated. A telegram appeared in his name in the St. Petersburg *Birzheviye Vedomosti* on 3 July 1914[197] and in *Rech* the next day. By that time, Trufanov had hurriedly left his home in a chauffeured vehicle (said to have belonged to Grand Duke Nikolai Nikolayevich) right under the eyes of the *Okhrana*. The following is a partial excerpt from that published telegram that reveals Trufanov's determination:

> *"Khioniya Guseva, a Tsaritsyn 30 year old* meshanka (middle class), *is very intelligent and decisive. I saw her 7-10 months ago. She knew a lot and knew how Rasputin had behaved in Tsaritsyn ... She believed that he was a dangerous ... liar. She had often stated what her thoughts were about Rasputin as a religious and state criminal ... which role Grishka played in the matter of ruining the Tsaritsyn monastery ... She was convinced that the elimination of Grishka was God's Holy Will. As far as I am aware, she spoke with other maidens who were offended by Rasputin ... that she wanted to destroy him one year ago. ... Then she gave her word to God that she would do this, in her mind, a great holy thing the next time."*[198]

Trufanov's words reveal several matters. Firstly, Guseva believing her dealing with Rasputin was "God's Holy Will" was Trufanov's projection to justify his own duplicitous conduct in conspiring in a murder. [On 12 July, *Rech* reported that Guseva acted because Rasputin had raped her two adult daughters.[199]] Secondly, Trufanov tried to distance himself from blame by inferring God sanctioned the murder. The article assuredly exposes Trufanov's pathologic mindset.

On 12 October 1914, after the Tyumen Court investigator declared that Sergei Trufanov was guilty of inciting murder, while the local *procurator* suspended further action against him. Notably, the court backdated its declaration to 15 July 1914. Evading arrest, Trufanov absconded by crossing the Russian border into the Duchy of Finland dressed as a woman, the same attire used whilst hiding from the *Okhrana*.[200] In Russia throughout 1915, Trufanov's manuscript appeared in chapter format in one Moscow newspaper, which was applauded by Maxim Gorky, who gladly facilitated its printing.[201] After the October revolution, the Bolsheviks published the book in *Golos Minyvshago* (*Voices of the Past*) as part of their campaign to smear the former imperial family and the former regime. After settling in the United States, Trufanov published his book that disparaged his greatest enemy, Rasputin. The *Metropolitan Journal* in New York rewarded Trufanov handsomely for his effort.[202] Though Trufanov's book failed to interest most émigrés in Paris or Berlin, it found a receptive audience who believed his story that persists to this day. Still, in his second book, *Martha of Stalingrad*, Trufanov admits his part in planning Rasputin's murder and that Guseva had willingly volunteered to commit the crime at his behest.[203] After the assault, Maklakov (Minister of Internal Affairs) directed General-Major Vladimir Djunkovsky to place a surveillance team using four *Okhrana* agents, two of whom were to act undercover.[204]

The Third Attempt Against Rasputin's Life

On the morning of 6 January 1915, Rasputin very nearly lost his life when a cart lost its load of large logs on Kamenoostrovskii *Prospekt*. The logs cascaded from the conveyance that was in front of the car in which Rasputin and his secretary Simanovich were sitting. Fortunately, the oncoming vehicle swerved to the side to avoid a catastrophe. A peasant woman was knocked down in the mêlée and the offenders, taking advantage of the confusion, attempted to run but were caught by the security team who were shadowing Rasputin. During the interview, the *Okhrana* found out the offenders came from Tsaritsyn, which happened to be the same city where Trufanov maintained ties. At Rasputin's insistence, the offenders left Petrograd without being charged, having earlier admitted that Trufanov was behind this attempt on Rasputin's life.[205] As for the injured peasant woman, the *Okhrana* agents drove her to a nearby infirmary and left her with some rubles to soften her injuries. This incident necessitated strengthening the security, who worked in two shifts, in addition to a 'chauffeur.'

The *Okhrana* and the British Step In

Sometime in 1908[206] (Director of Police General Kurlov supposed that it was during the winter of either 1909 or 1910[207]), the imperial court commandant, Vladimir Dedyulin, spoke to the Head of the *Okhrana*, General Alexander Gerasimov. Dedyulin told him that Rasputin might be a "disguised terrorist." Since the emperor and empress often visited Anna Taneeva's home to chat with Rasputin, Gerasimov did not understand why Rasputin was worming his way into the palace. Dedyulin's conversation set off a chain of events that brought Prime Minister Pyotr Stolypin into the circle. Stolypin set the process into motion by directing Kurlov to assign gendarmes to shadow Rasputin.[208] The exercise lasted only for a few days when Nikolai II requested Stolypin to terminate the surveillance. Before Stolypin met with the emperor, the surveillance detail had to have a diary, noting his movements. Furthermore, a police agent would watch over happenings in Pokrovskoye,[209] and submit a report about Rasputin's lifestyle. The first surveillance report revealed that Rasputin was forced to leave for St. Petersburg because of his lurid affairs with girls and married women and that he was implicated in theft and other unspecified criminal activities.[210] Stolypin brought that 'evidence' to Nikolai II, who disliked any invasion into Rasputin's private life. According to Gerasimov, the emperor agreed not to meet Rasputin again because the material that Stolypin and Gerasimov presented that day had revealed that Rasputin was "not a reputable person for the Tsar to be associated with." Instead, Nikolai II asked that Stolypin "never again mention Rasputin."[211] Misinterpreting their emperor's response, Stolypin and Gerasimov, whilst returning to St. Petersburg, presumed that no further meetings would take place with Rasputin. To be on the safe side, instead of ending the surveillance as the emperor had expected, Gerasimov strengthened it. The *Okhrana* agents learned that not only did Rasputin carry on visiting Taneeva's cottage, but they also sighted the empress there at the same time, yet overlooked the obvious: palace security surrounded her at all times.

Fearing for the emperor's safety, General Gerasimov and Stolypin co-signed a secret order in October 1910, authorizing Stolypin to use his executive power to banish Rasputin. The plan failed after they saw Rasputin, returning from Tsarskoe Selo, getting into Grand Duke Pyotr Nikolayevich's car. It transpired later that Rasputin had returned to Pokrovskoye, saving Stolypin and Gerasimov from the embarrassment of executing the arrest warrant.

That arrest order remained active until Stolypin's assassination in September 1911 and with his death, the order became void.

One day after Bishop Hermogen's banishment, on 23 January 1912, the emperor sought a surveillance team to protect Rasputin[212] following the incident at the Yaroslavskii Synodal House. The team recorded his daily movements and contacts. Today, these reports are valuable to examine; not so much for the fabrications they contained, but showing how the *Okhrana* tended to operate (after Stolypin's death). In 1912, those 'reports' served another purpose. Stepan Beletsky (Director of Police from 14 December 1911[213]) deliberately asked for the upkeep on a dossier so that he had material to compromise Rasputin and permanently drive him out of town.[214] The dossier remained in Beletsky's office rather, than as required by procedure, passed on to the minister of justice (Makarov).

The author(s) of the reports accused Rasputin of hiring prostitutes, accosting female passers-by, visiting suspect bathhouses and creating public mischief.[215] However, were these reports, parts which are archived in G.A.R.F.[216] and Tobolsk, truthful? Platonov discovered what should have been identical proved otherwise, demonstrating how the scheme to discredit Rasputin operated in 1912. The agents used the codename *Temnii* (Dark One) for Rasputin, which was an expression used against individuals who steadfastly held onto a bygone era for which superstition and old traditions were considered supreme.

The surveillance diaries, from the period 1 January 1915 to 10 February 1916, were housed in two folders. Glaring discrepancies included the typing (the reports should have been handwritten), and pages left unsigned. Also, the folders did not have all the original back-up papers containing the individual police agents' field reports.[217] Significantly, the diary entries coincided with the period when Khvostov and Beletsky were in charge of the Internal Affairs Department. No entries existed after Beletsky lost his position as the Director of Police. How were the reports modified? The two police agents, Daniel Terekhov and Pyotr Svistunov, passed on their observations routinely to the Tobolsk gendarme unit, where its chief, Colonel Vladimir Dobrodeev, signed and sent off his report (marked SECRET) to General-Major Djunkovsky in Moscow. Using standard administrative procedure, Dobrodeev retained the second copy.[218] Despite the local safeguarding, the copy kept in Moscow was different, whereby the parent report did not contain compromising material. One entry revealed that Rasputin donated five hundred rubles to the local society on 11 June 1915. Years later, in exile, Beletsky confirmed that a journalist, using the pseudonym 'Veniamin Davidson,' modified the Tobolsk reports. Moreover, 'Davidson' naively retained the same journalistic style that he used in his series articles about Rasputin in *Birzheviye Vedomosti* (*The Stock Exchange Record*)[219] during Beletsky's period of office. The diaries were initially published in the Soviet journal *Krasnii Arkhiv* (*Red Archives*) in 1924.[220] When this material became accessible to biographers in the West, it seemingly provided an accurate account of Rasputin's day-to-day activities. However, none of this material was truthful.

After 30 June 1914, Maklakov, the justice minister, assigned the *Okhrana* to again watch over Rasputin. General Spiridovich controlled one set of agents, Terekhov and Svistunov, who would act as Rasputin's personal bodyguards.[221] Alexei Khvostov (Minister of Internal Affairs) appointed a second set of agents.[222] The operation passed to the newly appointed chief of the Petrograd *Okhrana*, General Konstantin Globachev, though gendarme General-Major Mikhail Komissarov received instructions to take charge of Rasputin's security in the field. Until 1909, Komissarov had experience with surveillance matters concerning "foreign embassies, foreigners and military agents,"[223] but more significantly, he was well acquainted with Beletsky. Globachev later realized that Komissarov fostered Rasputin's trust by visiting the apartment on a daily basis, then reporting to Beletsky and Khvostov.[224]

Unofficially, there was a third surveillance team. In his deposition before the Extraordinary Commission of Inquiry in 1917, Alexei Khvostov revealed that there was a group of Jewish bankers (Manus and Rubenstein[225]) who were always "hanging around" to protect their own interests, which meant that close to ten individuals were protecting Rasputin at any one time.[226] The reason why so many different operative forces existed had more to do with distrust between palace security and the *Okhrana*. Given

Russia's alliance with Britain during wartime, it was not surprising to learn from Samuel Hoare (Chief of British Intelligence Mission 1916) that the British also maintained their own special interest in Rasputin's activities.[227] Possibly the most surprising element about the surveillance agents was the one revealed by Khvostov: Aron Simanovich was a police agent.[228] The police files indicate that in 1915 the agents[229] who guarded Rasputin received the following posts:

1. One agent was usually posted inside Rasputin's apartment; unless Rasputin asked him to leave, the agent would stay near the door close to the staircase.

2. Another remained by the front door dressed as a porter (but not at the back door).

3. The third agent interacted with the internal and external posts.

4. An agent acted as the chauffeur on permanent standby (in a car provided by the *Okhrana*[230]).

Furthermore, all of Rasputin's correspondence was subject to covert examination by the *Okhrana*, which in this case involved all court connections,[231] the very practice that compromised Grand Duchess Elizaveta Fyodorovna (**Chapter Seven** and **Appendix B**).

Who Else Wants to Eliminate Rasputin?

1. The Dumbadze Telegram

In 1913 (from 14 August to 17 December), the imperial family was staying at their Livadia estate on the Crimean coast.[232] The Yalta Governor General, Ivan Dumbadze, who was also the curator of Livadia, became irritated that Rasputin was once more staying in 'his' town (at the Yalta Hotel) and that locals saw him being chauffeured around in one of the court vehicles. (Nikolai II's diary reveals that they had invited Rasputin on two occasions during their vacation in Crimea.[233]) The governor decided it was up to him to look after the emperor's majestic image during their stay.

[Radzinsky claimed that Dumbadze approached Nikolai II, but his diary does not mention that such a meeting happened.] In 1917, Stepan Beletsky explained what actually occurred. Dumbadze sent him a telegram marked *lichno* (personal), which conveyed the following message:

> "*Permission requested to eliminate Rasputin during his transportation on the launch boat from Sevastopol to Yalta.*"[234]

Dumbadze transmitted this communication in all sincerity. He, however, failed to appreciate that Beletsky would not be the only person who would read it. Upon arrival at the St. Petersburg Post Office, the typed telegram passed the desk of decipherer A. N. Mitrofanov, in the Black Chamber section. Because of its tenor, he notified Beletsky using the minster's only telephone, saying it was "interesting." Before passing on the facsimile, Beletsky wrote, "by hand only to N. A. Maklakov" (Minister of Internal Affairs). Maklakov solved Dumbadze's appeal in two ways. To remove all traces, he destroyed the communiqué and instructed Mitrofanov to "rip up the original." Since Beletsky did not get the telegram back (for his archive), he asked Maklakov if he had sent a reply, which meant that he did not intend to respond to Dumbadze's appeal. The governor's request failed to embrace its intended importance. When Beletsky travelled to Yalta (to present his regular report to the emperor), he asked the local gendarme, Colonel Trotskii, if he knew anything about a "murder during a sea transfer." Understanding the import of the question, Trotskii replied that he was aware that Dumbadze hinted about a vague plan, which involved taking Rasputin to a cliffside castle from which the *strannik* would plummet into the water below.

Rasputin was able to stroll around Yalta. Since no criminal act had taken place and no one wanted to initiate legal action against the governor, the follies Dumbadze created came to nothing. Dumbadze was to live three more years, passing away shortly after a failed operation. When General Alexander Spiridovich replaced him, he closed his eyes to the former governor's indiscretion, preferring to remember Dumbadze as "a faithful servant to the emperor and to the Motherland."[235]

2. The Khvostov-Beletsky Schemes

Oleg Platonov describes Alexei Khvostov and Stepan Beletsky as confidence tricksters[236] who were both careerists at the pinnacle of the State apparatus. Though both believed that they were Russian patriots, they used their connections to gain advantage. General Spiridovich thought that Alexandra Fyodorovna had confidence in their expertise to protect Rasputin,[237] particularly since both ministers had told her they supported Rasputin.[238] Following the successful lobbying efforts of Prince Andronikov, on 28 September 1914, the emperor appointed Alexei Khvostov to handle the internal affairs portfolio. He replaced Prince Nikolai Shcherbatov (appointed on Grand Duke Nikolai Nikolayevich's recommendation), even though he had only held that position since June.[239] Spiridovich recalled that from that day, he began to hear the rising waves of public dissension against the emperor and empress.[240] Khvostov's appointment revealed that this promotion caused many aristocrats to presume that a grubby *muzhik* was influencing the monarch.

a. When Drunkenness Can Help One's Survival

Since Khvostov and Beletsky had Rasputin under their control, the circumstances were favorable for them to purge Rasputin from Petrograd. It proved rather comical if one ignores the tragedy of their desperate attempts to eliminate him.

The first scheme developed sometime before 23 November 1914.[241] Khvostov and Beletsky decided that Rasputin should not be in the capital before the Duma reconvened. Khvostov, with cunning on his part, approached the emperor and suggested that Rasputin would enjoy, at government expense, an excursion to see holy places, which would show Rasputin's religiosity during wartime and help appease the rising dissent in the Duma.[242] Their plan centered on Rasputin's friend, *Igumen* (Father Superior) Martemian, who headed the Tyumen Troitsky Monastery. To give some credibility to their scheme, Bishop Varnava was also invited to Petrograd, and like Martemian, to stay at Prince Andronikov's apartment on Fontanka, 54.[243] Beletsky wanted Martemian to act as a travelling companion during their visit to monasteries around Russia. The justification for this lavish trip was to bring back an icon depicting St. Pavel Obdorskii for the imperial family.[244] Irrespective, Martemian wanted to benefit from this arrangement. Thus to cement the deal, he imposed one condition before this excursion was to begin: the Synod must approve his appointment to the rank of Archimandrite.[245]

When Rasputin heard about the offer of a trip, he sensed that there was more unsaid about this unprecedented generosity. On the day, Rasputin pretended to agree to the proposal. At Andronikov's apartment, a festive meal was laid out. The police department thoughtfully provided Madeira for the key guest (and wine for Martemian) from their stores. Fortuitously (or was it planned by Rasputin?), Martemian's enjoyment for alcohol had shone through before their 'departure' and everything fell apart.

Later on, Beletsky was asked why Rasputin acted in the way he had, to which he replied that Taneeva was against the trip, and Grigorii had understood that Martemian was not the trip's organizer.[246] Using the cunning of a *muzhik*, Rasputin had foiled the preparations by relying on Martemian's social habit. The expenses for the journey (to be handed to Martemian) would have been five thousand rubles, plus three thousand rubles for a manservant. In the end, two people gained from the agreement: Beletsky gave Andronikov ten thousand rubles for his generosity in accommodating the visiting clergy (whom he beforehand never met), and Martemian received his promotion.[247] Khvostov later admitted to Spiridovich that the purpose of the trip was to throw Rasputin off the moving train.[248]

b. The Hounds Begin to Circle

Khvostov and Beletsky's scheming advanced to a new level — not to demonstrate their loyalty to the monarch but to achieve professional advantage. The urgency in getting rid of Rasputin had reached its peak. The Duma, despite political differences between the party factions, consolidated its power to fight Rasputin and his perceived influence on the podium. Rasputin's death would placate the mood of the Duma and elevate its role in the public's mind.[249] During his conversation with Palace Commander General-Major Voyeikov at Tsarskoe Selo, Beletsky found out that the military was mulling over similar issues about

Rasputin's influence. Voyeikov apparently thought that palliative measures would be ineffective in the long-term and that 'other measures' ought to be considered. Voyeikov suggested that he, Beletsky, ought to pay special attention to the matter and that it was imperative to conclude it.[250] [Voyeikov omitted this conversation in his memoirs.]

By now, Khvostov and Beletsky began to consider other strategies to "liquidate Rasputin."[251] Khvostov had set up a secret fund to cover expenses for that purpose. The next idea under discussion involved enticing Rasputin from his home using the pretense of an invitation from a woman. Just as he was to enter the building, Komissarov's agents would drag him into a nearby dark blind alley and strangle him with a rope. They would either then discard his corpse into the Neva River out on the islands or perhaps bury the body under snow and rocks, near the Gulf of Finland. However, this idea proved hard to implement because Globachev's surveillance team remained in place and prevented the success of their plan. Furthermore, finding a suitable woman who was known to Rasputin and able to entice him into a car was rather problematic. Khvostov apparently became more paranoid in his determination to harm Rasputin. At one point, Khvostov showed his Browning revolver, indicating he was prepared to use it. Ideas flowed from one to the next. Finally, the conspirators settled on using Komissarov's agents, who would punch Rasputin after his return to Mikhail Snarsky's (a.k.a. Otsup-Snarsky) apartment on Kazachy *Pereulok* (Lane)[252] and end with entertainment provided by two theater women. Snarsky was an itinerant journalist whose articles appeared in many city newspapers. The next plan involved attacking Rasputin near the dimly lit entrance. The noises from the fracas would attract the concierge, after which that person would be compelled to register the incident with the local police. The assault was supposed to be a firm message for the palace, which had to concede that Rasputin ought to leave Petrograd for his own safety.

On the night when the entrapment was set, Rasputin declined to get into the car. The disappointment of this second failure caused Beletsky and Khvostov to play their own hands against each other to achieve their goals.[253] The secret rivalry between the two ministers now created an atmosphere of distrust and excessive competiveness. Khvostov was completely dissatisfied with the current state of affairs and began to plan Rasputin's murder in earnest with Komissarov but without Beletsky.

Chasing Tails Bring No Reward

Khvostov's next idea was to send a case of poisoned Madeira wine as if it came from the banker Dmitri Rubenstein, a trusted regular visitor to Rasputin's apartment. Khvostov disliked Rubenstein and was therefore unfazed in implicating this man. Komissarov obliged by bringing back some powder in a small flask following his trip to Saratov.[254] However, the tables were turning. Although Komissarov told Khvostov that he had successfully tested the substance on a cat,[255] Beletsky was told that not only was the cat story was false, the powder was a regular pharmaceutical product. It was a game of cat and mouse. Komissarov failed in his mission to eliminate Rasputin and after he lost his position,[256] the scheming became irrelevant. [Globachev mused that under his watch, "if Rasputin had been found murdered ... then all the blame would fall on me."[257]]

The Rzhevsky Matter

Without Beletsky's knowledge, Khvostov enlisted the services of an old journalist acquaintance from Nizhny-Novgorod, where he was beforehand the governor. Before his arrival in Petrograd, Boris Rzhevsky was a minor official with the Red Cross, but Khvostov recruited him as an agent[258] with a monthly stipend of five hundred rubles.[259] Khvostov sent Rzhevsky to meet the former monk, Trufanov (Iliodor), now ensconced in Christiana (later renamed Oslo) in Norway. The pretext involved the cancellation of a deal to purchase Trufamov's manuscript *Holy Devil*.[260] Djunkovsky allowed Trufanov's wife to travel abroad in order to take her husband's papers. That gesture allowed Trufanov to continue writing his manuscript that provided reproductions of the falsified love letters supposedly written by Alexandra Fyodorovna that would humiliate the imperial family and dishonor Rasputin. Khvostov, aware that Trufanov failed to murder Rasputin in 1914, thought that with his present financial impoverishment, he would be responsive in accepting this 'assignment' to eliminate his nemesis. Financial support in the form of sixty thousand rubles would flow from Khvostov's private fund to Trufanov to seal the deal.[261] The generous fee also included five false internal passports for Trufanov's clique to travel from Tsaritsyn to St. Petersburg.

During the first week of February 1916, Beletsky found out what Khvostov was up to (following Rzhevsky's rowdy border incident with a gendarme at a railway station). Beletsky had Rzhevsky searched and questioned before returning to Petrograd with his documents, which would be used against Khvostov and force him to admit his culpability. Grabbing hold of Khvostov's messenger, Beletsky proceeded to betray his superior. Unfortunately for Rzhevsky, before leaving for Norway, the journalist boasted to Vladimir Gein at the Journalist's Club that he was about to go on an important mission on behalf of Khvostov, showing him a foreign money order and adding that there was more to come.[262] When Rzhevsky returned to Petrograd, he received a series of telegrams[263] from Trufanov informing him that:

"The brothers agree." *"The brothers have been summoned."* *"The brothers have arrived."*

Simanovich found out about the plot from Gein on 4 February and told Rasputin before visiting Taneeva, who of course notified Alexandra Fyodorovna. Since Nikolai II was on military duty in Mogilev, the empress handed the matter over to General Mikhail Belyaev. After Belyaev finished speaking with Simanovich, he ordered Rzhevsky's immediate arrest. The *Okhrana* went to search Rzhevsky's apartment on Zhukovskaya *Ulitsa*, 47.[264] Even though they questioned Rzhevsky, the material Beletsky was interested in was missing. According to Globachev, Beletsky needed more evidence against Rzhevsky. Two weeks later, the arrest took place after the apartment underwent a second, more meticulous search.[265] This time they found a packet addressed to Khvostov that contained a credit note for six thousand rubles, five revolvers,[266] and a petition for mercy in case of his arrest.[267] Belyaev, who would later become the Minister of War, was finally able to telephone the empress that the matter was resolved.

As payback for his interference, Khvostov arrested Simanovich[268] outside his home after he alighted from Stürmer's car after giving evidence[269] and detained him in an *Okhrana* cell for sixteen days.[270] It was Khvostov's peculiar way to sway Rasputin's secretary to join his cause. Simanovich claimed that he feared for his life because he refused to yield to Khvostov. At the end of the detention period, Simanovich was given twenty-four hours to leave Petrograd with his family and advised to travel to the Narymsky region, a place where political offenders were often exiled. [Narym is a marshy, damp place situated on the Ob River, east of Tobolsk.[271]] Rzhevsky was sent to the same place on 27 February. As soon as the empress found out about Simanovich's relocation, she promptly revoked Khvostov's exile order.[272]

Given that Simanovich was a surveillance agent, it helps to explain why Khvostov wanted to exploit him and why the empress demanded his safe return from exile. *Okhrana* agents escorted Simanovich back to Petrograd so that Khvostov would not attempt to eliminate him along the way. Meanwhile, Khvostov began to point fingers at Beletsky's underhand activities. Their former friendship in tatters, Beletsky and Khvostov successfully betrayed each other. Interestingly, Globachev claimed that Beletsky was a man "wholeheartedly loyal to his monarch" but like Khvostov, he used men who "totally lacked principles."[273] The games the two government officials played out was over.

Unexpected Consequences Emerge After the Stürmer Investigation

Nikolai II asked Stürmer to investigate Khvostov's involvement in latest assassination attempt on Rasputin. Stürmer, a competent bureaucrat, knew about a plot to murder Rasputin. Both Beletsky and Rzhevsky had exposed Khvostov, though Beletsky admitted in his memoirs that he 'failed' to tell Stürmer of his own involvement in the conspiracy. In his deposition, Rzhevsky admitted that while he was going to act as the chauffeur, his wife would sit in the back and try to entice Rasputin with her charms to enter into the car, after which others would kill him and his corpse was to end up in the Neva River.[274]

When Spiridovich questioned Khvostov, the minister blamed Beletsky, by justifying his actions in maintaining his trumped-up story that Rasputin was a German spy. Spiridovich asked Khvostov to provide evidence to support his suspicions to General Leontiev of the Intelligence High Command so that he could take action and arrest the espionage group, along with Rasputin. Hearing these words, Khvostov became speechless and their meeting ended rapidly. Spiridovich was unable to reconcile that the man sitting in front of him, a senior government minister, had acted like a common street bandit with a huge personal agenda.[275] The matter did not end there. An official letter of demand sent from the chancellery requested that Khvostov submit the information in his possession that indicated that Rasputin was a German spy and which measures he had taken as minister of internal affairs. The predictable response was Khvostov's admission that there was no information.[276] The significance of this interaction was that it was on file. However, Khvostov's rumor would provoke a different group of conspirators to take action.

The Fourth Duma session opened with prayers on 9 February 1916 at the *Tavricheskii Dvoretz* (Taurida Palace).[277] It was also on this occasion when Nikolai II stepped inside the State Duma for the first - and what would prove to be the last - time. The emperor's attention brought confidence among the deputies, at least temporarily. On the other hand, Khvostov was about to experience a break in their support.[278]

Beletsky decided to set one more mousetrap. He suggested to Khvostov that it would be useful to find the police surveillance records bearing Komissarov's signature that would form part of a future report that should adversely reflect against Rasputin. Beletsky gave two copies of the completed report to Khvostov so it would form part of Khvostov's overall *doklad* (report) to the emperor at his next audience. After Khvostov returned from Tsarskoe Selo, Beletsky did not believe Khvostov's statement that the audience went well. He went into Khvostov's office, found the executive briefcase and opened it, finding it still contained both copies of his report and noting that neither copy had the usual notations indicating the emperor sighted them. Clearly, Khvostov did not submit Beletsky's report and instead chose to follow up with his own duplicitous plan. Rather than criticizing Rasputin as Beletsky had anticipated, Khvostov accused Beletsky of scheming against him and conspiring to murder Rasputin. Revealing his amity towards Rasputin, Khvostov recommended that Beletsky ought to be dismissed from his commission and as a concession, the emperor could offer him a gubernatorial post in Irkutsk (in Siberia). Trusting Khvostov, an *Ukaz* gave effect to that request on 13 February 1916.[279]

Days later, Boris Stürmer, after returning to Tsarskoe Selo on 18 February,[280] submitted his report to the emperor, which exposed Khvostov's criminal link to Rzhevsky. Imperial action moved swiftly. When Khvostov returned home on 3 March, he found his letter of instant dismissal, giving subversion as the reason. To complete his undignified termination, the chancellery requested the return of all awarded medals and that Khvostov must vacate his premises that same evening. Added instructions advised that Khvostov visit his rural estate for six months.[281] Khvostov promptly left Petrograd for Ryazan[282] by train. Stürmer had the task to nominate three suitable candidates to replace Khvostov.[283] In the end, Nikolai II appointed Stürmer as the new Minister of the Interior on the same day of Khvostov's departure. Stürmer concurrently retained his presidency of the Council of Ministers.[284] Stürmer was a legally trained conservative who many thought was disinterested in the political environment into which Russia was heading, concentrating instead on the minutiae of administration.[285] Spiridovich thought Stürmer was a smart bureaucrat,[286] who later proved to be of weak character,[287] because he failed to stand up against his rivals, like Rodzianko, who in turn labelled Stürmer a "dictator with full powers."[288]

Beletsky likewise suffered from the emperor's portfolio shuffle. One day after Nikolai II read through the conclusions in Stürmer's investigation, Beletsky responded to an invitation at the prime minister's apartment where Stürmer gave him an *Ukaz* requesting that he not take up the governor's office in Irkutsk. Beletsky could remain a senator, with an income of eighteen thousand rubles. To settle the dust, Stürmer advised Beletsky to leave Petrograd for a brief period.[289] Knowing where he stood, Beletsky accepted the proposal. As for General Komissarov, who managed to retain good relations with both Beletsky and Khvostov to the last moment, he became the new governor of Rostov-on-Don.[290]

Clearly, the Beletsky-Khvostov schemes conflicted with the very essence of their duties as law-abiding ministers. It was not until 20 December 1916 when the media reported some details about this sordid affair. The article revealed that Iliodor, initially a friend of Rasputin, had become his enemy to the point that he gladly planned his murder. The journalist hinted towards Khvostov's connection to the episode and that with his and Beletsky's dismissal, the episode was suppressed at the highest level.[291]

Andrei Amalrik (a former Soviet dissident) emphasized in his unfinished work on Rasputin[292] that Alexei Khvostov had undergone a remarkable conversion after becoming a government minister. Khvostov became a would-be murderer who was also a liar and a thief. Prince Andronnikov's recommendation proved to be a failure. Mikhail Rodzianko was unimpressed with Khvostov's dismissal, believing that the ex-minister had "broken his neck in combating Rasputin's clique."[293] [At the 1917 Extraordinary Commission of Inquiry, Khvostov[294] admitted that he had conspired to murder Rasputin, and Komissarov confirmed that was so[295] but was silent about his participation.]

French Ambassador Maurice Paléologue had wrongly implicated Rasputin as being the instigator of Khvostov's downfall.[296] He assumed that Stürmer's appointment relied on Alexandra Fyodorovna's recommendation.[297] Paléologue had no idea how principled the emperor was and how he administered the government behind the scenes. From the emperor's position, it would have been morally inconceivable to permit Khvostov to retain his portfolio after he chose to conspire to commit a crime.

Chapter One Photos

Счетъ ро- дившихся.	Мѣсяцъ и день.	Имена родив- шихся.	Званіе, имя, отчество и фамилія родителей, и какого вѣроиспо- вѣданія.	Званіе, имя, отчество и фамилія воспріемниковъ.
			Sloboda Pokrovskoye, Efim	**Titles, names, patronymics**
February		**Grigorii**	**Yakovlevich and Anna Vasilievna present, both Orthodox**	**and surnames of Godparents**
Male	**D.O.B** ↑ **Date Baptised**			

DOCUMENT No. 1: Published for the first time, this page
from the 1869 Pokrovskoye Church Register, confirms Grigorii
Rasputin's birthdate. The author has inserted translations.

PHOTO 1: SLOBODA POKROVSKOYE. The Rasputin's
family home (on the corner of the street), 1912.

PHOTO 2: SLOBODA POKROVSKOYE. This photograph, taken by
Anna Taneeva shows Grigorii and his wife Paraskeva Rasputina, 1914.

PHOTO 3: TSARSKOE SELO. Grigorii Rasputin
with Alexandra Fyodorovna, Alexei, his sisters,
Olga, Tatiana, Maria, Anastasia and the
children's carer, Maria Vishnyakova, 1908.

PHOTO 4: ST. PETERSBURG. Grigorii Rasputin,
Bishop Hermogen and the monk Iliodor, 1911.

PHOTO 5: Police photograph of Khioniya Guseva
soon after her arrest, 29 July 1914.

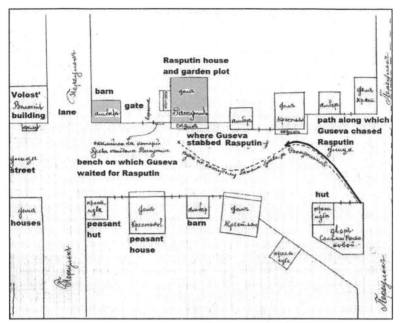

DOCUMENT No.2: Police sketch of the crime scene (modified by author) in Pokrovskoye, showing the path taken by Guseva before stabbing Rasputin in the street in front of his home, 29 July 1914.

PHOTO 6: TYUMEN. Rasputin recovering in the hospital after an attempt on his life, 1914.

CHAPTER TWO
Social and Political Intrigues

The High Ideals of St. Petersburg Society
Clash with the Modest Rasputin

The salons of the nobility were notorious for making or breaking State careers and reputations. Among those considered the most influential were the salons of Grand Duchess Maria Pavlovna (the elder) and Elizaveta Naryshkina. The men's equivalent was the Imperial Yacht Club, located close to *Dvortsovaya Ploschad* (Palace Square), which began operations in 1903.[298]Its exclusive membership list boasted top government officials, most of whom belonged to the nobility, and foreign diplomats who were trusted to mix with the imperial members. The club facilitated networking whereby social and political opinions evolved and schemes devised. Much of the gossiping would find its way to Nikolai II, some of which ran against the imperial couple. Indeed, Grand Duke Nikolai Mikhailovich, caring little about the consequences, often stoked the revolutionary flames at the club. One of his closest friends, Ambassador Sir George Buchanan, considered the duke to be a comrade who distinguished himself as a liberal-minded man.[299]

Notwithstanding the censorship on publishing the Romanov family's private matters, gossip inside the salons and the Yacht Club also served as the main vehicles for conveying information, whether credible or not; its contributors were more interested in being entertained. Indeed, two political reformers, Peter Stolypin and Sergei Witte (banned from applying for membership to the club), were not immune from their verbal attacks. When Rasputin became the focus of the club's attention, they spoke as if they knew everything about the *strannik*, when in reality no one knew anything about his private life.[300] A few of these members would have an impact on Rasputin's fate because of their incessant gossip.

Since the imperial family favored the Siberian *strannik*, notwithstanding his poor literacy skills, unpolished manners and blunt speech, Rasputin was, at first, welcomed into the salons. Aristocrats viewed Rasputin as engaging and modest, traits that allowed him to mix amongst them. Despite his clothing and unusual appearance, it was his sincerity that appealed to them. His pragmatic thoughts became wisdom, which contrasted with the esoteric mysticism that pervaded high society. The problems stemmed from rumors that spoke of Rasputin's divine gift of healing and prophesizing. Those supposed qualities made him immensely popular. However, within a few years, many of his noble admirers began to question why such an uncultured *muzhik* entered the palace. Association with Rasputin or naming him in conversation brought feelings of revulsion. Although Ambassador Buchanan admitted he never met Rasputin, he bluntly condemned him as a cunning peasant who delved in self-interest and believed in his powers.[301]

The Welcome Mat is Withdrawn and the Scuttlebutt Begins in Earnest

After Peter Stolypin's death, the toxicity against Rasputin was unleashed in the media. By 1911, the media campaign against Rasputin had amplified. Two newspapers stood out against Rasputin: *Rech* and *Russkoye Slovo* (*Russian Word*), which were controlled by Vasilii Maklakov, Gessen, and the Dolgorukov brothers.[302]

The fact that Rasputin favored traditional home remedies and distrusted commercially prepared medications would generate spiteful remarks against him. His adverse opinion about the efficacy of pharmaceuticals had aggravated Feofan when the cleric was ill. That clash, concerning modern city attitudes and the simpler rural customs, caused a rift between them in 1910, and subsequently brought their asinine conflict into the open. After Feofan recovered, wanting to disgrace the primitive-minded *strannik*, he set up a meeting with the Third Duma President, Alexander Guchkov, and a colleague from the Moscow Theological Academy, Mikhail Novoselov.[303]

Novoselov composed the first malicious exposé about Rasputin using an assumed name. Titled *The Holy Tour of Grigorii Rasputin*, it appeared on 2 March 1910.[304] A follow-up article, *More nothing about Grigorii Rasputin,*[305] appeared on 30 March. It called out to the Synod, asking when they would act against the "sex maniac." Novoselov's third assault followed in 1912 with a supplement, *Grigorii Rasputin and Mystical Debauchery,*[306] which he passed to Guchkov for publication in his brother's newspaper, *Golos Moskvy* (*Voice of Moscow*). The author accused Rasputin of belonging to the *Khlyst* sect by featuring the 'true confession' of a recently widowed woman who was defiled by Rasputin. The details were extracted from the Tobolsk Consistory File, which was archived by the St. Petersburg Synod.

Unpleasant as it was, Nikolai II had to act because of what Guchkov did. Avoiding a direct challenge, he asked Minister Makarov[307] (Stolypin's successor) to initiate police surveillance on both Rasputin and Guchkov. For the second time, the censors confiscated all unsold papers.[308] It was a futile move, which had no practical effect, because Novoselov's article was mentioned from the Duma podium. To give it additional exposure, the obliging Duma secretary and member of Guchkov's *Soyuz* 17 October Party, Mikhail Iskritskii, on 25 January 1912, posed the delegates these questions:

> *"Why are the Bishops silent, who know the activities of the insolent deceiver and seducer very well? Why are they silent ... when in their letters some of them openly call this servant a lying* Khlyst, *erotomaniac and charlatan? Where is his 'holiness?'"* [309]

The material caused a volatile reaction inside the Duma. Requesting permission to speak, Guchkov then reinforced the questions asked by Iskritskii using a different emphasis that bordered on treason: "Where are the protectors of these sacred matters: the sacred altar and sacred throne?" His final point involved a plea for the freedom of (his brother's) "independent press" to have the right "to raise its voice."[310] Iskritskii's (and Guchkov's) contrived disclosures produced the desired effect. All party factions gleefully applauded, yet offended that because the newspapers were confiscated by the *Okhrana*, the public was deprived from reading the 'truth' about Rasputin. Notably, not one party expressed an opposing view or bothered to question the veracity of the Novoselov material. Guchkov had foreseen that no one would challenge an academic of religious studies who received support from the elite clergy of the church. Just before their morning recess, Prince Georgii Lvov wanted to know "who this strange individual Grigorii Rasputin, who was isolated from ordinary laws on publishing?" [311]

Whatever copies of the printed material remained on hand commanded huge sums of money. To counteract the difficulty of the previous day, additional leaflets were printed and passed hand-to-hand the following day. Guchkov had succeeded in his quest. Practically every publishing house protested against government censorship and started to create their own articles about a man who was a complete stranger to them. As soon as the censors penalized the wrongdoers and once the newspaper businesses paid the exorbitant fines, the more swiftly they reappeared on the city streets. It did not take long before the empire would hear the name *Grigorii Rasputin*. Alexander Guchkov delivered his first calculated political blow against the monarchy with immense success, naming Grigorii Rasputin in the Duma[312] for the first time. Having activated unrest among the delegates, Guchkov did not stop with just one assault.

A File Like No Other

The newly-installed president of the Third Duma (which sat until 9 June 1912), Mikhail Rodzianko, gathered the leaders of all party factions and tried to convince them that all the compromising material, better identified as 'the facts,' should be collated and that he, as the president, would present the dossier to the emperor.[313]

It is important to step back a little now in order to understand what Rodzianko's dossier contained. Earlier, when Iliodor was visiting Rasputin in Pokrovskoye, he removed a set of letters (one written by the empress and two written by a grand duchess) from Rasputin's bedroom. Iliodor passed copies to Dr. Pyotr Badmaev (specialist in Tibetan medicine), who, acting as an intermediary, handed them over to his patient Alexander Protopopov (an *Oktobrist* in the Duma). In Iliodor's hands, the number of letters increased to seven. The text of the original letters required adjustments to stress the empress' infatuation for Rasputin.[314] One such letter ran with these sentiments:

*"My beloved, my memorable teacher, savior and mentor,
How wearying for me to be without you. My soul is only at
peace, resting, when you, teacher, are sitting by me, and I
kiss your hands and I lean my head against your blessed
shoulders. Oh how easy, easy it becomes for me. Then I
wish one thing: sleep, sleep forever on your shoulders, in
your embrace. Oh what joy to feel your presence next to
me ... For me it is so difficult, such anguish in my heart
... do not tell Anya about my sufferings without you. I wait
for you, and am suffering ... seeking your holy blessing
... M."*

This fabricated letter demonstrates how psychologically impaired
the former monk Iliodor was and does not reflect Alexandra
Fyodorovna's writing style, while the inclusion of Anna (Taneeva)
in the text was an absurdity. The letter appeared in *Russkaya Volya*
(*Russian Will*)[315] and later in Trufanov's book *Svyatoi Chert* (*Holy
Devil*). Accordingly, the fiction about Rasputin's sexual exploits
provided a titillating attack against the empress.

The day of 25 January 1912 proved to be cataclysmic for the
Romanov family. Nikolai II's sister, Grand Duchess Ksenya
Alexandrovna, noted in her diary:[316 317]

*"I went to see Alix, whom I found in bed ... We talked
about Hermogen, Iliodor, and importantly about Grigorii
Rasputin. The papers are banned from writing about him
– but for two days his name appeared again in several
of them, and these editions were confiscated. Everyone
already knows and talks about him, and what things they
say about him, i. e. about Alix and all, which is happening
in Tsarskoe. The Yusupovs came to tea – always the same
conversation — and at Anichkov [the Dowager's Palace]
during the evening and at dinner I repeated everything
that was heard. How will this all end? Horror!"*

The diary extract is astonishing in what it fails to reveal. Grand
Duchess Ksenya Alexandrovna evidently confronted Alexandra
Fyodorovna but seemingly failed to confront her brother, Nikolai
II. The other disturbing aspect is that Ksenya accepted what she
heard about her sister-in-law. It was not until 10 March that her
sister Grand Duchess Olga Alexandrovna spoke about the nature

of Alexei's real illness and that Alix had become seriously ill because of that circumstance.[318]

In relation to Novoselov's letters, Kokovtsov and Makarov met to discuss what action to take, convinced that the letters affected the prestige of the regime. Makarov was at a loss of what to do and Kokovtsov was uneasy. At first, the emperor did not address the impropriety shown by the media with his prime minister.[319] Nikolai II waited until 29 January to approach Makarov during a luncheon at the Winter Palace, saying, "I simply fail to understand, is it possible that there is no way to carry out my Will?"[320] Nikolai II blamed Guchkov and asked that Kokovtsov, Makarov and Sabler resolve the matter. Makarov received a note from Nikolai II to "once and for all to stop the persecution against Rasputin and request that my order shall be carried out."[321] Maklakov delegated that responsibility to Alexander Belgard, the head of the Government Printing division (until 1912), who said that the imperial order had nothing to do with him and asked not to become involved.[322] Makarov and Kokovtsov decided to take the easiest option, thinking it would be best that someone persuade Rasputin that he must return to Pokrovskoye.[323]

Makarov's report to Nikolai II on 3 February was unproductive. The minute Makarov raised the Rasputin incident, the emperor changed the flow of conversation, saying, "I need to think properly about this detestable gossip and we shall discuss this in more detail … but I nevertheless fail to understand in what manner it is not possible to put an end to all this dirt." After hearing about Makarov's lackluster audience, Kokovtsov's audience two days later (5 February) returned a similar result.[324] Much later, Kokovtsov learnt from Sabler that Nikolai II had something in mind. He instructed Rodzianko to act in a manner that promised to convey his conclusions.

Nikolai II asked Sabler to obtain the Tobolsk Ecclesiastical Consistory File from the Synodal Archive and hand it to Palace Commander General-Lieutenant Vladimir Dedyulin, who was to give it to Rodzianko for his evaluation. Thus, it was up to Rodzianko (the Duma) to terminate this very public affair. Rodzianko sought help from Guchkov, Badmaev, and Hermogen's aide Rodionov for an entire month. Rodzianko felt that the forces he faced "were unequal" since Alexandra Fyodorovna was "strong-willed and despotic ... and supported by the Court Clique."[325]

As soon as Dowager Empress Maria Fyodorovna learnt from Felix Yusupov (senior) that Rodzianko was preparing a file about Rasputin, she invited him to call in. The visit took place a few days before the audience with Nikolai II, at eleven o'clock in the morning. Her interest lay in the fact the file involved her own son. The dowager examined the file before Rodzianko told her everything he knew about the case. Though the dowager admitted that she knew the details in advance, sighting the 'evidence' caused her to vent, "this is terrible, this is terrible."[326] Irrespective of this audience, Maria Fyodorovna had purposefully indicated to Rodzianko her acceptance about the veracity of the material before approaching her son. Her public action was inappropriate. Likewise, Rodzianko's presentation of the file for the dowager's scrutiny, in advance of him presenting it to Nikolai II, was improper. Even so, the audience with Rodzianko identifies one lamentable issue: The dowager was the one person who had the power to put an end to the scurrilous gossiping but instead fell into the same trap set by Alexander Guchkov.

What's more, in violation of executive practice, Mikhail Rodzianko showed Zinaida Yusupova all the material before he drove off to Tsarskoe Selo for his audience at six o'clock in the evening on 26 February.[327] When Rodzianko was received by Nikolai II, he expressed concern about Rasputin, that he was "surrounded by Russia's enemies who were undermining the church and the monarchy." Rodzianko relied on broad 'evidence' that included the Synodal letters, the fabricated Novoselov letters (outlining that Rasputin was a debaucher who was interfering with the Synod) and a couple of photographs. One photograph showed Rasputin wearing a ring on his little finger, which only the clergy were permitted to wear.[328] Two other photographs, taken by the police agents, showed Rasputin standing with a group of young (fully dressed) females, and another with unidentified youths. Another photograph showed Rasputin clutching a Bible allegedly containing *Khlyst* text (the page was not shown), and lastly, two women standing next to Rasputin. The only accurate detail was Rodzianko's remark that Rasputin's "proximity to the imperial family was alarming everyone." Rodzianko declared that all of "this is lowering society and lowering the court,"[329] then ended with the remark that Rasputin was an enemy of Russia. Nikolai II thanked his minister and acknowledged that Rodzianko confirmed his loyalty to the Duma. Rodzianko, not realizing the import in the last remark, felt that he held the emperor's confidence and left.

Basking in his apparent triumph, Rodzianko headed straight to the Tavricheskii Palace[330] to gloat in front of the waiting Duma delegates. Rodzianko boasted to anyone who would listen that "with his report it was his destiny to save the monarch and Russia from Rasputin."[331] Hermogen sent his blessings through Rodionov, thanking him for "defending orthodoxy."[332]

Rodzianko was unaware that Nikolai II knew beforehand that no evidence would be forthcoming. Thus, he never responded to Rodzianko's report. Though Rodzianko thought he could deceive the emperor, he failed to recognize his fraudulence. After this episode, the emperor knew he could never expect loyalty from the president of the Duma,[333] and that Rodzianko and Guchkov were striving to get rid of Rasputin. To achieve that outcome, both were prepared to compromise their integrity and dishonor their Oath of Loyalty. Indeed, if Rodzianko honestly thought that the material he collected was accurate and that it was verifiable, then one could accept that Rodzianko presented his report in good faith. However, since Rodzianko knew that the material had contained misleading or incorrect information and he used it for the sole purpose to realize an ulterior motive, then without doubt, the man was guilty of deception. His mistake was to stand and face Nikolai II knowing he was acting deceitfully. The Ecclesiastic file was Nikolai II's way to show Rodzianko that Rasputin was held to be above suspicion. It was immaterial that the Duma representatives were offended because they assumed that Nikolai II failed to act on Rodzianko's findings.[334] To be sure, the emperor, favoring diplomacy, had acted by his silence, which was a powerful message indeed.

On 15 February 1912, the dowager decided it was time to confront what she believed to be the facts about Rasputin. To start the process, she requested that Kokovtsov visit her in the morning to discuss the matter more fully. Kokovtsov wrote in his memoirs that he held nothing back during the ninety-minute audience. He told her about the gossip on the streets that spoke of the most intimate details concerning the imperial family. Listening to these details, the dowager was unable to hold back her tears, promising Kokovtsov that she was ready to speak with her son. She ended the visit with these daunting words:

> *"My pitiful daughter-in-law fails to understand, that she is ruining the dynasty and herself. She is convinced by some passer-by, and we are powerless to divert the misfortune."*[335]

Shortly after that audience, the dowager confronted her son and his wife. Instead, Nikolai II attempted to assure his "dear mother" that all the rumors were lies and that Rasputin "was a simple and amazing person"[336] whom she should find the time to meet. Alexandra Fyodorovna concluded the conversation that left no doubt about her sincerity as a mother of a sick child:

> *"How can I not believe in him, when I see that* Malenkii (Little One) *is always better when he is near him or prays for him?"*

Grand Duchess Ksenya Alexandrovna this entry in her diary[337] on 16 February:

> *"Mama talked about her conversation yesterday. She is so pleased that she spoke out. Now they have heard and know what is being said, although Alix defended Rasputin. … Mama's only advice was to send him away now."*

Undesirably for Nikolai II, the main adversaries were emerging within his family,[338] who seized all the public gossip before pressuring him to send Rasputin away for their sake.

Finally, Makarov did what he should have done much earlier. He sought to obtain the original letters Iliodor stole from Rasputin's home. He also succeeded in getting hold of Guchkov's collection, which included one letter written to Rasputin by all four grand duchesses and one small letter written on plain postal paper that ended with the letter **A**. At his next audience, as soon as Makarov handed over the envelope containing the letters, Nikolai II wordlessly took one look at Alexandra's supposed signature and placed the envelope inside his desk drawer.[339] Makarov was dismissed on 16 December 1912 because of his laxity regarding the censorship issue. Nikolai II notified Kokovtsov that he would accept his advice and appoint a more "energetic person," Nikolai Maklakov.[340]

The Gossip Becomes Both Personal and Political

The minute Guchkov and his group introduced the "Rasputin matter" in the Duma in 1912, the *strannik* became a political creature. The Third and Fourth Duma sessions used much time in condemning Rasputin.

Evgenii Botkin, one of the family's physicians, remarked in 1913:

> *"If Rasputin did not exist, then the adversaries of the Imperial family and the preparationists of the revolution would have created him with their own babble from Vyrubova, if no Vyrubova, from me, from whoever you want."*[341]

Grand Duchess Olga Alexandrovna, a regular visitor to the palace, added this view:

> *"To judge by some of the absurdities written about him, you would imagine he practically lived at the palace."*[342]

Ivan Manasevich-Manuilov eagerly provided his readers at least one explanation why Rasputin indulged in erotic exploits. He wrote that Rasputin was bathed in his home sauna by seven naked females, with the intention that during the cleansing he was "becoming closer to God."[343] The absurdity of the tale exposed two fundamental issues. It conveniently ignored the fact that the Russian peasant sauna could never have accommodated so many people at any one time. More telling, his article only appeared to readers who lived too far away from any persons who could have challenged Manasevich-Manuilov's 'evidence.'

No matter what Makarov attempted to do, the press's freedom to publish material about Rasputin had prevailed over the emperor's requests. Following the administrative reforms that came after the 1905 October Manifesto was promulgated, the Minister of Internal Affairs no longer had the authority to restrain the media from writing about Rasputin and his exploits.[344] That was why

Belgard refused the minister's request and the media's assault against Rasputin kept on.

Georgii Sazonov, the Petrograd journalist and editor of *Rossiya*, who was also a member of the Holy Synod[345] (the first private citizen to offer Rasputin temporary accommodation in St. Petersburg), advised Rasputin that he should consider taking the newspapers to court to stop the salacious articles directed against him. However, the response to that suggestion was always the same: "What they are saying about me! God will forgive them."[346] Matrena said that although people judged her father, he did not judge anyone.[347] Given the nature of any litigation, it would have proved sensational in its own right. If Rasputin pursued that advice, the onus was on the plaintiff (Rasputin) to prove the information lacked the truth.

Alexandra Fyodorovna's friend Yuliya (Lili) Dehn wrote, "Rasputin's influence was purely mystical" and "there was absolutely no sensual attraction … such a monstrous thing never happened … her morals were the ultra-strict morals of her grandmother" (Queen Victoria). Dehn stressed here that she knew Alexandra Fyodorovna, whereas the dowager and those who frequented the court did not. At all times when the empress met with Rasputin, it was with the consent of her husband. Alexandra Fyodorovna was on friendly terms with Rasputin only because, for her, "Our Lord did not choose well-born members of Jewish society for His followers."[348] Never left alone, Alexandra Fyodorovna was perfectly frank with all her associations and always appeared with palace security and ancillary staff. Admittedly, she did demonstrate a naïve sense of duty towards the one person whom she believed had healing powers.

Although he was aware that Nikolai II had not forced him to leave St. Petersburg, Rasputin returned to Pokrovskoye in May 1912, disillusioned that the emperor seemingly lacked the strength to shield him from the gossip. In October, everything changed for Rasputin after he received a message from Taneeva telling him that Alexei was in a critical condition in Spala. On 5 October, he lay dangerously ill and this time was so close to death that he received the last anointing sacrament. Rasputin's telegraphic reply gave assurance that Alexei would survive this ordeal. Regardless of the message, Alexei's distraught parents failed to take in that there was already an improvement.[349] His temperature decreased with consequent pain reduction. The final doctor's report issued on 1 November implied the crisis had passed.[350] Alexandra Fyodorovna (like the attending physicians) failed to comprehend that Alexei's recovery was a natural process, preferring to accept that Rasputin had once again alleviated Alexei's suffering, this time from a great distance. Modern information about hemophilia reveals that Alexei's body responded with rest and in time, slowly healing itself in the same way it had after every other crisis. Fundamentally, no one at the time of the Spala crisis was in any position to argue against the psycho-emotional anguish of a mother who thought her son was dying. After that incident, no one could challenge her steadfast beliefs.

The jubilee year, 1913, was the final year of peace and national celebration for the Russian Empire. The entire nation celebrated the tercentenary of the Romanov dynasty. However, the tribute in the Kazan Cathedral on 21 February had proved to be more than just an impressive commemorative occasion for Rasputin. Rodzianko went outside the cathedral to get some fresh air when he was approached by Baron Ferzen, who told him a man was spotted inside, standing in front of the area designated for Duma delegates and when asked, he refused to leave. Rodzianko returned inside and saw the *strannik,* who was seen wearing a dark raspberry-colored silk *kosovorotka* (Russian blouse) adorned by a large pectoral cross (worn by clergy only), wide black cloth trousers, with matching waistcoat and high, lacquered boots. Rodzianko asked, "why are you here?" to which Rasputin replied, "what is it to you … what do you want from me?" Rodzianko then asked the "despicable heretic" to leave. Rasputin said that he was "invited by the will of more important people than he was," showing his invitation. Uncomfortable with Rasputin's response and presence, Rodzianko insisted he leave. In order to avoid unpleasantness, Rasputin stepped outside, wearing his sable coat and alighted into his waiting *Okhrana* car.[351]

War in Europe Begins and Rasputin Fears for Russia's Future

Taneeva claimed that many hours after Germany had declared war on Russia on 19 July (1 August N. S.), the empress was oblivious of this event.[352] British Ambassador Buchanan noted that Russia did not mobilize until forced to do so. Despite the German army's readiness for battle, Russia, by contrast, was inadequately equipped.[353] Following a full day of intense deliberations, by the evening of 17 July, Nikolai II accepted that it was crucial to mobilize Russian forces, since Austria had already done so.[354] General Danilov, Grand Duke Nikolai Nikolayevich's adjutant, admitted that the Russian military began to mobilize on the night of 18 July 1914,[355] before the official public announcement.

On Sunday 20 July 1914, Nikolai II signed the *Manifest* [356] in the Nikolayevskii Hall of the Winter Palace, declaring war on Germany. Following a *moleben* (prayer service) with Father Alexander Vasiliev reading the *Manifest* to the imperial family, ministers, journalists and others, the emperor walked towards the balcony that faced Alexandrovskaya *Ploschad* (now Dvortsovaya Square). By three o'clock in the afternoon, thousands had gathered holding icons, banners, and portraits of the emperor to hear the news that Russia was at war. Seeing the sovereign standing on the balcony, men removed their headwear. Many in the crowd spontaneously knelt on the stones, others sang the hymn *Spasi Gospodi Lyudi Tvoya* ("God Save Thy Nation"), people wept.[357] The sovereign announced the coming war then lowered his head (Photo 7) before retreating inside.[358] It took only minutes. No one, of course, could predict that this was the last time the sovereign would face his people in this solemn way.

The crowds moved to Nevskii *Prospekt* sharing their patriotic enthusiasm, raising flags and placards of the sovereign and his heir while men began to enlist into the army. Much of the Russian nation supported their sovereign's response to the Kaiser and the army welcomed the "announcement calmly and with certainty."[359] Though Rasputin, together with Alexandra Fyodorovna, the Minister of the Imperial Court, Count Frederiks, and Sergei Witte were against the war, their objections muted amid the fervor that gripped the nation. Danilov noted that once again "the internal mood in our Motherland"[360] would influence the outcome of this new war. The Duma and State Council united like "all intelligent society greeted the news about the war."[361]

After the first few days of the war, on 23 July, the British Foreign Office informed their ambassador in Russia that England was a partner in the *Triple Entente*[362] with France and Russia. At the Yacht Club, the conversations had turned pessimistic; many believed that Austria and Germany had dealt a mortal blow against the monarchies of Europe.[363] Grand Duke Nikolai Nikolayevich became the Supreme High Commander[364] of the army and navy and departed for the front.

On 5 August, after Nikolai II declared Russia's respect for the alliance, the formalities in Moscow culminated in a special *liturgiya* (liturgy)[365] at the Uspenskii Cathedral in the presence of the imperial family, as well as the French and British ambassadors.[366] Under the blazing sunshine, church bells chimed as the crowd expressed its support. The officers thought this war would be short-lived.[367] Speaking with Sazonov, the Minister of Foreign Affairs (who received the German ultimatum in Kaiser Wilhelm's name declaring war on Russia[368]), said that they should recall what happened in 1905 (War with Japan). He said one of the reasons why peace came early had to do with Russia's domestic difficulties.

Within this milieu, Matrena explained why her father had an aversion to war:

> "*His horror of war and its cruelties, his pity for its innumerable victims, and his doubts as to the outcome of such a massacre – in short, from all that is the very essence of true pacifism. … He had the outlook of a peasant who understands the reality of life.*" [369]

Given Matrena's clarification, it makes sense why Rasputin sent the emperor a letter (DOCUMENT No. 3) from his Tyumen hospital bed. Rasputin's message indicated his fears about the pointless death of Russian men and the inevitable devastation of land and Russia itself. Although some have construed Rasputin's words as prophecy, a closer look at the wording reveals that there was nothing prophetic about them. Danilov and Sazonov understood the internal dangers Russia was facing and that the nation would be doomed if she appeared politically unstable (to her enemies), a circumstance that could spark upheaval. Rasputin was familiar with the character of the ordinary people and it was this uncomplicated understanding of Russia's weaknesses and her strengths, which he had identified in the following way:

"Defeat will bring in its wake the ruin of the dynasty, and in consequence the ruin of all Russia."[370]

If Russia saw victory, then the emperor would enjoy strengthening of his reign, which would have curbed revolutionary fervor. Unfortunately, Russia's entry into the theater of war had exacerbated the domestic political turmoil.

Rasputin left St. Petersburg and returned at the end of August to the renamed city, Petrograd. In the first days of combat, hospitals barely coped with the numbers of wounded and the diseased. Military incursions into enemy territory during the first weeks proved devastating. The poorly-provisioned army was let down by mostly ill-trained, illiterate peasants, who were thousands of kilometers away from the familiarity of their village life and forced to fight an enemy they knew nothing about. Along with these tribulations, the men began to endure too many military failures. The losses were horrendous; one million had fallen in the first phase of the war.[371]

With the crisis on the Western Front, the former patriotic hysteria gave way to disillusion. Anti-German feelings spread across the city, with denunciations and many German-sounding businesses confronting rampant damage and burglary. The citizens shifted their abuse and pointed accusatory fingers towards Alexandra Fyodorovna and Rasputin, accusing them of conducting espionage for the Kaiser's side. Without doubt, espionage is problematic in any war, but the present flurry of rumormongering had escalated only because the masses accused the empress of being a *Nemka* (German). [By contrast, Alexandra Fyodorovna's sister, Grand Duchess Elizaveta Fyodorovna, suffered that accusation once in June 1915 during a protest outside her monastery. After listening to a warning to respect her vocation as an orthodox abbess of her religious order, the crowd dispersed.[372] Grand Duchess Maria Pavlovna, the elder, *née* Duchess Marie of Mecklenburg-Schwerin, successfully concealed her origins.]

At some point during 1915, the branches of the Romanov family referred to Rasputin and Alexandra Fyodorovna as the *German Party*. Among that group were Dowager Empress Maria Fyodorovna, Grand Duchess Elizaveta Fyodorovna, Grand Dukes Nikolai Nikolayevich, Nikolai Mikhailovich and Alexander Mikhailovich. The most prominent outsider was Zinaida Yusupova, who enjoyed a cordial relationship with Mikhail Rodzianko, as an extended family member (by marriage). The group's conversations centered on the idea that it may be best if the empress was secluded in a monastery for the duration of the war.[373]

The empress overcame her shyness and, accompanied by her two eldest daughters, Olga and Tatiana, they attended a two-month first aid course. They acquired their Sister of Mercy certificates in order to tend to the needs of the wounded in the infirmary they had set up in Catherine Palace at Tsarskoe Selo.[374] Two others in the extended family, Grand Duchesses Olga Alexandrovna and Maria Pavlovna the younger (Dmitri Pavlovich's sister), put on Sister of Mercy uniforms and confronted the dying and the suffering on a daily basis. Through the Red Cross, the empress established numerous infirmaries, which included the one in the Winter Palace in Petrograd, at the Fyodorovskii *Gorodok,* and at the Catherine Palace (referred to as the *Dvortsovii Lazaret* or infirmary, of which there were fifty in Tsarskoe Selo alone[375]). Some were strictly for officers and others accommodated ordinary soldiers.[376]

Rasputin was a regular visitor to these infirmaries. There he comforted the wounded soldiers and extracted information for the many relatives who sought details about their loved ones. Rasputin began to receive petitions in his Gorokhovaya *Ulitsa* apartment from the distressed relatives who sought news of their husbands, fathers, sons or family relatives who had become prisoners-of-war. Gone was the convivial parade of admirers who used to patronize the apartment.[377] The war's beginning had changed everyone. No one of consequence bothered Rasputin, instead leaving him with his undesirable pacifistic views. One other matter changed for Rasputin. He could no longer freely enter the palace. It took considerable effort to receive an audience with the emperor. One encounter took place on Monday evening, 25 August.[378] Again

Rasputin attempted to sway Nikolai II to stop the war, oblivious that Russia was in an alliance, rendering his pleading futile.

"In war Russian people die and when it ends, even victory will turn out to be defeat." [379]

Rasputin was trying to stress that the downside of Russia's victory relies on the death of too many Russians, which was an extreme price to pay. With considerable energies being directed towards the war effort, no one stopped to listen to Rasputin's words. Matrena explained that following his last meeting with the emperor, her father became so depressed from the shame of his rejection that he exposed "the darkness of his soul" by drinking more alcohol. He remained with his private thoughts about the immorality of war, notwithstanding that his prayers remained unanswered.[380]

A Disaster That Brought New Beginnings

During a snowstorm on 2 January 1915, a train driver, not noticing a railway marker,[381] caused his train to collide with an oncoming steam train.[382] The train was en route from Tsarskoe Selo to Petrograd with Anna Taneeva among its passengers sitting in the first carriage. One of Count Grabbe's *Konvoi* officers (Nikolai II's personal Cossack escort) pulled Taneeva out from the wreckage.[383] Both legs were badly injured (one was broken in two places) and there was bleeding from the mouth due to one shattered facial bone. Given it was minus twenty degrees outside, the officer carried her inside the railway storage building. She did not receive medical assistance because the rescuers assumed she was dying. Taneeva spent the next four hours covered by a *shinel* (long coat) before being conveyed unconscious to the Tsarskoselskii (Tsarskoe Selo) infirmary. Later, it transpired that Taneeva also sustained an injury to her spinal column.[384] Due to the severe blood loss, with little hope for her recovery, Taneeva received the last sacrament in Nikolai II's presence.[385]

Even so, when the palace summoned Rasputin, he gratefully returned to Tsarskoe Selo. General Voyeikov escorted Rasputin to the bedside of the comatose patient, as he started to pray whilst holding Anna's hand. Despite repeating her name, Anna failed to react. Rasputin turned around and said to those standing around him that Anna would live but would become a cripple.[386] Possibly because of his last drinking bout, in combination with overall fatigue and not eating proper meals, Rasputin collapsed in the adjacent room. Splayed out on the floor, his face became very pale as perspiration spread through his garments.[387] Despite this surprising leave-taking, Alexandra Fyodorovna again presumed that she had witnessed a miracle after hearing that her friend would survive. Rasputin's affiliation with the court appeared renewed after Alexandra Fyodorovna rang the apartment to enquire about his health. As for Taneeva, she became more devoted to Rasputin as the one who stimulated her recovery.[388]

Moscow Nights

The Yar Restaurant story has received prominence in all biographies of Rasputin. When Platonov researched the topic over a decade ago, his trail ended after he ascertained that one *Okhrana* document dated 26 March was missing in G.A.R.F. Trusting that result, he supposed the Yar incident was fictitious. Since then, it appears that the document exists, confirming that Rasputin did visit the Yar Restaurant.[389] [Favored past patrons were Alexander Pushkin and Lev Tolstoy.] Moreover, the *Okhrana* surveillance report reveals that his visit did not involve sexual antics as universally assumed by most biographers. As the story went, at eleven o'clock at night, a small group reserved a private room at the restaurant.[390] Rasputin entered the restaurant inebriated and insisted the female choir dance for him. After dancing the so-called "Russian," Rasputin became sexually psychopathic, exposing himself whilst conversing with singers from the hired chorus. Rasputin boasted that the kaftan he was wearing was made especially for him by the *starukha* (crude expression for an old lady, implying the empress). Some performers received ten or fifteen ruble bills, and at the end of his visit at two o'clock in the morning, Rasputin's young female companion paid their expenses before leaving.

The text of this story appears on official paper as a secret memorandum.[391] The chief of the Moscow Gendarmerie, Colonel Alexander Martynov, composed and typed the memo[392] four days after Djunkovsky spoke to Nikolai II, which in reality turned out to be two months after the described event. Djunkovsky repeated that story at the Commission of Inquiry in 1917, which was also included in his memoirs.[393]

The first surveillance report regarding the Moscow trip, dated 25 March, was telegraphed by Globachev[394] to Colonel Martynov in Moscow:

> *"Institute absolutely secret surveillance for Grigorii Rasputin surveillance nickname* Temnii (Dark One) *left for Moscow on Kourier No.1. .... Telegraph me on No.139."*

In response, the first Moscow surveillance report dated 26/27 March recorded Rasputin's activities. It states a vehicle collected three individuals at one o'clock in the morning and left them at the Yar Restaurant, where they remained some hours. Crucially, the *Okhrana* did not report anything out of the ordinary. So where did the alternate story evolve?

Djunkovsky, the Deputy Minister of Internal Affairs (to Maklakov), was also commander of the gendarmerie and police[395] stationed in Petrograd. He decided that Rasputin's visit to Moscow provided him the perfect opportunity to destroy him, even if an incident had to be concocted.[396] Yearning to halt the emperor's association with Rasputin, Djunkovsky spent one day preparing his material about a man who "was shaking the throne and threatening the dynasty."[397] This involved contacting Martynov in Moscow and asking for his urgent re-appraisal regarding the Yar visit two months earlier. Armed with his 'information,' Djunkovsy was ready to be received by Nikolai II at one of his regular audiences in Tsarskoe Selo. He, as normal, presented his *doklad* (report) about the disturbances on *Krasnaya Ploschad* (Red Square) and other parts of Moscow that began on 26 May,[398] explaining how the crowd yelled that the empress ought to spend her days in a convent and sought the emperor's abdication in favor of Grand Duke Nikolai Nikolayevich.[399] After finishing his oral account that included organizational issues, Djunkovsky sought permission to speak about a matter that "was not giving me peace." He promptly condemned Rasputin and included a story about his scandalous night at the Yar Restaurant. All throughout, the emperor stood silent. When Djunkovsky finished, Nikolai II requested the memorandum note linked to this oral exposé. Handing it over, Djunkovsky stressed that the memorandum was the only copy, before noticing that Nikolai II, without glancing at it, placed the paper inside his writing desk drawer. Nikolai II, lastly, invited Djunkovsky to let this matter remain with them, before politely thanking him. With the audience over, Djunkovsky felt pleased that he executed his duty well.[400] Afterwards, Nikolai II met Grigorii on 9 June, [401] whilst stepping back to see if Djunkovsky would disregard his final request.

Soon after, Djunkovsky spoke with Grand Dukes Nikolai Nikolayevich and Dmitri Pavlovich about his audience with Nikolai II, giving them a duplicate of his candid report. Djunkovsky's scheme proved most effective in another way; the sordid exposé gave the Romanov family one more reason to vilify Rasputin. Yet, despite his assistance, Djunkovsky played a duplicitous game against the grand dukes as well.

It did not take long before Alexandra Fyodorovna discovered that Dmitri Pavlovich discussed the contents of the Djunkovsky's exclusive report with others, writing to Nikolai II (at army headquarters):

22 June 1915. *"Ah dearest, he is not an honest man, he has shown that vile, filthy paper (against our Friend) to Dmitri who repeated it all to Paul and Ella. - Such a sin ... that you are bored with these filthy stories and wish that he* [Djunkovsky] *should be severely punished. ... At headquarters one wants him to be got rid of ... ah, it's so vile – always liars, enemies - I long knew Djunkovsky hates Grigorii, and the Preobrazhenskii clique therefore dislikes me ... And the Duma dare not broach this subject when they meet – Loman says they will, so as to force one to get rid of Grigorii and Anya* [Taneeva] *..."* [402]

As the former governor of Moscow, Djunkovsky had excellent connections. Now living in Petrograd, it was easy to get a sleazy story with Martynov's (the new chief of the *Okhrana* department) assistance.[403] Using the standard Moscow *Okhrana* letterhead, Martynov's task involved reshaping the 26 March report whilst bearing his signature. Carelessly, he dated his revised report on the day it was composed, 5 June 1915. Djunkovsky, failing to notice the discrepancy between dates, affixed Martynov's report to the file. The most amusing part in Martynov's rephrased report must be his inclusion of seventy-eight year old Reshetnikova partying with Rasputin late at night. **Sablin's Secret Inquiry**

Wanting to find out if there was any truth to Djunkovsky's Yar incident report, Nikolai II sent his former Commandant of the Imperial Yacht, *Shtandart*, Nikolai Sablin, to Moscow.[404] Sablin discovered there was no documentation to indicate Djunkovsky had authorized Martynov to conduct an investigation immediately following the alleged incident. No one, including the singers, had been asked to submit depositions.[405] Sablin, knowing that visiting the Yar Restaurant was pointless, had proven Djunkovsky's deception.

Two months passed before Djunkovsky was relieved of his duties on 15 August, when Minister of Internal Affairs Nikolai Shcherbatov temporarily took over his duties (until September).[406] The dismissal caused considerable uproar, all blaming the empress and Rasputin. Grand Duke Nikolai Nikolayevich's group was convinced that Djunkovsky's dismissal was a signal that Rasputin's influence had not diminished.[407] In support, Guchkov sent a letter to Djunkovsky on 17 August, saying:

"My soul is with you, I know that you are suffering. But do not grieve; rejoice about your liberation from prison. You see 'they' are doomed, no one can save them." [408]

After summoning Grand Duke Nikolai Nikolayevich and explaining the facts of the case, Nikolai II hoped that other interpretations on the matter would halt.[409]

Reservations and Revelations

Much later, former Moscow governor General Alexander Adrianov sent a letter to Anna Taneeva (through Beletsky) in which he admitted the Yar incident was a fabrication.[410] Beletsky explained that Adrianov attempted to see Rasputin, but he failed because, as Rasputin explained, "when he was the governor he should have looked at what Djunkovsky wrote about him." Not surprisingly, Martynov failed to mention the Yar incident in his memoirs, which were published posthumously in 1972 in the United States.[411]

Instead, he concentrated on the Moscow demonstrations and his association with Felix Yusupov (senior) and Governor Adrianov. Likewise, Djunkovsky only brought up his report and said nothing about Martynov's contribution.

Accordingly, Tatiana Mironova's assumption that a Rasputin look-alike (a double) had performed on the specified evening is an absudity.[412] This author failed to appreciate Globachev's remark in 1917 and the reason for his vigilance. Indeed, Mironova's speculation leaves this author asking why was the double used once and why only in Moscow?

There is one crucial aspect about this affair, which reveals why Nikolai II acted in the way he had. General Globachev testified to the Extraordinary Commission of Inquiry in 1917, that as the head the *Okhrana*, he always knew "who Rasputin saw and where he went" through his own special agent.[413]

The Supreme Dismissal

By August 1915, Rodzianko conceded that faith in Nikolasha's military leadership skills was waning and that General Alexeev must replace his chief of staff, General Yanushkevich, because of his incompetence.[414] Rodzianko was distressed about the rumor (stemming from Prime Minister Ivan Goremykin) that Nikolasha was facing dismissal and that Nikolai II was going to step in as the Supreme Commander. He presumed that the decision had to do with the empress' loathing for Nikolasha, claiming she wanted "to move the sovereign away from governing internal matters when he was located at Stavka," the new military headquarters in Mogilev, Minsk District, rather than leaving the position open for nomination. At the time of his audience with the emperor on 11 August, Rodzianko expressed dismay after hearing that the impending imperial decision was irrevocable. Possibly because of his visit, Rodzianko suffered a heart attack during his return from Tsarskoe Selo.[415] On 21 August, the Duma expressed its collective grievance against the imminent removal of Nikolai Nikolayevich.[416] Notwithstanding their position, Nikolai II issued an *Ukaz* on 23 August, designating himself as the new commander in chief. In reality, the majority of soldiers were satisfied with the change in supreme leadership.[417]

Grand Duke Andrei Vladimirovich reflected the feelings of most of the other members of the Romanov family regarding Nikolasha's dismissal. Ultimately blaming Rasputin, he wrote, "there is only one way now ... to finish off Rasputin."[418] One week later, he wrote this:

> **1915. 24 August:** *"In the afternoon I went to see Aunt Minnie* [the dowager] *... and found her in a despondent state ... She believes that his removal will lead to the inevitable death of N.* [Nikolai II]*, since they will not forgive him for this. ... blames Alix over everything."* [419]

Rodzianko, now fully recovered and not digressing from his plotting, approached Khvostov to demand Rasputin's arrest. The matter received attention at a government meeting on 24 August, but Khvostov said there was no reason to facilitate such a course of action.[420] Consequently, the Progressive Blok Party began its existence on the same day by signing a formal *Agreement*.[421] It was a coalition of leftist and centralist parties, the *Kadet* Party (reformists such as Vasilii Maklakov), the *Oktoberists* (Guchkov and Rodzianko), and the Nationalists, but it excluded the extremist left-wing faction. The policies of the party entailed the continuation of the war and a platform that would bring Russia a constitutional democracy.

The Final Chapter

On 5 September 1915, Grigorii sent a telegram to Anna Taneeva asking her to intercede with Alexandra Fyodorovna so that his only son, twenty-year old Dmitri, could be discharged from the Tyumen Rifles and made available "at the direction of the Tsarskoselskii military chief." Nikolai II ignored the request, since he could not be seen to favor one son over any other in wartime. Alexandra Fyodorovna instead forwarded the request through Colonel Loman to the new Minister of War, General Belyaev.[422] Dmitri joined the medical military train (No. 143) in October. The twenty-carriage train conveyed wounded soldiers from Evpatoria-Simferopol-Kursk-Moscow to the various hospitals in Tsarskoe Selo.[423] In this way, Dmitri could traverse the nation in relative safety and demonstrate his duty to the war effort.

Rasputin was beckoned one last time to pray over Alexei on 3 December 1915. This occurred after Alexei contracted a cold and his sneezing and coughing brought on a persistent nosebleed. Professor Fyodorov resolved the condition was serious enough for the emperor and his ailing son to discontinue their visit to the field and return to Mogilev headquarters.[424] The next day, after enduring considerable blood loss and an elevated temperature, Alexei became weaker. Reaching Mogilev at midday, the revised medical advice necessitated continuing on to Tsarskoe Selo. A second overnight train trip lay ahead. With his head resting on Klimentii Nagorny's (Alexei's carer) knees, the boy's condition fluctuated from bad to worse. Twice he lost consciousness along the way. The train stopped a number of times because of the jolting movements along the tracks. Rasputin sent a telegram at 6.20 in the morning, which read: "God will help, will recover." Despite Spiridovich's claim that the telegram's arrival had coincided with the cessation of bleeding, it resumed on the way to the palace.[425] Once in his bedroom, one of Alexei's nostrils was cauterized to stem the blood flow, a procedure that needed repeating the next day. [This proves the bleeding did not stop at 6.20 the previous day.] Though Nikolai II noted that the bleeding ceased before Rasputin's arrival on 6 December, Alexandra Fyodorovna still summoned him to the palace.[426] Taneeva's story—that once Rasputin prayed by Alexei's bed, the bleeding ceased—was wrong, but Rasputin was right to advise the boy's condition was not serious. Oblivious to the sequence of events, the empress reaffirmed her faith in Rasputin, whereby "she became unconquerable, like a granite cliff"[427] in her resolve that he perfomed God's work.

The Last Imperial Encounters with Rasputin

The last time Nikolai II met Rasputin was at Taneeva's house a few weeks before the murder. That occasion happened on Friday 2 December 1916, just two days before he and Alexei were to depart to Mogilev.[428] When the imperial couple rose to leave, the emperor asked Grigorii to bless them all (an orthodox custom when taking leave from the clergy —or from a *strannik,* in this case).[429] Rasputin responded, "No, today you bless me." [430] Some people have claimed that Rasputin was able to predict his own looming death. He certainly was aware that many wanted him dead and by December 1916, he had no doubt that the next assault on his life was imminent.[431]

Alexandra Fyodorovna met Rasputin a few more times at Anna's cottage and lastly on 5 December.[432] The next day, she wrote to her husband, saying:

"We spent yesterday evening comfortably and peacefully in the small house. Kind big Lili also came later, as did Munya Golovina. He was in a good and joyous mood. – It seems that he is always thinking about you and that everything will proceed well." [433]

On 11 December, the empress travelled by imperial train with the grand duchesses and Grand Duke Ioann Konstantinovich and Prince Andrei Alexandrovich to Novgorod for the day. Attended by the governor of Novgorod, they visited several infirmaries to offer their support to the wounded. At the Nobility House, the empress received five thousand rubles from the Women's Committee to assist the wounded soldiers. Alexandra Fyodorovna returned home with a number of icons (as gifts), one of which was to be given to Rasputin.[434] Radzinsky was wrong to say that Rasputin accompanied Alexandra Fyodorovna.[435] The letter to her husband reveals:

"My angel, yesterday we had lunch with our Friend at Anya's. Everything was so nice; we gave an account of our journey." [436]

The Final Days

Beletsky revealed that on 13 December, Aron Simanovich notified Taneeva that with his help, Rasputin had incinerated all letters and telegrams and deposited in the bank several thousand rubles in both of his daughters' names.[437] The next day, 14 December, Rasputin was in a jovial mood when Beletsky last saw him.[438] Nikolai II received a letter dated 17 December from Alix, which stated "our Friend these days was in a good mood, but nervous."[439]

Taneeva arrived at Gorokhovaya, 64, at 8 p.m. on the evening of 16 December, in order to present Rasputin with the special icon. The empress, the four grand duchesses, and Anna Taneeva signed the back of icon to mark the empress' visit to Novgorod. Thinking about the peculiarity of Rasputin's late night invitation to meet with Felix Yusupov's wife,[440] she allegedly stressed that if the invitation related to their embarrassment about Rasputin visiting the Yusupovs during the day, then it would be more dignified if he declined the invitation.[441] Returning to Tsarskoe Selo, Taneeva told Alexandra Fyodorovna about Rasputin's intention to visit the Yusupovs. She responded that there must have been some error because Irina was in Crimea with Yusupov's parents.[442] The significance of this conflicting information was ignored.

Matrena thought that Protopopov came to see her father at 7 p.m.;[443] in fact, his visit happened after 11 p.m., once the surveillance left at Rasputin's insistence.[444] Rasputin told Protopopov that he was going out later that evening, refusing to reveal what that appointment entailed. Protopopov left shortly after his arrival.

Ignoring Matrena's protestations, Rasputin calmly waited for Felix Yusupov to arrive. On this night, Rasputin paid considerable attention to his grooming. He dressed in his finest blue silk shirt, which the empress had sewn, black velvet trousers, and long leather boots. Felix entered into the kitchen and followed Rasputin into his bedroom, in which glowed the flame from the *lampada* (a special oil lamp used for permanently illuminating icons). The bed appeared as if Rasputin had recently rested on it. Yusupov sensed that Rasputin smelled of cheap soap. Before leaving his apartment after midnight,[445] Rasputin crossed himself as was customary before any departure, put on his beaver coat and *ushanka*[446] (fur hat with earflaps), and closed the back door behind him before descending the badly lit stairs into the courtyard with his friend. On this night, Rasputin's peasant instincts had betrayed him because he trusted people he liked.

Chapter Two Photos

PHOTO 7: St. PETERSBURG. The Emperor lowers his head after announcing Russia's entry into the War from the balcony of the Winter Palace while several people kneel with lowered flags, 20 July 1914.

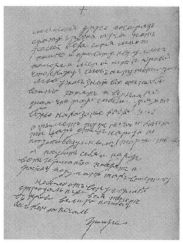

DOCUMENT No. 3. Copy of the letter Grigorii Rasputin sent to the Emperor expressing his concern about Russia's future in 1914.

TRANSLATION

Dear Friend, Once again I say a thunder cloud is above Russia, pity, much grief, darkness and no gleam of hope; tears now a sea and there are no measures, and blood? What to say? There are no words ... horror. I know, all want war from you and truly, not knowing, for the sake of destruction. God's punishment is heavy ... You are tsar, father of the people, do not allow the senseless to celebrate and destroy oneself and the people. Think, that everything is different ... everything drowns in great blood, destruction without end sadness.

Grigorii

CHAPTER THREE
Conspiracy to Commit Murder

On Saturday afternoon, 17 December 1916, at the northern limit of the city, two workers crossing the Petrovskii Bridge noticed stains on the fresh white snow which looked like blood. Their vigilance set off a cascade of events that would signal the beginning of the death throes of the Russian Empire. The gendarmes who swarmed onto the bridge all had the same thought. They had arrived at the site where Rasputin's corpse was most likely dumped into the part of the river that was not yet covered with ice.[447]

Due to media censorship, the Sunday evening Moscow newspaper *Russkiye Vedomosti* (*The Russian Gazette*), using the heading "Sensational Murder", hinted that there was the suspicion of a murder having taken place at one of the aristocratic residences in Petrograd.[448] Grand Duke Andrei Vladimirovich copied the following sentence from *Birzheviye Vedomosti* (*The Stock Exchange Gazette*):

> "*Today during the sixth hour of the morning, in one of the aristocrats' house in the center of the capital, after a reception, the life of Grigorii Rasputin-Novy ended unexpectedly.*"[449]

Various versions as to how the murder might have taken place appeared in newspapers around the country during the next couple of days, though none of the published information was accurate. The reason being that the investigators did not reveal how the murder was carried out.

The painstaking search for Rasputin's corpse came to a halt on Monday 19 December after one of the river policeman, who was sweeping the ice surface with his broom close to the riverbank, noticed a dark patch where he stood. With considerable effort, the corpse was raised to the surface by several policemen using gaffs and a wooden platform. The twine that originally bound the hands snapped, allowing them to separate as the corpse was uplifted onto the surface.[450] When the river debris was removed off the head, a battered and bloodied, swollen male face became visible;

everyone was glaring at Rasputin's corpse.

The popularly accepted version of Rasputin's murder was delivered by two self-confessed murderers, Prince Felix Yusupov and Vladimir Purishkevich. One intriguing aspect about this one hundred-year old criminal case is that the plan to murder Grigorii Rasputin involved many individuals from diverse backgrounds. It was carried out by monarchists, who decided it was time to release the emperor from his greatest political influence, Rasputin. By 1 November 1916, a definite plan materialized that involved government ministers, police officials, and a few members of the nobility.

From the time of the murder until now, few have tested the details of the crime published by two of Rasputin's murderers, Felix Yusupov and Vladimir Purishkevich. It was not a random act of violence, because its planning had taken several weeks. Two questions need to be addressed: How and why did eminent Russian men come together and calmly settle on murdering Rasputin?

Who was the Mastermind Behind the Murder?

Given that Purishkevich had no previous connection with the other two conspirators, it was necessary that something would bring the conspirators together. The coordinator had to be of such standing that the group would trust him and remain assured the matter of immunity from prosecution would prevail. That coordinator had to be so secure of his position that he enjoyed support from the Minister of Justice, whose cooperation would be needed before and after the murder occurred.

It was vital for the mastermind to have the wits and time to coordinate all the intricacies of carrying out Rasputin's murder. One person who possessed all these qualities was Grand Duke Nikolai Mikhailovich. Alexander Benois, the St. Petersburg law graduate who became an art historian and stage designer, wrote in his diary at the time of the episode that in his opinion Nikolai Mikhailovich had appeared to be the "actual mastermind."[451] Professor Alexander Kotsyubinsky also held that Grand Duke Nikolai Mikhailovich was the principal organizer of Rasputin's murder.[452] Closer to all events, Alexandra Fyodorovna believed that he was indeed responsible.

There is ample evidence that points to his culpability. Fuhrmann[453] wrote that "perhaps he [the grand duke] prodded Yusupov into action and advised him in some way," but then declared that circumstantial evidence is lacking. This belief was premised on Cockfield's biography that supposed the grand duke "knew nothing of the scheme until the first phone call came in the early morning" hours afterwards.[454] However, Cockfield did err in other areas, e.g. that Rasputin was poisoned.[455] Even if, as Fuhrmann advises, the grand duke was a "loquacious busybody," and with Smith agreeing[456] it was "unlikely that he would keep a secret,"[457] these perceptions fail to negate my assessment, because (seen later in this chapter and in Chapter Five) even a loquacious busybody can decide to be quiet when suited. The grand duke had already demonstrated his conspiratorial mindset by his intent to murder Alexandra Fyodorovna (and his involvement in other conspiracies, as discussed later in this chapter and in Chapter Four).

Details supporting my view that Grand Duke Nikolai Mikhailovich was the mastermind may be gleaned from the various remarks made by Felix Yusupov in his book *Konetz Rasputina* (*The End of Rasputin*).[458] The grand duke was an outspoken adversary of Rasputin. He detested Alexandra Fyodorovna, whom he believed dominated and controlled his younger cousin Nikolai II. It was the grand duke's confrontational personality and criticisms concerning the political direction into which Russia was seemingly heading which caused him to take measured steps. The grand duke regularly consulted with the dowager empress, who had apparently said to Felix Yusupov (the elder) that her son Nikolai II had to make the choice of either her or Rasputin.[459] Within the extended family, it was Grand Duke Nikolai Mikhailovich who had engaged in copious conversations with Grand Duke Dmitri Pavlovich and Felix Yusupov (the younger) after the murder. The grand duke was the first person whom Felix telephoned after he was forced to return from the railway station under a gendarme escort after he was prevented from leaving Petrograd.[460] It was Nikolai Mikhailovich who saw Dmitri Pavlovich off at the railway station on 23 December prior to boarding the train to embark upon his passage to Persia.[461] It is hard to believe that all of this happened because of "simple curiosity … encouraged by the murderers," then noting the family in Crimea used the grand duke as the "point man in the capital for the whole business."[462]

Shortly after Nikolai Mikhailovich's face-to-face warning to Nikolai II on 1 November 1916 (with the dowager empress' consent) and returning to Petrograd, he invited Duma delegates Vasilii Shulgin and Prince Georgii Lvov for a chat (most likely on 2 November). It was not a casual social event. He needed to tell them that he had just returned from Mogilev (the military headquarters where Nikolai II was positioned as the Supreme Commander of the military) and his reason for going there. It was an unusual step to make, bringing out his personal affairs outside of his reigning family. The Duma delegates listened while Nikolai Mikhailovich read out a confidential letter meant for Nikolai II's eyes only. Why would this have happened? The delegates learned how the grand duke implored Nikolai II to adjust his private life and warned him about his wife's interference in matters of State to Russia's detriment.[463] Although Shulgin claimed that he forgot most of what was said, he nevertheless acted on what he heard. As expected, Shulgin spoke in the Duma on 3 November, conscious of his words — "We have only one remedy, fight the government until it goes," and that "the State Duma is fighting with a sinister shadow, which has shrouded Russia"[464] — words that received approval from Grand Duke Nikolai Mikhailovich and Dowager Empress Maria Fyodorovna.

There appears to be two reasons why Nikolai Mikhailovich took that step. Firstly, Nikolai Mikhailovich deliberately alerted these two Duma delegates about the frustrations most members of the Romanov family (who were unable to go public) were feeling about the emperor's decision making. The second reason was he wanted to ensure that the Duma would maintain its political momentum that began with Pavel Milyukov's speech on 1 November. Nikolai Mikhailovich was not acting independently. He had the blessing of the dowager empress and others in the Romanov family, whom he consulted earlier in Kiev. Effectively, they were passing on their assent for the Duma to unveil the supposed wrongs of the government under Nikolai II's direction while at the same time warn the public about the menacing figure Rasputin and his influence over Alexandra Fyodorovna.

Nikolai Mikhailovich did not stop with Shulgin and Lvov. The same tactic was applied with Vladimir Purishkevich,[465] whom he invited to his palace in the early days of November.[466] Purishkevich presented his oration in the Duma on 19 November, in which he pleaded with the emperor to change his approach and get rid of Rasputin. The Romanov family's expectations were made clear after one grand duke telegraphed Nikolai Mikhailovich about the family's disgust concerning the issues that were publicly revealed by this accommodating Duma delegate.[467]

Given the public assault, there was one course left to end Rasputin's power and that involved eliminating him. After that eventuality, Nikolai Mikhailovich would then deal with Alexandra Fyodorovna.[468] Providing handwritten letters to specific individuals proved to be a very effective method, which Nikolai Mikhailovich used in order to achieve his objectives. He knew that each of the recipients who received his confidential information would act on his behalf. This pattern continued after the emperor abdicated. The activist journalist Vladimir Burtsev (editor of *Byloye* journal that was later subsidized by the Provisional Government[469]) was another one of the grand duke's chosen beneficiaries.[470][471] [During 1917, Burtsev was given permission to sift through the *Okhrana* archives that were not destroyed by fire, and gather evidence for the Extraordinary Commission of Inquiry.[472]] In fact, just days after the Provisional Government came to power, Nikolai Mikhailovich invited Professor Valentin Speransky to his palace. It was their first face-to-face meeting. Upon departure, Speransky was handed an envelope addressed to "His Imperial Majesty." Inside, four handwritten pages were enclosed, and bearing the grand duke's signature *Nikolai* on the last page. Speransky did exactly as predicted. He gave the envelope to new Minister of Justice Alexander Kerensky, then both read its message: "Avowing to You that I had no part in Rasputin's murder."[473] It was not a touch of latent conscience that caused Nikolai Mikhailovich to hand over his letter into the hands of a journalist who had experienced prison life during the imperial era. This letter was another signal how Nikolai Mikhailovich subtly maneuvered political matters with the changing circumstances. In this case, Nikolai Mikhailovich needed to be sure that Kerensky would release him from having to be questioned at the Commission of Inquiry under oath in front of a panel of common citizens.

Matters moved swiftly after Nikolai Mikhailovich spoke with the sovereign. Sometime between 4 and 6 November, he invited Vladimir Purishkevich and Felix Yusupov to come to his palace on the same day. When Purishkevich arrived, he found that Felix was already there enjoying breakfast. Purishkevich bragged that the grand duke extended him an open invitation to call at any time, day or night, after his return from the Front. [Purishkevich ran a three-carriage train to battlefields supplying books and pharmaceuticals to officers and soldiers.[474]] The topic the three men discussed focused on Rasputin and Alexandra Fyodorovna's influence over Nikolai II.[475]

At Nikolai Mikhailovich's instigation, Yusupov attended the Duma sitting that was held on 19 November. Though Yusupov said he went there for something to do, that atypical act was purposeful. The visit was a motivational exercise that would ensure Felix would be stirred by what he heard in Purishkevich's speech and in the subsequent speech that was uttered by his uncle Misha (Mikhail Rodzianko). Yusupov was driven by Purishkevich's speech, saying it was "creating an overwhelming impression," while Rodzianko's words proved outstanding.[476] Rodzianko undoubtedly knew why Felix was there, given that he told Felix after the Duma sitting, "there was one way out – to kill the scoundrel. But in Russia there is no one so fearless. If I was not so old, I would have finished him myself."[477]

One letter written by Felix's mother, Zinaida Yusupova, from her Crimean estate, dated 25 November 1916, confirms that Yusupov's attendance at the Duma was not by chance. Part of that letter reads:

> *"When I heard that you visited the House* [Duma] *... nobody believed it here and when your letter arrived Papa was very flustered by it. He did not like it, and I understand him. May you not be in military institute, this might be permissible, but this is bad and there may be unpleasantness ahead, when this reaches the Corps de Pages. – We must hope that this time it will come together.*

For God's sake do not take risks ..." [478]

Since Nikolai Mikhailovich was a member of the Yacht Club, he continued his tactics, knowing that Felix Yusupov and Dmitri Pavlovich were also regular visitors.[479] At the club, these young, impressionable men would have heard vigorous debates about Rasputin's supposed influence at Tsarskoe Selo. Their source of information came from the press and from foreigners expressing unease that Russia was seen to be heading towards the abyss. Diplomats from the allied nations were accepted as honorary guests and friendships developed within its walls. Ambassador Buchanan's daughter, Muriel, explained that her father considered Nikolai Mikhailovich his greatest friend in Russia.[480] Nikolai Mikhailovich, on 26 April 1917, wrote that during Nikolai II's reign, the Yacht Club was used for "a political gathering."[481] Elsewhere in the capital, the British tentacles had spread to the upper levels of the Sergievskii Palace, which Dmitri Pavlovich inherited from Grand Duchess Elizaveta Fyodorovna and where he now lived. Since 1916, it was also occupied by the British Embassy and the Anglo-Russian military hospital.[482]

Felix Yusupov's book about Rasputin's murder singled out Grand Duke Nikolai Mikhailovich, specifically praised his virtues, and expressed his regret that the grand duke was banished from Petrograd after Rasputin was murdered.[483] If the grand duke was not complicit in the crime, why did he race over to the Sergievskii Palace just to be the first to tell Dmitri and Felix that Rasputin's body had been found?[484] At each visit, Nikolai Mikhailovich showed immense interest about the specifics of the events as they unfolded after the murder. What's more, Nikolai Mikhailovich told Dmitri and Yusupov that the empress wanted them both shot immediately, but that she was persuaded to back off from the idea.[485] Such concern must surely indicate that the grand duke's role was far more than Yusupov was prepared to reveal. Nikolai Mikhailovich went to the railway station,[486] [487] and that act suggests his concern about Dmitri's wellbeing. Supportive to the last moment, he was the perfect mastermind.

Significantly, Nikolai II suspected Nikolai Mikhailovich's involvement in Rasputin's murder. The grand duke dodged a face-to-face cencounter with the emperor when Count Vladimir

Frederiks, Minister of the Imperial Court,[488] telephoned him. The grand duke promptly decided that he must seek fresh air on his Grushevka estate, though to begin with, he spent the evening of New Year's Day with Grand Duchess Maria Pavlovna (the elder) and the Vladimirovichi clan.[489] The following words in Nikolai Mikhailovich's diary, written in January 1917 while he was travelling to Kiev on the train to visit the dowager empress, give the clearest indication that he was involved in Rasputin's murder:

"Shulgin [Duma member] – *now he would have been useful, not of course for the murder, but for the uprising."*[490]

Countess Cantacuzene, whose daughter Zinaida had married General Handbury-Williams (British officer at Stavka), wrote in her memoirs[491] that she was told that Nikolai Mikhailovich "was implicated ... as an adviser and abettor." Before his departure, he "sent his resignation ... removed his aiguillettes and uniform once and for all" and "did not reappear in the life of Petrograd until just two months later ... on the eve of the revolution."

Recently, I came across the following telegram, which Felix's wife Irina Yusupova sent to Nikolai Mikhailovich, which was intercepted by the perlustration unit in the Petrograd Post Office.

Telegram No. 179 Grand Duchess Irina Alexandrovna Yusupov to Grand Duke Nikolai Mikhailovich:

Sent from st.(ation) Koreiz 19 December 1916 14h 16m by p.

Received MD 19 – 16h 3m by p.

"To Grand Duke Nikolai Mikhailovich.

Do not understand anything, (we) *do not know even if the fact completed. Awfully worried. Telegraph further, tomorrow everyone leaving. Kisses Irina."*[492]

The question lies, why would Irina Alexandrovna send this communiqué to Nikolai Mikhailovich?

The most compelling ingredient that motivated each co-conspirator was one of patriotism for Mother Russia. Dmitri Pavlovich repeated that idealistic sentiment in one his first letters to his father, saying "it was time to see the purer ray of light."[493]

A Prince Confides His Trepidations to a Lawyer

Felix did play a key role, but it was not in the manner he wanted to be identified with. A little known document offers the testimony of the former imperial senator Vasilii Maklakov that was taken down by Nikolai Sokolov in Paris on 19 September 1920.[494] To maintain the semblance of the well-established legal code of behavior, those who were asked to present their evidence to Sokolov were required to affirm in writing that what they had revealed was the truth. That action was Sokolov's personal guarantee that his witnesses were being truthful. Although Sokolov maintained his Russian designation as a *Sudebnii Sledovatel'* (Court Investigator), the reality was that the designation written below each Protocol he obtained did not carry legal weight in any foreign jurisdictions.[495] Likewise, Sokolov did not hold legal authority to continue with his investigation, which meant his work abroad had become a personal project.

Sokolov was the principal forensic investigator in Ekaterinburg who searched for the truth about the murder of the imperial family and their entourage on the night of July 16/17 1918. During the final years of his life as an émigré living in France, Sokolov expanded his investigation to include the political circumstances that lead to the death of the imperial family and its repercussions. The original investigation was authorized by General Kolchak of the Siberian Army in February 1919, and only concluded with Sokolov's premature death in 1924 at the age of forty-two.[496] The fourth volume of his dossier ended up in hands of the Soviet armed forces in May 1945 and was then handed over to the military procurator in the Soviet Union after Berlin was liberated in May 1945. The Sokolov dossier was marked SECRET and remained hidden inside the archive until 1991.[497] Among that series of papers, Maklakov acknowledged that he spoke with Nikolai Mikhailovich after Milyukov's speech on 1 November (recalling it was before 3 November 1916).[498] Despite several differences in his information, a large part of Maklakov's testimony was repeated in two articles he published in 1923 and in 1932.[499] The latter formed part of an extensive series of articles relating to Rasputin's murder that were written by Russian émigrés familiar with the Rasputin Case. To differentiate Maklakov's two papers, the 1920 testimony will be referred to as the Sokolov File.

In 1923, French editor Yakov Povolotskii planned to publish Purishkevich's 'Diary' to interest the huge number of Russian émigrés living in Europe. Possibly, to add wider appeal to the foreign edition, Maklakov was given the opportunity to respond to Purishkevich's previous edition. Maklakov wrote the preface for the first printing of the 'Diary' in the West, three years after Purishkevich's death. Lamentably, Maklakov never disputed Yusupov's 1927 book, *Konetz Rasputina*, which appeared in 1927. Using guarded language, Maklakov admitted that the first contact that he had about the "Rasputin matter" happened in early November 1916 through "another participant."[500] The encounter occurred shortly after the tumultuous 1-3 November 1916 Duma sittings, an occasion that coincided with the emperor's agreement to retire his prime minister, Boris Stürmer, before the news became public.[501] The initial consultation was arranged by one of Yusupov's staff, on either 6 or 7 November,[502] for 6 p.m. for the same day. Yusupov needed to seek legal counsel because he was confused as to what he should do. Maklakov admitted that he did have prior knowledge why Yusupov needed to speak with him through "another participant." This detail dismisses ideas that Purishkevich was responsible for arranging the first meeting between Maklakov and Felix. At all times maintaining his guard, Maklakov said that he nodded his head that he was receptive about the conspiracy to murder Rasputin.

Tracing Yusupov's movements prior to 4 November, we know that Felix passed through Moscow on 3 November 1916, where he visited his friend Grand Duchess Elizaveta Fyodorovna. Before he caught the evening train for Petrograd, he wrote a letter to his mother that was postmarked 'Moscow 3/11.1916.'[503] Sometime after Felix returned from Crimea to Petrograd, he was drawn into the conspiracy to murder Rasputin. Consequently, Purishkevich first saw Felix at Nikolai Mikhailovich's palace on 4 November.

Maklakov stressed the point that Felix was responsible for "organizing this murder"[504] at the Moika Palace, and that Purishkevich brought Dr. Stanislav Lazovert into the conspiracy circle.[505] Maklakov stated that he met Felix Yusupov for the very first time at that initial consultation.[506] During their conversation,

Felix told him: "I am not interested in personally killing him."[507] One legal piece of advice that Maklakov imparted to Felix was that hiring an assassin willing to kill Rasputin would bring the necessary end result.[508] Maklakov revealed that Felix had accepted the point that something had to be done about Rasputin but he was not as yet prepared to kill him. Accepting that Maklakov had nothing to gain from his disclosures, it is strange that Felix would bother visiting the lawyer unless there was a rationale to do so. The consultation ended with Maklakov advising Felix that if he "wanted to personally go with this," then he was welcome to return and be assisted in "being cautioned against needless errors."[509] Maklakov confessed his disappointment about the conduct of their meeting because "Yusupov had no plans."[510] Given this evidence, why did Smith echo Fuhrmann's view "that Felix Yusupov ... hatched the plot,"[511] saying "the idea to kill Rasputin began with Yusupov"?[512]

Between the time Felix left Nikolai Mikhailovich's palace and his appointment with Maklakov, Felix was unsure how Rasputin had to be dealt with – either bought off or killed by someone for a fee.[513] His rambling thoughts indicate that at this early date in November he had no desire to kill Rasputin. It would take another two weeks, after Purishkevich's impassioned speech, before Felix changed his mind. This renders Smith's assertion that Yusupov's mind crystallized "around the end of October" strange.[514] What or who altered Felix's attitude may be difficult to discover; however, Maklakov does provide a clue.

A few days after Purishkevich gave his speech in the Duma (on 19 November), he spoke to Maklakov in the Ekaterininskii (Catherine) Hall inside the Duma building during their break. Purishkevich told him that "it was decided that Rasputin was to be killed on 17/18 December,"[515] which was a Saturday night. [In his 1928 account, the date was corrected to 16/17 December.[516]] Purishkevich told him that he was aware of the substance of the consultation that Maklakov held with Felix two weeks earlier. Then adding, "there were no hired assassins in this matter, only intelligent people are participating."[517] As they sat "beside the bust of Alexander II"[518] (assassinated in 1881), Purishkevich disclosed the "five names of those who were actually privy to the matter."

In his 1923 rebuttal letter, Maklakov disclosed that both he and Purishkevich were "in conversation" with the same un-named participant.[519] Hence, the mastermind was not Purishkevich. After Maklakov was made aware *who* (this word was emphasized by Maklakov using italics) the intermediary was, he had agreed to meet Yusupov a second time.[520]

This *tête à tête* meeting exposes the fact that Purishkevich knew about Maklakov's involvement but Maklakov beforehand was unaware who else was actively involved in the "Rasputin matter" until Purishkevich revealed the name of their intermediary. In his 1920 sworn confidential statement, Maklakov listed the names of five men that were prepared to deal with Rasputin, but in the published letter (in 1923), in addition to the two successive journal articles, he stood silent about their identities. Those five individuals are known to history for what they did and are listed later in this chapter.

To understand why Maklakov had agreed to see Yusupov again, it is necessary to return to Maklakov's account of the first consultation (as described in the Sokolov File). Yusupov asserted that because "he was almost a member of the imperial family," he was unable to carry out the murder because if he did so, it would turn out to be "almost a revolution." Maklakov replied that revolutionaries, being enemies of the regime, "will not touch Rasputin" because he was already doing them a favor by bringing down the monarchy.[521] One person among the "five names who were actually privy to the matter" turned out to be Dmitri Pavlovich. It was a shrewd move on Nikolai Mikhailovich's part, to steer Felix Yusupov into reconsidering what was expected of him.

On 20 November 1916, Felix wrote a brief letter (**Document No. 4**) to Irina in *Koreiz*:

> "*I am awfully busy working over the plan about destroying R. This is now simply important, or else everything will end. ... Dmitri Pavlovich knows everything about it and is helping. All this will occur in the middle of December.*"[522]

Reading Maklakov's recollections, one can discern that the reason why Yusupov went to visit Purishkevich was not to praise the quality of his Duma speech nor to invite Purishkevich into the conspiracy.[523] It appears Yusupov had to find out whether Maklakov was willing to see Yusupov again, because by then Felix had decided to participate. Maklakov explained that his subsequent meetings with Yusupov involved giving advice within the framework that the person who sat before him had agreed to partake in an unlawful act – as a murderer.[524]

In 1917, Dmitri Pavlovich, wrote the following to his father:

"Finally, the final act upon my arrival in Petrograd was the full acceptance and premeditated participation in the murder of Rasputin, as the last attempt for the sovereign to openly alter his course, not taking upon myself the responsibility for the elimination of that person." [525]

Dmitri's words take on a special character when they are compared to Maklakov's instructions to Yusupov. The obliging lawyer stressed the necessity of "brushing away his tracks" and above all, not to take on "the role of a hero." To succeed, Maklakov advised that one should "mislead" when being questioned; otherwise, in the interests of Russia, the "murder would lose its significance and … justification." The most important legal advice tendered was that no one was to learn who the real murderer was, and in so doing, ensure the "impossibility that the murder would become a matter for the court."[526] That advice was carried out to the letter, as can be read in Dmitri's communication to his father.

The best evidence that identifies who masterminded the conspiracy to murder Rasputin can be read in Nikolai Mikhailovich's diary entry for 23 December 1916 (emphasis by this author):

"…it is essential to finish off Alexandra Fyodorovna and Protopopov. You see, again I have flashing thoughts of murder…or else it will be worse, than before…the task is almost complete." [527]

Chapter Four will show that other than Nikolai Mikhailovich and his clique, others were interested as to what was happening inside Russia, wondering how to improve Russia's tarnished political image abroad.

The Plot Has Been Revealed but did it Conform to the Truth?

The *strannik* was lured to the Yusupovskii Palace with the promise that he would meet Felix Yusupov's wife, Irina Alexandrovna, who was Nikolai II's niece. The room in the basement was prepared by the palace staff. The table was thoughtfully set with enticing finger food that included small almond cakes and alcohol that included a few bottles of Rasputin's favorite wine, Madeira. Prior to the guest's arrival, the Madeira and cakes that were intended for the guest were, by some accounts, laced with potassium cyanide. Much to Felix's chagrin and polite persuasion, Rasputin just sat in the armchair and failed to accept the small treats laid out for his benefit. Before long, we learn that he started to eat and to drink. With time passing, Rasputin remained seated, showing no ill effects from the poison he had ingested. He should have died by now. Instead, Rasputin became increasingly intoxicated from the alcohol he continued to drink. Felix, in a state of nervous panic, rushed upstairs to consult with his other guests. Dmitri, perhaps in somewhat of a panicky state, thought that Rasputin should return home, but Purishkevich insisted that Rasputin should not be allowed to leave the palace alive, as had been pre-arranged. Since the poison failed to do its work, the only alternative left was to shoot him. Felix returned to his abandoned guest armed with a weapon.

What really happened next is unclear, but one bullet fired from Yusupov's gun penetrated Rasputin's body. Due to the nature of the gunshot wound, Rasputin would have begun to bleed profusely and before long, become markedly disabled. Yusupov's victim became silent and motionless. The gunfire alerted the men upstairs, who ventured downstairs to view the body. Satisfied that Rasputin appeared to be dead, they returned upstairs. Left alone, Rasputin regained consciousness and knew that he had to flee (rather than accepting his fate as some writers have proposed). With his last bit of strength, Rasputin touched the small stairwell door. It was unlocked. Opening the door, he saw a small courtyard, but before he reached the gate, barely mobile, a second shot was fired. It entered his back. With his strength seeping away and losing consciousness, he fell onto the snow. Rasputin was dragged inside, dragged down the stairs and left lying on the granite[528] floor. A third shot was fired. Before long, his body, covered in fresh blood, was wrapped and placed into Dmitri Pavlovich's waiting car. Lazovert drove the car beyond the city limits and then the body was thrown from the Bolshoi Petrovskii Bridge into the icy water. Leaving the scene, they had all expected that the corpse would disappear with the flow of the river that opened into the Gulf of Finland.

In this brief account, it is apparent that there are gaps that give rise to many questions. If poison was used, why was it ineffective? Were other intervening factors involved that were never revealed? If one accepts Purishkevich's word that he shot Rasputin in the back, then how could Yusupov have accomplished the same feat? The forensic evidence shows that only one of them could have been right. The most glaring omission in the books written by the murderers is the one relating to the third gunshot wound. Why were both perpetrators silent about the third gunshot that was fired into Rasputin's forehead? That third gunshot wound exposes one striking truth. One of the conspirators on the night had the necessary calm to approach the supine victim, position his firearm on the mid-section of the forehead of the dying man, and pull the trigger. Why was it necessary? Was Rasputin dead before he reached the icy water or could he have survived for a short time?

A few answers to the questions just posed can be answered. My reconstruction of the crime will focus on what the photographs of the corpse are telling us today. The forensic photographs, together with the senior investigator's comments that were disclosed in 1917, indicate that the pre-meditated murder, which was not supposed to attract outsiders, had turned out to be a complex and very bloody affair.

Two conflicting eyewitness accounts provided by Felix Yusupov in *Konetz Rasputina* and the earlier authorship by Vladimir Purishkevich of *Dnevnik* (Diary), also published in abridged format as *Ubiistvo Rasputina* (*The Murder of Rasputin*[529]), deliberately obfuscated many details. Summaries from both books appear in Table No.1 at the end of this chapter.

Was a Foreign Power Part of the Conspiracy to Murder Rasputin?

Neither Yusupov nor Dmitri Pavlovich admitted joint liability for participating in the murder. By 1927 (after Yusupov's book was published), everyone knew the identities of the five people named by Purishkevich. However, Felix said that apart from the five identified persons engaged in the conspiracy, "those culpable of this disappearance [Rasputin's] had to remain ... unknown."[530] This admission leads one to wonder why Felix was always reluctant to say more.

Writer of the time Mohammed Essad-Bey held that Ambassador Buchanan did meddle in Russian politics.[531] He was described as a confidant of the liberal factions of the Duma. During his audience with Nikolai II, it became apparent that Buchanan did not represent King George V. In February 1916, Buchanan admitted that during his audience with Nikolai II, he made his "first serious attempt to induce the emperor to steer a more liberal course."[532] In a later audience, Buchanan discussed the "profound discontent" that prevailed all over the country owing to the disturbances in Petrograd. The ambassador did not conceal his hostility, adding that the peasantry was losing faith in autocracy "thanks to his Ministers' shortcomings."[533] Princess Paley revealed that "liberals like Prince Lvov, Milyukov, Rodzianko, Maklakov and Guchkov with them never left the embassy" where they plotted "the way to revolution."[534] Even so, Buchanan had stepped outside the boundaries of diplomacy by discussing the errors of the imperial government with "cold objectivity"[535] with anyone who would listen. Buchanan was so alarmed by the "German influence" that supposedly pervaded Russia, he communicated his concerns to the British Foreign Office on 18 October 1916. He wrote that German propaganda was spreading tactical disinformation whereby:

> *"Great Britain ... is forcing Russia to continue the war and forbidding her to accept the favorable peace terms which Germany is ready to offer ... and that Russia has nothing to gain by prolonging the war."* [536]

Then Buchanan enlightened his superiors with this comment:

> *"... before tendering advice to the Emperor ... and*

as her health failed her ... the strain of the war, anxiety about her son, and the overtaxing of her strength in hospital work ... she came more and more under his baleful influence." [537]

Buchanan was convinced that Rasputin was influencing the Russian monarchy, which gave the impression that the administration was inept.[538] Buchanan, blinded by his fear of a man (Rasputin) he had never met, never questioned if his information was true. It is impossible to verify if Buchanan was involved in the conspiracy to murder Rasputin. What is known is that British intelligence knew about the conspiracy through the friendship Buchanan had nurtured with Grand Duke Nikolai Mikhailovich, primarily to ensure the *Entente* Agreement would endure while the war played out in Europe. The friendship maintained between Felix Yusupov and his friend from their Oxford University days, Oswald Rayner, who was stationed in Petrograd as a British intelligence operative, aided that undertaking. Cook might be right that a British agent was present at the Yusupovskii Palace on the night of Rasputin's murder.[539] However, Cook, for reasons that will be explained in Chapter Five, was wrong to propose that Rayner was responsible for killing Rasputin. It is more credible to trust that Chief of British Intelligence in Petrograd Samuel Hoare only sanctioned Rayner to confirm that Rasputin was dead. Purishkevich, who was delegated to be in charge of the events at the Yusupovskii Palace, likewise determined that their scheme would end that night. If Rasputin lived, he would have told the palace about his latest torment (in the same way as he did in 1911).

Buchanan recognized that despite the many attempts to deliver Russia from the man that he described as an "evil genius," Rasputin's position appeared to be unassailable until "deliverance eventually came on the morning of December 30" (New Style).[540]

One of the most important details that Buchanan divulged in his memoirs was that he knew that Rasputin was not missing, but had died in the early hours of Saturday morning, 17 December. He was aware of that fact BEFORE Nikolai Mikhailovich, who learnt the news directly from the ambassador. This news could have waited until a reasonable hour, if the grand duke was a mere friend and not involved in the murder. Notably, both these men kept that secret to themselves (proof that Nikolai Mikhailovich can stay silent), many hours before the gendarmes initiated their investigation into what started out as a missing person's case.

Nikolai Mikhailovich's first diary entry for that day says that Buchanan telephoned him at 5.30, confirming that **Rasputin was dead** (my emphasis). Buchanan could only have known that Rasputin was no longer alive because Rayner was the silent partner at the Yusupov residence. Cook and Smith failed to understand that when Nikolai Mikhailovich wrote 5.30, it meant 5.30 in the morning. The reason being that he wrote events sequentially as they happened. Several lines down, the word *obed* (lunch) appears. Smith, critical of my reading of the time, named "Russian Diary" [Gibbs],[541] as the book confirming his belief, that the time was 5.30 p.m. However, Smith's claim is based on hearsay evidence from a book that has no acknowledged authorship. The "Russian Diary" discusses a different set of events, where at 5 p.m. a man called Seymour spoke to the anonymous diarist that Rasputin had been shot but it was not known if Rasputin was dead.

Favoring the British, the grand duke felt no obligation to inform the Petrograd governor to stop wasting time and call off the search for Rasputin and advise it might be best to look for a corpse.

SIS Accepts a Silent Role

Samuel Hoare began his Russian commission in January 1916 (he omits the exact date in his memoir). As head of the British Intelligence Mission[542] (also known as the SIS, or the Secret Intelligence Service) in Petrograd, he was responsible for intelligence gathering "about the Tsarist Empire."[543] His first duty involved making contact with the head of the *Okhrana*,[544] Globachev [who failed to mention Hoare in his memoirs]. Hoare does not impact on the Russian scene until towards the end of his posting in Russia.

On 1 November, Purishkevich was ablaze after Milyukov's speech was over. He sent Hoare "a message card" saying that he needed to talk to him urgently, in private. Both Buchanan and Hoare found that Purishkevich was composed when he said "he and his friends had resolved to liquidate the affair of Rasputin."[545] Hoare indicated that he was not shocked by Purishkevich's outburst and instead had given his endorsement. Though details about the true nature of this meeting are omitted, Hoare understood that Purishkevich "meant the assassination of an enemy." In this context, the enemy was a mutual one for the British and the Russians [Buchanan and Purishkevich failed to mention this encounter in their memoirs].

Hoare said that he first met Purishkevich in autumn 1916.[546] By November, Purishkevich knew Hoare well enough to know that Hoare would be interested enough to listen to what he had to say, even though Hoare would later describe Purishkevich as "a bigoted reactionary" possessing a "splendid stream of patriotic fervor."[547] The meeting indicates that the subject matter was not new for either of them. The idea to eliminate Rasputin evidently would not involve their other ally, the French, even though Paléologue shared Britain's opinion about Rasputin and the likelihood of his prompting a ceasefire between Russia and Germany.[548]

Hoare was concerned about the events that were exposed on the Duma floor. The Duma represented "public opinion"[549] and because government ministers were being dismissed too often, the public became concerned about the so-called 'dark forces.' The problem was that the reasons for their dismissal were not usually made public, which effectively sheltered the person who was dismissed. Each dismissal, however justified, reflected badly against Nikolai II rather than on the discharged minister. Hoare admitted that "it was humanly impossible to take a detached view, particularly as certain ... events [dismissal of ministers] were due to Rasputin's influence."[550]

One of Hoare's duties was to gather information about "Rasputin and his camarilla"[551] [the same expression, which referred to a secret cabal, was used by Ambassadors Paléologue[552] and Buchanan[553]], whom he believed were "the hidden power behind the anti-war parties."[554] Hoare's intelligence gathering was for the edification of the Director of Intelligence in London. However, Hoare admitted that he thrived on "any scandals that surrounded his [Rasputin's] name."[555] Practically every day "some rumor"[556] reached him regarding the "coarsely wicked" and "sinister man"; a person whom he had never set eyes on.[557] Hoare's opinion of Rasputin was certainly fixed after speaking with Purishkevich.

It was Purishkevich who gave the intelligence officer reason to be aware of "the evil influence that the Siberian peasant was exercising, not only upon the Russian Empire, but upon the whole course of the war."[558] Hoare explained why the British were discontent with Russia:

> "Let the Emperor only banish this man, and the country would be freed from the sinister influence that was striking down its natural leaders and endangering the success of its armies in the field."[559]

Samuel Hoare's reports relied on material gleaned from Petrograd newspapers such as *Birzheviye Vedomosti, Novoye Vremya, Russkaya Volya,* and *Rech.*[560] Intermittently, he received information from the police department.[561] Some of the details, such as the place where Rasputin's corpse was conveyed after it was found, are wrong, while his description of the autopsy findings is also incorrect. The series of reports bear out that he was not present at the Yusupovskii Palace on the night of the murder of Rasputin, a point that contradicts Oleg Shishkin's idea that Samuel Hoare killed Rasputin. The idea that Hoare lived "two steps away from Moika, 94" and that his dwelling "was not accidental"[562] ignores the fact the apartment was in the Internal Affairs Department building that was separated not by a road, but a canal. Recognizing that Hoare could not possibly have envisioned that an incident of 'special interest' to Britain would happen eleven months after his arrival, Shishkin's proposal is flawed.

When news of Rasputin's death reached Samuel Hoare, he stressed in his memoirs that his report was transmitted to London "within a few hours of the murder."[563] The media never covered up that the "British secret operative in Imperial Russia" had "almost immediate knowledge of the assassination."[564] On New Year's Day (New Style), Hoare sent this report to the chief of the foreign section of the Secret Intelligence Service, Commander Mansfield Cumming[565] saying (in part):

> "Gregory Efemovich Novikh (sic) – for Rasputin, 'the rake' …I do not wish to appear to meddle in Russian internal affairs …since Saturday I made it my business to discover as many details as I can about the murder… The result of my inquiries is as follows: Rasputin has not

been seen since the evening of Friday, the 29th December [New Style], *when he left his flat in company with an officer in a motor car. Prince Yusupov had a party on the same evening that was attended by one or two of the Grand Dukes. ... The details of the story vary. Some people say that Rasputin was got into a room and told to kill himself. ... The generally accepted story, however, is that he was shot. A motor is supposed to have taken the body to the islands, where it was thrown into the sea or one of the rivers. This story is generally supported in Petrograd. There is also general agreement that he was killed by either the Grand Duke Dmitri Pavlovich or by Prince Yusupov.*" [566]

The next day, 2 January (New Style), Hoare transmitted this memorandum (in part):

"I have received information that the body of Rasputin has been discovered in the river Nevka, near the Petrovskii Bridge. I received this information in the strict confidence from the Chief of the Department of Military Police in the General Staff. ... It is also certain that Rasputin was actually killed in Prince Yusupov's house and not in the motor ... there seems to have been a certain amount of promiscuous shooting, in which a dog was killed in the courtyard ..." [567]

Samuel Hoare's most interesting memorandum was composed on 5 January 1917 (New Style). He credited himself as being the first non-Russian to learn of the autopsy findings. His memorandum revealed the following details (provided in part):

"Late in the evening he [Rasputin] *sent away the detectives of the secret police, and told them that they were not wanted any more. Shortly afterwards, a motor with a cape cart hood arrived and someone came and knocked at the back door. This proved to be a boy who frequently visited Rasputin ... The two went off in the motor car in the direction of the Fontanka ... and was seen to the turn right. ... The* dvornik *[yard feepeer] at Prince Yusupov's house seemed either stupid or very clever ... admitted that the driver of the motor was in uniform ... supposed to*

have been Grand Duchess Irene's brother.

At 12.30 the gorodovoi *[policeman] outside the Ministry of the Interior in the Moika heard four shots. ... At 3.30 the* gorodovoi *standing outside Prince Yusupov's house was called into the house by a man in general's uniform... said 'Rasputin is destroyed'. ...two examining judges, Sereda and Zarvadtsky (sic), and the police, went round in the morning to Prince Yusupov's house. The only trace they could find of the murder was some blood stains on the snow outside the small door that leads into the bachelor rooms which Prince Yusupov used before he married. ... Prince Yusupov came out, and said ... that all that happened was that the Grand Duke Dmitri Pavlovich had shot a dog that had attacked him. ...*

...a galosh was discovered near the Petrovsky Bridge, it was taken to 64 Gorkhovaya for recognition. The Rasputin family at once recognized it as Rasputin's. ... on Monday morning ... found ... Rasputin's body, completely frozen into a block of ice. Both hands were raised, and one side of his face was badly damaged by the fall into the river. The body was ...taken to Vyborg Military Hospital. ... They found that Rasputin, although 46 years of age, had the look of a man of only 36. He was dressed ... as a Russian mujik *(sic). He was wearing however a pair of expensive boots and a blue shirt with yellow cornflowers sewn upon it. ...*

The examination showed that there were three wounds, one in his back and two in his head, all showing signs that they had been made by shots at a very close range.

... Throughout the autumn of 1916 it was the fashion amongst the reactionaries known as 'The Black Hundred' to connect British diplomats and officers with supposed intrigues against the Emperor... It was not surprising, that Rasputin's death should have been the occasion of a crop of wild rumors about British participation in the crime. ... Purishkevich ... gave a ready excuse to the anti-British clique of reactionaries to father the plot and even

the murder on me and my staff. I knew nothing of this outrageous charge until Sir George Buchanan told me of the rumors that were reaching him."[568]

If Hoare was responsible for murdering Rasputin, then why was Rayner also needed to be at the Moika Palace? The presence of two British agents would have been heavy-handed, at the very least. With a clear conscience, Buchanan strongly refuted that Rasputin was murdered "by British agent Hoare."[569] Likewise, Hoare's description of two separate bullet wounds to the head was not correct (see Chapter Eight), while details including the conspicuous facial disfigurement had escaped his interest. Hoare would not have obfuscated facts that would have been of interest to the War Ministry.

Once the Russians eliminated Rasputin, they allegedly steered back onto the correct [British] course and continued fighting the war. Buchanan admitted that Britain conducted a wave of propaganda in favor of keeping up the war.[570] However, Rasputin's murder forced Hoare to admit:

"I imagined that the murder would destroy the 'Dark Forces' and enable Russia to continue her war with a singleness of purpose that hitherto been impossible. I was too overconfident."[571]

After the Russian monarchy crumbled, Samuel Hoare wrote this:

"... when a political crisis is imminent, there is nothing so dangerous as an arresting crime. ... At a moment, when authority needed to be strengthened rather than weakened, an explosion occurred that shook the crazy structure of government to its very foundation."[572]

Hoare's belated admission can be understood to mean that the British Intelligence operation had unintended consequences. If the Kaiser was seeking a way out of the war with Russia, as suggested by Shishkin,[573] the emperor was not listening. To eliminate the possibility of a separate agreement with the Kaiser, Britain's egocentrism had struck at the one victim who openly promoted pacifist ideas who held no sway over Nikolai II.

The few revelations read in Hoare's memoirs are notable in a number of ways. Hoare admitted that the information he transmitted to London was largely based on local suspicions, conversations, and reading the local (heavily censored) newspapers. Some of the material that passed his way he considered to be authentic because it came "first hand."[574] However, it cannot be ignored that Hoare had disseminated the same rumors heard in the Duma, the salons, and in the newspapers. Thirteen years after Russia was taken over by the Bolsheviks, Hoare admitted:

> "...so far as the conduct of the war was concerned it would have been better if the murder had never taken place."[575]

Except the very few who received Grigorii Rasputin favorably, no one close to the throne expressed horror in Rasputin's passing. The majority thought that Rasputin's elimination was justified and that once half of the 'dark forces' were destroyed, Russia had the opportunity to continue fighting the war without hindrance, since "the danger of immediate peace has been for the moment removed."[576] Hoare trusted and believed Purishkevich, who warned him that something drastic had to be done to protect British war interests, because "the man [Rasputin] stood in the way of all the brave hopes and high ideals with which he and his friends had entered the war," which Hoare described as "treachery to the allied cause."[577] All in all, it is strange that Hoare (who had occasion to visit Stavka numerous times[578]) failed to see that Nikolai II, as commander in chief, never once expressed his desire to separately negotiate an end to the war. Likewise, the British military stationed at Stavka must have known that Nikolai II only anticipated victory for Russia. General Spiridovich said that Nikolai II "was highly principled and very fanatical about the alliance Russia had with France and England."[579] Belatedly, Samuel Hoare admitted that Nikolai II "never abandoned his Allies in arms."[580] There can be no dispute that Russia paid an incalculable price for her loyalty to the British.

Who Murdered Rasputin?

The individuals who forced their hands against Rasputin on the night of 16/17 December 1916 have always been correctly known to history. They were:

1. **Prince Felix Felixovich Yusupov II, Count Sumarokov-Elston,** Cadet in the *Pazheskii Korpus*, married to Nikolai II's niece.

2. **Sergei Mikhailovich Sukhotin,** Reservist in the Petrograd *Generalitet* Headquarters.

3. **Vladimir Mitrofanovich Purishkevich,** the leader of the right faction in IV State Duma, leader of the ultra-monarchist movement *Soyuz Russkogo Naroda* (Black Hundred).

4. **Dr. Stanislav Sergeyevich Lazovert,** senior doctor aboard Purishkrvich's Red Cross train.

5. **Grand Duke Dmitri Pavlovich,** cousin to Nikolai II, *Fligel*-Adjutant, *Shtabs Rotmeister*.

How did foreign dignitaries view the key players involved in Rasputin's murder? Paléologue described Grand Duke Dmitri as a "fervent patriot and capable of courage in the hour of battle." Prince Yusupov was a dilettante "who was too prone to perverse imaginings and literary imaginings and literary representations of vice and death," while Purishkevich's participation in the murder added to the extreme right-wing attitude of the "champions of autocracy," [581] who thought it necessary to act against the emperor to achieve their goal. Purishkevich's participation in the crime carried a political element because he was a founding member of the extremist right-wing organization, the *Chernosotentsi* (Black Hundred) Movement. This last credential explains why Purishkevich was interested in conspiring to murder Rasputin. Purishkevich and Alexander Dubrovin created the Black Hundred Movement, which rallied likeminded individuals against leftist forces. Extremist in their views, the group held deep grudges against persons of Jewish faith and any intellectuals who detested autocracy.[582] The Movement attempted to unify loyal Russians in a confronting manner; their street marches, with supporters bearing icons and orthodox crosses, large portraits of the emperor, and other symbols of patriotism were tolerated as much as the knuckledusters and other more persuasive implements. Furthermore, at the start of the war, Purishkevich became an "anglophile,"[583] a sentiment that proved useful for British intelligence.

Aside from the political nature of this crime, it also sent the public another, more profound message. It was impossible to escape the fact that Dmitri Pavlovich's attendance had thrust a blow — not against the monarchy, but against its reigning monarch.

The Reasons Why the Conspirators Preferred 16 December to Save the Motherland

English Professor Michael Hughes revealed that on 16 October 1915, Buchanan informed the London Foreign Office "the country is almost ripe for revolution."[584] Throughout 1916, Buchanan was concerned by the rapid turnover of government ministers and presumed that this was due "to the influences of the dark forces." Buchanan's report noted that Nikolai II "could never hope to regain his popularity as long as he allows himself to be influenced by Rasputin and other persons in the empress's entourage."[585] Buchanan feared that the support and trust shown by his government to Russia would be severely compromised. Towards the end of 1916, and particularly after the emperor failed to respond to the Duma speeches, Buchanan became alarmed "that the political instability might ruin Russia's war effort." Throughout those weeks, blaming Rasputin, the British Embassy noticed "the radical shift in the public mood."[586]

Felix renewed his acquaintance with Rasputin on 17 November,[587] two days before his second consultation with Maklakov. It now emerges that Yusupov's plans to murder Rasputin must have been thrashed out with his discussion group sometime before he began to cultivate Rasputin's trust. Purishkevich, as Maklakov revealed in 1923, was not shy in telling him the date of the murder.[588]

Two events occurred that indicate the conspiracy to murder Rasputin had materialized by 1 November 1916:

1. The first event, **the family trigger**, happened on 1 November, when Grand Duke Nikolai Mikhailovich (with the consent of the dowager empress and other family members) tried to convince Nikolai II to change his ways.

2. The second event, **the public trigger**, occurred on the same day. It developed when Pavel Milyukov presented his vitriolic speech in the Duma, which launched a series of speeches by other delegates, each expressing their stance against Nikolai II's form of governance and the 'dark forces' that were seen to influence his decisions. [Milyukov's speech was heard on the first sitting day of the Fourth Duma session. Rasputin was murdered on the night after the Duma session went into recess.]

Both lines of attack were premeditated, arranged to impact on the same day. In both instances, the target was the same: Nikolai II. Those triggers brought out the Romanov family's private concerns into the public sphere after Purishkevich, Shulgin, and Lvov were pressed to speak out on the matter in the Duma. Grand Duke Nikolai Mikhailovich ensured that the public condemnation of Rasputin and Alexandra Fyodorovna would generate a vigorous response that would strike incessantly from two quarters to the point that the dilemma severely affected Russia's global image.

It is now easier to understand why Hoare accepted Purishkevich's invitation on 1 November. That encounter brought the extremist-thinking politician and the receptive British SIS agent towards a common purpose. It was Milyukov's exposé which prompted Purishkevich to speak to Buchanan and Hoare at the Duma that he had decided to solve the dilemma Russia was facing. For an ultra-nationalist, humiliating the monarch would have been intolerable. At some point he would invite his colleague, Dr. Lazovert, to assist, who must have despised Rasputin enough to participate.

At the end of Tuesday's Duma sitting on 1 November and before Saturday 19 November 1916, the plan to eliminate Rasputin began to consume the players. The Duma was to go into recess for the Christmas holidays on Friday 16 December[589] [590] and that date became central to their planning. The recess would eliminate the otherwise predictable uproar from any of the Duma delegates at the Tavricheskii Palace had the murder been arranged a few days earlier.

Felix agreed that the proposed date was convenient. His wife and family were staying in Crimea and the renovtions at his residence would to be concluded by mid-December.[591] The newly revamped basement would offer the ideal venue, with his staff assisting, some of whom had a military background and understood the meaning of loyalty. In Yusupov's words, his role "in this matter [was] the role of a host preparing for the death of his guest."[592] [Most likely, Nikolai Mikhailovich brought Felix into the conspiracy because of the Yusupovskii Palace's layout, in addition to Zinaida and Irina Yusupov's absence.] Sukhotin, a friend of Zinaida Yusupova, was probably drawn into the conspiracy upon her encouragement. As a reservist with the *Generalitet* Headquarters since February 1916, Sukhotin was able to assist on any date.

It was easy enough to draw in Dmitri Pavlovich, who had spoken out at Stavka against Nikolai II's decisions. Dmitri was slated to return from Stavka between the 10th and 15th of December.[593]

Grigorii Rasputin accepted Felix's cordial invitation to the Yusupovskii Palace, notwithstanding the unusual late hour on Friday night.

With all the key players in place by 19 November, the deed would occur within one month. Perhaps the only setback that could have disrupted their plans would have been a whiteout that would have prevented the drive beyond the city limits. In Yusupov's words, 16/17 December was to become the night when they served their most decisive "duty to the Tsar and the Motherland."[594]

Noble Service on Behalf of the Emperor and Country

Felix Yusupov first met Rasputin in 1909[595] just before his departure for Oxford University in England. The Yusupov family hoped that Rasputin would cure their son of his homosexual penchant. Felix met Rasputin at Maria (Munya) Golovina's family apartment at the time when the *strannik* was among the most popular personalities in society. Yusupov re-established his acquaintance with Rasputin and continued meeting him in the Golovin apartment. For some undisclosed reason, their meetings transferred to Rasputin's own apartment on Gorokhovaya *Ulitsa*, which Nikolai Mikhailovich noted had occurred "almost daily."

Matrena testified at the Extraordinary Commission of Enquiry that Felix insisted that these daily visits were conducted in absolute secrecy. She explained that Felix would only arrive between 8 p.m. and 5 a.m.[596] when the *dezhurnaya* (house supervisor) was off duty. Felix would park his car on the Fontanka corner and walk up Gorokhovaya *Ulitsa*, pass through the front passageway of the building, walk across the courtyard and always use the back door that led to the stairs ascending to the Rasputin family apartment, just as Munya had shown him beforehand. Rasputin knew he could remove the chain and unlatch the door to allow his guests to enter.[597] Felix claimed these measures were necessary to prevent Taneeva from finding out and then telling Alexandra Fyodorovna about his visits.[598]

Grand Duchess Maria Pavlovna (the younger) gives the impression that her brother Dmitri was initially tormented by his participation. To alleviate his reservations, he travelled to Moscow and met with Grand Duchess Elizaveta (Ella) Fyodorovna. She was a logical choice because as his former legal guardian, she and Grand Duke Sergei Alexandrovich raised him at their Ilinskoye estate.[599] Their conversation convinced him that he should take part.[600] The duchess was prejudiced in her advice. She had despised Rasputin for many years. Narishkin-Kurakina noted that the grand duchess showed "passionate zeal" as she "urged and encouraged her nephew Dmitri to commit the murder."[601] It is difficult to grasp why as a nun running a religious order, Ella did not steer Dmitri away from the conspiracy that involved an immoral act.

Legal Advice That Recommends a Surprising Remedy

Maklakov said that he had offered legal advice to Yusupov more than twice after Yusupov had finally decided he would become involved in the conspiracy to murder Rasputin.[602] One aspect about those sessions was the disturbing finding that rather than informing Yusupov how the Imperial Criminal Code might affect him, instructions were given as to how best to take the life of a human being and then to cover one's tracks using the Criminal Code and related legal considerations that affected the nobility. Yusupov admitted he had sought Maklakov's advice,[603] not because of the Duma speech, but that they were arranged at the behest of

Nikolai Mikhailovich. These consultations expose Maklakov's role in the scheme, besides the prospect of receiving a telegram from Purishkevich informing him in Moscow that the conspiracy had reached its intended conclusion.[604] Maklakov would understand from Purishkevich's message that his services would be required again. The three consultations that Yusupov had with Maklakov expose how willingly this person had compromised his professional integrity. To add to his failing, he not only provided a weapon to facilitate the commission of a crime but he did nothing to prevent the commission of Rasputin's murder.

Maklakov never denied that he provided a weapon intended to harm Rasputin. This item, which lay on his desk, was an implement that could be used "just in case"[605] of difficulties. Both Yusupov and Purishkevich mentioned Maklakov's weapon.[606] [607] The object loaned to Yusupov was not just a rubber stick[608] or a weight.[609] It was a club made of tightly woven fiber that was shaped at either end into a sphere with a short bar connecting the outer spheres.[610] Maklakov had purchased the object as a souvenir when he was abroad. Although it is impossible to establish the truth of the matter, Maklakov stated that he handed the club to Yusupov at his insistence,[611] and not as Yusupov had inferred, that Maklakov offered the club as a parting gesture. [The relevance of Maklakov's truncheon will be better appreciated in Chapter Eight.] Maklakov, however, denied that he supplied cyanide to Yusupov, saying with all sincerity that had he done so, the poison would have been effective.[612]

Loose Ends

The vehicle chosen to convey Rasputin belonged to Dmitri Pavlovich, because his automobile was emblazoned with a regal emblem.[613] This distinctive feature would provide the necessary sanctuary should anyone attempt to stop them en route because of the night curfew in war time.

To ensure that there was a public record (if needed as evidentiary material), Yusupov asked his wife to send him a telegram on 16 December, notifying him of her illness and requesting his arrival in Crimea.[614] The telegram would provide the reason why he needed to leave Petrograd promptly.

Nikolai Mikhailovich explained why Yusupov had succeeded in getting Rasputin's confidence:

> *"How to explain the blind trust, which Rasputin had shown the young Yusupov, [when] actually [he] trusted nobody, always in fear of being poisoned or murdered? This leaves the proposition again something completely incredible, and that is – frightfully carnal love towards Felix, which overshadowed this robust man – debaucher that led him to the grave."* [615]

The grand duke's character analysis that Rasputin's erotic fantasies had played a fatal part is absurd thinking. After cultivating Rasputin's trust, Yusupov was confident that his seemingly innocent night-time invitation would be accepted. The lateness of the hour was not unusual for either of them, eliminating any feeling of mistrust.

Vasilii Maklakov's file reveals that the conspiracy to eliminate Rasputin was the first phase in the plan to create a constitutional monarchy. The second phase necessitated the banishment of the empress to a mental institution two weeks after Rasputin's death.[616] Grand Duchess Elizaveta Fyodorovna expressed the widespread view, saying she passionately felt that "Providence had selected Dmitri and Felix."[617]

It was no coincidence that both Nikolai Mikhailovich and later Felix Yusupov had referred to Rasputin as a dog.[618] Felix Yusupov always claimed when he lived in exile that he only killed a dog! For both of them, the life of an innocent human being was reduced to a creature that required extermination.

Table 1 is an outline of the murder, which Felix Yusupov and Vladimir Purishkevich described in their published books. It is split into two to help identify where there are similarities and where there are variations in their recollections. It should be recognized that Felix Yusupov may have had accessed Purishkevich's book before he decided to put pen to paper and offered his own interpretation of the events.

TABLE 1. The Evidence as Stated by Vladimir
Purishkevich and Felix Yusupov

Recollection of Purishkevich (1918)	Recollection of Yusupov (1927)
Maklakov gave Felix a rubber baton (*girya*)	Maklakov gave Felix a rubber baton
+ potassium cyanide (KCN) crystals	-
Felix gave Dr. Lazovert cyanide crystals (KCN) + rubber gloves → chopped KCN into powder on a plate → Lazovert added KCN powder to the top half of <u>pink</u> iced cakes, <u>two cut as if partially eaten.</u> → Disposed rubber gloves into the fireplace	Felix gave Dr. Lazovert cyanide sticks Lazovert puts on rubber gloves → dissolved the crystals into a *slurry* Lazovert added KCN powder to three <u>chocolate</u> iced cakes, 3 almond cakes were harmless -
P. places his Savage pistol on Felix's desk	-
Felix gave Purishkevich and Grand Duke Dmitri KCN liquid in vials to pour into two of four wine glasses; 15 minutes after, Felix left to collect Rasputin. → no gloves mentioned	Wine glasses laced later by person's unknown, if at all. → Felix not present when KCN was handled

Recollection of Purishkevich (1918)	Recollection of Yusupov (1927)
Field Hospital emblem on Purishkevich's car masked by paint purchased by Lazovert on 15 December	-
Felix was wearing a military fur coat; and Sukhotin in chauffeur uniform	Felix wearing a Siberian *Doha* (fur coat + fur hat); and Sukhotin in a chauffeur's uniform collect Rasputin.
Collect Rasputin at 12.30 a.m. in Purishkevich's car	
-	Felix spoke to *dvornik* (caretaker) at Gorokhovaya, 64; Felix uses back stairs, same stairs used on departure
Rasputin ate a few pink cakes, drank two glasses of wine	Rasputin drinks tea first, then eats cakes and drinks wine (amount unspecified), but first wine was not poisoned
Poison → NO EFFECT	**Poison → NO EFFECT**
Felix goes upstairs twice and admits to the group that the poison was not working	Felix comes up to his study once and admits to the conspirators that the poison was ineffective
Dmitri prefers to call it off	-
Purishkevich advocates for a conclusion	
	Felix now decides "shoot to kill"
Felix takes the rubber baton	
Felix takes his Browning pistol from his writing desk	Felix takes Dmitri's revolver (type not identified)
2 or 3 shots fired by Y.- R. falls on bear rug – face up	One shot fired, Rasputin falls onto bear rug - face up

Recollection of Purishkevich (1918)	Recollection of Yusupov (1927)
Rasputin **shot in chest** (no exit wound)	Rasputin **shot near heart** (entry wound)
Rasputin not bleeding Dmitri and Purishkevich move R. onto stone floor	Rasputin tiny blood stain on shirt (bleeding) Dmitri & Purishkevich move Rasputin onto granite floor, bleeding onto floor; Felix shakes Rasputin. Rasputin opens left eye, then both 'green' eyes Frothing from mouth, fight ensures then Rasputin collapses on his back. Locks door
Rasputin wore cream silk shirt, raspberry sash with tassels, velvet pants, boots	Rasputin wore a white shirt with cornflowers, raspberry sash with tassels, new high boots, combed hair
Sukhotin puts on Rasputin's beaver coat, gloves and boots over his military uniform.	Felix plans for others to go on a fictitious drive back to Gorokhovaya, 64. Sukhotin dressed in Rasputin's fur coat
Dmitri and Lazovert leave in Purishkevich's car to burn Rasputin's clothing in the hospital train stove (Mrs. Lazovert burns gloves & waistcoat (not oversized fur coat or galoshes)	Felix plans that others burn Rasputin's spare clothing in hospital train. Felix remains at the Moika Palace alone
Change cars at Sergievskii Palace, return to Moika to transport Rasputin's corpse from palace.	-
-	*Izvozchik* from Warsaw station to Sergievskii Palace, return in Dmitri's car to Moika Palace.

Recollection of Purishkevich (1918)	Recollection of Yusupov (1927)
Purishkevich removes his Savage from holster, goes to basement	Purishkevich removes Savage from holster, goes to basement.
-	Felix takes his revolver from holster and Maklakov's rubber baton
-	
Rasputin seen running towards the closed gate	Rasputin on all fours climbs stairs, runs outside
	Purishkevich stalls Rasputin near the gate
Purishkevich fired and missed twice.	Purishkevich fires at least twice and misses
Third shot entered Rasputin's back	Purishkevich fires - **hits Rasputin**
Rasputin still standing	
Fourth shot fired into Rasputin's *possibly head*	-
	Purishkevich rapid fires → **Body parts hit not identified**
Rasputin fell face down, shaking head	Rasputin falls on the snow
Purishkevich kicks Rasputin in the temple	Purishkevich kicks Rasputin - large gaping wound on left temple
Rasputin attempted to crawl on his abdomen over the snow, teeth clenched, then lay by the gate	Rasputin moves (near the gate) but unresponsive

Recollection of Purishkevich (1918)	Recollection of Yusupov (1927)
Two persons pass the fence – heard shots	*Gorodovoi* speaks with Felix - heard shots. Rasputin's body still in yard.
Purishkevich declares to Felix and Dmitri: *"I killed Grishka Rasputin, enemy of Russia and the Tsar"*	-
Felix's soldiers bring Rasputin's body inside – below the stairs in the lobby	
Purishkevich witnesses Felix retrieve rubber baton and wildly beats Rasputin downstairs, throws baton at Rasputin. Felix covered in blood spatter	-
Rasputin face up, breathing laboriously, pupil disappearing in open right eye	-
Rasputin covered head-foot in blue (curtain) material, tied up with rope. Purishkevich thinks Rasputin is now dead	-
Gorodovoi returns – Purishkevich converses, whilst Rasputin's body placed into car	*Gorodovoi* returns and enters Felix's study, Purishkevich converses, Rasputin's body placed on platform at the bottom of the stairs by Felix's *kamerdiner*
	Felix beats Rasputin's body using Maklakov's rubber baton
Felix washes off blood spatter, changes clothes and shoes	-

Recollection of Purishkevich (1918)	Recollection of Yusupov (1927)
Felix's staff soldier placed Rasputin's corpse into Dmitri's car, with a two pood weight + chains + beaver coat + galoshes	Dmitri, Sukhotin and Lazovert took Rasputin in a closed car (not stated whose) to dispose of the body on Petrovskii Island
- Dmitri drove, Sukhotin sat in front, behind sat Lazovert, Purishkevich and Felix's *kamerdiner*	
Motor running, lights out, car stopped at the left side bridge railing, Dmitri stood beside the car. The bridge guard slept in hut on the opposite side on the right.	
Purishkevich, the soldier, Lazovert and Sukhotin threw R.'s body over the rail, with weights + chain inside the beaver coat + one galosh.	
Second galosh + bloodied car carpet destroyed later by maid in Sergievskii Palace	
Purishkevich and Lazovert and Sukhotin returned to Warsaw station in separate *izvozchik* (coachman with carrier) at 6 a.m.	-

Recollection of Purishkevich (1918)	Recollection of Yusupov (1927)
-	Felix's *Kamerdiner* shot a dog (tied up in yard) with a revolver and threw it on the snow. Felix witnessed bloodied corpse passed over where Rasputin crawled to mask Rasputin's blood and destroy police tests. Poured camphor on visible blood stains.

Chapter Three Photos

DOCUMENT No. 4: Fragment of Felix Yusupov's letter
stating, "I am working out a plan to destroy R."

CHAPTER FOUR
Why Russian Society Wanted Rasputin Dead

Late on Friday night, 16 December 1916, the Duma went into recess.[619] During the day, Prince Felix Yusupov telephoned Rasputin and invited him[620] to come to his home at Moika, 94. The pretext of that invitation was to meet Felix's wife, Princess Irina Alexandrovna, who was Nikolai II's niece. It was agreed that Felix would collect Rasputin around midnight.

Fundamental Reasons that Lead to Rasputin's Murder

The strength of Imperial Russia came from the connection the sovereign had with his people. Once criticisms began against the emperor, it was impossible to ignore them while they intensified alongside the cries for a revolution. Political dissent after 1 November 1916 grew rapidly across the nation. Samuel Hoare said that the name *Rasputin* was on everyone's lips in Petrograd, "where not a day passed without some rumor ... of his influence."[621] Most saw Grigorii Rasputin as the root cause of Russia's despair. Aristocrats blamed Nikolai II and especially Alexandra Fyodorovna for causing a rift between the dynasty and the Russian people because of their closeness to Rasputin. On 3 August (New Style), Foreign Affairs Minister Sergei Sazonov confided to Paléologue:

> *"The Emperor is the sovereign, but it is the Empress who governs under Rasputin's guidance."*[622]

Sazonov's complaint clarifies why many wanted to be rid of the Siberian *muzhik*. Seven factors played their part in removing Russia's most despised domestic enemy.

FACTOR ONE: The Seclusion of the Imperial Couple in Tsarskoe Selo

The first factor concerned the self-imposed seclusion of Nikolai II and Alexandra Fyodorovna. That circumstance, well before the war began, had affected relationships with their extended family and the aristocracy. The privileged social class comprised descendants of eminent titled aristocracy, military officers and government ministers who, in the company of their wives, relished the constant cycle of invitations to attend grand receptions, banquets and balls. The Court of Nikolai II was in stark contrast to the lively Court of Alexander III. The dowager reproached her son Nikolai that his court lacked the luster of the previous court.[623] The loss of the gaiety, which society had become accustomed to enjoy, had promoted additional angst. This unwelcoming situation lead to extensive ill feeling against Alexandra Fyodorovna, whose social skills were insufficiently attuned to her primary, ceremonial role as the consort of the sovereign. The court only celebrated the essential festive days as stated in the court calendar.

Few were aware that Nikolai II and his wife's seclusion was to protect their son from the prying eyes of the nation. Both parents were desperate to impart the illusion of his well-being. The trauma of having to watch her son's painful episodes of debilitating ill health[624] only lessened when Rasputin offered solace to Alexandra Fyodorovna. The dowager empress paid little attention to the fact that her daughter-in-law preferred to be present during her son's hemophiliac crises, sitting long hours by Alexei's bedside. Narishkin-Kurakina watched how Alexandra "trembled for the life of her child every minute."[625] The last thing on her mind was to host a function just to gratify the dowager's vast social circle. Alexandra Fyodorovna tended to each of her children after their birth, unlike most of the aristocracy who employed nannies for that purpose. Children rarely saw their parents, not even at mealtimes. By contrast, Alexandra Fyodorovna enjoyed family life and that circumstance raised harsh criticism. The empress' attitude gave the impression that it was a deliberate act,[626] not helped by her failure to take delight in social chitchat.[627]

The poor relationship Alexandra Fyodorovna had with her mother-in-law, Dowager Empress Maria Fyodorovna also played a part in the seclusion. Privately, the dowager empress expressed annoyance about her daughter-in-law, which no doubt affected the way other family regarded the empress. Had she trusted her son's judgement about Rasputin, she and her court might have aligned dutifully with her.

These two diary entries illustrate the difficulties and the dowager empress' exasperation:

1915. 28 August. *"…she is a tiresome, strange person* [who] *speaks merrily about nothing as if everything is going well"* [628]

1916. 20 December. *"A*[lix] *sees everything incorrectly and with her obstinate viewpoint and willfulness which only amuses us all into the abyss of suffering."*[629]

However, the dowager's discontent also fell on Rasputin.[630] A schism had developed between the two courts. No matter what her daughter-in-law did or said, she was criticized. The dissimilarities between the two women in their separate courts was causing society to favor the dowager. The fact that protocol demanded Nikolai II's mother be given first place if both women were present at a function[631] added to Alexandra Fyodorovna's solitude. Everybody always saw Nikolai II escort his mother ahead of Alexandra Fyodorovna and her escort. General Alexander Mosolov (head of the imperial chancellery attached to the imperial court) was acquainted with matters involving court protocol. He explained the reason for this scenario had to with Nikolai II leaving his mother with all the prerogatives, which should have flowed to the consort of the ruling emperor.[632]

Rasputin was seen as an intruder, an outsider who in some way had manipulated his way into the court. No one understood why a *muzhik* gained favor with the sovereign's family, particularly as very few enjoyed open access. To counteract the insult to their pride was to vilify the empress. Mosolov explained that Grand Duchess Maria Pavlovna (the elder) was power hungry and disliked the new empress to the point she "began to behave with hostility towards her." According to his observations, the empress, from the very beginning of her life in Russia, not only experienced the dowager's court placing itself against hers, but Grand Duchess Maria Pavlovna's (the elder) court tended to influence St. Petersburg high society.[633]

Nikolai II knew that family members were creating a politically dangerous situation by their hostility. That hostility simmered from the Vladimirovich branch of the family ever since Nikolai II became the sovereign. The dissent resurfaced when Maria Pavlovna (the elder), widowed since 1909, began to circulate rumors against Alexandra Fyodorovna, which continued unrelentingly up to the last day of Nikolai II's reign (on March 2, 1917). The genesis of her venom came about after she married Grand Duke Vladimir Alexandrovich, who was Alexander III's brother and the progenitor of the Vladimirovich branch. In 1904, he "encouraged disloyalty to the emperor ... and led disturbances ... to satisfy his grasping ambition."[634] When Alexander III was alive, he disliked his brother's wife because of her "disposition to play a political role."[635] Upon Alexander III's death, an arrangement came into existence, which would prevent Vladimir Alexandrovich "from making any attempt to secure the throne on Alexander's death by means of a *coup de main*."[636] A special *Ukaz* decreed that the consort of the sovereign had to be orthodox. Vladimir Alexandrovich's wife was the only grand duchess who had steadfastly refused to convert from her Lutheran religion. She saw that imperial instruction as a direct affront. Cleverly, Alexander III sought assistance from his brother-in-law, the Prince of Wales, to come and stay and serve as his son's protector and mentor for a short time, to prevent Grand Duke Vladimir from seizing the throne in the British prince's presence and subjecting the British heir-apparent (who became King Edward VII after the death of his mother, Queen Victoria) to political "indignities." This "debt of gratitude" was always borne in mind by Nikolai II when he dealt with Britain.[637]

FACTOR TWO: Nikolai II Becomes the Supreme Commander of the Imperial Forces

Following the disastrous events in the war, when Kovno (now Kaunus, Lithuania) was captured by the Germans, Russia was embarrassed by its continuous military losses. Paléologue noted in his diary[638] that the disaster was placed on Grand Duke Nikolai Nikolayevich's shoulders, as the Supreme Commander. In an attempt to lessen further military embarrassment, the emperor dismissed the grand duke and took over as Supreme Commander of the Imperial Forces. He believed that as head of state it was his responsibility to assume command of his dispirited army, who were retreating rather than advancing towards victory.[639] Father Georgii Shavelsky, the military cleric at Stavka, knew that Nikolai Nikolayevich blamed Alexandra Fyodorovna for the dismissal because she detested him, a loathing spurred on by Rasputin.[640]

Dowager Empress Maria Fyodorovna provided a personal insight regarding her son's decision in her diary:

1915. 8 August. *"Pavel Benkendorf visited me after a long absence. We were both in despair about the terrible communication from the front and other events, which are occurring and about which are now spoken. Before everything it is, that the irate soul of Gr[igorii] has returned, and also A. [Alexandra Fyodorovna] wants Niki to take the Supreme Command for himself instead of Grand Duke Nikolai Nikolayevich; have to be mindless, to do that!"*[641]

[Yulia Kudrina, Maria Fyodorovna's biographer, provided the following sentence that is missing in the recent Russian edition, which was sourced from a Danish source:

"She must be psychiatrically insane, if she honestly believes this!" [642]]

1915. 12 August. *"… Yusupov arrived this afternoon and recounted all kinds of terrible things, which are spoken about in the city. Niki arrived with his 4 girls. He began to say himself that he will take over the command instead of Nikolasha, I was so horrified, that I nearly collapsed, and told him, that it was a huge mistake, [I] pleaded not to do it now, when everything is bad for us, and added that, if he does this, everyone will see, that this was Rasputin's Prikaz. I believe that this impressed him, because he became significantly red. He simply does not understand, what danger and suffering this may bring us and to the entire nation."*[643]

The dowager empress blamed her daughter-in-law[644] and in the same stroke implicated Rasputin as the main menace who shaped her son's decision. Failing to respect her son's decisions concerning military matters (a situation that was never tolerated by her late husband, Alexander III, when he was the emperor[645]), the dowager struggled to impress on her son that he ought to be in Petrograd.[646] She, like most of Petograd society, feared that Alexandra Fyodorovna through Rasputin would direct military strategy.[647] Baroness Buxhoeveden was perceptive enough to see that the real effect this change would bring to the empress was the "tragedy" of "the separation" but she "felt it was her duty to support him."[648]

Alexandra Fyodorovna wrote the following to her sister, Ella:

"Nicky will take over command ...and then he will constantly go and see the troops and know what's going on at last ...It's a heavy cross Nicky takes upon himself, but with God's help it will bring better luck." [649]

The emperor's decision was not setting precedent, nor was he duty-bound to stand at the head of his military forces. Peter the Great lived in Mogilev while he directed operations against the Swedes in 1704.[650] Grand Duke Andrei Vladimirovich noted in his diary that Alexander I in 1812 and Alexander II in 1877 headed their armies in battle. He conceded that the idea itself was a good one, which had the effect of elevating the "moral element of the army" (which also happened in 1915[651]). Grand Duke Andrei Vladimirovich reflected how the German and Italian monarchs in the past preserved the leadership of their armies without having the need to command them, whereby the "sovereign was persuaded not to travel to the army and become directly involved in matters of the high command."[652]

Dmitri Pavlovich, believing his close relationship with Nikolai II would help him whilst pleading with him to change his mind, sought military leave. His request was refused. Frustrated with the response, Dmitri complained to the dowager empress. Within a few days, Nikolai Nikolayevich received a telegram demanding that Dmitri's request be granted. He acceded to the dowager's request. Before Dmitri left, he met several generals who helped him formulate what he must say to Nikolai II.[653] Admiral Bubnov, the chief of staff of the naval forces at Stavka, confirmed that Dimitri's conversations at Stavka came about "in the name of saving Russia."[654] Dmitri left the military headquarters (located at the time in Baranovichi, Minsk District) and arrived in Tsarskoe Selo. Paléologue claimed he spoke with Dmitri and found out that

Dmitri wanted to speak up against the pending dismissal because it would cause a deplorable effect on the troops and it would pave the way for the empress (and Rasputin) to control the military.[655] Nicholai II rejected Dmitri's plea, apparently saying, "Stay calm, I am acting how my conscience is prompting me."[656] In April 1917, Dmitri, writing from Persia, told his father he was "correct to have pleaded with Niki not to take over the command of the army."[657]

The dowager empress attempted to discourage her son for about two hours in the Yelaginskii Palace garden (in Petrograd). After that meeting, she wrote in her diary:

1915. 18 August. "[I] *had the opportunity to speak with him, but without result.*"[658]

Three days later, she raised her concern with her son again:

1915. 21 August. "*I once more requested Niki to preserve the Supreme* [Command], *regretfully, probably, without any benefit.*"[659]

Two days later, on 23 August,[660] the emperor exercised his prerogative power and signed a *Prikaz* (Decree) to the army and navy, declaring that he was the Supreme Commander of the military forces. He immediately departed for Stavka, arriving at 3.30 in the afternoon.[661] Almost immediately upon arrival at his new headquarters at Mogilev, Nikolai II transmitted a telegram to King George at Windsor Castle[662] and one was sent to the President of the French Republic, Raymond Poincaré, as well as all the other allies, informing them of the new circumstance.

After Admiral Bubnov learnt of the change in command, he blamed it on "the insistence of the empress." who saw the grand duke as a future "threat to the Throne" With that thought, "the Empress was supported by all of the Rasputin camarilla who did not tolerate the grand duke."[663] Others like Narishkin-Kurakina argued that "on the advice of Rasputin ... the Empress finally decided to transfer the Grand Duke to the Caucasus."[664] While Pavel Milyukov supposed the "Empress together with Rasputin found a way to clear Nikolasha away supporting the Emperor's conviction that it was ... his holy duty."[665]

General Mosolov understood that Nikolai II "considered himself to be the premier professional militarist of his empire and did not permit any compromises in this matter. His duty was the duty of all serving soldiers."[666] Along those lines, at the risk of forfeiting his throne, Nikolai II reflected that his taking over of the supreme command would not only elevate the army's morale, it would also halt the Germans and lead to victory. Indeed, few of the dowager's clique believed that this change would lead to military success. Yet shortly afterwards, the 11th Armed Forces gained a significant victory in Galicia, taking two German divisions. Nikolai II attributed this success to his taking of the command and to "God's blessing."[667]

Just one day after the change in the supreme command of the military forces, the dowager empress empress expressed her utter despair, writing in her diary:

> **1915. 24 August.** *"Benckendorff came at 12, stayed until the afternoon. Finding him in despair about everything that is happening, like I. Incomprehensible to be so power hungry!"*[668]

General Danilov admitted that Nikolasha had accepted his dismissal calmly, but to his surprise, Dmitri Pavlovich now voiced his irritation about the emperor taking command,[669] and thus acted with "dry formality" towards him,[670] while the dowager empress blamed her son for Nikolai Nikolayevich's downfall. For her it was intolerable that a senior Romanov appeared to have fallen from public grace. Maria Fyodorovna's position suited the majority the Nikolayevich branch of the family. They fell in behind the dowager empress, indifferent to the fact that the majority at the Front, including many of the commanders, gladly accepted the change,[671] which saw the rejuvenation of the battle-weary troops.

The German newspaper *Fossische Zeitung* compounded public distress by publishing the following inflammatory article:

> *"The appearance of the Russian autocrat into the role of Supreme Commander will soon prove the impending disintegration of the army and the Empire. In any case the descent of the Grand Duke indicates political reasons, rather than military considerations."* [672]

Yusupov presumed that when Nikolasha was ensconced in the Caucasus, Rasputin made almost daily visits to Taneeva's cottage in Tsarskoe Selo to give advice on government matters.[673] Elsewhere, Nikolai Mikhailovich was leading the seditious charge within his social circles[674] looking for a way to place Nikolasha on the throne (Milyukov[675] and General Mosolov[676] confirmed this was indeed true). Since there was "nothing more dangerous than changing the chief during military operations," Mosolov concluded the emperor "did not make one wrong step to discredit the powerful high command."[677]

FACTOR THREE: The Accusation that Rasputin and the Empress Were Involved With Espionage Against Russia

Many years after the Bolsheviks seized power, Kerensky wrote in one of his memoirs that when Alexei Khvostov first became Minister of Internal Affairs, he told him that he was convinced that the Germans received military intelligence from the Imperial High Command Headquarters through Rasputin.[678] More revealing is the fact that Kerensky failed to act on that information. In 1917, Khvostov did not hold back his thoughts during his questioning session at the Extraordinary Commission of Inquiry. This is part of the Commission's questioning and responses:

> **President:** *"What do you consider was Rasputin's role?"*
>
> **Khvostov:** *"He was a convenient pedal for German spying. Though I never caught him spying, but logically I thought that he was a spy because it was very easy to discover, through him what was happening in Tsarskoe. ..."*
>
> **President:** *"In whose hands was he the instrument of espionage?"*
>
> **Khvostov:** *"I believe that he was in the hands of German agents. I tried to catch them, but this did not happen."*
>
> **Sokolov:** *"... did some kind of words of a political character emerge in Rasputin's speech or expressions? Did Germanophilic tendencies emerge in him?"*
>
> **Khvostov:** *"This I had no opportunity to find out. I believe that he was a naïve spy."*[679]

Kerensky explained that after the February Revolution, the

Provisional Government found out that the Germans had covertly gained Rasputin as one of their agents.[680] It is difficult to understand why Kerensky made such a spurious claim when the Commission he set up revealed that Rasputin did not influence Russian domestic affairs during the war. Rasputin's telegrams proved that although he abhorred the idea of war, it did not mean that he would have compromised one fighting Russian soldier, more so since the majority of soldiers came from rural villages similar to his own.

Admiral Bubnov said that during 1916, the "rumors about the Rasputin clique's links with secret German agents" had reached them in Stavka, from which there "emerged groundless ... blameworthiness of the empress a *Nemka* [German] by origin, of treason." Bubnov added that "under these conditions, the Empress's and the sovereign's stubborn protection of Rasputin and his clique insulted our nationalistic dignity and brought out among all of us ... profound offense."[681] By then, the pervasive negative feelings were impossible to neutralize.

Radzinsky claimed that it was the Germans who had spread the rumor that Rasputin was being told military secrets by the "debauched German tsarina." The German disinformation was supposed to demoralize the Russian army into defeat.[682] The disinformation had also affected Petrograd society, which accepted its veracity and used it to strike against Rasputin. Those falsehoods, after reaching Stavka, incited individuals like Dmitri Pavlovich to fear for Russia's future.

General Spiridovich stressed that the allegation about the empress' German sympathies was untrue, because he knew that Alexei Khvostov made up the espionage rumor in February 1916 and that he was responsible for leaking that story to the press.[683] Sergei Sazonov (Minister of Foreign Affairs until July 1916) knew the truth,[684] as did Nikolai Mikhailovich. Alexandra Fyodorovna was never a traitor and had never sabotaged the war effort,[685] but the grand duke's hatred for her was so toxic, he stayed silent.

Shortly after the war was announced, though Kerensky discovered that Alexandra Fyodorovna despired the Kaiser,[686] he argued the empress had sympathies towards the German people. Believing that she was linked to a German spy ring suited his political agenda. Felix Yusupov was no different, saying in 1927 that the German High Command had secured Rasputin with the help of money.[687] However, he became muddled after he questioned whether Rasputin "was actually a German spy or nothing at all."[688] Major-General Handbury-Williams, who spent time at Stavka, revealed that Rasputin was "never allowed to come to the Headquarters of the Armies in the Field."[689] In fact, Handbury-Williams never set eyes on Rasputin but had to admit that "the scandals [unspecified] which he had caused led to tales of worse ones, most of the latter being, however, without any foundation." Then, adding that "anyone who knew the Empress knew her full well and that she might have been spared many of the wicked accusations which were made concerning her dealings with him [Rasputin]."[690] Accordingly, it is puzzling why others at Stavka did not share similar impressions.

Rumors and disinformation proved to be the most effective domestic weapon that was launched against Nikolai II, using Rasputin as the projectile. Yet despite the rare praise imparted about the empress' sincere loyalty for her adopted country, few defended her at the time.

FACTOR FOUR: The Accusation that Rasputin had Demanded a Separate Peace Treaty Between Russia and Germany

Paralleling with the previous factor, the fourth factor concerned the allegation made by Nikolai Mikhailovich that Rasputin had declared that there were plans to sign a separate peace treaty with Germany in December.[691] Samuel Hoare imagined[692] that the "murder would destroy the 'Dark Forces' to enable Russia to continue with the war with a single purpose."

Purishkevich added to the gossip when he travelled on his hospital train and told anyone who would listen that Russia was preparing to sign a separate peace treaty.[693] His news was at odds with Nikolai II, who was a "fanatical supporter of the *Entente* with England and France."[694] The French government believed that this was indeed the Russian position, given that Paléologue wrote:

"The Russian people are more than ever determined to

continue the war to victory." [695]

Towards the end of November 1916, the dowager empress received a telegram that exposed the truth of the matter:

1916. 30 November. *"Shervash[idze] read the telegr[am] from Ger[many], in which is proposing peace, to which, I hope, not one of us shall go with."* [696]

The letter sent by Anna Rodzianko to Felix's mother, Zinaida Yusupova, presents the common view held at the time by Russian high society. Intercepted at the central Petrograd post office, one copy was passed on to the emperor. Her message conveyed the following (in part):

"... There is nothing pleasant to say about our existence: the whole country is in ferment it declares loudly and unanimously, through the Duma, the State Council and even through the united nobility that the motherland is in danger that the power is in the hands of dark forces and irresponsible persons, ... Most people are afraid that Rasputin might hasten the conclusion of peace, regardless of the Allies, now that the official communiqués suggesting peace negotiations with Germany and Austria have been published. ...The French and British diplomats complain to Misha ... and that Germany through A. F. is attempting to influence the tsar (sic) against the allies." [697]

This letter the dowager empress sent to Nikolai II at Stavka states:

1916. 3 December. *"We are all influenced by the German proposal* [offer for concluding peace: Yu. Kudrina]. *The entire time one thing or another, he* [German Emperor Wilhelm: Yu. Kudrina] *is striving to take the position of peacemaker and places all responsibility on us, if only they* [the proposals] *will not be accepted. I hope very much that no one will give in to this trick. I am absolutely certain, that we and our allies shall preserve the strength and unity and divert this «bighearted» extended hand."* [698]

This letter exposes that it was the Kaiser who wanted to act as the peacemaker. Kudrina (Maria Fyodorovna's biographer) believes the dowager empress did not to quash the rumor about Russia wanting a peace treaty with Germany because it suited her purposes to help get rid of Rasputin. Indeed, Alexandra Fyodorovna's principal court lady, Narishkin-Kurakina, professed the empress was "secretly in contact with the Germans and working with them towards a separate peace." Then added that "the situation had grown so alarming that the King of England wrote to the Tsar suggesting that he send the empress to Sandringham for a period of rest." But 'they' were astonished when Buchanan "declared categorically in the emperor's face that he had absolute proof of a conspiracy which aimed at making a separate peace, the trail of which led to the empress."[699] Not surprisingly, Nikolai II denied the accusation.

Baroness Sophia Buxhoeveden explained that although much "was made of her [the empress] German origins, the tales of her pro-German sympathies were invented and assiduously spread. Stories were circulated of her desire for a separate peace treaty"[700] and had gained acceptance. Those rumors were created in ignorance of her character, in that Alexandra Fyodorovna was very English. All of Alexandra Fyodorovna's published letters, diaries and conversations nowadays prove how much she rejoiced at the Allies' successes or followed with sympathy when there were losses, saying, "God will not leave our troops – they are so brave."[701] Kerensky had to concede in 1917 that Nikolai II never considered such a measure.[702] Speaking with Buchanan, Kerensky confessed that no compromising material was found to suggest that "either she or the Emperor had ever contemplated a separate peace treaty with Germany."[703]

General Mosolov said that the rumor that Rasputin wanted to influence the empress about the necessity to conclude a separate peace treaty was largely heard "in diplomatic circles."[704] Mosolov investigated whether there was any substance to that rumor, which meant "the troops were not to be demobilized but returned to Russia." What he found was interesting. The rumor had coincided with the period when the "high command were preparing for a spring offensive" when "there was general dissatisfaction in Russia … once it was clear that the dynasty was in danger."[705] Judging by the conversation Mosolov had with Rasputin, it appears that the year was 1915, because they spoke of Count Witte in the present (he died in the same year in March). When Mosolov asked Rasputin what he thought about the war, he answered:

"Before the war I was for friendship with the Germans. That was best for the Gosudar *[sovereign]. But when the war began, then one had to try for victory: otherwise it would be bad for the* Gosudar."[706]

Frank Golder[707] discovered that the Germans planned to cause internal trouble for Russia. It was easy for them to learn that there was discord between Nikolai II and Nikolasha. Using that information, German intelligence made up the separate peace treaty story and had it disseminated among the Russian troops, scattering propaganda leaflets over the battlefields. Collaterally, the Germans successfully contaminated Petrograd society, allowing them to accept their lie, who in turn blamed Rasputin and the empress. Additional proof came from the Russian career diplomat, Nikolai de Bazily [Basily]. He recorded a conversation that took place twelve years after the war had ended. In Berlin, Bazily met the former wartime German Minister of Foreign Affairs, Gottlieb von Jagow, who asked why the German offers for a separate peace treaty were rejected. Nikolai de Bazily replied:

"We had promised our allies to continue the war at their side. Neither the Emperor nor the imperial government had considered betraying Russia's allies in spite of all the dangers presented by the internal situation."[708]

Significantly, the socialist leaning Provisional Government chose to operate in the same manner after the forced abdication of the emperor, respecting the *Entente* arrangement, although not legally bound to do so, given that it was not a signatory to the original pact. Soon after, the newly installed Bolshevik government headed by Vladimir Lenin negotiated for a ceasefire. After learning of the Armistice negotiations that began in December 1917, the former emperor, now imprisoned in Tobolsk, wrote:

1918. 7/8 February: *"Judging by the telegrams ... at the front, we have nothing; the army has demobilized pieces of ordinance and munitions discarded arbitrarily to chance and advancing unpleasantries! Dishonor and horror!"[709]*

The bilateral negotiations between Bolshevik Russia and Germany ended with the signing of the Armistice at Brest-Litovsk (now Brest, Belarus) at the former Russian Officers Club,[710] which led to the Brest-Litovsk Treaty. The treaty with Germany was signed on 3 March 1918 (New Style), almost one year after the Romanov dynasty ceased to exist. It marked the withdrawal of the army from the war and the surrender of vast tracts of highly arable territory, which Russia had gained from the Swedes and Poland.[711] The treaty was a departure from what Imperial Russia had fought for up until February 1917. Lenin ordered Foreign Affairs Commissar Leon Trotsky to agree to all of Germany's terms, so that the Bolshevik centralists could concentrate on strengthening their political grip over the Russian people.

FACTOR FIVE: The Maternal Influence of Zinaida Yusupova

Felix was convinced that Rasputin had deceived their majesties into believing that he was a genuine man of God and argued that "he was unconsciously the first Commissar of bolshevism," whose proximity to the throne caused the supreme power to become paralyzed by his influence.[712] Felix praised his mother saying she was among the first to step forward against Rasputin. This move was precipitated by Zinaida's disassociation from the empress; not in 1910,[713] as Felix recalled, but on 9 March 1912, an incident that happened after Guchkov revealed the text of the Novoselov letters in the Duma on 25 January 1912.

Zinaida Yusupova confronted the empress, apparently soon after Elizaveta Fyodorovna did the same, telling her, "Rasputin must be banished. He is a *Khlyst* who is abusing his position against you."[714] The empress supposedly responded that people were "slandering a holy man."[715] After their exchange, the imposing socialite was asked never to return to the palace.[716] Zinaida was doing everything possible to expose Rasputin's influence in the court. Just prior to Nikolai II's announcement that he would become Supreme Commander, Yusupova went so far as to visit the dowager empress in mid-1915 to protest against Rasputin. On 16 December 1915, exactly one year before Rasputin was murdered, Felix's father wrote the following in his diary:

> "*I saw a huge change in her: in outlook and movement.*

Before me was not the same Tsaritsa who I knew, but some kind of creature, obviously nervous and unwell. I felt pity for her and those sweet Grand Duchesses who were with her. ... I pity her with all my heart. She is absorbed in power ...continues to drag it into a precipice, already at the edge ... How right my wife was when she arrived on Kamennii Ostrov to [see] *Empress Maria Fyodorovna, in the presence of Grand Duchesses Ksenya and Olga Alexandrovna, saying that the only remedy to save the Sovereign, the children* [the imperial Grand Duchesses] *and Russia – is to send the Empress to a sanatorium for the affected soul. Isolation, peace, a quiet life might still save her. ... My wife nevertheless went to her once more. The chat lasted one and half hours,* [my] *wife told her the whole truth, pleaded with her to change everything, but the Empress was reticent and was only irritated about this conversation.*"[717]

Rodzianko claimed that Zinaida had entreated the dowager empress to use her influence over her son's decision to dismiss Nikolasha as the Supreme Commander. Rodzianko further asserts with a touch of the melodramatic that after the formal announcement declaring the change in command, Zinaida came to see him and his wife Anna. She was in tears because that decision would "bring us to revolution."[718]

Felix Yusupov claimed that in 1915, when he spoke with his mother about Rasputin's depraved influence, thoughts of murder had fermentted in his mind.[719] Despite this exposé, Felix did not follow along with his mother's view until mid-November 1916. Revealing her torment, Zinaida sent Felix a letter on 21 September 1916 saying:

"I am frightened to see that you are thinking completely like Valide [the Empress], *turning away from the truth and believe the lies and those 'friends' who surround you with flattery and hypocrisy. ... Come to your senses, I implore you and do not give the impression that you do not understand my alarm."*[720]

[The word *Valide* derived from the Arabic for *Empress*.[721] It was used by the Tartar people settled in Crimea, where Zinaida spent much time.] Felix was unconvinced by his mother's message.

The letters that Zinaida Yusupova sent to her son Felix reveal how far her maternal loyalty extended. Of course, due to wartime censorship, the word 'murder' could not be written. After Nikolai II became Supreme Commander, Yusupova dreaded the thought that her only surviving son would be called up to the Front. She became agitated when Felix enrolled [all able-bodied males had to enlist in the military] into the *Corps de Pages* in September 1915.[722] Zinaida, shortly thereafter, assured Felix that Minister of War General Alexei Polivanov (also opposed Nikolai II's new responsibility[723]) gave his guarantee that he would not be called to the Front "for one year," until after December 1916 or perhaps even January of the following year.[724]

Zinaida introduced Sergei Sukhotin to Felix on 2 October 1915. Sukhotin (Zinaida's guest at the family residence, *Koreiz*, Crimea) hand-delivered a letter to Felix where he with his wife Irina were also staying. Sukhotin first encountered Zinaida when he spent time at the Yusupov *lazaret* (infirmary) in Petrograd. In the letter that was personally delivered to Felix, she added towards the end of her news: "Sukhotin is everything to us ... he is so nice ... I adore him very much."[725] Trusting his mother about Sukhotin, Felix invited him to help their cause in December 1916. Sergei Sukhotin and his brother (both worked at the Yusupov *lazarets* in Petrograd and Koreiz in Crimea) would prove valuable to both mother and son, because they secretly passed on candidly written letters to avoid the prying eyes of the censors.[726] [727] Despite the caution, some letters, written in code, were posted and hence did not escape the postal censors. After Rasputin was murdered, a series of letters written by Zinaida Yusupova were passed over by Protopopov (Minister of Internal Affairs from September 1916) to Nikolai II. The person *Misha* refers to in the letter is their uncle by marriage, Mikhail Rodzianko.

1916. 18 November. *"Unless the book* [Rasputin] *is not eliminated and* Valide [the Empress] *tamed, nothing can be done, tell that to Uncle Misha."*[728]

1916. 25 November. *"Now it is too late, impossible to avoid a scandal whereas then everything could have been saved, demanding the removal of the manager* [Rasputin] *for the duration of* [the] *war and* [the] *non-interference of* Valide [the Empress] *in matters of State. And now I repeat that until these two matters will not be liquidated, nothing can be accomplished in a peaceful way. Tell this to uncle Misha from me.*

Protopopov and Kurlov must go, and then it will be easier to liquidate those two problems about which I wrote above."[729]

By the beginning of December, Zinaida's pleas to her son became even more frantic:

1916. 3 December. *"...I wrote to Medvedev* [Rodzianko] *that until the managers will be curtailed and* Valide [Empress] *is rendered harmless, nothing will come of it and to render it harmless is very simple ... This is essential and with this* [one*] must hasten."*[730]

Despite how kindly history has described Zinaida Yusupova, the wealthiest socialite in Imperial Russia, who exemplified elegance and sophistication, there was a darker side to her personality. The first letter was written one day before Felix listened to Purishkevich in the Duma. Zinaida's advice to discuss the matter with Rodzianko, a staunch monarchist, widens the network of those who may have known or contributed effort in ensuring that the matter would, as Zinaida stated, be "liquidated." Both letters go part of the way in helping to identify what inspired Felix to act. Once Felix confirmed his role on 19 November (and telling Irina about it the next day, see his 20 November letter above), his mother's appeal had been met.

Yet, if one asks as to what promoted Zinaida to act so forcefully during 1916, the answer may lie in Buchanan's visit to their estate in Crimea in April.[731] Though Felix explained that he was taking on the task to murder Rasputin, it was not entirely due to his reaction about the Duma speeches. Once Maklakov gave Felix his professional assurance that everything would be fine, his client felt at ease to proceed with his mother's wish. In this way, Zinaida's incessant haranguing played a part in his final decision.

Ella travelled to Tsarskoe Selo to speak with her sister about Rasputin's 'evilness' one last time. On 3 December,[732] the sisters met at the palace. [Almedingen mistakenly claimed that their quarelling had been settled.[733]] Almedingen's speculation fails to align with Ella's future actions and with the tenor of Alexandra Fyodorovna's message to her husband:

"...*if* matushka *[mother superior] will write to you, remember that she is backed by the Michels* [the Mikhailovich branch of the family], *do not to pay attention and do not to take this close to heart.*"[734]

Ella attempted to speak about Rasputin, after which a "serious argument that ended in a fracture" ensued. Ella was told to "shut up and go away" and was escorted in silence by Alexandra Fyodorovna to the train station as protocol demanded.[735] [Elizaveta Fyodorovna mentioned the rift in her letter to Nikolai II on 29 December.[736]] Arriving in Petrograd, she headed to the Yusupovskii Palace where Zinaida and Felix "sat on tenterhooks," keen to hear about her visit. Felix remembered her saying, "she sent me out like a dog," then adding "poor Niki, poor Russia."[737] Though Ella travelled "from Moscow, offering advice,"[738] she was forced to return to Moscow without realizing her objective. Ella, like Zinaida, was no longer favored by the empress because of her hostility concerning a contentious topic. No doubt Felix felt assured that with this incident and his mother's exclusion from the court two years earlier, he had made the right decision.

FACTOR SIX: The Maneuverings of Grand Duke Nikolai Mikhailovich

George Katkov, an émigré Russian historian from Oxford University, thought that the role Nikolai Mikhailovich played during the pre-revolutionary period was hard to evaluate.[739] However, with the publication of the dowager empress' diaries, it became easier to draw conclusions regarding the real role Nikolai Mikhailovich had played. Nikolai Mikhailovich began to take charge of family politics following Nikolasha's dismissal in August 1915.

Shortly after the war broke out, the grand duke wrote to the dowager empress expressing his "fears for the future, that one needs to observe the [nationalistic] tendencies of various relatives of German origin" and that the most "harmful of all the Hessians ... is Alexandra Fyodorovna, who in her soul had remained a German, who was against the war until the last moment..."[740] Nikolai Mikhailovich (aware about the dowager empress' long held loathing of Germans) urged her that these considerations had to be kept in mind, because Sazonov told him that Alexandra Fyodorovna was not in favor of mobilizing troops. This remark caused Nikolai Mikhailovich to misinterpret the context of what he heard, thinking that she wanted to shield Germany from imminent harm. Thus Nikolai Mikhailovich decided the empress was the greatest villain in the empire, who was manipulated by Rasputin.

Nikolai Mikhailovich visited Alexandra Fyodorovna on 1 May 1916. Though Alexandra Fyodorovna failed to mention what transpired during their one-hour meeting in her letter to Nikolai II,[741] Cockfield revealed that Nikolai Mikhailovich spoke to the empress, hoping she understood the gravity of her words.[742] He was frustrated that she failed to ignore accusations about Rasputin's political interference. Failing to impress on the empress what he believed were her fundamental problems, controlling her husband and, in turn, Rasputin manipulating her, Nikolai Mikhailovich decided to change tactics and strike against Nikolai II head on.

Until now, all of Nikolai Mikhailovich's letters addressing Nikolai II were restrained in their content and his conversations with Alexandra Fyodorovna were cordial. Nikolai Mikhailovich began to act on behalf of the family's interests. Firstly, he visited the dowager empress in Kiev. Her diary reveals that they met at 12 o'clock on 29 September and that he told her "about a lot of things" and stayed for dinner.[743] Following this visit, Nikolai Mikhailovich began to compose his plea to Nikolai II. By happenstance, Nikolai II, together with Alexei, arrived in Kiev a month later, arriving on Friday afternoon 28 October.[744] Here, the emperor, with Alexei, attended an officer's graduation ceremony, after which they spent the remainder of the day with the dowager, and left the next day.[745] Nikolai II wrote to his wife saying, "Mama was very kind and loving."[746] It appears his mother gave him no sign about what he was going to face in a day or so.

With Nikolai II's permission, Nikolai Mikhailovich arrived at Mogilev headquarters on the afternoon of 1 November.[747] They spoke for a long time during the evening.[748] The visit, encouraged by the dowager empress and her two daughters, Grand Duchesses Olga and Ksenya,[749] happened on the same day when Milyukov spoke in the Duma. Thus, why did Nikolai Mikhailovich race from Kiev to Mogilev?

The main purpose of Nikolai Mikhailovich's visit was to disparage Alexandra Fyodorovna. Shavelsky revealed that the grand duke stressed that there was an impending "political catastrophe due to Rasputin's government and pleaded with him that it was not too late to save the situation."[750] He advised the emperor not to give in to her pressuring and that she was influenced by those close to her who were leading her astray. Then came the warning. Russia was "on the eve of massive agitation and even an attempt on his [the emperor's] life."[751] To reinforce his views, Nikolai Mikhailovich named five individuals who maintained the same opinions as his own, identifying Father Shavelsky, Generals Alexeev and Grabbe who were attached to the imperial suite at Stavka.

Not desiring to engage with Nikolai Mikhailovich, Nikolai II listened, politely re-lighting the nervous grand duke's cigarette.[752] At the conclusion of the monologue, Nikolai Mikhailovich announced his loyalty to the monarchy [but not to the monarch]. Before the grand duke left, he handed over two sealed letters. Indifferent to what was written on each envelope, Nikolai sent both letters to Tsarskoe Selo for his wife to read. In his covering letter he said that both would give her an understanding as to what Nikolai Mikhailovich said.[753] Both letters shaped what was to be the first warning from the family. It was a measured strategy to offend Nikolai II (and Alexandra Fyodorovna), which recommended that *Niki* take action considered appropriate by the family (principally by the dowager). The second letter was intended for Alexandra Fyodorovna to read. Deceitfully, to give the impression that each letter was written for the person reading the letter, the second letter did not refer to Nikolai II's wife by name but Nikolai's letter was critical of Alexandra Fyodorovna. The method used was simple. Nikolai Mikhailovich firstly sowed the seeds of discontent and then stood back to watch the drama unfold.

The first letter, intended for Nikolai II's stated (in part):

"You trust Alexandra Fyodorovna, which is easy to understand, but that which comes out of her mouth is the result of clever fabrication and not the truth. If you are [not] strong enough to remove these influences from her, [Rasputin] at least guard yourself against this steady and systematic interference by those who act through your beloved wife. ...grant a Ministry which is responsible to you and to constitutional institutions. This could be done simply, without any pressure from outside [Rasputin]... I finally decided to do so after being urged by your mother and sisters. You are at the beginning of a new era of disturbances ... at the beginning of attempts at assassination. Believe me in trying to loosen you from the chains that bind you, I do it from no motives of personal interest ... but in the hope and in the expectation of saving you, your throne and our dear motherland from serious and irreparable consequences." [754] [755]

The text of the second letter (meant for Alexandra Fyodorovna only), while less direct, included different criticisms, whereby Alexander Protopopov should not be a government minister and the elderly Count Frederiks was useless. These details were pointed out in the letter that Alexandra Fyodorovna wrote to her husband on 4 November. [756] It stated that if the emperor accepted these facts and ...

"... permanently eradicated all the dark forces issues it would uplift Russia immediately ... and he [Nikolai] would regain massive loyalty ..." [757]

Alexandra Fyodorovna described the grand duke's conduct in this way:

"I read the letter from Nikolai and I am terribly indignant of him ... He has always despised me and foolishly commented about me for 22 years, - and at the [Yacht] club ... but during the war and at such a time [he is] hiding behind your mother's back and sisters rather than coming out fearlessly to defend the wife of his emperor. This is loathsome and treacherous ... he feels ... that my opinions are taken in regard and this he cannot tolerate. He is the incarnation of hate ... He and

Nikolasha are my greatest enemies. ...they have no right to do this ...."[758]

Both letters failed to change anything. On 7 November,[759] again with the dowager empress' encouragement, a second verbal session took place at Stavka. The dowager empress wrote in her diary that she had an hour and a half conversation with Nikolasha before he left for Stavka with his brother Peter Nikolayevich. While waiting for news as to how 'Niki' responded to their pleading, the dowager commented in her diary:

1916. 9 November. *"...desiring, that the chats with Niki by four different people shall open his eyes ... Alexeev, Shavelsky* [the army priest], *Nikolai* [Mikhailovich] *and finally Nikolasha ... who told Niki the whole truth."*[760]

Nikolasha was abrupt and warned Nikolai II that he "may lose his crown."[761]

On 9 November, Alexandra Fyodorovna wrote to her husband informing him that she became aware of Nikolai Mikhailovich's antagonistic ranting at the Yacht Club and that he was in constant touch with "Rodzianko and his company" (Zinaida Yusupova).[762] Nikolai Mikhailovich declared that he was aware of Alexandra Fyodorovna's irritation regarding the criticisms and that some of its members, including Count Frederiks, had threatened to close the club's doors.[763] Regardless, its members listened to Nikolai Nikhailovich's "constant caustic criticisms" that "contributed [to] weakening the regime. With spineless sarcasm he continued to speak in society with agonizingly negative authority about tsarist power."[764]

FACTOR SEVEN: The Duma Contravenes its Fidelity to the Emperor

The Duma representatives who had vowed their allegiance to their emperor at the beginning of the war now began working on ending his reign by raising derogatory accusations against Alexandra Fyodorovna and Rasputin, in the Duma. Most of the grand dukes began to align themselves with Guchkov and Rodzianko and the reformist Progressive Bloc party that formed on 24 August 1915,[765] days after Nikolai II became the commander in chief. By

November it was difficult to find prominent individuals or interest groups who had failed to join in the clamor for political change. The common cry on the streets became "Save the monarchy from the monarch."[766] The media reported that the Progressive Bloc reflected what the public was supposed to be thinking.[767] Left-leaning newspapers promoted the treasonous ideas expressed in the Duma. The Progressive Bloc's program was to fight "from the inside" by opposing the "existing order."[768]

The Fifth, and what proved to be the final assembly, of the State Duma re-assembled in the White Hall on Tuesday afternoon, 1 November 1916. Some 450 delegates gathered for the opening session.[769] During his conversation with Pavel Milyukov two days earlier, Paléologue was told that "certain things will have to be said from the tribune. Otherwise we shall lose all our influence ..."[770] All the diplomats were invited to attend but Paléologue had been pre-warned by the President of the Council, Stürmer, that there would be a problem during the afternoon session.

Rodzianko's opening speech for the new session acknowledged the presence of the Diplomatic Corps who sat up in the gallery above the delegates. Rodzianko warned that "the government cannot go by means separate from the nation," adding that Russia gave its word that peace with their allied nations would only come through decisive victory, while "any thoughts for a separate peace will be rejected."[771] As soon as his highly patriotic, but anti-tsarist speech ended, Stürmer with other conservative members left the chamber amidst the raucous noise that erupted from the socialist faction. All attending diplomats, on cue, stood up and walked out of the chamber, to avoid being compromised by their presence.[772] The sitting continued at with many empty seats. In a matter of hours, the Duma began to attract the public's attention by the unusual boldness of the speeches that began to be heard from its chamber.

The leader of the Constitutional Democrat (Kadet) Party and Professor of Russian history Pavel Milyukov (Photo 8) made his momentous speech, deliberately and repeatedly posing the same question to his listeners "with stupidity or with treachery?", with predictable almost theatrical responses: "this is stupidity", "shameful" or "this is treason" erupting across the various factions. The speaker accused the 'dark forces' for all the ills of the government, who "direct … important State matters." Milyukov maintained, "this power has now descended lower than the level in which it stood in normal times in our Russian life." Setting off an unprecedented political drama, Milyukov, critical of the empress, linked her publicly with the word 'treason.' "I have already warned that a contaminated family is already causing suspicion (about a) flourishing harvest, which from corner to corner of the Russian land, dark forces are unraveling, in relation to traitors and treason … these rumors are taking possession highly and do not spare anyone." Milyukov then asked, "How will you refute the opportunities of such suspicion when the clutch of dark personalities rule in personal and immutable matters…?"

Stürmer's alleged transgressions were summed up using five German newspapers in an attempt to prove that he, like Rasputin, was "against England and against the continuation of the war." With few dissenters (except for the far-right faction) to obstruct his speech (Maklakov incorrectly claimed there were none[773]), Milyukov read out extracts of German disinformation, declaring that his examples offered "published impressions from abroad about Stürmer's appointment" with this censored piece: "This is the victory of the Court party grouped around that young Czarina."[774] Protopopov and Metropolitan Pitirim were not left out, both accused of belonging to the "Court party." The most provocative words revealed the party's platform: "we told this government, as stated in the Bloc's Declaration: we will fight you, we will fight with all the laws until you leave."[775]

At this first sitting, the Duma exploded into open revolt against the political system and revealed their fury against the fictional '*dark forces.*' Despite the intense quality of Milyukov's speech that was based on dishonesty,[776] some had considered that it was "too timid and platonic and wanted an open fight against the Government."[777] The most astonishing words in his speech must surely be that "one cannot step into battle with all living forces of the nation; one cannot conduct conflict within the nation if you are leading it to the front…."[778] Years later, Milyukov admitted that his speech had "established a reputation as an assault signal in the direction of the revolution."[779] Though in 1917, he testified "we had no idea what form that change would take."[780]

In her letter to Nikolai II, Alexandra Fyodorovna wrote, "Milyukov had taken Buchanan's words that Stürmer was a traitor."[781] The empress continued, "let them shout – we must show them that we do not fear them and that we are firm." Indeed, Nikolai II could never permit a 'responsible ministerial government' under these circumstances.

The enforcement of regulations governing censorship concerning what the newspapers were able to publish had two consequences. Knowing that Duma speeches were classified material, Miluikov boasted that this restriction "only strengthened their resonance." Copies were reproduced on "*ministerial* (department) and *Shtab* (headquarters) machines and distributed over the entire country." The second consequence allowed the circulation of Milyukov's speech via word of mouth, often with added flourishes to create a more vivid tone.[782] Although Rodzianko admitted that the "Duma stenograms had to pass through the censor with massive white spaces," revealing that the speeches the public read were "in a completely distorted form."[783] All that Count Frederiks could do was to send a directive to Stürmer, asking him to amend the official copy. The naming of newspapers cited by Milyukov was tolerayed, but the German phrases and the name of the empress was forbidden.[784]

Part of the Council of Ministers' agenda on 2 November was to have considered the merits of dissolving the Duma (to prevent further trouble-making speeches) and whether to request Milyukov's arrest.[785] No one except Protopopov (Minister of Internal Affairs) and Stürmer wanted to arrest Milyukov for his subversive remarks. Stürmer obtained an uncensored copy of the speech from Rodzianko and passed it over to Makarov but the minister of justice found that despite the defamatory allegations, there were no words in Milyukov's speech that warranted legal action. Milyukov was protected from prosecution by the Duma's national immunity. Nobody questioned why Milyukov used German propaganda in the Russian Duma to make his case. The apparent inaction by the Council of Ministers indicated that there was a tacit endorsement concerning Milyukov's allegations. This situation paved the way for Shulgin and Purishkevich to utter their toxic speeches.

On 4 November, Kerensky led the charge about the purpose of censorship by posing the question:

> "*What kind of staretz* (sic) *are they and who is this Grigorii Rasputin, which military censorship is protecting, i.e. censorship which should protect the nation during the course of hostility, conceal that which the enemy should not know about in the interests of military safety? It means there is a staretz* (sic) *with whom the nation must not be acquainted, because if the nation finds out, there will be insurrection and indignation.*"[786]

Following his return from Petrograd on the evening of 6 November, Shavelsky requested an audience with Nikolai II. Both sitting down in armchairs, facing each other, Shavelsky broached the subject about the Duma speeches (a meeting that was anticipated by the dowager empress). Setting the tone of the conversation, he began by revealing that numerous "honest" Duma delegates "who loved their *Rodina* (Homeland)" had approached him. After revealing that the Duma had identified Protopopov as being "insane," Nikolai II asked whether that opinion was arrived at before or after he became a minister. The conversation flowed in similar fashion, with Nikolai II rebutting everything Shavelskii attempted to tell him, including the cleric's statement that "they are calling us rotten and lying slaves who are concealing the truth from you." Then Shavelsky exclaimed:

> "*If you do not pity Russia, please pity yourself and your family. Know that the wrath of the nation shall first of all be brought down on you and your family. It is terrifying to say: You with your family may be torn to pieces.*
>
> *So far not much is asked of you: place people who are honest, serious politicals who understand the needs of the people and are ready to selflessly go to satisfy them!*"[787]

Taking his leave, Shavelskii asked for the emperor's forgiveness in expressing such harsh unpleasantness. It was a pathetic appeal. At his departure, Grand Duke Sergei Mikhailovich, who was standing immediately outside the room, praised the priest for telling Nikolai II how they both thought it was. The following day, Shavelsky reported to Nikolasha shortly after his arrival in Mogilev. They met up again before Nikolasha departed for the Caucasus front, but not before telling the dowager all about the meeting with '*Niki.*'

Not to be outdone by the impact received by the Milyukov speech, on 19 November, shortly after three in the afternoon, the flamboyant orator Vladimir Purishkevich plunged into his speech, which turned against Rasputin.[788] Prior to that event, the President of the Council of Ministers Alexander Trepov opened the sitting by reminding the delegates that it was "exactly 28 months since the actual war began." Purishkevich began his address saying, "Russia will leave the war renewed ... free of foreign influence and her elements." (Yusupov was up in the public gallery.[789]) Purishkevich demanded Protopopov's dismissal because he "lost ... his authority in the eyes of Russian society." Nearing the end of his lengthy speech, Purishkevich reached his core argument, saying that Protopopov was "not the root of the rage" but:

> "...*all that rage comes from those dark forces, from those influences, which move those or other persons and compel persons to fly into high posts, who should not hold them ... which are directed by Grishka Rasputin.*"

Purishkevich explained that when in the city he noticed "chaos" because "...every day one hears incredible rumors ... saying something new but all these threads lead to Grigorii Rasputin." Then he added that society was united in their rage because Rasputin was "corrupting Russian public life." He thought it was reprehensible how the "illiterate *muzhik*" placed demands on ministers, most often with Protopopov. In parting reflection, Purishkevich pleaded to the delegates, who sat mesmerized by what they heard.

> "*If the cabinet* [is] *really united then go to the Tsar and say that this [state of affairs] cannot persist any longer... If you are loyal ... your road* [is] *to go there to Imperial Stavka, throw yourselves at the Sovereign's feet and will* [him] *to open his eyes to this terrible reality, ask [him] to purge Russia of Rasputin and* [the] *Rasputin group large and small.*

... We must plead with the Sovereign ... so that Rasputin will not guide Russian internal public life."

Purishkevich implored that his words reflected what Russia believed, desiring the "Tsar's wellbeing, the Church and for the Russian people" but they now could only watch how Rasputin was "shaking the foundation of the Russian State." The speech was met by thunderous applause from the right, center and left factions with indiscriminate shouts of "bravo!" Not one cared that Purishkevich lacked proof to support his electric statements, based on his longstanding hatred of Rasputin that stemmed before the War,[790] in that Rasputin's activities were destroying the dignity of the monarchy. Purishkevich was convinced that their conflict was with domestic "German lackeys" who wanted to weaken the British alliance. Purishkevich was correct on one fact: Russia was heading towards revolutionary upheaval, a position towards which Purishkevich had contributed.

Zinaida admitted she and her clique were shaken by the Purishkevich's speech, writing to Felix:

> *"I am beginning to think that I am cleverer than I had supposed, since all the things that I have been saying for the last two years are reproduced word for word in these speeches, and the general trend of events is going in the direction which I have been predicting word-for-word ... Now it's too late ..."[791]*

A few days later a resolution was passed to acknowledge that the 'dark forces' must be restrained[792] at all cost. Still exhilarated by the speech, Yusupov met with Purishkevich and said:

> *"The Sovereign does not like it when his will is pressured, and the significance of Rasputin, we must recognize, will not only not diminish, but, on the contrary, will strengthen, thanks to his undivided influence over Alexandra Fyodorovna, [who] now runs the government, whilst his Majesty is occupied at Stavka with military operations." [793]*

After learning the specifics of Purishkevich's oration, the grand dukes were mortified. Shavelsky made the following notation in his memoirs: *"One of the Mikhailovich Grand Dukes telegraphed his brother Nikolai Mikhailovich in Petrograd on 22 November"* saying: *"Have read Purishkevich's speech... Wept. Ashamed!"*[794]

The Duma maintained its rigorous tempo striking against the Emperor and the 'dark forces,' sneering at anyone who was a conservative. The speech by Vladimir Dzubinskii of the *Trud* Party (Tobolsk District), represented the widespread attitude of the left-wing factions sitting in the Duma. Dzubinskii spoke just before the afternoon break, ahead of Purishkevich's speech. He pleaded for the abolition of the monarchy. Lacking facts, the speech relied on sheer emotion, asking the delegates as to why Milyukov's words, heard two weeks earlier, had failed to take effect:

> *"Instead of Goremykin* [second Prime Minister] *Stürmer appeared, you said thank God ... with Stürmer there will be a new government, a new trend. And what did you receive* [with] *these new trends? ...- German sympathy to your President Council of Ministers ... In this period your trust towards the power of dark forces seizing our nation and rule our nation, irresponsible forces, these forces have strengthened even more,* [who] *stood behind Stürmer's back and began control. You said down with Stürmer - Stürmer departs and instead of Stürmer appears another force. With this power there appears to be truth. Is this a power change? This change is only in the surname ... but the regime, the system remains the same, with those behind their backs we have the dark forces of Rasputin and other persons* [the Empress] *who push your nation into the abyss. ... The only way to rescue the nation is when the system changes* [and] *the regime changes, when a responsible government appears before the people* [with] *the supremacy of the State Duma. The authority is using* [the fact] *that our finest sons who are found in the trenches are unable to shield us."*[795]

Delegates expected the Duma speeches would have prompted Nikolai II to respond, but that expectation had the opposite effect. In the present milieu, the series of speeches were treacherous acts. The emperor responded, whether rightly or not, by maintaining his silence. He did want to indulge the Duma, defending his deeds or way of life. The public, on the other hand, was bewildered because they wanted to hear their sovereign deny the verbal surge of venom coming from the Duma. It would be fair to say that there was a morsel of truth regarding some of the questions the Duma had pronounced on a daily basis. In 1917, Milyukov admitted the Duma had strived "through all legal possibilities ... to create a (ministerial) cabinet."[796]

Vasilii Shulgin, a member of the Nationalist Party,[797] met Purishkevich outside the Tavricheskii Palace and was drawn into a bizarre conversation, in which he was asked to remember 16 December. Expressing interest, Shulgin asked what the date meant and was told:

> Purishkevich - *"You I can tell. On the sixteenth we are going to kill him."*
>
> Shulgin - *"Who?"*
>
> Purishkevich - *"Grishka."*

The conversation ended with Purishkevich announcing, "I'll kill him like a dog."[798] Perhaps not so peculiar, but this was exactly the same expression which Nikolai Mikhailovich used when he spoke with Shulgin very early in November.

The verbal attacks inside the Duma demonstrated the magnitude of private and public discontent regarding Rasputin and the empress. Nikolai II directed that Prince Golitsyn, the new President of the Council of Ministers, sign the *Ukaz*, which should have prorogued the Duma on 14 February 1917, but with the Duma's excessive use of their power, Protopopov and Prince Golitsyn failed to set the ruling into motion.[799] After Saturday morning dawned in Petrograd, Grigorii Rasputin was dead.

Deadly Opponents

Undercurrents were flowing inside the British embassy. Around October 1916, Buchanan was concerned about the rapid turnover of ministers, especially Sazonov's departure, who had commanded the trust of the Allies and "because he was seen as a force for modernization in domestic politics." He blamed those objectionable changes on the "dark forces at Tsarskoe Selo."[800] Buchanan supposed that a large section of the governing clique was

Britain's enemy.[801] He privately expressed alarm about it, fearing the "sullen indifference" of the population regarding political issues and the increasing anti-war sentiment would influence Nikolai II to seek a separate peace treaty with Germany. After hearing Milyukov's speech, Buchanan's sense of alarm increased. He began "calling for constitutional change."[802] He aggravation extended towards Nikolai II's intolerance whereby foreigners had to stay silent about perceived deficiencies in his governance.

To boost British sympathies, the Anglo-Russian Society was re-constituted in November 1916, with Rodzianko elected as its president.[803] The society (located on *Bolshaya Morskaya Ulitsa*, 36) was intent on promoting the importance of the *Entente* agreement among its Russian members. [Count Alexander Benckendorff was instrumental in signing the Anglo-Russian Agreement in 1907, which settled the "spheres of influence of the two countries ... that resulted in the Triple *Entente*."[804]] At the society's inaugural meeting, Buchanan concluded his reception speech saying:

"It is not only on the battlefields of Europe that the war must be fought out to a victorious end." [805]

Buchanan was referring to his battlefield against the "governing clique" which he thought were not favoring the British foreign policy that Russia must remain in the war. One of Buchanan's responsibilities in wartime Russia was to protect British interests. His friendship with Nikolai Mikhailovich involved more than quiet respect. The grand duke facilitated the British ambassador to secure a solution concerning the political difficulties. Like Purishkevich, Nikolai Mikhailovich began to spread the story that Russia was about to sign a separate peace treaty with Germany in December. It was a tactic that affected the ordinary soldier on the battlefield and ensured that Rasputin was viewed as Russia's vilest domestic enemy.

Thus, Purishkevich, the avid anglophile and ultra-monarchist, was led by the grand duke's plan that offered a solution. Purishkevich would be the one who would "save Russia" and preserve her absolutist monarchy, which he and his Black Hundred members extolled.

After Lvov told Buchanan in mid-December that he believed

that "we are drawing near the end and drifting into anarchy and revolution,"[806] there was very little time to waste. Reports reaching the British Embassy in Petrograd stressed that the Russian soldiers were becoming increasingly critical of the emperor and the empress.[807] The German propaganda that Milyukov identified was spreading on the city streets and on the battlefields. The idea of fighting for their sovereign was becoming a repugnant concept. Given these facts, the meaning behind Yusupov's words "those culpable of this disappearance (Rasputin's) becomes clearer,"[808] as does Samuel Hoare's[809] admission that safeguarding the *Entente* drove the British to destroy the 'dark forces.'

Secretary of War Lloyd George did not sanction the operation[810] [appointed prime minister in December 1916.[811]] because there was no need to approve an operation that involved willing Russian citizens to carry out the murder on their own territory. The British were only interested in the outcome. Hoare only needed to assure to his superior that the matter would end favorably.

Stephan Dorril revealed that MI6 preferred the use of third parties. (The SIS emerged as MI6 after WWI.[812]) For that reason, Secret Intelligent Service (SIS) agent Oswald Rayner's role on the night of 16/17 December was to act as an observer, ensuring the liquidation of a common enemy would be carried out on the designated night. His second duty would have been to confirm the result to his superior, who would have notified Buchanan. [Even though Smith failed to find Rayner in the active agent's list dated 24 December 1916, a British operative in Petrograd, Captain Steven Alley, wrote on 25 December 1916 that Rayner was "attending to loose ends."[813]] Choosing to notify Nikolai Mikhailovich at 5.30 in the morning, Buchanan knew in advance that Rasputin was dead. The received phonecall came hours before the Petrograd authorities were notified that Rasputin was missing.

Buchanan's audience with Nikolai II on Friday 30 December 1916 at 11 in the morning[814] was significant in that the emperor knew the British were involved (Buchanan used the word "concerned."[815]). This meeting was more formal previously. Rather than sitting in the study's armchairs, Nikolai II preferred to conduct the conversation standing. Buchanan told the emperor that it would be ideal to "break down the barriers that separate you from your people and to regain their confidence." He then added that the Germans were "pulling the strings and were using as their unconscious tools those who were in the habit of advising His Majesty as to the choice of his ministers."[816] Nikolai II interrupted the flow of words and explained that he chose the ministers.

Buchanan continued: "They indirectly influenced the Empress through those in her entourage … with the result that instead of being loved, as she ought to be, Her Majesty was discredited and accused of working in German interests." When Nikolai II asked for evidence, Buchanan responded, "there are no facts"[817] but in his defense asserted, "her [Alexandra's] politics are such that the masses draw that conclusion," adding, "Your Majesty must find a way to remove the Empress from politics" because "persistent rumors are afloat that the Empress is determined to have a peace treaty with Germany and that Protopopov is helping in the matter." In closing, Buchanan admitted[818] that he knew that Rasputin was going to be murdered, but for now he "treated it as idle gossip." His parting statement advised the emperor to take the path that "will lead you to victory and a glorious peace" rather than the path "to revolution and disaster."

What cannot be overlooked is Buchanan's admission that he had prior knowledge that Rasputin was to be murdered. Buchanan revealed in his memoirs that he and Nikolai Mikhailovich "frequently exchanged views on the internal information, in the hope that by our concerted action we might induce the Emperor to change his attitude."[819] Days before the publication of this book, I came across two telegrams that were transmitted by Buchanan to his superior in Britain, which are held in the United Kingdom's National Archives. In the first telegram, dated 31 December 1916, Buchanan declared "I was told about a week ago by a friend who is in close touch with some of the younger grand dukes that a member of the young officers had sworn to kill him (Rasputin) before the end of this year." The second telegram, dated 1 January 1917, exposed the detail that "Grand Duke Nicholas remarked to me that now that assassinations had been begun they would not stop with Rasputin." [820]

Samuel Hoare's 5 January 1917 (N. S.) intelligence report exposes why Purishkevich had intervened against the anti-British clique:

"It was not surprising, that Rasputin's death should have been the occasion of a crop of wild rumors about British participation in the crime. ... Purishkevich ... gave a ready excuse to the anti-British clique of reactionaries to father the plot and even the murder on me and my staff ... The British Ambassador had solemnly to contradict it to the Emperor at his next audience at Tsarskoe Selo." [821]

Lacking compassion for the victim, Samuel Hoare's final thought regarding the Rasputin matter now makes sense:

"...so far as the conduct of the war was concerned it would have been better if the murder had never taken place." [822]

Stephen Dorril described one central philosophy of MI6 planning in *MI6: Fifty Years of Special Operations.* [823] For the success of any of their operations, the following factors had to be observed:

1. The use of third parties to lessen the threat of the operation unscrambling that would reveal the sponsoring organization, and

2. Plausible deniability,

3. That during wartime the MI6 operations were more justifiable.

Each factor had played its part in the Rasputin Operation with minimal effort or expense to be incurred by the British government. Consequently, what transpired accorded with MI6 policy to the letter:

1. The third party was Grand Duke Nikolai Mikhailovich who had organized his group of willing Russian citizens, believing that they had acted in their country's interest.

2. Ambassador Buchanan officially denied that the British government was responsible.

3. The operation was carried out during wartime as part of Britain's strategy to continue with the war.

Though Nikolai Mikhailovich's diary was silent about Oswald Rayner's attendance at the Yusupovskii Palace, it does not imply that the Englishman was absent. The grand duke had no need to know that detail.

On 18 February 1917 (N.S.), Buchanan wrote a communiqué to the London Foreign Office concerning the "prospects of Russia continuing in the war," stating:

> "...the anti-British campaign has died out and Anglo-British relations were never better than at present. The Emperor, most of his Ministers and the bulk of the nation are all firm supporters of the Anglo-Russian Alliance. ... The Emperor, the supreme factor, is deplorably weak; but the one point on which we can count on his remaining firm is the war, more especially as the Empress, who virtually governs Russia, is herself sound on this question. She is not as is often asserted, a German working in Germany's interests, but a reactionary, who wishes to hand down the autocracy intact to her son. It is for this reason that she prompts the Emperor to choose, as his Ministers, men on whom she can rely to carry out a firm policy ...*
>
> I would sum up the situation as follows: ... the Emperor and the majority of his subjects are bent on fighting out the war to a finish... and my only hope is that she will be able to hold out to the end if we continue to give her the necessary assistance."[824]

Bruce Lockhart (Consul-General in Moscow) recognized Buchanan's mission this way:

> "...future generations will recognize how great was the work accomplished by Sir George Buchanan in helping to keep Russia in the war."[825]

In December 1916, Grand Duke Alexander Mikhailovich understood that Buchanan encouraged "plotters" to usurp the monarchist government for the sole purpose of "protecting the interests of the Allies."[826]

Persons knowingly concerned in the conspiracy to murder Grigorii Rasputin

A. **The British Group:**

- ► Ambassador George Buchanan – aware but not implicated
- ► Samuel Hoare – Petrograd Chief of SIS
- ► SIS agent Oswald Rayner - confirmed the murder to his superior

B. **The Russian Group:**

- ► Grand Duke Nikolai Mikhailovich – the go-between (associated with Buchanan)

These individuals contributed to Rasputin's murder and/or disposal of his remains:

- ► Grand Duke Dmitri Pavlovich
- ► Prince Felix Yusupov
- ► Sergei Sukhotin
- ► Vladimir Purishkevich
- ► Dr. Stanislav Lazovert

These individuals offered legal counsel to Felix Yusupov:

- ► Senator Vasilii Maklakov – 3 consultations, November 1916.
- ► Minister of Justice, Alexander Makarov – one consultation, 17 December 1916.

Chapter Four Photos

*PHOTO 8: PETROGRAD. Pavel Milyukov addressing
the State Duma, 1 November 1916.*

CHAPTER FIVE
DAY 1 of the GENDARME and Judicial INVESTIGATIONS

Saturday 17 December 1916

"In The Matter of the Disappearance of the Peasant Rasputin"

«Дело об исчезновении крестьянина Распутина»

The First Notice

Before 8 a.m., police officer Colonel Alexander Rogov notified his chief, *Politsmeister* General Georgii Grigoriev (*Kazanskii* District Police unit), that gunshots were heard at Moika, 94. Grigoriev telephoned Petrograd Mayor, Alexander Balk.[827]

The First Incident Report

Information that *gorodovoi* (city policeman) Stepan Vlasyuk passed to his supervisor (Grigoriev) after going off-duty at 6 a.m. activated the investigation into the disappearance of Grigorii Rasputin. Vlasyuk submitted his written statement to Rogov before they saw *Politsmeister* Grigoriev, allowing Vlasyuk to repeat his evidence.[828] Realizing its seriousness, Grigoriev contacted Mayor Balk, whose chambers and residence were on the corner of Admiralty *Prospekt* and Gorokhovaya *Ulitsa*, 2.[829]

Prior to contacting the governor, the district police in the zone where Rasputin's apartment building was located (Gorokhovaya, 64) telephoned the household to learn if Rasputin was home.

By eight o'clock in the morning, Chief of the Gendarme *Korpus*,

General-Lieutenant Nikolai Tatishev, Konstantin Globachev, Alexei Vasiliev (Director of the Police) and Alexander Protopopov received the news.[830] Balk told them that hours earlier Vlasyuk had been invited inside the Yusupov residence and was told by a man not known to him that Rasputin was dead. [Vlasyuk would later identify Purishkevich from a photograph shown to him by the Criminal Department.[831]]

The First Phase of the Investigation

General Arkadii Koshko, Head of Criminal Court Investigation in Russia, authorized Petrograd criminal police chief Arkadii Kirpichnikov to start searching for Rasputin. General Pyotr Popov (former head of the *Okhrana*[832], Photo 9) received instructions to search for Rasputin in the field, on the assumption that he was a missing person. Before the task began, police agents were heard to protest, "we do not need to search for all kinds of rubbish," as well as "Disappeared – well, thank God" and "since the *Okhranki* let him go, then they should now search for him themselves." Koshko noted that this was the first refusal by the ranks to "submit unquestioningly to authority." Nevertheless, he resolved the crisis and some fifty police agents started searching.[833] Based on past rumors about Rasputin's carousing habits, a contingent of police agents searched inside restaurants, *traktiri* (inns) and gypsy quarters.[834] Elsewhere, Vasiliev, aware of the importance[835] to inspect the courtyard adjoining the Yusupovskii Palace, firstly sought permission from Protopopov to enter the courtyard that faced the Moika canal, since that residence was off limits.

One Communication Misleads While Another Causes Anguish

Before his departure for the Front on his hospital train on Saturday morning,[836] Purishkevich sent a telegram to Maklakov in Moscow from the Duma post office. Maklakov never received the message confirming Rasputin's death. It was intercepted. Protopopov confirmed it read, "Everything is finished."[837] It was passed on to the emperor along with related telegrams sent by others[838] (see Appendix D).

The earliest forewarning the Alexandrovskii Palace received that something had happened to Grigorii Rasputin happened when one of Rasputin's daughter's telephoned, saying her father failed to return home by 7 a.m., adding that he left their apartment with Yusupov. Within moments, Alexandra Fyodorovna heard about that conversation. Protopopov rang soon afterwards, telling her the little he knew.[839] Their conversation ended with the empress imploring him to find Rasputin "alive or dead."[840]

Alarm Bells Ring at Gorokhovaya, 64

Ekaterina (Katya) Poterkina, the Rasputin family housekeeper, alerted Matrena and Varvara that their father failed to return home by seven o'clock in the morning.[841] Poterkina feared that "some evil had overtaken [their] father." Though they knew that his failure to return home was irregular, their first reaction involved waiting a little longer. Matrena, meantime, made a few telephone calls, hoping to learn about her father's whereabouts. Though Matrena said she phoned Felix first, this detail is problematic, in that the household would not have known that he was living temporarily at Grand Duke Alexander Mikhailovich's palace. More convincing is that she contacted Taneeva (a regular guest), who would have known how to contact Felix. Maria (Munya) Golovina was a longtime friend of Yusupov's and a regular visitor at the Rasputin apartment. Golovina told the police that after the daughters called her,[842] she attempted to assure them that their father was with the gypsies and that they were wrong to say that Felix had visited their apartment last night.[843] Once the daughters learned of their father's disappearance, Golovina arrived at their apartment in tears, but showed no sympathy, despite knowing the girls for several years.

Using standard procedure, Protopopov rang the Gorokhovaya apartment to find ask if Rasputin had returned home in the interim. Though Protopopov was a regular visitor at the apartment, he had to perfom as the minister in charge of the police and gendarmes.[844] In 1917, Zavadsky (the same person who was the procurator in this case during December 1916) asked Protopopov whether he went to the Rasputin apartment on Saturday morning. He replied, "Never, nothing of the kind," adding that it was the police who had done so.[845] It was Vasiliev's agents who had the duty to take all of Rasputin's personal papers. As it turned out later, no material that would have embarrassed the palace was found.[846] This response was necessary in order to avoid such material falling into the wrong hands. A brief notice appeared in *Birzheviye Vedomosti*, which incorrectly reported this incident happened two days later, on 20 December.[847]

In February 1917, the Petrograd District Court's Special Investigator (concerning Important Matters) Sereda revealed details of his conversation with Grand Duke Andrei Vladimirovich. Apparently Rasputin's secretary Simanovich had become anxious about the information he received, suggesting that Rasputin was going to be murdered within days. He approached Protopopov four days before the murder to no avail. Though Simanovich told Protopopov that when Rasputin left his apartment, he would always telephone and let him know the telephone number of the place where he was visiting.[848] On Friday night (16 December), before going out, Rasputin rang Simanovich, saying he "would ring again"[849] within the one hour to reveal his location, but the call never came.[850] Fearing the worst, Simanovich rushed to Protopopov's apartment.[851] [852] In spite of the effort taken to alert Protopopov, the minister did not react until he received Balk's phone call a few hours later.

Gendarmes Proceed but May Have to Step Back

Given that the Yusupov residence belonged to a member of the nobility, only the mayor could give permission for the police and the justice department to enter the property to search for evidence that a crime had taken place. The investigation would be run in parallel by both departments,[853] though consent was withdrawn by the afternoon. Vasiliev deployed the entire police apparatus. At 9 a.m. the police began their search in the front courtyard located at Moika, 94. The Yusupov family also owned the adjoining property that faces the courtyard, Moika, 92. Vasiliev knew that some six hours earlier, a series of gunshots resounded here.

Before Balk's call, Protopopov, aware that Rasputin had "stepped out and disappeared,"[854] became uneasy about possible consequences his information might introduce. Once Balk confirmed that news, Protopopov had to update the palace and approve all fieldwork. Staying in his office throughout the day, he kept phone contact with Vasiliev[855] and the Criminal Unit chief. Protopopov would maintain this routine for the next couple of days until the Rasputin Case ended, all the while hoping to escape a new 'scandal,'[856] given his refusal to act on Simanovich's fear. The investigation became **Case No. 573**.

According to the regulations governing personnel of the Criminal Department, dated 9 August 1910,[857] the head of the Criminal Unit had the legal capacity "to investigate and conduct an inquiry." It was standard procedure to categorize any person of interest by their social standing, because many residents in the city were immune by virtue of their nobility ranking. Given that Yusupov enjoyed this position, the search in the Yusupov courtyard could continue until Balk indicated otherwise.

THE INVESTIGATION

On 19 December 1916, just prior to the emperor's return from Stavka, Vasiliev, without giving a reason, told General Popov to stop his investigations. Popov's final task was to collate the fifteen depositions he had time to pursue and complete a summary report that would be dated 23 December. His folder was designated **Report No. 694**. Besides the copy Protopopov needed to hand deliver to the emperor,[858] a second copy would be held by the Director of Police.

The Judicial Department Makes Its First Move

Chief Procurator of the District Court (located on *Liteinii Prospekt*[859]) Fyodor von Nandelshtedt telephoned Procurator Sergei Zavadsky (head of the Petrograd Court Chambers) early in the morning and told him that during the night Rasputin had been murdered [not disappeared] and that the crime had "probably been carried out in the courtyard of the Yusupov residence."[860] Nandelshtedt directed Victor Sereda to accompany him on behalf of the juridical department. Sereda had to examine the crime scene and determine whether there was any human blood and if so, retrieve a sample for laboratory analysis.[861] Accompanied by the head of the Criminal Unit and the police photographer, the four of them drove the short distance to Moika, 94, arriving there at nine o'clock.[862] On arrival, Sereda focused on identifying the presence of physical traces left by the murderer(s) or by the victim in the courtyard.

There were a number of technical difficulties with this particular investigation. Firstly, it was supposed to be conducted in secrecy, which was impossible to achieve. The investigators arrived en masse, dressed in their uniforms, and alighted at about the same time from their chauffeured vehicles that could only be parked down the length of the Moika Embankment, right in front of private apartments. Secondly, the crime scene was located at the residence of a person directly related to Nikolai II (Yusupov's wife Irina Alexandrovna) and owned by a titled family. Keeping the Criminal Code regulations in mind, that the property belonged to Felix Yusupov (senior), who was in Moscow acting as the city's governor, Balk, as the chief administrator, gave the the police and the judicial investigators permission to enter the property and search for evidence. This circumstance also meant that Felix Yusupov (junior) was not compelled to offer any information. The investigators at the scene were limited to the morning hours and restricted in their movements. They were only allowed to enter the palace using the secondary front entry rather than the grander parade entrance.

Just like any other crime scene, it was important for the police to evaluate the primary scene and establish the "path of flight"[863] and determine if there were any secondary scenes, such as where the body might be found.

CRIME SCENE ONE - The Yusupov Residence at Moika, 94

The palace that originally belonged to Peter the Great's niece Praskovya Ioannovna and then reconstructed to its present two-story stone appearance was passed to the Yusupovs in 1830. It remained in the family until it was abandoned after the owner's son Felix Yusupov left Petrograd shortly after the February Revolution. Procurator Zavadsky described the Yusupov courtyard in this way:

"Prince Yusupov's palace is positioned on the very embankment and next to that lies the neighbor's yard with a railing instead of a fence: there is a special door that leads from the prince's study to that yard ... that was used during this winter's night."[864]

Felix Yusupov allowed the police to look at the study in the Yusupov residence and the courtyard. The first detail that was noticed before going inside was that the snow had been freshly swept in the small courtyard (**POLICE PHOTO No. 1**), which was common practice during winter. Escorted inside, they were led into a clean and tidy room.[865] Felix controlled all his visitor's movements and only allowed the investigators a polite cursory glimpse.[866] Vasiliev recalled how he and his men sat on tenterhooks in Yusupov's study, waiting to hear Felix explain what had happened during the night and for him to admit his culpability.[867]

A Dog's Tale

POLICE PHOTOS Nos. 2 and **3** show the blood trail that extends from the basement door, across the right side of the step, and runs into the courtyard. The blood spatter that was found in the courtyard alerted Sereda that the victim had moved away from the door and headed "into the courtyard," but not across it.[868] Balk's media representative, by contrast, said the blood was "by the side door."[869] This information tells us that Rasputin never reached the gate. Moreover, Sereda recognized that the blood trail indicated the victim "was carried"[870] back inside, no doubt because he saw foot imprints in the blood pool by the step (**POLICE PHOTO No. 4**). The foot impressions appear at one location, suggesting that Rasputin could not have moved much beyond that step. This was the victim's short 'flight path' that began inside the residence. The bleeding victim was picked up off the step and hauled inside through the small metal door. Yusupov did not refute the presence of blood near the porch, which had also penetrated into the substance of the stone step.[871] But he failed to give Vasiliev a rational explanation as to why there was blood on the step. The dense, smaller, discrete blood trail on the lefthand side of the step spreads a short distance beside the door, but the blood trail on the right side, which also originates from the inner side of the door, spreads partly across the step, runs along the edge of the step and flows down onto the snow. Sereda took a blood sample "at the place where Rasputin fell"[872] "in front of the exit door,"[873] as close as possible by the door in order to minimize contamination from another source. The blood spatter indicates its point of origin was inside the palace, which was a location he was not permitted to examine.

At the start of the investigation, neither the yard keeper nor the *kamerdiner* (valet) said anything about a dog (see Lazukov's Protocol, **Chapter Six**). That story emerged later during the day after the blood sample taken from the courtyard had confirmed that it was of human origin.[874] This result was reported in *Russkoye Slovo* on 20 December.[875] Vasiliev supposed afterwards[876] there was too much blood on the snow if it had seeped only from a 'domestic' dog. A deposition (of uncertain origin) was published in 1917, which did not appear with the set of statements published by *Byloye* journal, nor has it ever been cited by any Russian historians. In that 'statement,' Buzhinsky claimed that the dog "Frale was always chained and at nightfall was released to guard the palace."[877]

Yusupov provided a few contradictory reasons why the dog had to be sacrificed. Firstly, to explain the reason for the shooting that was heard resounding from his courtyard, he claimed that he decided it was necessary to shoot one of his dogs. The dog's corpse was supposed to have provided visual proof to any inquisitive authority that it had been killed just "for fun."[878] Yusupov revised this story, saying one of his departing, inebriated guests shot the dog.[879] Ivan Nefedov (a *kamerdiner*) acted strictly according to his employer's orders. Purishkevich knew that Yusupov was very upset that one of his "best dogs" had to be shot because of Rasputin.[880] The *kamerdiner* tossed the dead dog over to where Rasputin's body had been lying earlier, not far from the gate, "onto the snow behind the snow mound."[881] Recalling Yusupov's words that the morning search found the dog's remains "buried in the garden," his account that the dog was left in the courtyard is false. The real story about the dog will be revealed shortly.

Yusupov offered another explanation as to why the dog had to be sacrificed. He wrote that its bleeding body was also used to combine its blood with Rasputin's spent blood in the courtyard. Nikolai Mikhailovich was told the same story: the dog's blood was used "to confuse the traces of blood." The police who saw the blood pooled by the gate from the dog's corpse should have assumed that the blood spatter by the step was of the same origin. However, Yusupov enhanced the story after he claimed that the dog's corpse was "dragged" across where Rasputin "crawled" in the courtyard.[882] Sereda blew this myth apart after he described the presence of blood "drops," not "bloodied drag marks" on the snow. This suggests that someone had carried the dog's still-bleeding corpse to the area where it was about to be buried. Despite Yusupov's nefarious after-thought, the fresh blood pool by the door was undisturbed. It was likewise nonsensical to suggest that the dog's corpse was tossed over to the supposed problematic area.

Yusupov's third admission that the "step was layered with thick snow" and then smeared with "oil paint of similar color to that of the stone"[883] is also an absurd scenario. Neither Yusupov nor Purishkevich would have been bothered about such a triviality. It was ludicrous for Yusupov to write that he knew that the blood test result was positive for human blood and then later revise his published story that he and some unnamed person attempted to cover up human blood on the stone step using one method (the paint) and then masking the blood trail on the snow using dog's blood. If Yusupov's tale bore a scintilla of truth, then there should have been drag marks across the snow. When Yusupov wrote his tales, he never envisioned that the police photos that refuted his ideas would be published and scrutinized.

Dmitri Pavlovich told Grand Duke Andrei Vladimirovich on 19 December 1916 that the bullet which killed the dog was fired from his Browning.[884] The police veterinarian confirmed that a "Browning was used almost at point blank range, shattering the ribcage."[885] The story that Dmitri was provoked into killing the dog because he was attacked by it outside cannot be believed, in the same way that the *gorodovoi* who approached the fence was supposed to have seen the dog's corpse. Unfortunately, it was impossible to identify the caliber of the bullet that was extricated from Rasputin's corpse during the autopsy and compare it with the bullet removed from the dog because it was too deformed (see **Chapter 8**).

There is yet another version as to who killed the dog. The story in the *New York Times* said that Rasputin was given a revolver "to shoot himself" after being "told that he had been condemned to death." Instead, Rasputin "fired at the man who gave him the revolver and missed him, but killed the wolfhound that was standing by."[886]

It is doubtful that anyone thought about the possibility of the blood being tested to identify if it was of human or animal origin. The conspirators had no inkling that Sereda would arrive a few hours after the shooting. This means the canine sacrifice had nothing to do with blending blood types in order to contaminate the crime scene. The dog was to become the second victim at the Yusupovskii Palace only after *gorodovoi* Vlasyuk approached Felix and his butler (**Protocol No. 9, Chapter Six**) by the fence and enquired about the shooting. He was not shown a dead dog. Had he been shown the corpse he might have gone away, satisfied with the response. Aware that Vlasyuk had to, by law, report the shooting incident to his superiors, they panicked and only then did it become necessary to organize a suitable explanation why shooting was heard in the front courtyard. In his revised memoir, Felix admitted that this was indeed why the dog was sacrificed.

The Gunshots That Were Enclosed by Glass and Stone

Sereda provided a vital clue to help solve one mystery about the shooting. The basement windows were double-glazed ("dual winter frames"). Therefore, whatever shots were fired in the basement "behind closed doors" would not have been heard (by the *gorodovoi*) on the other side of the Moika at house No. 61.[887] This scenario exposes a new complexity. Sereda's revelation only helps to explain the blast from at least three if not four bullets had to have been fired as the basement exit door opened, one of which we know entered Rasputin's back (**POLICE PHOTO No. 13**). For reasons explained earlier, one of the gunshots heard by the *gorodovoi* would not have been directed at the domestic dog. As Yusupov admitted, he (and the conspirators) needed to work out how they could explain the shooting that was heard by the *gorodovoi*. It would have taken time to grasp the idea that one of the palace dogs had to be sacrificed. Grand Duke Nikolai Mikhailovich said that the dog was shot by a member of staff at 6 a.m. "inside the house,"[888] which was long after the murderers left the palace. The dog was shot in the only location where the sound of additional gunfire would not be heard, undoubtedly in the basement tunnel.

Statements submitted by the *gorodovoi* (who were former soldiers[889]) were more credible than those provided by Yusupov or by three of his employees. Indeed, both Vlasyukand and Efimov testified that they heard at least three or possibly four gunshots (**Protocols No. 9 and 8, Chapter Six**).

When Vlasyuk approached Yusupov and the butler Buzhinsky by the Moika courtyard fence, there was a strong denial about any shooting. Most significantly, Vlasyuk found nothing suspicious in the courtyard after the residents went back inside. Vlasyuk returned later with his supervisor and both men found nothing to arouse their suspicions. Since it was not known whether Vlasyuk would return to the palace or the courtyard, Yusupov left instructions that the dog had to be shot, aware that all *gorodovoi* nightshifts ended at a specific time, after which time Vlasyuk would report the night's incident to his supervisor. Koshko[890] and Globachev confirmed that a canine corpse was "brought to the police" by Yusupov's *denshik* (batman) to prove it had been shot by Dmitri.[891] This was a very unusual step. If the dog had been unintentionally shot dead (for fun), then all Yusupov had to do was show its corpse when the police came to investigate the reason for the shooting. Globachev revealed two very important details. No one at the time took any notice "of the boyish way out" of the predicament in which Felix found himself in. The other detail was that the dog had only recently been shot, because its corpse was still warm.

Grand Duke Andrei Vladimirovich spoke with Felix during the morning after the murder. Felix told him that he left instructions for the dog's corpse to be buried,[892] not mentioning his batman's special journey to Fontanka, 16. The batman returned to the palace and only then buried the dog's corpse where it was found by the police. Unfortunately, Sereda failed to say where the gendarmes found the dog's corpse but did reveal that it had been shot "into the heart,"[893] suggesting it was a calculated shooting by a knowledgeable marksman.

The Case of the Dots

POLICE PHOTOS Nos. 2 and 3 show dot points that start from the far corner of the step and continue some distance into the courtyard and then deflect over the snow mounds beyond a second pillar that is on the boundary of the property. Recalling what was said about the 'flight path' of the victim, the dots drawn on these photos do not reflect what Sereda described to Grand Duke Andrei Vladimirovich. This can only mean that whoever marked those photographs with purple ink did not attend this crime scene. Andrew Cook accepted that the dots were drawn by an investigator in 1916 and used them to enhance his argument.[894] Knowing that the police photographs disappeared until they were handed to the Political History Museum in 1992, one cannot rule out that someone tampered with these two photographs. The folder does not bear official signatures, stamps or coding as would be expected. Instead, the rough cardboard cover had an inscription, with similar handwriting alongside each photo. Hence, it would be unwise to rely on what appears to be aberrant pen markings on these photographs.

Synopsis of the forensic evidence found at the first crime scene

▶ The corpse of a dog was buried under the snow in the garden.

▶ The deceased dog was shot through the heart by a Browning.

▶ Traces of blood were found on the step and snow immediately beyond the step. The blood trailed over the step and ran partway into the courtyard.

▶ A random blood sample was analyzed and found to be of human origin.

A Warm Invitation that Lead to a Cold Departure

From the little information that is available today, it is possible to assemble a few details regarding Rasputin's last movements and some of the discussions that took place inside his apartment Friday.

Out of all the residents at Gorokhovaya, 64, Maria Zhuravleva,[895] the concierge, provided the most helpful information. She saw Rasputin returning from the sauna before 3 p.m., adding that no more than seven individuals visited the apartment between three o'clock and midnight, which was the time she locked the main entry gate before going off duty. Though not knowing the identity of Rasputin's visitors, Zhuravleva disclosed that they were not first time callers. One afternoon visitor was Anya Taneeva. She recalled that she stayed for fifteen minutes.[896] Her visit concerned passing on the empress' gift, which was one of a set of small icons that depicted the Mother of God. The icons were acquired at the Znamenskaya Church during the 12 December imperial visit to Novgorod (the other set was dispatched to Nikolai II at Stavka).[897] When Taneeva learnt that Rasputin was going out with Felix, she urged him to remain at home. Rasputin responded that it was his first visit to the Yusupovskii Palace and that everything would be fine, adding that Felix wanted the visit to be kept a secret because he did not want his parents to find out. Even though she was unhappy about the strange hour of that invitation, she left the apartment.

Bishop Isidor appears to have been another visitor. Isidor, hearing the rumor that the *strannik* was going to be murdered very soon, attempted to caution Rasputin not to venture out that night.[898] The last visitor was Protopopov. He arrived some time before midnight, after escorting his sister-in-law (Taneeva's eldest sister) to the railway station.[899] (Matrena incorrectly recalled the time as 7 p.m.[900]) Protopopov testified that his midnight visit to Rasputin's apartment was "by chance." Even so, Protopopov then gave a different excuse, saying that he wanted to calm Rasputin, believing that he was still infuriated after the fiancé of one of his daughters attempted to commit suicide a few days earlier. [This incident was reported in *Rech* on 21 December.[901]] Protopopov stayed ten minutes in the apartment, speaking only with Grigorii.[902]

As Minister of Internal Affairs (appointed on 18 September

1916[903]), it was his responsibility to ensure that Rasputin was protected at all times. Though Protopopov stated at the 1917 Inquiry he "rarely saw Rasputin,"[904] he concealed the fact that he was one of the most regular visitors. Nevertheless, Protopopov knew Rasputin well enough to know about his personal habit of turning in for the night before midnight. His 'chance' arrival at that hour indicates that he not only knew why Rasputin was awake, but that his life was in imminent danger. Hence, Protopopov's declaration that he did not react when he Rasputin opened the back door fully dressed is difficult to accept. Protopopov's edginess at the time most likely related to his conscience when he was on his way home. His apartment, it must be said, was located directly across the canal, overlooking the Yusupovskii Palace. It is plausible to consider that Protopopov intended to warn Rasputin not to leave; however, after entering the kitchen, he changed his mind during those critical ten minutes. His professional duty to Rasputin vanished, never to return.

It is worth mentioning here that Taneeva testified in 1917 that Rasputin treated Protopopov very well,[905] while Globachev said that Protopopov showed Rasputin "absolute respect."[906] Globachev noticed that Rasputin's murder did not cause much of an impression on Protopopov and that "his only worry - was to quickly locate Rasputin's corpse, only because that was what the *Gosudarinya* (Empress) wanted."[907]

Protopopov's subsequent conversations and actions, including handing over all the incriminating material to Nikolai II (see **Appendix A**) after this night, were a duplicitous façade. Reading through his numerous depositions,[908] one finds that he strived to disassociate himself from Rasputin and his associates. He went so far as to claim he did not meet Aron Simanovich (Rasputin's secretary) until after the murder,[909] even though Simanovich walked into the guarded Ministry building and entered Protopopov's apartment, which no stranger could have achieved, particularly during the early morning hours.

Recently, Yuri Rassulin claimed that Rasputin knew that he would die soon and understood why Felix's friendship was bound by an ulterior motive.[910] These are empty thoughts because Rasputin, as a pious person, would not have decided to do nothing to prevent such a transgression. Rasputin's decision to go with Felix centered on the level of trust that Yusupov had nurtured, visiting, as Matrena revealed, "practically every day during the three months that preceded the murder."[911]

A letter written by Alexandra Fyodorovna to Nikolai II on 15 December explained what proved to be Rasputin's final visit to Anna Taneeva's cottage in Tsarskoe Selo. It confirms that Rasputin was very guarded about where he went.

> *"Our friend was at her* [place], *I did not leave home.*
> *He has for some time not left his home* [and] *only comes*
> *here* [Tsarskoe Selo]."[912]

Despite the condition Felix imposed (see below), Rasputin never suspected that the invitation was a hostile act. None were outlandish, otherwise Rasputin might have suspected something untoward (like he did at Prince Andronnikov's dinner party in 1914).

The conditions Yusupov imposed on Rasputin before his visit:

▶ The assurance that Rasputin's bodyguards were dismissed (after the concierge had gone off duty).

▶ Not to tell anyone that he was going to the Moika Palace.

▶ Only the back stairs that lead directly to the back door of Rasputin's apartment were to be used.

▶ The outing must be after midnight (the *Okhrana* were to assume that Rasputin was asleep).

All the listed conditions were suggested by Maklakov after Felix told his advocate that he intended to participate in the plan to kill Rasputin.[913] The hour for Yusupov's visit was not unusual because that was the time when he used to visit the apartment on all previous occasions.[914] Globachev revealed that Rasputin often dismissed his security at 10 p.m. at night[915] and that certain visitors, like Protopopov and Yusupov, used the back staircase to gain entry into the apartment.[916] What was unusual on Friday night was Rasputin's departure at such a late hour.

As stated earlier, the British government also kept watch over Rasputin. *Russkoye Slovo* somehow got hold of the information that British agents saw a vehicle approach Rasputin's building, from which alighted "a young person. After sometime Rasputin was seen getting into the approaching automobile with the same young person." The agents immediately jumped into their own car and headed to the Department of Internal Affairs building,[917] where Samuel Hoare lived. Their information would have assured him that Yusupov had begun to carry out his assigned task.

Given the facts, Alexander Bushkov's suggestion that Rasputin was going to the Moika Palace because of a secret meeting to find out about the progress towards a separate peace treaty[918] is ludicrous authorship. Likewise, Matrena, who trusted Yusupov, inexplicably wrote some twenty-seven years after her father's death that before going to bed at 10 p.m., she pleaded for her father to stay home and even tried to hide his boots.[919]

Juridical Action and Reaction
This Morning in Petrograd Brings Mixed Responses

After Zavadsky returned from the Yusupov residence later in the morning, he had a less than edifying telephone conversation with Minister of Justice Alexander Makarov. It was obvious how far the indifference to work on the Rasputin case had extended (like the police earlier saying no to the search) when Makarov said, "What kind of funny situation are we to expect, if it is found that Rasputin was alive and was somewhere with the gypsies, while we had to alarm an important investigator just for the sake of a dog." Makarov advised Zavadsky that he perhaps should step back from the case, an invitation that was declined.

Shortly after midday, a member of staff announced that Yusupov wanted to see either Zavadsky or another court procurator and that this visitor had just been to see the city mayor.[920] Zavadsky walked to the reception room and saw a young military man whom he seemingly recognized from Valentin Serov's (1903) portrait of the prince with his little dog. Nandelshtedt recalled that he wore the *shinel* (long overcoat) of the Imperial *Pazheskii Korpus*.[921] Yusupov, looking incredibly pale, was pacing nervously "from corner to corner." The stranger initiated a conversation, saying, "We are both it seems here on the same matter. Permit me to introduce to introduce myself: Prince Yusupov." Entering the minister's office, Yusupov told his story, concluding that only a dog was killed and that incident had attracted the attention of the *gorodovoi*. Yusupov left after some ten minutes.[922] In his revised memoirs, Yusupov stated that after the gendarmes interviewed his staff, he felt compelled to seek legal advice (Maklakov was in Moscow).[923] However in his first memoir, Yusupov admitted that he needed to figure out what legal position he was in.[924] Feeling uncomfortable about confiding with these strangers, he left the chambers.

Makarov said that he believed "the young man," but Zavadsky responded that he did not believe what he just heard, feeling that Yusupov came to the court building because he was caught up in the affair. Indeed, why would Yusupov extend a personal visit to defend the shooting of a domestic dog? Nandelshtedt explained that Yusupov requested that "until the police discover Rasputin's whereabouts, the investigating authorities have no need to cause agitation in this matter."[925]

Later in the afternoon, Zavadsky telephoned the minister and told him that the dog was sacrificed in vain because Sereda had taken a blood sample and the *Uhlenhuth* Test had confirmed that the sample was of human origin. In frustration, Makarov mumbled, "How unpleasant that such a test is so revealing."[926] Makarov closed the case[927] after Yusupov demanded that the mayoral order to search his apartment be withdrawn. This step meant that Yusupov was free to join his family in Koreiz. It was premature to alter the status of the investigation (referring to it as murder case), which had now identified that a person had shed blood in the Yusupov courtyard.

After Makarov's astonishing remark, Zavadsky wrestled the knowledge that the conspiracy had ostensibly snared his superior and "those close to the throne."[928] Zavadsky feared for the future once he realized that the participants in this crime directed it against the monarch to bring about a "Court uprising." It fell into place after Zavadsky realized why Nikolai Mikhailovich invited him to his palace (with Grand Duke Alexander Mikhailovich present) seeking him to stop the investigation. Nikolai Mikhailovich (later telephoned Zavadsky's chambers about the same matter) showed immense interest about Dmitri's fate, while his brother, Alexander

Mikhailovich, was more interested about Felix's culpability. It left Zavadsky wanting to hear more from them, whilst leaving him to believe there was no court conspiracy. Both grand dukes were relieved to learn from Zavadsky that the first day of the investigation was progressing "at a tortoise pace."[929] Smith notes that Zavadsky believed that Nikolai Mikhailovich "knew little about the affair."[930] However, it must be said that the grand duke had no reason to divulge information and thus deftly mislead Zavadsky.

The police knew that Dmitri Pavlovich, Purishkevich and Yusupov were at the Moika residence for a few hours, which otherwise was undergoing extensive renovations. The wooden objects protruding through the snow in the courtyard (**POLICE PHOTOS Nos. 1, 2 and 3**) prove that the work was not yet complete. The peculiarity of holding an event at the Moika palace while Felix was temporarily living at Grand Duke Alexander Mikhailovich's palace did not escape the police.

During the morning, Grand Duke Alexander Mikhailovich's *Adjutant* entered the dining room in Gatchino (renamed Gatchina in 1944[931]) and notified the grand duke that Rasputin had been murdered. Hearing this news, the grand duke contacted the dowager empress. Both agreed that it was good that "Rasputin has been swept off the road."[932] Later, after he had arrived in Petrograd, Grand Duke Alexander Mikhailovich, Felix's father-in-law, spoke with Dmitri and reacted in the same way as most had, calling Dmitri and Felix "two national heroes" but he was no wiser as to who raised his hand against Rasputin after they "admitted to me that they had taken part in the murder, but that they refused to admit the name of the main murderer."[933]

The emperor, located far away at Stavka in Mogilev, reasoned that only if the body was found would it be necessary to return to Tsarskoe Selo and take action against the perpetrators.

Noontime Rumors in Moscow

On Saturday morning, Maklakov was participating at a judicial conference in Moscow. During his lunch break he was summoned to take a phone call from one of his Moscow acquaintances (whom he preferred not to name). The caller asked Maklakov whether the Petrograd rumor about Rasputin's death at the Yusupov house was true. Maklakov's lunch colleague rang the local *Okhrana* department and was told that there were indeed rumors circulating in Petrograd about Rasputin's (probable) fate. Despite those rumors, he thought that it was premature to admit that Rasputin was no longer alive, especially since Purishkevich had seemingly failed to notify him by telegram as had been agreed. Maklakov boarded the train back to Petrograd on Saturday night and noticed that in his carriage they were celebrating Rasputin's demise. Maklakov also heard passengers name those who were purportedly responsible. Setting foot on the Nikolayevskii station platform in Petrograd on Sunday morning, Maklakov remained uncertain if Rasputin was indeed missing.[934]

A Remarkable Expression of Loyalty

Since some of the guests on Friday night at the Yusupovskii Palace may have been members of the nobility, it introduced an impediment for the investigation. Director of Police Vasiliev was unable to ask the simplest of questions, such as who was present at the palace that night. There was, however, one item of information that most of Petrograd society knew and that related to Yusupov's wife, Irina. She was not in Petrograd.[935] General Popov could only invite Felix Yusupov, if he was willing, to provide his account of the events of Friday night.

Yusupov claimed that shortly after he arrived at the Sergievskii Palace, Dmitri attempted to contact the empress.[936] The telegram Alexandra Fyodorovna sent to Nikolai II (see **Chapter Six**) mentioned that Dmitri asked if he could visit on Sunday.[937] Alexandra Fyodorovna firmly refused to see Dmitri. She left an order with palace security that Dmitri was prohibited entry into the palace grounds.[938]

Felix placed his own call to the palace asking for Anna, in the hope that he would be allowed to come to Tsarskoe Selo to explain what had happened on Friday night. Taneeva left a message with her roommaid saying that Alexandra Fyodorovna did not allow her to approach the phone[939] and speak to Felix. The empress instead passed on a message that Felix could send a letter describing what happened. In the French edition of his memoirs, Felix claimed that Taneeva telephoned Felix, telling him that the empress was ill and because she was unable to receive him, it was better that he wrote an explanatory letter.[940] This alternative scenario, though tame, was probably written to conceal Yusupov's irritation that the empress refused to see or speak directly with him.

Although Felix[941] preferred to take credit for composing the text of the letter addressed to the empress, Purishkevich claimed that all three of them drew up the letter.[942] Felix admitted that it was an exercise, which assisted them all to get their story straight should they be asked any questions. Curiously in the revised Russian edition of his memoirs, Felix omitted to mention his phone calls to the palace and that he sent a letter to Alexandra Fyodorovna.[943] The letter reads:

"Your Imperial Majesty,
17 December 1916

I hasten to obey the commands of Your Majesty and to inform You what occurred in my place last night, to throw light on the dreadful accusation that is placed against me. On the occasion of a house warming on the night of December 16, I organized myself a supper to which I invited my friends, and a few ladies. Grand Duke Dmitri Pavlovich was also there. About 12 o'clock in the night Grigorii Efimovich, telephoned me to invite me to go with him to the gypsies I declined, saying, that I have my own evening, and asked, from where he called. He replied: " you want to know too much" - and hung up. When he spoke, many voices were audible. This is everything that I heard that evening about Grigorii Efimovich. Returning to my visitors, I mentioned my phone conversation, which caused careless remarks by them. You are aware, Your Majesty, that Grigorii Efimovich's name in many circles is rather unpopular. About three my visitors began to depart and, having said goodbye with the Grand Duke and two ladies, and with others I went into my study. Around me it seemed, that somewhere a shot resounded. I summoned a servant and ordered him to find out what was happened. He returned and stated, that a shot was heard, but it is not known from where. Then I myself went to the court yard and personally asked the caretaker and the policeman 'Who fired?' The caretakers said that they were drinking tea in the caretaker's lodge, and the policeman said that he heard a shot, but did not know who fired. Then I went home and sent for the policeman, and personally rang Dmitri Pavlovich, asking, whether it was he who fired. He replied to me laughing, that when leaving the house, he fired a few times at the watchdog and that one of the ladies had fainted. When I told him that the shots caused alarm, he replied to me, that it cannot be, as nobody else was there. I called my servant, who himself went to the court yard and saw one of our watchdogs, killed, near the fence.

Then I ordered the servant to bury it in the garden. At four everyone departed, and I returned to Alexander Mikhailovich's palace, where I live. On the following day, i.e. this morning, I learned of the disappearance of Grigorii Efimovich, which they are connecting with my evening. Then they informed me, that apparently I was seen at his place during the night, and that he drove away with me. This is a veritable lie as all evening I and my visitors never left the house. Then they told me that, he told someone that he would go one of these days to become acquainted with Irina. In it there is some truth, in that when I saw him the last time, he asked me to acquaint him with Irina, and asked if she was here. I told him that the wife is in the Crimea, but will arrive around the 15th or 16th December. On the evening of the 14th I received a telegram from Irina, in which she informed me that she became ill, and is requesting me to appear together with her brothers, who were leaving this evening.

I fail to find words, Your Majesty, which can express to You how shocked I am by all these happenings and up to what degree it appears to me monstrous accusations, which are raised against me.

I remain deeply devoted to Your Majesty.

Felix" [944]

The letter (attempting to vindicate its author whilst insulting the empress' intelligence) was meant to deceive her.[945] Left unanswered, it passed on to Protopopov, who forwarded a copy to Vasiliev.[946]

Protopopov received orders not to allow Felix to leave Petrograd.[947] General Voyeikov, the Palace *Commandant,* recognized that the empress was given a "double blow." The first blow was her realization that Rasputin was probably dead and the second blow was dealt by Dmitri Pavlovich.[948] The amiable bond Alexandra Fyodorovna had shared with Dmitri as he matured into adulthood and treated like a son by her family[949] was irreparably affected.

Dmitri's sister Maria Pavlovna was in Pskov assisting with the war effort. She was awoken in the morning by the sound of a telephone ringing. Not doubting what she heard, the grand duchess wrote in her memoirs that although she "was proud of him," she had a "feeling of unaccustomed estrangement" because Dmitri had failed to hint to her about his plans.[950] Loyal to her brother, the murder itself did not upset her. When she went to lunch, those who were there had heard the news and although no one spoke to her about the matter, she felt as if there was "hidden admiration in the looks given me."

Did Felix Yusupov Have Female Guests on Friday Night?

A number of authors have queried whether any women had also been invited to attend Felix's soirée on Friday night at the time when Rasputin was murdered. Paléologue dismissed the idea that ladies were invited to "the gathering."[951] Paléologue's remark becomes all the more significant since *Birzheviye Vedomosti*[952] alleged that two women were seen getting into a car that pulled up alongside the palace driveway entrance. The letter Felix sent to Alexandra Fyodorovna said "two ladies" were at the palace, a detail that he reiterated in his police deposition.

Recently, Shishkin wanted to find out more about the identity of the women who were supposedy Yusupov's guests on Friday night.[953] To support his idea, Shishkin published a *Spravka* (Certificate) that was addressed to "*Gospodin* Director of Police." That statement was made to resemble a surveillance report, giving details about Moscow resident Vera Karalli. Considered to be a talented ballerina, Karalli was visiting Petrograd around that time to give a ballet performance along with two other performers from the Moscow Imperial Theater. She was in Petrograd on Friday night because she received public acclaim for her evening performance in Saturday's edition of *Novoye Vremya* (*New Times*).[954] Nevertheless, did Karalli visit the Yusupov's Palace after giving her performance?

Shishkin's Certificate[955] contains several irregularities, four of which are:

► Only noted the month and the year but failed to give a specific day when it was co-signed.

► It lacked the customary professional courtesy of addressing General Vasiliev and instead used the vague term *Gospodin* (Mister).

► Naming the Hotel *Medved* (where Karalli allegedly stayed). The *Medved*[956] (Bear) was a restaurant favored by actors and theater goers but does not offering lodgings.

► The *Medved* was not located on *Konyushennaya Ulitsa* but on *Bolshaya Konyushennaya Ulitsa*, 27.[957] There are two streets in Petrograd using the name *Konyushennaya*, the second one being *Malaya Konyushennaya*.

The idea that Karalli was present at the Yusupovskii Palace came from Simanovich's memoirs. He alleged[958] that after Yusupov shot Rasputin "in the eye" and then as the victim began to fall, "everyone" began to shoot at him, except "Koralli (sic) refused and screamed: I do not want to shoot." Significantly, Simanovich did not witness the events at the palace. While it is true that Karalli was acquainted with both Felix and Dmitri,[959] such friendships were common between honored performers and members of the nobility. Accordingly, one must conclude that Paléologue did after all receive truthful information.

One anonymous publication that appeared in 1917 fancifully suggested that Princess Orbeliani, confined to a wheelchair and died prematurely on 2 December 2 1915,[960] and Baroness

Buxhoeveden (in Alexandra Fyodorovna's permanent service at the time) might have been Yusupov's guests.[961]

Who Will be the Next Victim?

After the events of Friday night, Taneeva claimed that she and the empress were to be Yusupov's next victims. Taneeva revealed this detail during her interview with the American journalist Rheta Child-Dorr in the summer of 1917.[962] Protopopov likewise testified in 1917 that there were rumors suggesting that Taneeva might be the next target.[963] There is one piece of evidence that someone planned to murder Taneeva. Protopopov handed over an anonymous letter to General Globachev, which was posted to Taneeva's home. It threatened she would receive "the same share."[964] Copies of the letter were placed inside the police, the governor's and the procurator's office files. Protopopov warned Spiridovich (head of palace security) that this threat[965] had to be taken seriously. By nightfall, Taneeva's house was surrounded by *Okhrana* agents. Solving the problem, Alexandra Fyodorovna ensured that Taneeva would, for the time being, live in the left wing of the palace.[966] An *Okhrana* agent would escort Taneeva around the palace, while medical *feldsher* Akim Zhuk accompanied her during all visits to the infirmary.[967]

Baroness Buxhoeveden confirmed that threatening letters addressed to the empress were received at the palace after Rasputin's death.[968] The Romanov family was certainly discussing what had to be done with Alexandra Fyodorovna, with Grand Duchess Maria Pavlovna (the elder) not shy in showing her hostility against the empress, letting it be known that such a drastic action was necessary.[969] Nikolai Mikhailovich wrote in his diary on 23 December that the "young people ... cleared the air, though - half measure, since it was vital to do away with Alexandra Fyodorovna and Protopopov."[970]

Nikolai II transmitted a telegram from Mogilev to the palace, which advised Alexandra Fyodorovna to seek Protopopov's guidance. At 10 p.m. Protopopov telephoned the palace that Yusupov was detained by the gendarme at the Nikolayevskii *Vokzal* (railway station) and then driven to Grand Duke Alexander Mikhailovich's palace where he was temporarily staying.[971] The empress responded to her husband's telegram with her own,[972] in which she said:

"*Kalinin* [Protopopov] *is doing everything possible. So far nothing found. F., intending to travel to Crimea, detained.*

Very much desire that you would be here.

May God help us."

While Makarov sat back, the empress summoned General Mikhail Belyaev (who was in her service[973]) to discuss matters with him.[974]

Mixed Feelings at Mogilev Military Headquarters

General Spiridovich described the general mood at Stavka after the first news regarding Rasputin's disappearance had reached military headquarters. After his breakfast, Nikolai II went for his morning walk (not a drive, as Spiridovich incorrectly recalled) into the local forest. He was handed a telegram from Alexandra informing him that Rasputin had disappeared. His outward demeanor did not change with this news, and then attended the military council meeting, at which he replaced General Alexeev with General Gurko. Nikolai II, always reserved in front of his subordinates, did not offer any opinion about the events unfolding in Petrograd.[975] By late evening a copy of the *Birzheviye Vedomosti* (*Stock Exchange Record*) had found its way into Stavka, which General Voyeikov handed over to the emperor. It was then that the emperor had apparently shown signs of unease, becoming agitated but tight-lipped.

Shavelsky, the Stavka priest, described the attitude of the officers after General Tatishev arrived to report the latest news from Petrograd directly to the emperor.[976] His appearance was an unusual event, which immediately alerted many officers that something was wrong. After speaking with the emperor, Tatishev, over breakfast in the officer's mess, revealed his news. Officers down to the lowest ranks rejoiced and many rose to kiss each other spontaneously on the cheek, as Russians normally do, each congratulating the other with such good fortune. It was obvious that Grand Duke Dmitri Pavlovich's placement at Mogilev and in the imperial suite was no longer tenable. By evening, numerous bottles of champagne had appeared, the corks popped and the alcohol flowed in the mess with shouts of *Ura* (Hooray).[977] Few officers or clergy expressed empathy. Nikolai II's diary for that day reveals nothing noteworthy.

Shadowy Agents

Paléologue was the first person to name an *Okhrana* agent who was allegedly an eyewitness to the shooting in the small Yusupov courtyard. Paléologue identified him only by the surname Tikhomirov. According to Paléologue, Tikhomirov was watching the Yusupovskii Palace at the Ministry of Interior building, across the Moika canal, and afterwards supposedly "pushed his way in" into the vestibule where he saw Purishkevich.[978] Did Tikhomirov see activity on the other side of the canal at night?

Paléologue's information is problematic. **Photo 10** shows a tall gas lamp close to the entrance of the Ministry of Internal Affairs building on *Bolshaya Morskaya Ulitsa*. On the opposite side of the canal, the courtyard bordering the Moika Embankment did not have illumination. Given the night setting, Tikhomirov's eyes would never be able to distinguish different military uniforms from his position. Yusupov told the truth when he said the courtyard was "in darkness."[979] Accordingly, Tikhomirov never existed. Paléologue seemingly confused the surname Tikhomirov with the *gorodovoi* Vlasyuk, who, invited inside the Yusupovskii Palace, did talk with a man wearing the khaki tunic of a State Councillor (Purishkevich).

Almost ten years ago, the text of a telegram was published, giving the impression it was the first notification received by Nikolai II that Grigorii Rasputin had disappeared. It was said to have arrived at Military Headquarters at 6 p.m. and addressed to a "Colonel Rotko."[980] The alleged dispatch published by Shishkin, however, is fictitious for the following reasons:

▶ Intended for the sovereign's attention, it was addressed to a low ranked officer rather than "Your Imperial Highness."

▶ "Colonel Rotko" is not listed as a member of staff stationed at military headquarters in December 1917.[981]

► General Tatishev's lengthy journey to speak confidentially with Nikolai II on the same matter would have accordingly rendered his visit superfluous.

► The text does not reflect the information that the gendarmes had in their possession:

- The statement that "a human cry was heard after which the sound of a motorcar was heard leaving." *Gorodovoi* Efimov stated in his deposition (not on Saturday when this telegram was supposed to have been transmitted, but on Sunday) that the sound he heard was "akin to a woman's scream" (see **Protocol No. 8, Chapter Six**).

- The *Okhrana* agents were dismissed by ten at night, not nine.

- The information that "the shooter wore a military field artillery uniform" implies that there was an eyewitness to the shooting. General Gurko recalled that he only heard rumors of Rasputin's alleged death because there was no communication to confirm that information at Mogilev military headquarters.[982]

Proving that Shishkin's telegram was fake, why do I mention it? The telegram raised the question about the uniform the eyewitness saw, a detail that Cook used to introduce his notion that a British agent shot Rasputin. Applying a poor translation of the description *v voenno-polevoi forme,* which translates as the "uniform of the artillery regiment" - for Cook, it became a "military field uniform."[983] Shishkin interpreted the uniform to be a long overcoat (*shinel*) that was adorned with fleece (an Australian "kangaroo") trim. Recognizing that Russian officers like the grand duke did not wear military overcoats adorned with fleece, but finding a photograph of Hoare wearing an overcoat with a fleece collar, Shishkin implicated the English operative as the last shooter (**Photo 11**).[984] Cook, however, took one step further, saying that British officers during the Russian winter wore "Russian army greatcoats over their tunics,"[985] but Russians wore "tunics" (*gymnasterki*) as their "formal uniform,"[986] not the "field uniform" worn when on active service. Purishkevich wore the green tunic of a State Counsellor (see **Protocol No. 9**), whereas Felix Yusupov wore the khaki cadet uniform of the Imperial *Pazheskii Korpus* with the shoulder boards of the imperial suite. Dmitri Pavlovich wore the uniform of a *Shtab-Rotmeister* and *Fligel-Adjutant* attached to the imperial suite (**photo 12**).

Cook postulated that the shooter wearing an overcoat was Oswald Rayner. It is absurd to envisage that Rayner, wearing a heavy winter coat, waited outside the Yusupovskii Palace (depicted in the Russian 2014 film, *Rasputin R*, with its accompanying book penned by Ilya Tylkin[987]). Supposing Rayner did so, why not wait in the main barricaded courtyard where Felix and his guests alighted unseen from their cars? Since the sounds of the shooting happened some two hours after Rasputin's arrival, how could Rayner anticipate the *strannik* would open a tiny auxiliary door facing the secondary courtyard that was normally locked? Indeed, why would Rayner wait outside at all?

The First Deposition in the Investigation

Protocols (Depositions) are general witness statements that assist with the reconstruction of a crime. The testimony provided by each person in the Rasputin Matter was a signed (if the person was literate) statement that contained opinions, expressions of hearsay and hard facts, which are composed in such a way that they enable the eyewitness to tell their story. Imperial law protected Dmitri Pavlovich and Felix Yusupov from participating, though the latter consented to do so.

Two Protocols were taken down on the first day of the investigation, the first was given by Yusupov's batman, Ivan Nefedov. Only one or two gendarme generals were authorized to take down the statements from key witnesses, which may explain why city policemen Efimov and Vlasyuk did not submit their Protocols until the next day (Sunday). Only a small window of opportunity became available to process Yusupov's staff. Once Yusupov rescinded his permission, General Popov was unable to return to the Yusupovskii Palace and question his employees. Nevertheless, two employees, normally located outside, were asked to give evidence. They were the watchman at Moika, 94 and the yard keeper of the adjoining house at No. 92.

The second Protocol was taken from Maria Golovina, whose bias was directed in favor of protecting Felix Yusupov. Golovina's Protocol will not be provided here because it adds nothing to this case. Golovina testified that Felix did not see Rasputin that evening because he was entertaining guests and thus had to decline Rasputin's invitation to visit the gypsies. Allegedly, it was Rasputin who telephoned the palace, even though Yusupov was not living there at the time.[988]

Though General Vasiliev concluded that Nefedov's Protocol was largely "insincere and false,"[989] he did confirm that Grand Duke Dmitri Pavlovich was at the palace and that all the guests left by four o'clock on Saturday morning.

PROTOCOL No. 1 - Ivan Grigoriev Nefedov

"My name is Ivan Grigoriev Nefedov. From birth I have 39 years, raised in the *Molokansky* sect. My rank is a peasant from Ryazan Province, Kasimov *Uezd*, Betnin *Volost*. I live in the city of Petrograd at the 2nd Reserve Battalion (I) am a batman for General-Adjutant Prince Yusupov Count Sumarokov-Elston.

On 16 December of this year around 5 o'clock in the evening young Prince Felix ordered me *"Today I will have guests, prepare the dining room downstairs with everything needed - by 10 in the evening"* and left, after that I did not see the prince until the night. I prepared the table with everything, that was needed – tea, wines, fruit for 7-9 persons, since that was the number the prince indicated to me. Everything was ready by 10 o'clock at night. I and the house supervisor, Buzhinsky were alternatively located at the parade porch of No. 94 exiting onto the Moika. During my presence during this night no one passed through the parade entrance into the dining room and the prince's study. Around 11 or 12 o'clock at night not long before I absented myself from the parade porch, when I returned, Buzhinsky told me that Grand Duke Dmitri Pavlovich had arrived and had gone down to the dining room below. I sat with Buzhinsky at the parade [entrance] until 4 o'clock in the morning and during that time neither one of us entered the dining room, because the Prince warned us, that there would be ladies and ordered us not to enter. Guests arrived by the side entrance from No. 92 and entered straight into the dining room, and from the Prince's study, only doors slamming and the gramophone playing were heard. Prince Yusupov always had the key to the side porch on him. In the past there were two-three such evenings for the Prince and the maid also did not go to the dining room and study. I did not hear shots in the dining room, nor in the street during the night of 17 December. Around 4 o'clock in the morning, the bell rang, to which I entered the Prince's study, where already there were no guests, and the Prince told me *"go into the yard, have a look, what has happened there"*. I went out through the side entrance into the yard of house No. 92 but no one was there anymore, and I did not notice anything, about which I informed the Prince. Within a few minutes he again rang for me and ordered that I check the yard again, because a slain dog was lying there. I exited through the side door into the yard of house No. 92 and this time I saw a dog lying by the railing, which I picked up and dragged it into the garden of Yusupov's house, where it lies for the present time. After that the Prince himself went out to the parade porch and ordered that (I) call the *gorodovoi*, which I carried out. The fetched *gorodovoi* went into the Prince's study, what conversation took place, I do not know. If there was anyone in the Prince's study at that time, I do not know. Besides, I went to bed and how the Prince left I did not see. On the morning of 17 December, the dining room was tidied by me, everything in the dining room was in order; *judging by the volume of the wine drunk,* the previous nights' guests must have left rather intoxicated. Prince Yusupov was also merry during that night. The slain dog - was a stray in the Yusupov house. (I have) nothing further to testify."

Signed: Ivan Grigoriev Nefedov

Countersigned: General-Major Popov[990]

It is perplexing that Nefedov was able to hear loud benign sounds such as music and slamming of doors but not able to hear any gunshots that were fired inside his building.

A Window That Revealed Different Views

It is unfortunate that Yusupov's butler Buzhinsky, who was also on duty at the Moika Palace on the night in question, did not submit a Protocol. Cook claims that Buzhinsky did speak with the police when they attended the crime scene.[991] However, Cook failed to reference his source about a conversation during which Buzhinsky pointed out a damaged window to the police.

An article in the morning edition *Birzheviye Vedomosti,* dated 21 December, reported that a broken window was willingly pointed out by a *dvornik* (yard keeper) to an approaching police officer who was accompanied by a *gorodovoi*. If so, this means that there was confusion as to whether the person was the butler (as Cook wrote) or a *dvornik*. The damage was supposedly caused by a stray bullet.[992] Although the published report contains a few incorrect details, the only part about that article that is relevant in the present discussion is the broken window.

The correspondent wrote that a *dvornik* gave his testimony to General Popel on 17 December. When the *gorodovoi* provided his statement on 18 December (not on 17 December as reported), Vlasyuk found nothing suspicious. He never heard the sound of glass shattering, a noise that he would have heard from his location. The mystery as to how the window became broken needs to be found elsewhere.

Importantly, while Sereda, with Zavadsky and General Vasiliev, inspected the courtyard and had it photographed, not one of them said that there was a connection between the broken window and the crime scene they were examining in daylight.

Yusupov revealed that he was living elsewhere because the palace, including the basement area, was undergoing renovation. It therefore seems likely that the damage to the window was caused during the renovations. Accordingly, none of the palace employees needed to comment about the window. If the damage had occurred on Friday night (as asserted by Cook), I doubt that it would have been patched up after six o'clock in the morning (once Vlasyuk's night shift ended) during the winter darkness and before the unanticipated arrival of the investigation teams after first light.

The windows to the left of the basement door shows the typical Russian style window composed of three separate sections. The two lower inner frames open individually outwards, which normally support either a single or multiple smaller window panes. POLICE PHOTO No. 1a shows that the main outer frame of the window has undergone some repair on three sides, while all the window panes appear intact. If a bullet had passed through the window it would have only gone through one of the window panes, leaving a discrete hole. If such an opening needed fixing, the repair work would not have involved three sides of the main window frame. As far as the *Birzheviye Vedomosti* article is concerned, it would have been typical for a journalist, seeing the patched up window from the public sidewalk, to draw their speculative conclusions.

CRIME SCENE TWO - The Bolshoi Petrovskii Bridge

On Saturday afternoon, the investigation had switched to a second location. The search was initiated 7.4kms from the city center, at the northwestern margins of the town on one of seven islands in the Neva delta. Petrovskii Island originally belonged to Peter I, on which in 1710 he built two wooden huts. By the end of the nineteenth century, a number of large-scale industries were constructed on the island and in 1896, the *Dom Veteranov Tseni* (House for Theater Veterans) made its appearance. By the turn of the century, few private houses existed. The main access road on the island is Petrovskii *Prospekt*.[993]

Course of Action in Finding Rasputin's Remains

At noon, the guards on duty changed shift with their fresh replacements on the Bolshoi Petrovskii Bridge. The original 1838 wooden structure was a drawbridge, which joined Petrovskii and Krestovskii Islands over the *Malaya Nevka* (Minor Neva) River. The mouth of the river is very close to the bridge and flows into the Finnish Gulf. In 1916, this bridge was located in a remote region (see **MAP No. 1, Chapter Seven**) and accommodated two-way vehicular traffic. After 1947, the bridge was upgraded and was measured to be 297 meters long and 18 meters wide;[994] however, these days a footbridge connects the two islands.

The new guard on duty at Post No. 2, Fyodor Kuzmin, walked once over the bridge span, seeing nothing suspicious. (Post No. 150, where Kuzmin sat on duty, was located around a bend which did not afford a view of the bridge.[995]) Two hours later, two unnamed passing workmen notified Kuzmin that they saw blood stains on the fourth bridge span (about forty paces from where the bridge began on the Petrovskii side[996]). Kuzmin walked over to the area and noticed that there was also blood on the bridge foundations below the carriageway. He immediately notified *gorodovoi* Vasilii Kordyukov, of the 4th Petrograd District, telling him that he had found traces of what appeared to be blood on the bridge panels, railing and bridge supports on the Krestovskii Island side of the bridge. Fresh powdered snow lay on top of these bloodstains.[997] Following the guard to the location, Kordyukov confirmed that Kuzmin was not mistaken before he contacted his superior, police supervisor Asonov.

According to Protocol No. 1740 (below), all three men returned to the location, by which time not only did they all agree that the stains were blood spatter but when a galosh was also spotted lying between two adjacent foundations, the matter became somber. The galosh (**DIAGRAM No. 1, Chapter Seven**) was retrieved and handed to Fyodor Kuzmin for temporary safe keeping (**Protocol No. 13, Chapter Six**). It was identified as a brown, men's size 10, *Treugolnik* brand. [*Birzheviye Vedomosti* incorrectly reported it was size 11[998]]. Though the *New York Times* inaccurately reported that "a pair of galoshes with suspicious red marks" was found near "a freshly made hole,"[999] the *Times* in London revealed that "in the snow near the bank was found a man's galosh," which was said to have been "stained with suspicious marks."[1000] Despite the ice forming over much of the river, from the bridge, nothing was seen in the water that still circled the bridge foundations below (POLICE PHOTO No. 9).

The London Times correspondent reported the police "discovered a newly cut ice hole."[1001] *Birzheviye Vedomosti* stated that a car had stopped close to the railing, leaving tire impressions in the snow. Footprints were also found close to the bridge railing.[1002] *Novoye Vremya* (*New Times*) reported that the tire tracks were so deep they left piles of snow along the bridge span. Below the bridge, the snow on one side of the bridge support had been disturbed. In that area, bloodstains could be seen that appeared "somewhat smeared." Their appearance "left the impression that a bloodied object had slipped" down the "vertical beam." More blood was found on the horizontal beam of the bridge support.[1003] General Popov notified Vasiliev that some bloodstains and one galosh had been found on the Bolshoi Petrovskii Bridge, as well as recent tire tracks that extended part of the way along the bridge span close to where the blood was sighted. Vasiliev then ordered the local police to secure the area and ensure that no traffic would pass,[1004] thereby escalating the investigation at this second location.

PROTOCOL No. 1740

- On the fourth panel of the bridge and on the wooden bridge supports and railing, traces of blood were found at a distance of 1 arshin (28 inches or 0.71 of a meter).

- A size 10 warm men's *Treugolnik* brand galosh (*botik*) was found in the gap between the supports.

[Signed] *Police Supervisor Asonov, Vasilii Kordyukov* (No. 1876)

Guard Fyodor Kuzmin.

- On duty since 12 noon, Kuzmin conducted his rounds on the bridge and failed to see the blood on the bridge.

- Whilst on the Krestovskii side of the bridge, Kuzmin was alerted by passing workers that there was blood on the fourth panel.

- Returning to that location, the workers showed Kuzmin the bloodstains on the panels, railings and between the supports, and below that between the supports lay a men's boot.

- No other object was found in the water that remained unfrozen.

[Signed] Guard Fyodor Kuzmin

[Counter-signed] Police Supervisor Asonov.[1005]

Vasiliev promptly notified Minister Protopopov of the finding, who then contacted the chief of the Petrograd River police and ordered that they must conduct a search at the Bolshoi Petrovskii Bridge using their divers. Protopopov had apparently ordered that the search was to be extended as far as the Kronshtadt Naval Base on Kotlin Island in case the corpse might have drifted in that direction.[1006] With twilight approaching after three o'clock,[1007] nothing new was found and the search had to be abandoned until the daylight of the following morning. The area was guarded overnight by the gendarmes and the river police. The footwear (later identified by the Rasputin daughters as belonging to their father[1008]) and the location where it was found indicated that Rasputin had met with a dreadful fate. *Birzheviye Vedomosti* reported that a portion of snow containing blood was sent over to the court investigator.[1009] By nightfall the blood was confirmed to be of human origin rather than from an injured bird.[1010]

It was not until after the revolution in February 1917, when a single page summary of what was known about the crime up to Sunday 18 December was found in the police department. The details from that summary were published. Most likely it was a draft, since it was handwritten in pencil by an unidentified individual. The text incorporated details that were sourced from a number of statements, mostly relying on what Vlasyuk and Yusupov said. The first paragraph provided part of Purishkevich's conversation with Vlasyuk announcing that Rasputin died (*pogib*). The author noted that it was this information, which initiated the (second) search. The outline appears to have been composed shortly after the after the galosh had been identified by Grigorii Rasputin's family. The communiqué was directed to Nikolai II, using the proper address "To Your Imperial Highness" and ended with the words: "further investigations are continuing."[1011]

Noble Conspirators are One Step Closer to Facing Their Destiny

Just like Purishkevich, Yusupov planned to leave Petrograd on the day of the murder. Instead, Felix was detained at the Nikolayevskii railway station by a colonel attached to the gendarmes, just he ascended the steps to board the train. Felix was accompanied by his brothers-in-law, Grand Dukes Fyodor Alexandrovich, Nikita Alexandrovich and Andrei Alexandrovich, as well as Rayner and another man identified as "Stuart."[1012] Nikita would continue his journey alone. An imperial order had been issued saying he was not permitted to begin his train journey. Yusupov was placed under arrest until the emperor would return to decide the prince's fate.[1013] Felix was politely urged to return to Grand Duke Alexander Mikhailovich's palace, which was primarily occupied by Felix's mother-in-law, Grand Duchess Ksenya Alexandrovna. One local newspaper managed to disclose on their front page that "Felix, who was preparing to leave … for Crimea… was compelled to delay his departure."[1014]

Felix telephoned Nikolai Mikhailovich around 10.30 p.m., insistent that he come over to his brother's place.[1015] [Felix claimed that the grand duke came over out of mere curiosity.[1016]] Nikolai Mikhailovich stayed with Felix for an hour and a half listening to his revelations "without sustained criticism."[1017] The next morning, Felix either decided or was urged to move into the Sergievskii Palace with Dmitri Pavlovich, but before that happened, he needed to sleep.[1018]

Seemingly in control of his emotions, Dmitri went to the Yacht Club after lunchtime and sat at another table away from Nikolai Mikhailovich, who noticed how "deathly pale" the young man appeared. Not surprisingly, Dmitri was asked about Rasputin and heard to respond that he "had either disappeared or was killed."[1019] His word choice was odd, considering they inferred that something had happened to Rasputin. Senator Alexander Trepov, replying to Nikolai Mikhailovich's question about the legality of Yusupov's detention, exclaimed that it was not only nonsense but that it was all due to "Protopopov's new provocation."[1020] Dmitri Pavlovich attended a performance to watch a comedy in prose by Emil Augier and Jules Sandeau: "*Le gendre de M. Poirier,*" presented by the permanently-based French Drama Troupe[1021] at the Mikhailovskii Theatre. According to Grand Duke Gavril Konstantinovich,[1022] Dimitri received a standing ovation.

One other person who appeared calm after the murder was Purishkevich. Andrei Shingarev, a medical doctor and Duma delegate,[1023] met Purishkevich at eight in the morning to discuss matters related to hospitals for the war-wounded. Earlier, Shingarev seemingly did not believe the rumor that Purishkevich was going to be involved in murdering Rasputin. Now after the murder had been committed, Shingarev faced a man who showed no outward signs that he had participated in such activity hours before.[1024]

After marrying Grand Duke Paul Alexandrovich, Princess Olga Paley became Grand Duke Dmitri's stepmother. Being close to the unfolding drama, she described in her memoirs that she never forgot that Saturday night after Rasputin was declared missing. During the evening she was preparing to attend a concert that was to be held at the Tsarskoe Selo Concert Hall. At 8 p.m., her son Vladimir rushed into her room and spoke excitedly that he had just received a call telling him that Rasputin had vanished. Not quite understanding the significance of Vladimir's information, instead of attentively listening to the orchestra, Princess Paley felt that all eyes had focused on her instead. During intermission she learnt why she became the main attraction.[1025] By the end of the night, Dmitri's name, along with the names Felix Yusupov and Vladimir Purishkevich, was on everyone's lips.[1026]

Is it Time to Celebrate or Commiserate?

The newspapers were quick to follow-up after the Petrograd evening *Birzheviye Vedomosti* had cunningly obtained information from the police and Rasputin's family in defiance of censorship regulations. It named the murderers in its pages. The police promptly confiscated all unsold copies, while in the salons the champagne bottles popped in celebration, matching the merriment that infected many passers-by who happened to hear the news on the streets.

Grand Duke Andrei Vladimirovich pasted a copy of the article from the evening edition of *Birzheviye Vedomosti*, dated Saturday 17 December, into his diary. Using the heading *"Smert'* (Death) of Grigorii Rasputin,"* it read:

> *"Today at 6 o'clock in the morning, following a reception, the life of Grigorii Rasputin-Novy came to a sudden end in one of the aristocratic houses in the center of the capital."*[1027]

Other Petrograd papers such as *Petrogradskaya Gazeta* (*The Petrograd Newspaper*), *Novoye Vremya* and *Vecherneye Vremya* (*Evening Times*) could only provide the barest details, reporting the event with cautious language like a "Mysterious Crime" or "Mysterious Event" which involved unknown persons in the Petrograd center.[1028] Another version of this story provided the vaguest details; however, it is helpful in demonstrating how censorship regulations ruined most journalistic endeavors. It offered the following:

> *"One person whose surname the newspaper is not naming was called late at night from his apartment into an automobile, in which there were two representatives of the capital's high society. According to what is heard circulating in the Tavricheskii Palace ... the assault occurred after the night in one aristocratic house to which all the former arrived in the automobile."*[1029]

Spiridovich explained that by the evening "all of the fashionable society in Petrograd, the diplomats, women's circles, newspapers and all the police" knew who was responsible.[1030] On the other hand, the only name which was mentioned in relation to this matter appeared in *Russkaya Volya* on Sunday on page 6[1031] was repeated in *Rech* on page 2 two days after the incident.[1032] Both newspapers cunningly announced that "near to Prince Yusupov Count Sumarokov-Elston's house on Moika, 94," a number of revolver shots had resounded. Despite the difficulties of publishing accurate information, *Russkoye Slovo* named Felix Yusupov and revealed that Purishkevich spoke to one of the *gorodovoi* at

Moika, 94.[1033]

Unlike Russia, the foreign press was not subject to the same censorship restrictions. *The New York Times* somewhat amusingly wrote that "a more lenient press censorship has allowed the newspapers here to publish all conceivable versions of the story of the death of the monk Gregory Rasputin...."[1034] An unidentified Petrograd correspondent for the *New York Times* named "Felix Prince Yusupoff" (sic) as one of "the high rank of the persons immediately concerned," adding that he was "29 years of age" and related by marriage to the "Czar" (sic). The same article also revealed "the name of a well-known and formerly reactionary Deputy is also mentioned in connection with the event [Purishkevich]."[1035] Across the Atlantic Ocean, the *Times* in London merely cited the Russian newspaper *Rech*. It was only able to state that "the tragedy ... appears to have been enacted at the Yussupoff (sic) Palace, on the Moika" and that "none of the names of the participants are mentioned."[1036] In the next day's edition, the *Times* repeated the same point that was published days earlier in Russia, in that "the names of those who took part in the deed are generally known." The participants would remain nameless in the British media as well. Nevertheless, that same article went on to claim that "it is no exaggeration to say that the whole of Russia breathes more freely for the removal of most hateful influence...."[1037] A few days later the, the *Times* incorrectly claimed that "Prince Yussupoff (sic) was present yesterday at an entertainment at the house of a prominent banker, where he received an enthusiastic ovation. The guests showered flowers upon him and carried him shoulder high."[1038]

Duma representative Vasilii Shulgin recalled[1039] that when the news reached Moscow that evening, theatre patrons asked the orchestra to play the national anthem. For Shulgin, the words "never had a deeper meaning" and was probably the last time that *Bozhe, Tsarya Khrani!* (God Save the Tsar!) was heard at least in Moscow. The new governor of Yalta, General Spiridovich, remembered that "everyone was pleased that Rasputin disappeared." He said that because Felix's family was living in Koreiz, he was careful "not to express his personal opinion" at functions. Apparently, two hundred and fifty guests, including counts, princes and representatives from various newspapers, had gathered at an unidentified house to party and play cards. The host allegedly exclaimed "about time" (*pora*).[1040] Milyukov, in his typical dry style, said there was "universal joy on the occasion of the heroic deed [made by] Felix...."[1041] Far away, Petrograders congratulated each other on the streets, "going insane" or "fainting from hysteria" that "the beast had been crushed." One was heard to cry out that Rasputin's "depraved soul was no more."[1042]

One of the most intriguing announcements that appeared in the media had appeared in *Den'* (*Day*) on 22 December.[1043] It reported that a group of (unidentified) statesmen from Moscow had sent Purishkevich a salutatory telegram for being a "fighter against dark forces that terrorized the Russian community and national identity," whereby Purishkevich was "the first to boldly tear away the veil that concealed the secret work of the enemies of the *rodina* (motherland) from all of Russian society." Given the timing of that communiqué, their heartfelt support for his most recent deed could not have been expressed in any other public way.

Regardless of the news that was spreading across the nation and around the world, in stark contrast, inside the Alexandrovskii Palace, Alexandra Fyodorovna and Anna Taneeva had begun to mourn.

As Night Falls, the Palace Fears the Worst

During Saturday Alexandra Fyodorovna composed a letter to Nikolai II that was obviously written at different times of the day. The last paragraphs revealed the following:

> "*We are sitting all together – can you imagine our feelings, thoughts – our Friend has disappeared. Yesterday A[nna] saw him, and he told her that Felix had asked to come over at night, and that he will come for him by automobile, so that he could meet Irina. The car came for him (an army vehicle) with two state Counsellors, and He left. This evening there is a huge scandal at the Yusupov home – mainly a meeting, Dmitri, Purishkevich and so forth – all are inebriated. The police heard shots. Purishkevich ran outside, yelled at the policeman, that*

our Friend was murdered.

The police ...search, and then the investigator went inside the Yusupov house – he was not permitted to do so earlier, because Dmitri was there. The Governor asked for Dmitri. Felix intended to go to the Crimea, I asked Kalinin [Protopopov preferred this name[1044]] *to detain him.*

Our friend was in a good mood during these days, but nervous ... Felix ... that he never went into the house and never invited Him. ... I am still seeking God's mercy, that He was driven somewhere. Kalinin is doing everything that he can. I am asking you to send Voyeikov. We, women are alone here with our weak heads. ... I do not want to believe, that He was murdered." [1045]

Pierre Gilliard, Alexei's tutor, noticed the empress' grief was inconsolable. Alexandra Fyodorovna's faith was fragmented, because the very one who she thought could save her son had died. For her it seemed that this was the beginning of a catastrophe that could not be overcome.[1046] At the time, Alexandra Fyodorovna not only feared for the fate of the Russian monarchy but for the effect this extraordinary loss would have on Alexei. It is not known whether Alexei became aware or was told by his father that something had happened to Rasputin. Russian author Haustova recently alleged that Alexei simply "guessed"[1047] and supposedly asked: "Who shall help me when I will be ill again?"

Grigorii Rasputin's disappearance had brought delight for many and uncertainties to just a few. In the end, Rasputin's elimination would prove to be a fateful event for Imperial Russia. The first day of the investigation turned up evidence which indicated that Rasputin probably had been murdered, but perhaps tomorrow, on Sunday, the truth of his disappearance would be revealed.

Chapter Five Photos

PHOTO 9: General-Major Pyotr Popov, c. 1916.

POLICE PHOTOGRAPH No. 1. CRIME SCENE ONE.
YUSUPOVSKII PALACE. The door to the basement is
on the right and the door with overhead lintel leads to
the ground level of the Palace, 17 December 1916.

POLICE PHOTOGRAPHS No. 2 and No. 3. CRIME SCENE ONE. YUSUPOVSKII PALACE. Blood spatter radiates out from the stone step. Purple dots appear on both photos, which start near one corner of the step and extend just beyond the second pillar, 17 December 1916.

POLICE PHOTOGRAPH No. 4. CRIME SCENE ONE. YUSUPOVSKII PALACE. The step at the basement entrance. Pools of blood have penetrated into the snow. Shoe imprints are visible, two of which face the door.

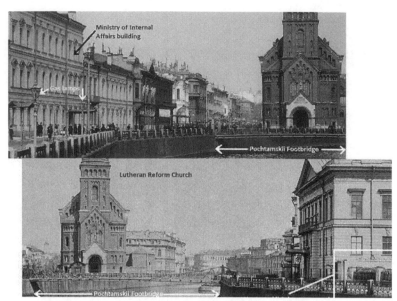

PHOTO 10: PETROGRAD. The building belonging to the
Ministry of Internal Affairs on Bolshaya Morskaya Ulitsa, 61
with its awning entry faces the Yusupovskii Palace courtyard
on the opposite side of the Moika canal. The Pochtamskii
footbridge connects both thoroughfares, pre 1916.

PHOTO 11: PETROGRAD. Samuel Hoare (left) and
Grand Duke Dmitri Pavlovich wearing winter coats.

PHOTO 12: PETROGRAD. Felix Yusupov (left),
Dmitri Pavlovich and Vladimir Purishkevich.

POLICE PHOTOGRAPH 1a: An enlarged image of police photo No. 1,
showing the repair work around the frame of the window on the right.

CHAPTER SIX
DAY 2 of the GENDARME and Judicial INVESTIGATIONS

Sunday 18 December 1916

"In The Matter of the Disappearance of the Peasant Rasputin"

"Дело об исчезновении крестьянина Распутина"

The second day of the unvestigation had dawned in Petrograd and Rasputin was still officially declared as missing. Sunday proved hectic for General-Major Popov and his assistant, Colonel Popel. Much of the day was devoted to taking down statements from key individuals in the case. In the northwestern outskirts of Petrograd, around the area of Petrovskii Bridge, the search was to be resumed in the hope Rasputin's corpse would be found.

A Lawyer Confronts a Few Truths

After returning from Moscow in the early morning, Vasilii Maklakov's first visit was to the communications bureau in the Duma building. He wanted to find out why he had not received Purishkevich's telegram (it arrived in Moscow twenty hours after it was expected[1048]). Maklakov learnt that it had been sent, but its delay had to do with the telegram being held back in the perlustration section. Somewhat defensively, Maklakov claimed that he was unable to prevent Purishkevich from going ahead with this arrangement.[1049] In an effort to show Purishkevich's frame of mind after he "crossed the line of uprightness," he was amazed that, despite the "turmoil of the fatal night,"[1050] Purishkevich managed to send a telegram, about which they spoke of three weeks earlier. Nevertheless, on his way to the communications center, Maklakov met Kerensky, who took the "position of revolutionaries in this matter," and said "do you really not understand that the 'murder' will strengthen the monarchy?'"[1051]

Maklakov's second stop was at the Ministry of Justice where Alexander Lyadov, the Director of the First Department of the Criminal Branch (in the Ministry of Internal Affairs), told him about the previous night's events. At the conclusion of their meeting, they recognized that because Dmitri Pavlovich was implicated, there could never be a trial and that only the emperor had the power to deal with the matter. Nevertheless, the police still had to continue with the investigation despite the legal complexity Purishkevich caused by what he said to the *gorodovoi* Vlasyuk. It was probably why Lyadov "laughed" self-assuredly and said to Maklakov that when the *gorodovoi* will be shown "a particular portrait of Purishkevich, that he will not in any way identify him."[1052] Lyadov was proved wrong because Vlasyuk recognized the man in the photograph. It was the same man Vlasyuk spoke to briefly inside Yusupov's study. Even though Vlasyuk correctly identified Purishkevich, his time and effort was wasted because neither Purishkevich nor anyone else would be charged with any criminal acts perpetrated against Grigorii Rasputin.

The Russian Imperial Eagle is Wounded

As was customary on Sunday morning, Nikolai II attended the Sunday service with his son Alexei and the imperial suite at the Military Headquarters chapel.[1053] There is some confusion about *Fligel*-Adjutant Anatolii Mordvinov's recollection about that morning's events. He claimed that the emperor received the "news of Rasputin's murder" at Stavka "after our breakfast," which was not possible, because, although it was understood that Rasputin had become a victim of foul play, he was still officially missing. Nearly everyone, except for the emperor, believed that he was dead. After their meal, Nikolai II went on his usual morning walk with Mordvinov. They discussed many subjects but Nikolai II never brought up the news from Petrograd for the entire two hours. Upon his return, the emperor received Dmitri's father, Grand Duke Pavel Alexandrovich. Returning from the walk, officers asked Mordvinov about the emperor's reaction to the news, but he only stressed there was nothing to explain to the curious throng. Because the emperor did not appear agitated or alarmed, Mordvinov decided that for the sovereign, Rasputin "did not play a large role in his inner world."[1054]

Lunch followed with a few of the officers and everything at the dining table appeared normal. Shavelsky explained the scene at the Mogilev railway station. When he arrived onto the platform at 3.15 in the afternoon, the emperor had already arrived with his son. Despite the cold, the emperor was dressed only in his *gymnasterka* (field tunic) and held onto his walking stick after just having returned from a stroll in the forest with General Voyeikov.[1055] General Vasilii Gurko approached Nikolai II and then they both walked along the platform talking about the forthcoming Allied Conference. Gurko did not detect any change in the emperor's demeanor.[1056] Shavelsky saw that the emperor held himself "upright, often looking at Gurko directly in the face," while Gurko's right hand was seen waving in all directions during their conversation.[1057] From this distance, not a single word or movement had betrayed the emperor's inner thoughts. Generals Voyeikov, Dolgoruky and Mordvinov would accompany Nikolai II back to Tsarskoe Selo. At precisely four o'clock, the imperial train departed for Tsarskoe Selo, leaving all military matters with his new chief of staff commander, General Gurko,[1058] whose appointment would last four months.[1059]

Count Alexander Grabbe, the commander of the emperor's *Konvoi*, who was also waiting at the platform, was not told why he was returning to Tsarskoe Selo. Grabbe said that he did not suspect anything at the time and only learned of Rasputin's probable murder on the train.[1060] Fortunately at this time of year, during the winter months, there were no serious military operations that needed to be reviewed. After they farewelled their commander in chief, the Stavka generals returned to their headquarters building to discuss the number of reinforcements in men the armies would need during 1917.[1061] During the train journey, Nikolai II continued to maintain the same demeanor. His calm exterior during such pressing times was always similar and not unlike that witnessed during the near tragic medical crisis Alexei had experienced in 1912 in Spala.[1062] The emperor, always appearing calm in public, only showed his true feelings in front of his wife, and "for everyone else, he was their sovereign – a monarch."[1063]

Meantime, the emperor received Alexandra Fyodorovna's telegram with the following message:

"Ordered Maksimovich under your name to forbid Dmitri to leave his home until your arrival, Dmitri wanted to see me today, I refused. He is involved. The body so far not found. When will you be here?"[1064]

At 8 p.m., Alexandra Fyodorovna received a reply from Stavka, which Nikolai II sent from the railway station before his departure:

"Only now read your letter. Indignant and shaken. Prayers and thoughts are with you. Arrive tomorrow at 5 o'clock."[1065]

After Nikolai II read his wife's telegram en route in Orsha, General Spiridovich noticed that for a brief moment he became "unnerved" by what he read.[1066]

Elsewhere, in Kiev, the dowager empress wrote this note into her diary:

"So far there is no official news about this unbelievable event. ... Dmitri and Felix are named in connection with this dreadful story."[1067]

By nightfall, nothing more was found at the Bolshoi Petrovskii Bridge. Protopopov rang the palace and told Alexandra Fyodorovna that the police search would resume at daybreak.

The Sergievskii Palace Parade

On Sunday morning, Felix Yusupov moved into the Sergievskii Palace that is located on the corner of Nevskii *Prospekt*, 41 and the Fontanka canal. Grand Duchess Elizaveta Fyodorovna allowed Dmitri to use the palace after her husband was assassinated in 1905.[1068] Felix's change in living arrangements must have happened shortly after General-Major Popov arrived at Grand Duke Alexander Mikhailovich's palace at Moika, 106 to take down Felix's testimony. General Spiridovich understood that the real reason behind the relocation had more to do with Grand Duke Dmitri's status, in that Felix wanted to "protect himself inside a residence that belonged to Dmitri Pavlovich."[1069] This explanation is flawed because, during the previous evening, Felix was escorted back to the palace that belonged to his Romanov in-laws. In any case, Felix's knew that he was safe from prosecution no matter where he lived or what he told the police.

Dmitri anticipated that he would be able to return to Mogilev Headquarters at the end of his leave,[1070] as if nothing had changed. The call that was put through to Dmitri in the early morning[1071] from General-Adjutant Konstantin Maksimovich changed everything. Maksimovich, a former military commander, was now acting as one of the assistants attached to the imperial suites department.[1072] This morning he was acting under the authority of its minister, Count Frederiks.[1073] The telephone call may have been a polite forewarning of his impending visit. As soon as Maksimovich arrived at Sergievskii, he was immediately escorted into the study. Facing Dmitri, Maksimovich said that it was his duty to inform him that Her Majesty requested that Dmitri must not leave the palace.[1074] On hearing this unexpected news, Dmitri returned to the dining room and as Felix explained, he seemed "very upset."[1075] Nevertheless, he complied with the order (at least for the short term, believing that this situation would be resolved in his favor). Both men sat and discussed the meaning of this unforeseen turn of events. Dmitri apparently argued against Alexandra Fyodorovna's power, saying that only the emperor had the authority to request his arrest,[1076] because he submitted his Oath of Allegiance in the name of "His Majesty" and not to "Her Majesty."[1077] While the emperor was at Stavka, his wife had legitimately delegated the day-to-day administrative affairs of state, but that entrustment did not include exercising the Criminal Code.

Despite the arrest order, Dmitri was not prevented from sending a telegram to Grand Dukes Kirill Vladimirovich, Andrei Vladimirovich, and Prince Gavril Konstantinovich, telling them about his predicament. Shortly after that communication, Grand Duchess Maria Pavlovna (the elder), Andrei Vladimirovich's mother, demanded the police send her a copy of the Protocol explaining the reasons for Dmitri's detention. The family found it hard to believe that Nikolai II had sent Alexandra Fyodorovna a telegram giving instructions for Dmitri's detention. Dmitri's relatives were convinced that Alexandra Fyodorovna acted alone,[1078] but they could do nothing until the emperor returned from Mogilev.

The gendarmes guarding the main entrance to the Sergievskii Palace only allowed family members to enter Dmitri's apartment. Trepov ordered the extra security because of the wave of threats allegedly voiced by Rasputin's former devotees wanting to end Yusupov's life.[1079] In response to Dmitri's message, Grand Dukes Kirill Vladimirovich, Andrei Vladimirovich, and Prince Gavril Konstantinovich arrived together. They found Dmitri rather morose but grateful for their moral support. Felix was acting "calmly,"[1080] and then told Dmitri's guests that because of Rasputin, he "renounced Nikolai and Alix and that he no longer visited them." He was not telling the truth, since the last time he and Irina had tea with Alexandra Fyodorovna at the palace was on 14 August.[1081] In fact, Alexandra Fyodorovna noted how *"very nice and at ease they had conducted themselves"* during their visits. Dmitri's sister, who was staying at Sergievskii (after her arrival from Pskov), said that Felix appeared "intoxicated by his importance of the part that he had played"[1082] in the murder. Neither Dmitri nor Felix said much more, other than revealing that Purishkevich was with them on Friday night.[1083] [1084] Before their departure, the grand dukes assured Dmitri that no matter what happened, he could rely on their support. Nikolai Mikhailovich arrived next and appeared "most agitated."[1085]

Many members of the imperial family who remained in Petrograd for the winter visited the Sergievskii Palace during the course of the day. Perhaps it was out of inquisitiveness or perhaps it was to just to express their despair over Dmitri's detention. Felix claimed that the visitors who came in their carriages wanted to share their concerns because they were so riled by Alexandra Fyodorovna's provocative interference.[1086] Felix was probably truthful after he admitted that Dmitri and he were both pleased when the parade of guests stopped calling. Dmitri was profoundly affected during those "difficult minutes," but Felix alleged he was "fortunate" that he could go to Dmitri's place and share his "enforced loneliness." This last detail may explain why Nikolai Mikhailovich, always attentive about Dmitri's wellbeing, had advised Felix to go to Dmitri's residence.

Gracious Congratulations for a Job Well Done

During the evening, Grand Duke Dmitri Pavlovich received a telegram from Grand Duchess Elizaveta Fyodorovna (Ella), which was composed in English[1087] (see **Appendix A**). It was an extraordinarily careless gesture, because the message revealed two things. Firstly, that she was aware that the murder was to take place, and secondly, she knew who was going to commit that particular crime. The real eye-opener was that Ella unmistakably endorsed the actions of those murderers by her congratulations. This telegram was copied by the telegraph office and passed on to Protopopov, who in turn forwarded a second copy to Alexandra Fyodorovna.[1088] It was the moment when the empress became aware that her own sister had moved against her and the emperor by being involved in the conspiracy to liquidate Rasputin.

The telegram which Dmitri received was not the only one that Ella sent during the day. A second congratulatory telegram (see **Appendix A**) was sent to Felix's mother Zinaida Yusupova in Crimea. This second telegram was composed in French. Ella let Zinaida know that her prayers had surrounded them all. This, as it turns out, was during the moment when Felix was actively engaged in extinguishing the life of a human being. Her characterization that the murder was a "patriotic act" would be used by Felix in his 1927 memoirs.

Inside the shelter of the Convent of the Holy Trinity and of St. Seraphim (in the village of Diveyevo), recognized as amongst Russia's holiest places because it holds the relics of one of Russia's most venerated saints, St. Seraphim Sarovskii, Ella was on her knees in prayer seeking God to "protect" the murderers.[1089] She later wrote to Dmitri that she had just returned (to Moscow) on Saturday evening from the wilderness near *Nizhnii* Novgorod after one week of praying. [Ella also sent the emperor a letter, dated 16/17 December, in which she attempted to mitigate Felix's deed, because for her, his "patriotism…to save the sovereign and the nation…from the suffering of all…" was like a "duel" (see **Appendix A**).] The most disturbing aspect about Ella's messages is that she did nothing to prevent the commission of this crime. Her communiqués prove that she knew beforehand that Rasputin was going to be murdered.

It will never be known if she felt the burden of taking such a position after Rasputin was murdered by persons familiar to her, since she must have recognized the immorality of taking an innocent life. In fact, one of her biographers, Lubov Miller, explained this contentious aspect of her spiritual life by offering the suggestion that it was only "later" that the "Grand Duchess learned that Dmitri was involved in the murder" and when she did, Ella "could not bring herself to harshly judge him or the other conspirators" since "Rasputin was a devil incarnate." Ella's position regarding the 'patriotic act' was explained, not in political terms, but that it was a matter of divine intervention (the word "Providence" was used), which had "chosen Dimitry (sic) and Prince Felix Yussoupov (sic) to execute the sentence of heaven on Rasputin." Miller's speculative discussion ignored many documented facts, such as the time when Ella spoke at length with Dmitri about the planned murder (see Chapter Four). While Miller admitted that Ella believed that Rasputin's murder was justified, she strove to present Ella's sense of piety in a better light.[1090]

Ella's telegrams, the intercepted letter addressing the sovereign, and other related correspondence were handed over to Nikolai II soon after his arrival in Tsarskoe Selo. The text left no doubt as to the identity of the murderer, but then she did not know about Purishkevich's participation on the day she wrote her letter. She was expecting that Felix was going to be the solitary murderer. Even so, Felix admitted that Ella's "telegrams had severely compromised us."[1091]

Dark Shadows Descend Across Petrograd

Paléologue wrote that he attended the Mariinskii Theatre during the evening to watch Tchaikovsky's ballet performance of "Sleeping Beauty" and that the only topic of conversation was yesterday's drama at the Yusupovskii Palace[1092] News from the warfront took back stage. Petrograd high society was still rejoicing on Sunday. Unsubstantiated rumors suggested that the Sergievskii Palace was partying after it was noticed that carriages began arriving. In reality there was little merriment inside. What should have been rejoicing on their part had turned into gloominess and circumspection.

WITNESS TESTIMONIES

Note by the Author:

All Protocols are translated by the author. In some cases, the construction of the sentences or language may appear peculiar to the English reader. The language structure and punctuation used by each of the persons deposed over ninety years ago is followed as closely as possible. With the exception of a few Protocols, the majority are offered in unabridged form.

A. The Residents of Gorokhovaya *Ulitsa,* 64, Petrograd

PROTOCOL No. 2 - Maria Vasilievna Zhuravleva [the concierge]

Zhuravleva, aged twenty-eight, formally of Gdovsk region (near Pskov), was the resident concierge at the four-story stone building located on *Gorokhovaya Ulitsa*, 64. She confirmed that the building was locked overnight, preventing ordinary entry into the building after hours. Although Zhuravleva saw Rasputin only once during the entire course of the day after he had returned to his apartment on Friday afternoon from the bathhouse, she assumed that he was too inebriated during the morning to receive visitors.

"In house No. 64 along Gorokhovaya Ulitsa I have served for about 12 years, and for the last two I have undertaken the duties of a concierge. On 16 December, I saw Grigorii Rasputin only one time, when he at three o'clock in the afternoon returned from the baths, from whereto he set off by the back entrance. From the morning he did not receive anyone, because he was extremely drunk. Even so, returning from the baths in not a completely sober condition. From 3 o'clock to 12 at night no more than 7 persons came, who were here previously. Only at 10 in the evening one lady came, whom I had not seen before, and was with Rasputin until 11 o'clock, left.

Features of this lady: blonde, aged 25, average height, average build. Wearing a coat "flared" dark brown color and the same color only slightly darker boots, on her head a black hat without a veil. When I locked the parade entrance door at 12 o'clock at night, Grigorii Rasputin was home. When and with whom he left home - I do not know, since [he] passed by the back stairs."

Read. [Stated that Zhuravleva was illiterate therefore the protocol was not signed]

Countersigned: Lieutenant-Colonel Popel.[1093]

PROTOCOL No. 3 - Fyodor Antonovich Korshunov [*dvornik* - a caretaker]

Fyodor Korshunov was aged thirty when he submitted his statement before Lieutenant-Colonel Popel. He was the resident caretaker, who originally came from Ivantsevo village (Tver District). Korshunov confirmed that he saw a man arrive by car and then enter the building. After some time, Rasputin was seen leaving with the man during the night of 16/17 December. Korshunov proved to be an uncommonly sharp eyewitness. He confirmed that that the "unknown person" was familiar with the out-of-hours circumstances of the building.

"I am a *dvornik* at house No. 64 on Gorokhovaya *Ulitsa*. On the night of 17 December I was on duty and was located on the street by the gate of this house. Approximately at the beginning of the beginning of the second hour at night a large military grey motor automobile with a waterproof hood and mica glass windows arrived; at the back a spare wheel was attached. The automobile came from the Fontanka direction and, turned around in the same direction, (and) stopped. From the automobile alighted a man unknown to me, who headed straight for the gate. To my question, "*To whom are you going?*" [he] replied "*To Rasputin*". I opened the gate and said "*Here is the parade door*" but the unknown replied that he will go by the back entrance. There upon he quickly and directly headed to this entrance. It was obvious, that this person knew the layout of this house very well. In some 30 minutes the unknown came out with G. E. Rasputin and seated into the automobile, drove away in the direction of the Fontanka. This person I have never seen before.

Distinctive features of the unknown: He was taller than average, average build, 30 years of age, with a small black moustache, without a beard and possibly without eyeglasses, was wearing a (large) long reindeer coat with fur on the outside, on his head a black cap which I did not examine well. On his feet high boots were worn.

The driver appeared slightly older than the unknown; he was around 35, with average sized black moustache without a beard: wore a black coat with wool collar, a fur hat and long red gloves.

After having left, G. E. Rasputin did not return home."

Read. Korshunov

Signed: Lieutenant-Colonel Popel.[1094]

The Residents of Apartment Number 20

All the family and other members of the household who lived in the Rasputin apartment (Photo 13) were interviewed by General-Major Popov. The most interesting detail, which emerged from the different testimonies, was that the young, seventeen-year-old niece knew Maria Golovina well enough to call her *Munya*. In the same way, the daughters knew Golovina's telephone number and felt confident enough to be received inside the Golovin apartment, which belonged to her parents. This information bears out that Maria Golovina could not have visited their apartment on only two occasions.

PROTOCOL No. 4 - Ekaterina Ivanovna Poterkina [Housekeeper]

Ekaterina Poterkina [Pecherkina] was said to be a twenty-nine-year old woman (Pecherkina's 1908 statement stated she was twenty-four] who followed Rasputin from Siberia to carry out the duties of a housekeeper in his apartment. She declared that she arrived from Lanbin village located in the Tobolsk region. Her statement indicates that she could describe Rasputin's appearance but failed to recognize the guests who were known to have visited the apartment after 7 p.m. on Friday 16 December. She was equally short on recalling how often Felix Yusupov, using Grigorii Rasputin's adopted name *Malenkii* (Little one), visited their apartment. She was sharp-eyed about Yusupov's facial features but failed to take note of his clothing.

Her evidence was crucial for two reasons. Firstly, she confirmed that Rasputin expected to leave the apartment with Felix Yusupov, and secondly, she saw both men leave the apartment together. Unlike the employees of their building complex, Ekaterina recognized that Yusupov was not an unfamiliar person in their apartment. From a forensic perspective, the housekeeper described the clothing Rasputin wore on Friday night, which corresponded with the Special Investigator Sereda's description of the clothing found on the body at the Bolshoi Petrovskii Bridge. It is of some interest that the *Okhrana* had apparently gained entry into the family apartment on Saturday morning, without ringing the front door bell to announce their arrival.

"16 December of this year there was not a large reception [of guests] at Grigorii Rasputin's, none were strange persons, over the day there were no more than 10 people; of the callers for Rasputin on this day I only remember Maria Evgenievna Golovina, who came around 12 o'clock in the day, and left around 9 o'clock in the evening and went home. At 9 o'clock in the evening, apart from Grigorii Efimovich and his family, no one else was in the apartment. Around 11 o'clock in the evening Rasputin's children – daughters Maria and Varvara Rasputin and niece Anna began to prepare for bed, while Rasputin himself lay on his bed dressed in boots. When I asked Grigorii Efimovich – "*What you are not undressing?*" to that he replied "*Tonight I am going out to pay a visit.*" When I asked "*To whom*", Rasputin replied "*to Malenkii, he is coming for me*" and ordered me to go to bed. By name *Malenkii* I did not know of before, only heard from Grigorii Efimovich, that *Malenkii* - the husband of Grand Duchess Irina Alexandrovna, after Rasputin's disappearance during the last two days I learnt that the surname of *Malenkii* was Prince Yusupov. This *"Malenkii" was* in the apartment twice – around November 20, on the day of the "Presentation of the Blessed Virgin icon" [church celebration], and during the first days of December of this year 1916, approximately one week before Rasputin's disappearance. Both times he came with Maria Evgeniyevna Golovina by the back stairs and in mufti. Although Grigorii Efimovich ordered me to go to bed, I went into the kitchen, but did not fall asleep. Rasputin put on a blue silk shirt embroidered with cornflowers, but was unable to do up the buttons on the collar and came to me into the kitchen, I did up his buttons. At that time a bell rang from the back entrance, Rasputin opened the door himself. The *'enterer'* asked *"So no one here?"* to which Grigorii Efimovich replied *"No one here and the children are sleeping, come in Malenkii."* Both came through the kitchen past me, into the rooms, while I was at that time behind the maid's kitchen barrier and, moving the curtain, saw that it was *Malenkii* i.e. known to me as the husband of Irina Alexandrovna. What coat and hat *Malenkii* had on, I did not notice, and only recognized him by his face, unable to say, if his coat collar was raised or not. Before long Rasputin began to leave through the kitchen, I at that time was already lying in bed. Grigorii Efimovich quietly said that he locked the front door, will leave by the back door, and will use this entry on his return, and ordered to lock the door after him. During all these orders I was lying in bed and replied *"Good"* and when they left, I locked the door. Since then I never saw Grigorii Efimovich. On 17 December, about 8 o'clock in the morning the Okhrana police appeared in the apartment and began asking *"Where is Grigorii Efimovich?"* Then the whole family became worried and began to phone Maria Golovina, who at first replied, that she did not know anything, but asked [us] not to worry. At 11 o'clock Golovina appeared at the Rasputin apartment, asked to wait until 12 o'clock, ran to the fruit store to talk on the telephone, and later [she] spoke on the telephone from Rasputin's apartment with someone in English. Later she left, saying, that she would find out everything there and will return. Golovina returned about 1 o'clock during the day with her mother and declared that *Malenkii* said that he did not come for Rasputin and that Rasputin did not visit him. When I began to say why *Malenkii* was in denial when I myself saw his arrival for Grigorii Efimovich, Golovina said *"Perhaps you and Grigorii Efimovich were mistaken and that someone else who looked like Malenkii came instead?"* After this incident Maria Evgeniyevna Golovina did not come to us again.

Distinguishing features of *Malenkii* are the following: reasonably tall, slim, thin face, straight nose, dark hair, no moustache or beard, bluish circles under the eyes."

Declared: *"Everything is written correctly from my words"*.

[Poterkina was illiterate; by her own request Anna Nikolayevna Rasputina was the signatory.]

Countersigned: General-Major Popov.[1095]

PROTOCOL No. 5 - Matrena Grigoriyevna Rasputina

Matrena, aged nineteen, was Grigorii Rasputin's eldest daughter. She stated that she was originally from Pokrovskoye and confirmed that her father was expecting Yusupov later during the night. The impression received from this statement is that the family must have discussed earlier as to what they should reveal to the police because of the similarity of the omissions and the details that were revealed. Both sisters' statements were of little value or filled with irrelevancies, which may relate to their immaturity and not knowing what the gendarme had required from them.

"16 December 1916, at seven o'clock in the evening I left the apartment and returned around 11 o'clock in the evening. When I was going to bed, father told me that during the night he was going to visit *Malenkii*. Under the name *Malenkii* father thought it up for Prince Yusupov, he always called him that. Later I went to bed and did not see – whether Malenkii came or left with father. Speaking of this visit to Yusupov, father ordered me not to say anything about this trip to Maria Evgeniyevna Golovina. Father explained to me that Golovina might link up with him, but Yusupov did not want Maria Evgeniyevna to go to him. On the morning of 17 December the security police appeared and began to ask *"Where is* [your] *father?"* We all became concerned and started to ring Maria Evgeniyevna Golovina. The latter replied, that if father left with *Malenkii* then there was nothing to worry about, seems they are sleeping and Grigorii Efimovich will return home soon. At 11 o'clock Maria Evgeniyevna came to us, many callers had already gathered at our place; so as not to make known about father's disappearance, I went with Maria Evgeniyevna to the fruit shop and from there I began to ring Prince Yusupov, but the later had already left home. Around 12 o'clock in the day or 1 o'clock in the day Prince Yusupov telephoned the apartment, I recognized him by his voice. Maria Evgeniyevna spoke with him in English. After that conversation Maria Evgeniyevna was very worried and went home, saying, that the prince would come to her [place]. After one hour had passed, I and my sister went to Golovina's apartment, where the latter told us, that prince Yusupov swore, that [he] did not come for [our] father and on the night of 17 December father was not at his place. After that Maria Evgeniyevna came to the apartment with her mother and both wept. Prince Yusupov I saw once in our apartment – approximately 5-6 days ago, around 12 December of this year.

The distinctive features of the Prince are the following: taller than average height, slim, pale, long face, under the eyes large dark circles, brown hair, do not remember, if a mustache and beard."

Signed: Matrena Grigoriyevna Rasputina

Countersigned: General-Major Popov.[1096]

PROTOCOL No. 6 - Varvara Grigorievna Rasputina

Varvara was Grigorii Rasputin's youngest daughter. She was only sixteen and submitted a very brief statement, which failed to disclose anything significantly different to her older sister, Matrena. It is hard to believe that the daughters failed to realize that *Malenkii* was Prince Yusupov, since Golovina would have used his correct name during her conversations with Matrena and Varvara.

"16 December of this year I with my sister Matrena went to visit and returned around 11o'clock in the evening. Father said nothing to me, that on this night he was preparing to go to visit somewhere. We found father home, then we went to sleep, and I did not see, with whom and where to father had actually gone. I know Prince Yusupov, before he was known to me under the nickname *Malenkii* that is how father called him, I only knew that "*Malenkii*" was married to Grand Duchess Irina Alexandrovna, and about his surname I only found after father disappeared.

17 December, when father did not return home, we began to worry, began to ring Maria Evgenievna Golovina, she came to us and we were at her apartment, at first she consoled us, and later, after speaking with Prince Yusupov, she worried. I know nothing more about this matter."

Signed: Varvara Rasputina-Novaya

Countersigned: General-Major Popov.[1097]

PROTOCOL No. 7 - Anna Nikolayevna Rasputina [Grigorii Rasputin's niece]

Anna Rasputina was aged seventeen and also came from Pokrovskoye. She was Grigorii Rasputin's niece and lived in the Rasputin family apartment. Since Yusupov preferred to visit the apartment late at night, it is not surprising that the young girl might not have been aware or interested as to which guests her uncle entertained in the very late evening.

"16 December around 1 p.m. my uncle Grigorii Efimovich returned from the baths and went to sleep. On this day not many people who came before, came. At 10 o'clock in the evening a plump blonde arrived, who was called *Sister Maria*, although she was not a sister of mercy [a nurse]. Just after midnight, uncle lay on the bed and did not undress. I and our permanent resident, *Katya* (Ekaterina Ivanovna Poterkina) approached uncle and asked him, why he was not changing. To this uncle replied: "*Today I am going to Malenkii*". After that I went to bed and did not hear, when and who with uncle left. Uncle called Prince Yusupov *Malenkii*, who was here two or three times. The next day at 8 o'clock in the morning I rang *Munya*, Maria Evgenievna Golovina and asked her, where was uncle, since he had still not returned home from *Malenkii*'s and asked if she could ring there, since I did not know his phone number. [Around] 11 in the morning, M. E. Golovina came to us and said that she rang Prince Yusupov, but they are still sleeping there. After about half an hour we again rang Prince Yusupov, but from there they said he had already gone. Around 12 or 12.30, someone rang us at the apartment and asked for M. E. Golovina. She approached [took the telephone] and spoke in English. With whom she spoke we do not know, but assume that it was Prince Yusupov. [Around] 2 o'clock in the day M. E. Golovina left our place. At 5 o'clock in the day M. E. Golovina arrived with her mother; they were agitated and cried.

Read and signed: Anna Nikolayevna Rasputina

Countersigned: Lieutenant-Colonel Popel."[1098]

Analysis of the submitted Protocols (I)

▶ Felix Yusupov arrived at the Rasputin apartment on the night of 16/17 December, using the 'black' stairs.

▶ One eyewitness saw Rasputin willingly leave his apartment building.

► Rasputin and Yusupov were seen leaving together in a chauffeured automobile that headed in the direction of the Fontanka canal.

► Yusupov was known to the Rasputin family and their housekeeper, confirming that Yusupov had visited their apartment on several occasions.

► Not one single family member said that Rasputin intended to visit Irina Yusupova.

► Grigorii Rasputin failed to return home.

B. The Petrograd City *Gorodovoi*

The city's ever-present *gorodovoi* (Photo 15) were posted on patrol duty day and night, on street corners, around public parks, churches and public buildings, on six hour shifts. Primarily they were engaged in overseeing public order. There were seven thousand *gorodovoi* employed in Petrograd. They were noted for their physical strength and came from an army background, usually wearing their medals whilst on duty.[1099]

PROTOCOL No. 8 - Flor Efimovich Efimov

Flor Efimov was fifty-nine years old and lived on Morskaya *Ulitsa*, 61. Not only was the same building occupied by the Ministry of Internal Affairs, but it was also the telegraph address of General Trepov.[1100] Efimov was on night duty at one of the sectors of the 2nd Admiralty District, standing adjacent to his home address. His night watch area was just west of the German Reform Church (Photo 10), flanking the Moika canal, diagonally opposite the two buildings owned by the Yusupov family, Moika, 92 and 94.

"On the night between 16 and 17 December I was standing on duty on Morskaya *Ulitsa* near house No. 61. At 2h 30m at night I heard a gunshot, after 3-4 seconds 3 more gunshots one after another. The sound appeared to come from the house on Moika, 92. After the first gunshot a not so loud akin to a woman's scream resounded. No noises were heard. Over the course of the next 20-30 minutes after the shooting no automobiles or *izvozchiki* passed by. After 30 minutes had elapsed, some kind of automobile traveled along the Moika from the *Sinii* Bridge (next bridge after Pochtamskii) towards the Potseluyev Bridge, which did not stop anywhere.

Concerning the gunshots, I telephoned and informed the 3rd Kazanskii District police, and I walked in the direction of the shots. On Pochtamskii Bridge I saw duty *gorodovoi* Vlasyuk, who also heard the shots, and thought, they originated on Morskaya *Ulitsa*, [he] walked towards me to meet with the purpose to know, where and who was shooting. I said that the gunshots originated in the region of No. 92 on Moika. After that I returned to [my] post and no longer saw or heard anything. I remember, from the time, after the gunshots resounded, until 5-6 o'clock in the morning I did not see other automobiles, driving along the Moika, except for the above mentioned. There is nothing more I can say."

Read and signed: Efimov

Countersigned: Lieutenant-Colonel Popel.[1101]

PROTOCOL No. 9 - Stepan Fedosiev Vlasyuk

Stepan Vlasyuk, aged forty-eight, came from the Kiev region. He lived on Ofitserskaya *Ulitsa* (today known as *Ulitsa* Dekabristov[1102]) in building 28, apartment 16. Vlasyuk's home address was also the headquarters of the Petrograd criminal police and the residence of its chief, Arkady Kirpichnikov.[1103]

Vlasyuk's watch was the corner of Prachechnii *Pereulok* and Maksimilianovskii *Pereulok* (today known as *Pereulok Pirogova*, which was one block away from where he lived). The placement was designated the 3rd Kazanskii District (see Map No. 1, Chapter Seven), by the side of the building that faced the Moika canal, which was house No. 90. The Yusupov buildings followed on after Moika, 90, to the west of Vlasyuk's post. Vlasyuk, at the end of his shift, gave his report initially to his division supervisor, Colonel Rogov, at around 6 a.m. on Saturday. More than twenty-four hours would pass before Vlasyuk repeated his observations to Lieutenant-Colonel Popel.

"On the night from 16 to 17 December I stood on duty on the corner of Prachechnii and Maksimilianovskii lanes. Around 4 o'clock I heard 3-4 gunshots quickly following one after the other. I looked around, everything was quiet. I heard the shots resounded from the right side of the German Church [located on the other side from where he stood on the corner of Bolshaya Morskaya *Ulitsa* and the Moika Embankment], therefore I approached Pochtamskii Bridge and called duty *gorodovoi* Efimov, who stood at [his] post along Morskaya *Ulitsa* by house No. 61. To my question, where were the gunshots, Efimov answered, that they were shooting on *"your side"*. Then I approached the caretaker of house No. 92 on Moika and asked him, who was shooting. The caretaker whose name I do not know, but his face was familiar to me, replied, that he heard no gunshots. At this time, I saw through the fence railing two persons in military uniform and without caps, walking across the courtyard of this house in the direction of the gate. When they approached, then I recognized Prince Yusupov and his butler Buzhinsky. The latter I also asked; who was shooting; about this Buzhinsky stated that he did not hear any gunshots, but maybe, *"from fooling around someone might have shot from a cap gun"*. I think, that Yusupov said, that he did not hear gunshots. After that they left, and I remained here and looked over the yard through the fence and the street and did not find anything suspicious, returned to my post. About the incident I so far have not informed anyone, as I heard earlier several times similar sounds of bursting automobile tires. Some 15 -20 minutes after I returned to my place and the above mentioned Buzhinsky approached me and told me that Prince Yusupov demanded to see me. I followed behind him and he brought me past the parade porch of house No. 94 into the Prince's study. Barely had I stepped over study step (located on the left of the Moika entry), when Prince Yusupov and an unfamiliar person dressed in a khaki tunic, with epaulettes of an active State Counselor, with a small ginger beard and moustache approached to greet me. If he had hair on his head, or was bald, and also if he had eyeglasses or not, - I did not observe. This unknown addressed me with questions:

Purishkevich - *"Are you an Orthodox person?"*

Vlasyuk - "That is so."

Purishkevich - *"You a Russian person?"*

Vlasyuk - *"That is so."*

Purishkevich - *"Do you love the Sovereign and the Motherland?"*

Vlasyuk - *"That is so."*

Purishkevich - *"Do you know me?"*

Vlasyuk - *"No I do not know you."*

Purishkevich - *"Of Purishkevich have you heard anything?"*

Vlasyuk - *"I have heard."*

Purishkevich - *"Here I am myself."*

Purishkevich - *"About Rasputin have you heard or know of him?"*

Vlasyuk - *"I do not know him, but I have heard of him."*

Purishkevich - *"Well he* [Rasputin] *has died and if you love the Tsar and the Motherland, then you must remain silent about this and not tell anyone anything."*

Vlasyuk - *"I hear you."*

Purishkevich - *"Now you may go."*

I turned around and went to my post. In the house it was completely quiet and except for the Prince, the unknown and Buzhinsky, I saw no one. I do not know Purishkevich and have never seen him before, the unknown was somewhat similar to the photo of Purishkevich which the Head of the Criminal Police showed me yesterday (17 Dec.) in some journal. I again searched the street and the yard, but as before everything was quiet and no one was visible. In about 20 minutes the rounds police officer Kalyadich approached my post, to whom I told everything that happened. After that I with Kalyadich returned to the parade door of this Moika, 94 house by the porch we saw a motor "at the ready." We asked the chauffeur, who requested the motor and he replied *The Prince*. After that, Kalyadich went on [his] rounds and ordered me to stay here and see who was going to leave. I remember that when we approached No. 92, Kalyadich entered the yard keeper's room and questioned him about something. When he went out from the yard keeper's, then I went with him to house No. 94. From where the motor was provided I do not know exactly. From the parade door (No. 94) Prince Yusupov exited alone and drove in the direction towards Potseluyev Bridge. When the Prince drove away I told Buzhinsky, who took leave of the Prince, that he wait for Kalyadich, but he (Buzhinsky) notified me that he had not slept the night, and would speak with Kalyadich tomorrow (i.e. 17 Dec.). I waited for a bit longer near this house and not seeing anyone anymore, again returned to my post. This was already after 5 a.m. Some 10-15 minutes later, Kalyadich returned from rounds, I told him, what I had seen, and we again went to house No. 94. Apart from the duty caretaker we saw no one there. Thereupon he went to the district, and I remained in [my] place. Around 6 o'clock he again came to me and called me to [go to] District officer Colonel Rogov, to whom we reported all the events. After that I went home. The motor was the Prince's personal [car], in which he always rode. This motor I know well, it is not large, brown color. Signs of any murder I for the whole time did not notice, but the conversation in the Prince's study with the unknown I explained to myself as it was a kind of test from their side about [my] knowledge of my service, i.e. how I act after receiving such information. I did not notice any nervousness or embarrassment on the part of the Prince and the unknown during the time of my conversation in the study, only that the unknown "spoke quickly". If they were not in a sober state, I cannot definitely say. [There] is nothing more I can say."

Read: S. Vlasyuk

Countersigned: Lieutenant-Colonel Popel.[1104]

Sometime during the previous day (Saturday), Director of the Criminal Police Department Lyadov showed Vlasyuk a photograph taken from a journal in order to confirm the identity of the person to whom Vlasyuk had spoken in Yusupov's study. All the same, it was Vlasyuk's verbal report to the Colonel Rogov at the district police station which triggered a series of events that would lead Imperial Russia into political upheaval.

Why Was This Evidence Ignored?

Two days after the murder, at least two newspapers in Petrograd, *Rech*[1105] and *Den'*,[1106] reported that a *gorodovoi*, who was not identified, stood on duty on Ofitserskaya *Ulitsa* in the Kazanskii sector (see **MAP No. 1, Chapter Seven**). He heard "screams and noise" coming from the garden of property No. 21 on Ofitserskaya *Ulitsa*. That building (facing a **T** intersection) sits alongside the main (vehicular) entrance into the Yusupovskii Palace, which leads to the rear courtyard. The report did not cover up the fact that the house belonged to Prince Yusupov, but it did disclose the *gorodovoi* "saw a few people coming out from the garden gates from No. 21" and "shortly thereafter a car entered into the garden, which left in a few minutes." *The New York Times* largely repeated what was published locally in *Rech* and *Den'* but claimed that "several persons"[1107] were seen leaving around three o'clock in the morning.

C. Statements by the Employees and Occupant at the Yusupovskii Palace

PROTOCOL No. 10 - Julian Ivanov Bobkov [a Watchman]

Julian Bobkov declared that he was twenty-two years old. He originally came from Volno village located in the Minsk district and was now living at Moika, 94. He was employed as a watchman at the same address. Although challenged by poor eyesight as a result of a recent war injury, he was able to submit a brief. Bobkov was a privately employed watchman who was on night duty close to Moika, 94. His testimony should not be discounted, because he provided a useful timeframe, and significantly, because his hearing would have been more acute, his claim that he did not hear any human sounds following the gunshots is credible.

"I am a watchman at Prince Yusupov's house [at] No. 94. From 9 o'clock in the evening to 6 o'clock in the morning from 16 to 17 December I was on duty near No. 94. Around 3 o'clock at night I heard two quiet gunshots from the Prachechnii *Pereulok* side. I did not pay any attention to these sounds, thinking, that it was the screech of a motor or water pipes. At the time, when the gunshots or screech resounded, I was near No. 96 and now I went to house No. 94. Checked the street near this house and the yard of No. 92 through the fence and found nothing suspicious, I again began to walk along the panels from house No. 94 to No. 96. Until 6 o'clock in the morning I did not see any automobile arrive or leave from the parade entrance of No. 94. My eyesight is very bad, because I am wounded from the war. I did not hear any scream, after the likely gunshots resounded. I cannot say anything more."

Read: Bobkov

Signed: Lieutenant-Colonel Popel.[1108]

PROTOCOL No. 11 - Akim Kirillovich Lazukov [Yard keeper]

Akim Lazukov, aged nineteen, lived at Moika, 92. He was employed by the Yusupov family as their yard keeper. He was born in the village of Vish-Gorod (Ryazan Province).

"On the night of 17 December from 2 o'clock at night I began cleaning the panel near this house. Around 3 o'clock at night I heard 2 gunshots that were not loud that appeared to have come from Maksimilianovskii *Pereulok*; this shooting was not near No. 92 or No. 94 houses; [there] was no automobile near these houses at this time. After some time, a duty *gorodovoi* approached me and asked me, if the shooting was from here. I answered, that I did not hear shooting from here, but the sound had carried from the Maksimilianovskii *Pereulok* side. While I spoke with the *gorodovoi*, Prince Yusupov with Buzhinsky did not approach us and the *gorodovoi* did not speak with them. Not able to depose anything more."

Read. Illiterate

Signed: Lieutenant-Colonel Popel.[1109]

PROTOCOL No. 12 - Felix Felixovich Prince Yusupov-Count Sumarokov-Elston

Felix Yusupov, aged twenty-nine, said that his present address was the palace of Grand Duchess Ksenya Alexandrovna. A copy of his Protocol was forwarded to Mayor Balk and General Vasiliev, who noted that Yusupov maintained his story that a dog was the only fatality that night.[1110] He admitted that Grand Duke Dmitri Pavlovich, Purishkevich, and a group of unnamed officers were with him that night. Even though Yusupov hinted that ladies were present at his gathering, Sereda held "it was doubtful that the ladies were present during the commission of the murder."[1111] [Yusupov did not mention he had been deposed by the police in his original or revised memoirs.]

"I made the acquaintance of Grigorii Efimovich Rasputin some five years ago in Maria Golovina's home. In recent years I met him twice at the Golovin home. This year 1916, I met him in November also at the Golovin [apartment] in fact he made a much better impression upon me, than in previous years. Since I suffer from chest pains and medical treatment does not offer me any relief, I spoke about this matter with Maria Evgenievna Golovina and she advised me to drive to Rasputin's apartment and speak with him, since he has cured many and could be useful for me. At the end of November, I went to Rasputin together with Golovina, Rasputin made passes over me, after which I thought, that perhaps there was some relief of my condition. During my final visits to Rasputin, the later in fact told me: *"We will cure you forever, only you must go as well to the gypsies, there you will see nice women and your ailment will completely disappear."* These phrases from Rasputin made an unpleasant impression upon me. Around December 10, Rasputin called me on the telephone and suggested [we] drive to the gypsies, but I declined under the pretext, that on the next day I should have examinations. During the meetings Rasputin brought up the conversation about my wife, where and how we live, and expressed a desire to make his acquaintance with my wife, to which I said evasively, that when my wife returns from the Crimea, it might be possible to meet her, but I myself did not want to bring Rasputin into my home. I was hurriedly re-decorating my premises on Moika, 94 and Grand Duke Dmitri Pavlovich suggested that I should hold a small evening housewarming evening party. It was decided to invite Vladimir Mitrofanovich Purishkevich, a few officers and ladies of society. For completely understandable reasons I do not want to give the surnames of the ladies [who] were at the evening party. [I] do not want name the officers, attending the evening, since this may stir some kind of rumors and ruin these officers', literally not guilty of anything, service. The evening party was set for 16 December. So as to not embarrass the ladies, I ordered the servants to prepare everything for tea and dinner, and later not to come in. Most of the guests were to arrive not by the parade porch of house No. 94 on Moika, but by the side entrance from house No. 92, the key to that entry I had personally. I arrived home around 10 o'clock in the evening and probably, [I] do not firmly remember, [I] entered the apartment from the side entry from house No. 92. In the dining room and study everything was correctly prepared for the guests. At around 11.30 in the evening Grand Duke Dmitri Pavlovich, arrived by the parade porch, and later the others guests arrived. All the ladies arrived, of course, by the side entrance of house

No. 92, as to how the men arrived, I do not remember. The assembled drank tea, played the piano, danced and dined. At around 12.30-1 o'clock at night approximately I went up to my study and was in this place when the telephone rang. It turned out that Rasputin was speaking on the phone, and invited me to come to the gypsies, to which I replied, I was unable, because I had guests. Rasputin suggested that I should leave my guests and go, but I refused. Regarding my question to Rasputin "*from where he was speaking*" he did not want to tell me. I asked Rasputin this question because during our conversation on the telephone voices, noise and even squealing female voices, were heard, from which I concluded that Rasputin was speaking not from home, but from some kind of gypsy restaurant. Following this conversation, I went down to the dining room to the guests and told them: "*Ladies and gentlemen Rasputin spoke with me and invited* [me] to *go to the gypsies*", after which followed jokes and witty remarks from the guests, about the suggestion to go, but everyone remained and continued to dine. About 2½-3 o'clock at night two ladies wanted to go home and left by the side entrance, Grand Duke Dmitri Pavlovich departed with them. When they went out, I heard a gunshot in the yard, [which is] why I rang [the bell] for some one of the servants to look. Returning the servant reported, that everyone had driven away and there was nothing in the yard. Then I went myself outside into the yard and in the yard I saw lying by the railing a dog that was slain. On my way out into the yard from the dog some fellow, walked quickly onto the street [who was] wearing a grey shirt, like a military uniform, slender, [I was] unable to check him out properly in the dark. Returning into the apartment, I ordered the servant to remove the dog from the yard. Here I connected with Grand Duke Dmitri Pavlovich by telephone, and began to tell him about the slain dog, to which His Imperial Highness replied, that he killed the dog. On my objection, that there was no need to do that, because a noise occurred, the police appeared and my evening party with the ladies is becoming known publicly,

Dmitri Pavlovich replied, that these are trifles - not worth paying attention to. After that I ordered the *gorodovoi* to come off the street, to whom I told, that if asked about the gunshots – say, that my friend killed a dog. Purishkevich was in my study at the time started to say something to the *gorodovoi,* what he said, I failed to hear fully, only heard *"I am a member of the State Duma, Purishkevich"* waving his hands. Speaking about the slain dog, Grand Duke Dmitri Pavlovich by the way said that, when he fired, one of the ladies who were with him became nauseous. I do not remember which way Purishkevich left from me. I left home from No. 92 on Moika about 4 o'clock in the morning by automobile to the palace of Grand Duchess Ksenya Alexandrovna where I live.

On the morning of 17 December, intending to leave for the Crimea to my sick wife, I wanted to inform Maria Evgenievna Golovina about this. During the conversation on the telephone, she asked me *"where is Grigorii Efimovich"* to which I replied, I do not know, since I had not seen him, but only spoke to him on the telephone and that he had invited me to go to the gypsies. Then Golovina informed me, that Rasputin's maid confirmed that around 1 o'clock in the night I drove Rasputin away from his apartment. But this is a profound mistake, since on 16 December not during the day, nor during the evening was I at Rasputin's [place], and [that] all night on 17 December I spent in my home on Moika No. 92, which my servant and guests who visited me can attest. All the above mentioned, to avoid grave errors I thought it necessary to inform the local *Politsmeister* and the Petrograd Governor and the Minister of Justice on 17 December. From the *Politsmeister* I learnt, that from the *gorodovoi's* Protocol, Purishkevich, who was in my study, said some kind of phrase regarding the death of Rasputin. For this reason, I spoke in regard to the matter with Purishkevich on the telephone, and he explained, that he did say something to the *gorodovoi* about Rasputin, but, as he was extremely drunk by then, [he] does not now remember, what he actually said. I believe that the persons, who organized Rasputin's murder, if indeed that had occurred, intensely considered the murder plan and have intentionally connected my name and the evening at my place with this crime."

Signed: Prince Felix Felixovich Yusupov-Count Sumarokov

Countersigned: General-Major Popov.[1112]

The news that a number of individuals were asked to give evidence in this investigation appeared in the morning edition of *Birzheviye Vedomosti* on 21 December.[1113] The article revealed that a number of *gorodovoi*, caretakers, and a servant within an unidentified private residence had been questioned. The article mistakenly stated the "owner of the private residence" had invited the "officials to go down into the basement and form their appropriate conclusions."

Analysis of all Submitted Protocols (II)

Grigorii Rasputin's departure from Gorokhovaya *Ulitsa*

▶ The resident concierge locked the entrance to the building at midnight.

▶ Yusupov arrived by car around midnight.

▶ Yusupov seen leaving and getting into the same car with Rasputin, which headed towards the Fontanka canal.

The Gunfire
City policemen

▶ Policeman Efimov heard 1 - 3 gunshots at 2.30 a.m. from Moika, 92.

▶ Policeman Vlasyuk heard 3 or 4 gunshots at 4 a.m. from the right of the Lutheran Church.

Witnesses - on duty in the Yusupovskii Palace

▶ Lazukov (yard keeper at Moika, 92) heard

2 gunshots at 3 a.m. from the direction of Maksimilianovskii Pereulok (Lane) but nothing in front of Moika, 92 or 94.

▶ Bobkov (watchman at Moika, 94) heard 2 gunshots at 3 a.m. from Prachechnii Pereulok area (to his right).

Witnesses – Residents in the Yusupovskii Palace

▶ Yusupov heard one shot at 2.30-3.00 a.m.

▶ Nefedov (batman to Yusupov) did not hear gunfire.

▶ Buzhinsky (butler to Yusupov) did not hear gunfire.

1. Which Route Did Yusupov's Chauffeur Use to Arrive at the Yusupovskii Palace?

The vehicle was seen heading in the direction of the Fontanka canal. There is no reason to doubt that the car travelled anywhere else except directly towards the Yusupovskii Palace. The car drove the short distance, using a "circuitous route" before it "stopped at the smaller porched entrance"[1114] (**Photo 16**) of the building. The car turned right off Ofitserskaya *Ulitsa* (now Dekabristov) and entered the property through the high gated triumphal arch that was bounded by tall walls, just beyond the *Sadovii* (Garden) Pavilion.[1115] This entry was unlike to the "smaller ... entrance" alongside the Moika Embankment. Leading to the rear courtyard, its design concealed all outside movements. Thus, no outsider would see Rasputin walking through the porched entry. Given the size of the open space, it accommodated several vehicles, allowing guests to drive in and out unhindered. One of those vehicles parked in the courtyard belonged to Dmitri Pavlovich, and the second vehicle, driven by Lazovert, would have been military issue.

Though Yusupov testified that Dmitri arrived at the main parade entrance around 11.30 p.m., that could not have happened because no one knew that the grand duke was at the palace until Felix revealed that detail to the police and the court procurator at the

Justice Department Chambers. Yusupov and Purishkevich would have known (similar to all government buildings throughout the city) an *Okhrana* guard was always posted outside its building, one which happened to be located on the other side of the Moika canal.

2. What Time Did the Shooting Begin?

The problem with Vlasyuk's evidence (**Protocol No. 9**) is that he heard a volley of three or four gunshots around four o'clock in the morning. The timing is not supported by the events that preceded those shootings (see below). Efimov, on the other hand, thought the shooting began at 2.30 (**Protocol No. 8**). Because both timings varied by and hour and a half, it may suggest that they had no time pieces.

Nighttime presents numerous problems when attempting to identify and locate sudden noises, more so if one is surrounded by stone structures of variable density and with a frozen water canal coursing nearby. The guard, Bobkov, demonstrated how this physical characteristic operates when he testified that he heard "either a motor or water pipes" (**Protocol No. 10**). Sounds, including voices, would have been magnified during the night and might not have been easy to distinguish, particularly if the person was not attentive.

If the shooting began at four o'clock in the morning, then Yusupov would have had to endure entertaining Rasputin in the basement for over two hours.[1116] The host offered red wine, followed by sweet Madeira and cyanide-laced nibbles but there was no ill effect.[1117] In **Chapter Eight**, I discuss the perils of exposure when handling cyanide, which negates the myth that poison was added into the food or alcohol. [Besides, his daughter Matrena stressed her father did not eat sweets.] Yusupov then strummed his guitar and sang at Rasputin's request.[1118] This drawn-out scenario indicates that Yusupov planned to intoxicate Rasputin with his favorite Madeira wine. Since Yusupov had to give Rasputin the impression of being the gracious host, serving full glasses of alcohol would be realistic. Knowing that Rasputin enjoyed alcohol (a widespread habit in Russia), that habit was used to the conspirators' advantage. As soon as Rasputin slumped over, Yusupov ran upstairs and announced to his fellow conspirators that they should "finish Rasputin."[1119] It was now time to use weaponry to complete the assignment.

Remembering what Sereda had discovered about the soundproofing properties of the basement, it is impossible to fix the exact time when Felix fired his weapon. Likewise, it is impossible to find out how many gunshots were fired in the basement because with the courtyard door closed on the next level, not one of those gunshots would have been heard outside.

When Was the Shooting Heard Outside?

Despite poor lighting, Vlasyuk saw Yusupov and Bushinsky exiting through the larger door with its overhanging V-shaped lintel (**POLICE PHOTO No. 1**) soon after he approached the fence railing and spoke with the caretaker of Moika, 42. By using that door, Yusupov and Bushinsky avoided walking over Rasputin's spent blood that was trailing from inside the basement stairs and into the courtyard. The brief encounter with the policeman must have happened around three o'clock. At the time, Vlasyuk did not see anything unusual. [In the interim, between the shooting and this meeting, Yusupov had washed off Rasputin's blood that would have sprayed in his direction and have ample time to put on a fresh uniform.]

Within the hour, after Vlasyuk accompanied his area supervisor, Kalyadich, back to the perimeter of the Yusupovskii Palace, they saw a chauffeured vehicle parked outside the main parade entrance. Nikolai Mikhailovich wrote in his diary that the basement rendezvous had concluded at "3 o'clock."[1120] [This detail confirms that others left the palace via the Ofitserskaya *Ulitsa* access.] Ivan Nefedov, however, stated (**Protocol No. 1**) that the visitors left by four o'clock. Yusupov, knowing that he remained under the watchful eyes of the *gorodovoi*, had no reason to fabricate the time he left (at four o'clock in the morning, **Protocol No. 12**), in that way verifying Nefedov's statement concerning the last visitor, Felix Yusupov.

Thus, Efimov was correct to say that he heard gunshots at 2.30 in the morning (see **Protocol No. 8**). Sereda, trusting that time estimate, subsequently repeated that detail to Grand Duke Andrei

Vladimirovich.[1121] Therefore, it was Vlasyuk who mistook the time of the shooting.

An Explanation About the Probable Shooting Sequence: A Reconstruction

Vlasyuk believed that he heard gunshots "quickly following one another," while Efimov thought he heard one single gunshot followed by three more "one after another." Why such a discrepancy? According to Professor Kosorotov's expert medical opinion, the number of shooters could not be verified. The same point was recognized by Professor Zharov and his team in 1993 (see **Chapter Eight**).

Both Vlasyuk and Efimov testified they heard four gunshots. Common sense indicates that if all outside gunshots had been fired in rapid sequence at Rasputin, by different shooters, it would have been reckless. Hence, Cook's idea that Rasputin, with wrists bound, was "propped in a sitting position against a snow heap"[1122] and then shot by two persons is absurd and ignores the gunshot wound in the back.

Though it is impossible to say there was blood elsewhere in the courtyard area, **POLICE PHOTOGRAPHS Nos.** 2 and 3 suggest the snow further afield is uncontaminated, because Professor Kosorotov revealed in *Russkaya Volya* (*Russian Will*), in March 1917, that the abdominal gunshot wounds would have caused extensive blood loss. Had Rasputin progressed towards the gates by one snow heap (as claimed by Yusupov[1123] and Purishkevich[1124]), then it becomes difficult to explain why these photos do not show an obvious blood trail from the step to the gate. Recognizing the second bullet entered Rasputin's back and would have immobilized him immediately, Rasputin collapsed where he was. Since Sereda concluded the victim "was carried" back inside,[1125] the body was not dragged, otherwise it would have left bloody drag marks.

1. The First Bullet

It is time to revisit the memoirs written by the conspirators in conjunction with Nikolai Mikhailovich's notes. Purishkevich and

Yusupov agreed that Felix grabbed a gun before returning to his guest in the basement. Rather than reaching for his own familiar weapon, Felix said[1126] that he took Dmitri's revolver; the same detail is found in Nikolai Mikhailovich's diary.[1127] Why did Felix not grab his own gun?

Felix insisted that by the time he returned downstairs, Rasputin's head had slumped forwards and that he was breathing heavily,[1128] giving the impression that he was in a drunken stupor or asleep. This portrayal is not symptomatic of cyanide poisoning. [Kosorotov confirmed that Rasputin was inebriated at the time of his death, but was not poisoned.] Yusupov continued with his story, saying that Rasputin recovered, got up and began to walk around, gulping more Madeira and began to talk. Meeting Princess Irina Yusupova was all but forgotten, or was it? Instead we learn that Rasputin asked to visit the gypsies,[1129] a detail was not mentioned in the revised memoir. [Matrena revealed that her father did not venture out to the gypsies because he feared crowds after the 1914 attempt upon his life.] If meeting Irina Yusupova was the reason for the invitation, it is remarkable that not one Rasputin family member revealed that detail in their police depositions. Years later, Felix denied in the U. S. Supreme Court that Rasputin came to meet Irina.

Yusupov fired at Rasputin, who was "standing in front of him" when both stared into each other's faces.[1130] This meant that Rasputin would not have had time to react defensively and that Yusupov was controlling the moment. However, was Felix telling the truth? Yusupov's explanation about the first gunshot wound does not correlate with the forensic findings. Nikolai Mikhailovich wrote that Felix "sat" particularly close to Rasputin before he fired "one shot almost pointblank" and that the bullet had "passed through the liver."[1131] [Nikolai Mikhailovich relied on Felix for these details.]

The second version reveals that when Yusupov ventured downstairs with Dmitri's weapon in his hand, Rasputin remained slumped over in the same position as Yusupov had left him minutes earlier. Yusupov approached, and stood over Rasputin to check for a response. Family photographs indicate that Yusupov used his right hand to write and no doubt would have used the same hand to fire a gun. The police photo showing the abdominal entry wound indicates that Yusupov did not stand facing his victim. If Yusupov did stand face Rasputin when he fired the gun, then the bullet would have entered the front of the body and (might have) exited the back. POLICE PHOTOGRAPH No. 13 (in Chapter Eight) shows that the first bullet entered the abdominal cavity a few inches below the left nipple at close range, proceeded through and through (in one side and out the opposite side), and exited on the right side of the body (see POLICE PHOTOGRAPH No. 12). The bullet's trajectory indicates that Yusupov could only have been by Rasputin's left side, close enough to fire the gun at close range. The bullet passed through Rasputin's body from left-to-right, not front-to-back.

Photograph 17 show the "cozy"[1132] *Garsonerka* (Bachelor's quarters), which Felix described in this way:

"The newly renovated room formed part of the wine cellar. It was in half darkness, dreary, with granite floors with grey facing stone walls and with a low arched ceiling. Two small narrow windows, level with the ground, looked out onto the Moika. Two low form arches divided the space into two halves, one was somewhat narrow, the other was large and wide and was intended as a dining room. From the narrower part of the room, the exit door led to the spiral staircase, from which off the first landing there was an exit into the courtyard, while higher along the steps - an entry onto the first level.

The spiral staircase leading to the study was wider and made of dark wood.

Entering the new premises by this way, first of all [you] come into its narrow division. Here in the shallow niches there were two big Chinese porcelain vases which ...livened up the somber grey walls ...

There were dark leather chairs black wooden cupboards ... massive oak armchairs with high backs and here and there small tables covered with colored fabrics and on them elephant ivory and various art objects.

[I] especially remember among these objects one

cupboard with encrustations, inside which was an entire labyrinth of mirrors and bronze columns. On this cupboard stood an ancient crucifix made of crystal and silver workmanship of the 17th century.

In the dining room there was a large open fireplace of red granite, on which were ... plates ... a set of black wooden sculptures. ... On the floor lay a large Persian carpet and in the corner where the cupboard with labyrinths and crucifix stood there was a huge white bear skin.

In the middle of the room we placed a table at which Grigori Rasputin was to drink his last tea."[1133]

Purishkevich described the basement area more simply, saying:

"All of it was divided into two halves, one of which closest to the fireplace, from which glowed a bright cozy fire, giving the impression of a miniature dining room, and the other, at the back, something between a living room and boudoir, with soft armchairs with a refined deep divan in front of which lay a massive exquisitely white carpet skin from a white bear. By the wall below the windows in the shade a smallish table was located on which on a tray stood four corked bottles with Marsala, Madeira, Sherry and port wine and behind these bottles there could be seen a number of dark glassed wineglasses. On the fireplace between the groups of ancient artworks there was a crucifix of marvelous workmanship, I believe chiseled from an elephant bone.

The place was arched in the style of an ancient decorated Russian tent." [1134]

Felix purposefully approached his guest and waited for a response, which did not happen. He then sat down in the adjacent armchair to Rasputin's left, brought out Dmitri's gun, aimed, and pulled the trigger. Nikolai Mikhailovich says Felix was responsible for Rasputin's first gunshot wound. The same point was conceded by Purishkevich,[1135] therefore confirming that Felix was telling the truth.

Purishkevich came downstairs from the study to find that

Rasputin was lying on his back over the bear skin. Rasputin was left lying there, bleeding from two wounds (entry and exit) while Purishkevich and Felix returned upstairs.[1136] [1137] Since Rasputin was seated in the armchair when he was shot, he would have either remained slumped backwards or forwards. Either way, he could not have fallen across the bearskin and ended up on it on his back, while Felix stood there holding the discharged weapon.[1138] Kosorotov revealed that Rasputin would have been bleeding profusely from his abdominal wounds. If Yusupov was truthful, neither Purishkevich nor Dmitri moved the bleeding body. Yusupov had staff to do that. Similarily, it was absurd for Purishkevich to suggest that. After they realized Rasputin was still "breathing ... in agony,"[1139] they opted to return upstairs to the study and wait for Rasputin to die while they began to "congratulate Yusupov." Yusupov's failure to kill Rasputin was not a matter for praise but a setback.

2. The Second Bullet

In all likelihood, Yusupov panicked, and ran up the stairs to ask Purishkevich for help.[1140,1141] In Nikolai Mikhailovich's absence, as stated elsewhere, Purishkevich was the de-facto leader on this night and thus it was necessary for him to take the matter back into his control. Purishkevich had to intervene in order to cover Yusupov's ineptitude. During the minutes the conspirators remained upstairs debating their next move, Rasputin opened his eyes and realized his predicament. His only thought was to flee, which would have been a natural response. Gathering strength to raise himself, he moved towards the small passageway that led off the room he was lying in. The distance was not great – only several feet. After a few steps, Rasputin reached the landing. Bearing the intense abdominal pain, he grabbed hold of the first door handle he could see and realized that the door opened outwards (**Photo 18**).

Judging by the noises resonating from the stairwell into the study, it was not only obvious that Rasputin was still alive, but that he was moving. One of the men reacted and ran from the study towards the first flight of stairs and saw Rasputin opening the small courtyard door.

Nikolai Mikhailovich said that Purishkevich was the second shooter.[1142] To avert disaster, Purishkevich responded quickly. Acting instinctively, he removed his Savage pistol[1143] [1144] from its holster and "by the exit" (in the stairwell), "fired twice: one bullet into the occiput and the second into the leg."[1145] [It would have been challenging to shoot Rasputin had he been running.]

We know that Vlasyuk and Efimov heard four gunshots fired "one after the other" (Protocol No. 9). Neither Purishkevich, who said that "an extraordinary loud noise from my revolver carried into the air,"[1146] nor Yusupov denied that there was a "loud echo"[1147] in the small courtyard. The courtyard was surrounded on three sides by the solid stone walls of the adjoining buildings. Purishkevich said that he initially missed his target twice before one bullet entered Rasputin's back,[1148] and then, as Nikolai Mikhailovich wrote, "Rasputin fell by then onto the ground into the yard."[1149] This reconstructed scenario supports the fact that Purishkevich missed three times, not twice, which backs up what the *gorodovoi* heard.

There is no reason to disbelieve that it was Purishkevich's gunfire that Vlayuk heard. Though Purishkevich discharged his weapon, it did not happen as he described. Rasputin would have had to turn around and stare directly into his killer's eyes at the very instant he collapsed. Recalling Sereda's words that the victim never reached the gate, it implies there never was a shooter in the courtyard. This reasoning explains why the police never found a spent cartridge in the courtyard. The fact is, Rasputin would have become debilitated more or less immediately after the second bullet entered his back. Yusupov alleged Purishkevich caught up with Rasputin, fired his gun for the third time and followed up by discharging his weapon once more before watching Rasputin collapse beside the snow mound by the gates.

3. The Third Gunshot

Purishkevich used a curious set of words when he said that he fired his Savage "possibly into the head."[1150] Professor Kosorotov said that a bullet was fired into the victim's head. However, it was not into the occiput as described by Nikolai Mikhailovich,[1151] but into the frontal lobe (POLICE PHOTOGRAPH No. 10, Chapter

Eight). Remebering that Rasputin would have been immobilized, the third gunshot wound indicates that he was lying face up when he received the third bullet. It will never be known who was responsible for the third gunshot wound, though Purishkevich's use of the word "possibly" may attract assumptions.

None of the three gunshot wounds can be described as being more crucial than the other. The gunshot wound to the head just happened to be the last one inflicted and it is the most conspicuous wound on the corpse. The scenario described by the conspirators involved in this crime, although often tortuous and confusing, cannot be discounted as fiction. They do contain elements of truth. Professor Helen d'Encausse stated that in cases where the perpetrators of a crime recount their crime, the details are altered in the course of time.[1152] This opinion can be expanded to include memoirists who claim they knew the perpetrator and thus gained unique knowledge about the commission of that particular crime.

A Scenario Based on Forensic Evidence

Professor Kosorotov clearly explained that the victim died from a gunshot wound to the head that was caused by a revolver. To restate the effect of the second gunshot injury on the victim, after the second bullet hit Rasputin, he would have become disabled within seconds as a result of the injury caused by the bullet.[1153] All eyewitnesses must have assumed that Rasputin, covered in blood, was dead. He was carried inside, through the basement[1154] alcove and briefly left lying on the floor of the wide underground service tunnel shown in **Photo 19** (that runs from the alcove) until the items needed to take the body out of the building were made available. These tunnels, parts of which are accessible to the public, interconnect to various sections of the building complex. However, before the body was removed from the premises, two unforeseen events intervened.

The first unforeseen event was described by Purishkevich,[1155] and retold in more graphic detail by Nikolai Mikhailovich.[1156] He wrote that Yusupov was so overpowered by bestial rage that he beat Rasputin's corpse with a "stick," which "smashed his nose" and "disfigured the entire face." The police photographs of the head show that the face, including the right eye, had sustained physical injuries but the weapon that used to bring about those injuries was not Maklakov's truncheon (**Photo 20**). It is impossible to know whether Yusupov intended to use the truncheon that night, but to vent his frustration, he struck at Rasputin's face with the tip of his military boot. He rammed it towards the right eye and then struck him again around the head, shattering the nasal bone. Maklakov revealed in his 1920 Deposition that Yusupov, in a fit of madness, smashed Rasputin's skull,[1157] but did not say how Yusupov did that.

It will never be known why Purishkevich told Nikolai Mikhailovich that the truncheon, which Maklakov had so generously loaned to Yusupov, was used. Purishkevich wrote about the incident in his 'Diary'; the same detail was repeated by Yusupov a decade later. It can only be guessed that because Yusupov's final actions were so atrocious, they all felt it was best not to reveal too much about the young prince's unexpected pathological conduct towards their victim. Nikolai Mikhailovich, not witnessing the assault, wrote that Yusupov's "rage" over Rasputin took place until "his soul was no more."[1158] The reality was that Felix's physical abuse over Rasputin's body added a macabre element to the overall dehumanization of a human being. The most shocking aspect about Felix's physical assault is that his paroxysmal outburst involved, by his own admission, his interfering with a corpse.

Purishkevich revealed that Felix became "expressionless ... in an unresponsive state ... senselessly" headed towards his parents' section of the house without really seeing anyone,[1159] possibly in a state of shock. However, Yusupov added a melodramatic note to the episode, saying he lost consciousness after his furious attack on the "corpse," after seeing fresh blood flowing on his victim's disfigured face.[1160] It was a horrifying scene, which Yusupov walked away from, leaving his staff to carry out the plan to its finality.

Nikolai Mikhailovich described that Yusupov had to wash and change his uniform because, as Purishkevich admitted,[1161] Felix Yusupov was covered with blood. He would have been the only one of the conspirators who was able to change from what he was wearing that night before departing the palace. Yusupov was assisted by his "servants" to wash and discard his ruined military uniform and then put on a freshly laundered clothing and clean boots, which Purishkevich described fittingly as changing "from head to toe."[1162] Before long, he and Buzhinsky would encounter the inquisitiveness of policeman Vlasyuk.

The second unforeseen event would have occurred very shortly after the first, because Kosorotov explained that Rasputin had a maximum of some twenty minutes to survive after his body sustained the first gunshot wound. Knowing that Yusupov was changing clothes, in the meantime, Purishkevich instructed the house staff (confirming my hypothesis that he was in charge of the evening proceedings) to remove the corpse from the palace. At least two servants had to lug the bloodied body to the car using sturdy material that would also serve to cover it up. Rope and a wide piece of dark blue[1163]-colored broadcloth (*sukno*)[1164] served that purpose. [Maklakov incorrectly said it was floor carpet (*kovyer*).[1165]] These items were easy to gather because of the ongoing renovations. The body was placed onto a piece of wool fabric and the wrists and then the legs of the body were "tied tightly together"[1166] using twine. The outer wrap was bound with rope.[1167]

What happened next is conjecture on my part but it seems to offer the most likely explanation. When the time arrived to handle the body, at that instant, Rasputin must have made some kind of involuntary movement. The person(s) who noticed it assumed the victim's life had not been extinguished. One of them reacted instinctively, removed his firearm from its holster, knelt alongside the body, placed the muzzle firmly on the forehead, and pulled the trigger. The bloodied, battered corpse was ready to be taken away.[1168] The bulky woollen fabric would not only have concealed the body but it would have helped to absorb the flow of blood seeping into the hair and down the face. The house servants carried their load along the lit underground corridor and brought it up to the main courtyard. Given the cold, Dmitri, the nominated driver, was waiting to depart, with the car engine running to keep it warm.

Globachev, the former Petrograd chief of the *Okhrana*, revealed in 1922 that their investigation had established that Yusupov and Purishkevich murdered Rasputin.[1169] Samuel Hoare seemed troubled when he later came into contact with Purishkevich, who he knew "took a human life."[1170] It is possible that one other person contributed to Rasputin's death. What is certain: the person used a Russian military weapon.

Was Grand Duke Dmitri Pavlovich Involved in the Shooting?

Rasputin's bundled up corpse was placed into the car that was waiting in the rear courtyard. Both Purishkevich[1171] and Nikolai Mikhailovich said that Dmitri ended up as the driver because the designated person, Dr. Lazovert, was too ill to drive.[1172] When Grand Duke Andrei Vladimirovich spoke to Dmitri on Sunday morning, he learned that the Dmitri never saw Rasputin. One is left to assume that Dmitri drove out with the covered load onto Ofitserskaya *Ulitsa* without looking behind.

Dmitri's later admission to his father refutes Yusupov's claim that Dmitri handled Rasputin's bleeding body[1173] after he was shot the first time. I contend that Dmitri was kept well away from the events that were occurring elsewhere in the palace. Recalling that Dmitri avowed to his father that "your son is clean from actual blood stains,"[1174] but did accept his "premeditated participation in murdering Rasputin,"[1175] what was his contribution?

A letter Yusupov sent to his mother dated 2 January 1917 from the family's Rakitnoye estate spoke guardedly about Dmitri's presence. He wrongly believed that if he addressed the envelope to Grand Duchess Ksenya Alexandrovna, living in Crimea,[1176] the police would not intercept it. The communication that should have passed on to Zinaida Yusupova declared:

> "*I can absolutely definitely say that he was not the murderer, instead he was only the supervisor of the performance ...*" [1177] [1178]

Despite the fact that Dmitri did not reveal anything of consequence about the night to his relatives, he never denied that he was present in the Yusupovskii Palace while Rasputin was fighting fo his life, telling them that he was there to have dinner.[1179] At first glance, it appears that Dmitri's presence had been almost superfluous. However, Dmitri played two important roles that night.

Dmitri provided the necessary items for the night's undertaking. His vehicle would be used to convey Rasputin's body away from the murder site, and he brought a Browning revolver for Felix's use. Nikolai Mikhailovich and Grand Duke Andrei Vladimirovich repeated the same detail, after he questioned Dmitri on Saturday.[1180] In 1920, Yusupov told Maklakov that he used a revolver,[1181] implying it did not belong to him and also confirming his involvement in the murder. The only reason why Dmitri must have brought an extra gun with him had to do with ensuring that Felix would not use his military-issued firearm, which was part of a cadet's equipment. It seems logical to conclude that nothing would jeopardize Felix's upcoming class examinations.[1182] Dmitri's primary role had to do with him being a Romanov. His presence ensured that no one would be singled out.

Using the Potseluyev Bridge (Photo 21), Dmitri's car crossed over the Moika canal with three other passengers, Purishkevich, Sukhotin and Lazovert, to the site thought to have been ideal to dump the body. As the car advanced along the Bolshoi Petrovskii Bridge, Sukhotin directed the driver to inch his way along the middle of the bridge span before veering left and stopping beside the fourth bridge support,[1183] where he knew the partially frozen river still flowed out to the gulf. Thus, Sukhotin did have a role, albeit a minor one. One person was needed to take hold of the bundle and help prop it against the railing.[1184] One or two others helped to propel the hefty bundle over the bridge railing (POLICE PHOTOGRAPH No. 8, Chapter Seven). While Purishkevich stressed that "Dmitri stood watch,"[1185] the import of his words suggests that Dmitri sat looking straight ahead. With the car's engine running, Dmitri may not have heard the thud of the corpse smashing against the solid timber bridge support before it splashed into the flowing riverwater. The car then crossed the bridge on to Krestovskii Island before returning to the city.

Dmitri, as one of the willing conspirators, was not an innocent bystander. He always had the occasion to back off. He came to the palace knowing what was going to happen. He supplied the weapon to shoot Rasputin and drove his car to the place where the corpse had to be disposed of. Aside from the criminality of Dmitri's premeditated actions, from a religious perspective, while initially troubled by what he was going to do, he failed to respect the precepts of the church in which he was raised. Dmitri Pavlovich accepted what Ella (his former legal guardian) advised him and, comforted by her convictions, he willingly participated in this crime. It cannot be overlooked that even though Dmitri did not stain his hands with Rasputin's blood, he did reveal his disloyalty to the sovereign.

Summary of the sequence of events at CRIME SCENE ONE

▶ Yusupov and Rasputin arrive at the Yusupovskii Palace shortly after 1.30 a.m.

▶ The deliberate intoxication of the victim facilitated the use of a firearm.

▶ One bullet was fired into Rasputin's body.

▶ FOUR gunshots were heard in the vicinity of the Yusupov residence about 2.30.

▶ One bullet penetrates Rasputin's back.

▶ Rasputin's face is disfigured with injury to the right eye.

▶ One bullet was fired into Rasputin's head.

▶ Vlasyuk talks to Yusupov (and Buzhinsky) at the Moika, 92 courtyard around 3 a.m.

▶ In Yusupov's presence, Purishkevich discloses to Vlasyuk that Rasputin is dead.

▶ Only Yusupov was observed leaving by car from the front entry of Moika, 94 at 4 a.m.

▶ One bullet killed a dog (body shown at the police department, bullet not retrieved).

Foreign Disclosures

The scenario just described is not unlike the evidence that was offered by Yusupov in the New York Supreme Court in 1965.[1186] Yusupov, aged seventy-eight, testified that he did bring Rasputin to the Moika Yusupovskii Palace. He admitted he shot Rasputin in the basement, and that after the wounded victim "ran outside the room," he was "chased to the courtyard. Rasputin fell down in the snow. Purishkevich shot Rasputin."

One newspaper article reporting on the American court case revealed that the defense attorney, Carleton Eldridge, insisted that "Rasputin had expected to meet the princess, niece of Czar Nicholas II (sic) at the palace." Yusupov, according to this article, "vehemently"[1187] denied this statement.

In Andrew Dobson's book on the subject of Yusupov's various trials and other tangential matters, Felix declared in the U. S. Court "that he had shot Rasputin not once, but twice."[1188] The *New York News* article from which Dobson quoted also revealed that Felix never said "precisely how or where the almost indestructible monk (sic) died."[1189] Asked by his legal counsel, Herbert Zelenko, what happened to the body, Yusupov replied: "He was thrown into the river by Duke Dmitri."[1190] Dmitri died in 1942 and was unable to respond to this public accusation, and Yusupov enjoyed the rare fortune to consider himself immune from prosecution in a foreign jurisdiction. Never forgetting Maklakov's counsel decades earlier, he obfuscated the details, knowing that not one person alive would test his words.

During an earlier trial that was heard before the British Court system in 1937 (because the film company MGM was sued for libel in London), Yusupov was asked by his barrister, Sir Patrick Hastings, K. C. (King's Counsel), a series of questions, two of which appear below.

QUESTION: *"Where was Rasputin killed?"*

REPLY: *"He was killed in the Moika Palace ... in the cellar below the drawing room."*[1191]

QUESTION: *"Would it be wrong to say that after Rasputin was dead you so lost control of yourself and fell into a paroxysm of rage that you proceeded to beat the body?"*[1192]

REPLY: *"That happened just at the moment when he died."*

Yusupov then added: "*Purishkevich had fired three shots and still Rasputin was not dead.*"

Irina Yusupova was also asked to take the stand and this was part of her exchange with the Defense counsel, Sir William Jowitt:

QUESTION: "*I am suggesting that your husband fired the first shot, which did not kill Rasputin and that Rasputin got up and as he was making his way out of the place Purishkevich came up and fired four shots, two of which hit him.*"

REPLY: "*If he was dead before he was pushed into the ice it was Purishkevich who finally killed him.*"

Irina Yusupova's response is attention grabbing in that she identified that Purishkevich was the murderer and not her husband. The problem with Irina's response is that her testimony was hearsay evidence and in the majority of jurisdictions, a wife cannot be compelled to testify against her husband. The reason for this disqualification relates to the partner's direct interest in the outcome of the case.[1193] Indeed, Felix told Grand Duchess Ksenya Alexandrovna in January 1917 that "Irina sees this, just as I do."[1194] Irina Yusupova failed to accept that although the motive for her husband and Purishkevich to murder Rasputin was similar, she selectively disconnected her husband's actions away from those attributed to Purishkevich.

At the end of this court hearing, Yusupov was reported as saying to the British *Daily Express* that his "cross examination was a great trial" for him. He was particularly annoyed that the defense "had the audacity to suggest that I, Prince Yusupov did not kill Rasputin, when I suffered ever since for doing so."[1195] [Dmitri refused to give an interview about the London case.[1196]]

Dobson mentioned that following Felix's brother's tragic death (as a result of a duel) in 1908, Yusupov contemplated suicide.[1197] Felix admitted that, after the incident, he became severely depressed (and demonstrated erratic behavior that was disapproved by his mother).[1198] If Dobson is correct, there may have been a psychological link to Yusupov's excessive conduct against Rasputin.

Despite the conspirators' 1916 oath to preserve confidentiality[1199] and Yusupov's 1927 memoirs, the American law court finally heard some facts. Notwithstanding the numerous photographs and paintings that show a genteel aristocratic image of Felix Yusupov, often seen holding one of his pet dogs, the truth about his sinister persona was concealed from the public. Living as an émigré in Europe and occasionally visiting the United States, Felix Yusupov remained free to act and speak as he pleased, becoming a public curiosity among the disparate Russian communities. Felix's wife, Irina Alexandrovna, steadfastly remained with Felix until his death as a result of a stroke.[1200]

Even so, the final words should still remain with Yusupov. In 1927, he said that the "silent stone walls would always conceal the truth."[1201] Indeed, those walls became a silent witness to the events in the palace when a group of Russians tackled their enemy. Perhaps one century later, some of those stones are starting to crumble under the weight of the truth.

The Mastermind's Assessment of the Crime

While ensconced in his Grushevka estate, on 14 February 1917, Nikolai Mikhailovich offered this opinion about the two persons who were among the most influential women in Felix Yusupov's life at the time:

> "*What can one say about Irina and his mother Zinaida Nikolayevna Yusupova, who are in wild raptures, that Felix – was Rasputin's murderer!*"[1202]

He continued his exasperation over Yusupov's unprovoked assault on Rasputin with the following:

> "*Why such anger, why such pessimism ... over the dying sacrifice?*"

Nikolai Mikhailovich expressed more concern about Yusupov's unforeseen pathological behavior than for the victim. There are two other elements that may be interpreted from Nikolai Mikhailovich's choice of words. The first word "sacrifice" defined the motive as to why Rasputin was murdered. It also proves that the murder was pre-meditated.

In 1920, Maklakov revealed this facet about Yusupov:

"Yusupov was very determined to say that out of all the five participants, no matter how strange it is, he was the most coldblooded ..."[1203]

Sunday became a day of contemplation for two young noblemen and intense grief for the women in the Alexandrovskii Palace. For many, Dmitri had become a hero overnight. Grand Duke Andrei Vladimirovich reflected "that the more Dmitri was going to be pursued" about this matter following his arrest, it would only increase the dissent "against Tsarskoe Selo" brought on "by all of Russia and the army which would stand with Dmitri like a rock."[1204]

Recalling how proudly Purishkevich proclaimed "I killed Grisha Rasputin, the enemy of Russia and the Tsar,"[1205] it now appears that his outburst might not be an exaggeration. The Black Hundred political activist and fervent anglophile carried out the promise given to Samuel Hoare and Ambassador Buchanan. Indeed, the British were most satisfied with the outcome. It was, however, disastrous that more lives continued to be lost on the battlefield. By contrast, the *strannik*'s pacifism had no place in such a milieu, where a few men had decided that Grigorii Rasputin had to forfeit his life for the future common good of Russia. For the British, Rasputin's death would ensure the preservation of the *Entente*. The next few months proved that the Russians miscalculated badly.

Chapter Six Photos

PHOTO 13: PETROGRAD. GOROKHOVAYA ULITSA. View of the apartment building and the Rasputin apartment windows on the third floor that face the main courtyard. The 3 central windows looked out from the reception room, while the two windows to the right, opened from Grigorii Rasputin's bedroom.

PHOTO 15: PETROGRAD. A Gorodovoi wearing his winter uniform with military medals (pre-1916).

PHOTO 16: YUSUPOVSKII PALACE. The large inner courtyard and access off Ofitserskaya Ulitsa shows the porched entrance into the building, 1920's.

PHOTO 17: YUSUPOVSKII PALACE BASEMENT.
The Garsonerka, after 1917.

PHOTO 18: YUSUPOVSKII PALACE. The arrows
indicate Rasputin's flight path from the basement, up
a couple of steps, then out into the courtyard.

PHOTO 19: YUSUPOVSKII PALACE. The underground
network of tunnels below the Palace.

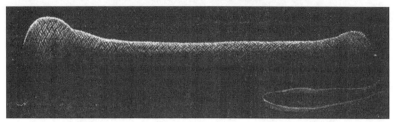

PHOTO 20: The rubber truncheon Maklakov gave
to Felix Yusupov. It is covered with a layer of plaited
thread. This photo offers crucial forensic evidence.

PHOTO 21: PETROGRAD. Potseluyev Bridge spanning across the
Moika canal. The Ministry of Internal Affairs building is just visible on
the left and the Yusupovskii Palace is the right side (Postcard c. 1916).

CHAPTER SEVEN
DAY 3 of the GENDARME and Judicial INVESTIGATION

Monday 19 December 1916

"In The Matter of the Murder of the Peasant Grigorii Efimovich Rasputin"

"Дело об Убийстве крестьянина Григория Ефимовича Распутина"

The third week of the Christmas Lenten period had begun. The city was hearing the news that Rasputin's corpse had probably been found in the outlying islands.

During the day, Nikolai Mikhailovich had travelled a mile or so to reach the Sergievskii Palace, where upon arrival he announced, *"Messieurs les assassins, je vous salue."*[1206] His visit gave Felix, with Dmitri, the opportunity to explain what had transpired at the Yusupovskii Palace on Friday night.[1207] Afterwards, Nikolai Mikhailovich wrote that on Friday night, Yusupov arranged "the upper level with tea and *zakuski*," while downstairs, the fare for Rasputin comprised "a cold table with drinks."[1208] The evening was not a social event because all the conspirators waiting in the study stayed sober. This revelation means that the nighttime episode was attended by only men and that Rasputin alone drank alcohol that night. [Russians at social gatherings only drink with their friends, never with their enemy.] This set up shows that Felix did not drink with Rasputin in the basement.[1209]

The Depositions of the Guard and His Supervisor at the Bolshoi Petrovskii Bridge

Although two individuals provided their testimonies on Sunday 18 December 1916, it is appropriate that their statements should appear in this section, which focuses mostly on the events that followed after the Bolshoi Petrovskii Bridge guard reported seeing blood on the bridge on Saturday. *Birzheviye Vedomosti* informed its readers that the guards posted on the bridge were asked to provide statements.[1210]

PROTOCOL No. 13 - Fyodor Kuzmin [bridge guard]

Fyodor Kuzmin was employed as a guard on the Bolshoi Petrovskii Bridge. He was forty-eight years old, and gave his address as Petrovskii *Prospekt*, 11/1 apartment No. 11. He originally came from Lyanino village (Novgorod District).

"On 17 December at 12 o'clock during the day I went on duty on the B. (sic) Petrovskii Bridge. Around 2 o'clock during the day two workers unknown to me approached me and told me that they saw blood stains on the bridge. I went with them and saw blood stains on the panels and on the wooden beams, and also on one of the supports there were blood stains; in addition to that; on the ice near the bridge support I saw a dark brown galosh. On the support *small drops* of blood, and not stains could be seen. At 2 o'clock during the day I on the orders of policeman Asonov, retrieved the galosh and took it for safekeeping until 12 o'clock at night, when it was demanded by the 4th Petrograd Division. I with *gorodovoi* Kordyukov carried it there.

Read and signed: Fyodor Kuzmin

Countersigned: Lieutenant-Colonel Popel."[1211]

PROTOCOL No. 14 - Vasilii Fyodorovich Kordyukov [*Gorodovoi*]

Vasilii Kordyukov was thirty-six years old and lived nearby on Petrovskii *Prospekt*, 8 (the main road on Petrovskii Island). Originally Kordyukov came from Ivanovskii village (Tver Province). He was a local *gorodovoi* stationed at the 4th Petrograd Division.

"On 17 December at 12 o'clock during the day I

went on duty, which was on Petrovskii Prospect opposite house No. 8. At the start of 2 o'clock during the day the bridge guard Fyodor Kuzmin, told me that he discovered blood stains on the panels and railings of the 4th span of the Bolshoi Petrovskii Bridge. I walked over there at that time and saw more blood stains on one of the bridge foundations; while in-between that support and the adjoining support, a men's dark-brown boot lay on the ice. I notified the 4th Petrograd Division about what (I) saw and to local police officer Asonov who set-up a protocol. At 2 o'clock during the day bridge guard Kuzmin in my and Asonov's presence used a gaff to retrieve this boot which was taken to the Division. I cannot depose anything more."

Read and signed: Vasili Kordyukov

Countersigned: Lieutenant-Colonel Popel.[1212]

Procurator Zavadsky sought permission from Trepov and Makarov to ensure that General-Major Popov terminate his parallel investigation in order to prevent him interfering with his investigator, Sereda. Permission given, General Vasiliev instructed Popov to stop questioning witnesses.[1213] Popov assembled the 15 Protocols into one folder, which contained other papers, including diagrams, photographs, maps, as well as Protocol 1740 and a police *Spravka* (Official document), which confirmed that the first object found at the bridge was identified by the family. The file was handed to Alexander Protopopov as Report No 694,[1214] on 23 December. The *Spravka* reads as follows:

Spravka

"A brown No. 10 boot *Treugolnik* brand was found under the Bolshoi Petrovskii Bridge on the Neva, which on this day at 3 o'clock at night was shown to the daughters of the missing Grigorii Rasputin-*Novy*, Maria and Varvara Rasputin-*Novy*, living at house No. 64 on *Gorokhovaya Ulitsa*; and which they recognized as the boot belonging to their father by its size and its external appearance. The boot was also recognized as that belonging to Rasputin-

Novy by two agents of the Okhrana Division, the porter and *gospodin* Semonovich (sic)."

18th December, 1916.

Supervisor of the Criminal Police: Mikhailov.[1215]

THE MORNING

Petrovskii Island

The harbor police divers renewed their search at first light.[1216] Hoare wrote in his report that it was very cold and that the unwelcome conditions made the task more difficult.[1217] At 8.40 in the morning, *gorodovoi* Andreev began to sweep the icy surface with a broom and before long noticed an abnormal dark coloration below the ice layer. He cut the ice and tugged at the object, which snapped off. It appeared to be a fur cuff. *Novoye Vremya*[1218] (*New Times*) and *Russkoye Slovo*[1219] (*Russian Word*) reported the cuff was made of beaver. Andreev immediately informed General Alexander Naumov, head of the river police. Naumov ordered the police to quarantine that area. At first, several men cut the ice before breaking it up.[1220] [*Novoye Vremya* reported the corpse found below the ice platform had not sunk to the bottom of the river,[1221] while *Russkoye Slovo* alleged that corpse was at "the bottom of the riverbed."[1222]] Several men placed large wooden planks underneath the corpse and using gaffs, after fifteen minutes, lifted the frozen body and placed it immediately adjacent to the excavation site (**POLICE PHOTOGRAPHS No. 5** and **6**). [*Rech*[1223] incorrectly reported on Tuesday: "Rasputin's corpse found washed up on the riverbank."]

General Koshko judged the body was located 140 meters away from the bridge, closer towards the Petrovskii Island riverbank.[1224] As soon as it was photographed without the beaver coat and river debris, "in the midst of the arrival of the designated high ranking administrators, the corpse was then covered over by two pieces of black material."[1225] This was done to thwart the growing number of inquisitive onlookers who began to "unceasingly approach in their automobiles." The main access road, Petrovskii *Prospekt*, had to be blocked to prevent unauthorized entry.

When this location was selected, the river was flowing. Grand Duke Gavril recorded this:

> "*Approximately one week before the murder, Dmitri had lunch with A. P.* [ballerina Antonina Rafailovna Nesterovskaya[1226]] *on Kamennostrovskii ...*
>
> *After lunch Dmitri ... drove by car to the outskirts of Petrograd on some kind of task. Of course we had no idea, ... he drove to find a place where Rasputin's body could be hidden, whom prince Felix was preparing to murder.*"[1227]

None of the conspirators realized that the *Malaya Nevka* River was freezing over and the slowing winter currents might prevent the corpse from being carried a great distance. That was why the corpse had lodged in the ice. At the time of retrieval, the middle of the river was flowing.

From the nearby Home for Veteran Artists on Petrovskii *Prospekt*, 13 (Petrovskii Island), a telephone call was placed to Protopopov (who stayed in his city office), telling him that Rasputin's remains had been found. Within fifteen minutes, all the hierarchy of the gendarmerie, the police, and government officials arrived en masse and walked across Petrovskii Bridge (POLICE PHOTOGRAPH No. 7 and list below). Some arrived dressed in their full parade uniforms[1228] to inspect the corpse.

List of individuals who attended Crime Scene Two

1. General-Major Pyotr Popov (Head of the field Investigation and photographer)
2. Alexander Balk (Mayor of Petrograd)
3. General-Lieutenant Pavel Kurlov (Deputy Minister of Internal Affairs)
4. Minister of Justice Alexander Makarov
5. Fyodor Nandelshtedt (Procurator in Petrograd)
6. Deputy to F. Nandelshtedt
7. Special Juridical Investigator Victor Sereda (Procurator Department)

8. Senior Procurator Sergei Zavadsky (Head of the Petrograd Criminal Chambers)

9. General Arkadii Koshko (Chief Criminal Court Investigations of the Empire)

10. Alexei Vasiliev (Director of the Police)

11. Arkadii Kirpichnikov (Head of the Criminal Department of the Police)

12. The Head of the Petrograd Criminal Department of the Gendarmerie

13. General-Major Konstantin Globachev (Head of the Petrograd *Okhrana*)

14. General-Lieutenant Sergei Khabalov (Chief of Petrograd Military District)

15. General-Major Vladislav Galle (*Politsmeister* of the Petrograd 4th District)

16. General-Lieutenant (Naval) Alexander Naumov (Head of the City River Police)

Sereda arrived shortly after with Procurator Nandelshtedt in order to document the appearance of the corpse while Popov photographed the area and the frozen body. Koshko explained that due to the severe frost, the authorities sought the hospitality of *Gospodin* (Mr.) E. V. Atamanov,[1229] whose house was located on Petrovskii Island. Kosho noticed that Makarov and Protopopov were "angrily nervous about the fact that Rasputin's corpse was found." Popov sought Protopopov's instructions about the removal of the corpse from the crime scene.[1230] By eleven o'clock, the corpse had been carried to the hut at the end of the bridge, where Sereda checked the pockets of the clothing for any contents.[1231] This process and the writing up of a new Protocol, according to *Den* (*Day*) dragged on until five o'clock in the evening. Police agent Mikhailov made a drawing (**DOCUMENT No. 5**), which showed the place where the galosh had been spotted earlier by bridge guard Fyodor Kuzmin. One Petrograd newspaper published an accurate image of Crime Scene No. 2 (**DOCUMENT No. 6**).

The next step in the investigation after the retrieval of the corpse involved the formal identification of the body. With the body's retrieval, the inquiry became a murder investigation.

The Procurator's Investigation

Soon after the investigation shifted to the Bolshoi Petrovskii Bridge area, Zavadsky re-enacted the journey that was used to dispose of the body. He wanted to know how long it would have taken to to reach the bridge from the Yusupovskii Palace. Zavadsky travelled from Moika, 94 down the Moika Embankment, turned right at Potseluyev Bridge, before crossing onto Nikolayevskii Bridge, then over Tuchkov Bridge to end the journey at the Bolshoi Petrovskii Bridge (see MAP No. 1[1232]). During daytime, it took about fifteen minutes. While his trip encountered traffic and pedestrian movement, the nighttime journey would have taken less time.[1233] Though Zavadsky wrongly supposed the vehicle started from the front of Moika, 94, the difference in time would have been negligible. The Yusupov residence is located inside the area labeled "**3 KAZ**" (Kazanskii District), which was one of twelve police districts in the city.[1234]

Identification of the Remains

The head of the corpse was cleared of most of the river debris to partially reveal the facial features. Protopopov had sent a car for Matrena and her sister Varvara.[1235] Arriving at noon, they were led to the shed where the corpse was laid out. *Rech* incorrectly reported that both daughters had arrived much earlier so that they could watch their father's corpse being uplifted from the river.[1236] Matrena recognized her father straight away. Observing police procedure, Matrena was asked whether she recognized the deceased, to which she replied: "Yes that is my father, Grigorii Efimovich Rasputin."[1237] [1238] She noticed that "his face was almost unrecognizable; clots of dark blood had coagulated in the beard and hair."[1239] Once Protopopov learned from Vasiliev that the corpse had been positively identified, his next duty involved informing the palace.[1240,1241] The empress immediately sent Nikolai II a telegram,[1242] stating: "Corpse found in the water." Elsewhere in Petrograd, Nikolai Mikhailovich rushed to the Sergievskii Palace to pass on the news to Dmitri Pavlovich and Yusupov.[1243]

Returning home, the daughters of the deceased noticed that the *Okhrana* was still guarding their building. While Simanovich failed to mention in his memoirs that he also went to the Petrovskii Bridge crime scene, journalist Kobil-Bobil[1244] noted that he had arrived with Bishop Isidor. Simanovich boasted that his "son Simon who found Rasputin's galosh" and the "fur coat on him had gunshot holes in eight places."[1245]

A Special Letter of Condolence

The Buriat Mongol, Dr. Peter Badmaev (Djamsaran Batma[1246]), treated many members of the imperial court and government officials with his exotic Tibetan herbal medicaments. His association with the branches of the imperial family spanned many decades. Rasputin had visited his pharmacy on Poklonnaya *Ulitsa* on a number of occasions[1247] following his close-to-death assault in 1914. Badmaev's son claimed that although his father was not sympathetic towards Rasputin when he was alive, he nonetheless extended his sympathies to Alexandra Fyodorovna by letter as soon as he heard the news.[1248]

THE AFTERNOON

In 1917, Sereda revealed many details[1249] about what he saw at the Bolshoi Petrovskii Bridge. His examination of the tire tracks embedded in the snow on the bridge revealed several forensic details:

► The vehicle came from the direction of the city and headed towards Krestovskii Island.

► At first the vehicle travelled in middle of the bridge (**POLICE PHOTOGRAPH No. 7**). Approaching the fourth bridge support, it veered to the left and stopped alongside the railing (next to a control box).

► Blood was found around the base of railing and on the support below, extending almost 1 arshin [28 inches or 0.71 meters].

► Judging by the blood spatter pattern, one person

removed the corpse from the vehicle, leaning it against the railing, then by the legs, pushed it over (**POLICE PHOTOGRAPHS No. 8 and 9**).

▶ The head of the corpse hit the bridge support before entering the water below (**POLICE PHOTOGRAPH No. 10**).

Though Sereda prepared a report that recorded his findings, it is now lost. Instead, the only journalist permitted on site, Ivan Kobil-Bobil, published an account on Tuesday 20 December 1916 in *Den* (*Day*, with the notice of Rasputin's death, **Document No. 7**) which was updated in 1917.[1250] At least three other papers, *Novoye Vremya*, *Russkoye Slovo* (see below) and *Birzheviye Vedomosti* printed similar versions.

These are Kobil-Bobil's on-site observations:

> "*On viewing the corpse, Rasputin received three bullet wounds, of which one was in the head, another into the chest and the third into the side. The first of these wounds, into the head, raises some doubt, in that on the head a significant amount of blood flow was found, which it seems, occurred because the corpse was thrown head first, before it fell into the water, after hitting against the bridge* [support]. *This is in fact confirmed by the bloodied stains on the beams. The fur coat was not worn by the corpse, he was simply covered by it, being also wrapped in fairly wide dark colored piece of broadcloth, approximately three arshin* [1 arshin is 28 inches or 0.71 meters] *in length. The legs of the corpse turned out to be bound with thin twine. It appears that the arms of the corpse were bound, but the twine unwound during its ascent and the corpse stiffened with raised arms. Apart from the fur coat, the corpse wore a long Russian upper shirt with attractive embroidery and bluish colored pants and boots without galoshes.*"[1251]

Zavadsky published his account in 1923, saying:

> "*...a blue silk shirt with embroidered gold grain ears: around the neck hung a large sized pectoral cross on which was inscribed:* "Спаси и Сохрани" [Save and

Preserve], *and on the arm there turned out to be a gold and platinum bracelet with a clasp, on one side of which there was an image of the double-headed eagle, and on the other – the letter **H** [Russian 'N'] with the Roman figure **II**. A sizeable portion of the shirt was covered in blood, which quickly began to decompose contaminating the air.*"[1252]

The blue embroidered shirt described by Ekaterina Pecherkina (Protocol No. 6) corroborated with Zavadsky's on-site observation. A few days later, the empress requested of newly appointed Minister of Justice General-Procurator Nikolai Dobrovolskii[1253] that the items found on the corpse were to be brought to the palace. These items included the blue shirt, which the empress embroidered with her own hands and had given to Rasputin as a gift,[1254] jewelry, and a pectoral cross. It was not until 28 December when the articles were brought to her for safe keeping. [1255]

Vasiliev managed to take with him into exile a duplicate copy of the Rasputin file containing all the police Protocols. A good deal of the text was translated from Russian into French and published posthumously in 1930. The following details were provided about the appearance of the corpse:

"His hands and feet were bound with ropes and, as well, the murderers out of precaution fastened a chain, so that it would keep the body under the water. Examination of the body indicated that the murdered [person] had many injuries from gunshots and slashes from a knife."[1256]

Sereda noted[1257] the fur coat was fastened by two hooks and that the feet were tied by a weight – "a bag made from thin fabric filled with a load" (the nature of that load was not described). As soon as the cloth became saturated with river water, it tore open and released its load. The empty bag remained tied to the body. It was made from material consistent with that seen at the Yusupovs' "apartment." [This fabric connected Felix Yusupov directly to this crime.]

As the body was falling down towards the water below, head down, a series of chance events occurred. Firstly, the beaver coat opened below the two hooks and formed something akin to a buoyancy vest (the original words used: "formed an air bell"). This prevented the corpse, at the point of impact, from sinking to the bottom of the river and enabled it to float along the surface of the water. Instead of floating out towards the gulf (as the murderers anticipated), it drifted left towards the edge of the ever-increasing ice mass forming out from the river bank. The splayed out beaver coat touched the ice and froze to it. "Icicles scattering above covered the corpse from above and formed an outer layer to which he froze." The cuff of the coat was close enough to the surface for it to be seen by *gorodovoi* Andreev. The second chance happening was that the head of the corpse hit the bridge support when it was in freefall.

On 20 December, *Russkoye Slovo* published these details:

▶ One eye was hit hard.

▶ The hands and legs were tightly bound with rope.

▶ The body was covered by a beaver coat that was not worn, but it was only thrown over the shoulders.

▶ The hands were clenched.

▶ The beard had frozen to the clothing.

▶ The head was damaged, presumably when the corpse was thrown over the bridge.

▶ The hair on the head was torn off in clumps in a few places.

▶ The face was covered with congealed blood.

▶ Examining the clothing, both galoshes were missing.

▶ The preliminary, on-site examination revealed two gunshot wounds: one on the left side of the chest and the other in the area of the neck.[1258]

Sereda thought the corpse was thrown over the bridge railing by one person. This opinion was based on two observable facts. Firstly, there must have been only one set of footprints by the bridge railing, and secondly, by the pattern of blood stains[1259] left by the corpse on the snow at the spot where it was believed to have been thrown over (**POLICE PHOTOGRAPHS No. 8 and 9**).

Heading Towards the Final Journey

Everyone present at the crime scene understood that the autopsy had to be performed under secrecy. Minister Protopopov stood firm[1260] in his opinion that it was risky to allow the corpse to remain in Petrograd. Considering the earlier drama about refusing to search for Rasputin, this time Protopopov feared the "workers would go on strike"[1261] rather than deal with Rasputin's remains. Koshko said that after much loud deliberation,[1262] the decision was made to transport the corpse to a quiet distant location so that the autopsy could be carried out. Rather than transporting the corpse to the Vyborg Clinic as proposed by Protopopov (and later incorrectly reported by *Rech*[1263]), the morgue in the Chesmenskii Almshouse that had its own church (**Photo 22**) would accept the body.[1264] Mayor Balk telephoned the Head of the Military Medical Academy, General Volkonskii, at four o'clock in the afternoon to organize the receipt of the corpse.[1265] The fact this facility lacked an electricity supply was disregarded, though it would prove challenging when the time came to conduct the autopsy.[1266] The Chesmenskii Almshouse was located seven and half kilometers from the southern city limit of Petrograd.[1267] The Almshouse not only offered a secure place to curtail public attention,[1268] it was close to the Tsarskoe Selo access road.[1269]

Matters began to move slowly, however. A coffin was requested from the Petrov Funeral Bureau, which was delivered within the half hour. It proved rather farcical that the raised frozen arms made it impossible to close the coffin lid. Therefore, a new wooden container was rapidly cobbled together by the funeral parlor and that second container[1270] provided a better result. A covered Red Cross sanitary automobile was secured from their central garage in order to transport the corpse to the Almshouse (not the "Nikolayevskii Naval Almshouse" as Protopopov incorrectly recalled in 1917), under armed police escort.[1271] The Red Cross driver was told to go to Petrovskii Bridge but as soon as he reached the site, he was directed to the side, away from where the corpse might be seen. The police used a sled to shift the parceled body, then covered with a tarpaulin and a bast mat.[1272]

At 6 p.m.,[1273] two vehicles left the bridge and travelled along Petrovskii *Prospekt* using a circuitous route to reach their intended destination. The gendarme escort was accompanying two boxes, one contained the corpse and the second one stored the beaver fur coat.[1274] General Koshko incorrectly recalled the corpse was firstly taken to the Vyborg district where it was photographed, before its transportation to the Almshouse.[1275] But his seemingly faulty memory might have arisen after he heard one of the police officers shout to the Red Cross driver to take the deceased to the military-clinical hospital on the Vyborg side of the city.[1276] Due to the ever increasing number of spectators, that instruction was used as a diversionary tactic. All clear, the police removed the security cordons to let regular bridge traffic to resume crossing over to Krestovskii Island.[1277]

Protopopov, acting on behalf of the empress, left instructions with the gendarmes that no one other than the relatives of the deceased were allowed to enter the Chesmenskii chapel where the body was laid out. The chapel precinct was guarded by three officers of the gendarmerie. During that period, the body continued to thaw and was later washed. There is no reason to mistrust Koshko,[1278] who wrote about two sullen women sitting in silence, undisturbed, near the corpse for several hours on the eve of the autopsy procedure. To be sure, Zavadsky[1279] claimed that an unidentified female, whom he believed may have been the empress, arrived at the chapel dressed in a medical nurse's uniform. Grand Duke Andrei Vladimirovich heard that the empress and Taneeva visited the Almshouse to pray over Rasputin's body.[1280]

There is one scene described in a book that offers reliable texts of documents in combination with excerpts from various memoirs relating to the political police of Imperial Russia. That publication revealed how the empress supposedly reacted after seeing Rasputin's corpse lying in the chapel. Nikolai II, who it was said had accompanied her, asked General Spiridovich to lift her back onto her feet. The empress then turned to her husband and asked, "How could you remove the *Okhrana* from Grigorii Efimovich?" The question did not receive a response. If this doubtful scenario happened, it is difficult to fathom why the palace security agents under Spiridovich's command failed to watch over Rasputin's wellbeing.

Accompanied by Aron Simanovich and Bishop Isidor, both Rasputin girls and Laptinskaya came to pay their respects.[1281] The palace granted Isidor permission to conduct a memorial service[1282] because the Petrograd Metropolitan Pitirim declined to become involved.[1283] Sereda revealed that Nikolai II left Makarov instructions to facilitate the carrying out of the autopsy,[1284] even though the relatives of Grigorii Rasputin opposed the procedure.[1285]

Later, during Monday, Sereda sent Professor Dmitri Kosorotov, who was the most eminent pathologist in the city, a note that he had to be prepared to conduct an autopsy on Wednesday morning at the Chesmenskii Almshouse. Fourteen people were also invited to attend.[1286] However, because the deceased had thawed sufficiently, the time of the autopsy was brought forward.

The Mastermind Upholds His Obligations

Without faltering, Nikolai Mikhailovich transmitted Felix Yusupov's father, who had recently moved from Moscow to Koreiz (Crimea), a number of telegrams,[1287] two of which are provided below:

> **19 December 1916.** *"Consider your arrival here is highly desirable. See Felix every day, quite, in control ..."*

> **19 December 1916.** *"Happy* [that you are] *coming.* [I] *shall tell you everything that I can on the way. Corpse found this morning under the ice close to Petrovskii Bridge. Felix is calm, see him often. Goodbye."*

These two telegrams indicate that Felix Yusupov (senior) was fully aware of what his son had done. Felix's father left Crimea, but he never reached Petrograd as planned due to unexpected intervening events that are discussed in **Chapter Ten**.

The Night Approaches

The telegram which Alexandra Fyodorovna sent earlier relaying the tragic news had arrived at two o'clock in the afternoon at Malaya Vishera railway station, while the emperor was en route to Tsarskoe Selo. At 5 p.m., the emperor and Alexei were met by the rest of the family at Tsarskoselskii railway station.[1288] As customary, their arrival was published among other "notices of the day" section of the *Rech*.[1289] The family returned to the palace using two vehicles. Spiridovich noticed that the empress was so agitated that he could clearly make out her facial flush and tightened lips.[1290]

Fligel-Adjutant (rank used for members attached to the imperial suite) Anatolii Mordvinov accompanied Nikolai II back from Stavka and remained the duty officer during the evening. His observations are interesting. The emperor and empress sat at the dining table "looking very tired" and were "only concerned with their own thoughts." The grand duchesses, on the other hand, were more animated showing their "typical cheerfulness" and invited him to join them after dinner in the upper level of the palace. Although they were all affected that "this person was no longer alive," no one mentioned Rasputin by name.[1291] Alexei's reaction to Rasputin's murder is unknown.

Spiridovich described what happened during the evening. Nikolai II asked General Voyeikov to telephone Protopopov and request his presence at Tsarskoe Selo. At 9.30 that evening, Protopopov was received by the emperor. The minister brought the emperor up to date with all the pertinent details. During that audience, Protopopov handed copies of two telegrams, which were sent by Grand Duchess Elizaveta Fyodorovna. Protopopov then passed on a summary of record[1292] that was dated 19 December 1916. That report provided a day-by-day account of the Rasputin Case, commencing with the information that the *gorodovoi* heard four gunshots being discharged at Moika No. 94 and concluded with the statement that the corpse was found during the morning. His report revealed that the corpse had sustained two gunshot wounds. [Information about Tikhomirov, who supposedly saw a shooter wearing a "military field uniform" in the Yusupovskii Palace courtyard, was absent.] Protopopov lastly admitted that many people of position had openly encouraged the murder of not only Rasputin but the empress as well.[1293] Being thoroughly informed, nothing about the verbal report was news to the emperor.

After Protopopov's departure at midnight, the next matter to be discussed related to Rasputin's burial. Once Voyeikov was summoned, Alexandra Fyodorovna asked him where Rasputin should be buried. Voyeikov suggested that it was best that he be transported to Siberia and buried in his *"rodina"* (homeland), because that was what the family of the deceased wanted. Taneeva preferred somewhere in Tsarskoe Selo but argued the grave "will be defiled."[1294] As it transpired, Voyeikov did not know what the Rasputin family wanted regarding this matter. The empress, aware that Paraskovya Rasputina was en route from Pokrovskoye,[1295] caught Voyeikov lying in her presence. Her demeanor changed towards Voyeikov. Spiridovich noted that Voyeikov failed to be sympathetic about the stress the empress was experiencing at this time. For the empress, it was impossible to imagine that someone would attempt to carry out an unspeakable act against Rasputin's gravesite. Voyeikov likewise failed to recognize her "mysticism" and, like many others, wanted to believe that "with his physical disappearance Rasputin's influence would cease." Spiridovich recognized that Voyeikov's next remarks began to show the empress his true feelings that evening, after he raised issues not related to his responsibilities. Voyeikov criticized Protopopov's conduct, saying that he appeared *"boastful"* after his police had effectively performed their duties. Not surprisingly, all that General Voyeikov was able to recall about this difficult evening was that the emperor never showed his feelings, and that he attempted to persuade Nikolai II not to attend the funeral.[1296]

Before Protopopov's audience with the emperor, Voyeikov visited him and told him about his annoyance that the corpse was found in such a short period.[1297] He was also annoyed that Protopopov "had not feared the high status of the culprits despite the passivity of the General-Procurator, the Justice Minister." What this episode exposed was that, even in death, Rasputin's name was still drawing reactions among government officials. This tragedy had created a very depressing atmosphere in the palace. Whenever a person closely acquainted with Nikolai II passed away, he faithfully recorded the date of their death in his diary, but for some reason Rasputin's death was not noted down.

Before retiring for the night, in the early morning hours Their Majesties decided they would bury Rasputin in Tsarskoe Selo, close to the palace grounds as soon as the autopsy was completed and after the burial site was prepared to receive the coffin. At the end of the day, Nikolai II's eldest daughter, Grand Duchess Olga Nikolayevna, wrote these extraordinary words into her diary:

> "*Conclusively found out that father Grigorii was murdered, must have been by Dmitri, and* [he] *was thrown from the bridge at Krestovskii. He was found in the water. It is so difficult to write, not worth it.*"[1298]

It is useful to mention here that Radzinsky made a number of assumptions (repeated by Oleg Shishkin[1299]) in order to explain why Olga Nikolayevna mentioned Dmitri in her diary entry about the murder. Radzinsky assumed that Rasputin had ruined her chance of being betrothed to Dmitri and thus in revenge Dmitri had "come with a revolver" to the Yusupovskii Palace.[1300] Radzinsky ignored the fact that officers always carried their military-issued pistols as part of their uniform. More pointedly, there is no evidence to support the idea of betrothal between those two persons was ever contemplated. Though one *New York Times* article, dated 8 September 1912, reported about the 'possibility' of an engagement, that event was never noted in Nikolai II's diary. It is impossible to figure out why Olga blamed Dmitri.

Tuesday 20 December 1916

Ministerial Dismissals

This day proved very difficult. The emperor was alert to the fact that Makarov was involved in hindering the investigation, allowing it to languish "at a tortoise pace"[1301] and the reason for doing so. Zavadsky saw that Makarov's problem stemmed from his inability to make firm decisions. It was on Stürmer's recommendation[1302] that Makarov had become the new Minister of Justice in July 1916.[1303] In this case, Makarov had shown favor towards the perpetrators rather than taking a neutral stance. It was indefensible that he allowed Yusupov to leave Petrograd before the emperor's return. Nikolai II had no alternative except to sign an *Ukaz* seeking Makarov's instant dismissal on 20 December.[1304] The next day, the *Ukaz* was published in the newspapers.[1305] Makarov's involvement in the conspiracy and expression of regret about the results of the blood assay only came to light recently.

Senator Nikolai Dobrovolskii recommended earlier by Ivan Sheglovitov,[1306] was received by the emperor at four o'clock in the afternoon in relation to his appointment as Makarov's replacement. This administrative change was announced by means of another *Ukaz*, published in *Russkoye Slovo* simultaneously with the first *Ukaz*. This notice also mentioned Dobrovolskii's brief résumé. Two hours later, at six o'clock,[1307] Prime Minister Alexander Trepov arrived for his meeting with the emperor. He was dismissed, not so much because he attempted to "buy Rasputin" (after replacing Stürmer on 9 November[1308]), but because after "Rasputin's murder he finally compromised himself in the Emperor's eyes."[1309] Senator Sheglovitov accepted the sudden vacancy and became the president of the Council of Ministers. [He was among the first group of government officials arrested on 27 February, after which time he would be executed by the Bolsheviks in 1918.[1310]]

Nikolai II quietly spent what was left of the evening with his family.[1311] Only several hours remained before the imperial family would secretly pay their final respects to Grigorii Rasputin.

Family Hindrances Continue

Dmitri's father, Grand Duke Pavel Alexandrovich, was received by the emperor at eleven o'clock at night. The grand duke wanted to know what right Alexandra Fyodorovna had to act in the way they all believed she had, seeking Dmitri's house arrest. The emperor gladly obliged Pavel's request with a copy of the telegram he sent to Alexandra on the following morning, offering proof that they were all mistaken. The text of the telegram said:

> "*I cannot change the house arrest until the investigation has been completed. I pray to God that Dmitri will walk away clean from this event which lured him.*"[1312]

For Nikolai II, it became transparent that his relatives had readily accepted all the malicious gossip and preferred to take comfort in their own lies rather than seek out the truth. The brutal murder of a simple Russian man of the earth who always demonstrated his genuine loyalty to his monarch and to his country had caused a deep political chasm among the elite of Imperial Russia.

Soon after the war commenced, Rasputin sent this telegram to Nikolai II. The powerful words and imagery they communicate are worth mentioning.

> *"Kind friend,*
>
> *Once again I say: a thunder cloud is above Russia, pity, there is much grief, darkness and no glimmer of hope; tears now a sea and there are no measures, and blood? What can I say? There are no words ... horror. I know, they all want war from you, and truly, not knowing, it's for the sake of destruction. God's punishment is heavy ... You are tsar, father of the people, do not allow the senseless to celebrate and destroy oneself and the people. Think, that everything is different ... everything is drowning in much blood, destruction without end, what sadness.*
>
> *Grigorii"*[1313]

Chapter Seven Photos

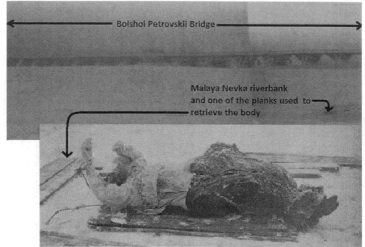

POLICE PHOTOGRAPHS No. 5 and 6. CRIME SCENE TWO. The relationship between the Bolshoi Petrovskii Bridge and the location where the body was retrieved, which is lying on a wooden plank by the Malaya Nevka riverbank. Rope binds the beaver coat to the corpse and the hands were tied with twine that snapped after retrieval, 19 December 1916.

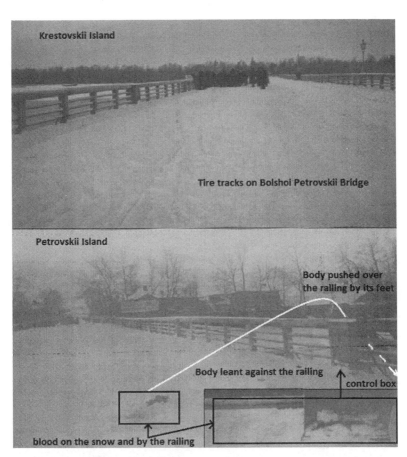

POLICE PHOTOGRAPHS No. 7, 8 and 9: Gendarmes, police
and government officials standing by the 4th bridge span. Frozen
tire tracks veer from the center of the bridge towards the 4th
bridge span on the left side (when looking towards Krestovskii
Island). Blood spatter (boxed) appears at two sites on the bridge
where the body leant against the railing before it was held by
the legs then pushed over the railing, 19 December 1916.

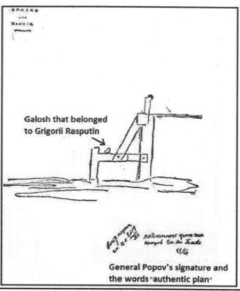

Galosh that belonged to Grigorii Rasputin

General Popov's signature and the words "authentic plan"

КРЕСТОВСКІЙ ОСТРОВЪ.

МАЛАЯ   НЕВКА.

ПЕТРОВСКІЙ ОСТРОВЪ.

✚ Мѣсто, гдѣ найденъ трупъ.	Location where the corpse was found.
Дворецъ кн. Бѣлосельскихъ к.	Prince Beloselskii's Palace.
Убѣжище сцен. дѣятелей.	Retreat for honored artists.
Старый Петровскій дворецъ.	Old Petrovskii Palace.

DOCUMENT No. 5: Criminal police agent Mikhailov drew the location of the brown galosh that was found on the bridge support. It was identified as authentic by General Popov on 19 December.

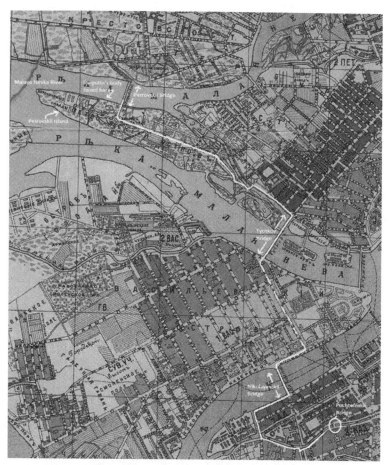

MAP 1: The route taken from the Yusupovskii Palace, in the police district "3 KAZ" (Kazanskii Number 3) to the Bolshoi Petrovskii Bridge that spans across two islands.

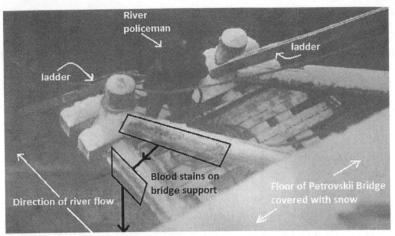

POLICE PHOTOGRAPH No. 10: The bridge pylon is
covered with blood and dislodged snow, indicated by the
two boxed inserts. A river policeman is standing on the
horizontal support next to one ladder, 19 December 1917.

PHOTO 22: PETROGRAD. The Chesmenskii military Almshouse, 1914.

Вторникъ, 20 декабря 1916 г. № 350

Конецъ Григорія Распутина.

Сегодня, 19-го декабря, утромъ, около Петровскаго моста
найденъ прибятымъ къ берегу трупъ Григорія Распутина. След-
ствіе производится судебными властями.

DOCUMENT No. 7: Den' dated Tuesday 20 December 1916
reported: "Today 19th December, Grigorii Rasputin's corpse
had been found near the Petrovskii Bridge this morning.
Investigations are being conducted by the court authorities."

CHAPTER EIGHT

The Autopsy Conducted on Rasputin's body and the Forensic Evaluation

Most biographers omit indepth discussion about the injuries that Rasputin's body sustained. Several assure readers that Rasputin was alive when he was thrown into the water and that his frozen right hand was poised as if he was about to offer his blessing at the moment of his death.[1314,1315,1316] This myth was advanced with the suggestion the empress did not want an autopsy to be carried out because it prevented the church deliberating about his sainthood. In 2006, French journalist Alain Deceaux[1317] wrote about enigmas around the world. In one sketch, he spread the mythmaking, saying that after Rasputin was raised from the ice, "his lungs were filled with water ... this indicates that Rasputin died by drowning." Shamefully, such myths disregard the forensic evidence that was published in Russia in 1917.

Preliminary Preparation

Given that it took two hours before a doctor arrived at the second crime scene, "during that time the corpse froze completely,"[1318] it needed time to thaw sufficiently before an autopsy could take place. The next day, Tuesday, at around 9 p.m., the arms of the deceased could be lowered;[1319] therefore, Professor Kosorotov was immediately notified that he was to conduct the autopsy procedure.

After the remains were identified on Monday 19 December, Sereda sent a letter to Professor Kosorotov instructing him to prepare for a special secret forensic examination on a corpse that would be conducted on 21 December.[1320] During the next day, Tuesday, Kosorotov arranged that his instruments and fresh solutions would be sent from the Imperial Military Medical Academy where he worked to the Chesmenskii Almshouse.[1321] At 7 p.m., Kosorotov received a telephone call telling him the autopsy had to be performed without further delay. Zavadsky and Sereda collected Kosorotov in their own vehicle from the function he was attending. It was not until ten o'clock when Professor Kosorotov

(Photo 23) was able to begin the autopsy. The purpose of that procedure was to ascertain Rasputin's cause of death. To maintain secrecy,[1322] the autopsy could not be deferred until daytime. The dissection took roughly four hours, ending early on Wednesday morning, 21 December. To help with the thawing process, the room in which the autopsy would be conducted had to be heated to 20°Ré or 25C/77F. [The Réaumur scale was widely used in Europe at the time.]

The Credentials, the Professor of Forensic Medicine

Kosorotov completed his studies at the Medical-Surgical Academy in 1879. Within eight years, in 1887, he was appointed assistant to the St. Petersburg Military Clinic Hospital. During that period, he proved to be a prolific author, editing the Russian Medical Journal, and in 1900, published "*Fundamental guide for compiling forensic-medical reports for the post-mortems*" and followed that work with his textbook "Toxicology" in 1911. In 1898, he became chaired professor of Forensic Medicine and toxicology at the St. Petersburg Imperial Military Medical Academy, then the chief dissector. From the beginning of the twentieth century, Kosorotov was recognized as one of the leading forensic experts in Russia. During the war, Kosorotov lectured at both at Petrograd University and at the Alexandrovskii Military Medical Academy. In 1914, he published the "Manual of Forensic Medicine" and regularly instructed gendarme officers from the criminal department.[1323] In recognition for his academic accomplishments, he held the civil rank of State Councillor.

The Published Conclusions of the Forensic Expert Professor Kosorotov

After the Provisional Government came to power on 3 March 1917, Professor Kosorotov granted his time to the journalist Kobil-Bobil from *Russkaya Volya* (*Russian Will*).[1324] The text of that article was reproduced into his book, titled *Vsya pravda o Rasputine* (*The Whole Truth About Rasputin*). In the second article, Kosorotov shared his personal impressions concerning the autopsy on Rasputin's corpse. His official report to the procurator is yet to be found, so these two publications are the only records that are available today. Kosorotov explained the nature of Rasputin's injuries and offers his conclusions. The overall impression gained from his account is that Kosorotov may not have known prior to this day about the identity of the deceased.

This first-time translation of the text describes the specifics that Professor Kosorotov recalled three months after he conducted the autopsy. Several preceding sentences in the published article described unrelated events and hence have been omitted. Due to the importance of what was described, the sentences are separated for ease of reading.

> *"By extraordinary decree, the autopsy was performed during this night and continued for about four hours. During the autopsy numerous extensive injuries were found, many of which were caused posthumously.*

> *The entire right side of the head was smashed and flattened following injury to the corpse at the time of falling from the bridge.*

> *Death was consistent with considerable hemorrhaging owing to a firearm wound into the abdomen. The shot was produced, based on my conclusion, almost pointblank, from left to right, through the stomach and liver with shattering of the latter in the right half. Bleeding was extensively profuse.*

> *On the corpse there was also a firearm wound into the back, in the vertebral region, with shattering of the right kidney, and another wound point-blank, into the forehead,* (possibly [when] *dying or dead*).

> *The chest organs were intact and were examined superficially; but there was no evidence of death by drowning. The lungs were not inflated, and in the respiratory tract there was no fluid, nor foamy liquid. Rasputin was thrown into the water when already dead.*

> [I] *shall remind* [you] *by the way; that the examination of the corpse was under very inconvenient surroundings, under kerosene lamps, in fact for inspecting the chest cavity and abdomen it was necessary to bring the lamp*

into the actual cavity."

Professor Kosorotov's Personal Impressions

"It has often been necessary for me ... to conduct various difficult and unpleasant autopsies. I – am a person with strong nerves and as can be referred to, I have seen sights. But seldom did I have to experience such unpleasant moments, such as during this terrifying night. The corpse gave me an unpleasant impression. It was the goatish facial expression, this enormous wound on the head was severe even for my experienced eye. In particular, what produced an impression on me was the haste whilst proceeding with the autopsy. ... About this I was also asked by the investigatory authorities, but I found it vital to conduct my work methodically and with honesty.

In my opinion, Gr. Rasputin was killed by a gunshot from a revolver. One bullet was extracted, the other gunshots were made at close range and the bullets passed straight through, thus it is impossible to give a conclusion as to how many persons were shooting.

Gr. Rasputin was of sturdy build: he was only 45 years old, and I recall, how during our conversation among us, sharing impressions, saying that he would have lived as much again. Without a doubt that Rasputin has been killed in a state of intoxication: the corpse gave off cognac. His brain hemispheres were of normal volume and did not bear any traces of pathological changes." [1325]

Sereda attended both crime scenes, which would have helped him to advance an understanding as to what the circumstances were to bring about the victim's death. Since the death was not due to natural causes, Sereda responded by viewing the body within the surroundings where it was found. The icy conditions and the wooden bridge from which the body was thrown helped to explain not only the external condition of the corpse but also explain some of the mechanical injuries, which were seen later by Kosorotov. The American Chief Medical Examiner, Vincent DiMaio, stresses the importance of a forensic investigator being present at crime scenes. That person assists with the interpretation of particular findings at the autopsy.[1326] This was Sereda's role on behalf of the chief procurator.

Procurator Zavadsky's Summary of the Autopsy Results

▶ Rasputin received fatal wounds affecting the stomach, liver, kidney and the brain.

▶ After the first wounding, Rasputin could not have survived more than 20 minutes.*

▶ All three gunshot wounds were inflicted when Rasputin was alive.[1327]

▶ *Although Professor Kosorotov did not mention the 20-minute time frame, there is no reason to doubt that fact. A 1917 report stating that "death would have resulted within 10-20 minutes," after the first gunshot was discharged, revealed these details:

▶ The body was thrown into the water after the victim's death.

▶ One gunshot wound went through the stomach and liver. It was fatal.

▶ A second gunshot wound on the right side of the waist. Also fatal.

▶ The bullet to the head went through the brain. Wounding occurred when the victim was lying down. Fatal.

▶ Rasputin was not wearing his coat at the time he was shot.

▶ Impossible to determine whether one kind of revolver was used.

▶ All the other injuries were post-mortem.[1328]

Grand Duke Andrei Vladimirovich's Diary

Whilst "taking the cure" in Kislovodsk (northern Caucasian region), Sereda spoke with Grand Duke Andrei Vladimirovich on 15 February 1917.[1329] Having attended the Petrograd Military Juridical Academy,[1330] Andrei Vladimirovich maintained a professional interest in legal affairs. The opportunity to speak with Sereda about his most recent case in Petrograd gave Andrei Vladimirovich the unique opportunity to learn about details that were never made public (provided here for the first time). Cast to memory, there is no reason to distrust the details in his diary, which appear nowhere else:

▶ The **first bullet** entered the left side below the heart and exited from the right side [through and through].

▶ The **second bullet** entered the back and lodged into the vertebral column.*

▶ The **third bullet** went through the bone in the forehead and passed through the brain.

▶ *A jacketed bullet was retrieved from the spine. It was deformed, making it impossible to conclude the type of weapon used.

A Modern Forensic Review

The police photographs that are held at the St. Petersburg Political History Museum (located at Kamenoostrovskii *Prospekt,* 2) came from an unknown source. The folder appears homemade and consists of several thick green fading cardboard pages holding twenty photographs. The album did not have signatures or other inclusions identifying it had originated from a specific government entity. Someone, using black ink, penned basic descriptions below each photograph.

In 1993, a group of Moscow forensic experts[1331] headed by the Chief of the Bureau of Forensic Medicine in Moscow and academic Professor Vladimir Zharov[1332] and his team examined Kosorotov's report and the twenty police photographs. The team published the following:

▶ The wound (from BULLET ONE) to the abdomen was inflicted **at close range**.

▶ The second gunshot could have been fired from either a pistol or from a revolver. The **distance from which it was fired cannot be estimated**. No gunshot residue.

▶ The THIRD BULLET into the forehead showed gunshot residue surrounding the wound. There is a visible standsmark* indicating the bullet was **fired at point blank range**.

   • The THIRD BULLET (into the forehead) was the last one fired into the body. Otherwise, the shooting sequence is impossible to determine.

▶ The mechanical (not gunshot) injuries to the head were caused by repeated blows by hard object(s). These injuries were not caused when the body hit the bridge pylon or against the ice (not posthumous). Use of a rubber truncheon** is not excluded.

▶ The facial bruising cannot be distinguished if it occurred before or after death.

▶ The injury on the back was caused by a sharp cutting weapon, possibly from the blade of a knife or razor blade. Unable to determine if this injury was inflicted before death or posthumously.

▶ After the gunshot wound (entered) into the ribcage, with damage to the stomach and liver, Rasputin could have could have engaged in purposeful, coordinated activity (walking, running and rendering resistance) during the next 5-15 minutes.

▶ Following the gunshot injury to the head, Rasputin's ability for purposeful co-ordination is doubtful.

▶ The gunshot wounds that were inflicted on

the body corresponded with what Professor Kosorotov described in 1917.

• The calibers and weapon types cannot be determined from the photographs. It is likely that the caliber of the [first] weapon was analogous to 6.35mm.***

CAUSE OF DEATH → HEAD WOUND with injury to the brain matter.

*A standsmark is the impression left by the muzzle of a gun in a contact shot when the muzzle of the gun is pressed against the victim's body.

Zharov was not given the photograph of the truncheon (Photo 20, Chapter Six**). I determine that it was not used, because there are no plaited impression marks on the body.

***The weapon that Dmitri handed to Yusupov was a Browning. [The Russian military at the time used 6.5mm bullets.[1333]]

Author's note: Although the conclusion provided by Professor Zharov's team differs from that given by Professor Kosorotov in 1917, it is fair to point out that today's approach has changed. This difference does not suggest that Kosorotov was incorrect. The first gunshot wound sustained by the body would have, in the long run, been fatal; even so, the gunshot to the forehead caused instant death.

The Impact of the Firearms Used to Kill Rasputin

The **First Entry Wound** (into the abdominal region) may have been caused by a revolver **fired at close range**.

The zone (or ring) of seared skin surrounding a bullet hole wound is seen when a handgun is discharged at near contact from a range of less than 10mm.[1334] (The band of blackened skin is wider than that seen in contact wounds.) The close distance and the appearance of the ENTRY WOUND agrees with the description given in Chapter Six that Yusupov most likely sat alongside Rasputin before firing his handgun. The searing pattern on the skin (POLICE PHOTOGRAPH No. 11) indicates that the weapon was pointed slightly to the left rather than straight ahead. When there is evidence of a "powder tattooing" around the entrance wound, the range would have been "intermediate range." This detail was described by Special Investigator Sereda, who also saw "sooting on the embroidered shirt"[1335] worn by the victim.

Most forensic experts today agree that the EXIT WOUND is typically larger than the ENTRY wound. This type of wounding causes the newly broken skin to split arbitrarily to form skin flaps that lie outwards from the wound site and are ragged in appearance. The relationship between the size of the wounds in POLICE PHOTOGRAPHS Nos. 11 and 12 is unknown. Rasputin was dressed when he was shot, which meant that he first bullet passed through clothing and soft tissue. The bullet would have remained intact after it exited the body. It is known that if the EXIT WOUND appears irregular, that effect is caused by multiple layers of tight clothing, or even the wearing of a belt.[1336] The caliber of a bullet cannot be determined from an entrance wound in the skin by measuring the diameter of the wound.[1337]

The **Second Entry Wound** (into the back) was **fired from some distance**.

A pathologist today would class such an injury as a "distance gunshot wound."[1338] POLICE PHOTOGRAPH No. 13 shows an irregular abrasion margin which indicates that BULLET No. 2 had impacted the skin at an angle. Owing to the impression left, Zharov did not discount the likelihood that the second gunshot wound was inflicted by a pistol. A 1915 model Savage pistol had a caliber of 7.65mm.[1339]

The size of the **Third Entry Wound** cannot be estimated from photographs because of parallax error (an optical phenomenon that affects angles relative to the observer). If a ruler was placed immediately above or below and at one side of the head wound and the photograph was taken directly above that wound, only then would we have been a better idea about the caliber (not the make) of the weapon that was used. POLICE PHOTOGRAPH No. 14 shows

a contact wound to the head. The muzzle of the gun was pressed against the skin at the time of discharge. [Given Kosorotov's precise language and the appearance of this entry wound, why did Furhmann and Smith both say "the final shot" was fired "at close range"?[1340]] The ENTRY WOUND has a muzzle imprint around it with stellar tearing that radiates out from the wound. A contact wound, such as the one seen on the forehead, if caused by a revolver, produces a specific muzzle imprint on the skin. The impression on the skin is round while that from a bullet discharged from a pistol has a tendency to be "rectangular or rhomboid."[1341]

If a weapon discharged a bullet from a considerable distance, it is impossible to distinguish which type of handgun was used. However, if a pistol was one of the weapons responsible, a cartridge casing, which is always expelled by the action of the firearm, should have been found. This vital detail was not pointed out by any investigator (suggesting all shots were fired inside the building).

Jacketed vs. Unjacketed Bullets

In 2005, British author Andrew Cook proposed that a British operative discharged his military-issued Webley weapon into Rasputin's head. These weapons used unjacketed bullets. In contrast, the Russian imperial forces used jacketed bullets as standard issue. The soft lead in jacketed bullets is surrounded by a second metal, usually copper, which allows the bullet to penetrate a target more easily. The Hague Convention of 1899 forbade the use of expanding, deformable bullets in wartime. Therefore, military bullets had metal jackets around the lead core. If an unjacketed bullet was used, the injury to the head would have been considerable, with extensive fragmentation of the bone[1342] and overlying skin. **POLICE PHOTOGRAPH No. 14** does not show widespread bone fragmentation; instead, the entry wound was well defined. Andrei Vladimirovich recorded in his diary that the retrieved bullet **was jacketed**. With full metal jacketed bullets entering bone, the entrance wound in the bone will be the same size as the diameter of the bullet.[1343]

In 2005, Professor Derrick Pounder of Dundee University, Scotland, was commissioned to provide an independent ballistics report to author Andrew Cook. Pounder concluded that the entry wound on the forehead "was about 6mm true diameter."[1344] This finding corresponded with Zharov's calculation (6.35mm). Therefore:

▶ How can a Webley firearm (British military issue), having a caliber of **11.56mm**, firing unjacketed bullets, **create a discrete, 6mm diameter wound?**

The forensic findings and police photographs do not support the premise that the gunshot to the head was caused by a Webley firearm.

Was Grigorii Rasputin Poisoned?

Yusupov and Purishkevich claimed that cyanide was ingested by Rasputin. Their story leads to the question as to why did the poison allegedly administered by Dr. Lazovert fail to act? To provide an answer, the nature of cyanide and its effect on the body needs to be understood. Potassium cyanide[1345] (chemical formula: KCN) has a perceptible, bitter almond odor, although not everyone can detect it. It is a highly corrosive, white crystalline substance that acts on the body by inhibiting respiration. It is toxic if inhaled, ingested, or comes into contact with the skin. In high concentrations, it will bring about a coma with convulsions, leading to cardiac arrest within minutes. It burns the esophagus and abdomen. Death follows in a matter of several minutes. If low dosage was applied, then the person who has ingested the substance will become weak, have a headache, become confused and will experience respiratory distress. The sufferer will progress towards unconsciousness and finally, they will go into cardiac arrest within the hour. The skin color changes perceptibly from pink to red.

▶ Rasputin did not experience any of these symptoms.

Had Lazavort handled cyanide, he would have been mindful of its toxicity. For protection, he would have required not only "rubber gloves" but a facial mask as well. Yusupov's claim that they watched Lazovert work[1346] is incredulous because of the lethalness of cyanide when it is exposed to the air, let alone its naked addition in food. [Matrena disclosed her father loathed sweet food.[1347]]

▶ Maklakov stressed that he never handed over cyanide to Yusupov.[1348]

When Grand Duke Andrei Vladimirovich spoke with Dmitri on the Saturday following the murder, Dmitri told him that Rasputin did not "drink poison,"[1349] though Nikolai Mikhailovich assumed "a solution of cyanide" failed to act.[1350] Even so, why did Rappaport (in 2014) endorse the myth that Rasputin was "plied ... with cream sprinkled with cyanide"[1351]?

▶ The autopsy indicated that **no food was consumed** and there was **no poison in the body**.

Synopsis of the Investigation

The following process was used in 1916, to determine the circumstances and cause of Rasputin's death:

▶ Interviewing eyewitnesses or persons previously known to the deceased.

▶ The investigation of two crime scenes:

- Firstly, in the courtyard contiguous with the Yusupovskii Palace on the morning of Saturday 17 December 1916.

  o Inspection and photographing the area of interest.

  o Taking a blood sample for analysis.

- Secondly, from noon Saturday until Monday 19 December 1916, on and in the vicinity of the Bolshoi Petrovskii Bridge.

  o Inspection and taking photographs of evidence found on the bridge.

  o Taking of a blood sample for analysis.

  o Photographing the deceased at the uplift site (the *Malaya Nevka* River) on Monday 19 December.

▶ The medical examination of the body of the

deceased on 20/21 December 1916. (Report published 3 March 1917).

- Studying the ballistics evidence by observing all gunshot wounds.

- Distinguishing other injuries.

It is now necessary that Nikolai Mikhailovich states his closing remarks:

> "*Finally, Yusupov himself frenzied before the slain corpse and the final blows with a synthetic rubber plait over his previously helpless sacrifice. Why such malice, why such cynicism, such perverse feelings – over a suffering, dying sacrifice? ... If Rasputin was an animal [a dog], what does it say about the young Yusupov?*"[1352]

► **Had the truncheon (Photo 20) been used, the imprint of the distinctive pattern would have been visible on Rasputin's skin.** There is no such impact injury to be found in the police photographs.

Professor Kosorotov never stated that there were other external impact injuries EXCEPT those sustained by the body after it hit the bridge. The pathologist found that the right cheek was shattered when the body was thrown from the bridge. This finding could be explained by a closed *contrecoup* injury sustained by the brain (an observation that subsequent examinations could not make). If that truncheon had been used, traces of blood would never have been efficiently removed from it. The truncheon that was returned to the owner appears spotless. Since Kosorotov said that all the mechanical injuries that he saw on the head were those caused when the body hit a stationary object posthumously, his professional opinion must be accepted.

Additional Comments

When Sereda arrived at the second crime scene to examine the corpse, it was already lying on the ice surface. He was told by the assistant of the head of the River Police that Rasputin, "at the same time when he was dying he formed his hand in blessing."[1353] The suggestion that Rasputin's right hand was held in benediction was first reported in *Rech*[1354] under the heading *Novii Muchenik* (*New Martyr*). It followed after a brochure that said "this debauched holy person ... should be revered as a martyr." Even so, Matrena was one of few people who saw the retrieved remains. This is her description (in 1934) as to what she saw in December 1916:

> "... *completely frozen, wrapped in his fur lined coat and his ankles bound in rope. ...The face was almost unrecognizable, clots of dark blood had coagulated in the beard and hair, one eye was almost out of its socket, and on the wrists were deep marks left by the bonds that my father had succeeded in breaking in his death-struggle, probably when, reanimated by the sudden shock of the freezing water, he made a supreme effort to escape from his prison of ice. His hand still lay beneath his chin, contracted in a last sign of the cross.*"[1355]

Was Matrena truthful? The first image in **Photo 24** shows both arms outsretched and the right and left hands were clenched. Keeping in mind that Kosorotov said that Rasputin was "already dead" when his body entered the water, the police photograph negates Matrena's memory. By way of comparison, the second image shows Rasputin's right hand in benediction when he was alive.

The other issue raised by Matrena concerned the eye, which was supposedly "almost out of its socket." **POLICE PHOTOGRAPHS No. 14** and **15** show that the right eye had sustained substantial trauma with evidence of significant hemorrhaging. Neither photograph shows ocular extrusion, a circumstance where the eyeball had partially come out from its orbit (bone structure).

Yusupov's description of the body is exceptionally informative and addresses Rasputin's violent death:

> "*The investigative authorities saw the disfigured corpse of Rasputin; the head of the deceased was damaged in a few places and the hair on it was torn off in clumps here and there ... the beard had frozen into the clothes; coagulated clots of blood were visible on the face and chest, one eye was black. ...The arms and legs*

were tightly bound with rope; in fact the right hand of the deceased was clenched hard."[1356]

Akayemov (in 1917) noted that one of those attending the scene said, "You will see someone will begin to say that he appeared to have died with hand in blessing."[1357] It is lamentable that Cook accepted the myth about the right eye,[1358] while others believe Rasputin attempted to cross himself moments before dying.

Towards the Final Journey

At the conclusion of the autopsy procedure, a police physician who assisted Kosorotov with the autopsy embalmed the body before it was sewn up. Protopopov supplied Laptinskayu with a chauffeured vehicle to bring her to the Chesmenskii chapel.[1359] Akulina Laptinskaya washed and dressed the body, using a silk shirt and black trousers (**POLICE PHOTOGRAPH No. 16**) that the Rasputin girls brought with them,[1360 1361] while Taneeva provided a shroud for the corpse.[1362, 1363] The only other outsiders permitted inside the chapel were Maria Golovina and Simanovich, who was accompanied by Bishop Isidor. The cleric chanted prayers for the soul of the deceased.[1364] The body was placed into a zinc coffin,[1365] and at four o'clock in the morning, the coffin (attended by Laptinskaya) was conveyed to the Fyodorovskii Cathedral[1366] in Tsarskoe Selo to await burial. Two newspapers reported the remains would be transported to Siberia,[1367] before the burial in the family's *rodina* (homeland).[1368]

After five intense days, Sereda's job was over. With all the secrecy surrounding this case, he was not told where the corpse would be taken after the autopsy concluded.[1369]

Chapter Eight Photos

PHOTO 23: Professor Dmitri Kosorotov, pre-1917.

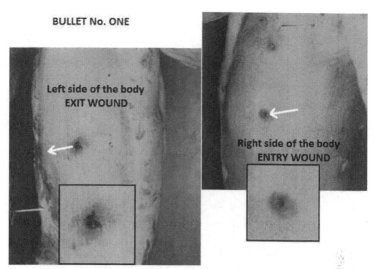

BULLET No. ONE

Left side of the body
EXIT WOUND

Right side of the body
ENTRY WOUND

POLICE PHOTOGRAPH No. 11. (Left) The ENTRY wound on the left side of the body. POLICE PHOTOGRAPH No. 12. (Right) The EXIT wound on the with radial splits in the skin on the right. The white arrows show the probable slightly downward trajectory of the discharged bullet.

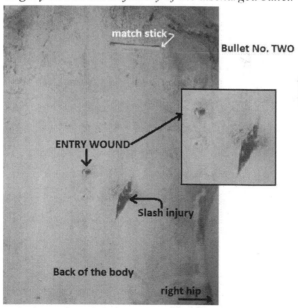

match stick

Bullet No. TWO

ENTRY WOUND

Slash injury

Back of the body

right hip

POLICE PHOTOGRAPH No. 13: BULLET TWO was fired near the lower part of the back at close range. The ENTRY wound lies over the vertebral column. A slash injury is evident to the right of the spine.

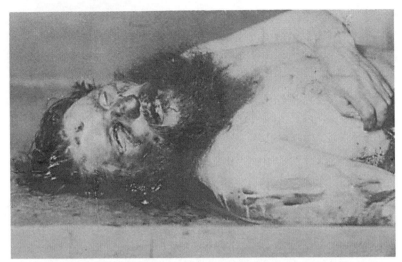

POLICE PHOTOGRAPH No. 14: BULLET No. 3 was fired
at point blank range. The entry wound is located midline
on the forehead. The right side of the head shows multiple
injuries. The undershirt is torn along the right arm.

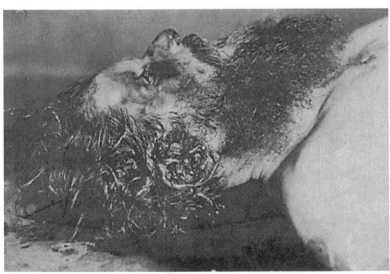

POLICE PHOTOGRAPH No. 15: The head has been
rotated to its normal position. Multiple injuries are
visible on the right side of the face and ear.

PHOTOGRAPH No. 24: The fingers of the right hand were clenched rather than held together as if in blessing. The second image shows how Rasputin placed held his fingers in benediction in life.

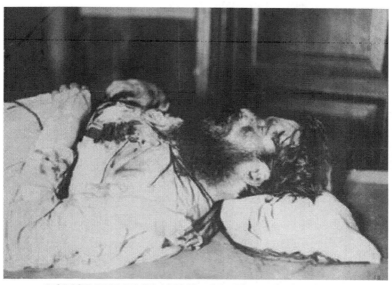

POLICE PHOTOGRAPH No. 16: This is the last known photograph of Grigorii Rasputin. There is a package and a small spray of flowers on his chest.

CHAPTER NINE
The *Muzhik* is Buried but the
Aftermath Turns Fiery

Towards The Final Journey

On Saturday 5 November 1916, while the emperor was at Stavka military headquarters with Alexei, the empress invited Grigorii Rasputin to attend a special ceremony. The event in Alexandrovskii Park (Tsarskoe Selo) was celebrated by Bishops Isidor, Melkhisedek and Alexander (Photo 24). During that morning, they, with the four grand duchesses,[1370] witnessed the laying of the foundation stone on the site of Taneeva's proposed church[1371] in the name of St. Serafim Sarovskii.[1372] This consecrated site would be part of the new hospital complex for military invalids.[1373] [The church was never completed.]

Due to military censorship,[1374] most details about the Rasputin investigation were suppressed. After the February Revolution, *Russkaya Volya* (*Russian Will*) published a series of articles, using the title *Rasputiniada*. This term was used to discuss the influences that existed over individuals whom Rasputin knew, in particular the former empress and Taneeva. Brief details about Rasputin's funeral were also published after the emperor's abdication on 3 March 1917. Though a few attendees wrote about the funeral, neither Alexandra Fyodorovna nor Taneeva recorded their impressions about that occasion.

Before the embalmed remains were conveyed to Tsarskoe Selo, Matrena and Varvara placed a small icon on the chest[1375] of the corpse, which depicted the *Znameniye Bogomater* (The Sign [or apparition] of Mother of God) from which the faithful sought intercession.[1376] The significance of this icon (Photo 24) related to its spirituality. Its image was venerated throughout Siberia,[1377] more so because it was considered to be one of the oldest 'miracle working' icons in Russia. Penciled on the reverse side were the names (lacking patronymics) Alexandra, Olga, Tatiana, Maria and Anastasia. In the right corner, the name Anna was also inscribed.[1378] Dated 11 December 1916, this icon happened to be the gift that Taneeva presented to Rasputin on behalf of the empress as a reminder of their visit to Velikii Novgorod, on the very last night that she saw him alive. Excluding a petite posy of fresh flowers and a pillow to rest the head, no other items were placed inside the coffin before it was sealed.

The Secret *Panihida* (Memorial Service)

During the pre-dawn hours of Wednesday morning, 21 December, a hole was being dug close to where the foundation stone of Taneeva's proposed new church had been laid in November. Grand Duchess Olga Nikolayevna noted in her diary that it was located "to the left of the proposed church."[1379] Under Colonel Vladimir Maltsev's command, soldiers of the Aerial Artillery Regiment prepared the gravesite. Maltsev told his men that the hole was to hold "refuse."[1380] One guard said it was to be "a store for forest material."[1381] Despite the mystery, Maltsev's men grasped that this was where Rasputin was to be buried, because of the recognizable dimensions of the hole being dug. Once completed, the site was guarded to ensure that the imperial family was able to gain safe passage to the gravesite at the designated hour.

There is conflicting information as to where the vehicles transporting the coffin had proceeded to after leaving the Chesmenskii Almshouse sometime after four in the morning. Two sources claimed that the coffin was brought inside the Fyodorovskii Cathedral[1382][1383] because it offered a secure place until the nearby gravesite was ready to receive it. One newspaper alleged that the car with four police, the driver and Laptinskaya arrived at their destination by the roadside,[1384] while the gravesite nearby was still being dug. It was reported that there was a slight problem when it was time to lower the coffin into the ground. Not enough ropes had been brought to allow the coffin to descend properly. It had to be lowered carefully until it hit "the frozen ground." Laptinskaya apparently remained at the gravesite throughout the night. After the grave diggers finished their task, they were given the huge sum of one hundred rubles for their effort and their silence.[1385]

Just before midnight (Tuesday 20 December), the empress contacted Father Alexander, leaving instructions that he would officiate at Rasputin's funeral. He telephoned Colonel Dmitri

Loman, the *ktitor* (fundraiser) of the church, to get hold of a small number of church items that included a gold-plated incense burner (*kadilo*) and candles that would be needed for the service.[1386] Father Alexander and Loman were the first to arrive at the gravesite at 8.30 in the morning. Taneeva and her maid[1387] followed soon after, with Lili Dehn arriving alone. Loman was not invited to stand at the gravesite service but was able to watch from a distance and hear Deacon Ishenko chant prayers in the absence of a choir.[1388]

In 1917, Akim Zhuk, the *feldsher* (doctor) from Taneeva's infirmary, provided a few sketches concerning the conversations he heard around the gravesite. Just before the imperial family appeared, Laptinskaya described how Rasputin had been dressed and laid out inside the coffin. Taneeva apparently asked if the lid of the coffin could be raised (customary at orthodox funerals), but Laptinskaya rejected the suggestion. As soon as the imperial party arrived,[1389] everybody became silent. Some reports claimed that Nikolai II, along with Protopopov, Voyeikov and Count Frederiks (the last three persons did not attend), carried the coffin to the gravesite.[1390] This myth is accepted by some writers to this day.[1391] [1392]

Nikolai II's diary[1393] gives the most accurate account about the funeral. At nine o'clock on a grey and frosty morning, a brief *Panihida* (Memorial service) was solemnized by Archbishop Alexander Vasiliev. The coffin was already lowered into the ground by the time the imperial family appeared. In order to preserve the secrecy of this event, few mourners were invited to attend. According to *Russkaya Volya*,[1394] the coffin was smothered with fresh-cut flowers. The list of attendees, excluding the Palace *Okhrana*, is provided below. Even among this small group, few were true mourners. It was said that Nikolai II threw a single rose into the grave at the conclusion of the service.[1395] Alexandra Fyodorovna clutched white flowers throughout the service and at the end of the service, handed one, stem first, to her daughters and then to the other women.[1396] Silently, one by one, the mourners tossed their single flower onto the coffin along with a small morsel of frozen earth. The emperor bowed respectfully then silently, not showing emotion, turned around and walked towards his waiting vehicle.[1397] Rasputin's remains were committed to the earth. All the mourners left the gravesite before it was painstakingly covered by frozen earth. The imagery that Alexandra Fyodorovna *"fell to her knees and pressed her ear over the over the freshly covered grave hearing his voice"* was a preposterous supposition for Gerasimov to have made.[1398] The imperial family returned to the palace[1399] straight after the burial service, which lasted fifteen minutes.[1400] Despite its simplicity, it seemed most fitting.

List of persons who attended Grigorii Rasputin's burial on 21 December 1916

1. Emperor Nikolai II
2. Empress Alexandra Fyodorovna
3. Grand Duchess Olga Nikolayevna
4. Grand Duchess Tatiana Nikolayevna
5. Grand Duchess Maria Nikolayevna
6. Grand Duchess Anastasia Nikolayevna
7. Anna Taneeva
8. Akilina Laptinskaya
9. Yuliya Dehn
10. Alexander Yakovlev (Tsarskoe Selo architect)
11. Father Alexander Vasiliev (imperial family confessor and resident priest at the Fyodorovskii Cathedral)
12. The monk Dosifey (Razumov, from Taneeva's infirmary)
13. Ishenko (psalm chorister and assistant deacon at the Fyodorovskii Cathedral)
14. Akim Zhuk (*feldsher* from Taneeva's infirmary)
15. Fedosiya Voinova (Taneeva's maid)
16. Lieutenant-Colonel Dmitri Loman (*ktitor* at the Fyodorovskii Cathedral and representative of the empress's medical train)
17. Colonel Vladimir Maltsev (Commander of the Aerial Artillery Regiment stationed at Tsarskoe

Selo)[1401]

Grand Duchess Maria Nikolayevna wrote in her diary[1402] that her brother Alexei was bed-ridden with an abdominal complaint (worm infestation) and therefore remained at home. No one from the Rasputin family nor Bishop Isidor attended the burial. The reason as to why Matrena and Varvara failed to attend is unknown, though their mother, Praskovya, was still in transit to Petrograd. Praskovya's reaction to her husband's death was never documented. Matrena only revealed her "sorrow and anguish weighed heavily" upon her during the morning of her bereavement.[1403]

The little Dehn mentioned about the *Panihida* (that did not begin at eight o'clock in the morning)[1404] was mostly inaccurate, though she did recall that planks were laid out over the snow as a footpath. Dehn incorrectly said the oak coffin (it was zinc sheeting[1405]), adorned with the customary orthodox cross on its lid, was taken out of the police van in front of them. When the American journalist Rheta Childe Dorr interviewed Taneeva from the prison hospital in 1917,[1406] she pointed out that the coffin was already lowered into the ground before her arrival.[1407]

Matrena raised the issue about transporting her father's body to Pokrovskoye with Protopopov, but the request was denied.[1408] Laptinskaya likewise preferred the burial to take place in the Rasputin home village, but the empress intervened.[1409]

After the funeral service, the day progressed ordinarily. Grand Duchess Olga Nikolayevna and the empress went to their infirmary to tend to their nursing duties,[1410] while Grand Duchess Maria Nikolayevna was given a history lesson. Nikolai II went for a stroll on his property[1411] before receiving government ministers.[1412] Later in the day, Grand Duchess Maria Nikolayevna, with her mother, went to Taneeva's cottage, where they "saw Matrena, Varya and Akilina."[1413]

The Time For Quiet Contemplation Shall Be Brief

After the grave was filled with earth, Colonel Maltsev received orders (from Voyeikov) that his regiment must guard the road that led to the gravesite.[1414] This arrangement allowed the empress (at times with Laptinskaya and Taneeva) to visit the gravesite daily.

On 27 December, a *Panihida* (customarily marking the tenth day after death) was observed at the site. A second service was held on 2 January 1917 to recognize Taneeva's recovery, which she believed resulted after Rasputin's intercession.[1415]

Despite *Russkaya Volya*'s (*Russian Will*) account,[1416] none of the Rasputin family members were allowed to visit the gravesite. Matrena never spoke about this matter. Likewise, it is not known if young Alexei was given an opportunity to pay his final respects. Instead, the Rasputin girls were invited to Taneeva's cottage a few times after their father's burial.[1417] [1418] One such occasion happened on Christmas Day, where "the entire family of 'father' Grigorii: Paraskovya Fyodorovna, Mitya [Dmitri], Matrena and Varya were present."[1419] Grand Duchess Olga Nikolayevna saw the Rasputin daughters, for what would prove to be the final time, at Anna's place on 9 February 1917.[1420]

When Nikolai II left for Military Headquarters on 22 February 1917 at 2 p.m.,[1421] the empress continued to raise Rasputin's name in her correspondence. Her letters show that she had elevated Rasputin's status after his death, using capitalization when referring to "Him." This is what she wrote, on the same day her husband left Tsarskoe Selo:

> "*Our Friend in the other world is also praying for you – thus He is more close to us. Still wanting to hear His calming and reassuring voice!*"[1422]

Four days later, on Sunday 26 February 1917, Alexandra Fyodorovna's commitment regarding Rasputin's illusory beyond-the-grave power was clearly evident in these two sentences:

> "*I have brought this fragment of wood from His grave, where I stood on my knees. .... He died so as to save us.*"[1423]

Alexandra Fyodorovna had detached a small fragment from the temporary wooden cross (traditionally placed on a fresh gravesite). At the end of Alexandra's last letter to Nikolai II, dated 2 March 1917,[1424] the following was added after her signature:

> "*Wear His [Rasputin's] cross, even if uncomfortable, for my peace of mind.*"

The Imperial Veneration is Withdrawn

On 15 March, Matrena, aged eighteen, and her younger sister Varvara, aged sixteen, were arrested and sent to the Minister's Pavilion at the Tavricheskii Palace.[1425] Their arrest, described as an administrative error, was corrected within a few days, once it was recognized that both girls did not know anything.[1426] After one year, the capital was no longer the city to which her father had brought Matrena and her sister to receive an education.[1427] They left Petrograd by train on 29 March 1918,[1428] taking only what they were able to carry. At that time, they were living in an apartment on Kolomenskaya *Ulitsa*, 9,[1429] since Matrena had married (in October 1917). Matrena grabbed the notebooks that Dunya compiled for several years, describing Grigorii's life in Petrograd.[1430] Taneeva said that the family was needy after Grigorii's death,[1431] since all donations had evaporated. The arrests of the imperial family and Taneeva[1432] prevented them from arranging welfare to the family. *Russkaya Volya* discovered that money was given to the daughters.[1433] The Petrograd Jewish community donated 50,000 rubles to the daughters in appreciation for their father's former lobbying on their behalf.[1434]

The military guarded Rasputin's gravesite[1435] until the morning of 2 March 1917, after which the sentries were ordered to abandon it. Rasputin's gravesite was protected for less than three months.

The Russian Turning Point and the Seemingly Powerless Become Empowered

On 28 February, Pavel Milyukov claimed "there was no tsar in the capital, no Duma or a Council of ministers" and that "the disorder had taken on the appearance of a downright revolution."[1436] Thus, he thought it was timely to announce in the Duma, in front of a crowd composed mostly of workers and soldiers, that the Temporary Duma Committee had been created. People had spilled into the adjoining Ekaterininskii Hall and out into the grounds of the Tavricheskii Palace. Milyukov declared that the Duma Committee held exclusive authority and that it was vital that everyone submitted to it "and no other authority"[1437] and that this committee was headed by Rodzianko with Kerensky acting as its deputy.

Skillfully taking advantage of the broader masses' political naivety, he tempered his action by introducing the new political word 'Provisional,' which deliberately masked the treasonous character of this new arrangement. Milyukov conceded that he devised his "own line," even though it was incompatible with his party's platform. He later admitted that his primary goal was "to oust Nikolai II from the throne,"[1438] which meant that he and his cluster of conspirators had to first "take power into their hands,"[1439] even if it meant that Nikolai II had to be liquidated.[1440] Milyukov told the crowd that the Provisional Committee members from the State Duma were taking "measures" that were forced upon them due to "difficult circumstances of the internal collapse of the old government" to "restore state and public order" with the help of the army. Mikhail Rodzianko signed a Declaration that there was a change in power.[1441] This notice came days before Nikolai II was pressured into abdicating. Alexandra Fyodorovna, unaware of the gravity of the political situation, noted that "troops were positioned in the garden" of the palace.[1442] At around eight o'clock in the evening, the former Tsarskoselskii Garrison left the palace grounds, shooting their rifles into the air in the darkness (the streets were not lit) and shouting, while the *Marseillaise*, the symbolic anthem of western revolutionaries, could be heard in the distance.[1443]

During the following morning, on 1 March, the Petrograd Soviet resolved to stay apart from the Provisional Committee. To fortify their public façade, they printed and pasted leaflets on the streets and had them distributed among the soldiers (but not to officers[1444]) at the Front. The Soviet released its divisive *Prikaz* (Decree) No. 1. The *Prikaz* had two primary effects. It removed authority from officers and demoralized the army. Admiral Virena, like many hundred officers after him, was murdered at the Kronshtadt naval base.[1445] Rather than streaming towards a new unified government, a diarchy (or dual power) situation had evolved and continued until the Bolsheviks took power in October. After the crowd learnt about the more 'radical' commands in *Prikaz* No. 1, "a shot was fired" and Milyukov watched as the rebellious crowd "carried out a Duma officer from the *Okhrana* by his arms and legs ... guilty that he wore an [imperial] uniform."[1446] Nobody protected the hapless victim from his fate. That incident at the Tavricheskii

Palace became a tangible symbol of revolutionary triumph. Petrograd was in the hands of rebels and the wave of terror and disorder persisted into the night.

The Russian Eagle is Brought Down Off Its Perch

A number of key events took place on 1 March. The first was the appearance of a *Manifest*[1447] that was signed by Grand Dukes Mikhail Alexandrovich, Kirill Vladimirovich and Pavel Alexandrovich. In this document, three Romanov family members declared their wish that a "new State order should preside on the day the war ends" because "our former government is considered to be undesirable." They urged that a "constitutional order" must be offered to the Russian nation "without delay." To complete their treacherous affront against Nikolai II, a copy of the *Manifest* was sent to the Duma Committee, which Milyukov countersigned.

At 4.15 in the same afternoon, Grand Duke Kirill (wearing a red band) brought his regiment to the Duma and declared their allegiance.[1448] [1449] Ambassador Buchanan noted that Kirill was the first Romanov "to recognize the revolution and to hoist the red flag."[1450] Countess Kleinmichel said that it was believed that Kirill had acted on Buchanan's advice.[1451] On the following day, Dmitri's father, Pavel Alexandrovich, expressed "horror" that Mikhail might now become the regent, saying "this is prohibited and impossible," after which he proceeded to accuse Mikhail's wife of meddling "to preserve the throne."[1452] Rather than aligning behind Nikolai II, Kirill concurred with Pavel by claiming that he was "completely alone in shouldering all the responsibility before Niki (Nikolai II) and Russia, saving the situation, recognizing the new regime."[1453] One lawyer, Nikolai Karabchevsky, who happened to be a close colleague of Kerensky, viewed the grand dukes' collective inclination for the Provisional Government with cynicism.[1454] Undeniably it was an incongruous act on the part of the grand dukes, considering that the media began to pour dirt over the entire Romanov family in their effort to sway public opinion.

The second matter concerned the appearance of a joint Declaration, signed by Ambassadors Buchanan and Paléologue. They informed Rodzianko that "the governments of France and Britain are entering into official relations with the Temporary Executive

Committee of the State Duma, as the expression of the true will of the people and the sole lawful government of Russia."[1455] This Declaration could not be published until Nikolai II had been removed. Their statement demonstrates the betrayal by these two allies, not knowing what Nikolai II would carry out. The British had no sympathy for the Tsarist regime. This tribute was published four days later in *Birzheviye Vedomosti*, on 5 March.

The Provisional Committee, composed of former State Duma delegates, met to discuss Nikolai II's fate and whether the monarchy should endure as their form of government under somebody else. The unanimous position they reached held that the emperor must be forced to abdicate. Rodzianko contacted General Ruzskii at Stavka and stressed the urgency of carrying out that resolution.[1456] Without the military generals' collective input, the implementation of the Committee's scheme remained tenuous. To achieve their political objective, the imperial train was detained and stood isolated on a railway track outside of Pskov. This confinement prevented Nikolai II from transmitting or receiving communications. Everything had to pass through General Alexeev in Mogilev. Alexeev composed a petition and sent it to all the Front commanders. Two commanders refused to comply with the dispatches, which required a swift assenting response. Many telegrams arrived that afternoon, each expressing the same: they had lost confidence in the emperor's authority and keenly sought his removal as their commander in chief.[1457] Nikolasha was among those who consented to the line of attack Alexeev crafted. Separate to this episode, two committee members, Shulgin and Guchkov, left Petrograd in order to 'persuade' the emperor to abdicate.[1458] The emperor always believed that the *Gen-Shtab* (Generals' Headquarters) always stood behind him and therefore political revolt was unconceivable. Alexeev changed that point of view after he drew the emperor's attention to the bundle of telegrams in his hand, telling the sovereign that he must now consider abdicating and urging that "it would give peace and an acceptable outcome from this more than critical situation."[1459] Ruzskii entered the green salon in the imperial train, where the sovereign was sitting and showed Nikolai II another batch of telegrams seeking his removal.[1460] The realization that his commanders had indulged in political intrigue rather than deliberate solely over their military duties was a matter of utter treachery. There was no way out of this engineered impasse after it became clear that his commanders aligned behind their *Shtabs*-Commander, General Alexeev and the President of the Duma Mikhail Rodzianko.

Guchkov and Shulgin arrived in Pskov at 9.45 p.m. and were escorted away from the platform to the imperial train that was standing on a siding track. The emperor listened attentively, while Guchkov, not looking at the emperor, spoke about events in Petrograd.[1461] This two-man delegation was competing for supreme power.

By 2 March, as can be read in the minutes of their first meeting, the Provisional Government considered that it was the lawful authority of the nation..[1462] Neither Stavka nor the officers at Pskov knew about this.[1463] Initially, the Duma needed the sovereign to provide a regency role to his brother Mikhail Alexandrovich, but after taking in Guchkov's address hours earlier, Nikolai II had time to think. He rephrased his Abdication Manifesto, submitting the crown to his brother Mikhail Alexandrovich. Nikolai II passed the newly signed document to Guchkov saying, "Here is the text."[1464] [Spiridovich[1465] and Maklakov[1466] thought that had the emperor refused to abdicate, he would have been killed. Guchkov found military officers willing to accomplish that deed.[1467]] Guchkov and Shulgin promptly transmitted a telegram to Rodzianko explaining the new situation.[1468] As soon as Rodzianko received the telegram, he read it out at the member's meeting. A shrewd legalist, Milyukov understood what Nikolai II had done: he did not break his Coronation Oath. Should the opportunity arise, he could rescind his flawed manifesto.[1469]

Nikolai II did not hand over his son, as had been expected. In practical legal terms, the manifesto had far more reaching implications. Nikolai II responded to the usurpers' unlawful demand with his own improper response. Signed in pencil and not addressing anyone, it was a piece of paper, which had no legal force. Having in hand what they wanted, not one lawyer cared to question it. Nikolai II understood that the circle of betrayal had closed around him, writing these words in his diary:

"Кругом измена, и трусость, и обман"

"All around treachery and cowardice and betrayal."[1470]

Rodzianko announced to those present in the Duma that "Mikhail Alexandrovich's accession [to the throne] was not possible." According to Kerensky, no one demurred, everyone "instinctively realized – at this stage of the revolution a new tsar was unacceptable."[1471] Milyukov provided a different scenario, saying there was initial doubt as to what should be done and their basic concern was "how the grand duke would respond to his nomination."[1472] Rodzianko, Milyukov, Guchkov and Kerensky formed the influential group of Provisional Committee representatives who had the duty to dissuade Mikhail Alexandrovich. Shulgin later said, "If the … emperor had to abdicate, Mikhail could renounce the throne."[1473] Nikolai Johnson, Mikhail Alexandrovich's secretary, revealed that the grand duke had initially accepted his role and was thinking about an appropriate response to the Duma delegation, which he was expecting to receive.[1474] So much so, a Thanksgiving liturgy was held in the Pskov Cathedral for the new Russian emperor, which was attended by Maria Pavlovna (the younger). Prayers were offered "for the prolongation of the days of the new tsar."[1475]

Given the wrath embedded in Milyukov's words on 2 March ("As for the old autocratic regime which during two years of war, was unable to bring final victory to Russia – let it be buried in oblivion."[1476]), it is impossible to accept that one day later, Mikhail Alexandrovich's renunciation was premised on the belief that he *might* be asked and offered the throne by popular consensus via a future Constituent Assembly.[1477] Kerensky, exposing his pro-republic position, told Mikhail Alexandrovich "assuming the throne you will not save Russia. Rather the opposite. I know the mood of the masses."[1478] Likewise, guided by Rodzianko's ealier speech (**Chapter Four**), I do not accept the refusal was predicated on the uncrowned emperor's future security.[1479] In fact, Guchkov later revealed that "outside of Petrograd there was ample possibility of gathering the military force required for the protection of the grand duke,"[1480] though Milyukov believed it was risky for Mikhail to face the public right now in Petrograd. The real concern involved the prospect that Mikhail would sign a peace treaty with Germany.[1481] In the end, the "final decision was made in favor of the opinion defended by the president of the State Duma."[1482] No one told Mikhail about the committee's prior approval of the Soviet Executive resolution, which sought Mikhail's "actual arrest"[1483] if his decision was adverse for them.

Mikhail Alexandrovich agreed to support the new regime. Months before, Kerensky revealed his hand in the Duma, saying "the only way to save the nation was to create a new authority,"[1484] not the same one with a new identity. Accordingly, for Kerensky, Rodzianko, Milyukov and Guchkov, their mission in Prince Putyatin's apartment on *Millionnaya Ulitsa,* 12 where Mikhail Alexandrovich was staying,[1485] proved to be a grand success. A manifesto (which Nikolai Nekrasov, a representative of the 4th Duma, brought with him,[1486] drafted on 28 February) needed adjustment, omitting the customary imperial definitions: "We ... Mikhail II, Emperor and Supreme Monarch of All Russia ..."[1487] It was worded to reflect Mikhail's future intentions and was signed "Mikhail." The signature appeared as if it was signed by an untitled ordinary citizen, and was now dated 3 March 1917.[1488]

The instant Mikhail Alexandrovich finished signing his name on the manifesto, the three-hundred-year old absolute monarchic rule became Russia's past. At the same moment, all the executive and legislative powers passed from Mikhail Alexandrovich and became vested with the Provisional Government. This process brought the political change these Duma delegates sought all along. Mikhail failed to demonstrate fortitude, which General Danilov described tactfully as a character flaw[1489] and fervently assert the inherent powers passed to him by his brother. Instead, he acceded to the revolutionary influences. Remarkably, Mikhail would become the first Romanov to be sacrificed for the Bolshevik cause on 12/13 July 1918 in Perm.[1490] Whatever turmoil the former sovereign must have felt by this unexpected turn will never be known, though he noted that evening:

> *"Misha abdicated ... God only knows who suggested for him to sign such filth!"*[1491]

The Provisional Government acted promptly to remove the symbols and links relating to the former imperial regime. Pamphlets appeared on 3 March announcing Nikolai II's abdication. The media followed with their announcement of the double abdication. Astonishingly, Nikolai II, on learning what Mikhail did, changed his mind and asked Alexeev to transmit a telegram to Petrograd, declaring his agreement that his son Alexei would accept the throne.[1492] It was too late; Alexeev no longer recognized the former emperor's authority, and refused to follow this order. With that, Russia, her allies, and wartime enemies learnt about the dissolution of the monarchy.

The Tormenting Effects of Change

On 3 March, Rodzianko told the Duma:

"A great event has taken place: the old regime, which was destroying Russia, has collapsed." [1493]

The social and political fabric of the nation was transformed. The elite who were connected with the old regime and persons who played an active political and economic role in government were affected by the euphoric state of affairs. In major cities and towns, the defenders of "liberty" began to arrest and detain any individuals considered to be the opposing forces. Property became a commodity for the taking.[1494] The Committee's Order, dated 2 March, declared that those guilty of harboring "supporters of the old regime would be court-martialed."[1495]

In Petrograd, the District Court (from which Zavadsky and Sereda were appointed to investigate the Rasputin Case) was set alight along with its files.[1496] Elsewhere in the city, all the files held in the gendarmerie criminal department on Fontanka, 16 were destroyed by fires created by the few remaining senior officers[1497][1498] before they fled Petrograd. Similar chaotic scenes had erupted at the police headquarters located on Furshtadskaya *Ulitsa* and before spreading to all city police districts.[1499] Countless loyal officers died whilst attempting to protect the many secrets held inside the criminal police divisions. Another victim was seventy-eight-year old Count Frederiks, because his name appeared on Nikolai II's Abdication Manifesto. His home on Pochtamskaya *Ulitsa*, 23, was torched.[1500] Frederiks was arrested[1501] not long after he left the imperial train[1502] and sent to the Tavricheskii Palace with other former imperial personages. General Alexeev mockingly declared that "in this revolutionary time, which we are suffering, the nation needs sacrifices. Speaking with Rodzianko and Guchkov we are of the opinion that the Count (and Voyeikov) must be those sacrifices."[1503] Guchkov also agreed they needed "sacrifices" from the old order.[1504] The morning edition of *Birzheviye Vedomosti* on 5 March published the headline "*REVOLUTION*".[1505]

At the Peter and Paul Fortress inside the Trubetskoi Bastion, the cells filled with former top imperial government officials, generals and members of the imperial suite: notably, the only female, Anna Taneeva,[1506] Palace Commander Vladimir Voyeikov[1507] and head of palace security, General Alexander Spiridovich. The decree, dated 7 March,[1508] authorized the arrest of all persons attached to the gendarmerie (including this author's grandfather, the head of the criminal and juridical department) was enforced strictly. Others imprisoned were Protopopov, Maklakov, Stürmer, Kurlov and the former mayor, Alexander Balk. Heads of various authorities, such as governors and the chief of staff of the navy, Admiral Alexander Rusin,[1509] were summarily dismissed because they once served the imperial government. Aron Simanovich, his wife, and daughter[1510] were arrested inside the family apartment. Judges, senators, and key administrators including the Metropolitan of Moscow[1511] and Stavka priest George Shavelsky[1512] were detained.[1513] The men's *gymnasia* (secondary school), which was located adjacent to the Tsarskoselskii Town Hall, was filled to capacity with many former security agents and gendarmes, as well as members of the imperial suite attached to the palace, including General Tatishev.[1514] Every day the media listed the names of those arrested; at other times it just listed the number of people sent to the detention center at the Tavricheskii Palace. Each detainee had two traits in common: they "opposed the revolution"[1515] and were the cream of the Imperial Russia society.

This ruthless political transformation signaled a bizarre paradox. All the prisoners in Petrograd, who were incarcerated for their criminal or religious activities, as well as those who had committed acts of terrorism against the former empire, were liberated,[1516] including those who had participated in anti-tsarist political uprisings.[1517] The Provisional Committee signed an *Ukaz* on 3 March that provided "immediate" and "unconditional and immediate amnesty" to all individuals who were accused of "crimes of a political character."[1518] Duma members Skobelev and Volkov visited every prison to check that all the cells were vacated for the incoming 'enemies of the Provisional Government.' Among the pardons were those extended to Dmitri Pavlovich (*in absentia*) and Felix Yusupov,[1519] who was now at liberty to return to Petrograd. Nikolai Mikhailovich returned to Petrograd on 1 March.[1520] One pardon of note was given to Khioniya Guseva, which declared her sane, thus enabling her to leave the Tyumen psychiatric facility on 15 March, where she had been detained since March 1915.[1521] Clutching her security pass that was signed by the new Tobolsk District Commissar Vasilii Pignatti[1522] (socialist party member), Guseva received money and a train ticket to Tobolsk.[1523]

At Tsarskoe Selo, under General Kornilov's orders, the *Okhrana* that guarded the perimeter of the Alexandrovskii Palace was replaced. A few men from the original group who confirmed loyalty to the new cause were mixed with the revolutionary forces.[1524] Some three hundred soldiers from the 3rd Rifle's Regiment ensured that no one left the palace and all communications were cut,[1525] except in the duty officer's room.[1526]

At the 5 March Provisional Government meeting, the second item on the agenda confirmed that the Winter Palace had become nationalized property.[1527] Whilst the former emperor remained in Mogilev,[1528] the decision concerning the "arrest of the former Imperatritsa Alexandra Fyodorovna" was deliberated.[1529] Guchkov, the new war minister, informed Alexandra Fyodorovna that the Alexandrovskii Palace would become the responsibility of the Provisional Government.[1530] His visit occurred at 1.30 on the morning of 6 March, indicating his disdain for the former empress.[1531] By limiting and controlling all of her movements, Kerensky devised a strategy to ensure that his government could enforce the next phase of his insidious plan. Two days later, on 7 March, the Provisional Government decided the former emperor and his wife would be deprived of their liberty, and in so doing, ensure Nikolai II's return to Tsarskoe Selo.[1532]

On 8 March, Kornilov with Guchkov (who administered all orders[1533]) and Colonel Evgenii Kobylinsky walked into the palace. Kornilov told Alexandra Fyodorovna that she and all palace residents, including the children, were deprived of their liberty[1534] and that Colonel Kobylinsky, who was introduced to her, was, as of that moment, the new chief of palace security.[1535]

The next day, *Birzheviye Vedomosti* published these lines:

"Alexandra Fyodorovna deprived of liberty

Chief of the Stabs Gendarmes Korpus arrested

Palace Commandant Voyeikov arrested."[1536]

On 9 March, the former sovereign arrived at the Imperatorskii Pavilion railway station. Not looking at anyone, he quickly walked to the waiting black car and arrived inside the palace grounds at 11.45 in the morning.[1537] Langansky wrote that the accompanying suite members headed to their "court carriages and also hurriedly and shamefully hide from view behind the gates of the Alexandrovskii Palace."[1538] Nikolai II saw the changes[1539] at the outset. Entering through the main gates, he confirmed his identity as "Nikolai Romanov." Not one guard, now wearing red bands,[1540] saluted as the former emperor passed by. They stared at citizen Romanov, entering the building that was no longer his home. Though *Birzheviye Vedomosti* claimed that no one cared about the former sovereign's arrival,[1541] it neglected to say that those who might have shown support were either in detention or had fled.

Kerensky recognized that as the former head of state, Nikolai II "could not remain at liberty" because that circumstance was "a psychological prerequisite during the first days of the revolution,"[1542] a position that was endorsed by the worker's Soviet.[1543] They issued a 'Protocol' stipulating that "Nikolai Romanov should not be permitted to depart for England" and ought to be sent to the Trubetskoi Bastion prison.[1544] The Soviet refused his departure because for the revolution to succeed, Nikolai II could not be seen "fleeing to England."[1545] After assuring the Petrograd Soviet of the arrest, Kerensky admitted that it was done in the national interest.[1546]

Kerensky's Inquiry Takes Shape

During the Provisional Government's 11th Sitting held on 8 March, the ministers announced the creation of the Extraordinary Commission of Inquiry. Its portfolio was to investigate the criminal activities of the former regime. The secret inquiry, headed by Kerensky, was given legal force on 11 March[1547] to examine correspondence[1548] besides the archives extracted from the Winter, Alexandrovskii and Peterhof Palaces,[1549] surveillance records and existing police files.[1550] It would question former government ministers, the heads of government and military personnel about their activities under the former regime. According to Kerensky's colleague, Karabchevskii, the inquiry's real objective was to bring to trial former ministers and responsible persons who would be accused of various (unspecified) administrative wrongdoings. The inquiry would be headed by Kerensky's trusted ally from Moscow,[1551] Nikolai Muravyev, and chaired by Senator Mikhail Zavadsky,[1552] along with a panel of interchanging jurists and academics. Alexander Blok would make stenographic records,[1553] [which would be published from 1923-1930]. In total, 59 persons were questioned (Alexei Khvostov was the first, on 18 March[1554]) from March to October 1917.[1555]

Special attention also focused on Rasputin's activities and personality and what influences the imperial family had with the German imperial family.[1556] Using the Imperial Criminal Code Statute No. 108 as his reference, Kerensky wanted to know whether the former emperor and his consort were guilty of treason against the State.[1557] Preempting his own inquiry, Kerensky alleged the "Rasputin clique" was involved with the German high command and that the elite knew about Alexandra Fyodorovna's treasonous actions,[1558] aside from his belief that she and Rasputin moved against the Duma.[1559]

By 1920, Kerensky had changed the direction of his refrain, when he told Sokolov that he fervently believed that even if Rasputin was not necessarily a German agent, it was "more correct to say that he was that figure around whom Germanophiles and also German agents worked." Kerensky did not doubt that "these Manasevich-Manuilovs, Rubensteins [Rasputin's banker], Simanovichs and other gentlemen who were near him ... were agents of the Germans,"[1560] while pinpointing that Purishkevich "never concealed that he killed, foremost, a traitor." He praised Khvostov, saying he should not be forgotten for "openly fighting with Rasputin as being the central figure of the German agentura ... Rasputin favored Germans to benefit the Germans." Kerensky stayed convinced that "the Tsaritsa with Rasputin had fought the people, the army, the grand dukes, and all of Russia."[1561]

In the end, Kerensky's eagerness to prove that the former sovereign and Alexandra Fyodorovna had acted against the State failed. Rudnev, whose role was to investigate the former imperial couple and "its circle," found that there was no case to answer.[1562] Alexander Blok, perhaps irked about the inquiry's formalism, claimed the "revolutionary essence was absent."[1563] Despite the months of questioning and amassed evidence, the inquiry was a futile exercise because it failed to enact its own legislation and misguidedly applied a defunct imperial statute to operate (sitting until 25 October 1917). Many who had vigorously defended their employment during the imperial regime remained prisoners at the will of the Bolsheviks.

Notwithstanding Kerensky's remark that he wanted to prevent Rasputin's gravesite from becoming a pilgrimage site,[1564] the exhumation had little to do with the government's zeal to extend a new image. The decision had aligned with Kerensky's own retaliation against the imperial order and the so-called "dark forces." His final target was Rasputin's corpse. To succeed in his mission, the body had to vanish. To add to his woes, Kerensky heard from former palace "employees" that there was "massive destruction of documents that proved the betrayal and dealings with the enemy Rasputin, Vyrubova ... and the Imperatritsa."[1565] Alexandra Fyodorovna wrote in her diary on 8[1566] and 9 March[1567] that they "burnt papers with Lili." Nikolai Alexandrovich did likewise[1568] on the morning of 10 March, the same day as the "archives of the court security police [*Okhrana*] went up in flames."[1569]

A Former Commander is Forced to Walk Away a Second Time

In order to rectify what was believed to have been a wrongful dismissal, Alexeev promptly sent Grand Duke Nikolai Nikolayevich a telegram asking when he would return to Stavka as commander in chief.[1570] During the evening of 3 March, Nikolasha sent his response from Tiflis, in the Caucasus, that "it was impossible to leave for Stavka at the present time."[1571] With this unexpected turn of events, Prince Georgii Lvov, the new president of the first Council of Ministers,[1572] hoped that Nikolasha would know that he had to decline his former commission.[1573] The Soviet faction[1574] argued that members of the Romanov family who still retained their commissions as military officers were offending the revolutionary cause. The revolutionaries wanted to arrest Nikolasha when he was to return to Petrograd.[1575] The Soviet signed a resolution to ensure "strict surveillance over him during his journey."[1576] Kerensky appeased the Soviets with a guarantee that Nikolai Nikolayevich would not resume his supreme command.[1577]

Setting his own political scenario, Nikolasha sent a telegram to Lvov in Petrograd on 12 March, which was published in *Vestnik* on 14 March 1917. It announced that he offered his loyalty to the "new State order."[1578] Alexander Mikhailovich (Felix's father-in-law) declared in his own message that the Mikhailovich branch of the family supported the Provisional Government. The Konstantinovich branch represented by Nikolai, Dmitri, Gavril and Igor were happy to regard themselves as "free citizens." The most surprising message came from Elizaveta Fyodorovna. Her communication, published in *Russkii Invalid* (*Russian Invalid*) on 15 March 1917, announced: "Recognizing the importance for all to support the new government, I announce that from my side I fully support it."[1579] Consequently, all three branches of the Romanov family publicly exposed their hostility towards the former sovereign. In so doing, they rejected their imperial birthright.

Unaware about the withdrawal of his command, Nikolasha arrived at Mogilev on 24 March. Lvov, foreseeing this event, passed on a message asking him not to proceed with his intentions.[1580] One day earlier, Buchanan received a telegram from Lvov saying that Nikolasha's appointment was opposed by "revolutionary elements."[1581] Nikolasha finally understood. Not setting foot at Stavka, he traveled to Yalta. His replacement, on 1 April 1917,[1582] was General Alexeev, who once strived for Nikolasha's return.

Perfidy Has Many Faces

Influenced by the appearance of *Prikaz* (Decree) No. 1, the Provisional Government enacted a law that abolished the use of superior military titles, which were recognized since Peter the Great created the system in 1722.[1583] Yusupov's imperial suite designation of *Fligel-adjutant* [1584] became irrelevant. [The law was modified by the Bolsheviks on 8 November of that year to include the elimination of all imperial civilian, military titles and ranks.[1585]] During the first month of the Provisional Government's existence, all the grand dukes who held an active military commission were discharged.[1586] No city or town in Russia was immune from political revision. On 1 April, a decree proclaimed that Romanov, the Northern Sea settlement, was renamed Murmansk.[1587] This was the route that was touted to be the exit point by the former imperial family, had they been permitted to leave Russia for England.[1588]

This message written by Lloyd George on 23 March 1917 (N. S.) was published in the *Times*:

"... *sentiments of the most profound satisfaction that the peoples of Great Britain and of the British Dominions ... have learned that their great Ally Russia now stands with the nations which base their institutions upon responsible government. ... I believe that the revolution whereby the Russian people have based destinies on the sure foundation of freedom is the greatest service which they have yet made to the cause, for which the Allied peoples have been fighting since August, 1914.*"[1589]

The final betrayal came from the partners of the *Entente*, Great Britain and France, who refused to provide safe passage to the imperial family to live in exile. [Buchanan "renounced his right to shelter fugitives" who "were in danger of their lives" inside the British Embassy, with the French Embassy applying the same approach.[1590]] The British Parliament accepted the agitation of their "workers," as had the French, who did not want a former sovereign to live among them. Buchanan tendered the formal apology to Foreign Minister Pavel Milyukov, saying that it was better not to create problems for Britain.[1591] Buchanan, sympathetic with the revolutionary cause, argued "the real promoters of the revolution were people like Rasputin, Protopopov and Mme Wyrobouwa" (sic).[1592]

The imperial family's presence in Tsarskoe Selo became

politically awkward, therefore Kerensky decided they must leave.[1593] Buchanan's telegram to Arthur Balfour (the British Foreign Secretary) on 12/25 July 1917, revealed why the relocation was necessary. It was "the fear of counter-revolution among the socialists."[1594] The relocation had nothing to do with safeguarding the imperial family. Kerensky selected Tobolsk, a city where he had spent his formative years. The city's remoteness, where Decembrists from the failed 1825 uprising and recent revolutionaries were sent, reinforced its "special geographic circumstance."[1595] Once the imperial family had re-settled, Kerensky was no longer answerable for their welfare. Upon reflection, he accused Rasputin for directing "the tormented path ... of the imperial family"[1596] but then argued, once the Bolsheviks took control, they were culpable for the family's fate.

The Dead Cannot be Allowed to Rest in Peace

When Alexandra Fyodorovna was told on 2 March that her movements would be restricted, she grasped her visits to Rasputin's grave had ended. At about the same time, Koshko found out from Procurator von Nandelshtedt that after Purishkevich spoke to Kerensky about the Rasputin Case, the case was dropped.[1597] That happening was reported by *Russkaya Volya*[1598] and *Birzheviye Vedomosti* (*Stock Exchange Record*).[1599] It is possible that Purishkevich's plea may have driven Kerensky to destroy Rasputin's corpse.

On 4 March 1917, during its first meeting, the Provisional Government brought into effect a series of new laws. The Alexandrovskii Palace with its land had come under its control.[1600] The nationalization included Taneeva's infirmary and the construction site that was to be the Serafimovskii Sanctuary Chapel. Of the seven regulations raised, Item 4 of the new palace "Instructions"[1601] stipulated that all movements of the family were restricted to small supervised areas in the palace grounds. This ruling meant that no one would visit Rasputin's gravesite.

At the time of Nikolai II's seclusion in Pskov, the military forces in Tsarskoe Selo joined the socialist uprising. Among the first to be arrested on 3 March was Commander Maltsev, whose men protected the Alexandrovskii grounds from the air.[1602] He was accused of being an "enemy of the military high command."[1603] The accusation came after Maltsev assured Alexandra Fyodorovna that despite the nearby gunfire, no one would interfere with the palace or its grounds, otherwise he would take action.[1604] Maltsev's communication had exposed his allegiance did not lie with the mutineers in his unit. By then, talk began as to where Rasputin's body might be buried. One report claimed it was in Pokrovskoye,[1605] another decided it was in one of the Petrograd cemeteries. The intercepted letter written by Anna Rodzianko to Zinaida Yusupova revealed that Alexandra Fyodorovna "goes to the gravesite and everyday finds her *couverte d'ordures* (covered rubbish)."[1606] That information had revealed that Rasputin's body was buried in Tsarskoe Selo.

At the Provisional Government's sub-branch meeting on 6 March 1917, Colonel Matsnev, the new Tsarskoe Selo commandant, announced that soldiers with Capitan found a metallic coffin in the Alexandrovskii Park.[1607] It was thought it contained Rasputin's corpse.[1608] Consensus was sought as to what should be done. The attendees elected that General Kornilov, the new commander in chief of the Petrograd Garrison (that included Tsarskoe Selo), had to be told. [Kornilov only acted with Kerensky's consent.[1609]]

Sometime after Captain Klimov returned from the Front in December 1916, he was instructed to find Rasputin's grave in Tsarskoe Selo. Klimov knew that one of the officers in his garrison, Maltsev, was part of the secret contingent guarding something in the remote part of the Alexandrovskii Park. Following one long road in a military vehicle, he was stopped en-route by gendarmes, who prevented him proceeding further. Reversing his vehicle, he headed towards Tsarskoe Selo. Along the way he passed a sled, which carried the empress. Klimov's inquisitiveness intensified. He decided to walk. Beyond the road, he noticed a track which entered into the depths of the forest. Clear of the thick vegetation, he reached a wooden construction site but failed to make out its purpose. By this time, Colonel Maltsev notified the empress that Klimov was seen wandering around the area and within the hour, Klimov was relocated to another section of the town and warned against further trespass.[1610] Taking advantage of the political disorder in March, Klimov arrested Maltsev and took his place.

He resumed his search.[1611]

Lydia Bogutskaya reported Klimov's finding this way. Klimov returned to the wooden construction site on 6 March, which was still guarded by soldiers. The guards told him that Maltsev always escorted Alexandra Fyodorovna to this site, which happened regularly. Klimov learnt that the material "belonged to the palace" rather than the Aerial Battery unit. The guards did not know what they had to protect. During these visits the troops were ordered to leave and tend to something insignificant nearby. The construction workers received unusual treatment when working on the site of the proposed chapel. They always arrived and left as one group and all their movements were controlled. Surveying the building site, Klimov worked out where the proposed altar was to have been and noticed a pile of rocks that were inconsistent with the rest of the site. With considerable effort, the soldiers moved the rocks and dug down to reveal a coffin. Hacking into one section the metallic coffin lid, Klimov recognized that it was Rasputin's corpse lying inside. Klimov left and straightaway notified his superior, Commandant Matsnev (just prior to the party meeting).[1612]

Two days later, on 8 March at six o'clock in the evening, Bogutskaya, with two colleagues (Evgenii Lagansky from *Russkaya Volya* and V. Filatov of *Russkoye Slovo*), rode in Captian Klimov's car until they reached an unsealed track. The rest of the trip was on foot. The tour was not arranged to solve Kerensky's "delicate request" to the Duma journalists to find Rasputin's remains.[1613] I believe Bogutskaya and her colleagues accompanied Klimov to ensure that there would be a public record of the discovery.

This is how Bogutskaya described her excursion:

> *"Passing by the Alexandrovskii palace in Tsarskoe Selo, the car rushed past the fence of the palace park, then turned to the right to forest park. In the depths of the forest we stopped the car. Here a small track began opened by Captain Klimov. The track wound between old spruces … Walking ¼ versts, we saw gates sawn from young birches, and further – little bridges, from both sides there were railings also constructed from young birches. The bridges ended at the edge of the forest, at an unfinished wooden chapel construction. … Approaching*

the chapel, we walked around it and came out to the western wall. The altar should have been here. Below this proposed altar Rasputin [This detail is incorrect] *was buried. Crawling under the wall, we saw a kind of pit 4 arshin deep* [280cms]. *Inside the pit can be seen the upper lid from a zinc coffin. This lid was cut, which turned out to be an opening approximately a ½* arshin in diameter [35cms] *right over the head of Rasputin.*

Under our self-lit flare, the beard and thick hair of the 'staretz' was clearly seen. His face had blackened. On the temple – a small opening, plugged with a piece of cotton wool. Here a bullet entered, ending Rasputin's life.

Near the chapel when we arrived there were 5 persons, soldiers. They all with curiosity crawled under the wall, leant over the coffin, while a few [soldiers] lowered themselves to the bottom of the well, to look at the face of the deceased. One of them in front of us extended his hand into the opening near the head and pulled out a small wooden icon 'Znameniye Bogomater' [Mother of God]. …

After inspecting the gravesite, we went back. On the track there were already tens of soldiers and citizens from Tsarskoe Selo hearing about the opening of the gravesite wanting to glance at the person who over the past years practically ruled Russia.

…. At 8 o'clock in the evening the Commandant of Tsarskoe Selo gave the order for a regiment of soldiers to go to the gravesite and to dig up his coffin and bring it back to a sealed place until instructions came from the provisional government."[1614]

Lagansky's article for *Russkaya Volya* published on the same day (9 March) gave a different slant. To set the right tone, Lagansky used Klimov's 6 March report. Lagansky placed himself as the initiator of the assignment, saying that Klimov had agreed to assist. Lagansky asserted that he acted on local rumors, and was able to discover Rasputin's gravesite.[1615] Lagansky added that it was he who pulled out the icon from inside Rasputin's coffin, going so far as to gloat that "my find made an immense impression over the soldiers," and that he was so "sorry to part with this historic document" after Klimov asked him "to hand over" what was actually an icon. Years later, he expanded his story into a two-part article for the journal *Ogonek* (*Small Flame*)[1616] [1617] to mark the tenth anniversary date of Rasputin's murder. The revised account aligned with Soviet policy to disparage an imperial military officer; in this case, Colonel Maltsev. [Lagansky originally used the term "unpopular" but altered the word to "detested."] Nothing can hide the fact that Klimov identified Rasputin's remains, three days before Lagansky published his original story.

Despite Lagansky's version of events, he did corroborate Bogutskaya's description of the deceased. [Bogutskaya's husband was a medical doctor.[1618]] Lagansky wrote that Rasputin's "face had completely blackened" and "the dark long combed beard and hair had clumps of frozen earth" and on the forehead there was a "black opening caused by a bullet wound."[1619] In 1926/7, Lagansky wrote that "on the temple – a dark mark from a blow. The head rested on a laced silk pillow," which was "of imperial origin."[1620] [Lagansky became a Bolshevik party publicist and was executed in 1937.[1621]]

A contemporary article stated that Klimov "by happenstance" saw a coffin below the ground inside the uncompleted chapel and "found a glass opening" on the lid (which in fact was solid zinc). Using insulting emotional language (including the use of the name of the deceased with undue familiarity), Konstantinov wrote that Klimov bent over and "looked at him, at what appeared to him, a live Grishka Rasputin."[1622] Perhaps the 1917 booklet that spoke of an opening on the coffin[1623] inspired Konstantinov to repeat it.

Neither Bogutskaya nor Lagansky described a glass component on the coffin. Though Lagansky said the zinc coffin lid had been designed to be opened at the chest of the deceased.[1624] When Bogutskaya saw the coffin in the pit, she noted that the lid had been "cut," leaving a half-arshin (35cm) opening over the head of the deceased. The soldiers had to prise open the lid so that the remains could be identified. That undertaking undoubtedly explains why Lagansky noticed soil debris on the head of the corpse.

Soon after, photographs similar to Photo 26 were published, locals began to mill around the gravesite, seizing wood splinters, snow and morsels of frozen earth from the construction site,[1625] which was assumed to have surrounded the coffin. [After the coffin was transported to the *Gorodskaya Ratusha* (Town Hall), the souvenir hunting resumed.[1626]] It is doubtful these events happened.

Lagansky returned to the gravesite early on the morning of 9 March. His mission was twofold: to report on the former emperor's return to Tsarskoe Selo, and then visit the freshly exposed gravesite.[1627] In the first of two related articles, he claimed the exhumation prevented unwelcome prying on the site.[1628] Yet, in his follow-up article, Lagansky did not know the coffin had been transported to the Town Hall overnight.[1629] Though claiming he saw countless foot impressions, made by "locals,"[1630] Lagansky knew the impressions were left by soldiers who disintered the coffin the previous evening.

The First Flames Raised by the Provisional Government

When the journalists left the gravesite, Matsnev ordered the soldiers to uplift the coffin from its frozen resting place.[1631] Under Ensign Bavtadze's supervision, the uplift took around half[1632] to one hour.[1633] [The *"Znameniye Bogomater"* icon would be brought to Kerensky.[1634]] The coffin was transported on a "Benz truck" [1635] to the Tsarskoselskii Town Hall, by which time a huge curiosity-driven crowd had gathered outside. Although the coffin had been damaged during the uplift, it remained intact. With better illumination, someone verified that they had the correct corpse. One eyewitness described how Rasputin's body looked:

> *"Rasputin's body as it turned out was wrapped in thin muslin, which was sewn up in linen. The head* [lay] *on a laced silk pillow. The arms were crossed over the chest and the left side of the head was shattered and disfigured. The body had blackened."*[1636]

The next process involved writing up a Protocol that was signed by a Tsarskoselskii Temporary Committee member. The Protocol confirmed that the remains in the coffin were checked and the coffin was placed inside a wooden crate that was sealed before transporting it to the Tsarskoselskii Railway Station (on 9 March).

Since the building adjacent to the hall was serving as a detention center, the route was secured from inquisitive onlookers. *Russkaya Volya* reported the next day (perhaps as a diversionary measure) that the remains were buried at the Volkov Cemetery.[1637] Another paper reported that the body "would be buried in one of the cemeteries in Petrograd."[1638]

General Kornilov telephoned Colonel Kobylinsky's apartment at 2 a.m. and ordered him to be at the Tsarskoselskii Railway platform at eight o'clock. On arrival, Kobylinsky saw Kornilov standing beside his Adjutant. To prevent others hearing their conversation, Kornilov used a railway carriage to bring Kobylinsky up to date. Kobylinsky's first duty was to accompany Kornilov to Tsarskoe Selo where the general would notify Alexandra Fyodorovna that she was under arrest. Then Kobylinsky learnt that he was to take immediate charge of the Tsarskoselskii garrison.[1639] His reassignment meant that it was his responsibility to oversee the soldiers who guarded the goods wagon that temporarily stored Rasputin's remains.[1640] Bizarre as it appears, the former sovereign arrived at the same station on the morning of 9 March, while Rasputin's remains were secured in a railway wagon close by.

The Folly of Liquidating a Dead Enemy

Back in Petrograd, Lvov and Commissar (the new political definition adopted from the Petrograd Soviet's political strategy) Fillip Kupchinsky debated how to destroy the remains.[1641] Kupchinsky was a former war correspondent with the *Rus'* newspaper during the Russo-Japanese War (1904-05). During his stint as a journalist, he was considered a traitor against the Russian imperial forces at Port Arthur and was arrested for espionage.[1642] At some point during the February Uprising, he began to work for *Petrogradskii Listok* and was also installed as a Duma representative.[1643] When Lvov proposed that the remains could be buried outside of Tsarskoe Selo in front of two witnesses, Kupchinsky suggested that "cremating by fire was best of all because it was difficult to dig frozen earth and [would take] a long time and someone might notice."[1644] However, his plan needed a day or so to organize. With Lvov's (and Kerensky's) approval, Kupchinsky travelled to Tsarskoselskii Railway Station and after showing his credentials to Kobylinsky, he ordered the wagon (with the corpse secured inside) sitting on the reserve track to proceed to Pavlovsk 2, Railway Station. Firstly, he "withdrew the soldiers from the commandant's quarters," then as soon as the sealed wagon with its cargo moved further down the line, a similar wagon headed on the parallel track towards Petrograd. This served to confuse possible onlookers, who would have expected the steam train to travel by that rail corridor. Kupchinsky then drove to Pavlovsk 2, with a truck following behind him, which would transport the cargo to Petrograd by road.

The next day, *Russkaya Volya* revealed that "Rasputin's corpse was at first directed to Pavlovsk 2, station and from there to Petrograd."[1645] At Pavlovsk 2, the coffin was placed into the truck, but before the coffin was driven to its next designated location, Kupchinsky had the contents opened to verify he had received the correct goods. Due to the intense snowfall, the tires often skidded along the route. [1646] Finally, at one o'clock in the morning, Kupchinsky and his men arrived at the former imperial stables building (Photo 27) in the center of Petrograd. The truck, with its cargo, was driven straight through and parked inside. Days after the transfer, *Birzheviye Vedomosti* reported "the coffin sat the entire day until the night next to the regal nuptial carriage."[1647] [Purishkevich repeated the same detail in his 'Diary'.[1648]]

After locking the stables, Kupchinsky told Lvov that Rasputin's remains were in Petrograd.[1649] Kupchinsky then met with the Petrograd governor, Vadim Yurevich (former professor at the Medical Military Academy), who, during the February Uprising, became a political activist and was given the role of commandant at the Tavricheskii Palace.[1650] Yurevich was asked to supply a reliable person who would act as their witness during the cremation process.[1651] Yurevich offered *Rotmeister* Kogadeev's (Kochadeev[1652]) services.

By Friday night, everything was ready for Rasputin's corpse to make its final journey. Kupchinsky sat in the leading vehicle with Kogadeev and one unnamed 'student.' Despite the night curfew, the drivers were given passes, which had to be shown at regular intervals along their drive north of the city limits. Kupchinsky's fleet proceeded northeast (see MAP No. 2) and headed towards the Petrograd Polytechnic Institute of Emperor Peter the Great (Photo 28, opened in 1902[1653]). The diminutive university town, Lesnoi, with its numerous dachas, was connected by one sealed road. Under normal circumstances, the journey to Lesnoi in 1917 took under one hour to reach,[1654] but Kupchinsky claimed he used a series of wretched roads, which contradicts the way seen on the map. Purishkevich claimed that the corpse was set alight near where Dr. Badmaev's house once stood on Poklonnaya Gora, which was the village immediately north of Lesnoi. Most of Badmaev's property had been razed to the ground during the first days of February because it was located close to the breeding ground of Bolshevik political activism at the institute. *Russkaya Volya* correctly reported that the exhumed corpse was transported in a truck "close to Piskarevka village not far off Vyborgskoe Shosse in Lesnoi."[1655]

Many Versions of the Truth

Kupchinsky most likely failed to identify the cremation site in order to avoid others knowing it. Yurevich's expertise proved useful, once he revealed where human remains could be cremated. The corpse was destroyed by fire, "after which the zinc coffin was thrown in, which quickly melted."[1656] The same detail appeared in one 1917 brochure, which revealed "it was decided to melt down the metallic coffin."[1657] The coffin was made from zinc sheet metal. Zinc in that form becomes malleable at temperatures of 100-150°C and has a melting point of 420°C.[1658] The institute suited Kupchinsky's needs by its remoteness, yet feasible driving distance from Petrograd. Crucially, it had furnaces that provided an effective disposal method. The smoke that would have emanated from one of its chimneys would not raise suspicion.

The Act (DOCUMENT No. 8) confirming the corpse had been destroyed by fire was signed by everone involved in the task. One copy was given to the governor and the second copy was handed to Lvov. Copy No. 2, first published by Lagansky in *Ogonek* in 1926, these days is displayed in the Political History Museum in St. Petersburg. The Act, not divulging the location of the cremation, was co-signed by six students attached to the Polytechnical Institute militia acting as witnesses. The date "10/11

March" identifies that the process had began overnight (at 3 a.m.) and ended before daybreak at "7 in the morning."

Since there was a proper facility under the government's control to destroy the remains, it seems absurd that Kupchinsky chose to invent a story by saying he painstakingly destroyed a corpse in a forest fire (restrained by snow), a process taking ten hours that not only extended into daylight but was seen by a casual observer.[1659] At least three persons associated with the institute knew the cremation happened at the institute. Among them was the dean of the Polytechnic Institute and foundation professor of electro-technology Mikhail Shatelin,[1660] and Professor (of theoretical electro-technology) Vladimir Mitkevich.[1661] The third person, Ivan Bashilov (a student and party secretary), held that "on that night Rasputin's corpse was brought to the Polytechnic Institute and incinerated in the melting cauldron."[1662]

How did Kupchinsky manage to rally a group of students to assist him? By Sunday 26 February 1917, most of the academic activities of the Polytechnic Institute were disrupted by political turmoil. The city authorities lost control most noticeably in the Vyborg District, close to where the Institute was located, before upheaval overtook the city center. The focal point, where events became most violent, occurred in Znamenskaya Ploschad, opposite the Nikolayevskii railway station, after the soldiers began to shoot in a vain attempt to maintain civil order. The worker's demonstration and its ensuing scuffles caused deaths, a situation that triggered a mutiny by disheartened soldiers, who began to hold their fire. Anarchy ensued and the nightly curfew was no longer observed.[1663] At night, some three thousand aggrieved soldiers and workers occupied and met in the main wing at the Polytechnic Institute to form the Petrograd Soviet of Workers and Soldiers.[1664] This revolutionary gathering was not unusual, because the Institute was politically active during the 1905 uprising on Bloody Sunday.[1665] Within this setting, as a commissar clutching special permits to gain entry into Lesnoi, Kupchinsky had pre-arranged the services needed to accomplish his assignment. Notwithstanding his disinformation, Kupchinsky always intended to travel directly to the Polytechnic Institute with his load and have others carry out the grim task. The facility had a sheltered building that housed heavy-duty cauldrons (Photo 29) that could destroy human remains. But then Kupchinsky's claim that he brought back the zinc coffin and left it with a political operative[1666] must be seen as an absurdity. Granting that *Petrogradskii Listok* offered a reason for the coffin's preservation, saying that the zinc would be recycled,[1667] the story denies Kerensky's objective, whereby everything related to Rasputin must disappear. *Den* (DOCUMENT No. 9) reported that the Minister of Justice had directed "the former correspondent Kupchinsky to cremate Rasputin's body, which had been carried out."[1668] Kerensky subsequently confessed that "Rasputin was actually cremated."[1669]

Lagansky's final remarks now draw added significance:

> *"Now look for the grave of the staretz (sic). ... Not water or earth as it is said accepted him. Thankfully the fire helped."*[1670]

He Shall Never Be Forgotten

The rumor-mongering did not cease with Rasputin's death. *Birzheviye Vedomosti* reported that the apartment which once belonged to Rasputin was searched by a team of undisclosed persons on 18 March. It was alleged that the searchers found "interesting correspondence of a political character ... pornographic literature and a particularly large number of pornographic photographic cards."[1671] This was a scurrilous piece of journalism, which ignored the fact that the apartment was searched within hours of Rasputin's reported disappearance and nothing compromising was found.

Kupchinsky wrote that he visited the cremation site sometime before May 1917 where Rasputin's corpse was supposedly burned. On one birch tree he saw a notice, appended to it, written in German: *"Hier ist der Hund begraben"* (The dog is buried here). This sketch provided a bizarre conclusion, which like the rest of his story, was composed to astonish readers.

While no one of note had expressed concern about the former imperial family's welfare at the time, a columnist noted that "there was nothing left of Rasputin except agonizing memories."[1672]

Chapter Nine Photos

PHOTO 24: TSARSKOE SELO. Grigorii Rasputin's remains were brought to the Fyodorovskii Cathedral before burial that was officiated by the resident cleric, Father Alexander Vasiliev, 1916.

PHOTO 25: Znameniye Bogomater icon that was found inside Rasputin's coffin. The reverse was inscribed by Alexandra Fyodorovna, her four daughters. Anna (Taneeva) added her name and included the date of the Velikii Novgorod visit, 11 Dec. 1916.

PHOTO 26: The partial construction of the Serafimovskii Sanctuary Chapel. The opened grave by the northern wall of the proposed chapel is to the right of the "X" and the pile of rocks that once overlay the grave are now scattered over the area. Published in Petrogradskaya Gazeta, March 1917.

PHOTO 27: The rear view of the Imperial stables building (facing the Moika canal) shows the row of doors, one of which was used to conceal the coffin containing Rasputin's remains, c. 1916.

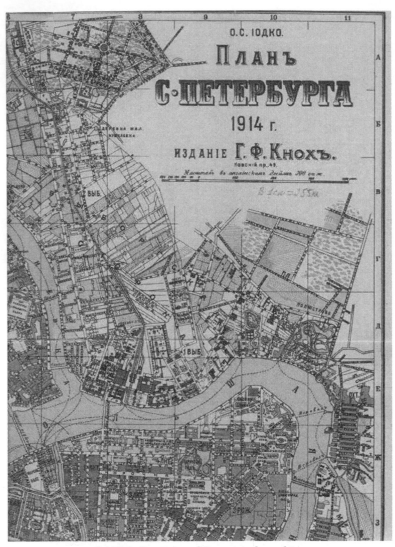

MAP 2. Lesnoi and Petrograd outskirts

*The Polytechnic Institute complex at Lesnoi can be seen
in Grids 'A 6-9'. A direct road led to the facility from
Petrograd after crossing the Bolshaya Neva River.*

PHOTO 28: LESNOI. Aerial view of the Polytechnic Institute (of Emperor Peter the Great). The side road on the left led to the furnaces, where the two chimney stacks are visible, pre 1916.

PHOTO 29: LESNOI. The cauldrons at the Polytechnic Institute, where Grigorii Rasputin's remains were destroyed on 10/11 March 1917.

Сожженіе трупа Распутина.

Министромъ юстиціи было поручено уполномоченному по реквизиціи придворнаго вѣдомства бывшему корреспонденту Купчинскому сжечь тѣло Распутина, что и было исполнено.

DOCUMENT No 9: Newspaper notice dated 14 March reveals that Rasputin's body was cremated.

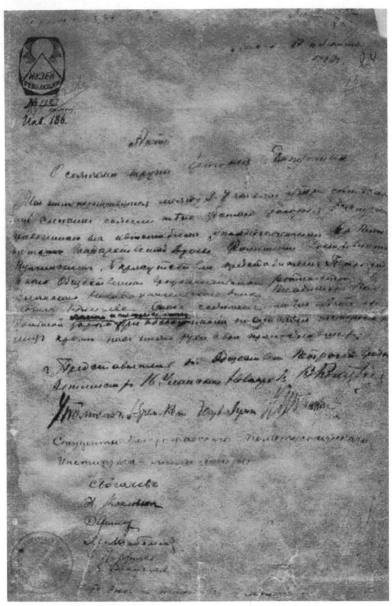

DOCUMENT No. 8: The Report that provides evidence
that Rasputin's corpse was cremated on the night of March
10/11, 1917 near Lesnoi, in the Petrograd region.

CHAPTER TEN
"No one has the right to commit murder"

A twenty-three-year old officer, Semyon Popov was one of many wounded patients recovering in the No. 3 Palace Infirmary. On Christmas Day (four days after Rasputin's burial), he detected that the empress no longer smiled and seemed gloomy.[1673] Rodzianko instead supposed the empress "saw enemies in everyone."[1674]

On 29 April 1917, Dmitri Pavlovich wrote to his father:

> *"Finally, the final act upon my arrival in Petrograd was the full acceptance and premeditated participation in the murder of Rasputin, as the last attempt for the sovereign to openly alter his course ..."*[1675]

This chapter discusses whether Dmitri's expectations materialized after Grigorii Rasputin's death.

Nikolai II Initiates Action Against Rasputin's Murderers

Felix Yusupov assumed the emperor would protect him from prosecution because of Dmitri Pavlovich's immunity.[1676] To place Dmitri on an equal legal footing with Felix or Purishkevich, Nikolai II would have to sign a special *Ukaz* to take away Dmitri's imperial prerogatives. With the exception of Purishkevich, none of the conspirators, in 1916, admitted their participation in killing Rasputin or disposing of his remains. Finding a person willing to indict Purishkevich and Felix was impossible. Thus, one part of Maklakov's counsel was taking effect.

The first administrative adjustment related to the Rasputin Matter happened within twenty-four hours of Nikolai II's return to Tsarskoe Selo on 19 December.[1677] Makarov became the first minister who faced dismissal. The second dismissal happened after the new Minister of Justice, Senator Nikolai Dobrovolskii,[1678] asked Sereda to hand over all the material related to the Rasputin case, including the "silk shirt with the bullet hole worn by Rasputin the gold cross and chain."[1679] Sereda refused, even though Alexandra Fyodorovna wanted all the items found on Rasputin's body to be sent to her. Thus, Dobrovolskii released Sereda from the investigation. His replacement, Vladimir Stavrovskii,[1680] forwarded the items to the palace.[1681]

Given that Dmitri was involved in the murder, only the emperor could act. Dobrovolskii applied for a "Plea for a settlement" (*Isprosheniye razresheniya*),[1682] so that the District Court could terminate its side of the investigation that was activated on 17 December 1916.

An Accusation of Guilt by Association

A few days after Rasputin's burial, the empress requested Protopopov to search Baroness Marianna von Derfelden's premises. She underwent home detention during the search. Derfelden, a twice-divorced twenty-six-year-old woman, was Countess Paley's daughter from her first marriage, and following her mother's remarriage, she became Dmitri's stepsister. Though Nikolai II had settled the judicial investigation, the police investigation remained active. The empress wanted to know whether Dmitri had involved his stepsister into the conspiracy.[1683] Marianna, on friendly terms with Dmitri,[1684] was not a Romanov, hence the police had no restrictions regarding her dwelling.

On 25 December, Marianna sent a message to her mother, explaining that she visited Dmitri one hour before his banishment and within twenty-four hours, Protopopov ordered her detention.[1685] Though the police did not find incriminating material, General Popov did pass one letter to Vasiliev.[1686] Failing to understand why her daughter was detained, Paley and Dmitri's sister arrived at Marianna's place to offer support. By day's end, though Derfelden was no longer detained, her mother blamed Protopopov for her daughter's plight.[1687]

As One Walks Away, Others Wait Their Turn

On 21 December, *Rech* reported that Rodzianko denied having had conversations with either Trepov or Makarov on Monday 19 December regarding the "arrest of the popular member of the State Duma" [Purishkevich].[1688] Notwithstanding the rumors, Purishkevich was exclusively concerned with continuing his war effort as head of the Red Cross at the Front. He left Petrograd on Sunday 18 December with his wife Alexandra, Lazovert, (Photo 30) and Sukhotin's wife, Irina (both women were Sisters of Mercy). Purishkevich enjoyed liberty seemingly because of his "prestige among the rural masses and his enormous influence ... as one of the 'Black Bands' made the emperor reflect that it was dangerous to strike at him."[1689] Spiridovich recalled that no one mentioned Purishkevich.[1690]

Alexandra Fyodorovna became agitated that Dmitri dared to go against the imperial family and, having committed treason, he breached his Oath of Allegiance. Though Felix was muttering "*the Court will never go against society,*"[1691] he failed to grasp that Petrograd society had wronged the imperial court.

Globachev explained that for a few former devotees, Rasputin's death had:

> "*...attained the oreal of a martyr, but for people like Yusupov and Purishkevich and with the co-participation with Grand Duke Dmitri Pavlovich it further severed common respect towards Superior power, placing it into two ambiguous circumstances. From one side, the law demanded the punishment of the murderers and from the other, it was not allowed to place the matter before the court carrying the name of Grand Duke Dmitri.*"[1692]

Dmitri's silence protected Felix and Purishkevich from judicial prosecution. Since Purishkevich thought that he did the right thing, this explains why he appeared calm at the railway station a few hours after the murder. Purishkevich, with clear conscience, knew that no one would hinder his career, which had nothing to do with his perceived popularity in the Duma.[1693]

When asked, Dmitri never concealed the fact that he was at the Yusupovskii Palace on the relevant night. He accepted that his attendance would offend the sovereign, who by happenstance intended to prove his high regard for Dmitri. *Petrogradskiye Vedomosti* (17 December) reported that Dmitri was to receive the St. Vladimir Order (4th class) "for outstanding efforts against the enemy."[1694] While Dmitri's sister Maria thought her brother's act was "rash"[1695] yet a "monstrous self-sacrifice," his stepmother repeated his explanation this way:

"I wanted to open the Tsar's eyes about the state of affairs, and that with my participation I would have helped His Majesty whereby he would not have to banish the staretz himself ... So I thought that to send away his influence, his Majesty would notice the root of all the considerable misery ..."[1696]

Felix instead boasted about his impending freedom, while staying at the Sergievskii Palace with Dmitri.

The Family Pleads to no Avail

Dmitri sent the dowager empress a letter saying he would never forget how badly Alexandra Fyodorovna had treated him when he tried to see her one day after the murder. Blaming her daughter-in-law for Dmitri's present plight, her diary for that day showed her mood when writing the words "**she**" and "**her**."[1697] Maria, Dmitri's sister, felt that since the "empress was under the influence of her recent sorrow," it caused her "to oppose any concession."[1698]

After consulting with the family in Kiev, under the banner of family honor, Grand Duke Alexander Mikhailovich sought permission to travel to the capital "to defend" Dmitri and Felix.[1699] In Petrograd, on 21 December, the family gathered at Grand Duke Gavril Konstantinovich's place to discuss what could be done. Having received the promised communication from Nikolai II (after the previous day's audience), Grand Duke Pavel Alexandrovich read it out:

"Unable to remove Dmitri's house arrest until the investigation has been completed. Praying to God that Dmitri, where his fervor was lured will come out of this incident clean."[1700]

Pavel Alexandrovich told the family that when he visited Dmitri (at the Sergievskii Palace), his son declared "over an icon and his mother's portrait that the blood of that person did not stain his hands."[1701] Regardless, everyone understood that Nikolai II was not going to release anybody, though "Dmitri's arrest shows his co-participation in the matter concerning Rasputin's murder." Grand Duke Andrei Vladimirovich felt confident that by "going against Tsarskoe Selo, all of Russia and the army would stand by

Dmitri."[1702] For his part, Gavril Konstantinovich presumed that because he knew Dobrovolskii, the Justice Minister would view the matter favorably and "soften Dmitri's involvement." Gavril's request was denied, not as presumed that Dobrovolsky "was not wishing to help Dmitri,"[1703] but because the minister wanted to preserve his job.

Arriving in Tsarskoe Selo on 22 December, Grand Duke Alexander Mikhailovich and his oldest son, Prince Andrei Alexandrovich, entered Nikolai II's study. After exchanging pleasantries, Grand Duke Alexander Mikhailovich plunged into a "passionately defensive speech in defense of the guilty asking that Yusupov and Dmitri Pavlovich would not be treated as ordinary murderers but as patriots, who stood agreeably on a deceitful path ... wanting to save Russia." The emperor complimented the grand duke upon his fine speech[1704] and ended the audience saying that he "promised to be compassionate regarding his choice of punishment."[1705] Alexander Mikhailovich, feeling disconsolate, sent a telegram to the dowager empress pleading for her mediation. She promptly sent her son a telegram requesting him to stop his action against Dmitri. It was a challenging impasse for Nikolai II to resolve, with his wife wanting justice and his mother demanding cessation. Much to her relief, Nikolai II responded to his mother's plea at the end of the same day[1706] saying that he would terminate the matter.

The next day, Friday 23 December, Nikolai II signed the "plea for a settlement" that Dobrovolskii handed to him. In so doing, the procurator's investigation terminated.

Three days after Rasputin's burial, Nikolai Mikhailovich sent the dowager empress this message:

> "*All of Russia knows that the deceased Rasputin and A. F. are one and the same. The first has been murdered, now the other must disappear.*"[1707]

The dowager's reaction cannot be assessed since her diary is silent about this communication. Meanwhile, Sandro approached Nikolai II once more, without success.[1708]

One Call Brings a Sense of Foreboding For Two

On 23 December at ten o'clock at night, Andrei Vladimirovich learnt from Gavril's call that Dmitri was leaving for Persia in four hours' time.[1709] Though a few grand dukes belatedly approached Rodzianko and Trepov, this tactic failed.[1710] Thus, adhering to Protopopov's instruction, Dmitri Pavlovich arrived at Maksimovich's office with his *Adjutant*, General Laiming. Both learned that General Nikolai Kutaisov would escort them to Persia where Dmitri would join General Baratov's First Caucasian Cavalry Division, which was unified with the British forces.[1711] At the time, Kutaisov was on medical leave after sustaining a head wound and the loss of his right eye. At 7 p.m., the emperor (as the Supreme Commander), summoned Kutsaiov and told him about his assignment. Maksimovich provided Kutsaiov with details for the journey to Kasvin (in Persia), where Baratov's headquarters was positioned near the Russian border. Nikolai II transmitted a telegram to Baratov saying Dmitri was not to return to Russia.

Despite the hour, Nikolai Mikhailovich,[1712] Andrei, Kirill, Gavril, Sandro, and Maria Pavlovna arrived at the Nikolayevskii train station to see Dmitri off before his 2 a.m. departure.[1713] Though no one mentioned that Dmitri's father remained in Tsarskoe Selo, the dowager empress wrote about Grand Duke Pavel Alexandrovich's despair, because he was "unable to offer his blessing" for his son's journey.[1714]

The proximity of Nikolasha's location in the Caucasus to Persia proved convenient for the family. Nikolasha sent Baratov a telegram, stating, "You will answer with your head for Grand Duke Dmitri Pavlovich's life commissioned to your billet." To guarantee Dmitri protection, Nikolasha sent two Ingushetian soldiers from his own security team. Both Laiming and Kutaisov (killed in 1918[1715]) returned to Petrograd once they were satisfied that Dmitri was safe.[1716]

During the same evening phone conversation, Andrei also learned that Felix was being sent to his family's estate at Rakitnoye, in the Kursk District of Southern Russia. To prevent his communicating with Dmitri, Felix had to leave ninety minutes earlier. Alexander Mikhailovich thought it appropriate to drive Felix to the railway station, even though an *Okhrana* agent sat in the back. After boarding the train at 12.30 a.m., Felix alighted in Kursk, where he met his father. Together they travelled to Rakitnoye.[1717] Alexander

Mikhailovich arrived shortly afterwards in his car,[1718] no doubt to see his daughter Irina, who had also arrived from Crimea with Zinaida Yusupova. The grand duke stayed overnight before leaving for Kiev to confer with the dowager empress. Following their discussion, the dowager wrote (in part):

"Waited nervously all day for Sandro, who arrived only after 3 in the afternoon ... Everything is so terrible. Good that he went to Petersburg, there simply – just simply a madhouse head by this fury [фурией].*"*[1719]

Life during the first few days proved serene for the Yusupovs in the countryside,[1720] while numerous loved ones helped lessen the annoyance of Felix's exile. Felix wrote to Grand Duchess Ksenya Alexandrovna on 2 January, admitting "we are content with our fate."[1721]

Dmitri's Fate Draws Tension

The family thought the "distribution of punishment was utterly unjust" and that Dmitri, "the least guilty," received "the only sentence of consequence."[1722] Maria Pavlovna (the younger) saw her brother's exile as one of "vengeance of Rasputin's partisans," while Purishkevich appeared to have "enjoyed impunity."[1723] Maria Pavlovna ignored one crucial point. Had the emperor not acted, it would have shown the public that the presence of a Romanov at any crime scene would circumvent the legal process and, in this case, indicate that the primary culprits would avoid punishment. Her expectation that Dmitri (and Felix) ought to be free of all legal responsibility must be seen as an egotistical reflection.

Though Purishkevich thanked God because "the hand of the Grand Duke Dmitri Pavlovich was not stained by the filthy blood [of Rasputin],"[1724] his outburst is puerile because he knew what Dmitri's role involved, which had nothing to do with absorbing culpability for his own participation in the murder.

Pavel Kovalevsky's[1725] submission in 1917 that Rasputin's murder had created the "final split of relations between the Grand Dukes and the Emperor"[1726] was accurate. However, by placing all the blame on the emperor's shoulders and accusing Alexandra Fyodorovna besides Rasputin for Russia's turmoil, Kovalevsky failed to grasp that the grand dukes had maneuvered against the sovereign since the day he became the Supreme Commander in August 1915.

The Decrees That Concluded the Rasputin Case

Zavadsky[1727] thought the emperor did not have the capacity to suspend the criminal investigations. His opinion was based on the *Sudebnii Ustavi* (Court Regulations) promulgated on 20 November 1864. Those regulations constrained a sovereign from interfering with court matters. That law preserved the authority of the Law Court as a separate institution, though the sovereign retained the right to grant specific decrees bearing his signature. Zavadsky's superior, Dobrovolskii, believed that it was correct to extinguish the case, since a juridical prosecution did not affect members of the imperial family that were sheltered by imperial prerogatives. This condition distinguished them from all other citizens, who were subject to the full force of the Criminal Code. Just as with the Rasputin Case, if a criminal matter affected a member of the imperial family, only the emperor had the capacity to close the matter.[1728] This was Nikolai II's approach.

Prosecutor Nikolai Chebyshev published material in 1916 based on Criminal Law cases, saying that because "Petrograd was under conditions of war ... the five main perpetrators, G. D. Dmitri Pavlovich ... Yusupov, Purishkevich, Lazovert and Sukhotin" could have been brought before a military tribunal. This action could have come about if the "*Imperial* authority ... deprived G. D. Dmitri Pavlovich of his grand ducal prerogative, his title ... create the possibility for him be prosecuted in the same way as the other accused."[1729] Of course, this alternative, though feasible, was perilous.

Koshko agreed with procurator Nandelshted's view that since Dmitri knew about the wrongdoing beforehand he could not be pardoned.[1730] Though correct, both had overlooked the harm a legal process would bring to the Romanov dynasty itself, more so in time of war.

Procurator Pavel Pereverzev (Minister of Justice in the Provisional Government) understood the emperor used Regulation No. 16 of the *Ustav ugolovnogo sudoproizvodstva* (The Regulations of the Criminal Court),[1731] which stipulated:

16. A court prosecution in relation to the criminal liability of the accused cannot be brought and (a court prosecution) begun is subject to termination:

(1) following the death of the accused;

(2) following the expiration of time;

(3) following the reconciliation of the accused with the victim in the designated case law and

(4) following an Imperial Decree or general Manifesto of Clemency, granting a pardon.[1732]

Nikolai II did two things:

1. He chose not to distinguish between the wrongdoers; and at the same time,

2. Ensured that Rasputin's murder would never become a matter for the court.

His action ensured that certain issues would not become a matter of public record. In the event of terminating legal proceedings, the Criminal Code provided two avenues of relief. The emperor, taking the administrative route, needed to resolve whether to grant a Decree of Pardon or sign a Manifesto of Clemency. Morally unable to offer his pardon, which would have had the legal effect of releasing the offenders from punishment, Nikolai II signed the decree that offered the offenders a reprieve.[1733] Responding to Dobrovolskii's "plea for a settlement," the sovereign granted clemency, as provided by Statute 16(4).

Both Dmitri Pavlovich and Felix Yusupov received identical Decrees allowable under the law. Without favoring one wrongdoer over the other, Nikolai II followed the law to the letter. Once the Decrees were signed, they had the same effect as a judgement handed down in a law court. In this way, not only had the prosecutorial machinery stopped, but no one would be indicted with Rasputin's murder and brought before a court to answer any charges.

Justice Must be Served

Nikolai II took the matter one step further, by leading the Romanov family in the direction they failed to predict. Weighing up the issues, on the one hand, he needed to satisfy the community (and his wife) that justice would be done and that Dmitri and Felix would not remain without some kind of reprimand, (which he was morally obliged to hand out). On the other side, he wanted to indulge his mother's appeal. With moral fortitude, Nikolai II undoubtedly held the same conviction as his wife that it was impossible to agree to the spilling of blood, no matter who the guilty were.[1734]

Grand Duke Alexander Mikhailovich understood this reality, given that he admitted that "Nicky in his quality of Supreme Protector of Justice was duty bound to punish the assassins, particularly as they happened to be members of his family."[1735] The granting of the Manifesto of Clemency and the banishments that followed did not settle the matter.

It is possible that Nikolai II was unwilling to grant a full pardon to Dmitri for another reason. The emperor, as the Supreme Protector of the Orthodox Church,[1736] knew that Dmitri Pavlovich had violated his Oath of Allegiance to the sovereign, which was affirmed on the day he attained his majority age, in his twentieth year.[1737] This violation was beyond the scope of the Criminal Code. Accepting Gavril Konstantinovich's remark that Dmitri did not go to confession because "he believed himself not deserving of receiving the Sacrament"[1738] strengthens my belief that the Oath that bound all "Grand Dukes and also Grand Duchesses of Imperial blood" to be 'loyal to the Emperor, his heir' and to the Homeland (*Otechestvo*)[1739] had affected Dmitri. Members of the family not born into the Imperial House (but like Felix entered it by way of marriage) did not give this Oath. Nikolai II, unable to forgive the killing of a man, reflected that Dmitri had breached his Oath. This may explain why Dmitri believed he became *nedostoinim* (undeserving) to seek forgiveness from the church through the rite of confession and so unable to receive earthly absolution for his transgression.

This is the interview Grand Duke Alexander Mikhailovich gave to *Le Matin Paris* journal in 1923, which was also published by *Time* magazine:

> "*Perhaps you do not know that one of the assassins is the husband of my adored daughter. I do not doubt that the motives that impelled these men to kill a person whose influence was in certain respects fatal were highly patriotic; but the act itself, the means employed, and the fear of discovery are beneath all Christian ethics and morality. For that reason I disavow this murder with all the strength of my soul and I pray that its authors may repent, and may find the peace of a purified conscience.*"[1740]

Throughout his life, Dmitri stayed silent about the conduct of the murder. That resolve took precedence over easing his conscience and ostensibly assisted his uttering his allegiance to Britain.

The Mastermind Plays His Last Card in Petrograd

On 29 December, Nikolai Mikhailovich visited the Vladimirovichi family. Appearing agitated, he explained that Count Frederiks had telephoned him at the Yacht Club and asked that he come to his home office and discuss a matter though "unpleasant ... it was not unexpected." Nikolai Mikhailovich discovered that the Minister of the Court, acting on Nikolai II's note, had to "pass on that he ceases gossiping otherwise he would be forced to take measures accordingly." Frederiks required an immediate response. Supplying pen and a blank sheet of paper, the grand duke wrote disingenuously: "In recent times as it happens, I rarely visit the yacht-club. Rarely eat there, sometimes (I) want to play cards and I do not stay after 11.30 in the evening."[1741]

The fact that Nikolai II did not wish to talk with Nikolai Mikhailovich underlined the disconnect within the Romanov family. Before his eviction from Petrograd, the grand duke spent New Year's Eve with the Vladimirovich family. En route to Grushevka (Ekaterinoslav Province) he visited the dowager empress in Kiev,[1742] where he disclosed "masses of interesting things."[1743] Though Nikolai Mikhailovich was not upset about his exile,[1744] the *New York Times* claimed he was banished for telling "the Czar the truth."[1745]

Defending Nikolai Mikhailovich, Paléologue said "the Emperor obviously intended to frighten the family" by "wreaking his vengeance on the Grand Duke," who did not deserve such "indignity."[1746] These were unforgiving words, considering that Paléologue noted the "kind and natural" emperor had congratulated the Diplomatic Corps as was customary on the first day of the New Year.

The Petition That Fails

Maria Pavlovna (the younger) described what happened next. One day after Dmitri's departure, she visited Maria Pavlovna (the elder), who proposed the family write a petition seeking Nikolai II's pardon or mitigation of the sentence.[1747] Using Maria Pavlovna's draft, Olga Paley refined the text before sending the final copies for signatures[1748] (DOCUMENT No. 11). At first, Olga held back, thinking her signature might breach her Oath of Allegiance.[1749] By the evening of 29 December,[1750] the petition, bearing sixteen signatures, was sent by courier to Nikolai II, seeking his favorable ruling. [Grand Duke Alexander Mikhailovich, who was not a signatory, thought it was "a silly letter."[1751]] The recurring reference to "Your Imperial Majesty" (using larger script) indicates the tenor in which the plea was written. Here is the first-time translation:

> *Your Imperial Majesty*
>
> *All of us whose signatures You will read at the end of this letter fervently and strenuously plead with You to soften Your severe decision concerning the fate of Grand Duke Dmitri Pavlovich. We know that he is physically in poor health and is deeply traumatized and morally depressed. You, as his Supreme guardian and Supreme carer, know of his deep love from the bottom of his heart towards You and to our Motherland. We plead with Your Majesty in view of his youth and the genuine weak health of Grand Duke Dmitri Pavlovich to permit him to reside either in Usov or in Ilinskoye. Your Imperial Majesty must be aware what grave conditions our troops are found in Persia in view of the absence of dwellings, epidemics and other social scourges, placement there for Grand Duke Dmitri Pavlovich will be equivalent to his complete*

ruin and (the) heart of Your Majesty shall awaken by compassion towards the youth whom You loved, who from childhood had the good fortune to be frequently and often beside You and for whom You were always like a kind father.

May the Lord God inspire Your Majesty to change Your decision and replace your wrath with mercy.

The co-signatories were: Olga Konstantinovna (Dmitri's grandmother), Maria Pavlovna (the elder), Kirill, Viktoria, Boris, Andrei, Pavel (Dmitri's father), Maria Pavlovna (Dmitri's sister), Elizaveta Marikevna, Ioann, Elena, Gavril, Konstantin, Igor, Nikolai Mikhailovich, and his brother, Sergei.

Two days later, on 31 December 1916, the family received a response, which was written at the top of the returned petition:

"No one has the right to commit murder; I know that for many their conscience does not give peace, since not only Dmitri Pavlovich is involved in this. Astonished by your appeal to me. Nikolai"

Maria Pavlovna (the elder) sent Dmitri a copy of the petition with the emperor's response. Refering to the petition, Dmitri told his father, "resolution was completely unexpected," whereby "the phrase '*No one has the right to commit murder*' somehow places the family into the position of a gang of criminals." Dmitri then advised they "must now calm down completely and no longer ask for anything." Although the family's argument related to his welfare and the unsuitability of Persia as a destination, Dmitri said that his health was "excellent" and his "mood was peaceful and calm."[1752]

After Grand Duke Alexander Mikhailovich spoke to Nikolai II, when he restated "no one had the right to kill, be it a Grand Duke or a peasant,"[1753] he understood that he had not only curtailed a public scandal, but that Felix and Dmitri "were not punished at all." The dowager and most of her family overlooked this fact. Instead, they had created a new scandal that was directed against the reigning monarch after Nikolai Mikhailovich distributed copies of the petition (with response) at the Yacht Club as his parting gift while Maria Pavlovna (the elder) "angrily showed it to everyone."[1754]

Meriel Buchanan, the British ambassador's daughter, speaking about her father's copy, aligned with her father's conviction that the emperor "was more than ever determined to maintain a policy of rigid and unbending autocracy."[1755] Paléologue took note of the substance of the sovereign's reply[1756] but unlike other issues that crossed his path, he stood silent about this one. Years later, Alexander Mikhailovich admitted that the family's "ravings and cruelty nauseated" him, as if expecting that the emperor would "decorate his two relatives for having committed a murder."[1757] Grand Duchess Olga Alexandrovna (Nikolai II's sister) thought the "foul murder was the greatest disservice to the one man they had sworn to serve - I mean Nicky. The involvement of two members of the family did nothing but reveal the appalling decadence in the upper social strata."[1758]

Since Grand Duchess Elizaveta Fyodorovna was in Moscow on 29 December, she wrote her own plea to Nikolai II, stating (in part):

> *"Returning* [from Diveyevo Monastery], *I know that Felix killed him, my little Felix, whom I have known as a child, who feared to kill a living being and did not want to become a soldier, so as not to spill blood. I imagined that he needed to overcome, in order to carry out this deed, and like him, prompted by feelings of patriotism, decided to rid his sovereign and the nation from the source of misfortune. I telegraphed Dmitri, not knowing where the lad is now, but did not receive a reply, and since then everything is covered by some kind of silence. (I) do not want to know the details, they say many are involved, all sent away to distant corners. A crime remains a crime, but this one is a special kind, akin to a duel or a matter of patriotism, and for these deeds the law, I believe softens the punishment."*[1759]

Both Alexander Mikhailovich and Spiridovich were wrong to think "the guilty ... remained unpunished."[1760] Nicholai II's measures carried a shrewd twist. Dmitri was transferred from his undemanding presence at Stavka headquarters, surrounded by relatives and officers he knew. His military transfer also meant that he was detached from the imperial suite. Felix, on the other hand, could not complete his final military examinations and consequently was deprived of the honor of graduating from the prestigious *Pazheskii Korpus* (Corps des Pages). By contrast, Rodzianko believed the emperor's stance against the Grand Dukes Dmitri and Nikolai Mikhailovich were "repressive measures." The suggestion that Dmitri's treatment was cruel[1761] served to mock the sovereign's moral values. With no evidence to support the story, another author suggested that because Dmitri did not want to marry one of the daughters in defiance of the emperor's expectation, he retaliated by deviously accusing Dmitri. The critic implied the emperor had abused his power by finding a way to strike at Dmitri because of "Alexandra Fyodorovna's loss."[1762]

Conversations Can be Fraught With Difficulties

Interestingly, the dowager empress met two of the would-be co-conpirators because of their link with the Russian Red Cross Society, of which she was the patron. On 9 December 1915, Vladimir Purishkevich and Dr. Lazovert were part of a group which presented Maria Fyodorovna a commemorative album,[1763] which showed their hospital train and nursing staff.

As soon as Maria Pavlovna (the younger) arrived in Kiev, she handed Maria Fyodorovna a letter that was written by her father. Her diary entry that day emphasized her disgust:

> *"Niki did not even receive Paul* (Pavel*), because he cannot decide anything because of her, that, who despises everyone ... This is how this bitter year ends!"*[1764]

Because of her need to be appraised about matters relating to Rasputin and Alexandra Fyodorovna, the dowager empress played an unintentional part in his downfall. She was confident that Rasputin influenced her son and daughter-in-law, after taking note of prejudiced informers that included Rodzianko, Nikolai Mikhailovich and Zinaida Yusupova. When Maria Fyodorovna learnt from Grand Duke Alexander Mikhailovich that Rasputin was murdered, she stated:

> *"Thank God, Rasputin has been removed ... But we now are facing an even larger misfortune."*[1765]

Like most of her family, the dowager did not think that Dmitri had wronged the family by partaking in Rasputin's killing. Most of the family protested that Dmitri's exile to Persia was too severe. It was not until 17 February 1917, when the dowager appealed to her son's sense of religiosity by reminding him:

> "*Since we are now fasting ... one must ... forgive everyone and seek forgiveness from those who we have insulted. I am certain that you sense that your brusque reply to the family deeply offended them in that you without justification have thrown a dreadful accusation against them.*"[1766]

Maria Fyodorovna blamed her son for the family rift. Conversely, the family did not seek forgiveness for their spiteful letters and judgements that Alexandra Fyodorovna must be either liquidated or locked up in a secluded monastery for the duration of the war. Instead of heeding his mother's rebuke, Nikolai II revealed an inner strength by reaching a just compromise that should have satisfied everyone. The dowager failed to see that her son could not allow Dmitri to continue his military life in the imperial suite as if nothing had passed between them. Believing that Rasputin's murder was justified, Dmitri knew he could never return to Mogilev Headquarters nor remain in the imperial suite. Conceivably the dowager's discontent arose because of this outcome, which exposed his downfall.

The Consequence of Nikolai II's Response

Taneeva overheard the emperor privately declare:

> "*I am ashamed before Russia that the hands of my relatives are stained with the blood of this peasant (muzhik).*"[1767]

Nikolai II's response on the petition had alienated all branches of his family, to the point that when the February Uprising erupted, most of them openly welcomed the Provisional Government before the sovereign was aware that the Duma and the *Generalitet* sought his abdication.

When One Murder is Not Enough to Resolve One's Difference of Opinion

With Rasputin out of the way, Rodzianko, the grand dukes and Purishkevich anticipated a progressive political change. But that was not to be. Sergei Oldenburg, as an observer, remarked, "if Rasputin had the meaning that was attributed to him, his murder should have pacified their fears." Instead, the realization was that their discontent was not about the *strannik* at all. The habitual gossipers turned their heads in the direction of new scapegoats. Some began to accuse Protopopov of having undue influence over the court.[1768] Anna Rodzianko telling Zinaida Yusupova that present-day political affairs had not altered in the way they had all expected following Rasputin's murder, whereby:

> *"Now it is clear that Alexandra Fyodorovna alone is not to blame for everything, but as the Russian Tsar he is more of a criminal."*[1769]

Time to Sweep Away Another Nuisance

Paléologue mentioned that because of Dmitri's participation in murdering Rasputin, Grand Duchess Maria Pavlovna (the elder) spoke "of nothing less than saving tsarism" from the current sovereign. Her strategy involved gaining the loyalty of several regiments under Dmitri's direction and "seize" the monarch and proclaim his son Alexei as the new Tsar "under the regency of Grand Duke Nicholas Nikolayevich."[1770] Maria Pavlovna (the elder) trusted Paléologue and must have known that he favored revolutionary dogma. Paléologue's father, Alexandru Paleologu (born with the surname Văcărescu), had been banished from Romania in 1848 for plotting to kill one princely member of the monarch family during the Wallacian (now a region of Romania) Revolution.[1771] General Spiridovich, as one concerned with security issues, knew about the French ambassador's family history,[1772] which is seldom mentioned nowadays.

Grand Duke Alexander Mikhailovich wrote a very long letter that warned Nikolai II:

> *"We are suffering the most dangerous moment in the history of Russia. ...some kind of internal forces in Russia are leading you and invariably Russia towards inevitable death."* [1773]

Nikolai II's responded by thanking Sandro for sending the letter from Kiev.[1774]

New Convictions Must Replace Old Allegiances

In an attempt to understand possible motives, which each of the conspirators believed in to defend Rasputin's murder, this narrative needs to advance a few months. Following his return to Petrograd, Felix Yusupov gave a series of interviews to the media. Vladimir Samoilov from *Russkaya Volya* published this discourse on 13 March 1917:

> QUESTION: *"By whom and how and for what reason was Rasputin killed?"*
>
> REPLY: *"Rasputin is dead – what difference does it make by whom and how. ...In Petrograd as far as I can remember no one questioned me. In Rakitnoye - the Court investigator came to visit."*
>
> QUESTION: *"What was his name?"*
>
> REPLY: *"Can't remember, there were a few of them."*
>
> QUESTION: *"You Prince are apprehensive to give the surnames of the investigators. However, the investigation has stopped and not to offer that secret is pointless."*
>
> REPLY: *"Since the investigation has stopped, then there is no reason to talk about it. ...Please note that I never belonged to any political party. I was educated in England and I liked the political system of that country. With regard to Russia, for the present moment I kneel before the members of our new government and consider that all citizens have the duty to submit without dissent to this true savior of the Motherland."* [1775]

This interview shows that Felix Yusupov favored the British monarchic system over the former autocratic imperial system in Russia. His remarks lend to the question as to what factors prompted his political conversion. The following may explain his new position:

> *"One word from the Emperor, one of his summons towards a new life and also to new sacrifices for the*

benefit of Russia – everything would have been forgotten, everything forgiven."[1776]

There is one sentence worth mentioning in Dmitri Pavlovich's letter to Felix that reveals that their past conversations focused on the political turmoil in Imperial Russia during 1916:

> *"Yes! It has happened! It happened, the possibility of which we together so believed in. Because of an empty and shortsighted obstinacy of one woman – the final catastrophe happened, which even swept away 'Tsarskoe'* [the Emperor] *and all of us in one, for the surname «Romanov» is now a synonym for all kinds of dirt ... for all kinds of filth, obscenities and indecency."* [1777]

Given the tenor of conversations and letters that were exchanged among the extended family, it is not surprising to find that Dmitri also blamed his former guardian's wife, Alexandra Fyodorovna, for much of Russia's internal political ills. Dmitri appeared unfazed by Nikolai II's abdication. He, like Felix, changed his allegiance with ease, telling his father that "with honor for the created situation without doubt called for the complete allegiance to the Provisional Government."[1778] His hatred for the imperial system came after Nikolai II took on the Supreme Command in 1915. It intensified to the point that he seized the opportunity to offend Nikolai II and myopically did not consider the heir to the throne, Alexei Nikolayevich.

Giving another interview, Felix Yusupov provided this insight in April 1917:

> *"During the final years he [Nikolai II] suffered a great evolution and literally became unrecognizable. Associated with this, one cannot deny that the fatal role in the life of the dynasty, was the former 'gosudarinya' [the Empress], who believed in Grigorii Rasputin's miracles and for him and his accomplices she sacrificed the nation's approval and national interests."*[1779]

It seems that it was easy for idealistic young men like Dmitri (aged twenty-five) and Felix (aged twenty-nine) to align with the charismatic dominance of Nikolai Mikhailovich and the highly persuasive Duma delegate Vladimir Purishkevich. Unlike the Romanov family members, Purishkevich, the outsider, irate over the ineptitude of the sitting monarch, fitted into Nikolai Mikhailovich's scheme effortlessly.

All the Russian co-conspirators had three elements in common:

► They detested Alexandra Fyodorovna.

► They believed that Grigorii Rasputin was Russia's most destructive political element, corrupting Russian public life (as stated by Purishkevich on 16 November).

► They became preoccupied "to purge Russia of Rasputin and the Rasputin group."[1780]

Grand Duke Alexander Mikhailovich pointed out that the extended family's animosity towards Alexandra Fyodorovna was so intense that they needed to draw on the dowager empress' assistance to achieve their objective:

"What concerns D. P. [Dmitri Pavlovich] and F. [Felix] that is all proceeding as I had predicted and within days it will all be finished ... I deliberately did not touch on the question about you [Nikolai Mikhailovich], nor D. P. and F., not wanting to add anything further. Misha does not see any other way out except to send her to Livadia, but the question is – how to do this, he will never agree to this, and yes, she will not go. I shall try and convince Mama to go to Stavka, when N. will travel there."[1781]

This message reveals why the dowager empress made the long train journey from Kiev. Backed by the family, her mission was to convince her son to part from his wife, at least for the duration of the war. By the time the dowager reached Mogilev on 4 March, both of her sons had relinquished the throne. When mother and eldest son met, their facial expressions gave nothing away.[1782] The dowager wrote in her diary, "Niki was unbelievably calm and imposing despite this dreadfully humiliating state of affairs."[1783] The former emperor clutched a wad of telegrams signed by his generals in the field that demanded his abdication and showed Alexander Mikhailovich the one sent by Nikolasha, saying "even he." [1784]

In 1925, Soviet author David Zaslavsky suggested that Purishkevich was quite prepared to restrain Nikolai II, if only to save the crown.[1785] Why so? In December 1919, Purishkevich revealed that he despised the Romanov state politics, because a "Russian autocratic Tsar" had to "treat the Russian nation" as if he was a "beast."[1786] Purishkevich and all the individuals who knew about or were directly concerned with Nikolai Mikhailovich's conspiracy circle concluded (retrospectively after they murdered Rasputin) that Nikolai II was Russia's real political problem.

On 8 March, Nikolai II's train moved away from the platform while his mother, standing by the *coupe* window from her train, watched her son's expressionless face for what would prove to be the very last time. Maria Fyodorovna's prophetic words said only months before, "he will remain completely alone"[1787] seemed more appropriate on the day the emperor abdicated.

Narishkin-Kurakina revealed that "knowing quite well that the Tsar would never consent to be an accomplice to such treason [the alleged separate peace treaty], the conspirators used their efforts to bring about the Emperor's abdication."[1788] The schemers referred to by Narishkin-Kurakina were very different to the conspirators who were involved in Rasputin's murder. Neverteless, both groups, determined to create political turmoil, had succeeded in bringing down the monarch. Rasputin's murderers primarily wanted to protect the monarchy, but once the regime collapsed, both groups welcomed it. Few mourned Nikolai II's downfall.

Felix Yusupov, the 'heroic' murderer, revelled in his new freedom, as evidenced in his statement given to *Novoye Vremya* (*New Times*) in April 1917:

> "*I am pleased that the criminals, who surrounded the Romanov House, are sitting in the Fortress. All these people - the Protopopovs, Sheglovitovs, Voyeikovs and others – deserve the most severe punishment. They sold Russia.*"[1789]

Without doubt, Grand Duchess Elizaveta Fyodorovna's encouragement gave Dmitri and Felix the momentum needed that they were on the right path to safeguard Russia's future, since she reasoned "there was no other way."[1790] She, like many of her family and friends, thought the autocrat had fallen under his wife's influence (who in turn was manipulated by the charlatan Rasputin). Under these circumstances, it was easy to justify Rasputin's murder and just as easy to watch Nikolai II being "swept away."[1791] Thus, Anna Taneeva rang true after she asserted the court was "rotten,"[1792] after "they" plotted political change and the murder of persons to resolve their differences. Rasputin's murder was immoral; its manner was brutal. That the murderers could have judged that by murdering Rasputin, their action would have solved the wide-ranging political issues that plagued much of Nikolai II's reign, can only be judged as bizarre. If Nikolai II acquiesced to the demands of his family, then what kind of dangerous signal would he as the sovereign have sent out to the broader community? Indeed, had Russian society sunk so low that the death of a *muzhik* was to be commended?

Chapter Ten Photos

PHOTO 30: Vladimir Purishkevich, first on the left and
Stanislav Lazovert (wearing two St. George Cross 4th Class
medals) in one of Purishkevich's Red Cross trains, 1915.

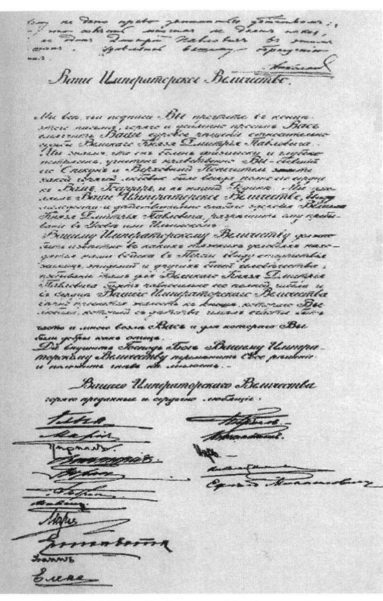

DOCUMENT No. 11: One copy of the Romanov Family
petition forwarded to Nikolai II with the 16 signatures. The
sovereign's response appears at the top of the page, 1916.

CONCLUSION

Until an earlier version of this book appeared in 2010, many details about Grigorii Rasputin's life and the manner of his death was unknown, leaving the path clear to craft falsehoods, not unlike during his lifetime. Despite common belief, Rasputin was not a monk, nor had the Siberian *muzhik* lead a life of depravity. This book has dismissed countless myths about Rasputin. It has shown that the hatred directed at him was not held by the ordinary soldiers fighting on far-flung battlefields, nor was it voiced by the majority of the population. The loathing was uttered by individuals who dominated Russian society. Given their lofty position, their contrived stories gained the tenor of truthfulness, which the media disseminated. Allegations flowed about Rasputin's improper relationship with the imperial family. Interconnected with this scenario was the political conspiracy that began once Nikolai II took on the Supreme Command during the war. The military and government ministers blamed Alexandra Fyodorovna for meddling in that decision and accused Rasputin of finding a way to direct the Supreme Command.

The conspiracies linked after Pavel Milyukov spoke in the Duma on 1 November 1916. By his own admission, his reactionary speech steered the nation towards the revolution in order to obliterate the monarchy. The constant barrage of insinuations and conjectures by Duma representatives destabilized the imperial government. Grigorii Rasputin was caught up in a devious battle for power. His name proved convenient for the various political factions to discredit the emperor. Within this setting, the public, vexed by the Duma announcements, began to act upon its fears, accusing Rasputin of being pro-German and not wanting the war to continue. Despite the coercive actions taken by the battlefront generals who forced Nikolai II to abdicate, the political shift most likely delayed the end of the war. Had the field commanders remained loyal to the emperor and to their Oath of Allegiance and focused solely on military matters, the Duma would not have succeeded in its quest for change. Instead, the Duma accommodated its domestic activists and, with the endorsement from the cabal formed by some grand dukes, the autocratic regime was left undefended.

The silence emanating from the church hierarchy in protecting the guardian of their church cannot be overlooked.

I have revealed that the attacks against Rasputin were coordinated and specious. I make evident that Nikolai Mikhailovich abetted Grigorii Rasputin's murder and at whose behest. Once Rasputin's corpse was found, the forensic evidence proved beyond reasonable doubt that he died at the hands of Russian citizens. Rasputin **did not drown**. Rasputin **did not ingest poison**. Though the 2014 Russian film *Rasputin R* drew on material first described in 2005 that a British spy killed Grigorii Rasputin, my ballistics evidence proves this is not so. I also prove that Felix Yusupov and Vladimir Purishkevich turned out to be cold-blooded murderers. The murder was brutal, it was heartless and above all, an immoral, premeditated act.

Few, including the church, condemned Rasputin's murder. His death as advocated by Grand Duchess Elizaveta Fyodorovna was not a special kind. There was nothing heroic about shooting an unarmed man and then inflicting physical abuse on the victim's corpse. The murder called to question moral standards, which Nikolai II alluded to, following his relatives' pleas for leniency for one of their own. Although the murderers supposed that Rasputin's death would alter the political course, they failed to get their gruesome message across.

In 1917, the Provisional Government was unable to find one document indicating that Rasputin was involved with espionage, or influenced the court politically, notwithstanding the accusations thrust at him by the Duma or the extended imperial family. Within a year of its coming to power, the Bolshevik Government set aside the *Entente* document co-signed by imperialists (in 1914) to sign a peace treaty with Germany. Grand Duke Alexander Mikhailovich conceded that by that time, "nobody cared to remember that the former Russian Empire had fought on the side of the Allies."

To understand Grigorii Rasputin, it is best to refer to the explanation Nikolai II gave to his son Alexei:

> *"When I had anxiety, doubts, unpleasantness, it was enough to speak five minutes with Grigorii, so that at that time I could feel strengthened and pacified. He was*

always capable of telling me that which I needed to hear."

As this book confirms, Grigorii Rasputin was a *muzhik* (as identified by Nikolai II), who practiced his faith, was respected by the monarch and was loyal to his homeland - three immutable qualities which Russian society struggled to defend.

***

On Saturday 14 April 1918, when the former sovereign, his wife and their daughter, Grand Duchess Maria Nikolayevna, were transiting from their place of detention in Tobolsk to another in Ekaterinburg, these words were written in their diaries:

> **Nikolai II**: *"In Pokrovskoye village there was changeover, stood a long time right across Grigorii's house and saw all his family, staring through the window."*

> **Alexandra Fyodorovna**: *"Around 12 arrived in Pokrovskoye, changed horses. We stood for a long time in front of the house of our Friend. Saw his family and friends, watching from the windows."*

Grand Duchess Maria Nikolayevna left a noteworthy record in her book. It is a drawing of Grigorii Rasputin's home that is similar to the first photograph in this book (**Photo 31**).

PHOTO 31: Grand Duchess Mariya Nikolayevna's drawing of Grigorii Rasputin's house and yard, 1918.

3

Letters and Telegrams given to Nikolai II on Monday 19 December 1916

▪ **Letter from Zinaida Yusupova to her son Felix - 25 November 1916**

"Now it is too late to avoid without a scandal whereas it was only possible to save all, by demanding the removal of the manager [Rasputin] for the duration of [the] war and [the] non-interference of Valide [the Empress] in matters of State. And now I repeat that until these two matters will not be liquidated, nothing can be accomplished in a peaceful way. Tell this to uncle Misha from me."

▪ **Letter from Anya Rodzianko to Zinaida Yusupova - 1 December 1916**

"All assigned to change the destiny of the Duma peace talks are in [the] hands of [the] deranged German, Rasputin, Vyrubova, Pitirim and Protopopov."

▪ **Letter from Grand Duchess Elizaveta Fyodorovna to Nikolai II - 16/17 December1916**

[Written at the Convent of the Holy Trinity and posted in Moscow 18 December 1916]

"...The news arrived here that Felix murdered him [Rasputin], my little Felix, I knew him as a child, who all his life was afraid to even kill animals, who did not want to become a military [person], so that he could never have the occasion to spill blood. And I imagine myself, as to what he must have gone through, in order to carry out such a deed, and how, moved by patriotism, he decided to save his sovereign and the nation from what caused the suffering of all. I telegraphed

Dmitri, not knowing, where the lad was, but received no answer, and since then some kind of silence lingers. I do not want to know all the actions, which are said, to be involved. All have been sent to different parts; and thank God, that is so – a crime remains a crime, but this, for the future may be counted as a duel and looked upon as an act of patriotism, and for such duels the law, I believe, is lenient...."

▪ **Telegram from Grand Duchess Elizaveta Fyodorovna to Zinaida Yusupova**

Koreiz, No. 18117, 18/12, transmitted at 9h 52' [In French]

"All my profound and fervent prayers surround you all for the patriotic act of your son. May God protect you. Have returned from Saratov and Diveyeva where I spent ten days in prayer. Elisabeth"

▪ **Telegram from Grand Duchess Elizaveta to Dmitri Pavlovich**

Petrograd from Moscow, No. 18017, 18 December 1916, transmitted at 9h 30' [In English]

"Just returned late yesterday evening after having been over a week at Saratov [in Russian] *and Divyev* [in Russian] *prayed for you all darlings. Please give me detailed news by letter. May God strengthen Felix after the patriotic deed he fulfilled. Ella."*

▪ **Letter from Anna Rodzianko to Zinaida Yusupova - 24 December 1916**

"Despite all gloom enveloping us I firmly believe that we shall emerge victorious similar to the struggle against the external enemy and with the internal [enemy]. *Holy Rus' cannot perish against* [the] *gang of deranged and lowly people: too much noble blood has spilt for* [the] *glory and honor of Russia for* [the] *devil's power to ascend."*

APPENDIX B
Encounters between Nikolai II
and Grigorii Rasputin

[The dates and comments are sourced from Nikolai II's diaries]

1905

[Visit took place at the Lower Dacha, Peterhof]

1 November: "At 4'clock we drove to *Sergievka*. Drank tea with Militsiya and Stanok. We were introduced to a man of God – Grigorii from the Tobolsk Province."

1906

[Both visits took place at the Lower Dacha, Peterhof]

18 July: "During the evening we were at *Sergievka* and we saw Grigorii!"

13 October: "Grigorii arrived at 6.15 and brought us a St. Simeon *Verkhoturye* icon. He saw the children* and chatted with us until 7.15."

1907

[Both visits took place at the Alexandrovskii Palace]

6 April: "After tea we went to the other side upstairs and there we had the joy to see and speak with Grigorii!"

15 November: "After tea Grigorii arrived unexpectedly!"

1908

[Most visits took place at Taneeva's cottage, Tsarskoe Selo]

12 March: "Saw Grigorii with Feofan. It was so good!"

10 May: "During the evening saw Grigorii at Anya V's and chatted about two hours."

23 May: "After dinner had a ride and went over to Anya V's, where [we] saw Grigorii and spoke to him for a long time."

4 August: "Arrived at Peterhof at 6½. Alix at that time was talking to Grigorii, with whom I also saw for half an hour!" [At the Lower Dacha, Peterhof]

31 October: "Saw Grigorii, with whom [we] sat for a long time."

6 November: "Saw Grigorii and chatted for a long time."

27 December: "Drove over to Anna V's, where we saw Grigorii."

1909

[4 February-26 April: visits took place at the Alexandrovskii Palace, 23 June-5 August: visits took place at the Lower Dacha, Peterhof]

4 February: "At 6 o'clock, Archbishop Feofan and Grigorii came to [see] us. He also saw the children."

24 February: "After dinner drove to Anna's and sat with Grigorii for one and half hours."

28 February: "Grigorii came at 2½ [2.30] whom we received with all the children. It was so good to listen to him with all of the family."

3 April: "Feofan and Grigorii came at 6 o'clock. Sat together for almost one hour."

26 April: "Saw Grigorii with Olga between 6 and 7½."

27 April: "In the afternoon …went to Anna's and saw Grigorii."

23 June: "After tea Feofan, Grigorii and Makarii came over." [At the Lower Dacha, Peterhof].

5 August: "Saw Grigorii." [At the Lower Dacha, Peterhof]

13 August: "Evening had the pleasure to see Grigorii." [At the Lower Dacha, Peterhof]

15 August: "During the evening chatted with Grigorii for a long time." [At the Lower Dacha, Peterhof]

1910

[All visits took place at the Alexandrovskii Palace]

3 January: "Saw Grigorii between 7 and 8 o'clock."

6 January: "Grigorii came to see Alix, with whom we sat and chatted for a long time."

27 January: "Saw Grigorii for half an hour after dinner."

1 February: "Saw Grigorii briefly."

3 February: "Chatted with Grigorii for a long time."

8 February: "Saw Grigorii."

12 February: "Saw Grigorii after dinner."

14 February: "Saw Grigorii; bid him farewell."

1911

12 February: "…drove to Anna's, where we chatted a long time with Grigorii."
[At Anna V's house, Tsarskoe Selo]

4 June: "After lunch [we] had the joy to see Grigorii after his return from Jerusalem and Athos." [At the Alexandrovskii Palace]

4 August: "Grigorii arrived afterwards and sat with us until 11½."
[At the Lower Dacha, Peterhof]

24 August: "Saw Grigorii during the evening]." [At the Lower Dacha, Peterhof]

25 November: "After dinner received Grigorii, who arrived in Yalta today." [Livadia in Yalta, Crimea, FIRST VISIT]

28 November: "Grigorii came to see us once more." [Livadia in Yalta, Crimea]

1912

No visits recorded.

1913

[Unless otherwise stated, most visits took place at the Alexandrovskii Palace]

18 January: "At 4 o'clock we received kind Grigorii, who stayed with us 1¼ hours."

15 February: "Grigorii arrived and was with us for over an hour."

18 April: "After tea, we sat for a long time with Grigorii."

1 June: "After tea [we] received Grigorii."

17 July: "Grigorii arrived at 7 o'clock, stayed briefly with Alix and Alexei*, [then] spoke with me and [my] daughters and left." [At the Lower Dacha, Peterhof]

6 August: "After tea saw Grigorii for a minute." [At the Lower Dacha, Peterhof]

23 September: "Saw Grigorii during the evening." [Livadia in Yalta, Crimea, SECOND STAY]

5 October: "After tea we received Grigorii at home, who stayed until 7¾." [Livadia in Yalta, Crimea]

1914

[Unless otherwise stated, most visits took place at the Alexandrovskii Palace]

2 January: "During the evening had the joy of seeing Grigorii."

20 January: "During the evening [we] sat and drank tea with Grigorii."

2 February: "Grigorii arrived in the afternoon, chatted together one hour."

18 February: "During the service I saw Grigorii in the altar." [Fyodorovskii Cathedral, Tsarskoe Selo]

20 February: "Saw Grigorii, who was at the evening service." [Fyodorovskii Cathedral]

14 March: "During the evening we sat with Grigorii."

18 May: "Saw Grigorii." [Livadia in Yalta, Crimea, THIRD STAY]

21 May: "[We] saw Grigorii and bid him farewell." [Livadia in

Yalta, Crimea]

17 June: "During the evening Grigorii sat with us."

Russia enters the War on 20 July

[August – November: all visits took place at the Alexandrovskii Palace]

22 August: "After dinner saw Grigorii for the first time since his injury."

25 August: "[We] saw Grigorii during the evening."

5 September: "During the evening we had the comfort of speaking with Grigorii from 9.45 until 11.30."

14 September: "Yesterday we waited a long time for Grigorii's arrival. Then we sat with him for a long time."

19 September: "During the evening [we] briefly saw Grigorii."

28 September: "During the evening we saw and chatted with Gr. a long time."

7 October: "During the evening [we] had a good discussion with Grigorii." [At the Alexandrovskii Palace]

17 October: "Only this evening after the calming influence of discussions with Grigorii, [my] soul became stable."

4 November: "This evening we had consoling discussions with Grigorii before his departure for his homeland."

1915

[Unless otherwise stated, most visits took place at the Alexandrovskii Palace]

2 January: "Later Grigorii arrived."

9 January: "After lunch Grigorii came to us from Anna's and stayed for tea."

20 January: "Grigorii came to us during the evening."

7 February: "During the evening Grigorii sat with us."

27 February: "Spent half an hour with Grigorii at Anna's." [At

Anna Taneeva's home]

22 March: "Grigorii arrived briefly at 6 o'clock."

1 April: "The three of us sat with Grigorii."

27 April: "We spent the evening with Grigorii at Anna's." [At Anna Taneeva's home]

4 May: "After dinner [we] saw Grigorii who blessed [me] for the road (first visit to Baranovichi *Stavka*)."

18 May: "After dinner Grigorii arrived to [see] us."

31 May: "[We] saw Grigorii this evening."

9 June: "[We] sat with Grigorii during the evening."

31 July: "Arrived [by car] at Anna's place where we saw Grigorii and his son [Dmitri]." [At Anna Taneeva's home]

4 August: "This evening Grigorii arrived, to chat with us and [he] blessed me with an icon."

Nikolai II becomes the Commander-in-Chief of the Imperial army and navy on 23 August

[All visits in December took place at the Alexandrovskii Palace]

28 September: "[We] spent the evening well at Anna's with Grigorii." [At Anna Taneeva's cottage]

21 November: "During the evening sat at Anna's with Grigorii." [At Anna Taneeva's cottage]

6 December: "After lunch Grigorii arrived, [we] sat together by Alexei's bed*."

11 December: "After tea we briefly saw Grigorii."

26th December: "Grigorii sat with us until vespers."

1916

[20 January – 23 April: visits took place at the Alexandrovskii Palace, 21 October – 2 December: visits took place at Taneeva's cottage]

20 January: "Grigorii sat with us for an hour."

26 January: "After lunch we saw Grigorii."

24 February: "[We] saw Grigorii."

23 April: "[We] saw Grigorii."

21 October: "Around 10 drove to Anna's – saw Grigorii, drank tea together."

26 November: "During the evening [we] sat at Anna's with Grigorii until 11 o'clock."

2 December: "This evening [we] spent at Anna's in conversation with Grigorii."

*Rasputin saw Alexei three times: 13.10.1906, 17.07.1913 and 6.12.1915; the latter two visits were due to the *Tsesarevich*'s ill-health.

APPENDIX C
Impressions and one Judgment

Grand Duchess Olga Alexandrovna [Nikolai II's youngest sister] -

"I never liked the man. ... All the children seemed to like him. I found him rather primitive. His voice was very rough and uncouth ...Rasputin was and always remained a peasant ...He was always respectful... Rasputin's reputed influence was non-existent where Nicky was concerned..."[1793]

Sergei Witte [Prime Minister until 1906] -

"What we see as a result of the decay of the church are people like Rasputin ..."[1794]

"He knows Russia better than anyone, its soul, aspirations and historic intentions."[1795]

Peter Stolypin [Prime Minister 8 July 1906 to 5 September 1911], observation made in 1906:

A cunning peasant, who presented *"a moral impression"*, was nevertheless asked to *"voluntarily leave Petersburg and return to your village and never re-appear here again."*[1796]

Captain Nikolai Sablin [Commander of the Imperial yacht *Shtandart*]

"The heir lives thanks to Rasputin's prayers. I completely refute the possibility that there was a physical closeness between Rasputin and the Empress."[1797]

Colonel Dmitri Loman [*ktitor* (fundraiser) of the Fyodorovskii Cathedral, Tsarskoe Selo]

"Rasputin left me with a very good impression. ... He approached people who were suffering spiritually and immediately guessed what that person was seeking, what concerned him. Simple in his attention and the kindness

which he showed to his discussion group ..."[1798]

Senator Stepan Beletsky [Director of Police], comment made in 1912:

"Rasputin possessed unusual instinctive mind, viewed practical life as a Siberian peasant ... ignored mockery and criticism ..."[1799]

Pierre Gilliard [Guardian and tutor to the *Tsesarevich*], observations made in 1913:

> *"Rasputin played a very insignificant part in the life of the Czarevitch (sic)."*

> *"I had a distinct impression that I was in the presence of a sinister and evil being."*

> *"His prophecies only confirmed the secret wishes of the Czarina."*[1800]

Alexander Protopopov [Minister of Internal Affairs], opinion given submitted at the K Commission of Inquiry 1917:

> *"...He was not completely normal in my opinion. A person, who certainly used his particular outlook; he could influence some, especially women and small children by hypnosis. ...*

> *...never hid that he was a close person there ... close to all of the* [imperial] *family.*

> *...clever, but not a mature person. ..."*[1801]

Yuliya Dehn [A companion to the Empress], opinion submitted at the Kerensky Commission of Inquiry in 1917:

> *"...the Empress never kissed Rasputin's hand. Rasputin did not change in her presence; he remained just as he was in our company and the discussion he led, were on the same topics as in our company ...in conversation she called him Grigorii ...the Empress believed that Rasputin's prayers create miracles ..."*[1802]

Professor Vladimir Rudnev [Procurator at the Extraordinary Commission of Inquiry from 11 March 11 to until August, 1917 that investigated *"the activities of the dark forces."*

"...Rasputin categorically declined any kind of monetary allowances ...deeply loyal to the Throne. The only thing Rasputin allowed himself that was payment for his apartment from His Imperial's Chancellery; he also accepted gifts for personal work for the imperial Family – shirts, belts etc.

...He possessed to a large degree some kind of inner strength that influenced the psyche of strangers, akin to a form of hypnosis."

...not withstanding that he was almost illiterate, he was far from ordinary person and differed with an innate sharp mind, immense resources, control and the ability to sometimes with incredulity markedly articulate, especially giving characterizations to individual persons. His outward rudeness and simplicity of responsiveness ... were undoubtedly imagined.

...the question about his association with the Khlyst sect was taken up at the invitation of Professor Gromoglasov...from Moscow Theology Academy ...he did not find any indication of his association with the khlyst ...studying all of Rasputin's writings concerning religious questions, Gromoglasovalso did not find Khlyst indicators.

In fact, ... the doors of his house were always open; through which thronged a varied group of people, [who] *ate at his* expense; *giving himself the oreiol of charity ... constantly receiving money from petitioners ... widely gave out this money to the underprivileged and in fact persons from the poor classes, sought some kind of favors from him even of a material character.*

His influence in the Court was undoubtedly enormous. Examples of his influence are numerous... searching in the chancellery [concerning] *the Court Commandant General Voyeikov a few letters were found with his name ... showing notes made in Voyeikov's hand ... letters were* [also] *found* [addressed] *to the former Council President Minister Stürmer ... However, all these letters dealt exclusively with the refusal of individual patronages ... who petitioned Rasputin.*

Examination of the Inquiry material draws one to the undeniable conclusion that Rasputin's influence within the Court was accorded with the intensely religious character of Their Majesties ... and prayers for the Sovereign ... that was observed by the Imperial Family and in individual cases ... on the psyche of those connected to the Court ... for example, bringing Gospazha Vyrubova [Taneeva] into consciousness, including the beneficial influence on the health of the Naslednik (Heir)...

This influence of Rasputin over the Imperial Family was naturally used by smart people ... In particular, this was vividly demonstrated by the activities of the former Minister of the Interior A. N. Khvostov and the Director of the Police Department, Beletsky, to consolidate their position within the Court...

Out of all State representatives, Khvostov was closest to Rasputin...

However, the Minister of Internal Affairs, Protopopov had the greater connection with Rasputin ...it must be said that Rasputin treated Protopopov with immense compassion...

It should be noted that in all the massive correspondence there was hardly any signs or interpretation on political issues: this correspondence carried a clearly intimate, domestic character. In those places in the correspondence which speak about Rasputin ... satisfactorily illuminates the attitude of the Empress towards this person, as if a provider of God's Word...

In all this correspondence extending almost ten years I did not find one letter using the German language... and questioning those associated with the Court I have established that the German language, long before the last war was not accepted by the Court.

...in fact there were no indicators established that the Imperial House dealt with the German [House] during

the war.

...the Empress was unable to objectively evaluate ...Rasputin's influence on the Heir's state of health and searched ...not in hypnotic power but in those Heavenly powers, which was provided by Her profound conviction ... in Rasputin.

...in the matter of Rasputin's advancement in the Court, during its time Grand Duchesses Anastasia and Militsiya Nikolayevni, confessor of the Majesties Bishop Feofan and Bishop Hermogen played a particularly fervent role. Because of this consideration Empress Alexandra Fyodorovna's association with Rasputin was from the first step favorably trusting and with the passage of time it was only strengthened...."[1803]

APPENDIX D

Key Personages

1. **Rasputin family and persons associated with them**

   Laptinskaya, Akilina Nikitina (1876-after 1920) –
   Lived with the Rasputin household in St. Petersburg
   working as his bookkeeper (1914-16). Sister of Mercy on
   the empress's hospital train (1916). Washed Rasputin's
   body after the autopsy (21.12.1916). Moved to Tobolsk.
   Married, two children, Agiya and Gleb. Her grandchildren
   live in Tyumen.

   Pecherkina, Ekaterina Ivanovna (1876-1956) – b.
   Derevnya Lambskoi, Tobolsk Province. Met through
   brother Dmitri Pecherkin (a priest in Afon). Worked as a
   housemaid in the Rasputin apartment in Pokrovskoye and
   in St. Petersburg. Lived in Tobolsk as a seamstress. Died
   aged 70 (29.04.1956).

   Pecherkina, Evdokiya Ivanovna (1869-1949) – b.
   Derevnya Lambskoi, Tobolsk Province. Niece to
   Ekaterina. Worked as housemaid in the Rasputin
   apartment in Pokrovskoye and St. Petersburg. Died in
   Tobolsk, aged 80 (21.08.1949).

   Rasputin, Dmitri Grigoriyevich (1895-1933) – b.
   Sloboda Pokrovskoye, Tobolsk Province. Son of Grigorii.
   Served most of the War on Hospital Train No. 143. Family
   home and contents were confiscated and being deprived
   of 'voting rights' after assessed as a *kulak*, for owning ten
   cattle (6 June 1920). NKVD sent the family to Obdorsk
   (on the Arctic Circle to help construct the Salehard fish
   canning factory (May 1930). Died from dysentery, aged
   38 (16.12.1933). Married Feoktista Ivanovna Pecherkina
   (1918). In exile, she worked as a fisherman. Died from
   tuberculosis, (September 1933). Daughter, Elizaveta, died
   days later (1927-1933).

Rasputin, Efim Yakovlevich (1841-1916) – b. Sloboda Pokrovskoye. Father of Grigorii. Tended horses and cattle and was a fisherman by trade. Married Anna Vasilievna Parshukova in 1862 (born in Usalki, Tyumen District). As a widower became the church's caretaker. Lived some time in Petrograd (1914). Died aged 74 in Sloboda Pokrovskoye.

Rasputina, Matrena [Matrona] **Grigoriyevna** (1898-1977) – b. Sloboda Pokrovskoye. Eldest daughter of Grigorii. Educated at the St. P. Steblin-Kamenski Preparatory School (1913-16). Arrested 15.03.1917. Fled Petrograd (29.03.1918). Returned to Pokrovskoye. Emigrated to France (1920). Died and buried in Los Angeles. Twice married. Memoirist.

Rasputina, Praskovya Fyodorovna (1867-1932) – b. Derevnya Dubrovino, Tobolsk Province. *Née* Dubrovina. Married Grigorii (1890). Had nine live births, two of whom, Grigorii and Feodosiya survived to adulthood. Present at Anna Taneeva's house on 25.12.1916 on the day the Imperial Family buried her husband (in her absence). Died in exile in Obdorsk (Arctic Circle), aged 70.

Rasputina, Varvara Grigoriyevna (1900-1925) – b. Sloboda Pokrovskoye. Youngest daughter of Grigorii. Lived and studied with her sister in St. Petersburg/ Petrograd (until 1916). Both arrested on 15.03.1917 by the Provisional Government but released soon after. Returned to Pokrovskoye from Vladivostok (1919). Stenographer in the Tyumen District law office (1919-22). Travelled to Moscow in the hope of emigrating. Caught typhus enroute and died soon after. Buried in the Novodevichi cemetery (Moscow). Never married.

Simanovich, Aron Samyilovich (1872-1944) – b. Vilnius, Latvia. Okhrana agent, acting as personal secretary to Rasputin. Memoirist.

2. **Personages implicated in Rasputin's murder and past offenders**

Dmitri Pavlovich (1891-1942) – b. Ilinskoye. Son from G. D. Pavel Alexandrovich's first marriage. After his guardian G. D. Sergei Alexandrovich died (1905), lived with the imperial family (until 1913). Shtabs-Rotmeister (1916). Banished to Persia then transferred to the British Expeditionary Forces.

Guseva, Khioniya Kuzminichna (b. 1881) – b. Syzran, Simbirsk Province. Worked as a seamstress in Tsarytsin. Placed into the Tyumen asylum. Amnesty (27.03.1917).

Illiodor [Sergei Mikhailovich Trufanov] (1880-1957) – b. Stanitsa Mariinskaya, Don Cossack Region. Completed the St. P. Theology Academy and tonsured a monk (1903). Banned from practicing (1907). Fled to Norway but returned to Tsarytsyn (1918). Author.

Lazovert (Lazavert), **Stanislav Sergeyevich** (1885-1936) – born in Poland. Senior army physician (Captain). Served on the Purishkevich's Red Cross hospital train during the War.

Purishkevich, Vladimir Mitrofanovich (1870-1920) – b. Kishinev, Bessarabian heritage. Delegate in II, III and IV Duma. In charge of the Red Cross army trains (from 1914). Author.

Rzhevsky, Boris Mikhailovich (d. 1919) – b. Nizhnii-Novgorod. Reporter (1909-10). Associated with the Red Cross (1914-17). Police agent (1916).

Sukhotin, Sergei Mikhailovch (1887-1926) – b. Kocheti, Tula region to Baronial parents. *Leib*-Guard Rifles Regiment (1915), Reservist at the Petrograd Generalitet (1916).

Yusupov-Sumarokov-Elston, Felix, the younger (1887-1967) – b. St. Petersburg. Prince and Count. Married G. D. Irina Alexandrovna (1914). Enrolled at *Pazheskii Korpus* but not completed (1915-16). Banished to Rakitnoe (1916). Memoirist.

3. **Members of the Imperial Family**

Alexandra Fyodorovna [Alix] (1872-1918) – b. Darmstadt. Last crowned Russian Imperial Empress and consort of Nikolai II (14.11.1894). Gave birth to one son and four daughters. Sister of Mercy (1914-16). Imprisoned by Provisional and Bolshevik governments. Murdered in Ekaterinburg (16/17.07.1918). Canonized as a passion bearer (2000).

Alexei Nikolayevich (1904-1918) – b. Peterhof. *Tsesarevic.* Fifth child and first born son to Nikolai II. *Efreitor* in the army (1915). Murdered in Ekaterinburg (16/17.07.1918). Canonized as a passion bearer (2000).

Maria Fyodorovna, Dowager Empress (1847-1928) – b. Copenhagen. Fourth child of King Christian IX of Denmark. Empress (1881-94). Consort of Alexander III.

Nikolai II (1868-1918) – b. Tsarskoe Selo. Eldest son of Alexander III. Last Emperor (from 20.10.1894). Supreme Commander (23.08.1915). Abdicated (02.03.1917). Murdered with all his family and their entourage, Ekaterinburg (16/17 July 1918). Canonized as a passion bearer (2000).

4. **Grand Ducal families**

Alexander Mikhailovich [Sandro] (1866-1933) – b. Tiflis. Grand Duke, fourth son of G. D. Mikhail Nikolayevich. Married **Ksenya Alexandrovna** (Nikolai II's sister, 1894). Admiral (1915). Daughter, **G. D. Irina Alexandrovna** married **Felix Yusupov**, the younger. Memoirist.

Anastasia Nikolayevna [Stana] (1868-1935) – b. *Cetinje* (Montenegro). Younger daughter of King Nikolai I. Second marriage, **G. D. Nikolai Nikolayevich, the younger** (1907).

Andrei Vladimirovich (1879-1956) – b. Tsarskoe Selo. Youngest son of G. D. Vladimir Alexandrovich. Graduate of the Alexandrovskii Military Juridical Academy (1908). General-Major (1915).

Elizaveta Fyodorovna [Ella] (1864-1918) – b. Darmstadt

(Alexandra Fyodorovna's sister). Married G. D. Sergei Alexandrovich (1884), who was assassinated (4.2.1905). Nun, established a religious order in Moscow. Murdered in Alapaevsk (1918). Canonized (1992).

Kirill Vladimirovich (1876-1938) – b. Tsarskoe Selo. *Kontr*-Admiral and *Fligel*-Adjutant. Commanded the *Gvardeiskii Ekipage* (1915). Memoirist.

Ksenya Alexandrovna (1875-1960) – b. St. Petersburg. Nikolai II's elder sister. Married G. D. Alexander Mikhailovich (July 1894).

Maria Pavlovna - the elder, [Miechen] (1854-1920) – b. Duchy Mecklenburg-Schwerin. Widow of G. D. Vladimir Alexandrovich (m. 1874). President of the Academy of Arts.

Maria Pavlovna - the younger, (1890-1958) – b. St. Petersburg. After father's morhanatic marriage, she and brother Dmitri cared by G. D. Sergei Alexandrovich and wife Ella. Memoirist.

Mikhail Alexandrovich (1878-1918) – b. St. Petersburg. Youngest son of Alexander III and brother of Nikolai II. *Fligel-Adjutant* (1899). Commander of the Caucasus Tuzemnaya Cavalry Division (1914). Renounced the Crown (March 1917).

Militsiya Nikolayevna (1866-1951) – b. *Cetinje* (Montenegro). Second daughter of King Nikolai I. Married **G. D. Peter Nikolayevich** (1889).

Nikolai Mikhailovich [Bimbo] (1859-1919) – b. Tsarskoe Selo, Grandson of Nikolai I. Graduate of the Nikolayevskii *Gen-Shtab* Academy (1885). Banished to his estate (01.01.1917). Author.

Nikolai Nikolayevich, the younger [Nikolasha] (1856-1928) – b. St. Petersburg. Grandson of Nikolai I. Supreme Commander at the start of War. Dismissed (August 1915). Viceroy in the Caucasus (1915-17). Married **G. D. Anastasia Nikolayevna**.

Olga Alexandrovna (1882-1960) – b. St. Petersburg.

Youngest daughter of Alexander III and sister of Nikolai II. A Sister-of-Mercy (1914).

Paley, Olga Valeryanovna (1865-1929) – b. St. Petersburg, *née* Karnovich. From first marriage, daughter, Marianna (Defelden). Second marriage to **G. D. Pavel Alexandrovich**. Memoirist.

Pavel Alexandrovich (1860-1919) – b. Tsarskoe Selo. Youngest son of Alexander II. Two children, Dmitri and Maria. Second marriage: **Olga Pistolkors** (Princess Paley, 1902). General-Inspector of the Guard Forces (September 1916-1917).

5. **Imperial Court personages**

Buxhoeveden, Sonya Karlovna [Isa] (1883-1956) – b. St. Petersburg. Baroness. *Freilina* to the Empress (1904-17). Memoirist.

Dehn, Yuliya Alexandrovna [Lili] (1888-1963) – *née* Bek-Smolsky. Friend to Alexander Fyodorovna. Memoirist.

Frederiks, Vladimir (1838-1927) – b. St. Petersburg. Boronial family of Swedish heritage. Minister of the Imperial Court (1897-1917) and Commander of the Imperial residence. Co-signed the Emperor's Abdication (02.03.1917).

Loman, Dmitri Nikolayevich (1868-1918) – b. St. Petersburg. *Shtab*-officer (1913-16) under Court Commmander. Khitor of *Fyodorovski Sobor* (1915). Worked on Empresses' hospital train No. 17 and headed *Lazaret* No. 73. Author.

Maksimovich, Konstantin Klavdiyevich (1849-1919) – Assistant to the Commander of the Imperial Apartments (1915-17).

Mordvinov, Anatolii Alexandrovich (1870-1938) – b. Novgorod. *Fligel*-Adjutant imperial suite (1913). Memoirist.

Mosolov, Alexander Alexandrovich (1854-1939) – b.

Smolensk District. Headed Chancellery of the Imperial Court (1900-16). Memoirist.

Narishkin-Kurakina, Elizaveta Alexeyevna [Zizi] (1838-1928) – b. St. Petersburg. *Ober-Gofmeisterina* to Alexandra Fyodorovna (until 1917). Memoirist.

Sablin, Nikolai Pavlovich (1880-1937) – b. Nikolayev. Captain 1st rank and Commander (1915). Discharged by the Provisional Government (24.03.17). Memoirist.

Spiridovich, Alexander Ivanovich (1873-1952) – b. *Kemi*, Arkhangelsk region. Commanded Imperial Court security (1906-16). Governor of Yalta (1916). Author.

Taneeva, Anna Alexandrovna [Vyrubova] (1884-1964) – b. St. Petersburg. Daughter of *Ober-Gofmarshal* Alexander Taneev (head of Imperial Chancellery). *Freilina* (1903). Sister of Mercy (1914-16). Memoirist.

Voyeikov, Vladimir Nikolayevich (1868-1947) – b. Tsarskoe Selo. Commandant Imperial Court (1916). Memoirist.

6. **Aristocrats**

Derfelden, Marianna Erikovna (1890-1976) – *née* Pistolkors. Daughter from Olga Paley's first marriage.

Golovina, Maria Evgenyevna [Munya] (1891-1972) – b. St. Petersburg. *N*ée Karnovich. Introduced Felix Yusupov to Rasputin. Lived with her parents on *Moika*, 104.

Yusupova, Irina Alexandrovna (1885-1970) – b. Peterhof. Only daughter of G. D. Alexander Mikhailovich and G. D. Ksenya Alexandrovna. Married **Felix Yusupov, the younger** (1914).

Yusupova, Zinaida Nikolayevna (1861-1939) – b. in St. Petersburg. *N*ée Yusupova. Princess. Socialite.

7. **Clerics and monks**

Fyodor [Afanasyevich, Chemagin] (1878-1959) – b. Pidjakovo Derevnya, Tyumen District. Ordained priest

(1905). Served as assistant cleric Sloboda Pokrovskoe (1905-10).

Khrisanf [Khristofor Petrovich Shetovskii] (1869-1906) – b. Stanitsa Velikoknyajeskaya, Don Cossack region. Ordained a priest (1891). Vicar in Kazan (1904) where he met Rasputin. Author.

Feofan [Vasilii Dmitriyevich Bistrov] (1872-1940) – b. Podmoshe, Novgorod Province. Rector St. P. Theology Academy (1909). Father confessor to the G. D.'s Militsia and Stana Nikolayeva and the imperial family. Bishop of the Tavrichesky Eparchy, Simferopol (1910).

Hermogen [Georgii Efremovich Dolganov] (1858-1918) – b. Kherson Province. Tonsured a monk (1890). Bishop of Saratov (1903). Excommunicated from the Synod (1912) and banished to Zhirovitskii Monastery (Smolensk District). Canonized (2000).

Ioann of Kronshtadt [Ivan Ilich Sergiev] (1829-1908) – b. Sura village, Arkhangelsk District. Archpriest, Andreevsky Sobor (Kronshtadt). Author.

Isidor [Pyotr Alexandrovich Kolokolov] (1866-1918) – b. St. Petersburg. Tonsured a monk (1888). Conducted a prayer vigil over Rasputin's remains at the Chesmenskii Almshouse (21.12.1916).

Martenmian [Bokarev] (b. 1875) – from Vologodsk District. Tonsured a monk Vologodsk Monastery. Visited Rasputin in Tyumen hospital (August 1914). Archbishop, Troitskii *Kalyazinsk* Monastery (Tversk, 1916-17).

Mitya [Dmitri Kozelsky or Kolyaba] (1868-1929) – b. Kozelsk village (Kaluga District). Diasabled and mute from birth. Brought to live at the Alexandro-Nevskaya *Lavra*. St. P. (1901). Attacked Rasputin (December 1911).

Pyotr Ioannovich Ostroumov (1878-?) – ordained priest from the Tobolsk Seminary School (1897). Served in the Sloboda Pokrovskoye church. Reported Rasputin (with Chemagin) to Bishop Antony (1907).

Pitirim [Pavel Vasilyevich Oknov] (1858-1920) – b.

Kokenhauzen, Latvia. Tonsured a monk (1883). Member of the Holy Synod (1914). Metropolitan of Petrograd (1915).

Sabler [Desyatovskii from 1915], **Vladimir Karlovich** (1847-1929) – b. Moscow. Completed the juridical faculty at Moscow University (1873). *Ober-Procuator* of the Holy Synod (1911-15).

Sergii [Ivan Nikolayevich Stragorodskii] (1867-1944) – b. *Arzamas, Nizhnegorodskoi* District. Rector St. P. Theology Academy (1899-1905). Member of the Synod (1911). Metropolitan (1918).

Shavelsky, Georgii Ivanovich (1871-1951) – b. Selo Dubokrai, Vitebsk District. *Protopresviter* for the military (1911); *Stavka* (1914-17). Memoirist.

Vasiliev, Alexander Petrovich (1869-1918) – b. Shepotovo, Smolensk District. Ordained (1892). Archpriest at Fyodorovskii Cathedral, Tsarskoe Selo (1913). Father confessor to the Imperial Family (1914). Officiated at Rasputin's funeral (21.12.1916).

Vostorgov, Ioann Ioannovich (1864-1918) – b. Stanitsa Kavkazkaya, Kubanskaya Oblast. Pokrovskoye priest. Canonized (August 2000).

8. **Gendarmes and Police**

Globachev, Konstantin Ivanovich (1870-1941) – b. Ekaterinoslav District. Director of Okhrana, Petrograd (1915). Memoirist.

Komissarov, Mikhail Stepanovich (1870-1933) – born to Yaroslav Cossack family. Assistant Chief Petrograd Okhrana (1915).

Koshko, Arkadii Fransevich (1867-1928) – b. Derevnya Brozhka, Minsk district. Head of St. P. Criminal Branch (1914-17). Author.

Kurlov, Pavel Grigoryevich (1860-1923) – Assistant Minister of Internal Affairs (1909) and Commander of the Gendarmes (1911). Assistant to Minister of Internal afffairs (until December 1916). Memoirist.

Martynov, Alexander Pavlovich (1875-1951) – b. Moscow. Moscow Okhrana Chief (1914). Memoirist.

Popel, Ivan Yulianovich (1879-after 1918) – Assistant commander of the Okhrana. Assisted with the 'Rasputin Case,' December 1916.

Popov, Pyotr Ksenofontovich (b. 1868) – Head of the Petrograd Okhrana (1914). *Stabs*-officer with in the Ministry of Internal Affairs (1915). Conducted the police investigation into Rasputin's murder.

Tatishev, Dmitri Nikolayevich (1867-1919) – b. St. Petersburg. Count. Gendarme Commander (1915).

Vasiliev, Alexei Tikhonovich (1869-1930) – b. Kiev. Director of Police (1916-03.03.1917). Involved in 'Rasputin Case.' Memoirist.

9. **Procurators and Court investigators**

Dobrovolskii, Nikolai Alexandrovich (1854-1918) – b. Novgorod region. Minister of Justice and Senate General-Procurator (20.12.16-28.02.1917). Terminated the 'Rasputin Case.'

Nandelshtedt, Fyodor Fyodorovich [or: von Nandelshtedt] (1870- after 1935) – born to a baronial family. Procurator, District Court (1914). Notified Zavadsky to activate the 'Rasputin Case.'

Pereverzev, Pavel Nikolayevich (1871-1944) – b. Fatezh (Kursk District). Member of the Petrograd District Court. Procurator in the Kerensky Commission (1917).

Sereda, Victor Nikolayevich (1877-1920) – Procurator of Special Matters (1911). Conducted legal processes for the 'Rasputin Case.' Dismissed (December 1916).

Sokolov, Nikolai Alexeyevich (1882-1924) – b. Mokshan, Penza District. Special Investigator, Omsk (1918). Investigated the murder of the imperial family.

Zavadsky, Sergei Vladislavovich (1870-1935) – b.

Kazan. Senior procurator, Petrograd District Court. Investigated Rasputin's murder (1916). Appointed to the Extraordinary Commission of Inquiry (March-May 1917). Memoirist.

10. Governors, Mayors and Ministers

Adrianov, Alexander Alexandrovich (1862-1918) – b. St. Petersburg. Moscow Mayor (1908-15).

Balk, Alexander Pavlovich (1866-1957) – Governor of Petrograd (10.11.1916-24.02.1917). Memoirist.

Beletsky, Stepan Petrovich (1873-1918) – b. Konotop, Chernigovsky District. Director of Police (1912-28.02.1914). Assistant Minister of Internal Affairs (28.10.1915 -13.02.1916). Memoirist.

Belyaev, Mikhail Alexeyevich (1863-1918) – b. St. Petersburg. Headed Gen-*Shtab* (April 1916). Minister of War (03.01.1917).

Dumbadze, Ivan Antonovich (1851-1916) – b. Tiflis, Georgia. Mayor of Yalta (1914-16).

Djunkovsky, Vladimir Fyodorovich (1865-1938) – b. St. Petersburg. Governor of Mocow (until 1913). Assistant Minister of Internal Affairs and Commander of the Gendarmes (January 1913-15). Memoirist.

Khvostov, Alexei Nikolayevich (1872-1918) – Minister of Internal Affairs and Commander of the Gendarmes (September 1915-March 1916).

Kokovtsov, Vladimir Nikolayevich (1853-1943) – b. Gorno-Pokrovskoe estate, Novgorod District. President of the Council of Ministers (1911-15). Memoirist.

Makarov, Alexander Alexandrovich (1857-1919) – b. St. Petersburg. Minister of Internal Affairs (1911-12). Minister of Justice 07 July to 20.12.1916.

Maklakov, Nikolai Alexeyevich (1871–1918) – b. Moscow. Minister of Internal Affairs (1912-1915).

Protopopov, Alexander Dmitrievich (1866-1918) – b.

Selo Marysovo, Nizhnenovgorod District. Minister of Internal Affairs (20.12.1916).

Rodzianko, Mikhail Vladimirovich (1859-1924) – b. Selo Popasnoye, Ekaterinoslav District. President of the Third and Fourth Duma (1911-17). President of the Temporary Committee, Prov. Government. Memoirist.

Sazonov, Sergei (1860-1927) – b. family estate, Ryazan District. Minister of Foreign Affairs (1910-1916). Memoirist.

Stürmer, Boris Vladimirovich (1848-1917) – b. Baikovo estate, Tver District. President of the Council of Ministers concurrently while Minister of Internal Affairs (7 July-10 November 1916).

Stolypin, Peter Arkadyevich (1862-1911) – born in Dresden, Germany. Minister of Internal Affairs and President of the Council of Ministers (1906-11). Assassinated in Kiev (01.09.1911).

Trepov, Alexander Fyodorovich (1862-1928) – b. Kiev. President of the State Council (10.11-27.12.1916).

Witte, Sergei Yulevich (1849-1915) – b. Tiflis, Georgia. President of the Council of Ministers (1905-6). Memoirist.

Yusupov–Sumarokov-Elston, Felix, the elder (1856-1928) – born in St. Petersburg. Moscow Mayor (May to 3.9.1915). Married to **Zinaida Yusupova**.

11. Politicians – Imperial and Provisional Government identities

Guchkov, Alexander Ivanovich (1862-1936) – b. Moscow. Founder Oktoberist Party (1905). President of the Third Duma (1910-11). One the first statesmen to rally against Rasputin. Accepted Nikolai II's abdication, Pskov (02.03.1917).

Kerensky, Alexander Fyodorovich (1881-1970) – b. Simbirsk. Delegate of the Fourth Duma. Minister of Justice (March-April 1917). Minister of War and Navy (May). Led the Prov. Government (6-11.1917). Memoirist.

Kupchinsky, Filipp Petrovich (1844-1927?) – War correspondent during Russo-Japanese War (1904-5). Provisional Government Commissar (1917). Responsible for cremating Rasputin's corpse (10/11.03.1917). Author.

Lvov, Georgii Evgenyevich (1861-1925) – b. Dresden. Prince. Kadet Party delegate, First Duma. Led the Provisional Government (March-July 1917).

Milyukov, Pavel Nikolayevich (1859-1943) – b. Moscow. Co-founded Kadet Party (1905). Delegate in Third and Fourth Duma (1907-17). Author.

Muraviev, Nikolai Konstantinovich (1870-1936) – b. Selo Sherbinino, Tver District. Moscow Duma (1916). Headed the Extraordinary Commission of Inquiry (March-October 1917).

Rudnev, Vladimir Mikhailovich – Assistant procurator Ekaterinoslav District Court (1915-17). Assistant investigator, Extraordinary Commission of Inquiry, Petrograd (from March 1917).

Shulgin, Vasilii Vitalyevich (1878-1976) – b. Kiev. Delegate, Second, Third and Fourth Duma. Accepted Nikolai II's abdication, Pskov (1917). Author.

12. Militarists

Alexeev, Mikhail Vasilyevich (1857-1918) – b. Vyazma, Smolensk District. Chief of Staff at Military Headquarters, Mogilev (23.08.1915). Advanced Nikolai II's abdication.

Bubnov, Alexander (1883-1963) – b. Warsaw, Poland. Naval Gen-*Shtab* (until June 1917). Memoirist.

Danilov, Yuri Nikiforovich (1866-1937) – b. Kiev. *Kvartirmeister, Baranovichi Stavka* (1914-15). Author.

Grabbe, Alexander Nikolayevich (1864-1947) – b. St. Petersburg. Commander of the Imperial *Konvoi* (1914-17).

Gurko, Vasilii Iosifovich (1864-1937) – b. Tsarskoe Selo. Commanded various army units (1914-16). Replaced

Gen. Alexeev (on sick leave) as Chief of Staff (10.1916-02.1917). Memoirist.

Klimov, – *Shtabs*-Captain. Took charge (from Maltsev) Aerial Security Battalion, Tsarskoe Selo (27.02.1917). Credited for finding Rasputin's gravesite.

Kobylinsky, Evgenii Stepanovich (1875-1927) – b. Kiev. Commandant, Alexandrovskii Dvoretz and its security (01.03.1917).

Kutaisov, Konstantin Pavlovich (1876-1918) – Commander of 3rd Cavalry Artillery Division (1916). After returning from Persia, resigned due to illness.

Maltsev, Vladimir Nikanorovich (15.09.1873-after 1920) – Commander *Otdelnii* Aerial Artillery Battery (security imp. palaces, Tsarskoe Selo (1915-27.02.1917).

Ruzskii, Nikolai Vladimirovich (1854-1918) – Commander of the South-Western Front (1914). Betrayed Nikolai II (1917). Executed (10.10.1918).

13. Diplomats and Foreign Agents

Buchanan, George (1854-1924) – b. Copenhagen. Ambassador to Russia (1910-17). Allied with Duma reformists. Diarist.

Hoare, Samuel Johhn (1880-1959) – b. London. Chief Petrograd Intelligence Service (1916). Author.

Paleologue, Maurice George (1859-1944) – b. Paris. Ambassador to Russia (1914-17). Author.

Rayner, Oswald Theodore (1888-1961) – b. Smethwick, U.K. Recruited by MI6 (1916). Implicated in Rasputin's death (1916).

14. Physician and healer

Badmaev, Peter Alexandrovich [Djamsaran] (1849-1920) – Alexander III's godson. Tibetan herbalist, established business (1893). Author/translator.

Kosorotov, Dmitri Petrovich (1956-1925) – b.

Novocherkassk. Chief Dissector and Professor of forensic medicine and toxicology, Imp. Military Medical Academy (1898). Conducted the autopsy on Rasputin (21.12.16). Executed by the NKVD, Petrograd. Academic author.

15. Journalists and authors

Andronnikov, Mikhail Mikhailovich (1875-1919) – Prince. Adventurist. Attached to the Synodal *Ober*-Procurator (1914-16).

Lagansky, Evgenii I. (?-1937) –Journalist, *Russkaya Volya* and in the Duma for the Provisional Government (1917). Wrote articles for *Ogonek* (until 1929).

Manasevich-Manuilov, Ivan Fyodorovich (1868/71-1918) – b. Kovno. Occasional journalist for *Novoye Vremya* (1906).

Novoselov, Mikhail Alexandrovich (1864-1938) – b. Babye Selo, Tver District. Academic at Moscow University. Authored letters to discredit Rasputin (1912).

APPENDIX E
A supplementary forensic evaluation

This supplementary forensic evaluation is this author's interpretation. Professor Kosorotov examined Rasputin's body, front and back, to assess the nature and extent of the injuries. He noted the type and location of the injuries to help differentiate between those that were inflicted ante-mortem (during life) and those that were post-mortem.

The body was photographed as a matter of record. There are no photographs of the back of the head, the front of the body, or below the abdomen. Given that Kosorotov was silent about these parts of the body in his published article in *Russkaya Volya*, it recommends that everything was normal.

The autopsy was conducted at the Chesmenskii Hospital morgue in Petrograd on the night of 20/21 December 1916, following a twenty-four hour period of thawing. The procedure, taking four hours, was conducted under poor lighting conditions.

The primary cause of death is defined as the injury (or disease) that initiated the morbid events leading directly to death, or the circumstances or violence that produced a fatal injury.

Name of the deceased: Grigorii Efimovich Rasputin-*Novy*

Nationality and gender: Russian male

D.O.B. 9 January 1869

Place of Birth: Sloboda Pokrovskoye, Tyumen District, Siberia.

Last known residential address: *Gorokhovaya Ulitsa*, 64, apartment 20, Petrograd,

Date of death: 17 December 1916.

Age of the deceased: 47 years.

Grigorii Rasputin in later life.

THE TIME of DEATH

There is no information that pin-pointed the exact time of death. A series of gunshots were heard at around 2.30 a.m. on Saturday 17 December at the Yusupovskii Palace on Moika, 94 (Protocol No. 8 submitted by *Gorodovoi* Efimov).

DESCRIPTION of the CADAVER

The body was thrown from the Bolshoi Petrovskii Bridge (of wooden construction).

The body was fully immersed in the near-frozen *Malaya Nevka* River.

Blood was found on the bridge and on two beams on one bridge support (POLICE PHOTO No. 10). The presence of this blood shows where the body was disposed.

The body was found 140 meters west of the bridge span, beneath the ice shelf close to the riverbank on the Petrovskii Island side.

It had been submerged for approximately fifty-five hours, at an unknown depth.

After uplift from the river, the retrieved frozen body was clothed and shod. The wrists and legs were bound (**POLICE PHOTO No. 6**).

The deceased presented as a healthy adult male with no known illnesses or definite forms of disfigurement.

Wounds Inflicted on Grigorii Rasputin's Body

EXTERNAL EXAMINATION

The cadaver exhibited minimal non-specific post-mortem changes.

The HEAD

1. The <u>head</u> has an entry wound located midline on the forehead and an exit wound at the back of the head caused by the trajectory from a single bullet (**POLICE PHOTO No. 14**).

2. The <u>right eye</u> – there was evidence of conjunctival hemorrhage that was identified by the solid dark red sheet of congealed blood over the surface of the eye. Injury was due to the rupture of the blood vessel in the conjunctiva. The hemorrhage was also associated with a black eye (**POLICE PHOTO No. 14**). This type of injury is due to the eye being struck by a blunt object (e.g. a boot).

3. The <u>left eye</u> – no injury observed.

   ▶ The nature of these injuries suggests that the victim was supine with the right side of the head facing the assailant during the physical attack.

4. <u>Face</u> - The right cheek is indented, indicating that the cheek bone is shattered, flattening the face. The nose is swollen, with contusion. The <u>nasal bone</u> is broken, giving it a deformed appearance (**POLICE PHOTO No. 14b**). These injuries were most likely

to have been sustained when the body was thrown off the bridge (the presence of three discrete blood stains on the same side of the bridge pylon leading down to the surface of the water are consistent with that event [**POLICE PHOTO No. 10**]).

5. The ears – There is evidence of hemorrhaging inside the right ear canal. The cause was due to the head injuries (**POLICE PHOTO No. 15b**). The margins of the right ear are intact. The left ear appears normal (**POLICE PHOTO No. 16**).

   ► When the body struck the water there were postmortem head injuries to the prominent points of the face and extremities.

6. The lower lip is bruised and swollen. The upper lip (concealed by beard hair) is not clearly visible. Mouth shows contusion and swelling (**POLICE PHOTO No. 14b**).

POLICE PHOTO No. 14b: The nasal bone is broken and the nose is swollen and bruised. The right eye shows retinal hemorrhage. The right cheek is battered and bruised. The lower lip is bruised and swollen.

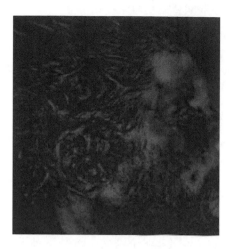

*POLICE PHOTO No. 15b: Hemorrhaging from the
right ear canal and bruising adjacent to the ear.*

7. <u>Hair</u> – The hair is matted with blood, due to the exit
gunshot wound at the back of the head. Just above
the right ear there is a bald patch, indicating that hair
might have been pulled out (**POLICE PHOTOS No.
14c and No. 15b**). The beard appears intact.

THE BACK of the BODY

<u>The cut on the back</u> below the gunshot wound was
caused by a sharp object which struck only once using
something like a knife or saber, etc. It is impossible to
say whether this mechanical injury was inflicted before
or after death (**POLICE PHOTO No. 13**). The wound
was inflicted through the clothing worn by the deceased.
The weapon responsible for this injury was unavailable
for examination.

THE FRONT of the BODY

There are no photographs of the front of the body or the
genitalia.

There are no photographs showing the right or left leg.

INTERNAL EXAMINATION

1. The brain hemispheres did not show pathological changes. One bullet passed through the brain matter but the nature of the damage caused was not described. The pathologist found that the right cheek was shattered when the body was thrown from the bridge. This finding could be explained by a closed *contrecoup* injury sustained by the brain (an observation that subsequent examinations could not make).

   ▶ No lead fragments were reported in the brain to indicate the bullet was unjacketed.

2. The respiratory passages did not contain any fluid or foam.

3. The lungs were clear.

   ▶ **Death by drowning is excluded.**

   The immersion of the body into the water indicated the final phase of a course of events that involved murder.

4. Liver - The right lobe of the liver was shattered. The smaller left lobe was not described.

5. Kidneys - The right kidney was shattered. The left kidney entire.

   There was extensive damage to the soft abdominal organs – the shattering of the right lobe of the liver and the right kidney, which together would have caused severe internal hemorrhaging.

   ▶ The massive loss of blood would have induced the victim to go into **shock,** leading to death.

6. The stomach showed injury as a result of the "through-and-through" penetration of the bullet, which entered from the left side of the body at CLOSE RANGE and exited out of the body on the right side (**POLICE PHOTOS No. 11** and **No. 12**).

GUNSHOT WOUNDS

Forensically, it is impossible to establish with confidence what the sequence of the shooting event was in the absence of reliable eyewitness accounts. It is also not possible to estimate the precise distance from which two bullets were fired, when not fired at pointblank range. For simplicity the gunshot wounds are distinguished as:

Bullet No. **1** = the gunshot wound into the abdomen (POLICE PHOTOS No. 11, No. 12),

Bullet No. **2** = the gunshot wound into the back (POLICE PHOTO No. 13),

Bullet No. **3** = the gunshot wound to the forehead (POLICE PHOTO No. 14).

The effects of each of the gunshot wounds were:

1. Bullet No. 1 – was fired at **close range** (or **near contact,** no more than ten millimeter range) and would not have been immediately disabling.[1804] An individual could still have retained the ability to walk and run using all his senses. Resistance could have been possible for the next 5-15 minutes. Bullet No. 1 would not necessarily have been immobilizing.[1805] This gunshot wound was perforating, a through-and-through passage by the bullet without interruption through the liver and exiting out of the body, left to right. The consequential **massive hemorrhaging** would have led to **cardiogenic shock and death**.

2. Bullet No. 2 – [jacketed] was fired at some distance and would have immediately incapacitated the victim if the spinal cord in the cervical vertebra was involved,[1806] either being lacerated or transected. The **distance gunshot wound** (no sooting around the wound) was penetrating – it remained in the body and was extricated from one of the vertebra. Therefore, there was no exit wound. The damage to the right kidney caused **extensive hemorrhaging, which** would have caused **cardiogenic shock and death**.

3. Bullet No. 3 – [jacketed] was fired at **point-blank**

range and would have caused immediate loss of coordination, not allowing the victim to act with purpose. It is not known whether both hemispheres were involved. The <u>exit wound</u> was not described, but from Kosorotov's language and **POLICE PHOTO No. 11c** and **No. 12b**, there is strong evidence to consider that there was an <u>exit wound</u>. The back spatter from the entry wound would have projected onto the shooter.[1807] Bullet No. 3 was immediately incapacitating[1808] because there was <u>direct trauma to the brain tissue,</u> resulting in tissue destruction, depriving the brain of oxygen caused by bleeding and diminution of blood pressure,[1809] leading to **rapid death**.

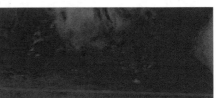

POLICE PHOTOS No. 12c and No. 14c: Blood stained fluid underneath the thawing head.

COMMENT

The bullet that was retrieved from the spinal column was jacketed.

It is likely that Bullet No. 1 that entered and exited the abdomen was also jacketed.

The absence of any expelled cartridges at CRIME SCENE No. 1 indicates that a pistol was not likely to have been fired in the courtyard.

▶ There is no ballistic evidence that proves or disproves that all three gunshot wounds were inflicted by the SAME WEAPON.

MICROSCOPIC FINDINGS

A blood precipitin assay - the _Uhlenhuth Test_ - was performed by the police laboratory on Saturday 17 December 1916. A sample of blood was removed from the step by the exit door[1810] at CRIME SCENE No 1 (Yusupovskii Palace, Moika, 94 Petrograd) by Special Investigator Victor Sereda. Blood samples were taken also taken from the second crime scene at the Bolshoi Petrovskii Bridge.

▶ The _Uhlenhuth_ Test was **POSITIVE for human blood** from both samples.

OTHER

▶ There was **no evidence of poisoning**. Death as a result of poisoning is excluded.

▶ There was evidence that the victim may have been **intoxicated**. The degree of intoxication was not described.

SUMMARY and COMMENTS

▶ Rasputin would have died following the overwhelming internal damage to the liver caused by the first bullet. The second bullet that resulted in renal damage before lodging into the vertebral column, was a contributing factor that would have accelerated death. However, because of the subsequent discharge of the third bullet, the forensic team under Professor Zharov in Moscow concluded in 1993 that it was the shot to the head, causing brain damage, which had the outcome of bringing about Rasputin's **immediate death**.

▶ The character of the attack to the right eye that was rendered by one (or more) was meted out with purpose.

There is strong forensic evidence that indicates **the killer(s) wanted to inflict the maximum punishment.**

CAUSE of DEATH

The contact gunshot wound to the head that caused significant damage to the brain.

Select BIBLIOGRAPHY

The majority of sources were published in
Russia in the Russian language

Akayemov, N., *"Kak nashli trup Rasputina"*, *Istoricheskii
Vestnik*, (1917), [Volume CXLIX], July-August

Alexander Mikhailovich,

– **Once a Grand Duke**, Cosmopolitan Book Co.,
New York, 1932

– *Velikii Knyaz Aleksandr Mikhailovich, Kniga
Vospominanii*, *Tsarskii Dom* Series, *Veche*, 2008

Alexandra Fyodorovna, *Pis'ma Imperatritsi Alexandri
Fedorovni k Imperatoru Nikolayu II*, *Slovo*, Berlin, 1920's

Alexandrov, A., *Rassledovaniye Tsareubiistva-
rassekrechenniye dokumenti*, *Chuvashkoe knizhnoye
izdatel'stvo, Cheboxary*, 2006

Almazov, B., *Rasputin i Rossiya*, *Grunkhut, Praga*, 1922

Almedingen, E., **An Unbroken Unity**, The Bodley Head,
London, 1964

Andrei Vladimirovich, *Voenni Dnevnik Velikogo Knyazya
Vladimirovicha Andrei Romanova*, *Sabashnikov* Press, *Moskva*,
2008

Anonymous (I), *"Zhizn i Pohozdheniye Grigoriya Rasputina"*,
M. E. Zaezdnag Typo-lithografia, Kiev, 1917

Anonymous (II), *"Temniye Sili: Tainy Rasputinskogo Dvora –
Rasputin"*, *Pechat* S. Yakovlev, Petrograd, 1917

Anonymous (III), [Ed. N. Kubikov], *"Kak Khoronili Rasputina
(I), Za Velikoknyazheskimi Kulisami"* (II), Dubovin Elektro-
Pechat, Kiev, 1917

Anonymous (IV), *"Taina Doma Romanovikh ili Pohozheniya
Grigoriya Rasputina"*, *Typographia* M. Brisker, Kiev, 1917

Arkhiv Noveishei Rossii, ROSSPEN, *Moskva*, 2001

– [Editor V., Khrustalev], *Skorbnii Put' Romanovikh* **(1917-18)**, [Volume III]

– [Editor B. Dodonov], *Zhurnali Zasedanii Vremennogo Pravitel'stva*, [Volume VII]

Astakhova, V., [Editor] **A. Blok**, [Volume II], *Portreti* Series, Terra, *Moskva*, 1997

Baryatinsky, V., *"Oshibka Istorii"*, *Illustrirovannaya Rossiya*, (1932), No 16

Batishev, *"Episodi moyei zhizni"*, *Minuvshee* Journal, (1998) No. 24, *Sankt Peterburg*

Bazily [Basily], N., **Memoirs**, Hoover Institute Press, Stanford University, 1973

Beletsky, S., *Grigorii Rasputin iz Zapisok*, *Byloye* Press, Petrograd, 1923

Benois, A., *Dnevnik* **1916-1918**, Zaharov, *Moskva*, 2007

Birzheviye Vedomosti:

– *"Pokusheniye na Gr. Rasputina"*, No. 14232, 2 July 1914

– *"K pokusheniyu na Gr. Rasputina"*, No. 14240, 6 July 1914

– *"V. M. Purishkevich i Gr. Rasputin"*, No. 14240, 6 July 1914

– *"Na Petrovskom Ostrove"*, No. 15995, Tuesday, 20 December 1916

– *"Posledniya Izvestiya"*, No. 15995, Tuesday, 20 December, 1916

– *"Posledniya Izvestiya"*, No 15997, Wednesday, 21 December 1916

– *"Soobsheniye oTainstvennom osobnyake"*, No. 15997, Wednesday, 21 December 1916

– *"Vskritiye Tela Gr. Rasputina"*, No 15997, Wednesday, 21 December 1916

– *"Revolutsiya"*, No 16120, Sunday March 5, 1917

– *"Likvidatsiya ubiistva Rasputina"*, No 16124, Wednesday 8 March 1917

– Arrest announcements, No 16126, Thursday 9 March 1917

– *"Arest protopresvitera o. Shavelskogo"*, No. 16126, Thursday 9 March 1917

– *"Sredi arestovovannoi Tsarskoi Sviti"*, Gan, L., No 16128, Friday, 10 March 1917

– *"Rasputin i Imperatorsky Dvor"*, No 16128, Friday, 10 March 1917

– *"Sozheniye Rasputina"*, No. 16133, 13 March 1917

– *"Obiisk v kvartire Rasputina"*, No. 16144, 19 March 1917

– *"Arest freilini Vyrubova"*, No 16150, Thursday, 23 March 1917

– *"Sud'ba zhertvi Rasputina"*, No 161176, 11 April 1917

Blok, A., *Posledniye Dni Imperatorskoi Vlasti*, Zaharov Press, *Moskva*, 1921 [reprinted 2005]

Botkina-Melnik, T., *Vospominaniya o Tsarskoi Semye*, Harvest, *Moskva*, 1921 [reprinted 2004]

Boyuvich, M. [Editor], *Chleni Gosudarstvennoi Dumi*, Sitin Publishing, *Moskva*, 1913, 4th Ed. 1917

Broitman, L., *Bolshaya Morskaya Ulitsa*, *Centerpoligraf, Sankt Peterburg*, 2005

Browder, R. and Kerensky, A., **The Russian Provisional Government 1917 Documents**, [Volume 1], Stanford University Press, California, 1961

Buchanan, G., **A Mission to Russia**, [Volume I and II] Little Brown & Co., Boston, 1923.

Buchanan, M., **The Dissolution of an Empire**, John Murray, London, 1932

Buckles, T., **Laws of Evidence**, Delmar Cengage Learning,

U.S.A., 2001

Burtsev, V., *"Rasputin v 1916 godu"*, *Illustrirovannaya Rossiya*, (1932), No. 17

Bushkov, A., *Rasputin Vistreli iz Proshlogo*, Neva, *Sankt Peterburg*, 2006

Bushkovitch, P., **Religion and Society in Russia: the 16th and 17th Centuries**, Oxford University Press 1992

Buxhoeveden, S., **The Life and Tragedy of Alexandra Feodorovna, Empress of Russia**, Longman Green and Co., London, 1930

Bokhanov, A.,

-     *Anatomiya Mifa*, ACT Press, *Moskva*, 2000

-     *Imperator Nikolai II*, *Russkoye Slovo*, *Moskva*, 2004

-     *Byl i Nebyl*, *Tsarskii Dom* Series, *Veche*, *Moskva*, 2006

Bubnov, A., *V Tsarskoi Stavke*, *Tsarskii Dom* Series, *Veche*, *Moskva*, 2008

Cantacuzene, J.,

-     **Revolutionary Days**, The Lakeside Press, Chicago, 1919 [reprinted 1999]

-     **My Life Here and There**, Charles Scribner's Sons, New York, 1923

Cheparukhin, V.,

-     *Krematsiya Tela G. Rasputina v Dni Fevralskoi Revolutsii 1917*, *Revolutsiya 1917 goda v Rossii Sbornik Nauchnikh Statei*, *Tretiya Rossiya*, *Sankt Peterburg*, 1995

-     *Grigorii Rasputin. Poslednyaya Tochka*, *Novy Chasovoi* J., 1995, No. 3, *Sankt Peterburg*

Chebishev, N., *"Navozhdeniye"*, *Illustrirovannaya Rossiya*, 1932, No. 20

Chernyshov, A.,

-     *"Religiya i Tserkov v Sibiri Sbornik nauchnikh*

statei i dokumentalnikh materialov", MI RUTRA, (1992) No. 11, Tyumen State University, Tyumen

‒   *"O Vozraste Grigoriya Rasputina i drugikh biographicheskikh detaliyakh"*, Otechestvenniye Arkhivi, (1992), No. 1

‒   *"V Poisk Mogili Grigoriya Rasputina"*, Rus' Journal, (1994), No. 13

Chernyshova-Melnik, N., **Mikhail Romanov Zhizn i Lyubov**, Enas Press, Moscow, 2009

Clay, C., **King, Kaiser, Tsar**, John Murray, London, 2006

Cockfield, J., **White Crow**, Praeger, Connecticut, 2002

Cook, A., **To Kill Rasputin**, Tempus, U. K., 2005

Crawford, R. and D., **Michael and Natasha**, Weidenfeld and Nicolson, London, 1997

Danilov, Yu.

‒   *Na puti k Krusheniyu*, Soglasiye Press, *Moskva*, 2000

‒   *Velikii Knyaz Nikolai Nikolayevich*, *Kuchkovo Pole, Moskva*, 2006

Damer, A., *"Rasputin vo Dvortse"*, *Illustrirovannaya Rossiya*, (1932), No 16

d'Encausse, H., **The Russian Syndrome**, Holmes and Meir, New York, 1992

de Jonge, A., **The Life and Times of Grigorii Rasputin**, Fontana, London, 1982

Den':

‒   *"Otyezd kn. F. F. Yusupova"*, No 349, Monday, 19 December 1916

‒   *"Otyezd V. M. Purishkevicha"*, No. 349, Monday, 19 December 1916

‒   *"K sluchayu na Moike"*, No. 349, Monday 19 December 1916

‒   *"Tainstvennoye Proishestviye"*, No. 349, Monday,

19 December 1916

– *"Proshestviye na Petrovskom Ostrove"*, No. 350, Tuesday, 20 December 1916

– *"Moskva – Privetstvennaya telegramma V. M. Purishkevichu"*, No. 352, Thursday, 22 December 1916

– *"Na Mogile Rasputina"*, No. 4, Thursday, 9 March 1917

– *"Sozzheniye trupa Rasputin"*, No. 8, 14 March 1917

Decaux, A., *Velikiye Zagadki XX Veka*, *Veche, Moskva*, 2006

Dehn, L., **The Real Tsaritsa**, Thornton Butterworth, London, 1922 [reprinted 1995]

Denikin, A., *Ocherki Russkoi Smuti, Krusheniye Vlasti i Armii, Fevral'-Sentyabr 1917*, *Nauka, Moskva*, 1991

DiMaio, V., **Handbook of Forensic Pathology**, Taylor and Francis, New York, 2006

Djunkovsky, V., *Vospominaniya*, [Volume II], *Sabashnikov Press, Moscow*, 1997

Dobson, C., **Prince Felix Yusupov: The Man Who Murdered Rasputin**, Harrap, London, 1989

Dorr, R., **Inside the Russian Revolution**, The Macmillan Co., New York, 1917

Dorril, S., **MI6 Fifty years of Special Operations**, Fourth Estate, London, 2000

Dorovatovsky, N., *Peterburg i ego Zhizn*, *Zhizn Dlya Vsekh*, St. Peterburg, 1914

Dorr, R., **Inside the Russian Revolution**, The Macmillan Co. New York, 1917

Essad-Bey, M., **Nicholas II**, Hutchinson and Co., London, 1936

Fedorchenko, F.,

– *Dvor Rossiiskih Imperatorov*, ACT, *Moskva*, 2004

–   *Svita Rossiiskih Imperatorov*, [Volume I, A-L and Volume II, M-Ya], ACT, *Moskva*, 2005

Fedorov, B., *Petr Stolypin: Ya Veryu v Rossiyu*, [Volume 1], *Limbus* Press, *Sankt Peterburg*, 2002

Figes, O., **A People's Tragedy**, Pimlico, London, 1996

Fuhrmann J. **Rasputin the Untold Story**, John Wiley and Sons, N. J., 2013

Fomin, S.,

–   *"Pravda o Grigorii Efimoviche Rasputine"*, *Russkii Vestnik*, Special Edition, (2002), No. 21-23

–   *Grigorii Rasputin: Rassledovaniye*, [Volume III], Forum Press, *Moskva*, 2009

Frantsev, O., *Grigorii Rasputin*, *Sovremenii Literator*, Minsk, 1998

Fülöp-Miller, R., **Rasputin: The Holy Devil**, The Viking Press, New York, 1928

Gavril Konstantinovich, *Vospominaniya*, Zaharov, *Moskva*, 2005

Gerasimov, V., *"Gde pokhoronen Grigorii Rasputin?"*, *Rus* J. (1993) Volume 8, No. 2, Rostov *Velikii*

Gilliard, P.,

–   **Thirteen Years at the Russian Court**, Ayer, Salem, 1994 Reprint

–   *Ryadom s Tsarskoi Semeyi*, *Tsarskii Dom* Series, *Veche*, *Moskva*, 2006

Glezerov, S., *Lesnoi, Grazhdanka, Ruchi, Udelnaya*, *Tsentrpoligraf, Sankt Peterburg*, 2006

Globachev, K., *Pravda o Russkoi Revolutsii*, ROSSPEN, *Moskva*, 1922 [reprinted 2009]

Genge, N., **The Forensic Casebook**, Random House, London, 2004

Golder, F., **Documents of Russian History 1914-1917**, The Century Co., 1927

Golos Moskvi: Suplemenet: *"Grigorii Rasputin i Mysticheskaya*

raspustvo", 12 February 1912

Grabbe, P and B., **The Private World of the Last Tsar**, Collins, London, 1985

Gurko, B., **War and Revolution in Russia 1914-1917**, The Macmillan Co., New York, 1919

Gusev, B., *Moi Ded Djamsaran Badmaev*, *Russkaya Kniga*, *Moskva*, 1995

Handbury-Williams, J., **The Emperor Nicholas II as I knew Him**, Arthur Humphries, London, 1922

Harclave, S., **The Memoirs of Count Witte**, M. E. Sharpe, Inc., New York, 1990

Heresch, E., *Rasputin Taina ego Vlasti*, OLMA-Press, *Moskva*, 2006

Hoare, S., **The Fourth Seal**, William Heinemann, London, 1930

Horvatova, E.,

– *Maria Pavlovna, Drama Velikoi Knyagini*, ACT Press, *Moskva*, 2005

– *Maria Fyodorovna, Sud'ba Imperatritsi*, ACT Press, *Moskva*, 2006

Hughes, M., **Inside the Enigma: British Officials in Russia, 1900-1939**, The Hambledon Press, London, 1997

Ikonikov-Galitsky, A.,

– *Khroniki Peterburgskikh Prestuplenii, Kriminalnii Peterburg* **1861-1917**, *Azbuka-Klassica, Sankt Peterburg*, 2007

– *Khroniki Peterburgskikh Prestuplenii* **1917-1922**, 2008

Ioffe, G., *Rasputiniada: bolshaya politicheskaya igra*, *Otchestvennaya Istoriya*, (1998), No. 8

Karabchevsky, N., *Chto glaza moi videli*, in: *Fevralskaya Revolutsiya*, [Volume 1], Inter-OMNIS, Perm, 1921 [reprinted 1991]

Kasvinov, V., *Dvadtsat Tri Stupeni Vniz*, Kazakhstan Press, Alma-Ata, 1989

Katkov, G., **Russia 1917: The February Revolution**, Collins, London, 1969

Kazarinov, M., "*Rasputinskii Schet*", *Illustrirovannaya Rossiya*, (1932), No. 22

Kerensky, A.,

– *Tragediya Dinastii Romanovikh*, *Tsentrpoligraf*, *Moskva*, 2005

– *Rossiya v Povorotnii Moment Istorii*, *Centerpoligraf*, *Moskva*, 2006

Khrustalev, V.,

– [Edited with Lykova, L.] *Skorbnii put' Mikhaila Romanova*: *ot prestola do golgofa*, *Pushka* Press, Perm, 1995

[Editor] *Dnevniki Nikolaya II i Imperatritsi Alexandri Fyodorovni*, [Volume 1], Vagrius, *Moskva*, 2008

– *Felix Felixovich Yusupov. Zagatka Ubiistvo Rasputina. Zapiski Knyazya Yusupova*, ACT, *Moskva*, 2014

Kirikov, V., et al., *Nevsky Prospekt, Arhitekturnii putevoditel'*, *Tsentrpoligraf*, *Sankt Peterburg*, 2002

Kleinmichel, M, **Memoirs of a Shipwrecked World**, Brentano's Press, New York, 1923

Kobylin, V., *Anatomiya Izmeni*, *Tsarskoe Delo*, *Sankt Peterburg*, 2005

Kokovtsov, V., *Iz Moego Proshlogo, Vospominaniya*, **1903-1919**, [Volume 2], *Nauka*, *Moskva*, 1933 [reprinted 1992]

Kochetova, A., [Editor] *Svyatoi Chert, Sbornik, Vospominaniya, Dokumenti, Materiali Sledstvennoi Kommisii* Knizhnaya Palata, *Moskva*, 1990

Konstantinov, V., "*Taina Alexandrovskogo Parka*", Tsarskoe Selo Journal, (1998) Volume 10, June 25

Koshko, A.,

– *Ocherki Ugolovnogo Mira Tsarskoi Rossii*, [Volume III], Paris, 1929

– *Uglovii Mir Tsarskoi Rossii*, *Veche*, *Moskva*, 2006

Kotsyubinsky, A., *Grigorii Rasputin Tainy i Yavny*, Limbus Press, *Sankt Peterburg*, 2003

Kotsyubinsky, D., [Editor] *Dnevnik Rasputina*, OLMA Press, *Moskva*, 2008

Kovalevsky, P., *"Grishka Rasputin"*, *Mokovskoye Izdatelstvo*, *Moskva*, 1917

Krasnii Arkhiv, Moskva,

–   Volume 4, (1923), *"K istorii ubiistva Grigorii Rasputina"*

–   Volume 5, (1924) *"Rasputin v osveshenii* 'okhrani': *Vipiska za Yanvarya 1 1915 do Fevralya 10, 1916"*

–   Volume 9, (1925), *"Pokazaniya A. D. Protopopova, 27 July 1917"*

–   Volume 14, (1926), *"K istorii poslednikh dnei Tsarskogo rezhima"*

–   Volume 30, (1928), *"Pisma D. P. Romanova k Otsu"*

–   Volume 49, (1931), *"Podrobnosti Ubiistva Rasputina"*

Krasnykh, E., *Za vse Blagodaryu*, RDL Press, *Moskva*, 2003

Krilov-Tolstikovich, A.,

–   *Bit' Russkoi Imperatritsei*, Gala Press, *Moskva*, 2003

–   *Poslednyaya Imperatritsa*, *Ripol* Classic Press, *Moskva*, 2006

Knodt, M., **Love Power and Tragedy**, Leppi publications, London, 1997

Kryukov, V., [Editor] *Grigorii Rasputin, Sbornik Istoricheskikh Materialov*, Terra, *Moskva*, 1997

–   Volume 2: Kobil-Bobil, I., *Vsya Pravda o Rasputine*, 1917

–   Kovalevskii, P., *Grishka Rasputin*, 1917

–   Volume 4: Zavadsky, S., *Na Velikom Izlome* (*Delo*

Ubiistvo Rasputina), 1923

Kryuchariantz, D., **Gatchina**, *Leninzdat*, Leningrad, 1990

Kudrina, Yu., *Imperatritsa Maria Fyodorovna Romanova*, OLMA Press, *Moskva*, 2001

Kulegin, A., *Zagrobeniye priklyucheniya 'svyatogo cherta'*, State Political History Museum Publication No. 3, Sankt *Petersburg*, (no date)

Kupchinsky, F., *Ya Zheg Grigoriya Rasputina*, [Editor V. Klaving], *Izdatelstvo, Sankt Peterburg Universitet, Sankt Peterburg*, 2001

Kurlov, P., *Gibel' Imperatorskoi Rossii*, Zaharov, *Moskva*, 1923 [reprinted in 2002]

Lagansky, E.,

– "*Kak Zhigali Rasputina*", *Ogonek*, (1926), Part 1, No 52, December, *Moskva*

– "*Kak Zhigali Rasputina*", *Ogonek*, (1927), Part II, No. 1, January, *Moskva*

Lieberman, A. [Editor] *Gibel Monarkhii*, *Fond* Sergei Dubov, *Moskva*, 2000

– Grand Duke Andrei Vladimirovich., *Dnevnik*, (1915-17)

– Grand Duke Nikolai Mikhailovich, *Zapiski*, (1917)

– Protopopov, A., *Pokazaniya*, (1917)

– Rodzianko, M., *Krusheniye Imperii*, (1929)

"*Lichnost' Nikolaya II i Alexandra Fyodorovni po svidetelstvam ikh Rodnikh i blizkikh*", (1917), Volume CXLIX, April

Lockhart, B., **Memoirs of a British Agent**, Pan, U. K., 1932 [reprinted 2002]

Maklakov, V., B. A.

– *Maklakov o svoem uchastii v zagovore*, *Illustrirovannaya Rossiya*, (1932), No. 12

– "*Tragicheskoye Polozheniye*", *Russkiye Vedomosti*,

(1915), No 221,

    – *"Nekotoriya dopolneniya k Vospominaniyam Purishkevicha i kn. Yusupova ob ubiistve Rasputina"*, *Sovremenniye Zametki*, (1928), No. XXXIV, Paris

    – *"O Knige B. Pares 'Padeniye Russkoi Monarkhii', Pro et Contra (P. Milyukov and S. Maklakov)"*, *Istoriya i Istoriki*, Journal, No. 1, 1939 [reprinted 2001]

    – *Posledniye Dni Rasputina*, Harvest, *Moskva*, 1923 [reprint 2005]

Marie Pavlovna, **Education of a Princess - A Memoir**, Blue Ribbon Books, New York, 1934

Maria Fyodorovna, *Dnevniki Imperatritsi Marii Fyodorovni*, Vagrius, *Moskva*, 2005

Maylunas, A. and Mironenko, S., **A Life Long Passion**, Weidenfeld & Nicholson, London, 1996

Melgunov, S., *Sud'ba Imperatora Nikolaya II Posle Otrecheniye*, *Veche*, *Moskva*, 1951 [reprinted 2005]

Meshaninov, M., *Serafimovsky Lazaret-Ubezhishche A. A. Vyrubovoi v Tsarskom Sele, Pravda o meste pogrebeniya Grigoriya Rasputina*, *Voskreseniye* Press, *Sankt Peterburg*, 2003

Miller, L., **Grand Duchess Elizabeth of Russia**, *Nikodemos* Orthodox Publication Society, Redding, California, 1995

Milyukov, P.,

    – *Vospominaniya gosudarstvennogo deyatelya*, Chalidze Publications, New York, 1955 [reprinted 1982]

    – *Vospominaniya*, Vagrius, Moskva, 1955 [reprinted 2001]

Mironenko, S. [Editor], *Dnevniki Imperatora Nikolaya II (1894-1918)*, [Volumes I and II, Part 1], ROSSPEN, *Moskva*, 2011

Mordvinov, A., *"Poslednii Imperator (Vospominaniya Fligel-Adjutanta A. Mordvinova)"*, *Otechestvenniye Arkhivi* Journal, (1993), No. 3 and No. 4, *Moskva*

Moskovskiye Vedomosti:

–   "*Dukhovnii gastroler Grigorii Rasutina*," No 49, 2 March 1910,

–   "*Yesho Nichto o Grigoriye Rasputina*, No.72, 30 March 1910

Mosolov, A., **Pri Dvore Poslednego Rossiiskogo Imperatora**, *Nauka, Sankt Peterburg*, 1932 [reprinted 1992]

Mourousy, P. *Alexandra Fyodorovna Poslednyaya Russkaya Imperatritsa*, *Veche, Moskva*, 2006

Multatuli, P., *Gospod' da Blagoslavit Resheniye Moe*, Status, *Sankt Peterburg*, 2002

Nadtochy, Vu., **Tobolsk Museum Preserve**, Mid Urals Publishing House, Sverdlovsk, 1988

Napley, D., **Rasputin in Hollywood**, Weidenfeld and Nicolson, London, 1989

Narishkin Kurakin, E., **Under Three Tsars**, Dutton and Co. Incorp. New York, 1931

Nazhivin, I., **Rasputin**, *Rosich* Press, *Moskva*, 1995

Nelipa, M.,

–   **Nikolai II and the Supreme Commander, Fighting on Two Fronts**, Sovereign J., No.2 (2016)

–   **The Tragedy of Nikolai II's Abdication**, Sovereign, No. 1, (2016), Toronto

–   **Alexei: Russia's Last Imperial Heir A chronicle of Tragedy**, Gilbert's Books, Toronto, 2015

–   **Alexander III: His Life and Reign**, Gilbert's Books, Toronto, 2014

–   and Azar, H., **An Inheritance No One Desired**, The European Royal History J., (2005),

        October [Part I] and December [Part II]

–   **The Murder of Grigorii Rasputin: A Conspiracy that Brought Down the Russian Empire**, Gilbert's Books, Toronto, 2010

Nikitenko, G., *Doma i Lyudi Vasilevskogo Ostrova*,

Tsentrpoligraf, Sankt Peterburg, 2007

Nikitin, A., "*Rasputina pokhoronili zhurnalisti*", *Zhurnalist* Journal, (2005), No. 4

Nikolai II,

-   *Dnevnik Imperatora Nikolaya II, 1894-1904*, [Volume I], ROSSPEN, *Moskva*, 2011

-   *Dnevniki Imperatora Nikolaya II 1905-1913, 1914-1918*, [Volume II, Part I and II]

Novy Plan Goroda Petrograda na 1915, *Ekateringofskoye Pechatnoye Delo*, Petrograd, 1915.

Novoye Vremya:

-   "*Vechernaya Khronika*", *Telegrama ot Matreni Rasputina*, No. 13757, 1 July 1914

-   "*Sobitiya dnya*", No. 13757, 1 July 1914

-   "*K pokusheniyu na Gr. Rasputina*", No. 13760, 4 July 1914

-   Letter to the Editor "*Vecher V. A. Karalli*", No 14651, 17 December 1916

-   "*K Tainstvennomu Ubiistvy*", No. 14654, Tuesday 20 December 1916

-   "*K smerti Grigoriya Rasputina*", No. 14655, 21 December 1916

Oldenburg, S., *Tsartsvovaniye Nikolaya II*, *Izdatelstvo* ACT, *Moskva*, 1940 [reprinted 2001]

O-vsky, [Ordovsky] V., "*Iz zapisok Politseiskogo Ofitsera*", *Na Chuzhoi Storone*, (1925), No. 9

Paléologue, M., **An Ambassador's Memoirs**, [Volumes I, II and III], George Doran, New York, 1925

Paley, O., *Vospominaniya o Rossii*, Zakharov, *Moskva*, 2005 and 2009

Patrick, U., **FBI Academy Firearms Training Unit: Handgun Wounding Factors and Effectiveness. U. S. Department of Justice**, Washington D. C., 1989

Pavlovsky, A., *Vseobshii Illustrirovannii Putevoditel po Monastiryam i Svyatim Mestam*, *Possev*, New York, 1907 reprinted 1988

Peregudova, Z., [Editor] *Okhranka, Vospominaniya Rukovoditelei Okhrannikh Otdelenii*, [Volumes 1 and 2], *Novoye Literaturnoye Obrazovaniye, Moskva*, 2004

    –   Gerasimov, A., *Na Lezvii s Terroristami*, (1934)

    –   Martynov, A., *Moya Sluzhba v Otdel'nom Korpuse Zhandarmov*, (1938)

    –   Vasiliev, A., *Okhrana, Vospominaniya Rukovoditelei Politseiskogo Siska*, (1930)

    –   Register of Names, pp 531-94.

Pereverzev, P., *"Ubiistvo Rasputina"*, *Illustrirovannaya Rossiya*, (1932), No. 21

Petrograd i ego Okrestnosti, M. Popov *Izdatelstvo, Sankt Peterburg*, 1915

Pikul, V., *Nechistaya Sila*, Veche, *Moskva*, 2003

Phillips, C., **Eyewitness Travel Guide St. Petersburg**, DK, London, 2004

Pipes, R., **The Russian Revolution**, Vintage Books, New York, 1991

Platonov, O.,

    –   *Zhizn za Tsarya*, *Voskreseniye, Sankt Peterburg*, 1996

    –   *Grigorii Rasputin i Deti Dyavola*, Algorithm, *Moskva*, 2005

    –   *Nikolai Vtoroi v Sekretnoi Perepiske*, Algorithm, *Moskva*, 2005

Polivanov, A., *Iz Dnevnikov i Vospominanii po Dolzhnosti Voennogo Ministra i Ego Pomoshnika 1907-1916*, [Volume 1], *Vyishii Voennii Redaktsionnii Sovet, Moskva*, 1924

Povolotsky, Y., [Editor] *Posledniye Dni Rasputina*, Harvest, *Moskva*, 2005

Povolyaev, V., *Rasputin Tsarskii Ugodnik*, Act Press, *Moskva*, 2005

Privalov, V., *Kamenoostrovsky Prospekt*, *Tsentrpoligraf, Sankt Peterburg*, 2005

Purishkevich, V.,

– *Dnevnik*, National *Reklama* Press, Riga, 1924

– *Ubiistvo Rasputina*, *Interbuk*, *Moskva*, 1918 [reprinted 1990]

Radzinsky, E.,

– *Gospodi ...Spasi i Usmiri Rossiyu*, Vagrius Press, *Moskva*, 1995

– **The Rasputin File**, Doubleday, New York, 2000

Rappaport, H., **Four Sisters**, Macmillan, London, 2014

Rasputina, M.,

– *"Moi otets Grigorii Rasputin"*, *Illustrirovannaya Rossiya*, 1932, No 13

My Father, Cassell and Co., London, 1934

– *Vospominaniya Docheri*, Harvest, *Moskva*, 2000

– *Vospominaniya Rasputin Pochemy?* , Zaharov, *Moskva*, 2000

Rassulin, Yu., *Vernaya Bogu, Tsarya i Ochestvu*, *Tsarskoe Delo, Sankt Peterburg*, 2006 [Includes: Taneeva, A. *Stranitsi Moyei Zhizni*, 1922]

Rech:

– *"Izvestiya za den'"*, No. 176 (2845), July 1, 1914

– *"Pokusheniye na zhizn Grigoriya Rasputina"*, No. 176 (2845), 1 July 1914

– *"Izvestiya za den"*, No. 177 (2846), Wednesday, July 2, 1914

– *"K Pokusheniyu na Rasputina"*, No. 179 (2848), Friday, 4 July 1914

 – *"Za nedelyu"*, No. 182, Monday July 7, 1914

 – *"Posledniya Izvestiya"*, No. 349 (3732), Monday, 19 December 1916

 – *"Posledniya Izvestiya: Smert' Grigoriya Rasputina"*, No. 350 (3733), Tuesday, 20 December 1916

 – *"Izvestiya za den"*, No. 350 (3733), Tuesday, 20 December 1916

 – *"A. N. Khvostov i Rasputin"*, No. 350 (3733), Tuesday, 20 December 1916

 – *"K smerti Grigoriya Rasputina"*, No. 351 (3743), Wednesday, 21 December 1916

 – *"Posledniya Izvestiya"*, No. 351 (3743), Wednesday, 21 December 1916

 – *"V. M. Purishkevich ..."*, No. 351(3743), 21 December 1916

 – *"Telegramma V. M. Purishkevicha"*, No. 351, 21 December 1916

 – *"Pismo Tsaryu"* (with comment by V. Iritsky), No. 58, 9 March 1917

 – *"Novy Muchenik"*, No. 60, 11 March 1917

 – *"Simanovich i Rasputin"*, No. 65, 16 March 1917

Riasanovsky, N., **A History of Russia to 1855**, [Volume 1], Oxford University Press, New York, 2005

Rodzianko, M., **The Reign of Rasputin**, Academic International Press, Florida, 1973

Ross, N., [Editor] *Gibel Tsarskoi Semyi*, Possev-Verlag, Frankfurt am Main, 1987

Roullier, A., *Raspoutine est innocent, France Europe Editions Livres*, Paris, 1998

Rudnev, V., *Pravda o Tsarskoi Semye i Temnikh Silakh*, Reproduced in: *Sbornik*, V. M. C. publishing, *Dornstadt bei Ulm*, U. S. Zone, 1949

Russkaya Volya:

- *"Strelba na ulitse"*, No. 4, 18 December 1916
- *"Pokhoroni Rasputina"*, No. 5, Wednesday, 8 March 1917
- *"Kak Nashli Mogilu Rasputina"*, Lagansky, E., No. 6, Wednesday, 9 March 1917
- *"Arestovanniye"*, No., 8, Friday, 10 March 1917
- *"Arest Nikolaya Romanova"*, Lagansky, E., No. 8, 10 March 1917
- *"Na Mogile Rasputina"*, Lagansky, E., No 8, Friday, 10 March 1917
- *"Vskritiye Telo Rasputina"*, Lagansky, E., No. 8, Friday, 10 March 1917
- *"Rasputiniada"*, Kobil-Bobil, I., No. 8, Friday, 10 March 1917
- *"Rasputiniada - Kak Khoronili Rasputina"*, No. 8, 10 Friday, March 1917
- *"Telo Rasputina"*, Evening edition, No. 9, Friday, 10 March 1917
- *"Kak byl vyslan Dmitri Pavlovich"*, No 8, 10 March 1917
- *"Rasputiniada"*, No 10, Saturday, 11 March 1917
- *"Rasputiniada- Esho o pohoronakh Rasputina"*, No. 10, Saturday, 11 March 1917
- *"Kto ubil Rasputina?"*, Samoilov, V., No 13, Monday 13 March 1917
- *"Sozheniye Tela Rasputina"*, No 14, Tuesday, 14 March 1917
- *"Arest sekretarya Rasputina Simanovicha"*, No. 18, Thursday, 16 March 1917
- *"Arest semyi Rasputina"*, No. 20, Friday, 17 March 1917
- *"Pismo Alexandri Fyodorovni Rasputinu"*, No. 23, 18 March 1917

   –   *"Department politsii ob ubiistvo Rasputina"*, No. 24, Sunday, 19 March 1917

Russkoye Slovo:

   –   *"Slukhi o konchini Rasputina"*, No. 150, 1 July 1914

   –   *"Tainstvennoye ischeznovaniye"*, No. 292, 18 December 1916

   –   *"Ubiistvo Grigoriya Rasputina"*, No 293, 20 December 1916

   –   *"Peremeni v Sovete Ministrov"*, No.294, 21 December 1916

Semennikov, V., [Editor], *"Nikolai II i Velikiye Knyazya Rodstvenniye Pisma k Polednemu Tsaryu"*, Gosudarstvennoye Izdatel'stvo, Leningrad, 1925

Simanovich, A., *Rasputin i Evrei*, Sovetsky Pisatel, Moskva, 1925

Sindalovsky, N., *Prizraki Severnoi Stolitsi*, Centerpoligraf, Sankt Peterburg, 2006

A. Shashkovsky [Editor], *Ves' Petrograd na 1916*, Novoye Vremya, Petrograd, 1916

Shavelsky, G., *Vospominaniye*, [Volumes I and II], Izdatel'stvo Imeni Chekhova, New York, 1954

Shchegolev, P., [Editor] *Padeniye Tsarskogo Rezhima*, [Volumes I-VII], Gosudarstvennoye Izdatelstvo, Leningrad, 1926

Shelley, G., **The Blue Steppes: Adventures among the Russians**, John Hamilton, London, 1925

Shelohaev, V., [Editor] *Gosudarstvennaya Duma Rossiiskoi Imperii*, **1906-1917**, [Volume 1], ROSSPEN, *Moskva*, 2006

Shepelev, L., *Chinovny Mir Rossii XVIII-nachalo XX* в, *Iskusstvo, Sankt Peterburg*, 1999

Shishkin, O.,

   –   *Ubit' Rasputina*, OLMA Press, *Moskva*, 2000

   –   *Rasputin Istoriya Prestupleniya*, *Yauza* Press,

Moskva, 2004

Shulgin, V., *Dni*, *Orfei* Press, Belgrad, 1920

Smirnov, V., *Neizvestnoye o Rasputine*, *Slovo* Press, Tyumen, 1999

Smirnov, V. and M., *Neizvestnoye o Rasputine R. S.*, *Tityl*, Tyumen, 2010

Smith, D., **Rasputin Faith, Power and the Twilight of the Romanovs**, Farrar, Straus and Giroux, N. Y. 2016

Sno, E., *"Kazan' Grishki Rasputina"*, *Almanakh Svobodi*, No. 1, Kiev, 1917

Sokolov, N.,

    –   *Gibel Tsarskoi Semyi*, [Volume I], Terra, *Moskva*, 1925 [reprinted 1996]

    –   *Ubiistvo Tsarskoi Semyi*, *Spasopreobrazhenskogo Valaamskogo Monastyr*, *Sankt Peterburg*, 1998

Soloviev, M., *"Kak i kem byl ubit Rasputin?"*, *Voprosi Istorii*, (1965), March, No. 3

Speransky, V., *"Istoricheskiye svideteli o Rasputine"*, *Illustrirovannaya Rossiya*, (1932), No. 19 (365), Paris

Spiridovich, A.,

    –   *Raspoutine*, *Payot*, Paris, 1935

    –   *Velikaya Voina i Fevral'skaya Revolutsiya*, Harvest, *Moskva*, 2004

Starikov, N., *Kto Ubil Rossiyu*, 1917 Series, *Yauza* Press, *Moskva*, 2007

Stenograficheskii Otchet, Gosudarstvennaya Duma,

    –   Third Duma Convocation, January 25, 1912

    –   Fourth Duma Convocation, November 1-16, 1916

Sveshnikova, G., **Yusupovsky Dvorets Sankt Peterburg Moika 94**, Art-Palace, *Sankt Peterburg*, 2005

Teffi, N., **Moya Letopis**, *Vagrius*, Moscow, 1932 [reprinted 2005]

Tereshuk, A., **Grigorii Rasputin Poslednii Staretz Imperii**, Vita

Nova, *Sankt Peterburg*, 2006

The New York Times:

- "Hint That Nobles Killed Rasputin Stirs Rasputin", No.21.529, Wednesday, 3 January 1917

- "Discuss Rasputin's Death", No. 21.531, Friday, 5 January 1917

- "Rasputin refused Suicide", No. 21.532, Saturday, 6 January 1917

- "Warned Nicholas of Wife's Intrigues, Grand Duke Nicholas Mikhailovich Banished by "Czar because of his Plain Talk", March, 1917

The New York News: "Rasputin's Killer Tells His Story", 21 October 1965

Times of London:

- "Rasputin Dead. Body recovered in the Neva", No. 41.366, Thursday, 4 January 1917

- "Echoes of Rasputin Case", No. 41.371, London, Tuesday, 9 January 1917

- "Obituary: Death of Count Benckendorff", No. 41.375, London, Friday, 12 January 1917

Tretyakova, V., [Editor], *Otrecheniye Nikolaya II, Taini Istorii* Series, Terra, *Moskva*, 1998

Trewin, J., **The House of Special Purpose**, Stein and Day, New York, 1975

Troyat, H., **Rasputin**, *Feniks* Press, *Moskva*, 1997

Trufanov, S., *Svyatoi Chert*, Inter-OMNIC, Perm, 1917 [reprinted 1991]

Tylkin, I., **Grigorii R**, Mars Media, *Moskva*, 1914

Varlamov, A., **Grigorii Rasputin**, *Molodaya Gvardiya, Moskva*, 2007

Vitala, E., *Bez Mifov i Legend*, Armada Press, *Moskva*, 2000

Vorres, I., **The Last Grand Duchess**, Key Porter Books, Toronto, 2001

Voeikov, V., *S Tsarem i bez Tsarya Vospominaniya Poslednego Dvortsogo Komendanta*, Harvest, *Moskva*, 2002

Volkov, A., *Okolo Tsarskoi semyi*, Ankor, *Moskva*, 1928 [reprinted 1993]

Vyrubova, A.,

- *Vospominaniya*, Harvest, *Moskva*, 2002
- *Freilina ee Velichestva*, Harvest, *Moskva*, 2002

Wycollar, F., **"A Secret Chapter of Russian History"**, Munsey's Magazine, (1904), Volume 31, No. 2, New York

Yelinsky, V., *Istoriya Ugolovnogo Siska v Rossii*, **(V- XX century)**, Infra-M Press, *Moskva*, 2004

Youssoupov, F., *La Fin de Raspoutine*, *Plon*, Paris, 1927

Yusupov, F., *Konetz Rasputina*, *Librarie Russe*, *Moskva*, Paris, 1927

Yusupov, F., *Memyari v dvykh knigakh*, Zaharov, *Moskva*, 1952 [reprinted 2004]

Zaharova, O., *Svetskiye Tseremoniali v Rossii* **XVIII-*nachalo* XX v.** *Tsentrpoligraph*, *Moskva*, 2003

Zalessky, K. *Kto byl kto v Pervoi Mirovoi Voine*, *Astrel* Press, *Moskva*, 2002

Zaslavsky, D., *Poslednii Vremenshik Protopopov*, *Knizhniye Novinki*, Leningrad, 1924

- *Ritsar' Chernoi Sotni V. V. Shulgin*, *Byloye Izdatelstvo*, Leningrad, 1925

Zemlyanichenko, M., **"Old Gentleman"** *Frederiks i Imperator Nikolai II*, *Biznes-Inform*, Simferopol, 2007

Zimin, I., *"Raneniye Rasputina"*, *Meditsinskaya Gazeta*, No. 9, 9 February 2001

Zuev, G. *Doma i Lyudi Ofitserskoi Ulitsi*, *Ostrov* Press, *Sankt Peterburg*, 2003

Zvereva, N. [Editor] *Avgusteishiye Sestri Miloserdiya*, *Tsarskii Dom* Series, *Veche*, *Moskva*, 2006

Zvyagintsev, A., *V Epohu Potryasenii o Reform Rossiiskiye*

Prokurori, ROSSPEN, *Moskva*, 1996

Journals and Newspapers

Most journals were published in Russia

Birzheviye Vedomosti, Petrograd, July 1914, December 1916, March-April 1917

Byloye Journal, Petrograd, July 1917

Den', Petrograd, December 1916-March 1917

Golos Moskvi, 1912

Illustrirovannaya Rossiya, Paris, 1932

Istoricheskii Vestnik, Petrograd, April /July-August, 1917

Istoriya i Istoriki, Moskva, 2001

Krasnii Arkhiv, Soviet Union, 1923, 1925, 1926, 1928, 1931

Meditsinskaya Gazeta, Moskva, 2001

Minuvshee, Sankt Peterburg, 1998

Moskovskiye Vedomosti, 1910

Munsey's Magazine, New York, 1904

Na Chuzhoi Storone, 1925

Neva, 2005

Novy Chasovoi, Sankt Peterburg, 1995

Novoye Vremya, Petrograd, July 1914, December 1916

Otechestvenniye Arkhivi, Moskva, 1992, 1993

Otchestvennaya Istoriya, Moskva, 1998

Ogonek, Moskva, December 1926, January 1927, 2003

Rech, Sankt Peterburg/Petrograd, July 1914, December 1916, March 1917

Rus', 1993, 1994

Russkaya Volya, Petrograd, 1917

Russkii Vestnik, Moskva, 2002, 2007

Russkoye Slovo, Petrograd, January 1910, July 1914, December 1916

Sovereign, Toronto, 2015

Stenograficheskii Otchet, Gosudarstvennaya Duma, Sankt Peterburg/Petrograd, 1912, 1916

Tsarskoe Selo, 1998

The European Royal History, San Fransisco, 2005

The New York News, 1965

The New York Times, 1917

Times, London, January 4 – 12, 1917

Zhurnalist, Moskva, 2005

Internet Sources

Most websites are in the Russian language

Ahkmirova, R., "*Rasputinskii Stul*", Sobesednik Journal, December 26, 2007,

See: http://www.sobesednik.ru/archive/sb/01_2008/rasputin_stul/

Amalrik, A., **Rasputin**, *Slovo* Journal, (1992), Moskva:

Preface: See: http://www.erlib.com/Андрей_Амальрик/Распутин/1/

Chapter IV, See: http://www.erlib.com/Андрей_Амальрик/Распутин/5/

Chapter XI, See: http://www.erlib.com/Андрей_Амальрик/Распутин/10/

Chapter XVIII, See: http://www.erlib.com/Андрей_Амальрик/Распутин/16/

Chapter XIX See http://www.erlib.com/Андрей_Амальрик/Распутин/17/

Chapter XXI, See: http://www.erlib.com/Андрей_Амальрик/Распутин/19/

Antonov, B., "*Pazheskii Korpus Ego Imperatorskogo Velichestva*", *Na Strazhe Rodini* Journal, December (1994), See: http://www.ruscadet.ru/kktoday/kk%20mo/sms_nmns/spbsvu/pk.htm

Blagotvoritelnost v Rossii: See: http://charity.lfond.spb.ru/aged/2.html

Chew, F., et al., **Muscular-skeletal imaging**, 2003
See: http://books.google.com.au/books?id=4N0DE6UU-3LIC&pg=PA19&lpg=PA19&dq=unjacketed+bullets&source=web&ots=1sAqAIM9NG&sig=bn0oR2E7yUyuGy-gEANff6riMw58&hl=en

Chumakov, V.,

- "*Rasputin, Kriminalnoye Chtivo*", *Ogonek*, (200), No. 51   See: http://www. ogoniok.com/archive/2003/4815/36-60-63/

- "*Rasputin Kriminalnoye Chtivo*", *Chas*, (2003), Latvian Daily   See: http://www.chas-daily.com/win/2003/10/11/lk001.html?r=41&

"*Delo V. F. Djunkovskogo*", *Otechestvenniye Arkhivi*, (2002), No. 5   See: http://www.rusarchives.ru/publication/djunk.shtml

Dregulyas, G., *Otkritiye Sankt Peterburgskogo politechnicheskogo instituta*, See: http://www.opeterburge.ru/history_147_242.html

Dvorets Beloselsky-Belozersky,
                   See: http://www.spbin.ru/encyclopedia/palaces/beloselsky.htm

Dvortsovy kompleks Yusupovih v Rakitnom",
See: http://yusupov.org/rakitnoe.html

Finkelshtein, K., *"Lechebniye Zavedeniya Tsarskogo Sela v Nachale XX Veka*", 2002, See: http://kfinkelshteyn.narod.ru/ Tzarskoye_Selo/hospital2b.htm

Fomin, S., *"Ubiistvo Rasputina: Sozdaniye Mifa*", *Russkii Vestnik*, (2007), January 8,
See: http://www.rv.ru/content.php3?id=6689

Fyodorovsky Sobor photo [Academic V. A. Pokrovsky],
See: http://www.rcio.rsu.ru/webp/class4/potok79/Web_79/ web_proskurin/web_sysoeva/vika5.htm

Gosudarstvennoye Pravo, **[1885-1886] Item 27,**
Grazhdanskiye Prava Chlenov Tsarstvuyushego Doma,
See: http://www.allpravo.ru/library/doc117p/instrum2817/ item2846.html

Green, Nesson & Murray - **Evidence**: Trammel v. United States, 445 U.S. 40 (1980), See: http:// isites.harvard.edu/icb/icb.do?keyword=k9840&pageid=icb. page36965&pageContentId=icb.pagecontent90797&view=view. do&viewParam_name=TrammelvUnitedStates.html

"Grigorii Efimovich Rasputin: geroi svoego vremeni"
See: http://www.ronl.ru/deyateli_istorii/14655.htm

Grigoriev, G., *"Grigoriya Rasputina Sozhgli v Pechke*", *Tyumenskiye Izvestiya*, (1999), No. 288
See: http://www.allrussia.ru/nowadays/Default.asp?HN_ ID=5&FlagR=4&vYear=2001&vMonth=12&vDay=24

Gutierez, S., **Blood Spatter Pattern and the Kennedy Assassination,**

See: http://www.jfklancerforum.com/sherryg/page03.html

Hutchins, G., **Practical Guidelines for Autopsy Reporting,** *Archives of Pathology and Laboratory Medicine* (1999), Vol. 123, No. 11, pp. 1085–1092,

See: http://arpa.allenpress.com/arpaonline/?request=get-document&doi=10.1043%2F0003-9985(1999)123%3C1085:PG FAP%3E2.0.CO%3B2

Isheev, P, *"Oskolki Proshlogo"*, Russian language Foreign Press Alibr.ru Catalog, 2008

See: http://content.mail.ru/arch/24812/1856679.html

Istoricheskaya Spravka Soyuz teatralnikh deyatelei Rossiiskoi Federatsii, Dom Veteranov

See: http://stdrf.ru/about/dvs/dom_savina/buklet/history/

Khronos biografiya [Biographical Index]
See: http://www.hrono.info/biograf/imena.html

Lepik D. and Vasiliev, L., **Comparison of injuries caused by different pistols at contact range, Russian Biomedical Journal,** 2003, Volume 4,

See: Medline.ru http://www.medline.ru/public/sudm/a2/art1-4.phtml

Likhacheva, A., *"Bolshoi Petrovsky Most"*
See: http://www.opeterburge.ru/bridge_448.html

Maurice Paléologue,

See: http://en.wikipedia.org/wiki/Maurice_Pal%C3%A9ologue

Mironova, T., *"Grigorii Rasputin: Obolgannyaya Zhizn, Obolgannyaya Smert"*, *Russkii Vestnik*, (2002), 11 October, *Moskva*

See: http://www.blagoslovenie.ru/client/New/83.htm

Muravyeva, N., *"Ubiitsi Grigoriya Rasputina terpet' ne mogli hamovatix gostei"*, *Kievskaya Rus'* Online Journal, (2007)

See: http://www.kievrus.com/index.php?action=razdel&razdel=15&subrazdel=69&art_id=9&lang=rus

Nalbandyan, L., *"Talisman Doma Romanovikh"*, *Russkaya Liniya*, (2005), March 11,

See: http://www.rusk.ru/st.php?idar=10490

"Ob Osvidetelsvtovanii v Umstvenikh Sposobnostyah Khionii Kuzminoi Gusevoi, Pokushavsheisya v Iyune 1914 goda na Grigoriya Rasputina",
    See: http://gato.tomica.ru/publications/region/2007shulga1

Osnovniye Gosudarstvenniye Zakoni [1906] *Glava 7*, **St. 64**,

See: http://monar.ru/index.php?download/tsar_orf/SZRI_Tom1_r1.html

"Petrovsky Ostrov", *Sankt Peterburg Encyklopediya*,

See: http://www.encspb.ru/article.php?kod=2803998841

Popov, S., *Moi Vospominaniya o Tsarskoi Semye*, 1930
See: http://kfinkelshteyn.narod.ru/Tzarskoye_Selo/hospital2c.
htm

Popovich, M., **"Permanent French troupe in St.
Petersburg, 19th and 20th centuries"**, *Le Bulletin
de l'Alliance Française*, (1999), No. 3, August
See: http://www.af.spb.ru/bull3/THEATRE.HTM

Potapov, A., *"Strasti Vokrug Ubiistvo Grigoriya Rasputina"*,
Neva Journal, (2005), No. 8   See:
http://magazines.russ.ru/neva/2005/8/po24.html

"Potassium Cyanide", **Material Safety Data
Sheet P5708- 21**, Mallinckrodt Baker Inc., 2007
See: http://www.jtbaker.com/msds/englishhtml/P5708.htm

Prilozheniye IV, **Prisyaga Dlya Chlenov Imperatorskogo Doma**
,   See:
http://www.monarchruss.org/library/prisyagi_tsar.htm

"Pro Pivo, Rossiiskoi Imperii", 2007
See: http://www.rupivo.ru/about_factory.php?id=9

Radio *Ekho Moskva*: **Interview with Sergei
Mironenko** by Evgenii Kiselev on August 5, 2007
See: http://www.echo.msk.ru/programs/all/53727/

Reynolds, P., **The Murder of Rasputin, 30 December** 2016, See:
http://blog.nationalarchives.gov.uk/blog/murder-rasputin/

*Yusupovskomu dvortsu vozvrashena vazhnaya chast'
vistavki o Rasputine*, *Rossiya* television, November 30, 2006

See: http://www.rtr.spb.ru/vesti/vesti_2006/news_
detail.asp?id=8792

Shakhanov, A., "*Moskva i tsentralniye gubernii:
organi politicheskogo siska, doznaniya i suda
(1826-1917)*", *Moskovsky Zhurnal*, (2006) No 1,
See: http://www.mj.rusk.ru/show.php?idar=801145

Shalmanov, S., *100 let SPbGTU: proshloe i Nastoyashee*,
See: http://www.techbusiness.ru/tb/archiv/number7/page07.htm

SIS Official website, History of the British Secret Service,
See: http://www.mi6.gov.uk/output/history-of-sis.html

Solzhenitsyn, A., "*Krasnoye Koleso*", Chapter 65,
Gosudarstvennaya Duma,
See: http://solzhenicyn.ru/modules/myarticles/article_
storyid_160.html

"*Sotrudniki Stavki i Chleni Imperatorskoi Sviti zhivushiye v
Mogileve v 1915-1917*"" See:
http://mogilevhistory.narod.ru/stavka/spisok.htm

Stepanov, A., "**Purishkevich, V.**", *Bolshaya Ensiklopediya
Russkogo Naroda, Russkii patriotism*
See: http://www.rusinst.ru/articletext.asp?rzd=1&id=6198

**The Russian Orthodox Church, Features and
Practices**, St. Petersburg Times, (1990), Florida
See: http://www2.sptimes.com/Treasures/TC.5.4.5.html

Time (U.S.A.):

"**A Vibrant Echo**", (1923), Volume X1, No. 14, Monday, 3 December,

See: http://www.time.com/time/magazine/article/0,9171,717062,00.html

"**Rasputin and the Record**", Foreign News, (1934), Volume XXII, No. 11, Monday, 12 March, See: http://www.time.com/time/magazine/article/0,9171,930156,00.html

"**The League: The Struggle for Peace**", (1935), Volume XXVI, No. 1, Monday, 23 September, See: http://www.time.com/time/magazine/article/0,9171,749065,00.html

Milestones, (1967), Volume 90, No. 14, Friday 6 October,

See: http://www.time.com/time/magazine/article/0,9171,844047,00.html

Tsvetkov, V., *Nuzhni ne rezkiye suzhdeniya, a ponimaniye i pokayaniye*, [Part III], (2008), 9 September See: *Russkaya Liniya*: http://www.rusk.ru/st.php?idar=424307

Ustav Ugolovnogo sudoproizvodstva **[1864]**, See: http://09403.khstu.ru/studentsbooks/othistory/historyist/ustav%20ugol%20sud.htm

Vladimir Zharov, Who is Who in Forensic Medicine in Russia See: http://www.med-pravo.ru/SudMed/WhoIsWho/WhoiswhoJar.htm

Maps

1. Fold out map in: *Peterburg i ego Zhizn,*

Dorovatovsky, N., Publ. *Zhizn Dlya Vseh, Sankt Peterburg*, 1914

2. **Plan of Saint Petersburg**, 1914, G. F. *Knoh* Press, *Nevskii Prospekt*, 49 *Sankt Peterburg*

END NOTES

1. Cook, A., **To Kill Rasputin**, Tempus, U. K., 2005

2. Purishkevich, V. (I), *Dnevnik*, National *Reklama* Press, Riga, 1918 reprinted in 1924

3. Blok, A., *Posledniye Dni Imperatorskoi Vlasti*, Zaharov, *Moskva*, 1919 [Reprinted in 2005]

4. Rudnev, V., *Pravda o Tsarskoi Semye i Temnikh Silakh*, reproduced in: *Sbornik*, V. M. C. publishing, *Dornstadt bei Ulm*, U. S. Zone, 1949, pp 14-35

5. *Pisma D. P. Romanova k otsu*, *Krasnii Arkhiv*, [Volume 30], 1928, *Gosudarstvennoye Izdatelstvo, Moskva*, pp 200-209

6. *Zapiski N. M. Romanova, Podrobnosti Ubiistva Rasputina*, *Krasnii Arkhiv*, [Volume 49], 1931, pp 97-105

7. Kasvinov, V., *Dvadtsat Tri Stupeni Vniz*, Kazakhstan Press, Alma-Ata, 1989

8. Radzinsky, E., *Gospodi ...Spasi i Usmiri Rossiyu*, Vagrius, *Moskva*, 1995

9. Radzinsky, E., **The Rasputin File**, Doubleday, New York, 2000

10. Nazhivin, I., **Rasputin**, *Rosich* Press, *Moskva*, 1995, pp 864

11. Pikul, V., *Nechistaya Sila*, Veche, *Moskva*, 2003

12. Amalrik, A., **Rasputin**, *Slovo* Journal, (1992), See: http://www.erlib.com/Андрей_Амальрик/Распутин/1/

13. Chernyshov, A., *O Vozraste Grigoriya Rasputina i drugih biographicheskikh detaliyakh*, *Otechestvenniye Arkhivi* Journal, No. 1, (1992)

14. Roullier, A., *Raspoutine est innocent*, *France Europe Editions Livres*, Paris, 1998

15. Nelipa, M., **The Murder of Grigorii Rasputin: A Conspira-**

cy That Brought Down the Russian Empire, Gilbert's Books, Toronto, 2010

16.   Chernyshov, A. (I), "*O Vozraste Grigoriya Rasputina i drugikh biographicheskih detaliyakh*", *Otechestvenniye Arkhivi*, (1992), No. 1, pp 112-114 [In March 2016, I accessed the Tyumen District State Archives and found the document declaring Rasputin's date of birth, see: *Fond* No. I-177, op 1, ed. hr, 109, list 3]

17.   Smirnov, V. and M., *Neizvestnoye o Rasputine R. S.*, *Tityl*, Tyumen, 2010, p 12

18.   Smirnov, V. and M., *Neizvestnoye o Rasputine R. S.*, p 14

19.   Rasputina, M. (I), **My Father**, Cassell and Co., London, 1934, p 27

20.   Nadtochy, Vu., **Tobolsk Museum Preserve**, Mid Urals Publishing House, Sverdlovsk, 1988, pp 240

21.   Nadtochy, Vu., **Tobolsk Museum Preserve**, p 238

22.   Smirnov, V. and M., *Neizvestnoye o Rasputine R. S.*, p 14

23.   Rasputina, M. (I), **My Father**, p 30

24.   Nalbandyan, L., See: http://www.rusk.ru/st.php?idar=10490

25.   Ahkmanova, O., [Editor] *Russkii Yazik*, *Moskva*, 1981, p 538

26.   Baryatinsky, V., "*Oshibka Istorii*", *Illustrirovannaya Rossiya*, 1932, No 16, p 6

27.   Buchanan, G., **A Mission to Russia**, [Volume I], Little Brown & Co., Boston, 1923, p 240

28.   Smirnov, V., *Neizvestnoye o Rasputine*, Appendix No. 2, pp 123-144

29.   Troyat, H., **Rasputin**, *Feniks* Press, *Moskva*, 1997, pp 5-6

30.   Smirnov, V., *Neizvestnoye o Rasputine*, Appendix No. 2, pp 123-144

31.   Smirnov, V. and M., *Neizvestnoye o Rasputine R. S.*, p 14

32.   Heresch, E., *Rasputin Taina ego Vlasti*, OLMA-Press, *Moskva*, 2006, p 14

33.   *Sibirskaya Torgovaya Gazeta*, 4 September 1915, reproduced in: Platonov, O. (II), *Zhizn za Tsarya, Voskresenie, Sankt Peterburg*, 1996, p 82

34.   Smirnov, V. and M., *Neizvestnoye o Rasputine R. S.*, p 15

35.   Chernyshov, A. (I), *O Vozraste Grigoriya Rasputina i drugikh biographicheskikh detaliyakh*, p 113

36.   *"Grigorii Efimovich Rasputin: geroi svoego vremeni"*, See: http://www.ronl.ru/deyateli_istorii/14655.htm

37.   Pavlovsky, A., *Vseobshii Illustrirovannii Putevoditel po Monastiryam i Svyatim Mestam*, Possev, New York, 1907 reprinted in 1988, p 687

38.   Platonov, O. (I), *Grigorii Rasputin i Deti Dyavola*, Algorithm, *Moskva*, 2005, p 56-57

39.   Smirnov, V. and M., *Neizvestnoye o Rasputine R. S.*, p 15

40.   Smirnov, V. and M., *Neizvestnoye o Rasputine R. S.*, p 15

41.   *Rech*, No. 45, October 1912, p 2, in: Smirnov, V. and M., *Neizvestnoye o Rasputine R. S.*, p 147

42.   Smirnov, V. and M., *Neizvestnoye o Rasputine R. S.*, Appendix No. 4, p 147

43.   Smirnov, V. and M., *Neizvestnoye o Rasputine R. S.*, Appendix No. 4, p 147

44.   Bokhanov, A. (II), *Byl i Nebyl, Tsarskii Dom* Series, *Veche*, *Moskva*, 2006, p 49

45.   Platonov, O. (II), *Zhizn za Tsarya*, p 177

46.   Rassulin, Yu., *Vernaya Bogu, Tsarya i Ochestvu*, *Tsarskoe Delo, Sankt Peterburg*, 2006, p 563

47.   Document 23, *"Protocol Doprosov: 2 Yanvarya*, 1908", reproduced in: Fomin, S., *Grigorii Rasputin: Rassledovaniye*, [Volume III], Forum Press, *Moskva*, 2009, p 586

48.   Smirnov, V. and M., *Neizvestnoye o Rasputine R. S.*, p 17

49.   Smirnov, V. and M., *Neizvestnoye o Rasputine R. S.*, p 23

50.   Bokhanov, A. (II), *Byl i Nebyl*, p 47

51.   Kotsyubinsky, A., *Grigorii Rasputin Tainy i Yavny*, p 94-96

52.   Smirnov, V. and M., *Neizvestnoye o Rasputine R. S.*, p 19

53.   Platonov, O., *Grigorii Rasputin i Deti Dyavola*, p 61

54.   Kotsyubinsky, A. (I), *Grigorii Rasputin Tainy i Yavny*, p 135

55.   Rasputina, M. (II), *"Moi otets Grigorii Rasputin"*, *Illustriro-vannaya Rossiya*, (1932), No 13, p 10

56.   Rasputina, M. (I), **My Father**, p 47

57.   Rasputina, M. (I), **My Father**, p 46

58.   Bokhanov, A. (I), *Anatomiya Mifa*, p 56

59.   *"K smerti Grigoriya Rasputina"*, *Novoye Vremya*, No. 14655, 21 December 1916, p 7

60.   *Stolichnaya Molva, Sankt Peterburg*, 19 May 1914

61.   Smirnov, V. and M., *Neizvestnoye o Rasputine R. S.*, p 26

62.   Dorovatovsky, N., *Peterburg i ego Zhizn, Zhizn Dlya Vsekh*, *Sankt Peterburg*, 1914, p 295

63.   Nikolai II, Diary excerpts, Monday 26 January 1904, p 787 and Wednesday 31 March, 1904, p 797, in: *Dnevnik Imperatora Niko-laya II, 1894-1904*, [Volume I], ROSSPEN, *Moskva*, 2011

64.   *Dnevnik Imperatora Nikolaya II*, Diary excerpt, Friday 30 July 1904, p 819

65.   Smirnov, V. and M., *Neizvestnoye o Rasputine R. S.*, p 34

66.   Decaux, A., *Velikiye Zagadki XX Veka*, *Veche, Moskva*, 2006, p 20

67.   *Petrograd i ego Okrestnosti*, M. Popov *Izdatelstvo, Sankt Pe-terburg*, 1915, p 171

68.   Sindalovsky, N., *Prizraki Severnoi Stolitsi*, *Centerpoligraf*, *Sankt Peterburg*, 2006, p 225

69.   *Petrograd i ego Okrestnosti*, p 172

70.   Platonov, O. (II), *Zhizn za Tsarya*, p 22

71.   Smirnov, V., *Neizvestnoye o Rasputine*, p 25

72.   Kotsyubinsky, A. (I), *Grigorii Rasputin Tainy i Yavny*, p 100

73.   Trufanov, S., *Svyatoi Chert*, Inter-OMNIC, Perm, 1917 reprinted in 1991, p 15

74.   Rasputina, M., **My Father** (I), p 50

75.   Frantsev, O., *Grigorii Rasputin*, Sovremenii Literator, Minsk, 1998, p 20

76.   Bokhanov, A. (I), *Anatomiya Mifa*, p 56

77.   Kotsyubinsky, A. (I), *Grigorii Rasputin Tainy i Yavny*, p 101

78.   Rasputina, M. (I), **My Father**, p 51-52

79.   Smirnov, V. and M., *Neizvestnoye o Rasputine R. S.*, p 27

80.   Simanovich, A., *Rasputin i Evrei*, Sovetsky Pisatel, Moskva, 1925, p 9

81.   Pavlovsky, A., *Vseobshii Illustrirovannii Putevoditel po Monastiryam i Svyatim Mestam*, p 280 and p 283

82.   Nelipa, M. (I), **Alexei: Russia's Last Imperial Heir A Chronicle of Tragedy**, Gilbert's Books, Toronto, 2015, p 16 and 34

83.   Kotsyubinsky, A. (I), *Grigorii Rasputin Tainy i Yavny*, p 104

84.   Nikolai II, Diary excerpt, 1 November 1905, in: *Dnevniki Imperatora Nikolaya II 1905-1913*, [Volume II, Part I], ROSSPEN, *Moskva*, p 68

85.   Nikolai II, Diary excerpt, 18 July 1906, in: *Dnevniki Imperatora Nikolaya II 1905-1913*, [Volume II, Part I], p 143

86.   Radzinsky, E., **The Rasputin File**, Doubleday, New York, 2000, p 71

87.   Bokhanov, A. (I), *Anatomiya Mifa*, p 59

88.   Sokolov, N.., *Ubiistvo Tsarskoi Semyi*, Spasopreobrazhenskogo Valaamskogo Monastyr, St. Petersburg, 1998, p 247

89.   Nikolai II, Diary excerpt, **13 October 1906**, in: *Dnevniki Im-*

peratora Nikolaya II 1905-1913, [Volume II, Part I], p 160

90.   Heresch, E., *Rasputin Taina ego Vlasti*, p 67

91.   Rasputina, M. (II), *"Moi otets Grigorii Rasputin"*, p 10

92.   Baryatinsky, V., *"Oshibka Istorii"*, p 6

93.   Platonov, O. (I), *Grigorii Rasputin i Deti Dyavola*, p 71

94.   Nikolai II, Diary excerpt, **29 March 1909**, in: *Dnevniki Imperatora Nikolaya II 1905-1913*, [Volume II, Part I], p 375

95.   Pereverzev, P., *"Ubiistvo Rasputina"*, *Illustrirovannaya Rossiya*, (1932), No. 21, p 9

96.   Kazarinov, M., *"Rasputinskii Schef"*, *Illustrirovannaya Rossiya*, (1932), No. 22, p 1

97.   **Document 45**, *"Raport Pokrovskogo ... Episkopu Aleksiyu"*, **9 November 1912**, reproduced in: Fomin, S., *Grigorii Rasputin: Rassledovaniye*, pp 638-639

98.   Tereshuk, A., *Grigorii Rasputin Polednii Staretz Imperii*, Vita Nova, *Sankt Peterburg*, 2006, p 252

99.   *Vechernee Vremya*, *Staretz Grigorii Rasputin – nynye Novikh*, 16 December, 1911

100.   Vorres, I., **The Last Grand Duchess**, p 134

101.   Platonov, O. (I), *Grigorii Rasputin i Deti Dyavola*, p 76

102.   Radzinsky, E., **The Rasputin File**, p 79

103.   Tereshuk, A., *Grigorii Rasputin Polednii Staretz Imperii*, p 75

104.   Bokhanov, A. (I), *Anatomiya Mifa*, p 42

105.   Smirnov, V. and M., *Neizvestnoye o Rasputine R. S.*, p 8

106.   Heresch, E., *Rasputin Taina ego Vlasti*, p 67

107.   Smirnov, V. and M., *Neizvestnoye o Rasputine R. S.*, p 15

108.   Chernishov, A., *O vozraste Grigoriiya Rasputina i drugikh biographicheskih detaliyah*, Otechestvenniye *Arkhivi* Journal, p 114

109.   Smirnov, V., Photograph of Grigorii Rasputin's Plea to Nikolai II, p 14

110.   Vorres, I., **The Last Grand Duchess**, Key Porter Books, Toronto, 2001, p 136

111.   Bokhanov, A. (I), *Anatomiya Mifa*, p 114

112.   Narishkin Kurakin, E., **Under Three Tsars**, Dutton and Co. Incorp. New York, 1931, p 195

113.   Kotsyubinsky, D., [Editor], *Dnevnik Rasputina*, OLMA Press, *Moskva*, 2008, p 121

114.   Trewin, J., **The House of Special Purpose**, Stein and Day, New York, 1975, p 22

115.   Botkina-Melnik, T., *Vospominaniya o Tsarskoi Semye*, Harvest, *Moskva*, 1921 reprinted 2004, p 38

116.   Gilliard, P., **Thirteen Years at the Russian Court**, Ayer, Salem, [1994 Reprint], pp 81-84

117.   Bokhanov, A. (III), *Imperator Nikolai II*, Russkoye Slovo, *Moskva*, 2004, p 289

118.   *Dopros* **A. A. Vyrubova** (Taneeva), **6 May 1917**, in: *Padeniye Tsarskogo Rezhima*, [Editor P. Shegolev], [Volume III], 1925, *Gos. Izdatel'stvo*, Leningrad, p 252

119.   Platonov, O. (II), *Zhizn za Tsarya*, p 51

120.   Kotsyubinsky, A. (I), *Grigorii Rasputin Tainy i Yavny*, p 120

121.   Bokhanov, A. (II), *Byl i Nebyl*, p 106

122.   Nikolai II, Diary excerpt, **6 April 1907**, in: *Dnevniki Imperatora Nikolaya II 1905-1913*, [Volume II, Part I], p 199

123.   Platonov, O. (I), *Grigorii Rasputin i Deti Dyavola*, p 76-77

124.   Document No. 3, Request by *Episkop* Antony, 1 September 1907, reproduced in: Fomin, S., *Grigorii Rasputin: Rassledovaniye*, [Volume III], p 552

125.   Smirnov, V. and M., *Neizvestnoye o Rasputine R. S.*, p 40

126.   Document No. 7, Report by Vishnevsky, 23 July 1906, repro-

duced in: Fomin, S., *Grigorii Rasputin*: *Rassledovaniye*, [Volume III], pp 560-561

127.   Document No. 23, *Protocol Doprosov*: *Dopros* Grigorii Rasputin-*Novii*, 2-3 January 1908, [Volume III], pp 585-586

128.   Document No. 23, Protocol: *Dopros* Efim Rasputin, [Volume III], pp 586-587

129.   Document No. 23, Protocol: *Dopros* Paraskovya Rasputina-*Novaya*, [Volume III], p 587

130.   Document No. 23, Protocol: *Dopros* Akilina Laptinskaya, [Volume III], pp 589-590

131.   Document No. 24, Protocol: *Doprosi*: Mikhail Ziryanov, Peter Bykov and Evdokiya Korneeva, January 4, 1908, [Volume III], pp 593-594

132.   Document No. 29, Protocol: *Dopros* priest Fyodor Chemagin, 4 January 1908, [Volume III], p 597

133.   Document No. 29, Protocol: Response of G. Rasputin to the Investigation, [Volume III], p 597

134.   Document No. 31, "*Schet sledovatelya ...*", [Volume III], p 598

135.   Document No. 40, "*Slushaniye Tobolskoi Duhovnoi Consistory Dela G. E. Rasputina-Novy*", 5 May 1908, [Volume III], pp 609-619

136.   *Tobolsk Eparkhal'niye Vedomosti*, 1908, No. 2, p 210, in: Smirnov, V. and M., *Neizvestnoye o Rasputine R. S.*, p 35

137.   Smirnov, V., *Neizvestnoye o Rasputine*, p 48

138.   Radzinsky, E., **The Rasputin File**, p 84-85

139.   Voeikov, V., *S Tsarem i bez Tsarya Vospominaniya Poslednego Dvortsogo Komendanta*, Harvest, *Moskva*, 2002, p 20

140.   Fuhrmann J. **Rasputin the Untold Story**, John Wiley and Sons, N. J., 2013, p 52

141.   Smirnov, V. *Neizvestnoye o Rasputine*, p 45

142.   Bokhanov, A. (I), *Anatomiya Mifa*, p 161

143.   Kotsyubinsky, A. (I), *Grigorii Rasputin Tainy i Yavny*, p 133

144.   **Document 37**, *"Pismo Tobolskogo Episkopa Aleksiya v Duhovnuyu Konsistoriyu"*, September 19, 1912, reproduced in: Fomin, S., *Grigorii Rasputin: Rassledovaniye*, [Volume III], p 633

145.   Bokhanov, A. (I), *Anatomiya Mifa*, p 160

146.   **Document 43**, *"Raport Pokrovskogo ... Episkopu Aleksiyu"*, 31 October 1912, reproduced in: Fomin, S., *Grigorii Rasputin: Rassledovaniye*, [Volume III], pp 636-637

147.   **Document 45**, *"Raport Pokrovskogo ... Episkopu Aleksiyu"*, 9 November 1912, [Volume III], pp 638-639

148.   **Document 46**, *"Ukaz Duhovnoi Consistory"*, **12 November 1912**, [Volume III], pp 639-642

149.   Kokovtsov, V., *Iz Moego Proshlogo, Vospominaniya*, **1903-1919**, [Volume II], *Nauka, Moskva*, 1933 reprinted in 1992, p 29

150.   Buchanan, G., **A Mission to Russia**, [Volume I], p 241

151.   Platonov, O. (II), *Zhizn za Tsarya*, pp 81-83

152.   Document No. 1, *"Zaveduishemy komnatoi veshestvennih dokazatelsv"*, 31 October 1917, [Petrograd], reproduced in: Fomin, S., *Grigorii Rasputin: Rassledovaniye*, [Volume III], p 551

153.   Bokhanov, A. (I), *Anatomiya Mifa*, p 299

154.   Trufanov, *Svyatoi Chert*, p 122

155.   Nikitenko, G., *Doma i Lyudi Vasilevskogo Ostrova*, *Tsentrpoligraf, Sankt Peterburg*, 2007, p 189

156.   Trufanov, *Svyatoi Chert*, pp 124-126

157.   D. Kotsyubinsky [Editor], *Dnevnik Rasputina*, **Endnote No. 79**, p 325

158.   Trufanov, *Svyatoi Chert*, pp 91-93

159.   de Jonge, A., **The Life and Times of Grigorii Rasputin**, Fontana, London, 1982, p 227

160.   Heresch, E., *Rasputin Taina ego Vlasti*, p 141

161.   Trufanov, S., *Svyatoi Chert*, p 126

162.   Kokovtsov, V., *Iz Moego Proshlogo, Vospominaniya*, 1903-1919, [Volume II], p 24

163.   Trufanov, S., *Svyatoi Chert*, p 128

164.   Kokovtsov, V., *Iz Moego Proshlogo, Vospominaniya*, 1903-1919, [Volume II], p 24

165.   Radzinsky, E., **The Rasputin File**, p 150

166.   Trufanov, S., *Svyatoi Chert*, p 128

167.   Trufanov, S., *Svyatoi Chert*, p 131

168.   Gerasimov, A., *Na Lezvii s Terroristami,* (1934), reprinted in: Peregudova, Z., [Editor] *Okhranka, Vospominaniya Rukovoditelei Okhrannikh Otdelenii*, [Volume 2], *Novoye Literaturnoye Obrazovaniye, Moskva*, 2004, p 331

169.   Radzinsky, E., **The Rasputin File**, p 149

170.   Gerasimov, A., *Na Lezvii s Terroristami*, p 332

171.   Platonov, O. (II), *Zhizn za Tsarya*, p 136

172.   Kokovtsov, V., *Iz Moego Proshlogo, Vospominaniya*, 1903-1919, [Volume II], p 27

173.   Trufanov, S., *Svyatoi Chert*, p 141

174.   Trufanov, S., *Svyatoi Chert*, p 163

175.   Kokovtsov, V., *Iz Moego Proshlogo, Vospominaniya*, 1903-1919, [Volume II], p 25

176.   *"Geroniya Nashikh Symerk,"* ISKRI, No 28, 20 July, 1914, p 223

177.   Platonov, O. (II), *Zhizn za Tsarya*, p 125

178.   *"Pokusheniye na Gr. Rasputina"*, *Birzheviye Vedomosti*, No. 14232, 2 July 1914, p 2

179.   Deposition of Nemkov, I., reproduced in: Platonov, O. (II), *Zhizn za Tsarya*, p 125

180.   *"Ob Osvidetelsvtovanii v Umstvennikh Sposobnostyakh Khionii Kuzminoi Gusevoi, Pokushavsheisya v Iyune 1914 goda na Grigoriya Rasputina"*, See: http://gato.tomica.ru/publications/region/

181. *Dopros* H. Guseva, June 29, 1914, reproduced in: Platonov, O. (II), *Zhizn za Tsarya*, pp 122-123

182. "*K pokusheniyu na Gr. Rasputina*", *Novoye Vremya*, No. 13760, 4 July 1914, p 2

183. Ivanov, A., "*Mneniye Bracha Tomskogo okruzhnoi lecheb-nitsi dlya dushevnobol'nikh, A. Ivanov o sostoyanii ... Kh. K. Guseva ...*", 1915, [Document held in GATO - State Archive Tomsk District, Fond 10. Op 2, D 441. L 8-10]

184. "*Izvestiya za den*", *Rech*, No. 176 (2845), 1 July 1914, p 1

185. "*Pokusheniye na zhizn Grigoriya Rasputina*", p 3

186. "*Slukhi o konchini Rasputina*", *Russkoye Slovo*, No. 150, 1 July 1914, p 2

187. Zimin, I., "*Raneniye Rasputina*", *Meditsinskaya Gazeta*, No. 9 (6137), 9 February 2001, p 15

188. "*Izvestiya za den*", *Rech*, No. 177 (2846), Wednesday 2 July 1914, p 1

189. "*Vechernaya Khronika*", [*Telegrama ot Matreni Rasputina*], *Novoye Vremya*, No. 13757, 1 July 1914, p 2

190. "*Sobitiya dnya*", *Novoye Vremya*, No. 13757, 1 July 1914, p 2

191. "*Za nedelyu*", *Rech*, No. 182, Monday 7 July 1914, p 2

192. Dubovskaya, E., *Tekutyevskaya bol'nitsa i yasnovidyashii Rasputin*, in: *Tyumenskaya Pravda*, 26 September 2013

193. "*K pokusheniyu na Gr. Rasputina*", *Birzheviye Vedomosti*, No. 14240, 6 July 1914, p 4

194. *Pokazaniya* Evdokiya Pecherkina, submitted 29 June 1914, reproduced in: *Zhizn za Tsarya.*, p 118

195. *Pokazaniya* Grigorii Rasputin-*Novy*, submitted 29 June 1914, reproduced in: *Zhizn za Tsarya*, pp 114-115

196. *Pokazaniya* Grigorii Rasputin-*Novy*, submitted 9 August 1914, reproduced in: *Zhizn za Tsarya*, p 130

197.   Platonov, O. (II), *Zhizn za Tsarya*, p 121

198.   "*K Pokusheniye na Rasputina*", *Rech*, No. 179 (2848), Friday 4 July, p 4

199.   "*Razniya Izvestiya*", *Rech*, No. 185 (2854), 12 July 1914, p 7

200.   Trufanov, S., *Svyatoi Chert*, p 174

201.   Platonov, O. (I), *Grigorii Rasputin i Deti Dyavola*, p 172

202.   Platonov, O. (I), *Grigorii Rasputin i Deti Dyavola*, p 175

203.   Radzinsky, E., **The Rasputin File**, p 258

204.   Zimin, I., "*Raneniye Rasputina*", *Meditsinskaya Gazeta*, p 15

205.   Simanovich, A., *Rasputin i Evrei*, Sovetsky Pisatel, Moskva, 1925, p 122

206.   Gerasimov, A., *Na Lezvii s Terroristami*, p 309

207.   Kurlov, P., *Gibel' Imperatorskoi Rossii*, Zaharov, Moskva, [1923 reprinted in 2002], p 192

208.   *Dopros* S. P. Beletsky, 19 May 1917, in: *Padeniye Tsarskogo Regima*, [Volume III], p 148

209.   Beletsky, S., *Grigorii Rasputin iz Zapisok*, Byloye Press, Petrograd, 1923, p 11

210.   Gerasimov, A., *Na Lezvii s Terroristami*, p 310-313

211.   Bokhanov, A. (I), *Anatomiya Mifa*, p 170

212.   Kotsyubinsky, A. (I), *Grigorii Rasputin Tainy i Yavny*, p 144

213.   *Dopros* S. P. Beletsky, 19 May 1917, in: *Padeniye Tsarskogo Regima*, [Volume III], p 257

214.   Bokhanov, A. (I), *Anatomiya Mifa.*, p 305

215.   Platonov, O. (II), *Zhizn za Tsarya*, p 144

216.   Platonov, O. (II), *Zhizn za Tsarya*, p 139

217.   Platonov, O. (I), *Zhizn za Tsarya*, p 145

218.   Bokhanov, A. (I), *Anatomiya Mifa*, p 319

219.   Platonov, O. (II), *Zhizn za Tsarya*, p 148

220.   *"Rasputin v osveshenii 'okhrani': Vipiska za Yanvarya 1 1915 do Fevralya 10, 1916"*, reproduced in: *Krasnii Arkhiv*, [Volume 5], 1924, pp 272-288

221.   Platonov, O. (II), *Zhizn za Tsarya*, p 138

222.   *Byloye* Journal, No. 1(23) July, 1917, Petrograd, p 59

223.   M. C. Komissarov, 4 May 1917, in: *Padeniye Tsarskogo Regima*, [Volume III], p 140 and p 150

224.   Globachev, K., *Pravda o Russkoi Revolutsii*, ROSSPEN, *Moskva*, [1922 reprinted 2009], p 99

225.   Globachev, K., *Pravda o Russkoi Revolutsii*, p 84

226.   *Dopros* A. N. Khvostov, 18 March 1917, in: *Padeniye Tsarskogo Regima*, [Volume I], 1926, p 53

227.   Hoare, S., **The Forth Seal**, William Heinemann, London, 1930, p 134

228.   *Dopros* A. N. Khvostov, 18 March 1917, in: *Padeniye Tsarskogo Regima*, [Volume I], p 53

229.   Platonov, O. (II), *Zhizn za Tsarya*, p 139

230.   Globachev, K., *Pravda o Russkoi Revolutsii*, p 83

231.   *Dopros* S. P. Beletsky, 19 May 1917, in: *Padeniye Tsarskogo Regima*, [Volume III], p 293

232.   Nikolai II, Diary excerpt, Wednesday 14 August 1913, *Dnevnik*, p 68

233.   Nikolai II, Diary excerpts, Monday 23 September and 5 October 1913, *Dnevnik*, pp 78 and 81

234.   *Dopros* S. P. Beletsky, 19 May 1917, in: *Padeniye Tsarskogo Regima*, [Volume III], p 150

235.   Spiridovich, A., *Velikaya Voina i Fevralskaya Revolutsiya*, Harvest, *Moskva*, 2004, p 360

236.   Platonov, O. (II), *Zhizn za Tsarya*, p 189

237.   Spiridovich, A., *Velikaya Voina i Fevralskaya Revolutsiya*, p

183

238.   Spiridovich, A., *Velikaya Voina i Fevralskaya Revolutsiya*, p 219

239.   Globachev., K., *Pravda o Russkoi Revolutsii*, p 95

240.   Spiridovich, A., *Velikaya Voina i Fevralskaya Revolutsiya*, p 190

241.   Spiridovich, A., *Velikaya Voina i Fevralskaya Revolutsiya*, p 222

242.   Beletsky, S., *Grigorii Rasputin iz Zapisok*, p 34

243.   "*Rasputin v osveshenii 'okhrani': Vipiska za Yanvarya 1 1915 do Fevralya 10, 1916*", reproduced in: *Krasnii Arkhiv*, Footnote 1, p 18

244.   *Pokazaniya* S. P. Beletsky, 24 June 1917, in: *Padeniye Tsarskogo Regima*, [Volume IV], (1925), 24 June 1917, p 176

245.   *Pokazaniya* S. P. Beletsky, 24 June 1917, in: *Padeniye Tsarskogo Regima*, [Volume IV], p 181

246.   Beletsky, S., *Grigorii Rasputin iz Zapisok*, p 37

247.   *Pokazaniya* S. P. Beletsky, 24 June 1917, in: *Padeniye Tsarskogo Regima*, [Volume IV], p 175, p 181 and p 187

248.   Spiridovich, A., *Velikaya Voina i Fevralskaya Revolutsiya*, p 223

249.   Beletsky, S., *Grigorii Rasputin iz Zapisok*, pp 73-74

250.   Beletsky, S., *Grigorii Rasputin iz Zapisok*, p 77

251.   Beletsky, S., *Grigorii Rasputin iz Zapisok*, p 76-77

252.   Pikul, V., *Nechistaya Sila*, p 540

253.   Beletsky, S., *Grigorii Rasputin iz Zapisok*, p 79

254.   Beletsky, S., *Grigorii Rasputin iz Zapisok*, pp 80-81

255.   Radzinsky, E., **The Rasputin File**, p 393

256.   Globachev, K., *Pravda o Russkoi Revolutsii*, p 99

257. Globachev, K., *Pravda o Russkoi Revolutsii*, p 99

258. *Dopros* A. N. Khvostov, 18 March 1917, in: *Padeniye Tsarskogo Regima*, [Volume I], p 41

259. Amalrik, A., Chapter XXI, *Vtoroi Triumvariyat, Okhota na Rasputina*, See: http://www.erlib.com/Андрей_Амальрик/Распутин/19/

260. Globachev, K., *Pravda o Russkoi Revolutsii*, p 102

261. Globachev, K., *Pravda o Russkoi Revolutsii*, p 100

262. Amalrik, A., [Chapter XXI], See: http://www.erlib.com/Андрей_Амальрик/Распутин/19/

263. Platonov, O. (II), *Zhizn za Tsarya*, p 193

264. O-vsky, [Ordovsky] V., *"Iz zapisok Politseiskogo Ofitsera"*, *Na Chuzhoi Storone*, (1925), No 9, p 146

265. O-vsky, [Ordovsky] V., p 100

266. Platonov, O. (II), *Zhizn za Tsarya*, p 193

267. Globachev, K., *Pravda o Russkoi Revolutsii*, p 101

268. Simanovich, A., *Rasputin i Evrei*, p 85

269. *"A. N. Khvostov i Rasputin"*, *Rech*, No. 350, Tuesday 20 December 1916, p 4

270. *"Arest sekretarya Rasputina Simanovicha"*, *Russkaya Volya*, No. 18, Thursday 16 March 1917, p 6

271. *Narymsky Krai, Slovopedia*, 2007, See: http://www.slovopedia.com/2/205/245892.html

272. *"Arest sekretarya Rasputina Simanovicha"*, *Russkaya Volya*, No. 18, Thursday 16 March 1917, p 6

273. Globachev, K., *Pravda o Russkoi Revolutsii*, p 103

274. Beletsky, S., *Grigorii Rasputin iz Zapisok*, p 91

275. Spiridovich, A., *Velikaya Voina i Fevralskaya Revolutsiya*, p 287

276. Spiridovich, A., *Velikaya Voina i Fevralskaya Revolutsiya*, p

289

277. Nikolai II, Diary excerpt, Tuesday, February 9, 1916, *Dnevnik*, p 302

278. Kotsyubinsky, A., (I), *Grigorii Rasputin Tainy i Yavny*, p 200

279. Spiridovich, A., *Velikaya Voina i Fevralskaya Revolutsiya*, pp 283-284

280. Amalrik, A., [Chapter XXI], See: http://www.erlib.com/ Андрей_Амальрик/Распутин/19/

281. Simanovich, A., *Rasputin i Evrei*, p 87

282. Platonov, O. (II), *Zhizn za Tsarya*, p 194

283. Spiridovich, A., *Velikaya Voina i Fevralskaya Revolutsiya*, p 295

284. Nikolai II, Diary excerpt, Wednesday 20 January 1916, *Dnevnik*, p 297

285. Globachev, K., *Pravda o Russkoi Revolutsii*, pp 105-106

286. Spiridovich, A., *Velikaya Voina i Fevralskaya Revolutsiya*, p 323

287. Spiridovich, A., *Velikaya Voina i Fevralskaya Revolutsiya*, p 395

288. Rodzianko, M., *Krusheniye Imperii*, (1929), reproduced in: *Gibel Monarkhii*, [Lieberman, A. Editor] *Fond* Sergei Dubov, *Moskva*, 2000, p 207

289. Beletsky, S., *Grigorii Rasputin iz Zapisok*, p 93

290. Globachev, K., *Pravda o Russkoi Revolutsii*, pp 102-103

291. "*A. N. Khvostov i Rasputin*", *Rech*, No. 350, Tuesday 20 December 1916, p 4

292. Amalrik, A., [Chapter XXI], See: http://www.erlib.com/ Андрей_Амальрик/Распутин/19/

293. Rodzianko, M., *Krusheniye Imperii*, p 195

294. *Dopros* A. N. Khvostov, 18 March 1917, in: *Padeniye Tsarskogo Regima*, [Volume I], p 73

295.   *Dopros* M. C. Komissarov, 4 May 1917, in: *Padeniye Tsarskogo Regima*, [Volume III], p 170

296.   Paléologue, M., Diary excerpt, Thursday 3 February 1916 (N. S.), **An Ambassador's Memoirs**, Volume II, George Doran, New York, 1925, p 165

297.   Paléologue, M., **An Ambassador's Memoirs**, [Volume II], p 166

298.   Broitman, L., *Bolshaya Morskaya Ulitsa*, Centerpoligraf, Sankt Peterburg, 2005, p 273

299.   Buchanan, G., **A Mission to Russia**, [Volume I], p 177

300.   Bokhanov, A. (I), *Anatomiya Mifa*, p 65

301.   Buchanan, G., **A Mission to Russia**, [Volume 1], p 242

302.   Platonov, O. (II), *Zhizn za Tsarya*, p 73

303.   Tereshuk, A., *Grigorii Rasputin Poslednii Staretz Imperii*, p 222

304.   Novoselov, M., *Dukhovnii Gastroler Grigorii Rasputina, Moskovskiye Vedomosti*, No 49, 2 March 1910

305.   Novoselov, M., *Yesho Nichto o Grigoriye Rasputina, Moskovskiye Vedomosti*, No.72, 30 March 1910

306.   Novoselov, M., "*Grigorii Rasputin i Mysticheskaya raspustvo*", Supplement in *Golos Moskvi*, 12 February 1912, p 3

307.   Beletsky, S., *Grigorii Rasputin iz Zapisok*, p 11

308.   Address to the Duma by Iskritsky, M., Third Duma Convocation, Session V, Sitting 54, 25 January 1912, reproduced in: *Stenograficheskii Otchet, Gosudarstvennaya Duma, Sankt Peterburg*, p 1014

309.   Address to the Duma by Iskritsky, M., Third Duma Convocation, Session V, Sitting 54, 25 January 1912, reproduced in: *Stenograficheskii Otchet, Gosudarstvennaya Duma*, pp 1013-1015

310.   Address to the Duma by Guchkov, A., Third Duma Convocation, Session V, Sitting 54, 25 January 1912, reproduced in: *Stenograficheskii Otchet, Gosudarstvennaya Duma*, pp 1015-1016

311.   Address to the Duma by Lvov II [Vladimir] Third Duma

Convocation, Session V, Sitting 54, 25 January 1912, reproduced in: *Stenograficheskii Otchet, Gosudarstvennaya Duma*, p 1016

312.   Address to the Duma by Guchkov, A., Third Duma Convocation, Session V, Sitting 54, 25 January 1912, reproduced in: *Stenograficheskii Otchet, Gosudarstvennaya Duma*, p 1014

313.   Tereshuk, A., *Grigorii Rasputin Poslednii Staretz Imperii*, p 222

314.   Bokhanov, A. (I), *Anatomiya Mifa*, p 176-177

315.   *"Pismo Alexandri Fyodorovni Rasputinu"*, *Russkaya Volya*, No. 23, 18 March 1917, p 3

316.   Ksenya Alexandrovna, Diary excerpt, 25 January 1912, reproduced in: Maylunas, A. and Mironenko, S., **A Life Long Passion**, Weidenfeld & Nicholson, London, 1996, p 350

317.   Bokhanov, A. (II), *Rasputin Byl i Nebyl*, *Tsarskii Dom* Series, *Veche, Moskva*, 2006, p 130

318.   Ksenya Alexandrovna, Diary excerpt, 10 March 1912, reproduced in: Maylunas, A. and Mironenko, S., p 351

319.   Kokovtsov, V., *Iz Moego Proshlogo, Vospominaniya*, 1903-1919, [Volume II], p 25

320.   Kokovtsov, V., *Iz Moego Proshlogo, Vospominaniya*, 1903-1919, [Volume II], p 27

321.   Zvyagintsev, A., *V Epohu Potryasenii o Reform Rossiiskiye Prokurori*, ROSSPEN, *Moskva*, 1996, p 167

322.   Zvyagintsev, A., p 168

323.   Kokovtsov, V., *Iz Moego Proshlogo, Vospominaniya*, 1903-1919, [Volume II], p 28

324.   Kokovtsov, V., *Iz Moego Proshlogo, Vospominaniya*, 1903-1919, [Volume II], p 29

325.   Rodzianko, M., *Krusheniye Imperii*, p 107

326.   Rodzianko, M., *Krusheniye Imperii*, p 108

327.   Rodzianko, M., *Krusheniye Imperii*, p 110

328. Tereshuk, A., *Grigorii Rasputin Poslednii Staretz Imperii*, p 226

329. Rodzianko, M., *Krusheniye Imperii*, pp 110-113

330. Rodzianko, M., *Krusheniye Imperii*, p 116

331. Kokovtsov, V., *Iz Moego Proshlogo, Vospominaniya*, 1903-1919, [Volume II], p 30

332. Rodzianko, M., *Krusheniye Imperii*, p 121

333. Platonov, O. (II), *Zhizn za Tsarya*, p 76

334. Tereshuk, A., *Grigorii Rasputin Poslednii Staretz Imperii*, p 235

335. Kokovtsov, V., *Iz Moego Proshlogo, Vospominaniya*, 1903-1919, [Volume II], p 31

336. Bokhanov, A. (II), *Rasputin Byl i Nebyl*, p 110

337. Maylunas, A. and Mironenko, S., p 351

338. Bokhanov, A. (II), *Rasputin Byl i Nebyl*, p 131

339. Kokovtsov, V., *Iz Moego Proshlogo, Vospominaniya*, 1903-1919, [Volume II], pp37-38

340. Zvyagintsev, A., *V Epohu Potryasenii o Reform Rossiiskiye Prokurori*, p 170

341. Botkina-Melnik, T., *Vospominaniya o Tsarskoi Semye*, p 38

342. Vorres, I., **The Last Grand Duchess**, p 135

343. Bokhanov, A. (I), *Anatomiya Mifa*, p 153

344. Tereshuk, A., *Grigorii Rasputin Poslednii Staretz Imperii*, p 355

345. Rasputina, M. (III), *Vospominaniya, Docheri*, Harvest, *Moskva*, 2000, p 143

346. Amalrik, A., [Chapter IV], *Prorok Prozorlivii*, See: http://www.erlib.com/Андрей_Амальрик/Распутин/5/

347. Rasputina, M. (III), *Vospominaniya Docheri*, p 146

348.   Dehn, L., **The Real Tsaritsa**, Thornton Butterworth, London, [1922 reprinted in 1995], pp 103-104

349.   Nelipa, M. (I), **Alexei: Russia's Last Imperial Heir A Chronicle of Tragedy**, p 90

350.   Nelipa, M. (I), **Alexei: Russia's Last Imperial Heir A Chronicle of Tragedy**, p 86

351.   Rodzianko, M., *Krusheniye Imperii*, pp 129-130

352.   Taneeva, A., *Stranitsi Moyei Zhizni*, 1923, reproduced by Rassulin, Yu., [Editor] in: *Vernaya Bogu, Tsaryu i Otechestvu*, *Tsarskoe Delo*, *Sankt Peterburg*, 2006, p 75

353.   Buchanan, G., **A Mission to Russia**, [Volume I], p 209

354.   Oldenburg, S., *Tsartsvovaniye Nikolaya II*, *Izdatelstvo* ACT, *Moskva*, [1940 reprinted 2001], pp 616-7

355.   Danilov, Yu. (I), *Na puti k Krusheniyu*, *Soglasiye* Press, *Moskva*, 2000, p 115

356.   Nikolai II, *Manifest*, Sunday 20 July 1914, in: *Dnevniki Imperatora Nikolaya II 1905-1913*, [Volume II, Part II], ROSSPEN, *Moskva*, 2011, p 47

357.   Grand Duke Andrei Vladimirovich, Diary excerpt, 20 July, 1914, *Voenni Dnevnik Velikogo Knyazya Vladimirovicha Andrei Romanova*, *Sabashnikov* Press, *Moskva*, 2008, p 50

358.   Rodzianko, M., *Krusheniye Imperii*, (1929), reproduced in: *Gibel Monarkhii*, [Lieberman, A. Editor] *Fond* Sergei Dubov, *Moskva*, 2000, pp 148-149

359.   Danilov, Yu. (I), *Rossiya v Mirovoi Voine 1914-1915*, p 112

360.   Danilov, Yu. (I), *Na puti k Krusheniyu*, p 116

361.   Danilov, Yu. (I), *Na puti k Krusheniyu*, p 117

362.   Buchanan, G., **A Mission to Russia**, [Volume I], p 212

363.   Buchanan, G., **A Mission to Russia**, [Volume II], p 67

364.   Danilov, Yu. (II), *Velikii Knyaz Nikolai Nikolayevich*, *Kuchkovo Pole*, *Moskva*, 2006, p 167

365. Nikolai II, Diary excerpt, Monday 4 August 1914, *Dnevnik*, p 161

366. Paléologue, M., Diary excerpt, Tuesday 18 August 1914 (N. S.), **An Ambassador's Memoirs**, [Volume I], p 90

367. Danilov, Yu. (I), *Na puti k Krusheniyu*, p 118

368. Danilov, Yu. (I), *Na puti k Krusheniyu*, p 115

369. Rasputina, M., **My Father** (I), p 81-82

370. Rasputina, M., **My Father** (I), p 82

371. Krilov-Tolstikovich, A., *Bit' Russkoi Imperatritsei*, Gala Press, *Moskva*, 2003, p 294

372. Paléologue, M., Volume II, Diary excerpt, Sunday 13 June 1915, (N. S.), **An Ambassador's Memoirs**, [Volume I], p 13

373. Kotsyubinsky, A. (I), *Grigorii Rasputin Tainy i Yavny*, p 221-222

374. Krilov-Tolstikovich, A., *Bit' Russkoi Imperatritsei*, p 293

375. Vilchikovsky, S., *Vsepredanneishii Doklad*, in: *Avgusteishiye Sestri Miloserdiya*, [Zvereva, N. Editor], *Tsarskii Dom* Series, *Veche*, *Moskva*, 1915 reprinted in 2006, p 333

376. Stepanov, I., (Date unknown) *Miloserdiya dveri Lazaret Ee Velichestva*, in: *Avgusteishiye Sestri Miloserdiya*, p 295

377. Rasputina, M. (II), *Vospominaniya Docheri*, p 253

378. Nikolai II, Diary excerpt, Monday 25 August 1914, *Dnevnik*, p 166

379. Rasputina, M. (II), *Vospominaniya Docheri*, p 255

380. Rasputina, M. (III), *Rasputin Vospominaniya Docheri*, p 263-264

381. Rasputina, M. (III), *Rasputin Vospominaniya Docheri*, p 270

382. Spiridovich, A., *Velikaya Voina i Fevralskaya Revolutsiya*, p 61

383. Grabbe, P and B., **The Private World of the Last Tsar**, Collins, London, 1985, p 163

384.   Rassulin, Yu., *Vernaya Bogu, Tsarya i Ochestvu*, p513

385.   Spiridovich, A., *Velikaya Voina i Fevralskaya Revolutsiya*, p 62

386.   Amalrik, A., [Chapter XVIII], *Yamshik ne goni loshadei*, See: http://www.erlib.com/Андрей_Амальрик/Распутин/16/

387.   Rasputina, M. (III), *Rasputin Vospominaniya Docheri*, p 270-271

388.   Beletsky, S., *Grigorii Rasputin iz Zapisok*, p 21

389.   Smith, D., **Rasputin: Faith, Power and the Twilight of the Romanovs**, Farrar, Straus and Giroux, N. Y. 2016, p 372

390.   Platonov, O. (II), *Zhizn za Tsarya*, pp 203-204

391.   Secret Memorandum No. 291834, 5 June 1915, reproduced in: *Zhizn za Tsarya*, Platonov, O. (II), pp 203-204

392.   "Register of Names": Martynov, A., *Okhranka*, [Volume 2], pp 567-568

393.   Djunkovsky, V., *Vospominaniya*, [Volume II], *Sabashnikov Press, Moskva*, 1997, pp 553-555

394.   Telegram, 25 March 1915, reproduced in: *Zhizn za Tsarya*, p 202

395.   "Register of Names": Djunkovsky, V. F., *Okhranka*, [Volume II], p 545

396.   Bokhanov, A. (I), *Anatomiya Mifa*, p 233

397.   Djunkovsky, V., *Vospominaniya*, [Volume II], pp 568-569

398.   Djunkovsky, V., *Vospominaniya*, [Volume II], p 559

399.   Paléologue, M., Diary excerpt, 13 Sunday June 1915, (N. S.), **An Ambassador's Memoirs**, [Volume II], pp 12-13

400.   Djunkovsky, V., *Vospominaniya*, [Volume II], pp 569-571

401.   Nikolai II, Diary excerpt, Tuesday 9 June 1915, *Dnevnik*, p 240

402.   Alexandra Fyodorovna, Letter to Nikolai II, 22 June 1915, reproduced in: Platonov, O. (III), *Nikolai Vtoroi v Sekretnoi Perepiske*,

Algoritm, *Moskva*, 2005, p 177

403. **"Register of Names"**: Martynov, A., *Okhranka*, [Volume 2], p 566

404. Amalrik, A., Chapter XIX, *Ne Posramim Zemli Russkoi*, See: http://www.erlib.com/Андрей_Амальрик/Распутин/17/

405. Platonov, O. (II), *Zhizn za Tsarya*, p 205

406. Bokhanov, A. (I), *Anatomiya Mifa*, p 252

407. Amalrik, A., [Chapter XIX], See http://www.erlib.com/Андрей_Амальрик/Распутин/17/

408. Bokhanov, A. (I), *Anatomiya Mifa*, p 255

409. Bokhanov, A. (I), *Anatomiya Mifa*, p 254

410. *Pokazaniya* S. P. Beletsky, 19 May 1917, in: *Padeniye Tsarskogo Regima*, [Volume III], p 151

411. Martynov, A., *Moya Sluzhba v Otdel'nom Korpuse Zhandarmov*, (1938), *Okhranka*, [Volume I], pp 29-408

412. Mironova, T., *"Grigorii Rasputin: Obolgannyaya Zhizn, Obolgannyaya Smert'*, *Russkii Vestnik*, 11 October, (2002), *Moskva*, See: http://www.blagoslovenie.ru/client/New/83.htm

413. Globachev, K., Deposition to the Extraordinary Commission of Inquiry, **6 August, 1917**, reproduced in: Globachev, K., *Pravda o Russkoi Revolutsii*, p 412

414. Rodzianko, M., *Krusheniye Imperii*, p 174

415. Rodzianko, M., Editor's comment, in: **The Reign of Rasputin**, Academic International Press, Florida, 1973, p 150

416. Rodzianko, M., *Krusheniye Imperii*, p 174

417. Spiridovich, A., *Velikaya Voina i Fevralskaya Revolutsiya*, p 174

418. Grand Duke Andrei Vladimirovich, Diary excerpt, 17 Monday August 1915, *Gibel Monarkhii*, p 293

419. Grand Duke Andrei Vladimirovich, Diary excerpt, 24 Monday August 1915, p 294

420.   Bokhanov, A. (II), *Rasputin Byl i Nebyl*, p 230

421.   Maklakov, V. (I), *"Tragicheskoye Polozheniye"*, *Russkiye Vedomosti*, No 221, 27 September 1915, p 198

422.   *Dopros* M. A. Belyaeva, 17 April 1917, in: *Padeniye Tsarskogo Regima*, [Volume II], (1925), p 172-173

423.   Finkelshtein, K., *"Lechebniye Zavedeniya Tsarskogo Sela v Nachale XX Veka"*, 2002, See: http://kfinkelshteyn.narod.ru/Tzarskoye_Selo/hospital2b.htm

424.   Nikolai II, Diary excerpt, Wednesday 3 December 1915, *Dnevnik*, p 285

425.   Nelipa, M. (I), **Alexei: Russia's Last Imperial Heir A chronicle of Tragedy**, p 151

426.   Nikolai II, Diary excerpt, Sunday 6 December 1915, *Dnevnik*, p 286

427.   Spiridovich, A., *Velikaya Voina i Fevralskaya Revolutsiya*, p 231

428.   Nikolai II, Diary excerpt, Friday 2 December 1916, *Dnevnik*, p 368

429.   Vyrubova, A. (I), *Vospominaniya*, Harvest, *Moskva*, 2002 Reprint, p 167-169

430.   Spiridovich, A., *Velikaya Voina i Fevralskaya Revolutsiya*, p 404

431.   Vyrubova, A. (I), *Vospominaniya*, p 168

432.   Bokhanov, A. (II), *Rasputin Byl i Nebyl*, p 325

433.   Alexandra Fyodorovna, Letter to Nikolai II, 6 December 1916, reproduced in: Platonov, O. (III), *Nikolai Vtoroi v Sekretnoi Perepiske*, p 670

434.   Alexandra Fyodorovna, Letter to Nikolai II, 12 December 1916, reproduced in: Platonov, O. (III), *Nikolai Vtoroi v Sekretnoi Perepiske*, pp 679-681

435.   Radzinsky, E., **The Rasputin File**, p 448

436.   Alexandra Fyodorovna, Letter to Nikolai II, 12 December

1916, reproduced in: Platonov, O. (III), *Nikolai Vtoroi v Sekretnoi Perepiske*, p 682

437.   Beletsky, S., *Grigorii Rasputin iz Zapisok*, p 23

438.   Beletsky, S., *Grigorii Rasputin iz Zapisok*, p 24

439.   Alexandra Fyodorovna, Letter to Nikolai II, 17 December 1916, reproduced in: Platonov, O. (III), *Nikolai Vtoroi v Sekretnoi Perepiske*, p 694

440.   Rassulin, Yu., *Vernaya Bogu, Tsarya i Ochestvu*, p 385

441.   Beletsky, S., *Grigorii Rasputin iz Zapisok*, p 23

442.   Grand Duke Alexander Mikhailovich, *Velikii Knyaz Aleksandr Mikhailovich, Kniga Vospominanii*, *Tsarskii Dom* Series, *Veche*, *Moskva*, 2000, p 273

443.   Rasputina, N., **My Father** (I), p 109

444.   Radzinsky, E., **The Rasputin File**, p 438

445.   Yusupov, F. (I), **Konetz Rasputina**, *Librarie Russe Moskva*, Paris, 1927, p 127

446.   Rasputina, M. (III), **Rasputin Vospominaniya Docheri**, pp 292-293

447.   Protocol No. 1740, in: **Byloye**, July, No 1 (23), Petrograd, 1917, p 65

448.   Tereshuk, A., *Grigorii Rasputin Poslednii Staretz Imperii*, p 454

449.   Andrei Vladimirovich, Diary excerpt, Saturday 17 December 1916, **Voenni Dnevnik Velikogo Knyazya Vladimirovicha Andrei Romanova**, *Sabashnikov* Press, *Moskva*, 2008, p 202

450.   Kobil-Bobil, I., *Vsya Pravda o Rasputine*, (1917), in: Kryukov, V., [Editor] *Grigorii Rasputin, Sbornik Istoricheskikh Materialov*, [Volume II], Terra, *Moskva*, 1997, p 61

451.   Benois, A., Diary excerpt, Tuesday 20 December 1916, **Dnevnik 1916-1918**, Zaharov, *Moskva*, 2007, p 56

452.   Kotsyubinsky, A. (I), *Grigorii Rasputin Tainy i Yavny*, p 225

453. Fuhrmann, J., **Rasputin: the Untold Story**, pp 200-201

454. Cockfield, J., **White Crow**, Praeger, Connecticut, 2002, pp 175-176

455. Cockfield, J., **White Crow**, p 175

456. Smith, D., **Rasputin: Faith, Power and the Twilight of the Romanovs**, p 627

457. Fuhrmann, J., **Rasputin the Untold Story**, p 201

458. Yusupov, F. (I), *Konetz Rasputina*, pp 246

459. Rodzianko, M., *Krusheniye Imperii*, p 109

460. Grand Duke Nikolai Mikhailovich, Diary excerpt, 18 December 1916, reproduced in: *Krasnii Arkhiv, "Podrobnosti Ubiistva Rasputina"*, p 98

461. Grand Duke Nikolai Mikhailovich, reproduced in: *Krasnii Arkhiv, "Podrobnosti Ubiistva Rasputina"*, p 101

462. Cockfield, J., **White Crow**, p 179

463. Shulgin, V., *Dni*, *Orfei* Press, Belgrad, 1920, p 118

464. Address to the Duma by Shulgin, V., Fourth Duma Convocation, Session V, Sitting 2, 3 November 1916, reproduced in: *Stenograficheskii Otchet, Gosudarstvennaya Duma*, pp 68 and 69

465. Purishkevich, V. (II), *Ubiistvo Rasputina, Interbuk, Moskva,* [1918 reprinted in 1990], pp 145-146

466. Purishkevich, V. (II), *Ubiistvo Rasputina*, p 143

467. Shavelsky, G., *Vospominaniya Poslednego Protopresvitera Russkoi Armii*, (1954), [Volume II], *Izdatel'stvo Imeni Chekhova*, New York, 1954, p 242

468. Grand Duke Nikolai Mikhailovich, Diary excerpt, Friday 23 December 1916, *Krasnii Arkhiv, "Podrobnosti Ubiistva Rasputina"*, p 102

469. Globachev, K., *Pravda o Russkoi Revolutsii*, p 149

470. Spiridovich, A., *Velikaya Voina i Fevralskaya Revolutsiya*, p 441

471.   Purishkevich, V. (II), *Ubiistvo Rasputina*, p 144

472.   Globachev, K., *Pravda o Russkoi Revolutsii*, p 149

473.   Speransky, V., *"Istoricheskiye svideteli o Rasputine"*, *Illustrirovannaya Rossiya*, (1932), No. 19, p 11

474.   Alexandra Fyodorovna, Letter to Nikolai II, 1 June 1916, reproduced in: Platonov, O., *Nikolai Vtoroi v Sekretnoi Perepiske*, p 500

475.   Purishkevich, V. (II), *Ubiistvo Rasputina*, pp 143-146

476.   Yusupov, F., Letter to mother Zinaida Yusupova, 20 November 1916, reproduced in: *Krasnii Arkhiv*, Volume 4, (1926), *K istorii poslednikh dnei Tsarskogo rezhima*, p 234

477.   Yusupov, F. (II), *Memyari v dvykh knigakh*, Zaharov, *Moskva*, 2004, p 176

478.   Yusupov, F., Letter to mother Zinaida Yusupova, 20 November 20 1916, reproduced in: *Krasnii Arkhiv*, *K istorii poslednikh dnei Tsarskogo rezhima*, p 237

479.   Radzinsky, The Rasputin File, p 425

480.   Buchanan, M., The Dissolution of an Empire, John Murray, London, 1932, p 49

481.   Grand Duke Nikolai Mikhailovich, (1917), *Kak vse oni predali ego*, in: *Gibel' Monarkhii, Fond* Sergei Dudov, *Moskva*, 2000, p 75

482.   Kirikov, V., et al., *Nevsky Prospekt, Arhitekturnii putevoditel'*, *Tsentrpoligraf, Sankt Peterburg*, 2002, p 254

483.   Yusupov, F. (I), *Konetz Rasputina*, p 195-196

484.   Yusupov, F. (I), *Konetz Rasputina*, p 205

485.   Yusupov, F. (I), *Konetz Rasputina*, p 202

486.   Grand Duke Nikolai Mikhailovich, Diary excerpt, Friday 23 December 1916, reproduced in: *Krasnii Arkhiv*, "*Podrobnosti Ubiistva Rasputina*", p 101

487.   Grand Duke Gavril Konstantinovich, *Vospominaniya*, Zaharov, *Moskva*, 2005, p 292

488.   Fedorchenko, F., *Svita Rossiiskih Imperatorov*, [Volume II,

M-Ya.], ACT, *Moskva*, 2005, p 375

489.   Spiridovich, A., *Velikaya Voina i Fevralskaya Revolutsiya*, p 441

490.   Grand Duke Nikolai Mikhailovich, Diary excerpt, 4 January 1917, reproduced in: *Gibel Monarkhii*, p 71

491.   Cantacuzene, J. (I), **Revolutionary Days**, The Lakeside Press, Chicago, 1919 [reprinted in 1999], p 222

492.   Telegram to Nikolai Mikhailovich, 19 December 1916, reproduced in: Khrustalev, V., *Felix Felixovich Yusupov. Zagatka Ubiistvo Rasputina. Zapiski Knyazya Yusupova*, ACT, *Moskva*, 2014, pp 133-134

493.   Grand Duke Dmitri, Letter to father: 14 January 1917, reproduced in: *Krasnii Arkhiv*, "*Pisma D. P. Romanova k Otsu*", p 202

494.   Protocol V. Maklakov, 19 September 1920, in: Alexandrov, A. [Editor], *Rassledovaniye Tsareubiistva- rassekrechenniye dokumenti*, *Chuvashkoe knizhnoye izdatel'stvo, Cheboxary*, 2006, pp 121-127

495.   Protocol V. Maklakov, 19 September 1920, in: Alexandrov, A., *Rassledovaniye Tsareubiistva- rassekrechenniye dokumenti*, p 14

496.   Protocol V. Maklakov, 19 September 1920, in: Alexandrov, A., *Rassledovaniye Tsareubiistva- rassekrechenniye dokumenti*, p 4

497.   Protocol V. Maklakov, 19 September 1920, in: Alexandrov, A., *Rassledovaniye Tsareubiistva- rassekrechenniye dokumenti*, p 8

498.   Protocol V. Maklakov, 19 September 1920, in: Alexandrov, A., *Rassledovaniye Tsareubiistva- rassekrechenniye dokumenti*, p 121

499.   Maklakov, V., B. A. *Maklakov o svoem uchastii v zagovore*, *Illustrirovannaya Rossiya*, (1932), No. 12 (358), Paris, Saturday 19 March 1932, pp 1-6

500.   Maklakov, V., (1923) Letter to the Editor Y., Povolotsky and Co., *Posledniye Dni Rasputina*, Harvest, *Moskva*, 2005, p 8

501.   Protocol V. Maklakov, 19 September 1920, in: Alexandrov, A., *Rassledovaniye Tsareubiistva- rassekrechenniye dokumenti*, p 121

502.   Maklakov, V., *Nekotoriya dopolneniya k Vospominaniyam Purishkevicha i kn. Yusupova ob ubiistve Rasputina*, in: *Sovremenniye*

Zametki, No. XXXIV, Paris, 1928, pp 261-262

503.   Footnote No. 2, in: *Krasnii Arkhiv*, *"K istorii poslednikh dnei Tsarskogo rezhima"*, p 231

504.   Protocol V. Maklakov, 19 September 19 1920, in: Alexandrov, A., p 124

505.   Grand Duke Nikolai Mikhailovich, Diary except, Monday 19 December 1916, reproduced in: *Krasnii Arkhiv*, *"Podrobnosti Ubiistva Rasputina"*, p 99

506.   Maklakov, V., *Nekotoriya dopolneniya k Vospominaniyam Purishkevicha i kn. Yusupova ob ubiistve Rasputina*, p 262

507.   Maklakov, V., *Nekotoriya dopolneniya k Vospominaniyam Purishkevicha i kn. Yusupova ob ubiistve Rasputina*, p 265

508.   Maklakov, V., *Nekotoriya dopolneniya k Vospominaniyam Purishkevicha i kn. Yusupova ob ubiistve Rasputina*, p 266

509.   Maklakov, V., *Nekotoriya dopolneniya k Vospominaniyam Purishkevicha i kn. Yusupova ob ubiistve Rasputina*, p 266

510.   Maklakov, V., *Nekotoriya dopolneniya k Vospominaniyam Purishkevicha i kn. Yusupova ob ubiistve Rasputina*, p 267

511.   Fuhrmann, J., **Rasputin: the Untold Story**, p 201

512.   Smith, D., **Rasputin: Faith, Power and the Twilight of the Romanovs**, p 571

513.   Maklakov, V., *Nekotoriya dopolneniya k Vospominaniyam Purishkevicha i kn. Yusupova ob ubiistve Rasputina*, p 263

514.   Smith, D., **Rasputin: Faith, Power and the Twilight of the Romanovs**, p 571

515.   **Protocol V. Maklakov**, 19 September 1920, in: Alexandrov, A., p 123

516.   Maklakov, V., *Nekotoriya dopolneniya k Vospominaniyam Purishkevicha i kn. Yusupova ob ubiistve Rasputina*, p 268

517.   Maklakov, V., *Nekotoriya dopolneniya k Vospominaniyam Purishkevicha i kn. Yusupova ob ubiistve Rasputina*, p 268

518.   Purishkevich, V. (II), *Ubiistvo Rasputina*, p 61

519.   Maklakov, V., Letter to the Editor, *Posledniye Dni Rasputina*, p 8

520.   Maklakov, V., *Nekotoriya dopolneniya k Vospominaniyam Purishkevicha i kn. Yusupova ob ubiistve Rasputina*, pp 267-268

521.   Protocol V. Maklakov, 19 September 1920, reproduced in: Alexandrov, A., p 123

522.   Yusupov, F., Letter to Irina Yusupova, 20 November 1916, reproduced in: Krasnykh, E., *Za vse Blagodaryu*, RDL Press, *Moskva*, 2003, p 411

523.   Purishkevich, V. (II), *Ubiistvo Rasputina*, p 39

524.   Maklakov, V., *Nekotoriya dopolneniya k Vospominaniyam Purishkevicha i kn. Yusupova ob ubiistve Rasputina*, p 269

525.   Grand Duke Dmitri Pavlovich, Letter to father, 23 April 1917, reproduced in: *Krasnii Arkhiv*, "*Pisma D. P. Romanova k Otsu*", p 206

526.   Maklakov, V., *Nekotoriya dopolneniya k Vospominaniyam Purishkevicha i kn. Yusupova ob ubiistve Rasputina*, p 270

527.   Grand Duke Nikolai Mikhailovich, Diary excerpt, Friday 23 December 1916, reproduced in: *Krasnii Arkhiv*, "*Podrobnosti Ubiistva Rasputina*", p 102

528.   Yusupov, F. (I), *Konetz Rasputina*, p 135

529.   Purishkevich, V. (II), *Ubiistvo Rasputina*, pp 158

530.   Yusupov, F. (I), *Konetz Rasputina*, p 122

531.   Essad-Bey, M., **Nicholas II**, Hutchinson and Co., London, 1936, p 241

532.   Buchanan, G., **My Mission to Russia**, [Volume II], Little Brown and Co., Boston, 1923, p 140

533.   Buchanan, G., **My Mission to Russia**, [Volume II], p 27

534.   Paley, O., *Vospominaniya o Rossii*, Zakharov, *Moskva*, 2005, pp 21-22

535.   Essad-Bey, M., **Nicholas II**, p 241

536.   Buchanan, G., **My Mission to Russia**, [Volume II], p 28

537.   Buchanan, G., **My Mission to Russia**, [Volume II], p 32

538.   Buchanan, G., **My Mission to Russia**, Volume II], p 86

539.   Cook, A., **To Kill Rasputin**, Tempus, U. K., 2005, p 216

540.   Buchanan, G., **My Mission to Russia**, [Volume II], p 36

541.   Smith, D., Notes in **Rasputin: Faith, Power and the Twilight of the Romanovs**, p 781

542.   Hughes, M., **Inside the Enigma: British Officials in Russia, 1900-1939**, The Hambledon Press, London, 1997, p 53

543.   Hughes, M., **Inside the Enigma: British Officials in Russia, 1900-1939**, p 55

544.   Hoare, S., **The Fourth Seal**, p 52

545.   Hoare, S., **The Fourth Seal**, p 68

546.   Hoare, S., **The Fourth Seal**, p 67

547.   Hoare, S., **The Fourth Seal**, p 67

548.   Paléologue, M. Diary excerpt, Saturday 19 August 1916, (N. S.), **Ambassador's Memoirs**, [Volume III], p 11

549.   Hoare, S., **The Fourth Seal**, p 107

550.   Hoare, S., **The Fourth Seal**, p 107

551.   Hoare, S., **The Fourth Seal**, p 108

552.   Paléologue, M., Diary excerpt, Saturday 19 August 1916, (N. S.), **Ambassador's Memoirs**, [Volume III], p 11

553.   Buchanan, G., **My Mission to Russia**, [Volume II], p 3

554.   Hoare, **The Fourth Seal**, p 108

555.   Hoare, S., **The Fourth Seal**, p 135

556.   Hoare, S., **The Fourth Seal**, p 134

557.   Hoare, S., **The Fourth Seal**, p 133

558.   Hoare, S., **The Fourth Seal**, p 135

559.   Hoare, S., **The Fourth Seal**, p 107

560.   Hoare, S., **The Fourth Seal**, pp 141-144

561.   Hoare, S., **The Fourth Seal**, p 147

562.   Shishkin, O., *Ubit' Rasputina*, OLMA Press, *Moskva*, 2000, p 116

563.   Hoare, S., **The Fourth Seal**, p 134

564.   **"The League: The Struggle for Peace"**, **Time**, Volume XXVI, No. 1, Monday 23 September 1935, See: http://www.time.com/ time/magazine/article/0,9171,749065,00.html

565.   **SIS Official website, History of the British Secret Service**, See: http://www.mi6.gov.uk/output/history-of-sis.html

566.   Hoare, S., **The Fourth Seal**, pp 135-139

567.   Hoare, S., **The Fourth Seal**, pp 147-149

568.   Hoare, S., **The Fourth Seal**, pp 149-157

569.   **"The League: The Struggle for Peace"**, Monday, 23 September 1935, See: http://www.time.com/time/magazine/article/0,9171,749065,00.html

570.   Buchanan, G., **My Mission to Russia**, [Volume II], p 140

571.   Hoare, S., **The Fourth Seal**, p 159

572.   Hoare, S., **The Fourth Seal**, p 159

573.   Shishkin, O., *Ubit' Rasputina*, p 43

574.   Hoare, **The Fourth Seal**, p 157

575.   Hoare, S., **The Fourth Seal**, p 160

576.   Hoare, S., **The Fourth Seal**, p 118

577.   Hoare, S., **The Fourth Seal**, p 135

578.   Hoare, S., **The Fourth Seal**, p 166

579.   Spiridovich, A., *Velikaya Voina i Fevralskaya Revolutsiya*, p 395

580.   Hoare, S., **The Fourth Seal**, p 176

581.   Paléologue, M., Diary excerpt, Thursday 31 December 1914,

(N. S.), **Ambassador's Memoirs**, [Volume III], pp 132-133

582.   Figes, O., **A People's Tragedy, The Russian Revolution 1891- 1924**, Pimlico, London, 1996, p 196

583.   *Khronos biografiya*, **Vladimir Purishkevich**, See: http://hrono.rspu.ryazan.ru/biograf/purishkev.html

584.   Hughes, M., **Inside the Enigma: British Officials in Russia, 1900-1939**, p 69

585.   Hughes, M., **Inside the Enigma: British Officials in Russia, 1900-1939**, p 74

586.   Hughes, M., **Inside the Enigma: British Officials in Russia, 1900-1939**, p 77

587.   Kotsyubinsky, A. (I), *Grigorii Rasputin Tainy i Yavny*, p 260

588.   Maklakov, V., Letter to the Editor, *Posledniye Dni Rasputina*, p 8

589.   Oldenburg, S., *Tsartsvovaniye Nikolaya II*, p 724

590.   Rodzianko, M., *Krusheniye Imperii*, p 229

591.   Yusupov, F. (I), *Konetz Rasputina*, p 126

592.   Yusupov, F. (I), *Konetz Rasputina*, p 125

593.   Spiridovich, A., *Velikaya Voina i Fevralskaya Revolutsiya*, p 73

594.   Spiridovich, A., *Velikaya Voina i Fevralskaya Revolutsiya*, p 163

595.   Yusupov, F. (I), *Konetz Rasputina*, p 43

596.   Kotsyubinsky, A. (I), *Grigorii Rasputin Tainy i Yavny*, p 263

597.   Yusupov, F. (I), *Konetz Rasputina*, p 91

598.   Yusupov, F. (I), *Konetz Rasputina*, p 95

599.   Grand Duchess Marie Pavlovna, **Education of a Princess - A Memoir**, Blue Ribbon Books, New York, 1934, p 22

600.   Grand Duchess Marie Pavlovna, **Education of a Princess**, p 28

601.   Narishkin-Kurakin, E., **Under Three Tsars**, p 215

602.   Maklakov, V., *Nekotoriya dopolneniya k Vospominaniyam Purishkevicha i kn. Yusupova ob ubiistve Rasputina*, p 269

603.   Yusupov, F. (I), *Konetz Rasputina*, p 122

604.   Maklakov, V., Letter to the Editor, in: *Posledniye Dni Rasputina*, p 10

605.   Maklakov, V., *Nekotoriya dopolneniya k Vospominaniyam Purishkevicha i kn. Yusupova ob ubiistve Rasputina*, Footnote at p 271

606.   Yusupov, F. (I), *Konetz Rasputina*, p 128

607.   Purishkevich, V. (II), *Ubiistvo Rasputina*, p 136

608.   Yusupov, F. (I), *Konetz Rasputina*, p 128

609.   Purishkevich, V. (II), *Ubiistvo Rasputina*, p 136

610.   Maklakov, V., *Delo ob Ubiistvo Rasputina, V. A. Maklakov o svoem uchastii v zagovore*, in: *Illustrirovannaya Rossiya*, p 5 (photo)

611.   Maklakov, V., *Nekotoriya dopolneniya k Vospominaniyam Purishkevicha i kn. Yusupova ob ubiistve Rasputina*, Footnote at p 272

612.   Maklakov, V., Letter to the Editor, *Posledniye Dni Rasputina*, p 11

613.   Yusupov, F. (I), *Konetz Rasputina*, p 127

614.   Bokhanov, A., *Rasputin, Byl i Nebyl*, p 325

615.   Kotsyubinsky, A. (I), *Grigorii Rasputin Tainy i Yavny*, p 236

616.   Pipes, R., **The Russian Revolution**, Vintage Books, New York, 1991, p 262

617.   Grand Duchess Marie Pavlovna, p 280

618.   Yusupov, F. (I), *Konetz Rasputina*, p 179

619.   *Pokazaniya* P. N. Milyukov, 7 August 1917, in: *Padeniye Tsarskogo Regima*, [Volume VI], (1925), p 350

620.   Yusupov, F. (I), *Konets Rasputina*, p 133

621.   Hoare, S., **The Fourth Seal**, William Heinemann, London, 1930, pp 134-135

622.   Paléologue, M. Diary excerpt, Thursday 3 August 1916 (N. S.), **An Ambassador's Memoirs**, [Volume II], p 310

623.   Mourousy, P. *Alexandra Fyodorovna Poslednyaya Russkaya Imperatritsa*, *Veche*, *Moskva*, 2006, p 322

624.   Nelipa, M. and Azar, H., **An Inheritance No One Desired**, The European Royal History Journal, (2005), [Part I]: October, pp 23-30; [Part II]: December, pp 31-35

625.   Narishkin-Kurakin, E., **Under Three Tsars**, p 196

626.   Mourousy, P., *Alexandra Fyodorovna Poslednyaya Russkaya Imperatritsa*, p 153

627.   Mordvinov, A., *"Poslednii Imperator (Vospominaniya Fligel-Adjutanta A. Mordvinova)"*, [Part II], in: *Otechestvenniye Arkhivi* Journal, *Moskva*, (1993), No. 4, p 65

628.   Maria Fyodorovna, Diary excerpt, Friday 28 August 1915, **Dnevniki Imperatritsi Marii Fyodorovni**, Vagrius, *Moskva*, 2005, p 91

629.   Maria Fyodorovna, Diary excerpt, Sunday 20 December 1916, p 164

630.   Kudrina, Yu., *Imperatritsa Maria Fyodorovna Romanova*, OLMA Press, *Moskva*, 2001, p 159

631.   Cantacuzene, J. (II), **My Life Here and There**, Charles Scribner's Sons, New York, 1923, p 253

632.   Mosolov, A., *Pri Dvore Poslednego Rossiiskogo Imperatora*, *Nauka*, *Sankt Peterburg*, [1932 reprinted in 1992], p 92

633.   Mosolov, A., *Pri Dvore Poslednego Rossiiskogo Imperatora*, p 92

634.   Wycollar, F., **"A Secret Chapter of Russian History"**, Munsey's Magazine, [Volume 31], No. 2, May, (1904), New York, p 171

635.   Wycollar, F., **"A Secret Chapter of Russian History"**, p 174

636.   Wycollar, F., **"A Secret Chapter of Russian History"**, p 175

637.   Wycollar, F., **"A Secret Chapter of Russian History"**, p 176

638.   Paléologue, M., Diary excerpt, Wednesday 18 August 1915, (N. S.), **An Ambassador's Memoirs**, [Volume II], p 53

639.   Nelipa, M. (II), **Nikolai II and the Supreme Commander, Fighting on Two Fronts**, Sovereign J., No.2 (2016), pp 77-113

640.   Shavelsky, G., *Vospominaniya Poslednego Protopresvitera Russkoi Armii*, (1954), [Volume I], p 313

641.   Maria Fyodorovna, Diary excerpt, Saturday 8 August 1915, *Dnevniki Imperatritsi Marii Fyodorovni*, p 88-89

642.   Kudrina, Yu., *Imperatritsa Maria Fyodorovna Romanova*, p 149

643.   Maria Fyodorovna, Diary excerpt, Wednesday 12 August 1915, *Dnevniki Imperatritsi Marii Fyodorovni*, p 89

644.   Grand Duke Andrei Vladimirovich, Diary excerpt, Wednesday 24 August 1915, *Voenni Dnevnik*, p 176

645.   Nelipa, M. (III), **Alexander III: His Life and Reign**, Gilbert's Books, Toronto, 2014, p 285

646.   Grand Duke Andrei Vladimirovich, Diary excerpt, Wednesday 24 August 1916, *Voenni Dnevnik*, p 176

647.   Kudrina, Yu., *Imperatritsa Maria Fyodorovna Romanova*, p 150

648.   Buxhoeveden, S., **The Life and Tragedy of Alexandra Feodorovna, Empress of Russia**, Longman Green and Co., London, 1930, p 208

649.   Buxhoeveden, S., **The Life and Tragedy of Alexandra Feodorovna**, p 209

650.   Spiridovich, A., *Velikaya Voina i Fevralskaya Revolutsiya*, p 158

651.   Nelipa, M. (II), **Nikolai II and the Supreme Commander, Fighting on Two Fronts**, p 104

652.   Grand Duke Andrei Vladimirovich, Diary excerpt, Monday 24 August 1915, in: *Voenni Dnevnik*, p 178

653.   Shavelsky, G., *Vospominaniya Poslednego Protopresvitera Russkoi Armii*, [Volume I], p 310

654.   Bubnov, A., *V Tsarskoi Stavke*, *Tsarskii Dom* Series, *Veche*, *Moskva*, 2008, p 125

655.   Paléologue, M., Diary excerpt, Thursday 2 September 1915 (N. S.), **An Ambassador's Memoirs**, [Volume II], p 66-67

656.   Shavelsky, G., *Vospominaniya Poslednego Protopresvitera Russkoi Armii*, [Volume I], p 314

657.   Grand Duke Dmitri Pavlovich, Letter to father, 23 April 1917, Kazvin, Persia, reproduced in: *Krasnii Arkhiv*, *"Pisma D. P. Romanova k Otsu"*, p 206

658.   Maria Fyodorovna, Diary excerpt Saturday 18 August 1915, *Dnevniki Imperatritsi Marii Fyodorovni*, p 89

659.   Maria Fyodorovna, Diary excerpt, Monday 21 August 1915, p 90

660.   Kobylin, V., *Anatomiya Izmeni, Tsarskoe Delo, Sankt Peterburg*, 2005, p 129

661.   Nikolai II, Diary excerpt, Sunday 23 August 1915, *Dnevnik*, p 258

662.   Clay, C., **King, Kaiser, Tsar**, John Murray, London, 2006, p 321

663.   Bubnov, A., *V Tsarskoi Stavke*, p 108

664.   Narishkin-Kurakin, E., **Under Three Tsars**, p 212

665.   Milyukov, P., *Vospominaniya*, p 508

666.   Mosolov, A., *Pri Dvore Poslednego Rossiiskogo Imperatora*, p 85

667.   Nikolai II, Letter to Alexandra Fyodorovna, 25 August 1915, reproduced in: Platonov, O. (III), *Nikolai Vtoroi v Sekretnoi Perepiske*, p 200

668.   Maria Fyodorovna, Diary excerpt, Monday 24 August 1915, *Dnevniki Imperatritsi Marii Fyodorovni*, p 90

669.   Danilov, Yu., *Velikii Knyaz Nikolai Nikolayevich*, p 356

670.   Shavelsky, G., *Vospominaniya Poslednego Protopresvitera Russkoi Armii*, [Volume I], p 340

671.   Danilov, Yu. (I), *Velikii Knyaz Nikolai Nikolayevich*, p 174

672.   Danilov, Yu. (I), *Velikii Knyaz Nikolai Nikolayevich*, p 363

673.   Yusupov, F. (I), *Konets Rasputina*, p 58-59

674.   Spiridovich, A., *Velikaya Voina i Fevralskaya Revolutsiya*, p 192

675.   Milyukov, P., *Vospominaniya*, p 504

676.   Mosolov, A., *Pri Dvore Poslednego Rossiiskogo Imperatora*, p 89

677.   Mosolov, A., *Pri Dvore Poslednego Rossiiskogo Imperatora*, p 87

678.   Kerensky, A., *Tragediya Dinastii Romanovikh*, *Tsentrpoligraf, Moskva*, 2005, p 44

679.   *Dopros* A. N. Khvostov, 18 March 1917, in: *Padeniye Tsarskogo Regima*, [Volume I], pp 60-63

680.   Kerensky, A., *Tragediya Dinastii Romanovikh*, p 43

681.   Kerensky, A., *Tragediya Dinastii Romanovikh*, p 204

682.   Radzinsky, E., **The Rasputin File**, p 355

683.   Spiridovich, A., *Velikaya Voina i Fevralskaya Revolutsiya*, p 286

684.   Spiridovich, A., *Velikaya Voina i Fevralskaya Revolutsiya*, p 385

685.   Cockfield, J., **White Crow**, p 164

686.   Kerensky, A., *Tragediya Dinastii Romanovikh*, p 45

687.   Yusupov, F. (I), *Konets Rasputina*, p 71

688.   Yusupov, F. (I), *Konets Rasputina*, p 101

689.   Handbury-Williams, J., **The Emperor Nicholas II as I knew Him**, p 140

690.   Handbury-Williams, J., **The Emperor Nicholas II as I knew Him**, p 142-143

691.   Grand Duke Nikolai Mikhailovich, Diary excerpt, Monday 19 December 1916, reproduced in: *Krasnii Arkhiv*, *"Podrobnosti Ubiistva Rasputina"*, p 99

692.   Hoare, S., **The Fourth Seal**, p 159

693.   Spiridovich, A., *Velikaya Voina i Fevralskaya Revolutsiya*, p 394

694.   Spiridovich, A., *Velikaya Voina i Fevralskaya Revolutsiya*, p 395

695.   Paléologue, M., Diary excerpt, Friday, 30 July 1915 (N. S.), **An Ambassador's Memoirs**, Volume II, p 38

696.   Maria Fyodorovna, Diary excerpt, Wednesday 16 November 1916, *Dnevniki Imperatritsi Marii Fyodorovni*, p 159

697.   Rodzianko, A., Letter to Zinaida Yusupova, 1 December 1916, reproduced in: *Krasnii Arkhiv*, *"K istorii poslednikh dnei Tsarskogo rezhima"*, pp 241-2

698.   Kudrina, Yu., Endnote No. 33, in: *Dnevniki Imperatritsi Marii Fyodorovni*, p 602

699.   Narishkin-Kudrin, E., **Under Three Tsars**, p 214

700.   Buxhoeveden, S., **The Life and Tragedy of Alexandra Feodorovna**, p 224

701.   Alexandra Fyodorovna, Letter to Nikolai II, 6 September 1915, reproduced in: Platonov, O. (III), *Nikolai Vtoroi v Sekretnoi Perepiske*, p 229

702.   Kerensky, A., *Tragediya Dinastii Romanovikh*, p 45

703.   Buchanan, G., **Mission to Russia**, [Volume II], p 77

704.   Mosolov, A., *Pri Dvore Poslednego Rossiiskogo Imperatora*, p 12

705.   Mosolov, A., *Pri Dvore Poslednego Rossiiskogo Imperatora*, p 13

706.   Mosolov, A., *Pri Dvore Poslednego Rossiiskogo Imperatora*, p 14

707.   Golder, F., **Documents of Russian History 1914-1917**, The

Century Co., 1927, p 40

708.   Bazily [Basily], N., **Memoirs**, Hoover Institute Press, Stanford University, 1973, p 101

709.   Nikolai II, Diary excerpts, Tuesday 7 and Wednesday 8 February 1918, *Dnevnik*, p 452

710.   Pipes, R., **The Russian Revolution**, p 576

711.   Pipes, R., **The Russian Revolution**, p 595

712.   Yusupov, F. (I), *Konetz Rasputina*, pp 37-38

713.   Yusupov, F. (I), *Konetz Rasputina*, pp 52-53

714.   Radzinsky, E. (I), **The Rasputin File**, p172

715.   Rodzianko, M., *Krusheniye Imperii*, p 119

716.   Dobson, C., **Prince Felix Yusupov The Man Who Murdered Rasputin**, Harrap, London, 1989, p 79

717.   Felix Yusupov (senior), Diary excerpt (1915), reproduced in: Krasnykh, E., *Za vse Blagodaryu*, p 373

718.   Rodzianko, M., *Krusheniye Imperii*, p 176

719.   Yusupov, F. (I), *Konetz Rasputina*, p 55

720.   Yusupova, Z., Letter to son Felix, 9 September 1916, reproduced in: Krasnykh, E., p 392

721.   Buxhoeveden, S., **The Life and Tragedy of Alexandra Feodorovna**, p 219

722.   Yusupova, Z., Letter to son Felix, 21 September 1915, reproduced in: Krasnykh, E., *Za vse Blagodaryu*, p 367

723.   Polivanov, A., *Iz Dnevnikov i Vospominaniii po Dolzhnosti Voennogo Ministra i Ego Pomoshnika 1907-1916*, [Volume 1], *Vyishii Voennii Redaktsionnii Sovet*, *Moskva*, 1924, p 235

724.   Yusupova, Z., Letter to son Felix, 29 September 1915, reproduced in: Krasnykh, E., *Za vse Blagodaryu*, p 368

725.   Yusupova, Z., Letter to son Felix, 2 October 1915, reproduced in: Krasnykh, E., p 371

726.   Yusupova, Z., Letter to mother, 20 November 1916, reproduced in: *Krasnii Arkhiv*, *"K istorii poslednikh dnei Tsarskogo rezhima"*, p 233

727.   Yusupova, Z., Letter to son Felix, 25 November 1916, reproduced in: *Krasnii Arkhiv*, p 238

728.   Yusupova, Z., Letter to son Felix, 18 November 1916, reproduced in: *Krasnii Arkhiv*, p 236

729.   Yusupova, Z., Letter to son Felix, 25 November 1916, reproduced in: *Krasnii Arkhiv*, pp 237-238

730.   Yusupova, Z., Letter to son Felix, 3 December 1916, reproduced in: *Krasnii Arkhiv*, p 238

731.   Buchanan, G., **Mission to Russia**, [Volume II], p 7

732.   Spiridovich, A., *Velikaya Voina i Fevralskaya Revolutsiya*, p 403

733.   Almedingen, E., **An Unbroken Unity**, The Bodley Head, London, 1964, p 101

734.   Alexandra Fyodorovna, Letter to Nikolai, 4 December 1916, reproduced in: Platonov, O. (III), *Nikolai Vtoroi v Sekretnoi Perepiske*, p 667

735.   Spiridovich, A., *Velikaya Voina i Fevralskaya Revolutsiya*, p 403

736.   Elizaveta Fyodorovna, Letter to Nikolai II, 29 December 1916, in: *Istochnik*, No. 4, 1994, pp 37-38

737.   Yusupov, F. (II), *Memyari v dvykh knigakh*, p 168

738.   Yusupov, F., Letter to Zinaida Yusupova, 8 December 1916, reproduced in: *Krasnii Arkhiv*, *"K istorii poslednikh dnei Tsarskogo rezhima"*, p 235

739.   Katkov, G., **Russia 1917 The February Revolution**, Collins, London, 1969, p 533

740.   Grand Duke Nikolai Mikhailovich, Diary excerpt, Thursday 17 November 1914, *Gibel Monarkhii*, p 44

741.   Alexandra Fyodorovna, Letter to Nikolai II, 1 May 1916, reproduced in: Platonov, O. (III), *Nikolai Vtoroi v Sekretnoi Perepiske*, p

479

742.	Cockfield, J., **White Crow**, p 166

743.	Maria Fyodorovna, Diary excerpt, Thursday 29 September 1916, *Dnevniki Imperatritsi Marii Fyodorovni*, p 147

744.	Maria Fyodorovna, Diary excerpt, Diary excerpt, Friday 28 October 1916, *Dnevniki Imperatritsi Marii Fyodorovni*, p 153

745.	Nikolai II, Diary excerpts, Saturday 29 October and Sunday 30 October 1916, *Dnevnik*, p 361

746.	Nikolai II, Letter to Alexandra Fyodorovna, Monday 31 October, 1916, reproduced in: Platonov, O. (III), *Nikolai Vtoroi v Sekretnoi Perepiske*, p 643

747.	Nikolai II, Diary excerpt, Tuesday 1 November 1916, *Dnevnik*, p 362

748.	Nikolai II, Letter to Alexandra Fyodorovna, Wednesday 2 November 1916, reproduced in: Platonov, O. (III), *Nikolai Vtoroi v Sekretnoi Perepiske*, p 649

749.	Spiridovich, A., *Velikaya Voina i Fevralskaya Revolutsiya*, p 392

750.	Shavelsky, G., *Vospominaniya Poslednego Protopresvitera Russkoi Armii*, [Volume II], p 217

751.	Spiridovich, A., *Velikaya Voina i Fevralskaya Revolutsiya*, p 392

752.	Spiridovich, A., *Velikaya Voina i Fevralskaya Revolutsiya*, p 392

753.	Nikolai II, Letter to Alexandra Fyodorovna, Thursday 3 November 1916, reproduced in: Platonov, O. (III), *Nikolai Vtoroi v Sekretnoi Perepiske*, pp 650-651

754.	*"Pismo Tsaryu"* (with comment by V. Iritsky), *Rech*, No. 58, 9 March 1917, p 3

755.	Grand Duke Nikolai Mikhailovich, Letter to Nikolai II, reproduced in: Golder, F., **Documents of Russian History 1914-1917**, pp 244-245

756.	Alexandra Fyodorovna, Letter to Nikolai II, 4 November

1916, reproduced in: Platonov, O. (III), *Nikolai Vtoroi v Sekretnoi Perepiske*, pp 651-652

757.   Varlamov, A., **Grigorii Rasputin**, *Molodaya Gvardiya, Moskva*, 2007, p 652

758.   Alexandra Fyodorovna, Letter to Nikolai II, 4 November 1916, reproduced in: Platonov, O. (III), *Nikolai Vtoroi v Sekretnoi Perepiske*, p 651

759.   Nikolai II, Diary excerpt, Monday 7 November 1916, *Dnevnik*, p 363

760.   Maria Fyodorovna, Diary excerpt, Wednesday 9 November 1916, *Dnevniki Imperatritsi Marii Fyodorovni*, p 155

761.   Spiridovich, A., *Velikaya Voina i Fevralskaya Revolutsiya*, pp 394-395

762.   Alexandra Fyodorovna, Letter to Nikolai II, 9 November 1916, reproduced in: Platonov, O. (III), *Nikolai Vtoroi v Sekretnoi Perepiske*, p 659

763.   Grand Duke Nikolai Mikhailovich, A Note, Wednesday 26 April 1917, *Gibel Monarkhii*, pp 75-76

764.   Mosolov, A., *Pri Dvore Poslednego Rossiiskogo Imperatora*, p 146

765.   Maklakov, V., *"Tragicheskoye Polozheniye"*, *Russkiya Vedomosti*, No 221, 27 September 1915, p 198

766.   Pipes, R., **The Russian Revolution**, p 246

767.   Maklakov, V., *"Tragicheskoye Polozheniye"*, *Russkiya Vedomosti*, No 221, 27 September 1915, p 199

768.   Globachev, K., *Pravda o Russkoi Revolutsii*, pp 64-65

769.   Solzhenitsyn, A., *Krasnoye Koleso*, Chapter 65, *Gosudarstvennaya Duma*, See: http://solzhenicyn.ru/modules/myarticles/article_storyid_160.html

770.   Paléologue, M., Diary excerpt, Saturday 11 November 1916 (N. S.), **An Ambassador's Memoirs**, [Volume III], pp 88-89

771.   Opening speech to the Duma by M. Rodzianko, Fourth Duma Convocation, Session V, Sitting No. 1, 1 November 1916, reproduced

in: *Stenograficheskii Otchet, Gosudarstvennaya Duma*, pp 1-6

772.　Paléologue, M., diary excerpt, Tuesday 14 November 1916 (N. S.), **An Ambassador's Memoirs**, [Volume III], p 91

773.　Maklakov, V., *"O Knige B. Pares 'Padeniye Russkoi Monarkhii', Pro et Contra (P. Milyukov and S. Maklakov)"*, p 312

774.　Rodzianko, M., *Krusheniye Imperii*, p 222

775.　Address to the Duma by P. Milyukov, Fourth Duma Convocation, Session V, Sitting 1, 1 November 1916, reproduced in: *Stenograficheskii Otchet, Gosudarstvennaya Duma*, pp 35-48

776.　Burtsev, V., *"Rasputin v 1916 godu"*, *Illustrirovannaya Rossiya*, (1932), No. 17, p 8

777.　Paléologue, M., Diary excerpt, Thursday 16 November 1916 (N. S.), **An Ambassador's Memoirs**, [Volume III], p 93

778.　Address to the Duma by P. Milyukov, Fourth Duma Convocation, Session V, Sitting 1, 1 November 1916, reproduced in: *Stenograficheskii Otchet, Gosudarstvennaya Duma*, p 46

779.　Milyukov, P., *Vospominaniya gosudarstvennogo deyatelya*, Chalidze Publications, New York, [1955 reprinted in 1982], p 277

780.　*Pokazaniya* P. N. Milyukov, 7 August 1917, in: *Padeniye Tsarskogo Regima*, [Volume VI], (1926), p 350

781.　Alexandra Fyodorovna, Letter to Nikolai II, 4 November 1916, reproduced in: Platonov, O. (III), *Nikolai Vtoroi v Sekretnoi Perepiske*, p 652

782.　Paléologue, M., Diary excerpt, Thursday 16 November 1916 (N. S.), **An Ambassador's Memoirs**, [Volume III], p 93

783.　Rodzianko, M., *Krusheniye Imperii*, p 227

784.　Rodzianko, M., *Krusheniye Imperii*, pp 222-223

785.　Paléologue, M., Diary excerpt, Tuesday 17 November 1916 (N. S.), **An Ambassador's Memoirs**, [Volume III], p 94

786.　Address to the Duma by A. Kerensky, Fourth Duma Convocation, Session V, Sitting 4, 4 November 1916, reproduced in: *Stenograficheskii Otchet, Gosudarstvennaya Duma*, p 179

787. Shavelsky, G., *Vospominaniya Poslednego Protopresvitera Russkoi Armii*, [Volume II], p 222

788. Address to the Duma by V. Purishkevich, Fourth Duma Convocation, Session V, Sitting 6, 19 November 1916, reproduced in: *Stenograficheskii Otchet, Gosudarstvennaya Duma*, pp 250-288

789. Yusupov, F., Letter to mother Zinaida Yusupova, 20 November 1916, reproduced in: *Krasnii Arkhiv, "K istorii poslednkh dnei Tsarskogo rezhima"*, p 233

790. *"V. M. Purishkevich i Gr. Rasputin"*, *Birzheviye Vedomosti*, No. 14240, 6 July 1914, p 4

791. Yusupova, Z., Letter to son Felix Yusupov, 25 November 1916, reproduced in: *Krasnii Arkhiv, "K istorii poslednkih dnei Tsarskogo rezhima"*, pp 236-237

792. Ioffe, G., *"Rasputiniada: bolshaya politicheskaya igra"*, *Otchestvennaya Istoriya*, (1998), No. 8, p 111

793. Purishkevich, V. (II), *Ubiistvo Rasputina*, p 39

794. Shavelsky, G., *Vospominaniya Poslednego Protopresvitera Russkoi Armii*, [Volume II], p 242

795. Address to the Duma by V. Dzubinskii, Fourth Duma Convocation, Session V, Sitting 6, 19 November 1916, reproduced in: *Stenograficheskii Otchet, Gosudarstvennaya Duma*, pp 246-247

796. *Pokazaniya* P. N. Milyukov, 7 August 1917, in: *Padeniye Tsarskogo Regima*, [Volume VI], p 364

797. Boyuvich, M., [Editor] *Chleni Gosudarstvennoi Dumi*, Sitin Publishing, *Moskva*, [1913, 4th edition 1917], p 51

798. Shulgin, V., *Dni*, pp 119-121

799. Milyukov, P., *Vospominaniya*, pp 551-2

800. Hughes, M., **Inside the Enigma: British officials in Russia, 1900-1939**, pp 74-75

801. Hughes, M., Buchanan Letter to Hardinge, 4 November 1916, in: **Inside the Enigma: British Officials in Russia, 1900-1939**, p 76

802. Hughes, M., **Inside the Enigma: British Officials in Russia, 1900-1939**, p 77

803.   Buchanan, G., **Mission to Russia**, [Volume II], p 29

804.   **"Obituary "Death of Count Benckendorff"**, Times (London), No. 41.375, Friday 12 January 1917, (N. S.), p 9

805.   Buchanan, G., **Mission to Russia**, [Volume II], p 29

806.   Hughes, M., **Inside the Enigma: British Officials in Russia, 1900-1939**, p 77

807.   Hughes, M., **Inside the Enigma: British Officials in Russia, 1900-1939**, p 78

808.   Yusupov, F. (I), *Konetz Rasputina*, p 122

809.   Hoare, S., **The Fourth Seal**, p 159

810.   Cook, A., **To Kill Rasputin**, p 230

811.   Hughes, M., **Inside the Enigma: British Officials in Russia, 1900-1939**, p 78

812.   Dorril, S., **MI6 Fifty years of Special Operations**, Fourth Estate, London, 2000, p 4

813.   Smith D., **Rasputin: Faith, Power and the Twilight of the Romanovs**, pp 630-631, Cook, A., **To Kill Rasputin**, p 217

814.   Nikolai II, Diary excerpt, Friday 30 December 1916, *Dnevnik*, p 373

815.   Buchanan, G., **Mission to Russia**, [Volume II], p 51

816.   Buchanan, G., **Mission to Russia**, [Volume II], pp 43-46

817.   Golder, F., **Documents of Russian History 1914-1917**, p 119

818.   Buchanan, G., **Mission to Russia**, [Volume II], pp 48-49

819.   Buchanan, G., **Mission to Russia**, [Volume II], p 50

820.   Reynolds, P., **The Murder of Grigorii Rasputin**, excerpts of **Telegram No. 1971** transmitted by G. Buchanan on 31 December 1916 (N. S.), U.K. National Archives catalogue reference: FO 371/2994 (705) and **Telegram No. 2 (K)** transmitted by G. Buchanan on 1 January 1917, U.K. National Archives catalogue reference: FO 371/2994 (1187), See: http://blog.nationalarchives.gov.uk/blog/murder-rasputin/

821.   Hoare, S., **The Fourth Seal**, p 133

822.   Hoare, S., **The Fourth Seal**, p 160

823.   Dorril, S., **MI6 Fifty years of Special Operations**, p 611

824.   Buchanan, G., **Mission to Russia**, [Volume II], pp 55-57

825.   Lockhart, B., **Memoirs of a British Agent**, Pan, U. K., 1932 [reprinted in 2002], p 121

826.   Alexander Mikhailovich, **Once a Grand Duke**, pp 280 and 281

827.   Vasiliev, A., *Okhrana, Vospominaniya Rukovoditelei Politseiskogo Siska*, (1930), in: *Okhranka*, [Volume II], p 433

828.   Shishkin, O. (I), *Rasputin Istoriya Prestupleniya*, *Yauza* Press, *Moskva*, 2004, p 25

829.   Ikonikov-Galitsky, A., *Khroniki Peterburgskikh Prestuplenii, Kriminalnii Peterburg* **1861-1917**, *Azbuka-Klassica, Sankt Peterburg*, 2007, p 47

830.   *Pokazaniya* XVII, A. D. Protopopov, 6 September 1917, in: *Padeniye Tsarskogo Rezhima*, [Volume IV], *Gosudarstvennoye Izdatelstvo*, Leningrad, 1925, p 104

831.   Protocol S. Vlasyuk, in: *Byloye* Journal, No. 1, (23) July, 1917, p 79

832.   Peregudova, Z., [Editor] *Okhranka*, [Volume II], Endnote at p 575

833.   Koshko, A., *"Kak bilo naideno telo Rasputina"*, in: *Ocherki Ugolovnogo Mira Tsarskoi Rossii* (1929), [Volume III], Paris, p 128

834.   *Pokazaniya* XVII, A. D. Protopopov, 6 September 1917, in: *Padeniye Tsarskogo Rezhima*, [Volume IV], p 105

835.   Vasiliev, A., *Okhrana, Vospominaniya Rukovoditelei Politseiskogo Siska*, p 437

836.   *"Otyezd V. M. Purishkevicha"*, *Den'*, No. 349, Monday 19 December 1916, p 1

837.   *Pokazaniya* XVII, A. D. Protopopov, 6 September 1917, in: *Padeniye Tsarskogo Rezhima*, [Volume IV], p 106

838.   Spiridovich, A., *Velikaya Voina i Fevralskaya Revolutsiya*, p

419

839.   Taneeva, A., *Stranitsi Moyei Zhizni*, p 103

840.   *Pokazaniya* XVII, A. D. Protopopov, 6 September, 1917, in: *Padeniye Tsarskogo Rezhima*, [Volume IV], p 105

841.   Rasputina, M., **My Father**, p 13

842.   *Dopros* M. Golovina, 17 December 1916, reproduced in: *Byloye* J., p 69

843.   Rasputina, M., **My Father**, p13

844.   Vasiliev, A., *Okhrana, Vospominaniya Rukovoditelei Politseiskogo Siska*, p 442

845.   *Dopros* A. D. Protopopov, **21 March 1917**, in: *Padeniye Tsarskogo Rezhima*, [Volume I], p 191

846.   Vasiliev, A., *Okhrana, Vospominaniya Rukovoditelei Politseiskogo Siska*, p 433

847.   "*Posledniya Izvestiya*", *Birzheviye Vedomosti*, No 15997, Wednesday 21 December 1916, p 4

848.   Grand Duke Andrei Vladimirovich, Diary excerpt, Wednesday 15 February 1917, *Voenni Dnevnik*, pp 226 and 235

849.   *Dopros* A. Simanovich, reproduced in: "*Zhizn i Pohozdheniye Grigoriya Rasputina*", Anonymous (I), M. E. Zaezdnag Typo-lithography, Kiev, 1917, p 21

850.   Grand Duke Andrei Vladimirovich, Diary excerpt, Wednesday 15 February 1917, *Voenni Dnevnik*, p 227

851.   *Pokazaniya* XVII, A. D. Protopopov, 6 September 1917, *Padeniye Tsarskogo Regima*, [Volume IV], p 105

852.   Simanovich, A., *Rasputin i Evrei*, p 134

853.   Zavadsky, S., Comment during A. Protopopov's *Dopros*, 21 March 1917, *Padeniye Tsarskogo Rezhima*, [Volume I], p 193

854.   *Dopros* A. D. Protopopov, 21 March 1917, in: *Padeniye Tsarskogo Rezhima*, [Volume I], p 192

855.   Vasiliev, A., *Okhrana, Vospominaniya Rukovoditelei Polit-*

seiskogo Siska, p 436

856.   *Dopros* A. D. Protopopov, 21 March 1917, in: *Padeniye Tsarskogo Rezhima*, [Volume I], p 192

857.   Yelinsky, V., *Istoriya Ugolovnogo Siska v Rossii*, (V- XX century), Infra-M Press, *Moskva*, 2004, p 66

858.   *Dopros* A. D. Protopopov, 21 March 1917, in: *Padeniye Tsarskogo Rezhima*, [Volume I], p 194

859.   Sindalovsky, N., *Prizraki Severnoi Stolitsi*, p 183

860.   Zvyagintsev, A., *V Epohu Potryasenii o Reform Rossiiskiye Prokurori*, p 178

861.   Zavadsky, S., *Na Velikom Izlome* (*Delo Ubiistvo Rasputina*), (1923), in: Kryukov, V., [Editor], *Grigorii Rasputin, Sbornik Istoricheskikh materialov*, Volume 4, Terra, *Moskva*, 1997, pp 231-232

862.   Grand Duke Andrei Vladimirovich, Diary excerpt, Wednesday 15 February 1917, *Voenni Dnevnik*, p 228

863.   Genge, N., **The Forensic Casebook**, Random House, London, 2004, p 3

864.   Zavadsky, S., *Na Velikom Izlome* (*Delo Ubiistvo Rasputina*), p 231

865.   Zavadsky, S., *Na Velikom Izlome* (*Delo Ubiistvo Rasputina*), p 239

866.   Grand Duke Andrei Vladimirovich, Diary excerpt, Wednesday 15 February 1917, *Voenni Dnevnik*, p 232

867.   Vasiliev, A., *Okhrana, Vospominaniya Rukovoditelei Politseiskogo Siska*, p 438

868.   Grand Duke Andrei Vladimirovich, Diary excerpt, Wednesday 15 February 1917, *Voenni Dnevnik*, p 228

869.   Akayemov, N., *"Kak nashli trup Rasputina"*, *Istoricheskii Vestnik*, (1917), Volume CXLIX, July-August, p 148

870.   Grand Duke Andrei Vladimirovich, Diary excerpt, Wednesday 15 February 1917, *Voenni Dnevnik*, p 228

871.   Yusupov, F. (I), **Konetz Rasputina**, p 184

872.	Zavadsky, S., *Na Velikom Izlome* (*Delo Ubiistvo Rasputina*), p 239

873.	Grand Duke Andrei Vladimirovich, Diary excerpt, Wednesday 15 February 1917, *Voenni Dnevnik*, p 228

874.	Grand Duke Andrei Vladimirovich, Diary excerpt, Wednesday 15 February 1917, *Voenni Dnevnik*, p 228

875.	"*Ubiistvo Grigoriya Rasputina*", *Russkoye Slovo*, No 293, 20 December 1916, p 3

876.	Vasiliev, A., *Okhrana, Vospominaniya Rukovoditelei Politseiskogo Siska*, p 437

877.	Anonymous (I), "*Zhizn i Pohozdheniye Grigoriya Rasputina*", 1917, p 19

878.	Yusupov, F. (I), *Konetz Rasputina*, p 173

879.	Yusupov, F. (II), *Memyari v dvyh knigah*, p 210

880.	Purishkevich, V. (II), *Ubiistvo Rasputina*, p 152

881.	Yusupov, F. (I), *Konetz Rasputina*, p 174

882.	Yusupov, F. (I), *Konetz Rasputina*, p 174

883.	Yusupov, F. (I), *Konetz Rasputina*, p 185

884.	Grand Duke Andrei Vladimirovich, Diary excerpt, 19 December 1916, Reproduced in: *Gibel Monarkhii*, pp 320

885.	Akayemov, N., "*Kak nashli trup Rasputina*", p 150

886.	"**Rasputin refused Suicide**", **The New York Times**, No. 21.532, Saturday 6 January 1917, (N. S.), p 9

887.	Grand Duke Andrei Vladimirovich, Diary excerpt, Wednesday 15 February 1917, *Voenni Dnevnik*, p 232

888.	Grand Duke Nikolai Mikhailovich, Diary extract, Monday 19 December 1916, reproduced in: *Krasnii Arkhiv*, "*Podrobnosti Ubiistva Rasputina*", p 101

889.	Ikonikov-Galitsky, A., *Khroniki Peterburgskikh Prestuplenii, Kriminalnii Peterburg*, **1861-1917**, pp 50-51

890.	Koshko, A., "*Kak bilo naideno telo Rasputina*", in: *Ocherki*

Ugolovnogo Mira Tsarskoi Rossii, p 129

891.   Globachev, K., *Pravda o Russkoi Revolutsii*, p 89

892.   Grand Duke Andrei Vladimirovich, Diary excerpt, Monday 19 December 1916, in: *Voenni Dnevnik*, p 204

893.   Grand Duke Andrei Vladimirovich, Diary excerpt, Wednesday 15 February 1917, *Voenni Dnevnik*, p 229

894.   Cook, A., **To Kill Rasputin**, p 211

895.   *Byloye* Journal, pp 72-73

896.   Taneeva, A., *Stranitsi Moyei Zhizni*, pp 102-103

897.   Alexandra Fyodorovna, Letter to Nikolai II, Monday 12 December 1916, reproduced in: Platonov, O., *Nikolai Vtoroi v Sekretnoi Perepiske*, p 681

898.   Heresch, E., *Rasputin Taina ego Vlasti*, p 260

899.   *Pokazaniya* A. D. Protopopov, 27 July 1917, reproduced in: *Krasnii Arkhiv*, [Volume 9], 1925, p 139

900.   Rasputina, M., **My Father**, p 109

901.   *"K smerti Grigoriya Rasputina"*, *Rech*, No. 351, 21 December 1916, p 4

902.   *Pokazaniya* A. D. Protopopov, 27 July 1917, reproduced in: *Krasnii Arkhiv*, p 139

903.   Zaslavsky, D., *Poslednii Vremenshik Protopopov*, *Knizhniye Novinki*, Leningrad, 1924, p 38

904.   *Dopros* A. D. Protopopov, 21 March 1917, in: *Padeniye Tsarskogo Rezhima*, [Volume I], p 199

905.   *Dopros* A. A. Vyrubova (Taneeva), 6 May 1917, in: *Padeniye Tsarskogo Rezhima*, [Volume III], p 242

906.   Globachev, K., *Pravda o Russkoi Revolutsii*, p 112

907.   Globachev, K., *Pravda o Russkoi Revolutsii*, pp 112-113

908.   Shchegolev, P., [Editor] *Padeniye Tsarskogo Rezhima*, [Volume V], 1926, pp 238-285

909. *Pokazaniya A. D. Protopopov*, 27 July 1917, reproduced in: *Krasnii Arkhiv*, p 142

910. Rassulin, Yu., *Vernaya Bogu, Tsarya i Ochestvu*, p 563

911. Rasputina, M., **My Father**, p 110

912. Alexandra Fyodorovna, Letter to Nikolai II, Thursday 15 December 1916, reproduced in: Platonov, O., *Nikolai Vtoroi v Sekretnoi Perepiske*, p 688

913. Maklakov, V., *Nekotoriye dopolneniya k vospominaniyam Purishkevicha i kn. Yusupov ob Ubiistvo Rasputina*, p 268

914. Yusupov, F. (I), *Konetz Rasputina*, p 95

915. Globachev, K., *Pravda o Russkoi Revolutsii*, p 87

916. Globachev, K., *Pravda o Russkoi Revolutsii*, p 112

917. *"Ubiistvo Grigoriya Rasputina"*, *Russkoye Slovo*, No 293, 20 December 1916, p 3

918. Bushkov, A., *Rasputin Vistreli iz Proshlogo*, Neva, *Sankt Peterburg*, 2006, p 379

919. Rasputina, M., **My Father**, p 12

920. Zavadsky, S., *Na Velikom Izlome* (*Delo Ubiistvo Rasputina*), p 235

921. Koshko, A., *"Kak bilo naideno telo Rasputina"*, in: *Ocherki Ugolovnogo Mira Tsarskoi Rossii*, p 129

922. Koshko, A., *"Kak bilo naideno telo Rasputina"*, p 130

923. Yusupov, F. (II), *Memyari v dvyh knigah*, p 215

924. Yusupov, F. (I), *Konetz Rasputina*, p 188

925. Koshko, A., *"Kak bilo naideno telo Rasputina"*, in: *Ocherki Ugolovnogo Mira Tsarskoi Rossii*, p 130

926. Zavadsky, S., *Na Velikom Izlome* (*Delo Ubiistvo Rasputina*), p 236

927. Spiridovich, A., *Velikaya Voina i Fevralskaya Revolutsiya*, p 416

928.   Zavadsky, S., *Na Velikom Izlome* (*Delo Ubiistvo Rasputina*), p 241

929.   Zavadsky, S., *Na Velikom Izlome* (*Delo Ubiistvo Rasputina*), pp 241-242

930.   Smith, D., **Rasputin: Faith, Power and the Twilight of the Romanovs**, p 627

931.   Kryuchariantz, D., **Gatchina**, *Leninzdat*, Leningrad, 1990, p 28

932.   Grand Duke Alexander Mikhailovich, *Kniga Vospominanii*, p 272

933.   Grand Duke Alexander Mikhailovich, *Kniga Vospominanii*, p 272

934.   Maklakov, V., *Nekotoriye dopolneniya k vospominaniyam Purishkevicha i kn. Yusupov ob Ubiistvo Rasputina*, p 276

935.   Grand Duke Alexander Mikhailovich, *Kniga Vospominanii*, p 271

936.   Yusupov, F. (I), *Konetz Rasputina*, p 199

937.   Spiridovich, A., *Velikaya Voina i Fevralskaya Revolutsiya*, p 422

938.   Damer, A., *"Rasputin vo Dvortse"*, *Illustrirovannaya Rossiya*, (1932), No 16, p 8

939.   Taneeva A., *Stranitsi Moyei Zhizni*, p 104

940.   Youssoupov, F., *La Fin de Raspoutine*, *Plon*, Paris, 1927, p 194

941.   Yusupov, F. (I), *Konetz Rasputina*, p 187

942.   Purishkevich, V. (II), *Ubiistvo Rasputina*, p 153

943.   Yusupov, F. (II), *Memoiri v Dvykh knigakh*, no page number

944.   Yusupov, F., Letter to Alexandra Fyodorovna, 17 December 1916, reproduced in: *Krasnii Arkhiv*, *"K istorii ubiistva Grigorii Rasputina"*, pp 425-426

945.   Spiridovich, A., *Velikaya Voina i Fevralskaya Revolutsiya*, p

416

946.   Vasiliev, A., *Okhrana, Vospominaniya Rukovoditelei Polit-seiskogo Siska*, p 443

947.   Spiridovich, A., *Velikaya Voina i Fevral'skaya Revolutsiya*, p 418

948.   Voyeikov, V., *S Tsarem i bez Tsarya Vospominaniya Poslednego Dvortsogo Komendanta*, Harvest, *Moskva*, p 164

949.   Voyeikov, V., *S Tsarem i bez Tsarya*, p 162

950.   Grand Duchess Marie, **Education of a Princess - A Memoir**, pp 254-255

951.   **An Ambassador's Memoirs**, [Volume III], p 142

952.   *"Soobsheniye oTainstvennom osobnyake"*, *Birzheviye Vedomosti*, No. 15997, Wednesday 21 December 1916, p 4

953.   Shishkin, O. (I), **Rasputin Istoriya Prestupleniya**, p 116

954.   Pleshev, A., Letter to the Editor *"Vecher V. A. Karalli"*, *Novoye Vremya*, No 14651, 17 December 1916, p 4

955.   Shishkin, O. (I), **Rasputin Istoriya Prestupleniya**, pp 117-118

956.   [No author] *Novy Plan Goroda Petrograda na 1915*, *Ekateringofskoye Pechatnoye Delo*, Petrograd, p 7 and 8

957.   [Editor: A. Shashkovsky], *Ves' Petrograd na 1916*, *Novoye Vremya*, Petrograd, 1916, p 1384

958.   Simanovich, A., **Rasputin i Evrei**, p 135

959.   Grand Duke Dmitri Pavlovich, Letter to Felix, 23 April 1917, reproduced in: *Krasnii Arkhiv*, *"K istorii poslednikh dnei Tsarskogo rezhima"*, p 249

960.   Alexandra Fyodorovna, Letter to Nikolai II, 2 December 1915, reproduced in: Platonov, O., *Nikolai Vtoroi v Sekretnoi Perepiske*, p 338

961.   Anonymous (I), *"Zhizn i Pohozhdeniye Grigoriya Rasputina"*, 1917, p 15

962.   Dorr, R., **Inside the Russian Revolution**, The Macmillan Co.

New York, 1917, p 122

963.　*Pokazaniya* XVII, A. Protopopov, 6 September 1917, in: *Padeniye Tsarskogo Regima*, [Volume IV], p 107

964.　*Dopros* K. Globachev, 6 August 1917, reproduced in: Globachev, K., *Pravda o Russkoi Revolutsii*, p 411

965.　Spiridovich, A., *Velikaya Voina i Fevralskaya Revolutsiya*, p 419

966.　Rassulin, Yu., *Vernaya Bogu, Tsarya i Ochestvu*, p 573

967.　Taneeva, A., *Stranitsi Moyei Zhizni*, p 107

968.　Buxhoeveden, S., **The Life and Tragedy of Alexandra Feodorovna**, p 243

969.　Rodzianko, M., *Krusheniye Imperii*, p 236

970.　Grand Duke Nikolai Mikhailovich, 23 December 1916, reproduced in: *Krasnii Arkhiv*, *"Podrobnosti Ubiistva Rasputina"*, p 102

971.　Spiridovich, A., *Velikaya Voina i Fevralskaya Revolutsiya*, p 418

972.　Spiridovich, A., *Velikaya Voina i Fevralskaya Revolutsiya*, p 419

973.　Zalessky, K., *Kto byl kto v Pervoi Mirovoi Voine*, *Astrel* Press, *Moskva*, 2002, p 55

974.　Taneeva, A., *Stranitsi Moyei Zhizni*, p 104

975.　Spiridovich, A., *Velikaya Voina i Fevralskaya Revolutsiya*, p 424

976.　Shavelsky, G., *Vospominaniya Poslednego Protopresvitera Russkoi Armii i Flota*, [Volume II], p 250

977.　Spiridovich, A., *Velikaya Voina i Fevral'skaya Revolutsiya*, p 425

978.　Paléologue, M., Diary extract, Saturday 6 January 1917, (N. S.), **An Ambassador's Memoirs**, [Volume III], pp 147-148

979.　Yusupov, F. (I), *Konetz Rasputina*, p 166

980.　Shishkin O. (II), *Ubit' Rasputina*, OLMA Press, *Moskva*,

2000, pp 151-152

981.   "*Sotrudniki Stavki i Chleni Imperatorskoi Sviti zhivushiye v Mogileve v 1915-1917*", See: http://mogilevhistory.narod.ru/stavka/ spisok.htm

982.   Gurko, B., **War and Revolution in Russia 1914-1917**, The Macmillan Co., New York, 1919, p 268

983.   Cook, A., **To Kill Rasputin**, p 215

984.   Shishkin, O. (I), *Rasputin Istoriya Prestupleniya*, p 264

985.   Cook, A., **To Kill Rasputin**, p 215

986.   Cook, **To Kill Rasputin**, p 215

987.   Tylkin, I., **Grigorii R**, Mars Media, 1914, p 313

988.   *Byloye* Journal, pp 69-70

989.   Vasiliev, A., *Okhrana, Vospominaniya Rukovoditelei Polit- seiskogo Siska*, p 437

990.   *Protocol* **Ivan Nefedov**, reproduced in: *Byloye* Journal, pp 77- 78

991.   Cook, A., **To Kill Rasputin**, p 206

992.   "*Soobsheniye oTainstvennom osobnyake*", **Birzheviye Vedomosti**, No. 15997, Wednesday 21 December 1916, p 4

993.   "*Petrovsky Ostrov*", in: **St. Petersburg Encyclopaedia**, See: http://www.encspb.ru/article.php?kod=2803998841

994.   Likhacheva, A., "*Bolshoi Petrovsky Most*", See: http://www. opeterburge.ru/bridge_448.html

995.   "*K Tainstvennomu Ubiistvy*", *Novoye Vremya*, No. 14654, Tuesday 20 December 1916, p 5

996.   "*K Tainstvennomu Ubiistvy*", p 5

997.   Akayemov, N., "*Kak nashli trup Rasputina*", p 151

998.   "*Na Petrovskom Ostrove*", **Birzheviye Vedomosti**, No. 15995, Tuesday 20 December 1916, p 4

999.   "Hint That Nobles Killed Rasputin Stirs Rasputin", The

New York Times, No. 21.529, Wednesday 3 January 1917, (N. S.), p1

1000. "Rasputin Dead. Body recovered in the Neva", Times (London), No. 41.366, Thursday 4 January 1917, (N. S.), p 8

1001. "Rasputin Dead. Body recovered in the Neva", Times (London), No. 41.366, Thursday 4 January 1917, (N. S.), p 8

1002. *"Na Petrovskom Ostrove"*, *Birzheviye Vedomosti*, No. 15995, Tuesday 20 December 1916, p 4

1003. *"Na Petrovskom Ostrove"*, p 4

1004. Vasiliev, A., *Okhrana, Vospominaniya Rukovoditelei Politseiskogo Siska*, pp 442-443

1005. Protocol No. 1740, reproduced in: *Byloye* Journal, p 65

1006. Zavadsky, S., *Na Velikom Izlome (Delo Ubiistvo Rasputina)*, p 237

1007. *"Na Petrovskom Ostrove"*, *Birzheviye Vedomosti*, No. 15995, Tuesday 20 December 1916, p 4

1008. *"Posledniya Izvestiya: Smert' Grigoriya Rasputina"*, *Rech*, No. 350, Tuesday 20 December 1916, p 2

1009. *"Na Petrovskom Ostrove"*, *Birzheviye Vedomosti*, No. 15995, Tuesday 20 December 1916, p 4

1010. Akayemov, N., *"Kak nashli trup Rasputina"*, p 152

1011. *"Department politsii ob ubiistvo Rasputina"*, *Russkaya Volya*, No. 24, Sunday 19 March 1917, p 7

1012. Yusupov, F. (I), *Konetz Rasputina*, p 193

1013. Vasiliev, A., *Okhrana, Vospominaniya Rukovoditelei Politseiskogo Siska*, p 177

1014. *"Otyezd kn. F. F. Yusupova"*, *Den'*, No 349, Monday 19 December 1916, p 1

1015. Grand Duke Nikolai Mikhailovich, Diary excerpt, Sunday 18 December 1916, reproduced in: *Krasnii Arkhiv, "Podrobnosti Ubiistva Rasputina"*, p 98

1016. Yusupov, F., *Konetz Rasputina*, pp 195-196

1017.   Grand Duke Nikolai Mikhailovich, Diary excerpt, Sunday 18 December 1916, p 98

1018.   Yusupov, F. (I), *Konetz Rasputina*, p 197

1019.   Grand Duke Nikolai Mikhailovich, Diary excerpt, Sunday 18 December 1916, reproduced in: *Krasnii Arkhiv*, *"Podrobnosti Ubiistva Rasputina"*, p 97

1020.   *"Podrobnosti Ubiistva Rasputina"*, p 97

1021.   Popovich, M., **"Permanent French troupe in St. Petersburg, 19th and 20th centuries"**, Le Bulletin de l'Alliance Française, No. 3, August, 1999, See: http://www.af.spb.ru/bull3/THEATRE.HTM

1022.   Grand Duke Gavril Konstantinovich, December 1916, p 288

1023.   Shelokhaev, V., [Editor], *Gosudarstvennaya Duma Rossiiskoi Imperii*, [Volume 1: **1906-1917**], ROSSPEN, Moscow, p 730

1024.   Burtsev, V., *"Rasputin v 1916 godu"*, *Illustrirovannaya Rossiya*, (1932), No. 17, p 8

1025.   Paley, O., *Vospominaniya o Rossii*, Zaharov, *Moskva*, 2009, p 15

1026.   Burtsev, V., *"Rasputin v 1916 godu"*, p 8

1027.   Grand Duke Andrei Vladimirovich, Newspaper clipping: *Birzheviye Vedomosti*, No. 15990, Saturday 17 December 1916, reproduced in: *Voenni Dnevnik*, p 202

1028.   Grand Duke Andrei Vladimirovich, Newspaper clippings, reproduced in: *Voenni Dnevnik*, p 32

1029.   *"Tainstvennoye Proishestviye"*, *Den'*, No. 349, Monday 19 December 1916, p 2

1030.   Spiridovich, A., *Velikaya Voina i Fevralskaya Revolutsiya*, p 419

1031.   *"Strelba na ulitse"*, *Russkaya Volya*, No. 4, 18 December 1916, p 6

1032.   *"Posledniya Izvestiya"*, *Rech*, No. 349, Monday 19 December 1916, p 2

1033.   *"Tainstvennoye ischeznovaniye"*, *Russkoye Slovo*, No. 292,

18 December 1916, p 3

1034. *"Discuss Rasputin's Death"*, The New York Times, No. 21.531, Friday 5 January 1917, (N. S.), p 2

1035. "Hint that Nobles Killed Rasputin Stirs Petrograd", The New York Times, No. 21.529, Wednesday 3 January 1917 (N. S.), p 1

1036. "Rasputin Dead. Body recovered in the Neva", Times (London), No. 41.366, Wednesday 3 January 1917, (N. S.), p3

1037. "Rasputin's Death. The End of a Nightmare", Times (London) No. 41.367, Thursday 4 January 1917, (N. S.), p 7

1038. "Echoes of Rasputin Case", Times (London) No. 41.371, Tuesday 9 January 1917, (N. S.), p 6

1039. Shulgin, V., *Dni*, p 122

1040. Spiridovich, A., *Velikaya Voina i Fevralskaya Revolutsiya*, p 382

1041. Milyukov, P., *Vospominaniya*, p 551

1042. Taneeva, A., *Stranitsi Moyei Zhizni*, p 105

1043. *"Moskva – Privetstvennaya telegramma V. M. Purishkevichu"*, *Den'*, Thursday 22 December 1916, p 4

1044. *Dopros* A. A. Vyrubova (Taneeva), 6 May 1917, in: *Padeniye Tsarskogo Rezhima*, [Volume III], p 248

1045. Chernishov, A., *Religiya i Tserkov v Sibiri Sbornik nauchnikh statei i dokumentalnikh materialov*, p 124

1046. Gilliard, P., *Ryadom s Tsarskoi Semeyi*, Tsarskii Dom Series, Veche, Moskva, 2006, p 218

1047. Haustova, R., *Delo ob Ubiistve Rasputina*, Geleos Press, Moskva, 2007, p 270

1048. Maklakov, V., *Nekotoriye dopolneniya k vospominaniyam Purishkevicha i kn. Yusupov ob Ubiistvo Rasputina*, p 277

1049. Maklakov, V., *Nekotoriye dopolneniya k vospominaniyam Purishkevicha*, Footnote at p 275

1050. *Nekotoriye dopolneniya k vospominaniyam Purishkevicha,*

Footnote at p 276

1051.   Maklakov, V., *Nekotoriye dopolneniya k vospominaniyam Purishkevicha*, p 277

1052.   Maklakov, V., *Nekotoriye dopolneniya k vospominaniyam Purishkevicha*, p 277

1053.   Shavelsky, G., *Vospominaniya Poslednego Protopresvitera Russkoi Armii*, [Volume II], p 249

1054.   Mordvinov, A., *"Poslednii Imperator (Vospominaniya Fligel-Adjutanta A. Mordvinova)"*, [Part II], p 51

1055.   Shavelsky, G., *Vospominaniya Poslednego Protopresvitera Russkoi Armii*, [Volume II], pp 251-252

1056.   Gurko, B., **War and Revolution in Russia 1914-1917**, The Macmillan Co., New York, 1919, p 269

1057.   Shavelsky, G., *Vospominaniya Poslednego Protopresvitera Russkoi Armii*, [Volume II], p 252

1058.   Nikolai II, Diary excerpt, Sunday 18 December 1916, *Dnevniki Imperatora Nikolaya II*, [Volume II, Part 2], p 271

1059.   Gurko, B., **War and Revolution in Russia 1914-1917**, p 273

1060.   Grabbe, P. and B., **The Private World of the Last Tsar**, Collins, London, 1985, pp 167-168

1061.   Gurko, B., **War and Revolution in Russia 1914-1917**, p 270

1062.   Nelipa, M. (I), **Alexei, Russia's Last Imperial Heir, A Chronicle of Tragedy**, p 96

1063.   Spiridovich, A., *Velikaya Voina i Fevralskaya Revolutsiya*, p 427

1064.   Chernishov, A., *Religiya i Tserkov v Sibiri Sbornik nauchnikh statei i dokumentalnikh materialov*, p 12

1065.   Chernishov, A., *Religiya i Tserkov v Sibiri Sbornik nauchnikh statei i dokumentalnikh materialov*, p 423

1066.   Spiridovich, A., *Velikaya Voina i Fevralskaya Revolutsiya*, p 427

1067.   Maria Fyodorovna, Diary excerpt, 18 December 1916, *Dnevniki Imperatritsi Marii Fyodorovni*, p 163

1068.   Kirikov, V., *Nevsky Prospekt, Arhitekturnii putevoditel'*, *Tsentrpoligraf, Sankt Peterburg*, 2002, p 254

1069.   Spiridovich, A., *Velikaya Voina i Fevralskaya Revolutsiya*, p 422

1070.   Yusupov, F. (I), *Konetz Rasputina*, p 73

1071.   Grand Duke Andrei Vladimirovich, Diary excerpt, 18 December 1916, *Voenni Dnevnik*, p 202

1072.   Footnote No. 396, In: *Voenni Dnevnik*, p 405

1073.   Spiridovich, A., *Velikaya Voina i Fevralskaya Revolutsiya*, p 422

1074.   Grand Duke Andrei Vladimirovich, Diary excerpt, 19 December 1916, *Voenni Dnevnik*, p 206

1075.   Yusupov, F. (I), *Konetz Rasputina*, p 200

1076.   Yusupov, F. (I), *Konetz Rasputina*, p 199

1077.   Shishkin, O., *Rasputin Istoriya Prestupleniya*, p 169

1078.   Grand Duke Andrei Vladimirovich, Diary excerpt, 21 December 1916, *Voenni Dnevnik*, p 206

1079.   Spiridovich, A., *Velikaya Voina i Fevralskaya Revolutsiya*, p 422

1080.   Grand Duke Gavril Konstantinovich, December 1916, p 289

1081.   Alexandra Fyodorovna, Letter to Nikolai II, Sunday 14 August 1916, reproduced in: Platonov, O., *Nikolai Vtoroi v Sekretnoi Perepiske*, p 572

1082.   Grand Duchess Marie Pavlovna, **Education of a Princess**, p 265

1083.   Grand Duke Andrei Vladimirovich, Diary excerpt, 19 December 1916, *Voenni Dnevnik*, p 205

1084.   Grand Duchess Marie Pavlovna, **Education of a Princess**, p 265

1085. Grand Duke Gavril Konstantinovich, *Vospominaniya*, December 1916, p 289

1086. Yusupov, F. (I), *Konetz Rasputina*, p 200

1087. Telegram to Grand Duke Dmitri, 18 December 1916, *Byloye* Journal, p 82

1088. Yusupov, F. (I), *Konetz Rasputina*, p 201

1089. *Byloye* Journal, p 82

1090. Miller, L., **Grand Duchess Elizabeth of Russia**, *Nikodemos* Orthodox Publication Society, Redding, California, 1995, p 185

1091. Yusupov, F. (I), *Konetz Rasputina*, p 201

1092. Paléologue, M., Diary extract, Sunday 31 December 1916, (N. S.), **An Ambassador's Memoirs**, [Volume III], p 133

1093. Protocol M. Zhuravleva, 18 December 1916, reproduced in: *Byloye* Journal, pp 72-73

1094. Protocol Fyodor Korshunov, 18 December 1916, reproduced in: *Byloye* Journal, pp 74-75

1095. Protocol Ekaterina Poterkina, 18 December 1916, reproduced in: *Byloye* Journal, pp 75-77

1096. Protocol M. Rasputina, 18 December 1916, reproduced in: *Byloye* Journal, pp 70-71

1097. Protocol V. Rasputina, 18 December 1916, reproduced in: *Byloye* Journal, p 71-72

1098. Protocol A. N. Rasputina, 18 December 1916, reproduced in: *Byloye* Journal, pp 71-72

1099. Ikonikov-Galitsky, A., *Khroniki Peterburgskikh Prestuplenii, Kriminalnii Peterburg*, **1861-1917**, pp 50-51

1100. Broitman, L., *Bolshaya Morskaya Ulitsa*, p 424

1101. Protocol F. Efimov, 18 December 1916, reproduced in: *Byloye* Journal, pp 80-81

1102. Zuev, G., *Doma i Lyudi Ofitserskoi Ulitsi*, *Ostrov* Press, St. Petersburg, 2003, p 2

1103.   Zuev, G., *Doma i Lyudi Ofitserskoi Ulitsi*, p 121

1104.   Protocol S. Vlasyuk, 18 December 1916, reproduced in: *Byloye* Journal, pp 78-80

1105.   *"Posledniya Izvestiya"*, *Rech*, No. 349, Monday 19 December 1916, p 2

1106.   *"K sluchayu na Moike"*, *Den'*, No. 349, Monday 19 December 1916, p 2

1107.   "Hint that nobles killed Rasputin stirs Petrograd", The New York Times, No 21.529, Wednesday 3 January 1917, (N. S.) p 1

1108.   Protocol J. Bobkov, 18 December 1916, reproduced in: *Byloye* Journal, p 73

1109.   Protocol A. Lazukov, 18 December 1916, reproduced in: *Byloye* Journal, pp 73-74

1110.   Vasiliev, A., *Okhrana, Vospominaniya Rukovoditelei Politseiskogo Siska*, p 446

1111.   Grand Duke Andrei Vladimirovich, Diary excerpt, 15 February 1917, *Voenni Dnevnik*, p 231

1112.   Protocol F. Yusupov, 18 December 1916, reproduced in: *Byloye* Journal, pp 66-68

1113.   *"Soobsheniye o Tainstvennom osobnyake"*, *Birzheviye Vedomosti*, No. 15997, Wednesday 21 December 1916, p 4

1114.   Yusupov, F. (I), *Konetz Rasputina*, p 148

1115.   Zuev, G., *Doma i Lyudi Ofitserskoi Ulitsi*, *Ostrov* Press, *Sankt Peterburg*, 2003, p 103

1116.   Yusupov, F. (I), *Konetz Rasputina*, p 155

1117.   Yusupov, F. (I), *Konetz Rasputina*, p 151

1118.   Yusupov, F. (I), *Konetz Rasputina*, p 154

1119.   Yusupov, F. (I), *Konetz Rasputina*, p 156

1120.   Grand Duke Nikolai Mikhailovich, Diary excerpt, Monday 19 December 1916, reproduced in: *Krasnii Arkhiv*, *"Podrobnosti Ubiistva Rasputina"*, p 93

1121.   Grand Duke Andrei Vladimirovich, Diary excerpt, Wednesday 15 February 1917, *Voenni Dnevnik*, p 229

1122.   Cook, A., **To Kill Rasputin**, p 211

1123.   Yusupov, F. (I), *Konetz Rasputina*, p 167

1124.   Purishkevich, V. (II), *Ubiistvo Rasputina*, p 133

1125.   Grand Duke Andrei Vladimirovich, Diary excerpt, Wednesday 15 February 1917, *Voenni Dnevnik*, p 228

1126.   Yusupov, F. (I), *Konetz Rasputina*, p 156

1127.   Grand Duke Nikolai Mikhailovich, Diary excerpt, Monday 19 December 19 1916, reproduced in: *Krasnii Arkhiv, "Podrobnosti Ubiistva Rasputina"*, p 99

1128.   Yusupov, F. (II), *Memyari v dvykh knigakh*, p 204

1129.   Yusupov, F. (I), *Konetz Rasputina*, p 157

1130.   Yusupov, F. (I), *Memyari v dvyh knigah*, p 205

1131.   Grand Duke Nikolai Mikhailovich, Diary excerpt, Monday 19 December 1916, reproduced in: *Krasnii Arkhiv, "Podrobnosti Ubiistva Rasputina"*, p 99

1132.   Yusupov, F. (I), *Konetz Rasputina*, p 140

1133.   Yusupov, F. (I), *Konetz Rasputina*, pp 135-137

1134.   Purishkevich, V. (II), *Ubiistvo Rasputina*, p 113-114

1135.   Purishkevich, V. (I), *Ubiistvo Rasputina*, p 125

1136.   Yusupov, F. (I), *Konetz Rasputina*, pp 160

1137.   Purishkevich, V. (II), *Ubiistvo Rasputina*, p 125

1138.   Yusupov, F. (I), *Konetz Rasputina*, p 159

1139.   Purishkevich, V. (II), *Ubiistvo Rasputina*, p 129

1140.   Yusupov, F. (I), *Konetz Rasputina*, p 166

1141.   Purishkevich, V. (II), *Ubiistvo Rasputina*, p 131

1142.   Grand Duke Nikolai Mikhailovich, Diary excerpt, Monday 19 December 1916, reproduced in: *Krasnii Arkhiv, "Podrobnosti Ubiistva*

Rasputina", p 100

1143.   Purishkevich, V. (II), *Ubiistvo Rasputina*, p 134

1144.   Yusupov, F. (I), *Konetz Rasputina*, p 130

1145.   Grand Duke Nikolai Mikhailovich, Diary excerpt, Monday 19 December 1916, reproduced in: *Krasnii Arkhiv*, "*Podrobnosti Ubiistva Rasputina*", p 100

1146.   Purishkevich, V. (II), *Ubiistvo Rasputina*, p 133

1147.   Yusupov, F. (I), *Konetz Rasputina*, p 166

1148.   Purishkevich, V. (II), *Ubiistvo Rasputina*, p 133

1149.   Grand Duke Nikolai Mikhailovich, Diary excerpt, Monday 19 December 1916, reproduced in: *Krasnii Arkhiv*, "*Podrobnosti Ubiistva Rasputina*", p 100

1150.   Purishkevich, V., *Ubiistvo Rasputina*, p 133

1151.   Grand Duke Nikolai Mikhailovich, Diary excerpt, Monday 19 December1916, reproduced in: *Krasnii Arkhiv*, "*Podrobnosti Ubiistva Rasputina*", p 100

1152.   d'Encausse, H., **The Russian Syndrome**, Holmes and Meir, New York, 1992, p 296

1153.   Patrick, U., **FBI Academy Firearms Training Unit: Handgun Wounding Factors and Effectiveness. U. S. Department of Justice**, 1989, p 9

1154.   Protocol V. Maklakov, 19 September 1920, reproduced in: Alexandrov, A., p 125

1155.   Purishkevich, V. (II), *Ubiistvo Rasputina*, p 137

1156.   Grand Duke Nikolai Mikhailovich, Diary excerpt, Monday 19 December 1916, reproduced in: *Krasnii Arkhiv*, "*Podrobnosti Ubiistva Rasputina*", p 101

1157.   Protocol V. Maklakov, September 19, 1920, (N. S.), reproduced in: Alexandrov, A., p 125

1158.   Grand Duke Nikolai Mikhailovich, Diary excerpt, Monday 19 December 1916, reproduced in: *Krasnii Arkhiv*, "*Podrobnosti Ubiistva Rasputina*", p 101

1159. Purishkevich, V., *Ubiistvo Rasputina*, p 131

1160. Yusupov, F., *Konetz Rasputina*, p 171

1161. Purishkevich, V. (II), *Ubiistvo Rasputina*, p 137

1162. Purishkevich, V. (II), *Ubiistvo Rasputina*, p 141

1163. Purishkevich, V. (II), *Ubiistvo Rasputina*, 140

1164. *"Proshestviye na Petrovskom Ostrove"*, *Den'* No. 350, Tuesday 20 December 1916, p 2

1165. Protocol V. Maklakov, 19 September 1920, (N. S.), reproduced in: Alexandrov, A., p 125

1166. Yusupov, F. (I), *Konetz Rasputina*, p 211

1167. Purishkevich, V. (II), *Ubiistvo Rasputina*, p 140

1168. Purishkevich, V. (II), *Ubiistvo Rasputina*, p 138

1169. Globachev, K., *Pravda o Russkoi Revolutsii*, p 89

1170. Hoare, S., **The Fourth Seal**, p 67

1171. Purishkevich, V. (II), *Ubiistvo Rasputina*, p 141

1172. Grand Duke Nikolai Mikhailovich, Diary excerpt, Monday 19 December 1916, reproduced in: *Krasnii Arkhiv*, *"Podrobnosti Ubiistva Rasputina"*, p 101

1173. Yusupov, F. (I), *Konetz Rasputina*, p 160

1174. Grand Duke Dmitri Pavlovich, Letter to father, 7 February 1917, reproduced in: *Krasnii Arkhiv*, *"Pisma D. P. Romanova k Otsu"*, p 203

1175. Grand Duke Dmitri Pavlovich, Letter to father, 23 April 1917, reproduced in: *Krasnii Arkhiv*, p 206

1176. Footnote No. 2, in: *Krasnii Arkhiv*, *"K istorii ubiistva Grigorii Rasputina"*, p 426

1177. Yusupov, F., Letter to Ksenya Alexandrovna, 2 January 1917, reproduced in: *Krasnii Arkhiv*, *K istorii ubiistva Grigorii Rasputina*, p 426

1178. Chernishov, A., *Religiya i Tserkov v Sibiri Sbornik nauch-*

nikh statei i dokumentalnikh materialov, pp 129-130

1179.   Grand Duke Andrei Vladimirovich, Diary excerpt, Monday 19 December 1916, *Voenni Dnevnik*, p 205

1180.   *Voenni Dnevnik*, Diary excerpt, Sunday 18 December 1916, p 202

1181.   Protocol V. Maklakov, 19 September 1920, (N. S.), reproduced in: *Rassledovaniye Tsareubiistva*, Alexandrov, A., p 125

1182.   Yusupov, F. (I), *Konetz Rasputina*, p 135

1183.   Grand Duke Andrei Vladimirovich, Diary excerpt, 15 February 1917, *Voenni Dnevnik*, p 229

1184.   Grand Duke Andrei Vladimirovich, Diary excerpt, 15 February 1917, *Voenni Dnevnik*, p 229

1185.   Purishkevich, V., *Ubiistvo Rasputina*, p 148

1186.   [No author], **"Rasputin's Killer Tells His Story"**, The New York News, 2 October 1965, p 1 and 18, column 7

1187.   Associated Press **"Rasputin's Slayer Loses"**, San Francisco Chronicle, Tuesday 9 November 1965, p 14

1188.   Dobson, C., **Prince Felix Yusupov The Man Who Murdered Rasputin**, p 191

1189.   [No author], **Rasputin's Killer Tells His Story**, The New York News, 2 October 1965, p 1 and 18

1190.   **Rasputin's Killer Tells His Story**, p 18

1191.   Napley, D., **Rasputin in Hollywood**, Widenfeld and Nicolson, London, 1989, p 190

1192.   **"Russian Prince tells court he killed Rasputin"**, American newspaper (unknown source) clipping, February 29, 1937

1193.   **Green, Nesson & Murray - Evidence:** Trammel v. United States, 445 U.S. 40 (1980), See: http://isites.harvard.edu/icb/icb.do?keyword=k9840&pageid=icb.page36965&pageContentId=icb.pagecontent90797&view=view.do&viewParam_name=TrammelvUnitedStates.html

1194.   Yusupov, F., Letter to Ksenya Alexandrovna, 2 January 1917, reproduced in: *Krasnii Arkhiv*, *"K istorii ubiistva Grigorii Rasputina"*, p 426

1195.   Napley, D., **Rasputin in Hollywood**, p 197

1196.   Foreign News: **"Rasputin and the Record"** Time, [Volume XXII], No. 11, 12 Monday March 1934, See: http://www.time.com/time/magazine/article/0,9171,930156,00.html

1197.   Dobson, C., **Prince Felix Yusupov The Man Who Murdered Rasputin**, pp 37-38 and p 41

1198.   Yusupov, F. (II), *Memyari v dvykh knigakh*, p 110

1199.   Grand Duchess Marie, **Education of a Princess**, p 265

1200.   **Milestones – Time**, Volume 90, No. 14, 6 Friday October 1967, See: http://www.time.com/time/magazine/article/0,9171,844047,00.html

1201.   Yusupov, F. (I) *Konetz Rasputina*, p 140

1202.   Grand Duke Nikolai Mikhailovich, Diary excerpt, Tuesday 14 February 1917, reproduced in: *Krasnii Arkhiv*, *"Podrobnosti Ubiistva Rasputina"*, p 103

1203.   Protocol V. Maklakov, 19 September 1920, (N. S.), reproduced in: Alexandrov, A., p 124

1204.   Grand Duke Andrei Vladimirovich, Diary excerpt, Wednesday 21 December 1916, *Voenni Dnevnik*, pp 206-207

1205.   Purishkevich, V. (II), *Ubiistvo Rasputina*, p 135

1206.   Grand Duke Nikolai Mikhailovich, Diary excerpt, Monday 19 December 1916, reproduced in: *Krasnii Arkhiv*, *"Podrobnosti Ubiistva Rasputina"*, p 98

1207.   *"Podrobnosti Ubiistva Rasputina"*, p 100

1208.   *"Podrobnosti Ubiistva Rasputina"*, p 99

1209.   Yusupov, F. (I), *Konetz Rasputina*, p 153

1210.   *"Na Petrovskom Ostrove"*, *Birzheviye Vedomosti*, No. 15995, Tuesday 20 December 1916, p 4

1211.   Protocol F. Kuzmin, reproduced in: *Byloye* Journal, p 75

1212. Protocol V. Kurdukov, p 81

1213. Zavadsky, S., *Na Velikom Izlome*, p 238

1214. *Byloye* Journal, p 64

1215. Mikhailov, *Spravka*, reproduced in: *Byloye* Journal, pp 65-66

1216. *"K Tainstvennomu Ubiistvy"*, *Novoye Vremya*, No. 14654, Monday 20 December 1916, p 5

1217. Hoare, S., **The Fourth Seal**, p 152

1218. *"K Tainstvennomu Ubiistvy"*, *Novoye Vremya*, No. 14654, Monday 20 December 1916, p 5

1219. *"Ubiistvo Grigoriya Rasputina"*, *Russkoye Slovo*, No 293, 20 December 1916, p 3

1220. *"Proishestviye na Petrovskom Ostrove"*, *Den'*, No. 350, Tuesday 20 December 1916, p 2

1221. *"K Tainstvennomu Ubiistvy"*, *Novoye Vremya*, No. 14654, Tuesday 20 December 1916, p 5

1222. *"Ubiistvo Grigoriya Rasputina"*, *Russkoye Slovo*, No 293, 20 December 1916, p 3

1223. *"Izvestiya za den"*, **Rech**, No. 350 (3733), 20 December 1916, p 3

1224. Koshko, A., *Uglovii Mir Tsarskoi Rossii*, *Veche*, Moskva, 1929 Reprinted 2006, p 293

1225. Kobil-Bobil, I., *Vsya Pravda o Rasputine*, (1917), in: Kryukov, V., [Editor], *Grigorii Rasputin Sbornik Istoricheskikh Materialov*, [Volume 2], p 60

1226. Khrustalev, V., *Felix Felixovich Yusupov. Zagatka Ubiistvo Rasputina. Zapiski Knyazya Yusupova*, p 119

1227. Grand Duke Gavril Konstantinovich, Diary excerpt, *Vospominaniya*, p 287

1228. Koshko, A., *Uglovii Mir Tsarskoi Rossii*, p 293

1229. Koshko, A., *"Kak bilo naideno telo Rasputina"* in: *Ocherki Ugolovnogo Mira Tsarskoi Rossii*, p 131

1230. Pokazaniya XVII, A. Protopopov, 6 September 1917, in: *Padeniye Tsarskogo Regima*, [Volume IV], p 453

1231. *"Proshestvie na Petrovskom Ostrove"*, *Den'* No. 350, Tuesday 20 December 1916, p 2

1232. **Plan of Saint Petersburg, 1914**, published by G. F. *Knoh* Press, Nevsky Prospekt, 49 [fold-out map]

1233. Zavadsky, S. *Na Velikom Izlome*, p 237

1234. Ikonikov-Galitsky, A., *Khroniki Peterburgskikh Prestuplenii, (1917-1922)*, p 48

1235. *"Ubiistvo Grigoriya Rasputina"*, *Russkoye Slovo*, No 293, 20 December 1916, p 3

1236. *"Posledniya Izvestiya: Smert' Grigoriya Rasputina"*, *Rech*, No. 350, Tuesday 20 December 1916, p 2

1237. Rasputina, M., *Vospominaniya Rasputin Pochemy?*, Zaharov Press, *Moskva*, 2000, p 304

1238. Kovalevskii, P., *Grishka Rasputin* (1917), in: Kryukov, V., [Editor], *Grigorii Rasputin, Sbornik Istoricheskikh Materialov*, [Volume 2], p 132

1239. Rasputina, M., **My Father**, p 16

1240. Spiridovich, A., *Velikaya Voina i Fevralskaya Revolutsiya*, p 423

1241. Vasiliev, A., *Okhrana, Vospominaniya Rukovoditelei Politseiskogo Siska*, p 443

1242. Chernishov, A., *Religiya i Tserkov v Sibiri Sbornik nauchnikh statei i dokumentalnikh materialov*, p 126

1243. Yusupov, F. (I), *Konetz Rasputina*, p 205

1244. Kobil-Bobil., I., *Vsya Pravda O Rasputine*, (1917), in: Kryukov, V., [Editor], *Grigorii Rasputin, Sbornik Istoricheskih Materialov*, [Volume 2], p 60

1245. Simanovich, A., *Rasputin i Evrei*, p 135

1246. Gusev, B., *Moi Ded Djamsaran Badmaev*, *Russkaya Kniga*, *Moskva*, 1995, p 5

1247.   Gusev, B., *Moi Ded Djamsaran Badmaev*, p 29

1248.   Gusev, B., *Moi Ded Djamsaran Badmaev*, p 36

1249.   Gusev, B., *Moi Ded Djamsaran Badmaev*, p 44

1250.   Kobil-Bobil, I., *Vsya Pravda o Rasputine* (1917), in: *Grigorii Rasputin, Sbornik Istoricheskikh Materialov*, [Volume 2], pp 62-63

1251.   Kobil-Bobil, I., *"Proshestvie na Petrovskom Ostrove"*, *Den'* No. 350, Tuesday 20 December 1916, p 2

1252.   Zavadsky, *Na Velikom Izlome* (*Delo Ubiistvo Rasputina*), p 240

1253.   Zavadsky, *Na Velikom Izlome*, p 240

1254.   Rasputina, M., **My Father**, p 60

1255.   Spiridovich, A., *Raspoutine*, *Payot*, Paris, 1935, p 402

1256.   Vasiliev, A., *Okhrana, Vospominaniya Rukovoditelei Polit-seiskogo Siska*, p 443

1257.   Grand Duke Andrei Vladimirovich, Diary excerpt, Wednesday 15 February 1917, *Voenni Dnevnik*, p 229

1258.   *"Ubiistvo Grigoriya Rasputina"*, *Russkoye Slovo*, No 293, 20 December 1916, p 3

1259.   Grand Duke Andrei Vladimirovich, Diary excerpt, Wednesday 15 February 1917, *Voenni Dnevnik*, p 229

1260.   Koshko, A., *Uglovii Mir Tsarskoi Rossii*, p 294

1261.   Grand Duke Andrei Vladimirovich, Diary excerpt, Wednesday 15 February 1917, *Voenni Dnevnik*, p 230

1262.   Koshko, A., *Uglovii Mir Tsarskoi Rossii*, p 294

1263.   *"Posledniya Izvestiya: Smert' Grigoriya Rasputina"*, *Rech*, No. 350, Tuesday 20 December 1916, p 2

1264.   Pokazaniya XVII, A. Protopopov, 6 September 1917, *Padeniye Tsarskogo Regima*, [Volume IV], p 106

1265.   Chernishov, A., *V Poisk Mogili Grigoriya Rasputina*, p 126

1266.   Grand Duke Andrei Vladimirovich, Diary excerpt, Wednesday

15 February 1917, *Voenni Dnevnik*, p 230

1267.   Koshko, A., *Uglovii Mir Tsarskoi Rossii*, p 294

1268.   Kobil-Bobil, I., *Vsya Pravda O Rasputine*, (1917), in: Kryukov, V., [Editor], *Grigorii Rasputin, Sbornik Istoricheskih Materialov*, Volume 2, p 60

1269.   Zavadsky, S., *Na Velikom Izlome*, p 237

1270.   *"Proishestviye na Petrovskom Ostrove"*, *Den'* No. 350, Tuesday 20 December 1916, p 2

1271.   Pokazaniya XVII, A. Protopopov, 6 September 6, 1917, *Padeniye Tsarskogo Regima*, [Volume IV], p 106

1272.   Kobil-Bobil, I., *Vsya Pravda O Rasputine*, (1917), in: Kryukov, V., [Editor], *Grigorii Rasputin, Sbornik Istoricheskikh Materialov*, [Volume 2], p 61

1273.   *"Proishestviye na Petrovskom Ostrove"*, in: *Den'* No. 350, Tuesday 20 December 1916, p 2

1274.   Chernishov, A., *V Poisk Mogili Grigoriya Rasputina*, p 126

1275.   Koshko, A., *"Kak bilo naideno telo Rasputina"*, in: *Ocherki Ugolovnogo Mira Tsarskoi Rossii*, pp 131-132

1276.   Kobil-Bobil, I., *Vsya Pravda O Rasputine*, (1917), in: Kryukov, V., [Editor], *Grigorii Rasputin, Sbornik Istoricheskih Materialov*, [Volume 2], p 61

1277.   *"Posledniya Izvestiya*: *Smert' Grigoriya Rasputina"*, *Rech*, No. 350, Tuesday 20 December 1916, p 2

1278.   Koshko, A., *Uglovii Mir Tsarskoi Rossii*, p 295

1279.   Zavadsky, S., *Na Velikom Izlome (Delo Ubiistvo Rasputina)*, p 238

1280.   Grand Duke Andrei Vladimirovich, Diary excerpt, Tuesday 3 January 1917, *Voenni Dnevnik*, p 222

1281.   Simanovich, A., *Rasputin i Evrei*, pp 136-137

1282.   Globachev, K., *Pravda o Russkoi Revolutsii*, p 89

1283.   *"Pokhoroni Rasputina"*, *Russkaya Volya*, No. 5, Wednesday

8 March 1917, p 3

1284.   Grand Duke Andrei Vladimirovich, Diary excerpt, Wednesday 15 February 1917, *Voenni Dnevnik*, p 230

1285.   Grand Duke Andrei Vladimirovich, *Voenni Dnevnik*, p 235

1286.   Grand Duke Andrei Vladimirovich, *Voenni Dnevnik*, p 230

1287.   Grand Duke Nikolai Mikhailovich, Telegrams to Felix Yusupov (senior), 19 December 1916, reproduced in: *Krasnii Arkhiv*, *"Podrobnosti Ubiistva Rasputina"*, p 240

1288.   Nikolai II, Diary excerpt, Monday 19 December 1916, *Dnevniki Imperatora Nikolaya II (1894-1918)*, [Volume II, Part 2], p 271

1289.   *"Izvestiya za den"*, *Rech*, No. 350, Tuesday 20 December 1916, p 3

1290.   Spiridovich, A., *Velikaya Voina i Fevralskaya Revolutsiya*, p 427

1291.   Mordvinov, A., *"Poslednii Imperator (Vospominaniya Fligel-Adjutanta A. Mordvinova)"*, [Part II], p 52

1292.   Chernyshov, A., *Religiya i Tserkov v Sibiri Sbornik nauchnikh statei i dokumentalnikh materialov*, pp 126-127

1293.   Spiridovich, A., *Velikaya Voina i Fevralskaya Revolutsiya*, pp 428-429

1294.   Spiridovich, A., *Velikaya Voina i Fevralskaya Revolutsiya*, p 430

1295.   *"Posledniya Izvestiya"*, *Birzheviye Vedomosti*, No. 15995, 20 December 1916, p 4

1296.   Voyeikov, V., *S Tsarem i bez Tsarya*, p 165

1297.   Spiridovich, A., *Velikaya Voina i Fevralskaya Revolutsiya*, pp 429-430

1298.   Grand Duchess Olga Nikolayevna, Diary excerpt, Monday 19 December 1916, *Avgusteishiye Sestri Miloserdiya*, p 236

1299.   Shishkin, O., *Rasputin, Istoriya Prestupleniya*, p 127

1300.   Radzinsky, E., **The Rasputin File**, p 480

1301.   Zavadsky, S., *Na Velikom Izlome (Delo Ubiistvo Rasputina)*, p 242

1302.   A. Makarov's Deposition (1917), reproduced in part in: Zvyagintsev, A., *V Epohu Potryasenii o Reform Rossiiskiye Prokurori*, ROSSPEN, *Moskva*, 1996, p 171

1303.   Zvyagintsev, A., *V Epohu Potryasenii o Reform Rossiiskiye Prokurori*, p 170

1304.   Copy of *Ukaz "Ostavka A. A. Makarova"*, 20 December 1916, reproduced in: *Voenni Dnevnik*, p 209

1305.   *"Peremeni v Sovete Ministrov"*, **Russkoye Slovo**, No.294, 21 December 1916, p 3

1306.   Spiridovich, A., *Velikaya Voina i Fevralskaya Revolutsiya*, p 431

1307.   Nikolai II, Diary excerpt, Tuesday 20 December 1916, *Dnevniki Imperatora Nikolaya II (1894-1918)*, [Volume II, Part 2], p 271

1308.   Nikolai II, Diary excerpt, 9 November 1916, *Dnevniki Imperatora Nikolaya II (1894-1918)*, [Volume II, Part 2], p 263

1309.   Spiridovich, A., *Velikaya Voina i Fevralskaya Revolutsiya*, p 431

1310.   *Khronos biografiya*, **Ivan Sheglovitov**, See: http://www.hrono.info/biograf/bio_sh/sheglovitov_ig.html

1311.   Nikolai II, Diary excerpt, Tuesday 20 December, 1916, *Dnevnik*, p 371

1312.   Grand Duke Andrei Vladimirovich, Diary excerpt, Wednesday 21 December 1916, *Voenni Dnevnik*, p 206

1313.   Kotsyubinsky, A., *Grigorii Rasputin Tainy i Yavny*, p 169

1314.   Nazhivin, I., **Rasputin**, p 510

1315.   Pikul, V., *Nechistaya Sila*, p 734

1316.   Povolyaev, V., *Rasputin Tsarskii Ugodnik*, ACT Press, *Moskva*, 2005, p 584

1317.   Decaux, A., *Velikiye Zagadki XX Veka*, p 54

1318.   Grand Duke Andrei Vladimirovich, Diary excerpt, Wednesday 15 February 1917, *Voenni Dnevnik*, p 230

1319.   Grand Duke Andrei Vladimirovich, Diary excerpt, Wednesday 15 February 1917, *Voenni Dnevnik*, p 230

1320.   *"K smerti Grigoriya Rasputina"*, *Rech*, No. 351, Wednesday 21 December 1916, p 4

1321.   *"Ubiistvo Grigoriya Rasputina: Vskritiye Telo"*, *Russkoye Slovo*, No. 294, 21 December 1916, p 3

1322.   Grand Duke Andrei Vladimirovich, Diary excerpt, Wednesday 15 February 1917, *Voenni Dnevnik*, p 235

1323.   Yelinsky, V., *Istoriya Ugolovnogo Siska v Rossii*, (V- XX century), p 50

1324.   Kobil-Bobil, I., *"Rasputiniada"*, *Russkaya Volya*, No. 8, Friday 10 March 1917, p 7

1325.   Kobil-Bobil, I., *Vsya Pravda o Rasputine*, *Sbornik Istoricheskikh Materialov*, [Volume II], pp 62-63

1326.   DiMaio, V., **Handbook of Forensic Pathology**, Taylor and Francis, New York, 2006, p 5

1327.   Zavadsky, S., *Na Velikom Izlome*, p 239

1328.   Anonymous (I), *"Zhizn i Pohozhdeniye Grigoriya Rasputina"*, 1917, pp 20-21

1329.   Grand Duke Andrei Vladimirovich, Diary excerpt, Wednesday 15 February 1917, *Voenni Dnevnik*, pp 230-231

1330.   Khrustalev, A, Editor's preface: *"Velikii Knyaz Andrei Vladimirovich i ego epokha"*, *Voenni Dnevnik*, p 15

1331.   Chumakov, V., *Rasputin Kriminalnoye Chtivo*, *Chas*, Latvian Daily, 2003, See: http://www.chas-daily.com/win/2003/10/11/lk001.html?r=41&

1332.   Vladimir Zharov, **Who is Who in Forensic Medicine in Russia – 20ᵗʰ Century**, See: http://www.med-pravo.ru/SudMed/WhoIsWho/WhoiswhoJar.htm

1333.   Karwan, C., **Guns Magazine** 12/1/99, "**Military Guns of the Century**", See: http://www.encyclopedia.com/doc/1G1-57006135.html

1334.   DiMaio, V., **Handbook of Forensic Pathology**, p 138

1335.   Grand Duke Andrei Vladimirovich, Diary excerpt, Wednesday 15 February 1917, *Voenni Dnevnik*, p 231

1336.   DiMaio, V., **Handbook of Forensic Pathology**, p 142

1337.   DiMaio., **Handbook of Forensic Pathology**, p148

1338.   DiMaio, V., **Handbook of Forensic Pathology**, p 140

1339.   **Pistols, Revolvers, Concealable Guns, Weapon's Table**, See: http://www.mclink.it/personal/MC4799/pulp/weapons/weapons_table. html

1340.   Fuhrmann, J., **Rasputin the Untold Story**, p 221 and Smith, D., **Rasputin: Faith, Power and the Twilight of the Romanovs**, p 610

1341.   Lepik D. and Vasiliev, L., **Comparison of Injuries caused by different pistols at contact range, Russian Biomedical Journal**, (2003), [Volume 4], p 10, See: Medline.ru http://www.medline.ru/public/sudm/a2/art1-4.phtml

1342.   Chew, F., et al., (2003) **Muscular-skeletal Imaging** See: http://books.google.com.au/books?id=4N0DE6UU3LIC&pg=PA19&lpg=PA19&dq=unjacketed+bullets&source=web&ots=1sAqA-IM9NG&sig=bn0oR2E7yUyuGygEANff6riMw58&hl=en

1343.   DiMaio., **Handbook of Forensic Pathology**, p 149

1344.   Cook, A., **To Kill Rasputin**, p 212

1345.   Mallinckrodt Baker Inc. **Material Safety Data Sheet P5708-21**, February, (2007), "**Potassium Cyanide**", See: http://www.jtbaker.com/msds/englishhtml/P5708.htm

1346.   Yusupov, F. (I), *Konetz Rasputina*, p 140

1347.   Rasputina, M., **My Father**, p 111

1348.   Maklakov, V., (1928) *Nekotoriya dopolneniya k Vospominaniyam Puriskevicha i kn. Yusupova ob ubiistve Rasputina*, *Sovremeniye Zapiski*, XXXIV, Paris, Footnote, p 272

1349.   Grand Duke Andrei Vladimirovich, Diary excerpt, Sunday 18

December 1916, *Voenni Dnevnik*, p 202

1350.   Grand Duke Nikolai Mikhailovich, Diary excerpt, Monday 19 December 1916, reproduced in: *Krasnii Arkhiv*, *"Podrobnosti Ubiistva Rasputina"*, p 99

1351.   Rappaport, H., **Four Sisters**, Macmillan, London, 2014, p 278

1352.   Grand Duke Nikolai Mikhailovich, Diary excerpt, Thursday 16 March 1917, reproduced in: *Krasnii Arkhiv*, *"Podrobnosti Ubiistva Rasputina"*, pp 104-105

1353.   Grand Duke Andrei Vladimirovich, Diary excerpt, Wednesday 15 February 1917, *Voenni Dnevnik*, p 230

1354.   *"Novy Muchenik"*, *Rech*, No. 60, 11 March 1917, p 6

1355.   Rasputin, M., **My Father**, pp 15-16

1356.   Yusupov, F. (I), *Konetz Rasputina*, pp 210-211

1357.   Akayemov, N., *"Kak nashli trup Rasputina"*, p 152

1358.   Cook, A., **To Kill Rasputin**, p 207

1359.   *Pokazaniya* XVII, **A.** Protopopov, 6 September 1917, in: *Padeniye Tsarskogo Regima*, [Volume IV], p 107

1360.   Simanovich, A., *Rasputin i Evrei*, p 137

1361.   *"Rasputiniada"*, *Russkaya Volya*, No 10, Saturday March 11, 1917, p 4

1362.   Chernyshov, A., *V Poisk Mogili Grigoriya Rasputina, Rus'* Journal, (1994), No. 13, p 127

1363.   Anonymous (II), *"Temniye Sili: Tainy Rasputinskogo Dvora – Rasputin"*, *Pechat* S. Yakovlev, Petrograd, 1917, p 12

1364.   Spiridovich, A., *Velikaya Voina i Fevralskaya Revolutsiya*, p 432

1365.   *Pokazaniya* XVII, A. Protopopov, 6 September 1917, in: *Padeniye Tsarskogo Regima*, [Volume IV], p 107

1366.   [Editor] Purishkevich, V., **Dnevnik**, *Facti i Sluhi*, [Part V], p 143

1367.   *"Posledniya Izvestiya"*, *Birzheviye Vedomosti*, No. 15995,

Tuesday 20 December 1916, p 4

1368. *"Posledniya Izvestiya"*, *Rech*, No. 350, Tuesday 20 December 1917, p 2

1369. Grand Duke Andrei Vladimirovich, Diary excerpt, Wednesday 15 February 1917, *Voenni Dnevnik*, p 235

1370. Meshaninov, M., *Serafimovsky Lazaret-Ubezhishche A. A. Vyrubovoi v Tsarskom Sele, Pravda o meste pogrebeniya Grigoriya Rasputina*, Voskreseniye Press, *Sankt Peterburg*, 2003, Introduction (no page number)

1371. Alexander Fyodorovna, Letter to Nikolai II, 5 November 1916, reproduced in: Platonov, O. (III), *Nikolai Vtoroi v Sekretnoi Perepiske*, p 653

1372. Meshaninov, M., *Serafimovsky Lazaret-Ubezhishche A. A. Vyrubovoi v Tsarskom Sele*, p 11

1373. Damer, A., *"Rasputin vo Dvortse"*, *Illustrirovannaya Rossiya*, p 8

1374. *"Rasputiniada- Esho o pokhoronakh Rasputina"*, *Russkaya Volya*, No. 10, Saturday 11 March 1917, p 5

1375. Rasputina, M., *Vospominaniya Docheri*, p 308

1376. Bushkovitch, P., **Religion and Society in Russia, The 16th and 17th Centuries**, Oxford University Press, 1992, p 104

1377. **Icon of the Mother of God** See; http://www.theophanes.com/writings/lives/nov/27.shtml

1378. Meshaninov, M., *Serafimovsky Lazaret-Ubezhishche A. A. Vyrubovoi v Tsarskom Sele*, p 15

1379. Olga Nikolayevna, Diary excerpt, Wednesday 21 December 1916, reproduced in: *Avgusteishiye Sestri Miloserdiya*, p 237

1380. *"Rasputiniada- Esho o pokhoronakh Rasputina"*, *Russkaya Volya*, No. 10, Saturday 11 March 1917, p 5

1381. Fomin, S., *"Pravda o Grigorii Efimoviche Rasputine"*, *Russkii Vestnik*, Special Edition, (2002), No. 21-23, p 4

1382. Editor's commentary, in: Purishkevich V. *Dnevnik*, [Part V], **Facts and Rumors**, p 143

1383.   Cantacuzene, J., **Revolutionary Days**, p 221

1384.   "*Rasputiniada- Esho o pokhoronakh Rasputina*", *Russkaya Volya*, No. 10, Saturday 11 March 1917, pp 4 and 5

1385.   "*Rasputiniada - Kak Khoronili Rasputina*", *Russkaya Volya*, No. 8, Friday 10 March 1917, p 7

1386.   "*Rasputiniada- Esho o pokhoronakh Rasputina*", *Russkaya Volya*, No. 10, Saturday 11 March 1917, p 5

1387.   Taneeva, A., *Stranitsi Moyei Zhizni*, p 105

1388.   Loman, D., *Vospominaniya*, reproduced in: Bokhanov, A., *Imperator* **Nikolai II**, pp 396-397

1389.   Radzinsky, E., **The Rasputin File**, p 485

1390.   Paley, O., *Vospominaniya o Rossii*, p 19

1391.   Gerasimov, V., "*Gde pokhoronen Grigorii Rasputin?*", *Rus'* Journal, (1993), Volume 8, No. 2, p 166

1392.   Konstantinov, V., "*Taina Alexandrovskogo Parka*", *Tsarskoe Selo* Journal, (1998), Volume 10 (109), June 25, p 2

1393.   Nikolai II, Diary excerpt, Wednesday 21 December 1916, *Dnevnik*, pp 271-272

1394.   "*Pokhoroni Rasputina*", *Russkaya Volya*, Evening edition, No. 8, Wednesday 8 March 1917, p 3

1395.   "*Pokhoroni Rasputina*", *Russkaya Volya*, Evening edition, Wednesday 8 March 1917, p 3

1396.   Spiridovich, A., *Velikaya Voina i Fevralskaya Revolutsiya*, p 433

1397.   Krilov-Tolstikovich, A., *Poslednyaya Imperatritsa*, p 253

1398.   Gerasimov, V., "*Gde pokhoronen Grigorii Rasputin?*", p 166

1399.   Spiridovich, A., *Velikaya Voina i Fevralskaya Revolutsiya*, p 433

1400.   Krilov-Tolstikovich A., *Poslednyaya Imperatritsa*, p 253

1401.   Meshaninov, M., *Serafimovsky Lazaret-Ubezhishche* **A. A.** *Vyrubovoi v Tsarskom Sele*, pp 24-25

1402.   Maria Nikolayevna, Diary excerpt, 21 December 1916, reproduced in: *Avgusteishiye Sestri Miloserdiya*, p 237

1403.   Rasputina, M., **My Father**, p 17

1404.   Dehn, L., **The Real Tsaritsa**, p 123

1405.   *"Rasputiniada- Kak Khoronili Rasputina"*, *Russkaya Volya*,
No. 8, Friday 10 March 1917, p 7

1406.   Dorr, R., **Inside the Russian Revolution**, The Macmillan Co.,
New York, 1917, p 110

1407.   Taneeva, A., *Stranitsi Moyei Zhizni*, p 105

1408.   Rasputina, M., **My Father**, p 17

1409.   Meshaninov, M., *Serafimovsky Lazaret-Ubezhishche* A. A.
Vyrubovoi v Tsarskom Sele, p 13

1410.   Olga Nikolayevna, Diary excerpt, 21 December 1916, reproduced in: *Avgusteishiye Sestri Miloserdiya*, p 237

1411.   Spiridovich, A., *Velikaya Voina i Fevralskaya Revolutsiya*, p
433

1412.   Nikolai II, Diary excerpt, Wednesday 21 December 1916,
Dnevniki Imperatora Nikolaya II (1894-1918), [Volumes II, Part 1], p
272

1413.   Maria Nikolayevna, Diary excerpt, Wednesday 21 December
1916, reproduced in: *Avgusteishiye Sestri Miloserdiya*, p 237

1414.   Spiridovich, A., *Velikaya Voina i Fevralskaya Revolutsiya*, p
433

1415.   *"Rasputiniada"*, *Russkaya Volya*, No. 10, Saturday 11 March
1917, p 5

1416.   *"Pokhoroni Rasputina"*, *Russkaya Volya*, No. 5, Wednesday
8 March 1917, p 3

1417.   Rasputina, M. **My Father**, p 114

1418.   Dehn, L., **The Real Tsaritsa**, p 125

1419.   Olga Nikolayevna, Diary excerpt, Sunday 25 December 1916,
reproduced in: *Avgusteishiye Sestri Miloserdiya*, p 238

1420.   Olga Nikolayevna, Diary excerpt, 9 February 1917, reproduced in: *Avgusteishiye Sestri Miloserdiya*, p 240

1421.   Nikolai II, Diary excerpt, Wednesday 22 February 1917, *Dnevniki Imperatora Nikolaya II (1894-1918)*, [Volumes II, Part 1], p 294

1422.   Alexander Fyodorovna, Letter to Nikolai II, 22 February 1917, reproduced as Document No. 1, in: *Skorbnii Put' Romanovikh* **(1917-18)**, [Volume III, Editor V. Khrustalev], *Arkhiv Noveishei Rossii*, ROSSPEN, Moscow, 2001, p 24

1423.   Alexander Fyodorovna, Letter to Nikolai II, 26 February 1917, reproduced as Document No. 7, in *Skorbnii Put' Romanovikh* **(1917-18)**, *Arkhiv Noveishei Rossii*, [Volume III]., p 33

1424.   Alexander Fyodorovna, Letter to Nikolai II, 2 March 1917, reproduced as Document No. 25, in: *Skorbnii Put' Romanovikh* **(1917-18)**, *Arkhiv Noveishei Rossii*, [Volume III], p 45

1425.   *"Arest semyi Rasputina"*, *Russkaya Volya*, No. 20, Friday 17 March 1917, p 6

1426.   *"Simanovich i Rasputin*, *Rech*, No. 65, 16 March 1917, p 5

1427.   Rasputina, M., *"Moi otets Grigorii Rasputin"*, p 8

1428.   Rasputina, M. Diary excerpt, 29 March 1918, reproduced in: Alexandrov, A., *Rassledovaniye Tsareubiistva- rassekrechenniye dokumenti*, p 48

1429.   *Peterburgskiye kvartiri Rasputina*, See: http://www.petersburg-mystic-history.info/ru/rasputin-adr_1.html

1430.   Rasputina, M., *Vospominaniya Docheri*, p 310

1431.   *Dopros* No. 5, A. Taneeva [Vyrubova], 14 October 1917, in: Rassulin, *Vernaya Bogu, Tsaryu i Otechestvu*, p 341

1432.   *"Arest freilini Vyrubova"*, *Birzheviye Vedomosti*, No 16150, Thursday 23 March 1917, p 5

1433.   *"Pokhoroni Rasputina"*, *Russkaya Volya*, Evening edition, No. 5, Wednesday 8 March 1917, p 3

1434.   Globachev, K., *Pravda o Russkoi Revolutsii*, p 85

1435.   Lagansky, E., *Kak Nashli Mogilu Rasputina, Russkaya Vo-*

Iya, No. 6, Wednesday 9 March 1917, p 5

1436.   Milyukov, P., *Vospominaniya gosudarstvennogo deyatelya*, p 290

1437.   Browder, R. and Kerensky, A., **The Russian Provisional Government 1917 Documents**, [Volume 1], Stanford University Press, California, 1961, p 51

1438.   Milyukov, P., *Vospominaniya gosudarstvennogo deyatelya*, p 284

1439.   Milyukov, P., *Vospominaniya gosudarstvennogo deyatelya*, p 293

1440.   Milyukov, P., *Vospominaniya gosudarstvennogo deyatelya*, p 309

1441.   *Izvestiya Petrogradskogo Soveta*, February 28, 1917, No. 1, p 2, reproduced as Document No. 13, in: *Skorbnii Put' Romanovikh (1917-18)*, *Arkhiv Noveishei Rossii*, [Volume III], p 36

1442.   Alexandra Fyodorovna, Diary excerpt, 28 February 1917, reproduced as Document No. 16, in: *Skorbnii Put' Romanovikh (1917-18)*, *Arkhiv Noveishei Rossii*, [Volume III], p 38

1443.   Khrustalev, V. [Editor] *Dnevniki Nikolaya II i Imperatritsi Alexandri Fyodorovni*, [Volume 1], Vagrius, *Moskva*, 2008, Footnote 7, p 222

1444.   Cantacuzene, J., **Revolutionary Days**, p 259

1445.   *"Protocol Sobitii Fevralskoi Revolutsii"*, Document 80, 27 February – 4 March 1917, reproduced in: Tretyakova, V., [Editor], *Otrecheniye Nikolaya II*, *Taini Istorii* Series, Terra, *Moskva*, 1998, p 314

1446.   Milyukov, P., *Vospominaniya gosudarstvennogo deyatelya*, p 294

1447.   *Manifest* of the Grand Dukes, 1 March 1917, reproduced as Document No. 18, in: *Arkhiv Skorbnii Put' Romanovikh (1917-18)*, *Arkhiv Noveishei Rossii*, [Volume III], pp 38-39

1448.   *"Protocol Sobitii Fevralskoi Revolutsii"*, Document 80, 27 February – 4 March 1917, reproduced in: Tretyakova, V., *Otrecheniye Nikolaya II*, p 311

1449. *Izvestiya Revoliutsionnoi Nedeli*, No. 4, 1 March 1917, p 1, reproduced as: Document No. 42, in Browder, R. and Kerensky, A., **The Russian Provisional Government 1917 Documents**, [Volume 1], p 64

1450. Buchanan, G., **Mission to Russia**, [Volume II], p 101

1451. Kleinmichel, M, **Memoirs of a Shipwrecked World**, Brentano's Press, New York, 1923, p 232

1452. Grand Duke Pavel Alexandrovich, Letter to Kirill Vladimirovich, 2 March 1917, reproduced as Document 23, in: *Skorbnii Put' Romanovikh* **(1917-18)**, *Arkhiv Noveishei Istorii Rossii*, [Volume III], p 42

1453. Grand Duke Pavel Alexandrovich, Letter from Kirill Vladimirovich, 2 March 1917, reproduced as: Document No. 24, in: *Skorbnii Put' Romanovikh* **(1917-18)**, pp 42- 43

1454. Karabchevsky, N., *Chto glaza moi videli*, in: *Fevralskaya Revolutsiya*, [Volume 1], Inter-OMNIS, Perm, 1921 reprinted 1991, p 178

1455. **"Official Recognition of the Provisional Government by England and France"**, reproduced in: Golder, F., p 284

1456. Milyukov, P., *Vospominaniya gosudarstvennogo deyatelya*, p 296

1457. Milyukov, P., *Vospominaniya gosudarstvennogo deyatelya*, p 313

1458. Spiridovich, A., *Velikaya Voina i Fevralskaya Revolutsiya*, p 605

1459. Danilov, Yu., *Na puti k Krusheniyu*, p 271

1460. Danilov, Yu., *Na puti k Krusheniyu*, p 273

1461. Shulgin, V., *Dni*, p 267

1462. Provisional Government Sitting No 1, 2 March 1917, reproduced as: Document No. 19, in: *Skorbnii Put' Romanovikh* **(1917-18)**, *Arkhiv Noveishei Rossii*, [Volume III], p 39

1463. Kobylin, *Anatomiya Izmeni*, p 298

1464. Shulgin, V., *Dni*, p 273

1465.   Spiridovich, A., *Velikaya Voina i Fevralskaya Revolutsiya*, p 387

1466.   Maklakov, A., *"Padeniye Russkoi Monarkhii: Pro i Contra"*, *Istoriya i Istoriki* Journal, *Moskva*, 2001, p 312

1467.   Spiridovich, A., *Velikaya Voina i Fevralskaya Revolutsiya*, p 477

1468.   Telegram of A. I. Guchkov and V. V. Shulgin *iz Pskova*, 3 March 1917, reproduced as Document No. 10, in: *Skorbnii put' Mikhaila Romanova*: *ot prestola do golgofa*, Khrustalev, V. and Lykova, L., [editors], *Pushka* Press, Perm, 1995, p 42

1469.   Milyukov, P., *Vospominaniya gosudarstvennogo deyatelya*, p 315

1470.   Nikolai II, Diary excerpt, Thursday 2 March 1917, *Dnevniki Imperatora Nikolaya II, 1914-1918*, [Volume II, Part II], p 296

1471.   Kerensky, A., *Rossiya v Povorotnii Moment Istorii*, *Centerpoligraf*, *Moskva*, 2006, p 211

1472.   Milyukov., P., *Vospominaniya gosudarstvennogo deyatelya*, p 315

1473.   Shulgin, V., *Dni*, p 270

1474.   Matveev, A.., *Vozrozhdeniye* XXIV (1952) pp 141-145, **The Refusal of Grand Duke Mikhail Alexandrovich to Accept the Throne**, reproduced as: Document No. 94, in: Browder, R. and Kerensky, A., **The Russian Provisional Government 1917 Documents**, [Volume 1], p 108

1475.   Grand Duchess Marie Pavlovna, **Education of a Princess**, p 293

1476.   *Izvestiya Revoliutsionnoi Nedeli*, No. 4, 1 March 1917, p 1, Appeal of the Officers to the Soldiers Reproduced as Document No. 39, in: Browder, R. and Kerensky, A., **The Russian Provisional Government 1917 Documents**, [Volume 1], p 63

1477.   Browder, R. and Kerensky, A., **The Russian Provisional Government 1917 Documents**, [Volume 1], p 25

1478.   Shulgin, V., *Dni*, p 300

1479.   Crawford, R. and D., **Michael and Natasha**, Weidenfeld and Nicolson, London, (1997), p 303

1480.   The Decision of Mikhail to Refuse the Throne, reproduced as Document No. 100, in: Browder, R. and Kerensky, A., **The Russian Provisional Government 1917 Documents**, [Volume 1], p 115

1481.   Crawford, R. and D., **Michael and Natasha**, p 306

1482.   The Decision of Mikhail to Refuse the Throne, reproduced as Document No. 100, in: Browder, R. and Kerensky, A., **The Russian Provisional Government 1917 Documents**, [Volume 1], p 116

1483.   *Protokoli*, pp 9-10, Resolution No. 1, Session of the Soviet Executive Committee of the Petrograd Soviet Demands the Arrest of the Romanovs, 3 March 1917, Resolution No. 1, reproduced as Document No. 142, in: Browder, R. and Kerensky, A., **The Russian Provisional Government 1917 Documents**, [Volume 1], p 177

1484.   Kerensky, A., Fourth Duma Convocation, Session V Sitting No. 6, 19 November 1916, reproduced in: *Stenograficheskii Otchet, Gosudarstvennaya Duma*, p 242

1485.   Kerensky, A., *Rossiya v Povorotnii Moment Istorii*, p 212

1486.   Matveev, A.., *Vozrozhdeniye* XXIV (1952), pp 141-145, The Refusal of Grand Duke Mikhail Alexandrovich to Accept the Throne, reproduced as Document No. 94, in: Browder, R. and Kerensky, A., **The Russian Provisional Government 1917 Documents**, [Volume 1], p 107

1487.   Chernyshova-Melnik, N., *Mikhail Romanov Zhizn i Lyubov*, Enas Press, *Moskva*, 2009, p 351

1488.   Nelipa, M. (II), **The Tragedy of Nikolai II's Abdication**, Sovereign, No. 1, (2016), p 79

1489.   Danilov, Yu., *Velikii Knyaz Nikolai Nikolayevich*, pp 416-417

1490.   Khrustalev, V. and Lykova, L., [editors] *Skorbnii put' Mikhaila Romanova*: *ot prestola do golgofa*, p 28

1491.   Nikolai II, Diary excerpt, Friday 3 March 1917, *Dnevniki Imperatora Nikolaya II, 1914-1918*, [Volume II, Part II], p 296

1492.   Denikin, A., *Ocherki Russkoi Smuti, Krusheniye Vlasti i Armii, Fevral- Sentyabr 1917, Nauka, Moskva*, 1991, p 54

1493.	*Izvestiya Revoliutsionnoi Nedeli*, No. 7, 3 March 1917, p 1, "Appeal of the Temporary Committee of the Duma", reproduced as: Document No. 52, in: Browder, R. and Kerensky, A., **The Russian Provisional Government 1917 Documents**, [Volume 1], p 69

1494.	Kerensky, A., *Rossiya v Povorotnii Moment Istorii*, p 215

1495.	*Izvestiya Revoliutsionnoi Nedeli*, No. 5, 2 March 1917, p 1, Order to the City of Petrograd, Reproduced as: Document No. 46, in: Browder, R. and Kerensky, A., [Volume 1], p 66

1496.	Nelipa, M. (II), **The Tragedy of Nikolai II's Abdication**, Sovereign, No. 1, (2016), p 77

1497.	*Izvestiya*, No. 1, Supplement, 28 February 1917, p 2, reproduced as Document No. 63, in: Browder, R. and Kerensky, A., **The Russian Provisional Government 1917 Documents**, [Volume 1], p 79

1498.	Ikonnikov-Galitsky, A., *Khroniki Peterburgskikh Prestuplenii* 1917-1922, *Azbuka-Klassica, Sankt Peterburg*, 2008, p 33

1499.	Ikonnikov-Galitsky, A., *Khroniki Peterburgskikh Prestuplenii* 1917-1922, p 34

1500.	Alexandra Fyodorovna, Letter to Nikolai II, 2 March 1917, reproduced as Document No. 25, in: *Skorbnii Put' Romanovikh* **(1917-18)**, *Arkhiv Noveishei Rossii*, [Volume III], p 44

1501.	Alexandra Fyodorovna, Letter to Nikolai II, 3 March 1917, reproduced as Document No. 31, in: *Skorbnii Put' Romanovikh* **(1917-18)**, *Arkhiv Noveishei Rossii*, [Volume III], p 53

1502.	Footnote 13, in *Dnevniki Nikolaya II i Imperatritsi Alexandri Fyodorovni*, [Volume 1], p 264

1503.	Zemlyanichenko, M., "**Old Gentleman** *Frederiks i Imperator Nikolai II*", *Biznes-Inform*, Simferopol, 2007, pp 145 and 147

1504.	Guchkov, A., "*V Tsarskom Poezde*", *Otrecheniye Nikolaya II*, p 185

1505.	"*Revolutsiya*", *Birzheviye Vedomosti*, No 16120, Sunday 5 March 1917, p 4

1506.	Provisional Government Sitting No. 5, 5 March 1917, Item No. 5, reproduced in: *Zhurnali Zasedanii Vremennogo Pravitelstva*, [Volume 1, March-April 1917], and in: *Arkhiv Noveishei Rossii*, [Volume VII], Editor B. Dodonov], p 34

1507.   Provisional Government Sitting No. 10, 7 March 1917, Item No. 3(1) and (2), reproduced in: *Arkhiv Noveishei Istorii Rossii*, [Volume VII], p 50

1508.   VVP, No. 2, March 7, 1917, Part I (1) and (4), reproduced as Document No. 35, in: Browder, R. and Kerensky, A., **The Russian Provisional Government 1917 Documents**, [Volume 1], p 61

1509.   Provisional Government Sitting No. 17, 13 March 1917, Item No. 9, reproduced in: *Zhurnali Zasedanii Vremennogo Pravitelstva, Arkhiv Noveishei Istorii Rossii*, [Volume VII], p 246

1510.   *"Arest sekretarya Rasputina, Simanovicha"*, *Russkaya Volya*, No 18, Thursday 16 March 1917, p 6

1511.   Provisional Government Sitting No. 19, 15 March 1917, Item No. 5, in: *Arkhiv Noveishei Istorii Rossii*, [Volume VII], p 100

1512.   Provisional Government Sitting No. 54, 14 April 1917, Item No. 3(1), in: *Arkhiv Noveishei Istorii Rossii*, [Volume VII], p 291

1513.   *"Arest protopresvitera o. Shavelskogo"*, *Birzheviye Vedomosti*, No. 16126, Thursday 9 March 1917, p 3

1514.   Gan, L., *"Sredi arestovovannoi Tsarskoi Sviti"*, *Birzheviye Vedomosti*, No 16128, Friday 10 March 1917, p 3

1515.   *"Arestovanniye"*, *Russkaya Volya*, No. 8, Friday 10 March 1917, p 3

1516.   Karabchevsky, N., *Chto glaza moi videli*, p 176

1517.   *"Protocol Sobitii Fevralskoi Revolutsii"*, Document 80, 27 February – 4 March 1917, reproduced in: Tretyakova, V., *Otrecheniye Nikolaya II*, p 306 and p 315

1518.   Kerensky, A., *Rossiya v Povorotnii Moment Istorii*, **Declaration of 3 March 1917**, Item No. 1, p 208

1519.   Zavadsky, S., *Na Velikom Izlome (Delo Ubiistvo Rasputina)*, p 242

1520.   Matveev, A.., *Vozrozhdeniye* XXIV (1952), pp 141-145, The Refusal of Grand Duke Mikhail Alexandrovich to Accept the Throne, reproduced as Document No. 94, in: Browder, R. and Kerensky, A.,

The Russian Provisional Government 1917 Documents, [Volume 1], p 107

1521. *"Sud'ba zhertvi Rasputina"*, *Birzheviye Vedomosti*, No 161176, 11 April 1917, p 7

1522. Platonov, O., *Grigorii Rasputin i Deti Dyavola*, pp 225-226

1523. *"Sud'ba zhertvi Rasputina"*, *Birzheviye Vedomosti*, No 161176, 11 April 1917, p 7

1524. Provisional Government Sitting No. 5, 5 March 1917, Footnote 3, reproduced in: *Zhurnali Zasedanii Vremennogo Pravitelstva, Arkhiv Noveishei Istorii Rossii*, [Volume VII], p 33

1525. *Ispolkom* Protocols, 9 March 1917, reproduced as Document No. 40, in: *Skorbnii Put' Romanovikh, Arkhiv Noveishei Istorii Rossii*, [Volume III], p 64

1526. Instructions to the chief of the Tsarskoe Selo garrison regarding security of the Alexandrovsky Palace, 17 March 1917, reproduced as: Document No. 45, in: *Arkhiv Noveishei Istorii Rossii*, [Volume III], p 68

1527. Provisional Government Sitting No. 5, 5 March 1917, Item No. 4b, reproduced in: *Zhurnali Zasedanii Vremennogo Pravitelstva, Arkhiv Noveishei Istorii Rossii*, [Volume VII], p 34

1528. Nikolai II, Diary excerpt, Thursday 2 March 1917, *Dnevniki Imperatora Nikolaya II, 1914-1918*, [Volume II, Part II], p 296

1529. Provisional Government Sitting No. 5, 5 March 1917, Footnote 3, reproduced in: *Zhurnali Zasedanii Vremennogo Pravitelstva, Arkhiv Noveishei Istorii Rossii*, [Volume VII], p 33

1530. Provisional Government Sitting No. 5, 5 March 1917, Footnote 3, reproduced in: *Arkhiv Noveishei Istorii Rossii*, [Volume VII], p 34

1531. Melgunov, S., *Sud'ba Imperatora Nikolaya II Posle Otrecheniye, Veche, Moskva*, 1951 reprinted 2005, p 64

1532. **Provisional Government Sitting No. 10, 7 March 1917**, Item No. 1(1), (2) and (3), reproduced in: *Arkhiv Noveishei Istorii Rossii*, [Volume VII], pp 49-50

1533. Melgunov, S., *Sud'ba Imperatora Nikolaya II Posle Otrech-*

eniye, p 64

1534.   Alexandra Fyodorovna, Diary excerpt Wednesday 8 March 1917, in: *Dnevniki Nikolaya II i Alexandra Fyodorovni 1917-1918*, [Volume I], p 340

1535.   Volkov, A., *Okolo Tsarskoi semyi*, *Ankor, Moskva*, 1928 reprinted 1993, p 68

1536.   Arrest announcements: *Birzheviye Vedomosti*, No 16126, Thursday 9 March 1917, p 3 and p 4

1537.   Alexandra Fyodorovna, Diary excerpt, Wednesday 8 March 1917, in: *Dnevniki Nikolaya II i Alexandra Fyodorovni 1917-1918*, Thursday 9 March 1917, [Volume I], p 366

1538.   Lagansky, E., *"Arest Nikolaya Romanova"*, *Russkaya Volya*, No. 8, 10 March 1917, p 6

1539.   Nikolai II, Diary excerpt, Thursday 9 March 1917, *Dnevniki Imperatora Nikolaya II, 1914-1918*, [Volume II, Part II], p 297

1540.   *Dopros* E. Kobylinsky, 6 - 10 April 1919, in: Sokolov, N., *Gibel Tsarskoi Semyi*, [Volume I], Terra, *Moskva*, 1925 reprinted 1996, pp 16-17

1541.   *"Rasputin i Imperatorsky Dvor"*, *Birzheviye Vedomosti*, No 16128, Friday 10 March 1917, p 4

1542.   Kerensky, A., *Tragediya Dinastii Romanovikh*, p 113

1543.   Kerensky, A., *Tragediya Dinastii Romanovikh*, p 114

1544.   *Ispolkom* Protocols, 9 March 1917, reproduced as Document No. 40, in: *Skorbnii Put' Romanovikh*, *Arkhiv Noveishei Istorii Rossii*, [Volume III], p 63

1545.   Melgunov, S., *Sud'ba Imperatora Nikolaya II Posle Otrecheniye*, p 72

1546.   Kerensky, A., *Tragediya Dinastii Romanovikh*, p 116

1547.   Provisional Government Sitting No. 15, 11 March 1917, Item No. 10 (Part I, a 1), reproduced in: *Arkhiv Noveishei Istorii Rossii*, p 79

1548.   Item No. 10 (Part II, 1), reproduced in: *Arkhiv Noveishei Istorii Rossii*, p 79

1549.   Kovalenko, N., *"Chrezvychainaya Sledstvennaya Kommissiya ... Delo 'Temnikh Sil'*, Vestnik* MGU, No 155, (2010), p 19

1550.   Almazov, B., *Rasputin i Rossiya*, Grunkhut, Praga, 1922, p 3

1551.   Karabchevsky, N., *Chto glaza moi videli*, p 183

1552.   Provisional Government Sitting No. 11, 8 March 1917, Item No. 7 (b), reproduced in: *Zhurnali Zasedanii Vremennogo Pravitelstva, Arkhiv Noveishei Istorii Rossii*, [Volume VII], p 54

1553.   Astahova, V., [Editor] **A. Blok**, [Volume II], *Portreti* Series, Terra, *Moskva*, 1997, p 163

1554.   *Dopros* A. Khvostova, 18 March 1917, in: *Padeniye Tsarskogo Regima*, [Volume I], pp 31-83

1555.   Varfolomeev, Yu., *Sedstvenniye Chasti Chrezvytchainoi Sled. Kommissii ...*, *Izvestiye Saratovskogo Universiteta*, 9, (2009), p 78

1556.   Rudnev, V., *Pravda o Tsarskoi Semye i Temnikh Silakh*, p 15

1557.   *Pokazaniya* A. Kerensky, 14-20 August 1920, reproduced in: Alexandrov, A., *Rassledovaniye Tsareubiistva- rassekrechenniye dokumenti*, p 137

1558.   Kerensky, A., *Tragediya Dinastii Romanovikh*, p 114

1559.   *Tragediya Dinastii Romanovikh*, p 56

1560.   *Pokazaniya* A. Kerensky, 14-20 August 1920, reproduced in: Alexandrov, A., *Rassledovaniye Tsareubiistva- rassekrechenniye dokumenti*, p 139

1561.   Kerensky, A., *Tragediya Dinastii Romanovikh*, p 64

1562.   *Pokazaniya* A. Kerensky, 14-20 August 1920, reproduced in: Alexandrov, A., *Rassledovaniye Tsareubiistva- rassekrechenniye dokumenti*, p 137

1563.   Astakhova, V., [Editor] **A. Blok**, [Volume II], p 169

1564.   Grigoriev, G., *Grigoriya Rasputina Sozhgli v Pechke, Tyumenskiye Izvestiya* (1999), No. 288, See: http://www.allrussia.ru/nowadays/Default.asp?HN_ID=5&FlagR=4&vYear=2001&vMonth=12&vDay=24

1565.   Kerensky, A., *Tragediya Dinastii Romanovikh*, p 117

1566.   Alexandra Fyodorovna, Diary excerpt, Wednesday 8 March 1917, in: *Dnevniki Nikolaya II i Alexandra Fyodorovni 1917-1918*, [Volume I], p 340

1567.   Alexandra Fyodorovna, Diary excerpt, Thursday 9 March 1917, in: *Dnevniki Nikolaya II i Alexandra Fyodorovni 1917-1918*, p 366

1568.   Nikolai II, Diary excerpt, Friday 10 March 1917, *Dnevnik*, p 388

1569.   Gan, L. *"Sredi arestovovannoi Tsarskoi Sviti"*, *Birzheviye Vedomosti*, No 16128, Friday 10 March 1917, p 3

1570.   Danilov, Yu., *Velikii Knyaz Nikolai Nikolayevich*, p 417

1571.   Telegram of Grand Duke Nikolai Nikolayevich to General Alexeev, 3 March 1917, reproduced as: Document No. 98, in: Browder, R. and Kerensky, A., **The Russian Provisional Government 1917 Documents**, [Volume 1], p 114

1572.   *Izvestiya Revoliutsionnoi Nedeli*, No. 7, 3 March 1917, p 1, reproduced as: Document No. 112, in: Browder, R. and Kerensky, A., **The Russian Provisional Government 1917 Documents**, [Volume 1], p 135

1573.   Danilov, Yu., *Velikii Knyaz Nikolai Nikolayevich*, p 421

1574.   *Izvestiya* No. 7, 6 March 1917, p 2, reproduced as Document No. 117, in: Browder, R. and Kerensky, A., **The Russian Provisional Government 1917 Documents**, [Volume 1], p 138

1575.   Danilov, Yu., *Velikii Knyaz Nikolai Nikolayevich*, p 423

1576.   Resolution No. 1, Session of the Soviet Executive Committee of the Petrograd Soviet Demands the Arrest of the Romanovs, *Protokoli*, 3 March 1917, pp 9-10, Resolution No. 3, reproduced as Document No. 142, in: Browder, R. and Kerensky, A., **The Russian Provisional Government 1917 Documents**, [Volume 1], p 177

1577.   Question regarding the Supreme Command, *Malenkaya Gazeta*, 10 March 1917, No. 58 (856), p 1 Reproduced as Document 43, in: *Skorbnii Put' Romanovikh, Arkhiv Noveishei Istorii Rossii*, [Volume III], p 67

1578.   Provisional Government Sitting No. 16, 12 March 1917, Item No. 2(a), reproduced in: *Zhurnali Zasedanii Vremennogo Pravitelstva,*

Arkhiv Noveishei Istorii Rossii, [Volume VII], p 83

1579.   Tsvetkov, V., *Nuzhni ne rezkiye suzhdeniya, a ponimaniye i pokayaniye,* [Part III], 2008, See: *Russkaya Liniya:* http://www.rusk.ru/st.php?idar=424307

1580.   Danilov, Yu., *Velikii Knyaz Nikolai Nikolayevich,* p 426

1581.   Danilov, Yu., *Velikii Knyaz Nikolai Nikolayevich,* p 423

1582.   Provisional Government Sitting No. 38, 1 April 1917, Item No. 16(1), reproduced in: *Zhurnali Zasedanii Vremennogo Pravitelstva, Arkhiv Noveishei Istorii Rossii,* [Volume VII], p 218

1583.   Shepelev, L., *Chinovny Mir Rossii XVIII-nachalo XX* в, *Iskusstvo, Sankt Peterburg,* (1999), p 135

1584.   Provisional Government Sitting No. 18, 14 March 1917, Item No. 2(I) and (II), reproduced in: *Zhurnali Zasedanii Vremennogo Pravitelstva, Arkhiv Noveishei Istorii Rossii,* [Volume VII], p 91

1585.   Shepelev, L., *Chinovny Mir Rossii XVIII-nachalo XX* в, p 448

1586.   Provisional Government Sitting No. 37, 31 March 1917, Item No. 5 Part IV (2), p 211_

1587.   Provisional Government Sitting No. 38, 1 April 1917, Item No. 2(b), reproduced in: *Zhurnali Zasedanii Vremennogo Pravitelstva,* p 213

1588.   *Russkoye Slovo,* No. 53, 8 March 1917, p 3, reproduced as Document No. 140, in: Browder, R. and Kerensky, A., **The Russian Provisional Government 1917 Documents,** [Volume 1], p 175

1589.   Message of Lloyd George to Prince Lvov, The Times (London), 23 March 1917, p 7, reproduced as Document 131, in: Browder, R. and Kerensky, A., **The Russian Provisional Government 1917 Documents,** [Volume 1], p 150

1590.   Kleinmichel, M., **Memoirs of a Shipwrecked World,** p 227

1591.   Kerensky, A., *Tragediya Dinastii Romanovikh,* pp 126-127

1592.   Buchanan, G., **Mission to Russia,** [Volume II], p 97

1593.   Kerensky, A., *Tragediya Dinastii Romanovikh,* p 126

1594.   Telegram from Ambassador G. Buchanan to Arthur Balfour, 12 (25) March 1917, reproduced as Document No. 59, in: *Skorbnii Put' Romanovih, Arkhiv Noveishei Istorii Rossii*, [Volume III], p 81

1595.   *Pokazaniya* A. Kerensky, 14-20 August 1920, reproduced in: Alexandrov, A., *Rassledovaniye Tsareubiistva- rassekrechenniye dokumenti*, p 134

1596.   Kerensky, A., *Tragediya Dinastii Romanovikh*, p 51

1597.   Koshko, A., *Uglovii Mir Tsarskoi Rossii*, pp 296-297

1598.   *"Rasputiniada"*, Kobil-Bobil, I., *Russkaya Volya*, No. 8 Friday 10 March, 1917, p 7

1599.   *"Likvidatsiya ubiistva Rasputina"*, *Birzhevlye Vedomosti*, No 16124, Wednesday 8 March 1917, p 7

1600.   Kerensky, A., *Tragediya Dinastii Romanovikh*, p 118

1601.   Instructions: Head of the Tsarskoe Selo Garrison about the Security of the Alexandrovsky Palace. Item 3, 17 March 1917, reproduced as Document No. 45, in: *Skorbnii Put' Romanovikh, Arkhiv Noveishei Istorii Rossii*, [Volume III], p 68

1602.   Anonymous (I), *"Zhizn i Pohozdheniye Grigoriya Rasputina"*, 1917, p 39

1603.   *"Sredi arestovovannoi Tsarskoi Sviti"*, *Birzheviye Vedomosti*, No 16128, Friday 10 March 1917, p 3

1604.   Gan, L., *"Zaklucheniye nizlozhenogo Imperatora v Tsarskoselsky Dvorets"*, *Birzheviye Vedomosti*, No. 16128, 10 March 1917, reproduced by Fomin, S., Footnote 3, p 4

1605.   *"K smerti Gr. Rasputina"*, *Den'*, No. 351, 21 December 1916, p 2

1606.   Rodzianko, A., Letter to Zinaida Yusupova, 7 January 1917, reproduced in: *Krasnii Arkhiv*, *"K istorii poslednikh dnei Tsarskogo rezhima"*, p 244

1607.   Bedun, *"Sozheniye trupa Rasputina"*, *Petrogradsky Listok*, No. 62, 14 March 1917, reproduced in: Fomin, S., *Pravda o Grigorii Efimoviche Rasputine*, p 2

1608.   *"Naiden trup Rasputina"*, *Vechernii Kurier*, No. 899, 10

March 1917, p 3, reproduced in: Fomin, S., p 2

1609.   Protocol G. Lvov, 6-30 July 1920, reproduced in: Alexandrov, A., p 149

1610.   Bogutskaya, L., "*Na Mogile Rasputina*", *Den'*, No. 4, Thursday 9 March 1917, p 3

1611.   "*Delo ob ubiistve Grigoriya Rasputina*", *Russkoye Slovo*, Thursday 9 March 1917, p 3, reprinted in: *Sbornik Istoricheskih Materialov*, Volume 2, Terra, *Moskva*, 1997, p 66

1612.   Bogutskaya, L., "*Na Mogile Rasputina*", *Den'*, No. 4, Thursday 9 March 1917, p 3

1613.   Kulegin, A., *Zagrobeniye priklyucheniya 'svyatogo cherta'*, State Political History Museum, No. 3, *Sankt Peterburg*, (no date), p 5

1614.   Bogutskaya, L., "*Na Mogile Rasputina*", *Den'*, No. 4, Thursday 9 March 1917, p 3

1615.   Lagansky, E., "*Kak nashli mogilu Rasputina*", *Russkaya Volya*, No 6, Thursday 9 March 1917, p 5

1616.   Lagansky, E., "*Kak Zhigali Rasputina*", [Part 1], *Ogonek*, No. 52, December 1926, (N. S.) p 1

1617.   Lagansky, E., "*Kak Zhigali Rasputina*", [Part II], *Ogonek*, No. 1, January 1927, (N. S.) pp 11-12

1618.   Footnote 1, in: Fomin, S., "*Pravda o Grigorii Efimoviche Rasputine*", p 3

1619.   Lagansky, E., "*Kak nashli mogilu Rasputina*", *Russkaya Volya*, No. 6, Thursday 9 March 1917, p 5

1620.   Lagansky, E., "*Kak Zhigali Rasputina*", [Part II], *Ogonek*, No. 1, January 1927, (N. S.), p 12

1621.   Nikitin, A., "*Rasputina pokhoronili zhurnalisti*", *Zhurnalist* Journal, (2005), No. 4, p 90

1622.   Konstantinov, V., "*Taina Alexandrovskogo Parka*", *Tsarskoe Selo* Journal, (1998), Volume10 (109), 25 June, p 2

1623.   Anonymous (I), "*Zhizn i Pohozdheniye Grigoriya Rasputina*", pp 41-42

1624. Lagansky, E., *"Kak nashli mogilu Rasputina"*, *Russkaya Vo-lya*, No. 6, Thursday 9 March 1917, p 5

1625. Lagansky, E., *"Kak nashli mogilu Rasputina"*, *Russkaya Vo-lya*, p 5

1626. Smirnov, V., *"Neizvestnoye o Rasputine"*, *Russkoye Slovo*, Friday 10 March 1917, reproduced in: Fomin, S., *"Pravda o Grigorii Efimoviche Rasputine"*, p 5

1627. Lagansky, E., *"Na Mogile Rasputina"*, *Russkaya Volya*, No 8, Friday 10 March 1917, p 6

1628. Lagansky, E., *"Kak nashli mogilu Rasputina"*, *Russkaya Vo-lya*, No. 6, Thursday 9 March 1917, p 5

1629. Lagansky, E., *"Na Mogile Rasputina"*, *Russkaya Volya*, No 8, Friday 10 March 1917, p 6

1630. Lagansky, E., *"Kak nashli mogilu Rasputina"*, *Russkaya Vo-lya*, No. 6, Thursday 9 March 1917, p 5

1631. Merkulov, P., *Rasputinskiye Chudesa*, *Petrogradsky Listok*, Monday 13 March 1917, p 3, reproduced in Fomin, S., *"Pravda o Grig-orii Efimoviche Rasputine"*, p 4

1632. *"Delo ob ubiistve Grigoriya Rasputina"*, *Russkoye Slovo*, Thursday 9 March 1917, p 3, reproduced in: Fomin, S., p 5

1633. Smirnov, V., *"Neizvestnoye o Rasputine"*, *Russkoye Slovo*, Friday 10 March 1917, reproduced in: Fomin, S., p 5

1634. Kerensky, A., *Tragediya Dinastii Romanovikh*, p 111

1635. Purishkevich, V. (I), *Dnevnik*, p 144

1636. Kovalevsky, P., *"Grishka Rasputin"*, *Mokovskoye Izdatelstvo*, *Moskva*, 1917, p 26

1637. *"Telo Rasputina"*, *Russkaya Volya*, Evening edition, No. 9. Friday 10 March 1917, p 3

1638. *"Rasputin i Imperatorsky Dvor"*, *Birzheviye Vedomosti*, No. 16128, March 10, 1917, p 4

1639. Protocol E. Kobylinsky, To N. Sokolov 6 -10 April 1919, reproduced as: Document No. 192, in: *Gibel Tsarskoi Semyi*, Nikolai Ross [Editor], Possev-Verlag, Frankfurt am Main, 1987, p 292

1640. *"Rasputin i Imperatorsky Dvor"*, *Birzheviye Vedomosti*, No. 16128, 10 March 1917, p 4

1641. Kupchinsky, F., *Ya Zheg Grigoriya Rasputina*, [Edited by V. Klaving], *Izdatelstvo Sankt Peterburg Universitet, Sankt Peterburg*, 2001, p 49

1642. General Stessel, A. M. (1907) *Moim Vragam, Sankt Peterburg*, pp 18-20, in: Fomin, S., *"Pravda o Grigorii Efimoviche Rasputine"*, p 6

1643. Glezerov, S., *Lesnoi, Grazhdanka, Ruchi, Udelnaya*, *Tsentrpoligraf, Sankt Peterburg*, 2006, p 182

1644. Kupchinsky, F., p 49

1645. *"Telo Rasputina"*, *Russkaya Volya*, Evening edition, No. 9, Friday 10 March 1917, p 3

1646. Kupchinsky, F., *Ya Zheg Grigoriya Rasputina*, p 52

1647. *"Sozheniye Rasputina"*, *Birzheviye Vedomosti*, No. 16133, 13 March 1917, p 2

1648. Purishkevich, V. (I), *Dnevnik*, p 144

1649. Kupchinsky, F., *Ya Zheg Grigoriya Rasputina*, p 52

1650. *"Protocol Sobitii Fevralskoi Revolutsii"*, Document No. 80, 27 February – 4 March 1917, reproduced in: Tretyakova, V., *Otrecheniye Nikolaya II*, p 299

1651. Kupchinsky, F., *Ya Zheg Grigoriya Rasputina*, p 52

1652. Fomin, S., Footnote No. 1, in: *"Pravda o Grigorii Efimoviche Rasputine"*, p 8

1653. Glezerov, S., *Lesnoi, Grazhdanka, Ruchi, Udelnaya*, p 31

1654. Glezerov, S., *Lesnoi, Grazhdanka, Ruchi, Udelnaya*, p 87 and p 106

1655. *"Sozheniye Tela Rasputina"*, *Russkaya Volya*, No 14, Tuesday 14 March 1917, p 6

1656. Purishkevich, V. (I), *Dnevnik*, pp 145-146

1657. Anonymous (II), *"Temniye Sili: Tainy Rasputinskogo Dvora*

– Rasputin", p 16

1658.   "Zinc, Physical Characteristics", See: http://en.wikipedia.
org/wiki/Zinc

1659.   Kupchinsky, F., *Ya Zheg Grigoriya Rasputina*, p 56

1660.   Cheparukhin, V., *Krematsiya Tela G. Rasputina v Dni Fe-vralskoi Revolutsii 1917*, in: *Revolutsiya 1917 goda v Rossii Sbornik Nauchnikh Statei*, Tretiya Rossiya, Sankt Peterburg, 1995, p 93

1661.   Cheparukhin, V., *Grigorii Rasputin. Poslednyaya Tochka, Novy Chasovoi* Journal, (1995), No. 3, *Sankt Peterburg*, p 35

1662.   Glezerov, S., *Lesnoi, Grazhdanka, Ruchi, Udelnaya*, p 184

1663.   Nelipa, M. (II), **The Tragedy of Nikolai II's Abdication**, Sovereign, No. 1, (2016), p 77

1664.   Kalmykov, A., *Politekniki v partiino-politicheskoi elite Rossii 1917*, in: Fomin, S., *"Pravda o Grigorii Efimoviche Rasputine"*, p 9

1665.   Dregulyas, G., *Otkritiye Sankt Peterburgskogo politechnicheskogo instituta*, See: http://www.opeterburge.ru/history_147_242.html

1666.   Kupchinsky, F., *Ya Zheg Grigoriya Rasputina*, p 58

1667.   Bedun, *"Sozheniye trupa Rasputina"*, *Petrogradsky Listok*, No. 62, Tuesday 14 March 1917, in: Fomin, S., *"Pravda o Grigorii Efimoviche Rasputine"*, p 11

1668.   *"Sozzheniye trupa Rasputin"*, Riss, P, *Den'*, No. 8, 14 March 1917, p 2

1669.   Kerensky, A., *Tragediya Dinastii Romanovikh*, p 131

1670.   Lagansky, E., *"Kak Zhigali Rasputina"*, [Part II], p 12

1671.   *"Obiisk v kvartire Rasputina"*, *Birzheviye Vedomosti*, No. 16144, 19 March 1917, p 4

1672.   *"Sozheniye Rasputina"*, *Birzheviye Vedomosti*, No. 16133, 13 March 1917, p 2

1673.   Popov, S., *Moi Vospominaniya o Tsarskoi Semye*, Bulgaria, 1930, See: http://kfinkelshteyn.narod.ru/Tzarskoye_Selo/hospital2c.htm

1674.   *Dopros* M. Rodzianko, 4 September 1917, *Padeniye Tsarsko-*

go Regima, [Volume VII], p 164

1675.   Grand Duke Dmitri Pavlovich, Letter to father, 23 April 1917, reproduced in: *Krasnii Arkhiv*, *"Pisma D. P. Romanova k Otsu"*, p 206

1676.   Spiridovich, A., *Velikaya Voina i Fevralskaya Revolutsiya*, p 435

1677.   Nikolai II, Diary excerpt, 19 December 1916, *Dnevniki Imperatora Nikolaya II, 1914-1918*, [Volume II, Part II], p 271

1678.   *"Peremeni v Sovete Ministrov"*, *Russkoye Slovo*, No.294, 21 December 1916, p 3

1679.   Zvyagintsev, A., *V Epohu Potryasenii o Reform Rossiiskiye Prokurori*, p 180

1680.   V. Stavrovskii, *Sudebniye Uchrezhdeniya poreformennogo perioda*, St. P Archives, See: https://spbarchives.ru/information_resources/-/archivestore/guide_page/2-162

1681.   Anonymous (I), *"Zhizn i Pohozhdeniye Grigoriya Rasputina"*, p 21

1682.   Zvyagintsev, A.., *V Epohu Potryasenii o Reform Rossiiskiye Prokurori*, p 180

1683.   *Pokazaniya VII*, **A. D. Protopopova**, <u>28 July 1917</u>, *Padeniye Tsarskogo Regima*, [Volume IV], p 144

1684.   Grand Duchess Marie Pavlovna, **Education of a Princess**, p 277

1685.   Paley, O., *Vospominaniya o Rossii*, p 20

1686.   Grand Duke Andrei Vladimirovich, Diary excerpt, 25 December 1916, *Voenni Dnevnik*, p 214

1687.   Paley, O., *Vospominaniya o Rossii*, p 21

1688.   *"V. M. Purishkevich ..."*, *Rech*, No. 351, 21 December 1916, p 4

1689.   Paléologue, M., Diary excerpt, Monday 8 January 1917 (N. S.), **An Ambassador's Memoirs**, Volume III, p 152

1690.   Spiridovich, A., *Velikaya Voina i Fevralskaya Revolutsiya*, p 435

1691. Horvatova, E., *Maria Pavlovna, Drama Velikoi Knyagini*, 2005, p 235

1692. Globachev, K., *Pravda o Russkoi Revolutsii*, p 90

1693. Spiridovich, A., *Velikaya Voina i Fevralskaya Revolutsiya*, p 435

1694. *"Vysochaishiya Nagradi"*, *Petrogradskiye Vedomosti*, No. 347, Saturday 17 December 1916, p 1

1695. Grand Duchess Marie Pavlovna, **Education of a Princess**, p 271

1696. Paley, O., *Vospominaniya o Rossii*, p 18

1697. Maria Fyodorovna, Diary extract, Wednesday 21 December 1916, *Dnevniki Imperatritsi Marii Fyodorovni*, p 164

1698. Grand Duchess Marie Pavlovna, **Education of a Princess**, pp 276-277

1699. Grand Duke Alexander Mikhailovich, **Once a Grand Duke**, p 278

1700. Grand Duke Andrei Vladimirovich, Diary excerpt, 21 December 1916, *Voenni Dnevnik*, p 206

1701. Grand Duke Gavril Konstantinovich, *Vospominaniye*, December 1916, p 291

1702. Grand Duke Andrei Vladimirovich, Diary excerpt, 21 December 1916, *Voenni Dnevnik*, pp 206-207

1703. Grand Duke Gavril Konstantinovich, *Vospominaniye*, December 1916, p 291

1704. Grand Duke Alexander Mikhailovich, **Once a Grand Duke**, p 279

1705. Spiridovich, A., *Velikaya Voina i Fevralskaya Revolutsiya*, pp 434-435

1706. Maria Fyodorovna, Diary excerpt, Friday 23 December 1916, *Dnevniki Imperatritsi Marii Fyodorovni*, pp 164-165

1707. Grand Duke Nikolai Mikhailovich, Letter to Maria Fyodorovna, 24 December 1916, [GARF]

1708.   Grand Duke Andrei Vladimirovich, Diary excerpt, 21 December 1916, *Voenni Dnevnik*, p 210

1709.   Grand Duke Andrei Vladimirovich, Diary excerpt, 21 December 1916, *Voenni Dnevnik*, p 210

1710.   Grand Duke Andrei Vladimirovich, Diary excerpt, 23 December 1916, *Voenni Dnevnik*, p 213

1711.   Zalessky, K., *Kto byl kto v Pervoi Mirovoi Voine*, pp 44-45

1712.   Grand Duke Nikolai Mikhailovich, Diary excerpt, 23 December 1916, reproduced in: *Krasnii Arkhiv*, *"Podrobnosti Ubiistva Rasputina"*, p 101

1713.   Grand Duke Andrei Vladimirovich, Diary excerpt, 23 December 1916, *Voenni Dnevnik*, pp 212-213

1714.   Maria Fyodorovna, Diary excerpt, Saturday 31 December 1916, *Dnevniki Imperatritsi Marii Fyodorovni*, p 166

1715.   Endnote No 406, in: *Voenni Dnevnik*, p 408

1716.   *"Kak byl vyslan Dmitri Pavlovich"*, *Russkaya Volya*, No 8, 10 March 1917, p 7

1717.   Yusupov, F., *Memyari v dvykh knigakh*, p 224

1718.   Yusupov, F., (senior), Diary excerpt, December 1916, reproduced in: Krasnykh, E., *Za vse Blagodaryu*, p 453

1719.   Maria Fyodorovna, Diary excerpt, Tuesday 27 December 1916, *Dnevniki Imperatritsi Marii Fyodorovni*, p 165

1720.   Yusupov, F., *Memyari v dvykh knigakh*, p 226

1721.   Yusupov, F., Letter to Grand Duchess Ksenya Alexandrovna, 2 January 1917, reproduced in: Krasnykh, E., *Za vse Blagodaryu*, p 454

1722.   Grand Duchess Marie Pavlovna, **Education of a Princess**, p 278

1723.   Grand Duchess Marie Pavlovna, **Education of a Princess**, p 271

1724.   Purishkevich, V., *Ubiistvo Rasputina*, p 79

1725.   Kovalevsky, P., *"Grishka Rasputin"*, p 23

1726.   Anonymous (III), [Ed. N. Kubikov], *"Kak Khoronili Rasputina* (I), *Za Velikoknyazheskimi Kulisami"* (II), Dubovin Elektro-*Pechat*, Kiev,1917, pp 8-9

1727.   Zavadsky, S., *Na Velikom Izlome*, p 240

1728.   Zvyagintsev, *V Epohu Potryasenii o Reform Rossiiskiye Prokurori*, p 180

1729.   Chebishev, N., *"Navozhdeniye"*, *Illustrirovannaya Rossiya*, (1932), No. 20, p 7

1730.   Koshko, A., *Uglovii Mir Tsarskoi Rossii*, p129

1731.   Pereverzev, P., *"Ubiistvo Rasputina"*, p 7

1732.   *Ustav Ugolovnogo sudoproizvodstva* [1864], See: http://09403.khstu.ru/studentsbooks/othistory/historyist/ustav%20 ugol%20sud.htm

1733.   Pereverzev, P., *"Ubiistvo Rasputina"*, p 7

1734.   Spiridovich, A., *Velikaya Voina i Fevralskaya Revolutsiya*, p 433

1735.   Grand Duke Alexander Mikhailovich, **Once a Grand Duke**, pp 278-279

1736.   *Osnovniye Gosudarstvenniye Zakoni* [1906] *Glava 7*, **St. 64,** See: http://monar.ru/index.php?download/tsar_orf/SZRI_Tom1_r1.html

1737.   *Gosudarstvennoye Pravo* [1885-1886] **Item 27,** *Grazhdanskiye Prava Chlenov Tsarstvuyushego Doma*, See: http://www.allpravo. ru/library/doc117p/instrum2817/item2846.html

1738.   Grand Duke Gavril Konstantinovich, *Vospominaniye*, **December 1916,** p294

1739.   *Prilozheniye IV, Prisyaga Dlya Chlenov Imperatorskogo Doma*, See: http://www.monarchruss.org/library/prisyagi_tsar.htm

1740.   **"A Vibrant Echo"**, **Time**, Volume X1, No. 14, Monday 3 December 1923, See: http://www.time.com/time/magazine/article/0,9171,717062,00.html

1741.   Grand Duke Andrei Vladimirovich, Diary excerpt, 29 December 1916, *Voenni Dnevnik*, p 216

1742.	Grand Duke Nikolai Mikhailovich, Diary extract, Diary excerpt, 4 January 1917, p 103

1743.	Maria Fyodorovna, Diary excerpt, 4 January 1917, *Dnevniki Imperatritsi Marii Fyodorovni*, p 169

1744.	Grand Duke Nikolai Mikhailovich, Diary excerpt, 31 December 1916, reproduced in: *Krasnii Arkhiv, "Podrobnosti Ubiistva Rasputina"*, p 102

1745.	*"Warned Nicholas of Wife's Intrigues, Grand Duke Nicholas Mikhailovich Banished by Czar because of his Plain Talk"*, **The New York Times**, March 1917, (no page number available)

1746.	Paléologue, M., Diary excerpt, Monday 15 January 1917, (N.S.), p 167

1747.	Grand Duchess Marie Pavlovna, **Education of a Princess**, p 278

1748.	Paley O., *Vospominaniya o Rossii*, p 19

1749.	Grand Duke Gavril Konstantinovich, *Vospominaniye*, December 1916, p 294

1750.	Grand Duke Andrei Vladimirovich, Diary excerpt, 29 December 1916, *Voenni Dnevnik*, p 218

1751.	Grand Duke Alexander Mikhailovich, **Once a Grand Duke**, p 278

1752.	Grand Duke Dmitri Pavlovich, Letter to father, 7 February 1917, reproduced in: *Krasnii Arkhiv, "Pisma D. P. Romanova k Otsu"*, p 203

1753.	Grand Duke Alexander Mikhailovich, **Once a Grand Duke**, p 279

1754.	Grand Duchess Marie Pavlovna, **Education of a Princess**, p 279

1755.	Buchanan, M., **The Dissolution of an Empire**, p 150

1756.	Paléologue, M. Diary excerpt, Saturday 13 January 1917, (N. S.), **An Ambassador's Memoirs**, Volume III, p 164

1757.	Grand Duke Alexander Mikhailovich, **Once a Grand Duke**, p 278

1758.   Vorres, I., **The Last Grand Duchess**, p139

1759.   Grand Duchess Elizaveta Fyodorovna, Letter to Nikolai II, 29 December 1916, reproduced in: *Istochnik*, No. 4, 1994, pp 37-38

1760.   Spiridovich, A., *Velikaya Voina i Fevralskaya Revolutsiya*, p 435

1761.   Anonymous (III), "*Kak Khoronili Rasputina* (I), *Za Velikoknyazheskimi Kulisami*" (II), 1917, p 10

1762.   Anonymous (IV), "*Taina Doma Romanovikh ili Pokhozheniya Grigoriya Rasputina*", *Typografiya* M. Brisker, Kiev, 1917, p 27

1763.   Maria Fyodorovna, Diary excerpt, 9 December 1915, *Dnevniki Imperatritsi Marii Fyodorovni*, pp 91-92

1764.   Maria Fyodorovna, Diary excerpt, Saturday 31 December 1916, *Dnevniki Imperatritsi Marii Fyodorovni*, p 166

1765.   Kudrina, Yu., *Imperatritsa Maria Fyodorovna Romanova*, p 160

1766.   Kudrina, Yu., *Imperatritsa Maria Fyodorovna Romanova*, pp 161-162

1767.   Taneeva, A, **Stranitsi Moyei Zhizni**, p 105

1768.   [Anonymous], "*Lichnost Nikolaya II i Alexandra Fyodorovni po svidetelstvam ikh Rodnikh i blizkikh*", p 150

1769.   Rodzianko, A., Letter to Zinaida Yusupova, 12 February 1917, reproduced in: *Krasnii Arkhiv*, "*K istorii poslednkh dnei Tsarskogo rezhima*", p 446

1770.   Paléologue, M. Diary excerpt, Friday 7 January 1917, (N. S.), **An Ambassador's Memoirs**, Volume III, p 140

1771.   **Maurice Paléologue** See: http://en.wikipedia.org/wiki/Maurice_Pal%C3%A9ologue

1772.   Spiridovich, A., *Velikaya Voina i Fevralskaya Revolutsiya*, p 296

1773.   Grand Duke Alexander Mikhailovich, Letter to Nikolai II, December 25, 1916-February 4, 1917, reproduced in: "*Nikolai II i Velikiye Knyazya Rodstvenniye Pisma k Polednemu Tsaryu*", [Editor V. Semennikov], *Gos. Izd-vo*, Leningrad, 1925, pp 116-122

1774. Grand Duke Alexander Mikhailovich, **Once a Grand Duke**, p 285

1775. *"Kto ubil Rasputina?"*, Samoilov, V., *Russkaya Volya*, No. 13, Monday 13 March (1917), p 3

1776. Yusupov, F., *Memyari v dvykh knigakh*, p 222

1777. Grand Duke Dmitri Pavlovich, Letter to Felix Yusupov, 23 April 1917, reproduced in: *Krasnii Arkhiv*, *"Pisma D. P. Romanova k Otsu"*, pp 247- 249

1778. Grand Duke Dmitri Pavlovich, Letter to father, 23 April 1917, reproduced in: *Krasnii Arkhiv*, *"Pisma D. P. Romanova k Otsu"*, p 207

1779. [No author], *"Lichnost Nikolaya II i Alexandra Fyodorovni po svidetelstvam ikh Rodnikh i blizkikh"*, Felix Yusupov interview in: *Petrogradskii Listok*, No. 62, reproduced in: *Istoricheskii Vestnik*, April 1917, pp 154-155

1780. Address to the Duma by Purishkevich, V., Fourth Duma Convocation, Session V, Sitting 6, 19 November 1916, reproduced in: *Stenograficheskii Otchet, Gosudarstvennaya Duma*, pp 250-288

1781. Grand Duke Alexander Mikhailovich, Letter to Nikolai Mikhailovich, January 1917, reproduced in: Krasnykh, E., pp 460-461

1782. Kudrina, Yu., *Imperatritsa Maria Fyodorovna Romanova*, p 163

1783. Maria Fyodorovna, Diary excerpt, Saturday 4 March 1917, *Dnevniki Imperatritsi Marii Fyodorovni*, p 176

1784. Grand Duke Alexander Mikhailovich, **Once a Grand** Duke, p 289

1785. Zaslavsky, D., *Ritsar' Chernoi Sotni V. V. Shulgin*, *Byloye Izdatelstvo*, Leningrad, 1925, p 46

1786. Stepanov, A., *Bolshaya Ensiklopediya Russkogo Naroda*, *Russkii patriotism*: Purishkevich, V., See: http://www.rusinst.ru/article-text.asp?rzd=1&id=6198

1787. Horvatova, E., *Maria Fyodorovna, Sud'ba Imperatritsi*, ACT Press, *Moskva*, 2006, p 510

1788. Narishkina-Kurakin, E., **Under Three Tsars**, pp 214-215

1789.   Felix Yusupov interview, *Novoye Vremya*, No 14726, April 1917, p 164

1790.   Horvatova, E., *Maria Fyodorovna, Sud'ba Imperatritsi*, p 497

1791.   Grand Duke Dmitri Pavlovich, Letter to Felix Yusupov, 23 April 1917, reproduced in: *Krasnii Arkhiv*, *"Pisma D. P. Romanova k Otsu"*, p 247

1792.   Taneeva, A., *Stranitsi Moyei Zhizni*, p 384

1793.   Vorres, I., **The Last Grand Duchess**, pp 131-135

1794.   Harclave, S., **The Memoirs of Count Witte**, M. E. Sharpe, Inc., New York, 1990, p 681

1795.   Grand Duke Andrei Vladimirovich, Diary excerpt, 17 September 1915, *Voenni Dnevnik*, p 184

1796.   Fyodorov, B., *Petr Stolypin: Ya Veryu v Rossiyu*, [Volume 1], Limbus Press, St. Petersburg, 2002, p 451

1797.   Bokhanov, A., *Anatomiya Mifa*, p 134

1798.   Bokhanov, A., *Anatomiya Mifa*, pp 151-152

1799.   Beletsky, S., *Grigorii Rasputin iz Zapisok*, p 19

1800.   Gilliard, P., **Thirteen Years at the Russian Court**, p 82, 84 and p 142

1801.   *Dopros* A. D. Protopopov, 21 March 1917, in: *Padeniye Tsarskogo Rezhima*, [Volume I], p 144, p 176 and p 199,

1802.   Vitala, E., *Bez Mifov i Legend*, p 126

1803.   Rudnev, V., *Pravda o Tsarskoi Semye i Temnikh Silakh*, pp 17, 18, 19-20, 21, 23, 33, 34 and 35

1804.   De Maio, V., **Handbook of Forensic Pathology**, p 151

1805.   De Maio, V., **Handbook of Forensic Pathology**, p 151

1806.   De Maio, V., **Handbook of Forensic Pathology**, p 151

1807.   Gutierez, S., **Blood Spatter Pattern and the Kennedy Assassination**, p 3, See: http://www.jfklancerforum.com/sherryg/page03.html

1808.   Patrick, U., **FBI Academy Firearms Training Unit: Handgun Wounding Factors and Effectiveness   U. S. Department of Justice**, Washington D. C., 1989, p 4

1809.   **FBI Academy Firearms Training Unit: Handgun Wounding Factors and Effectiveness   U. S. Department of Justice**, p 8

1810.   Grand Duke Andrei Vladimirovich, Diary excerpt, 15 February 1917, *Voenni Dnevnik*, p 228

Index